POE...

Leaving Certificate English Poetry

Higher Level 2022

Edited by Niall MacMonagle

Niall MacMonagle has taught English for the Leaving Certificate for many years. A well-known literary commentator on radio, he is the editor of several poetry anthologies, including the best-selling *Windharp: Poems of Ireland since 1916* (Penguin, 2015) and *TEXT: A Transition Year English Reader*. He writes a weekly art column for the *Sunday Independent*. In 2017, he was awarded a Doctorate of Letters, *honoris causa*, by UCD, for services to literature.

' . . . until everything
was rainbow, rainbow, rainbow!'

Elizabeth Bishop

First published in 2020 by
The Celtic Press

Ground Floor – Block B, Liffey Valley Office Campus, Dublin 22

ISBN: 978-0-7144-2777-5

Contents

John Keats (1795–1821)

Brendan Kennelly (b. 1936)

D.H. Lawrence (1885–1930)

William Butler Yeats (1865–1939)

Prescribed Poetry at Leaving Cert. Higher Level

Part II

Part III

Introduction

The Leaving Certificate student is already an experienced reader of poetry. For Junior Cycle, you were invited to read a great variety of poems on a wide range of subjects by many different poets. You will have realised that poets use language differently, that poetry is both challenging and rewarding, and in an age of soundbytes and mediaspeak it can hold its own and offer something unique and special; that poetry, in Allison Pearson's words, 'is not in the business of taking polaroids: it should be a long slow developer, raising images that we frame and keep'. You have also had experience of both seen and unseen poems. A similar challenge awaits you at Leaving Certificate level, but there are some important differences. Until now, you might have looked at three or four poems by different poets; in the Leaving Certificate, at Higher Level, you are being invited to read an interesting and representative sample of work by eight poets and you will also be given the opportunity to respond to unseen poetry.

It is worth remembering at the outset that the word for poet in English comes from the Greek word for maker. A good poem is language that has been carefully shaped and well made. Samuel Taylor Coleridge's definition of poetry in the nineteenth century as 'the best words in the best order' still holds. W. H. Auden has described poetry as 'memorable speech'. The *New Princeton Handbook of Poetic Terms* defines a poem as 'an instance of verbal art, a text set in verse, bound speech. More generally, a poem conveys heightened forms of perception, experience, meaning, or consciousness in heightened language, i.e., a heightened mode of discourse.'

But, whichever conception we accept, we will find definitions inadequate and less important than the unique and individual experience when we, as readers, allow ourselves to enter into the world of the poem that the poet has created for us on the page.

'The Voice You Hear When You Read Silently' by Thomas Lux reminds us of the unique, very private, pleasurable experience of reading poetry:

The Voice You Hear When You Read Silently

is not silent, it is a speaking–
out-loud voice in your head: it is spoken,
a voice is saying it
as you read. It's the writer's words,
of course, in a literary sense
his or her 'voice' but the sound
of that voice is the sound of your voice.
Not the sound your friends know
or the sound of a tape played back
but your voice
caught in the dark cathedral
of your skull, your voice heard
by an internal ear informed by internal abstracts
and what you know by feeling,
having felt. It is your voice
saying, for example, the word 'barn'
that the writer wrote
but the 'barn' you say
is a barn you know or knew. The voice
in your head, speaking as you read,
never says anything neutrally – some people
hated the barn they knew,
some people love the barn they know
so you hear the word loaded
and a sensory constellation
is lit: horse-gnawed stalls,
hayloft, black heat tape wrapping
a water pipe, a slippery
spilled chirr of oats from a split sack,
the bony, filthy haunches of cows . . .
And 'barn' is only a noun – no verb
or subject has entered into the sentence yet!
The voice you hear when you read to yourself
is the clearest voice: you speak it
speaking to you.

When we look at a poem for the very first time, we can appreciate and sense how that poem has been made and shaped. This does not only include its actual shape as printed text, though this in itself is extremely important; more importantly, it means that thought, idea, and feeling have been structured and the careful combination produces the living poem.

An open approach brings its own rewards. If we learn to understand how something complex works, then we are aware of its intricacies and can better admire the creative mind that made it possible. The Irish writer Michael Longley says that 'a poet makes the most complex and concentrated response that can be made with words to the total experience of living.' But he also admits that one of the things that studying literature taught him was 'the beauty of things difficult.'

It is an exciting challenge to stand before a painting and discover what it has to say to us, to listen to a piece of music and hear it for the first time, to read a poem unknown to us until that moment. And then to return to these works and to realise how our relationship with them changes and develops as we ourselves change and develop. As we grow and change, so does our response.

We can all remember instances and experiences which we found difficult and challenging initially, but with careful thought and an open, positive approach we gained insight and understanding. Stephen Booth puts it like this: 'Any reader superstitiously fearful that the magic of a poem will vanish with knowledge of its sources need not worry any more than a student of zoology need worry that gazelles will slow down if he investigates the reasons why they run so fast.' Helen Vendler also offers good advice when she says that a reader should not look at a poem 'as if you're looking at the text with a microscope from outside'. For Vendler, the close reader is 'someone who goes inside a room and describes the architecture. You speak from inside the poem as someone looking to see how the roof articulates with the walls and how the wall articulates with the floor. And where are the crossbeams that hold it up, and where are the windows that let light through?'

Poetry can sometimes be difficult and a challenge to understand. But if we reject challenges, our vocabulary, for example, would never grow; the enquiring mind would close down. We need challenges in our lives to sharpen our intellect and keep our minds from dozing off. Sometimes we fall into the trap of saying 'I like this poem because it is easy for me to understand' or 'Why doesn't the poet say what he or she wants to say in an easy-to-understand language?' If we adopt such a position, we are saying that we want a poetry that is at our level only, that if there is an unknown word or a difficult allusion, then the poem should be rejected. If we spoke down to little children throughout their childhood, they would never grow up. Most poetry is written by adults for other adults and as a Leaving Certificate student you are on the threshold of adulthood. Allow the poems in this antology to have their say and you will not be disappointed. And if you come upon a poem in a newspaper, magazine, book, the London Underground, the New York Subway or the DART, you should give that poem a chance. The poem might deserve it and so do you.

Some years ago, the Irish poet Paul Muldoon was asked to judge a poetry competition, in the north of Ireland, which was open to young people up to the age of eighteen. There were hundreds of entries and there were poems, short and long, on all the big subjects — famine, time, death, space travel, nuclear war. Muldoon awarded first prize to an eight-year old boy who wrote the following poem:

The Tortoise

The tortoise goes movey, movey.

There was 'consternation' when 'this little poem about a tiny little subject' was awarded the prize. Muldoon explains that a great deal of the consternation was in the minds of the school teachers in the audience: 'They were upset by the fact that there's no such word in the English language as "movey, m-o-v-e-y". I tried to point out that until recently that there'd been no such word as "movey", but there now certainly was such a word, and I would never again be able to think of a tortoise without seeing it go "movey, movey".' One teacher told Muldoon that the prize-winning poet was illiterate, forgetting that the same boy had an extraordinary fresh and alive imagination.

Consider the poem again. Say it aloud and its atmospheric rhythm is immediate:

The Tortoise

The tortoise goes movey, movey.

Professor Paul Muldoon now teaches creative writing at Princeton University and the first task he sets his students is to write a one-line poem that will change the way he looks at the world. When they have made their poem, he shows them 'The Tortoise', which, for him, does just that. It goes . . .

m-o-v-e-y, m-o-v-e-y.

There are many aspects to be considered when it comes to the poem on the page, but let us begin without any set ideas. Consider the following:

In a Station of the Metro

The apparition of these faces in the crowd;
Petals on a wet, black bough.

What have we here? A poem. How can we tell? One of the reasons we can identify it as poetry is by its physical arrangement on the page. Prose is presented within a right and left hand margin on the page, whereas poetry is written in lines, each one causing us to pause, however briefly, before we move on. When we read it through, we can sense a concentration and intensity, a focus, a way of looking, which is one of poetry's hallmarks. What have we here? Three lines, the first of them the title, then two lines separated by a semi-colon; twenty words in all. For accurate understanding, almost all you need is a dictionary: remember Elizabeth Bishop's advice: 'Use the dictionary. It's better than the critics'.

To ask 'What have we here?' is infinitely more rewarding than 'What is this poem about?' And this, I think, is by far the best way of approaching any text. 'What have I here?' means that I, in my own time, will interpret the poem. I will gradually build up an understanding of it in my own mind. A poem is not a static thing. It is in the poet Thomas Kinsella's words 'an orderly dynamic entity'. 'What is this poem about?' is an alienating way of looking at a text, implying as it does that there is only one way of looking at the poem and that I, as reader, must somehow crack some code.

We all bring different things to a text. My way of looking at a poem will be different from yours. The person who has walked Inniskeen Road on a July evening will read Patrick Kavanagh's poetry in a different light from the reader who has never been there. If you have been to Rathlin Island, on the north Antrim coast, then Derek Mahon's description of the place will have different resonances for you than for the person who has never seen the 'rock-face and cliff-top' of Rathlin, just as Emily Dickinson's poetry will be different for those who have been to Amherest, Massachusetts.

Similarly, if you have grown up on a farm you might find yourself reading Seamus Heaney's poetry from a different perspective to the urban dweller. One way is not necessarily better than the other. It is different. What does matter, however, is that interpretation and discussion of the text should be rooted in the text itself. There is such a thing as a wrong interpretation: one which does not take the details of the text into account.

In the short poem by Ezra Pound, the title – 'In a Station of the Metro' – gives us the setting of the poem.

In a Station of the Metro

The apparition of these faces in the crowd;
Petals on a wet, black bough.

We are in Paris, but the actual Metro stop is not named. The title is clinically factual; there is no word in the title to indicate an attitude or a tone. Yet the reader is immediately invited to imagine this particular scene: usually a crowded and very busy underground railway station. In many ways, it is a scene that sums up an aspect of twentieth-century life – urban, anonymous, busy, lacking individuality.

Then the first line of the poem itself speaks of the individual and separate faces in the crowd. Pound on seeing particular faces compares the event to that of experiencing an apparition. The faces are somehow supernatural or ghostly. In a world of concrete and steel, the human being is phantom-like. This is a sense impression. The poem for example has no verb. It is not so much concerned with making a definite statement as with capturing an immediate response to a situation at a particular moment in time.

The second and final line of the poem speaks about the natural world, petals on a tree. The tree itself is wet and black suggesting, perhaps, something unattractive; but the petals are wet too and therefore shiny. They stand out. There are many of them and yet each one is individual and unique. From the way the two lines are arranged on the page, and from the use of the connecting semi-colon, we can tell that Pound is making a link between the nameless faces of people moving through an underground station (with their bright faces) and the petals that stand out against the dull tree bough.

The train in the underground station is a hard, steel object and, it could be argued, bough-like in shape. The faces coming towards Pound are soft, living faces; the petals are soft against the hard surface of the tree, just as the faces are bright against the background of the Metro.

Ezra Pound has defined an image as 'an intellectual and emotional complex in an instant of time' and you can see how this poem is such an image. It captures the idea and the feeling, the intellectual and the emotional, and both are linked together within the one picture.

Pound himself has written of how he came to write this poem. He left the Metro at La Concorde and 'saw suddenly a beautiful face, and then another beautiful woman, and I tried all that day to find words for what this had meant to me, and I could not find any words that seemed to me worthy, or as lovely as that sudden emotion.' Later he wrote a thirty-line poem and destroyed it. Six months after that, he wrote a poem half that length; a year later, he made the haiku-like poem 'In a Station of the Metro'.

The above observations on this poem are far longer than the poem itself, but poetry is compression and intensity. So much is being said in such a short space that any discussion of a poem will require expansion and explanation. What is most important is that you feel comfortable and at ease with poetry. You speak the language in which it is written and this allows us to be closer to poetry and literature than any other art form; the words are ours already or, as we read, they become ours as well as the poet's. There may be no one single, definitive response, explanation or interpretation to a poem, but there are wrongheaded ones. Take care and then the private dialogue between you and the poem, the class discussion, the personal study of the text become rewarding and enriching experiences.

●

The philosophy behind this Leaving Certificate English course is 'knowledge made, not knowledge received'. In other words, you are expected to take an active, not a passive, part in the learning process. The knowledge, insight and understanding gained by you is more enjoyable and memorable than the knowledge presented to you by another. That is to say that if we had the time and inclination a library of books would educate us well if we were willing and enthusiastic readers. However, reality is otherwise. Most of us find a system and a structure, such as classroom and school, necessary, if not vital – initially at any rate. So we go to school and find ourselves in English class studying poems and poets and poetry.

Each year, young people worldwide study poetry in school. Poetry is an art form that exists in every known language. It is also known that only a small percentage of people continue to read poetry throughout their adult life, despite the fact that many enjoy it and remember it from school. But this is changing. Poetry readings now attract very large audiences. More poetry books are being sold; occasionally, poetry books even become best-sellers. *Birthday Letters* by Ted Hughes, for example, sold over 120,000 copies in one year, while 200,000 hardback copies of Seamus Heaney's translation of *Beowulf* were bought in 2000.

●

Silence and slow time are not things that we associate with the way we live today. Yet silence and slow time are probably the two most important things when it comes to the intensely private experience of reading poetry. There are specifically public poems as well of course. When President Mary McAleese was inaugurated, she quoted from Christopher Logue's poem 'Come to the Edge'. On 11 November 2004 in her Re-Inaugural speech, President McAleese ended with a quotation from a poem by Seamus Heaney, a poem which had been written especially to mark the expansion, six months earlier, of the European Union on 1 May: 'Move lips, move minds and make new meanings flare'. Michael D. Higgins, Ireland's ninth president, is himself a published poet. His *New and Selected Poems* was published in 2011.

Poetry does not offer easy answers or solutions, but it does allow us to experience emotions. It does not lessen our fear and confusions and anger, but it helps us to accept our anger, confusions and fears, and, in Richard Bernstein's words, we find in literature 'a difficult sort of comfort' because great literature 'refuses to provide comfort that is 'false' or 'saccharine''. Likewise, it heightens our experience of positive feelings and, at its best, is life-affirming.

In the film *Invictus*, Nelson Mandela, played by Morgan Freeman, tells the captain of the Springboks rugby team Francois Pienaar that his favourite poem is William Ernest Henley's 'Invictus'. When one remembers that Mandela was imprisoned for twenty-seven years for opposing apartheid, eighteen of which were spent on Robben Island, it is easy to see why such a poem sustained him during his imprisonment:

Invictus

Out of the night that covers me,
Black as the Pit from pole to pole,
I thank whatever gods may be
For my unconquerable soul.

In the fell clutch of circumstance
I have not winced nor cried aloud.
Under the bludgeonings of chance
My head is bloody but unbowed.

Beyond this place of wrath and tears
Looms but the horror of the shade,
And yet the menace of the years
Finds, and shall find me, unafraid.

It matters not how strait the gate,
How charged with punishments the scroll,
I am the master of my fate:
I am the captain of my soul.

William Ernest Henley (1849–1903)

This book provides you with the texts, the most important things of all. You may find the critical apparatus of some use, but absolutely nothing can replace the lively, engaged, discursive atmosphere in a classroom where poems and poets are discussed between teacher and student and student and student, or the careful reading of the poems and thinking done by you in private. It is hoped that you will return again and again to these wonderful poems and that long after you have left school, a poet's way of seeing, a poet's way of saying will remain with you. In an age such as ours, where we often demand and expect instant gratification, the reading and re-reading of poetry is sometimes viewed as an unusual and strange activity. It is also one of the most valuable, enriching and stimulating things you could do. And it can be, as Wallace Stevens reminds us, an adventure.

Niall MacMonagle

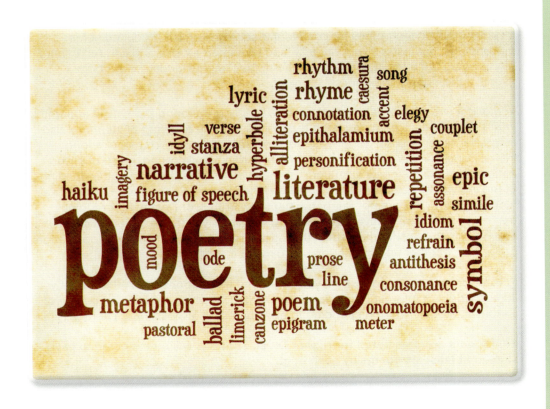

How To Use This Book

There are two compulsory poetry questions on **Paper II** of the Leaving Certificate English course: **Prescribed Poetry** and the **Unseen Poem**. Read the prescribed poems closely, preferably aloud. Then read the poems again (with the aid of the dictionary or glossary if necessary). Think about the poems and talk about the poems. Re-read the poems until you feel comfortable with them. There is no substitute for knowing the poems well; reading the poems and thinking about the poems is the most important of all. The questions beneath each poem will direct you towards some important aspects of the text. Later, you may wish to read the Biographical Notes and the Critical Commentary. These might help clarify your own thinking. Finally, you should find writing on the texts a very good way of finding out how much you understand.

There has been a long and interesting discussion regarding the relevance of biographical detail, glossary, background and so on to the poem. In 1929, I. A. Richards published an important and influential book called *Practical Criticism*. It was based on an experiment in which he gave his students at Cambridge a series of unsigned poems for comment. Such an exercise produced some misreadings, but in itself was valuable and promoted a close and careful reading of the poem. As a result, 'practical criticism' became a standard classroom exercise throughout the English-speaking world.

You might wish to adopt this method and, simply by ignoring the critical apparatus in this textbook, such an approach is possible. But the teaching of literature also allows for other approaches. If you met a person during the course of a long journey and that person withheld details regarding background, place of birth, nationality, religion, politics, influences, then your knowledge and understanding of the individual would be constrained and incomplete. So too with a poem. The more we know, the greater our understanding. Professor Declan Kiberd thinks that every text should have a context and that to stay with the 'practical criticism' approach is to become the ostrich that sticks its head in the sand and looks at one grain, then another and then attempts to make a connection between them.

For the Unseen Poetry question, you might find the response to 'A Blessing' by James Wright of interest. There is also an Appendix which includes an outline of various strategies when responding to any poem and a Glossary of Literary Terms.

Eight poets are prescribed for Higher Level. Students will be expected to have studied **at least six poems** by each poet.

American spelling has been retained where appropriate.

Prescribed Poets and Poems
at Higher Level
Part I

Elizabeth Bishop
(1911–1979)

Contents	Page

The Overview

These ten poems by Elizabeth Bishop reveal many of the most striking characteristics of her work: her eye for detail, her interest in travel and different places (Brazil; Nova Scotia; Worcester, Massachusetts), her apparently conversational tone, her command of internal rhyme, her use of repetition, her interest in strict poetic forms (the sonnet and the sestina), childhood memories, identity, loss.

The world which Bishop describes in her poetry is vivid and particular. Colm Tóibín says of Elizabeth Bishop that 'She began with the idea that little is known and that much is puzzling' (*On Elizabeth Bishop*, Princeton University Press, 2015). She is so intent on accurate description that often a detail is qualified and clarified within the poem. In Mexican-British poet Michael Schmidt's words, 'the voice affirms, hesitates, corrects itself; the image comes clear to us as it came clear to her, a process of adjusting perception until the thing is seen. Or the feeling is released.' For example, in 'The Fish' she tells us 'his gills were breathing in/ the terrible oxygen/ — the frightening gills,' fresh and crisp with blood,/ that can cut so badly' or that the eyes of the fish 'shifted a little', and then the more precise observation: ' — It was more like the tipping/ of an object toward the light'.

Bishop is a sympathetic observer and it has been remarked that she asks us 'to focus not on her but *with* her'. She looks at the fish, imagines its insides – 'the coarse white flesh/ packed in like feathers,/ the big bones and the little bones'; she sings hymns to the seal in 'At the Fishhouses'; she is concerned for the 'piercing cry/ and panic' of the armadillo; she finds love is present in the unlikely setting of a dirty filling station. When she uses 'I' in her poetry, it is never alienating or distancing. Somehow she makes the reader feel at ease. The poems as we read them are working out something.

The poetry is not always explicitly autobiographical but Bishop, an outsider for much of her life, writes indirectly in 'The Prodigal' of the outsider and later, in the explicitly autobiographical 'In the Waiting Room', she names herself ('you are an *Elizabeth*') and charts the sense of her child's mind realising her uniqueness and identity. 'Sestina' is also autobiographical, in that it tells of a home without a mother and father. Bishop only wrote about her childhood experiences late in life: 'Sestina', 'First Death in Nova Scotia', and 'In the Waiting Room' all date from when Bishop was in her fifties. She captures in them the confusion and complexities of childhood, its terror, panic and alienation. In 'First Death in Nova Scotia', she pieces together, as a child's mind would, the details, in order to understand them: 'Arthur's coffin was/ a little frosted cake,/ and the red-eyed loon eyed it/ from his white, frozen lake.'

Bishop preferred geography to history. It is significant that she remembers reading *National Geographic* in 'In the Waiting Room'. The title of her first book, *North & South*, contains the idea of opposites, but opposites that co-exist. Yet her descriptions of place are never just descriptions of place. Morality, history and politics are also evident in Bishop's landscapes. In 'Questions of Travel', Brazil and its otherness prompt Bishop to ask if it's right to watch strangers in another country. She dwells on the country's traditions ('In another country the clogs would all be tested'), religious influences ('a bamboo church of Jesuit baroque'), history ('the weak calligraphy of songbirds' cages').

Not only Bishop's eye but also her ear is finely attuned to the nuance of language. For example, she makes music in unusual and interesting rhyme patterns. In the closing lines of 'The Bight', the ear responds to sounds:

> and brings up a dripping **jawful** of marl.
> All the untidy activity continues,
> **awful** but cheer**ful**.

Rhyme (end rhyme, internal rhyme) and repetition are also used effectively. Bishop's tone is immediate ('Be careful with that match!'), often seemingly conversational ('There are too many waterfalls here'), relaxed ('He was curious about me. He was interested in music') or self-deprecating ('What childishness is it that while there's a breath of life/ in our bodies, we are determined to rush/ to see the sun the other way around?'). Bishop once wrote in a notebook that 'our nature consists in motion; complete rest is death.'

In Elizabeth Bishop's poetry, there is self-discovery, a sense of difference, moments of heightened awareness, a strong sense of here and now, an absence of any religious belief but a belief in the mystery of knowledge 'flowing and flown'. In 'At the Fishhouses', what begins as accurate and gradual description of landscape gives way to a downward movement towards the dark, cold centre of meaning, here imagined as deep beneath the ocean surface and something which we can never know or understand fully.

In Bishop, the act and the art of writing bring shape and order to experience. In 'Questions of Travel', she describes the traveller taking a notebook and writing. The use of 'we' in the poem and the way in which every traveller is contained in 'the traveller' allows everyone to enter into the experience. This record of thought and feeling is what Bishop herself does in her poems. She was interested in form: the sonnet and the sestina are very formal, but in other poems where the structure and rhythm may not be obvious at first, there is often a very fine command and control.

Biographical Notes

 An only child, Elizabeth Bishop was born on 8 February 1911, in Worcester, Massachusetts, and her father died of Bright's disease the following October, when she was eight months old. Her mother was deeply affected by the death and spent the following five years in and out of nursing homes and mental hospitals, moving between Worcester, Boston, and Great Village, her hometown, in Nova Scotia, Canada. In 1916, when Elizabeth Bishop was five, her mother was permanently confined in Dartmouth Hospital in Nova Scotia and she never saw her again.

Bishop was brought up by relatives. First by her maternal grandparents in Nova Scotia (from spring 1916 to September 1917, returning every summer for two months until 1923), and later by relations in Massachusetts.

Bishop's Nova Scotia childhood is captured in 'First Death in Nova Scotia' and 'Sestina', both written when she was in her fifties. Though 'Sestina' describes childhood anxiety, Bishop, elsewhere, has spoken kindly of her grandparents who were simple, loving and conservative people. Her grandfather was a deacon in the Baptist church and her grandmother used to sing hymns to the young Elizabeth. These were her first introduction to poetry. Later she stayed with her father's relations in Worcester and her aunt Maud, her mother's sister, in Boston. It was here that she first read the Victorian poets and learnt many poems by heart during the many days she spent ill in bed. It was here too, at the age of eight, that Bishop began to write poetry and prose. Looking back, she described her early years with relatives as a time when she was 'always a sort of guest', adding, 'I think I've always felt like that.'

As a child she had weak lungs and suffered from eczema, bronchitis and asthma. These and other lung-related illnesses were to bother her for much of her adult life. Her wealthy paternal grandparents paid for Elizabeth to attend boarding school but Bishop, when she stayed with them, was always uncomfortable in their luxurious home and it was here that she first suffered asthma attacks.

In 1928, Elizabeth Bishop published her first poems in the school's literary magazine. She was seventeen. In her school essays from this time she wrote about things that were to matter to her for the rest of her life: her love of the sea, islands, the seashore, and the need to travel. When she was twelve, Bishop won a $5 gold piece, awarded by the American Legion for an essay on 'Americanism'.

The opening sentence was quoted by Bishop in 1961 and she said of it that it seems to have been prophetic, indicating directions taken later in life and work: 'From the icy regions of the frozen north to the waving palm trees of the burning south....'

After high school, in the autumn of 1930, Bishop went to Vassar intending to be a composer but, at Vassar, music meant that you had to perform in public once a month and this terrified her. She gave up the piano and majored in English literature instead. Her other subjects included music, history, religion, zoology and Greek.

On 16 March 1934, the Vassar College Librarian arranged for Bishop, a young and enthusiastic admirer of Marianne Moore ('I hadn't known poetry could be like that; I took to it immediately'), to meet the poet on the right-hand bench outside the reading-room of the New York Public Library. It was the beginning of an important literary friendship. Moore became Bishop's mentor. She was, says one of Bishop's biographers, 'the most important single influence on Elizabeth Bishop's poetic practice and career'. What has been called Moore's 'meticulous taste for fact' was certainly an influence. The seventeenth-century poet George Herbert, Protestant hymns, Cowper and Wordsworth are other important influences. Like Wordsworth's, many of her poems contain a solitary figure, but George Herbert (1593–1633) was the poet she admired most and it is thought that Herbert strongly influenced Bishop's purity of line.

She left Vassar in June 1934 (Bishop's mother had died that May) and, determined to be a writer, moved to New York. She kept a notebook and that summer her entries record several trips to the sea and anticipate many of her poems, including 'The Fish' and 'At the Fishhouses'.

In December 1934, Bishop was so ill with asthma that she spent two weeks in bed. Alone on New Year's Eve she sat on the floor of her apartment, a map of the North Atlantic before her, and she wrote her poem 'The Map'. It is the first poem in her first collection, *North & South*, first in *The Complete Poems*, and it marks her first real signature as a poet.

Between 1935 and 1951, Elizabeth Bishop led an unsettled, restless life. In the poet Andrew Motion's words, Bishop was 'energetically nomadic'. Mark Strand, the American poet, says that for Bishop there was 'always the possibility of finding a place for herself', adding that 'if we have a home why travel?' She travelled to Europe (Belgium, France, England, Spain, Ireland, Italy), visited North Africa, spent a year in Washington as poetry consultant at the Library of Congress, lived in Key West in Florida, lived in Mexico and New York, but from 1952 to 1971 she considered Brazil her home, where she lived with her partner Lota de Macedo Soares. They lived in Rio de Janeiro and Petropolis, and Bishop eventually bought a house of her own in Ouro Preto. It was an eighteenth-century colonial house and she named it Casa Mariana after Marianne Moore.

She gave very few readings: once in 1947 at Wellesley College, two months after her first book appeared, when she was sick for days in anticipation; again in Washington in 1949, when she was sick again. And then she didn't read publicy for twenty-six years. She survived on grants, fellowships and the generosity of friends and, when she returned to the United States from Brazil in 1970, she took a teaching post at Harvard and later at New York University. She returned permanently to the United States in 1972, living for a time in Seattle and San Francisco. She spent her final years in Boston.

Bishop won the Pulitzer Prize in 1956, the National Book Award in 1969, and the Neustadt International Prize for Literature in 1976, but, in Eavan Boland's words, Bishop 'disliked the swagger and visibility of literary life'. In an interview in 1978 Bishop remarked that 'There's nothing more embarrassing than being a poet really... There must be an awful core of ego somewhere for you to set yourself up to write poetry. I've never felt it, but it must be there'. Her friend, the American poet James Merrill, speaking of Elizabeth Bishop, spoke of her 'instinctive, modest, lifelong impersonations of an ordinary woman, someone who during the day did errands, went to the beach, would perhaps that evening jot a phrase or two inside the nightclub matchbook before returning to the dance floor. Thus the later glimpses of her playing – was it poker? – with Neruda in a Mexican hotel, or pingpong with Octavio Paz in Cambridge, or getting Robert Duncan high on grass – "for the first time" – in San Francisco, or teaching Frank Bidart the wildflowers in Maine.'

Elizabeth Bishop, always a traveller, spent the last years of her life in her native Massachusetts, where she taught at Harvard. She was alone in her apartment on Lewis Wharf when she died of a cerebral aneurysm on 6 October 1979.

Elizabeth Bishop disapproved of biography; she considered it 'finally just unpleasant'. In Eavan Boland's words, she was 'shy and hidden' and preferred to remain that way. 'Elizabeth Bishop was known for not wishing to be known' was how Ian Hamilton put it; and Marianne Moore said that Bishop was 'spectacular in being unspectacular'. 'The shy perfectionist with her painter's eye' is how the writer Derek Mahon described her. Helen Vendler thought Elizabeth Bishop 'A foreigner everywhere, and, perhaps, with everyone.' But the poems are born of the life, and biographical details can deepen our understanding and appreciation of the poems and our admiration for the poet.

In one of Elizabeth Bishop's finest poems, 'Crusoe in England', she imagines Robinson Crusoe lonely for his island and Friday; and, remembering his time there, she writes:

> The sun set in the sea; the same odd sun
> rose from the sea,
> and there was one of it and one of me.

Here we have the voice of Robinson Crusoe, and the voice of Bishop, and the voice of all other lonely, observing, travellers. It is significant that Bishop was attracted to a figure like Crusoe, an isolate, someone ill-at-ease having returned to society. Bishop's sexuality and her struggle with alcohol were part of her own sense of isolation. In a letter written in 1948 to Robert Lowell, she said 'When you write my epitaph, you must say I was the loneliest person who ever lived.' Her later work suggests a happier person, but her life was never uncomplicatedly happy.

One other thing – read Bishop's poem called 'Poem' sometime. It maps a reader's experience of the reading of poetry itself – that initial distance between reader and poem, possibly indifference, then the gradual, awakening recognition and the final realisation that both reader and poet share a common humanity.

Bishop's *The Complete Poems 1927–1972* contains just over 140 poems and some thirty of these are translations from French, Spanish and Portuguese. She wrote very slowly, very carefully, sometimes pinning bits of paper on her walls, leaving blank spaces ('with gaps / and empties for the unimagined phrases' is how Robert Lowell described it in a poem for her), waiting for the right word. Some of her poems were several years in the making. She worked on 'The Moose' for over twenty-five years, yet it seems effortless as all good poetry does. She writes a poetry which echoes the rhythms of natural speech and her rhymes are not always easy to detect. End rhymes and cross rhymes or slant rhymes create a special and effective music. And what Yeats says of all true poetry is true of Bishop:

'A line will take us hours maybe;
Yet if it does not seem a moment's thought,
Our stitching and unstitching has been naught.'

POEMS

Dates refer to the year of composition. The poems as they are printed here, are in the order in which they were written.

The Fish

I caught a tremendous fish
and held him beside the boat
half out of water, with my hook
fast in a corner of his mouth.
He didn't fight.   5
He hadn't fought at all.
He hung a grunting weight,
battered and venerable
and homely. Here and there
his brown skin hung in strips   10
like ancient wallpaper,
and its pattern of darker brown
was like wallpaper:
shapes like full-blown roses
stained and lost through age.   15
He was speckled with barnacles,
fine rosettes of lime,
and infested
with tiny white sea-lice,
and underneath two or three   20
rags of green weed hung down.
While his gills were breathing in
the terrible oxygen
— the frightening gills,
fresh and crisp with blood,   25
that can cut so badly —
I thought of the coarse white flesh
packed in like feathers,
the big bones and the little bones,
the dramatic reds and blacks   30
of his shiny entrails,
and the pink swim-bladder
like a big peony.

I looked into his eyes
which were far larger than mine   35
but shallower, and yellowed,
the irises backed and packed
with tarnished tinfoil
seen through the lenses
of old scratched isinglass.   40
They shifted a little, but not
to return my stare.
— It was more like the tipping
of an object toward the light.
I admired his sullen face,   45
the mechanism of his jaw,
and then I saw
that from his lower lip
— if you could call it a lip —
grim, wet, and weaponlike,   50
hung five old pieces of fish-line,
or four and a wire leader
with the swivel still attached,
with all their five big hooks
grown firmly in his mouth.   55
A green line, frayed at the end
where he broke it, two heavier lines,
and a fine black thread
still crimped from the strain and snap
when it broke and he got away.   60
Like medals with their ribbons
frayed and wavering,
a five-haired beard of wisdom
trailing from his aching jaw.
I stared and stared   65
and victory filled up
the little rented boat,
from the pool of bilge
where oil had spread a rainbow

around the rusted engine   70
to the bailer rusted orange,
the sun-cracked thwarts,
the oarlocks on their strings,
the gunnels — until everything
was rainbow, rainbow, rainbow!   75
And I let the fish go.

📖 Glossary

Line 1 *tremendous*: it may seem unnecessary to explain the word tremendous, but poets are attuned to the nuance of words and the dictionary is a vital companion for the reader of poetry. Tremendous does not only mean immense; more accurately, it means that which excites trembling or awe from the Latin *tremere* to tremble, tremble at; awe-inspiring.

Line 8 *venerable*: worthy of reverence, aged-looking.

Line 9 *homely*: familiar or plain/ugly (in American English).

Line 17 *rosettes*: rose shaped patterns – knots of radiating loops of ribbon or the like in concentric arrangement.

Line 25 *crisp*: firm.

Line 31 *entrails*: the internal parts of the fish.

Line 33 *peony*: a large showy crimson or white globular flower.

Line 40 *isinglass*: a whitish semi-transparent gelatin substance used for windows, originally got from the swim bladders of some freshwater fish.

Line 45 *sullen*: showing irritation or ill humour by a gloomy silence or reserve.

Line 52 *leader*: short piece of wire connecting fishhook and fishline.

Line 53 *swivel*: a ring or link that turns round on a pin or neck.

Line 54 *five big hooks*: Bonnie Costello, in her book *Elizabeth Bishop: Questions of Mastery*, says, 'Five wounds on a fish make him a Christ figure but the epiphany he brings the poet has nothing otherworldly about it.'

Line 59 *crimped*: shrunk and curled.

Line 68 *bilge*: filth that collects in the broadest part of the bottom of a boat.

Line 71 *bailer*: bucket for scooping water out of the boat.

Line 72 *thwarts*: the seats or benches for rowers.

Line 73 *oarlocks*: a rowlock – metal devices to hold the oars, attached by 'string' to the boat itself.

Line 74 *gunnels*: or gunwale – the upper edges of a boat's side.

> In a letter, Bishop wrote: 'With "The Fish", that's exactly how it happened. It was in Key West, and I did it just as the poem says. That was in 1938. Oh, but I did change one thing; the poem says he had five hooks hanging from his mouth, but actually he had only three. Sometimes a poem makes its own demands. But I always try to stick as much as possible to what really happened when I describe something in the poem.'

? Questions

1. Between the opening line, 'I caught a tremendous fish', and the poem's final line, 'And I let the fish go', is a detailed and interesting account of Bishop's response to the incident. How does the speaker feel about catching this 'tremendous fish'? Which words and phrases, in your opinion, best capture her feelings? Comment on Bishop's use of 'him' and 'he'.

2. How does the fish react when caught this time? How and why does the poet empathise with the fish?

3. Comment on Bishop's use of language. What is the effect of repetition? Which lines or images are particularly vivid? Discuss images such as 'ancient wallpaper' and 'big peony' and say what they contribute to the poem.

4. 'I looked into his eyes …', says the poet in line 34. What happens?

5. How would you describe the speaker's tone? Look particularly at lines such as '— It was more like …' or '— if you could call it …'

6. What do you think Bishop means by 'victory' in line 66? How would you describe the poet's mood in the closing line?

7. Does the ending of the poem come as a surprise? Give reasons for your answer. Why do you think the speaker 'let the fish go'? What does this poem say about power and control?

At the Fishhouses

Although it is a cold evening,
down by one of the fishhouses
an old man sits netting,
his net, in the gloaming almost invisible,
a dark purple-brown,   5
and his shuttle worn and polished.
The air smells so strong of codfish
it makes one's nose run and one's eyes water.
The five fishhouses have steeply peaked roofs
and narrow, cleated gangplanks slant up   10
to storerooms in the gables
for the wheelbarrows to be pushed up and down on.
All is silver: the heavy surface of the sea,
swelling slowly as if considering spilling over,
is opaque, but the silver of the benches,   15
the lobster pots, and masts, scattered
among the wild jagged rocks,
is of an apparent translucence
like the small old buildings with an emerald moss
growing on their shoreward walls.   20
The big fish tubs are completely lined
with layers of beautiful herring scales
and the wheelbarrows are similarly plastered
with creamy iridescent coats of mail,
with small iridescent flies crawling on them.   25
Up on the little slope behind the houses,
set in the sparse bright sprinkle of grass,
is an ancient wooden capstan,
cracked, with two long bleached handles
and some melancholy stains, like dried blood,   30
where the ironwork has rusted.
The old man accepts a Lucky Strike.
He was a friend of my grandfather.

We talk of the decline in the population
and of codfish and herring   35
while he waits for a herring boat to come in.
There are sequins on his vest and on his thumb.
He has scraped the scales, the principal beauty,
from unnumbered fish with that black old knife,
the blade of which is almost worn away.   40

Down at the water's edge, at the place
where they haul up the boats, up the long ramp
descending into the water, thin silver
tree trunks are laid horizontally
across the gray stones, down and down   45
at intervals of four or five feet.

Cold dark deep and absolutely clear,
element bearable to no mortal,
to fish and to seals . . . One seal particularly
I have seen here evening after evening.   50
He was curious about me. He was interested in music;
like me a believer in total immersion,
so I used to sing him Baptist hymns.
I also sang 'A Mighty Fortess Is Our God.'
He stood up in the water and regarded me   55
steadily, moving his head a little.
Then he would disappear, then suddenly emerge
almost in the same spot, with a sort of shrug
as if it were against his better judgment.
Cold dark deep and absolutely clear,   60
the clear gray icy water . . . Back, behind us,
the dignified tall firs begin.
Bluish, associating with their shadows,
a million Christmas trees stand
waiting for Christmas. The water seems suspended   65
above the rounded gray and blue-gray stones.

I have seen it over and over, the same sea, the same,
slightly, indifferently swinging above the stones,
icily free above the stones,
above the stones and then the world.   70
If you should dip your hand in,
your wrist would ache immediately,
your bones would begin to ache and your hand would burn
as if the water were a transmutation of fire
that feeds on stones and burns with a dark gray flame.   75
If you tasted it, it would first taste bitter,
then briny, then surely burn your tongue.
It is like what we imagine knowledge to be:
dark, salt, clear, moving, utterly free,
drawn from the cold hard mouth   80
of the world, derived from the rocky breasts
forever, flowing and drawn, and since
our knowledge is historical, flowing, and flown.

Glossary

Line 4 gloaming: twilight, dusk.

Line 6 shuttle: an instrument used for shooting the thread of the woof between the threads of the warp in weaving.

Line 10 cleated: having pieces of wood nailed on to give footing.

Line 10 gangplank: a long, narrow, movable wooden plank/walkway.

Line 15 opaque: dark, dull, cannot be seen through, not transparent.

Line 18 translucence: when light shines through.

Line 24 iridescent: coloured like the rainbow, glittering with changing colours.

Line 28 capstan: a machine with a cylindrical drum around which rope is wound and used for hauling.

Line 32 Lucky Strike: an American brand of cigarette.

Line 37 sequins: small, circular, thin, glittering, sparkling ornament on a dress.

Line 52 total immersion: a form of baptism practised by certain Christian groups.

Line 63 associating: uniting.

Line 74 transmutation: a change from one form into another.

Line 77 briny: very salty water.

Line 83 historical: pertaining to the course of events.

? Questions

1. This poem begins with a particular place and then it becomes a poem which explores many complex and abstract ideas such as knowledge and meaning. Identify the words and phrases that allow the reader to picture the fishhouses in detail. Comment on Bishop's use of colour.

2. Can you suggest why Bishop has divided 'At the Fishhouses' into three sections? How would you sum up what is happening in each section? Which of the three sections is the most personal?

3. There are three solitary figures in the poem: the fisherman, the speaker and the seal. Imagine the poem without the fisherman and the seal and discuss what would be lost.

4. The poem moves from description towards meditation. Is it possible to identify where the poem becomes meditative or philosophical? Explain your answer.

5. 'Cold dark deep and absolutely clear,/the clear gray icy water . . .' (lines 60–61) refer not only to the ocean. What similarities, according to Bishop, are there between water and knowledge?

6. There are many religious references in the poem. Identify these and say whether you think the poem is religious or not.

7. What do you think Bishop means when she writes 'and then the world' (line 70)?

8. The poem ends with an image of knowledge. How would you describe Bishop's understanding of human experience as it is revealed to us in this poem?

The Bight
[On my birthday]

At low tide like this how sheer the water is.
White, crumbling ribs of marl protrude and glare
and the boats are dry, the pilings dry as matches.
Absorbing, rather than being absorbed,
the water in the bight doesn't wet anything,   5
the color of the gas flame turned as low as possible.
One can smell it turning to gas; if one were Baudelaire
one could probably hear it turning to marimba music.
The little ocher dredge at work off the end of the dock
already plays the dry perfectly off-beat claves.   10
The birds are outsize. Pelicans crash
into this peculiar gas unnecessarily hard,
it seems to me, like pickaxes,
rarely coming up with anything to show for it,
and going off with humorous elbowings.   15
Black-and-white man-of-war birds soar
on impalpable drafts
and open their tails like scissors on the curves
or tense them like wishbones, till they tremble.
The frowsy sponge boats keep coming in   20
with the obliging air of retrievers,
bristling with jackstraw gaffs and hooks
and decorated with bobbles of sponges.
There is a fence of chicken wire along the dock
where, glinting like little plowshares,   25
the blue-gray shark tails are hung up to dry
for the Chinese-restaurant trade.
Some of the little white boats are still piled up
against each other, or lie on their sides, stove in,
and not yet salvaged, if they ever will be,
        from the last bad storm,   30
like torn-open, unanswered letters.

The bight is littered with old correspondences.
Click. Click. Goes the dredge,
and brings up a dripping jawful of marl.
All the untidy activity continues,   35
awful but cheerful.

Glossary

Title The Bight: a bay formed by a bend in a coastline, a wide bay. The bight here is Garrison Bight in Key West, Florida.

Subtitle: 'on my birthday' – 8 February 1948 – Bishop was 37. Personal details in Elizabeth Bishop's poetry are rare and most often not explicitly expressed. By placing 'On my birthday' beneath a title that names a place, Bishop is suggesting both place and the passing of time.

Line 1 sheer: transparently thin; smooth, calm; bright.

Line 2 marl: deposit consisting of clay and lime.

Line 3 pilings: sharp posts or stakes, a heavy timber driven into the ground, especially under water, to form a foundation.

Line 7 Baudelaire: French poet (1821–1867).

Line 8 marimba: African xylophone adopted by Central Americans and Jazz musicians.

Line 9 ocher dredge: yellowish-brown machine used to scoop/draw up silt.

Line 10 claves: wooden percussion instruments; small wooden cylinders held in the hand and struck together to mark Latin American dance rhythm.

Line 16 man-of-war birds: the frigate-birds – large tropical sea bird with very long wings.

Line 17 impalpable: not perceivable by touch, imperceptible to the touch, not perceptible by the watching poet.

Line 17 drafts: currents of air.

Line 19 wishbones: forked bones in front of the breasts of some birds.

Line 20 frowsy: ill-smelling, offensive, unkempt.

Line 21 retrievers: dogs who have been trained to find and fetch.

Line 22 jackstraw: a short staff, usually set upon the bowsprit or at the bow of a ship on which the flag called the jack is hoisted.

Line 22 gaffs: hooks used especially for landing large fish.

Line 22 hooks: the hooks on a sponge-catching boat to hold the catch.

Line 25 plowshares: the part of a plough that cuts and turns the soil.

Line 27 Chinese-restaurant trade: shark tails are used in Chinese cooking. Shark-tail soup is a delicacy.

Line 29 stove in: broken — especially in the hull or lowermost portion.

Line 32 old correspondences: cf. line 7 — Baudelaire wrote a sonnet 'Correspondences' in which he speaks of man as one who, while wandering among Nature, wanders among symbols. Baudelaire says that the perfumes of Nature are as sweet as the sound of the oboe, as green as the prairies, as fresh as the caress of a child. Bishop responds in a similar way to the natural world in her poem. Baudelaire in his theory of correspondences promised connections or links by means of poetry between the physical and spiritual worlds.

This is a Bishop poem which, like 'At the Fishhouses', begins with objective description and gradually gives way to a more personal, private world. The objective and subjective are side by side in the poem's title and subtitle. A bight is a public place; a birthday is personal and an occasion for thinking more intensely about oneself, one's birth, one's life and death. In the poem, Bishop is on her own; she celebrates her birthday by celebrating the bight. The poem overall may not seem that personal, but the choice of subject matter, the way of seeing, the words used, the mood conveyed, all convey Bishop's personal view.

? Questions

1. Like 'At the Fishhouses', this is another place poem. What is usually associated with a birthday? Why do you think Bishop included the detail of her birthday here? Does it alter the poem? Explain.

2. In many of her poems, Bishop describes in an atmospheric way a particular place. Discuss how she does that in 'The Bight'. Pay particular attention to lines 7 and 8.

3. Is Bishop enjoying what she sees? Support your answer by reference to the text. Does it matter that she is alone in the poem?

4. Consider all the action and movement described in the poem. What is the significance of the dredge? What do you think Bishop means by the phrase 'untidy activity' in the closing lines?

5. Some sentences here are four or five lines long; others consist of one word. Examine and discuss how the sentence length and sentence organisation contribute to the poem's movement.

6. Is the bight in any way symbolic?

The Prodigal

The brown enormous odor he lived by
was too close, with its breathing and thick hair,
for him to judge. The floor was rotten; the sty
was plastered halfway up with glass-smooth dung.
Light-lashed, self-righteous, above moving snouts,   5
the pigs' eyes followed him, a cheerful stare –
even to the sow that always ate her young –
till, sickening, he leaned to scratch her head.
But sometimes mornings after drinking bouts
(he hid the pints behind a two-by-four),   10
the sunrise glazed the barnyard mud with red;
the burning puddles seemed to reassure.
And then he thought he almost might endure
his exile yet another year or more.

But evenings the first star came to warn.   15
The farmer whom he worked for came at dark
to shut the cows and horses in the barn
beneath their overhanging clouds of hay,
with pitchforks, faint forked lightnings, catching light,
safe and companionable as in the Ark.   20
The pigs stuck out their little feet and snored.
The lantern – like the sun, going away –
laid on the mud a pacing aureole.
Carrying a bucket along a slimy board,
he felt the bats' uncertain staggering flight,   25
his shuddering insights, beyond his control,
touching him. But it took him a long time
finally to make his mind up to go home.

Glossary

Title: The poem was originally referred to by Bishop as 'Prodigal Son'.

The Prodigal: A reference to the story of the Prodigal Son in the Bible as told by St. Luke, Chapter 15: A certain man had two sons and the younger of them said to his father, Father, give me the portion of goods that falleth to me. And he divided unto them his living. And not many days after the younger son gathered all together and took his journey into a far country, and there wasted his substance with riotous living. And when he had spent all, there arose a mighty famine in that land; and he began to be in want. And he went and joined himself to a citizen of that country; and he sent him into his fields to feed swine. And he would fain have filled his belly with the husks that the swine did eat: and no man gave unto him. And when he came to himself, he said, How many hired servants of my father's have bread enough and to spare, and I perish with hunger! I will arise and go to my father, and will say unto him, Father, I have sinned against heaven, and before thee, and am no more worthy to be called thy son: make me as one of thy hired servants. And he arose, and came to his father. But when he was yet a great way off, his father saw him, and had compassion, and ran, and fell on his neck, and kissed him. (King James Version).

Title prodigal: wasteful, extravagant.

Line 2 close: stifling, unventilated, oppressive.

Line 10 two-by-four: timber with cross-section, 2 inches by 4 inches.

Line 20 companionable: happily together.

Line 23 aureole: the halo or celestial crown round the head of a pictured martyr or divine figure.

Questions

1. What immediately comes to mind when the words 'prodigal' or 'prodigal son' are mentioned? (Bishop's original title was 'Prodigal Son'.)

2. Look at how the poem is organised and shaped (metre, line length, end-rhyme). Can you suggest a reason why Bishop chose this form?

3. How does Bishop imagine the life of the prodigal son in the first section of the poem? Is it all ugly and hopeless? Give reasons for your answer and quote from the text to support the points you make.

4. What is the effect of the use of 'But' in lines 9, 15 and 27?

5. Comment on the significance of 'sunrise', 'star', 'aureole' and the Biblical reference to the Ark.

6. What is meant by tone? How would you describe the tone in the opening lines? Is there a change of tone in the poem?

7. How do you respond and how do you think Bishop wanted her reader to respond to line 21: 'The pigs stuck out their little feet and snored' (a perfect example of an iambic pentameter)?

8. Comment on Bishop's choice of adjectives: 'enormous', 'glass-smooth', 'cheerful', 'overhanging', 'companionable', 'slimy', 'staggering', 'shuddering' and the power of the last word in the poem. Write a note on any four of these.

Filling Station

Oh, but it is dirty!
– this little filling station,
oil-soaked, oil-permeated
to a disturbing, over-all
black translucency.   5
Be careful with that match!

Father wears a dirty,
oil-soaked monkey suit
that cuts him under the arms,
and several quick and saucy   10
and greasy sons assist him
(it's a family filling station),
all quite thoroughly dirty.

Do they live in the station?
It has a cement porch   15
behind the pumps, and on it
a set of crushed and grease-
impregnated wickerwork;
on the wicker sofa
a dirty dog, quite comfy.   20

Some comic books provide
the only note of color –
of certain color. They lie
upon a big dim doily
draping a taboret   25
(part of the set), beside
a big hirsute begonia.

Why the extraneous plant?
Why the taboret?
Why, oh why, the doily?   30
(Embroidered in daisy stitch
with marguerites, I think,
and heavy with gray crochet.)

Somebody embroidered the doily.
Somebody waters the plant,   35
or oils it, maybe. Somebody
arranges the rows of cans
so that they softly say:
ESSO-SO-SO-SO
to high-strung automobiles.   40
Somebody loves us all.

Glossary

Line 5 translucency: shiny, glossy quality.

Line 8 monkey suit: dungarees, overalls.

Line 18 impregnated: saturated.

Line 24 doily: a small ornamented napkin, often laid under dishes (from Doily or Doiley, a famous haberdasher).

Line 25 taboret: a low seat usually without arms or back/a small drum.

Line 27 hirsute: shaggy, untrimmed.

Line 27 begonia: plant with pink flowers and remarkable unequal-sided coloured leaves.

Line 28 extraneous: of external origin, not belonging, not essential.

Line 31 daisy stitch: a design pattern.

Line 32 marguerites: ox-eye daisies.

Line 33 crochet: knitting done with hooked needle forming intertwined loops.

? Questions

1. What details immediately strike the reader on a first reading? Is this a typical or an atypical Bishop poem? Give reasons for your answer.

2. Lines 1 and 6 end with exclamation marks. How would you describe the tone of the opening stanza? Dismissive? Cautious? Both? Identify the other tones in the poem.

3. How does Bishop convince her reader that the place is indeed 'oil-soaked, oil-permeated' and 'grease-impregnated'?

4. Bishop has been described as a very accurate observer. Where in the poem is this evident? Quote from the poem in support of your answer.

5. Choose any stanza from the poem and show how Bishop creates an inner music in her use of language. Your answer should include a discussion of alliteration, assonance, slant or cross-rhyme.

6. Discuss Bishop's use of repetition in the poem, especially the repetition of 'why' and 'somebody'.

7. Were you surprised by the final line in the poem? How is the line justified within the context of the poem as a whole?

Questions of Travel

There are too many waterfalls here; the crowded streams
hurry too rapidly down to the sea,
and the pressure of so many clouds on the mountaintops
makes them spill over the sides in soft slow-motion,
turning to waterfalls under our very eyes.   5
— For if those streaks, those mile-long, shiny, tearstains,
aren't waterfalls yet,
in a quick age or so, as ages go here,
they probably will be.
But if the streams and clouds keep travelling, travelling,   10
the mountains look like the hulls of capsized ships,
slime-hung and barnacled.

Think of the long trip home.
Should we have stayed at home and thought of here?
Where should we be today?   15
Is it right to be watching strangers in a play
in this strangest of theatres?
What childishness is it that while there's a breath of life
in our bodies, we are determined to rush
to see the sun the other way around?   20
The tiniest green hummingbird in the world?
To stare at some inexplicable old stonework,
inexplicable and impenetrable,
at any view,
instantly seen and always, always delightful?   25
Oh, must we dream our dreams
and have them too?
And have we room
for one more folded sunset, still quite warm?

But surely it would have been a pity   30
not to have seen the trees along this road,
really exaggerated in their beauty,

not to have seen them gesturing
like noble pantomimists, robed in pink.
— Not to have had to stop for gas and heard   35
the sad, two-noted, wooden tune
of disparate wooden clogs
carelessly clacking over
a grease-stained filling-station floor.
(In another country the clogs would all be tested.   40
Each pair there would have identical pitch.)
— A pity not to have heard
the other, less primitive music of the fat brown bird
who sings above the broken gasoline pump
in a bamboo church of Jesuit baroque: 45
three towers, five silver crosses.
— Yes, a pity not to have pondered,
blurr'dly and inconclusively,
on what connection can exist for centuries
between the crudest wooden footwear   50
and, careful and finicky,
the whittled fantasies of wooden cages.
— Never to have studied history in
the weak calligraphy of songbirds' cages.
— And never to have had to listen to rain   55
so much like politicians' speeches:
two hours of unrelenting oratory
and then a sudden golden silence
in which the traveller takes a notebook, writes:

'Is it lack of imagination that makes us come
to imagined places, not just stay at home?   60
Or could Pascal have been not entirely right
about just sitting quietly in one's room?

Continent, city, country, society:
the choice is never wide and never free.
And here, or there . . . No. Should we have stayed at home,   65
wherever that may be?'

📖 Glossary

Title: Not only this particular poem but the title of Bishop's third collection.

Line 1 There: Brazil.

Line 11 hulls: framework or body of boats.

Line 22 inexplicable: unable to be explained.

Line 37 disparate: dissimilar, discordant.

Line 45 baroque: an exuberant kind of European architecture which the Jesuits in the seventeenth century introduced into Latin America.

Line 51 finicky: overdone.

Line 52 fantasies: fanciful design.

Line 54 calligraphy: a style of writing but here refers to the style of construction of the cages.

Line 57 unrelenting: persistent.

Line 57 oratory: public speaking.

Line 61 Pascal: French mathematician, physicist and philosopher (1623–1662) who in his *Pensées* wrote: 'I have often said that the sole cause of man's unhappiness is that he does not know how to stay quietly in his room'.

? Questions

1. In the opening section of the poem, Bishop describes a Brazilian landscape. How is a state of flux conveyed? How would you describe her response to it? Give reasons for your answer.

2. In the second section, she uses the pronoun 'we'. Who is she including here? Why is she uneasy about certain aspects of travel? Why does she think travel invasive and childish?

3. Which images do you find striking or interesting in the poem? Does the poem focus on the particular or the general or both? What is the effect of this?

4. 'But surely it would have been a pity ...' begins her justification for travel. Examine how she argues her point. Which details justify her point? Look at her use of the dash and repetition. Is the argument convincing? Why or why not? Is the speaker a sympathetic observer?

5. Bishop suggests that Pascal (line 61), who believed that 'the sole cause of man's unhappiness is that he does not know how to stay quietly in his room', might not have been entirely right. Which viewpoint would you agree with? Give reasons for your answer. Does Bishop put forward a convincing argument?

6. The poem's final italicised section takes the form of an entry in the traveller's notebook, written during 'a sudden golden silence'. What does the traveller conclude in this notebook entry? Why do you think the poem ends with a question mark?

The Armadillo

For Robert Lowell

This is the time of year
when almost every night
the frail, illegal fire balloons appear.
Climbing the mountain height,

rising toward a saint   5
still honored in these parts,
the paper chambers flush and fill with light
that comes and goes, like hearts.

Once up against the sky it's hard
to tell them from the stars —   10
planets, that is — the tinted ones:
Venus going down, or Mars,

or the pale green one. With a wind,
they flare and falter, wobble and toss;
but if it's still they steer between   15
the kite sticks of the Southern Cross,

receding, dwindling, solemnly
and steadily forsaking us,
or, in the downdraft from a peak,
suddenly turning dangerous.   20

Last night another big one fell.
It splattered like an egg of fire
against the cliff behind the house.
The flame ran down. We saw the pair

of owls who nest there flying up   25
and up, their whirling black-and-white
stained bright pink underneath, until
they shrieked up out of sight.

The ancient owls' nest must have burned.
Hastily, all alone,   30
a glistening armadillo left the scene,
rose-flecked, head down, tail down,

and then a baby rabbit jumped out,
short-eared, to our surprise.
So soft! — a handful of intangible ash   35
with fixed, ignited eyes.

Too pretty, dreamlike mimicry!
O falling fire and piercing cry
and panic, and a weak mailed fist
clenched ignorant against the sky!   40

📖 Glossary

Title: the armadillo is a chiefly nocturnal, burrowing animal whose body is encased in bony plates. It is found in southern United States and in Latin America. When captured it rolls itself into a ball and while curled tight it is protected from everything except fire. It is pronounced 'armadeeo' in Spanish. When this poem was first published – in *The New Yorker* on 22 June 1957 – it was called 'The Armadillo – Brazil'. Her friend the American poet Robert Lowell, to whom the poem is dedicated, considered the title wrong at first but later thought 'The Armadillo' right: 'the little creature, given only five lines, runs off with the whole poem'.

Line 1 time of year: June, particularly 24 June which is St. John's Day. This is the shortest day of the year in the Southern Hemisphere, a holy day, and as part of the celebrations balloons are released on St. John's Night and the nights before and after. These were fire balloons and supposedly illegal. The house mentioned in the poem is the house in Petropolis which Bishop shared with Lota de Macedo Soares.

Line 13 the pale green one: the planet Uranus, perhaps.

Line 16 kite sticks: the kite-like formation of the constellation.

Line 16 Southern Cross: constellation visible only in the southern hemisphere.

Line 35 intangible: cannot be touched/cannot be grasped mentally.

Line 37 mimicry: imitating, imitative, especially for amusement.

? Questions

1. The poem describes St. John's day, a religious feast in Brazil, and the practise of releasing fire balloons. Discuss how in the first five stanzas Bishop describes the balloons. Are they viewed as beautiful, or dangerous, or both?

2. Consider line length, stanza and rhyme. What is the effect of the short sentence at line 21 and the short line at line 30?

3. Does our attitude towards the fire balloons change when we read of the owls, the armadillo and the rabbit?

4. The balloons are described, at first, as 'paper chambers ... like hearts'. What does Bishop think of the balloons by the end of the poem? Where is this most evident?

5. Why do you think Bishop chose 'The Armadillo' as her title?

6. The armadillo and the other creatures have been interpreted symbolically as the oppressed, the victimised. Look particularly at lines 39–40. Do you think this is a valid interpretation? Give reasons for your answer.

7. What is being signalled, in your opinion, by the change to italics in the last stanza?

8. How would you describe the poet's tone? Does the tone change?

Sestina

September rain falls on the house.
In the failing light, the old grandmother
sits in the kitchen with the child
beside the Little Marvel Stove,
reading the jokes from the almanac,   5
laughing and talking to hide her tears.

She thinks that her equinoctial tears
and the rain that beats on the roof of the house
were both foretold by the almanac,
but only known to a grandmother.   10
The iron kettle sings on the stove.
She cuts some bread and says to the child,

It's time for tea now; but the child
is watching the teakettle's small hard tears
dance like mad on the hot black stove,   15
the way the rain must dance on the house.
Tidying up, the old grandmother
hangs up the clever almanac

on its string. Birdlike, the almanac
hovers half open above the child,   20
hovers above the old grandmother
and her teacup full of dark brown tears.
She shivers and says she thinks the house
feels chilly, and puts more wood in the stove.

It was to be, says the Marvel Stove.   25
I know what I know, says the almanac.
With crayons the child draws a rigid house
and a winding pathway. Then the child
puts in a man with buttons like tears
and shows it proudly to the grandmother.   30

But secretly, while the grandmother
busies herself about the stove,
the little moons fall down like tears
from between the pages of the almanac
into the flower bed the child   35
has carefully placed in the front of the house.

Time to plant tears, says the almanac.
The grandmother sings to the marvellous stove
and the child draws another inscrutable house.

Glossary

Title Sestina (meaning song of sixes): a rhymed or unrhymed poem with six stanzas of six lines and final triplet, each stanza having the same words to end its lines but in a different order. Lines may be of any length. The final three lines, the triplet, must introduce the six words which end the six preceding stanzas – in this instance, 'tears', 'child', 'almanac', 'stove', 'grandmother', 'house'. The sestina was supposedly invented by Arnaut Daniel in the twelfth century.

The order in which the end-words are re-used is prescribed by a set pattern which is very formal and it has been argued that such rules are so inhibiting that the poem becomes artificial and strained. But, on the other hand, if a poet chooses six key words or ideas or images, then they become vitally important throughout the poem and the accomplished poet can explore in great detail the important relation among all six. The six key words in Elizabeth Bishop's 'Sestina' are: house; grandmother; child; stove; almanac; tears, and many of these are highly charged, significant words in themselves. They become even more powerful in the context of what we know of Bishop's parents and early childhood. This poem was originally titled 'Early Sorrow'.

Line 5 almanac: a register of the days, weeks, months of the year, with astronomical events, anniversaries *et cetera*.

Line 7 equinoctial: at the time of the autumn equinox.

Line 37 inscrutable: that which cannot be searched into and understood.

? Questions

1. Having read the poem through a number of times, study the end word in every line. What is the effect of this? How does Bishop convey sorrow in 'Sestina'?

2. The sestina is a very strict poetic format. Try writing one yourself. What do you learn from the exercise?

3. The poem offers a view of the world from a child's perspective. What details are being pieced together in the child's mind? How can you tell that things are being seen from a child's point of view?

4. Of the six key words in the sestina, which would you consider more important? Give reasons for your choice.

5. The almanac becomes a sinister presence – it 'hovers'. What does this poem say about the passing of time? Why do you think Bishop uses the present tense throughout?

6. Choose any one example of very ordinary language (e.g. 'It's time for tea now') and one example of unusual language and comment on both.

7. What is the significance of the child's drawing in stanza 5? Why does the child draw 'another inscrutable house'?

8. What image of the grandmother emerges from the poem?

9. Discuss what is said and what is left unsaid in this poem.

First Death in Nova Scotia

In the cold, cold parlor
my mother laid out Arthur
beneath the chromographs:
Edward, Prince of Wales,
with Princess Alexandra,   5
and King George with Queen Mary.
Below them on the table
stood a stuffed loon
shot and stuffed by Uncle
Arthur, Arthur's father.   10

Since Uncle Arthur fired
a bullet into him,
he hadn't said a word.
He kept his own counsel
on his white, frozen lake,   15
the marble-topped table.
His breast was deep and white,
cold and caressable:
his eyes were red glass,
much to be desired.   20

'Come,' said my mother,
'Come and say good-bye
to your little cousin Arthur.'
I was lifted up and given
one lily of the valley   25
to put in Arthur's hand.
Arthur's coffin was
a little frosted cake,
and the red-eyed loon eyed it
from his white, frozen lake.   30

Arthur was very small.
He was all white, like a doll
that hadn't been painted yet.
Jack Frost had started to paint him
the way he always painted   35
the Maple Leaf (Forever).
He had just begun on his hair,
a few red strokes, and then
Jack Frost had dropped the brush
and left him white, forever.   40

The gracious royal couples
were warm in red and ermine;
their feet were well wrapped up
in the ladies' ermine trains.
They invited Arthur to be   45
the smallest page at court.
But how could Arthur go,
clutching his tiny lily,
with his eyes shut up so tight
and the roads deep in snow?

📖 Glossary

Title First Death: not only does the phrase suggest Bishop's first experience of death, but also the death of the very first person to die in the province of Nova Scotia.

Line 3 chromographs: pictures obtained by means of chromo-lithography – a method of producing coloured pictures by using stones with different portions of the picture drawn upon them in inks of different colours, so arranged as to blend into the complete picture.

Line 4 Edward: (1841–1910) Prince of Wales, eldest son of Queen Victoria and Prince Albert, later Edward VII.

Line 5 Alexandra: beautiful Danish Princess who married Edward VII in 1863.

Line 6 King George with Queen Mary: George V (1865–1936) and Mary (1867–1953), Queen consort of George V.

Line 8 loon: bird, the great northern diver.

Line 14 kept his own counsel: keeps to oneself secret opinions or purposes.

Line 28 frosted: iced.

Line 36 Maple Leaf: symbol of Canada. 'Maple Leaf Forever' is a phrase from the Canadian national anthem.

Line 42 ermine: a white fur (from the stoat's winter coat in northern lands).

Line 46 page: a boy attendant.

'First Death in Nova Scotia' was first published in *The New Yorker*, 10 March 1962, and was included in her third collection, *Questions of Travel*, in the section entitled 'Elsewhere'. The poem remembers a moment in Bishop's childhood, but she didn't write the poem until she was in her fifties. Elsewhere, Bishop wrote of other early deaths, many of them in Nova Scotia.

'First Death in Nova Scotia' remembers the winter funeral of Bishop's cousin Arthur (whose real name was Frank) circa 1914, when Bishop was almost four. It was first published when Bishop was fifty-one.

? Questions

1. What is suggested by the title of this poem? How does it capture a child's experience, a child's way of thinking?

2. In this poem, Bishop is remembering a winter funeral of a cousin almost half a century before. What details of the experience are being remembered here? How does Bishop give the sense of a child's confused mind? In your answer, you should discuss the significance of repetitions, confusions and connections.

3. Religion plays no part in the death of little cousin Arthur as it is described in this poem. What is the significance of the royal personages? Consider the colours and their clothes in your answer, quoting from the text to support your answer.

4. Identify and list all the references that give the poem a chilling quality.

5. How would you describe the speaker's mood in the closing stanza? What details help to create that mood? Do you think death is seen here as mysterious and frightening?

6. Compare the speaker's view of 'my mother' and 'Uncle Arthur' with the other adults mentioned in the poem – the figures in the chromographs.

In the Waiting Room

In Worcester, Massachusetts,
I went with Aunt Consuelo
to keep her dentist's appointment
and sat and waited for her
in the dentist's waiting room.   5
It was winter. It got dark
early. The waiting room
was full of grown-up people,
arctics and overcoats,
lamps and magazines.   10
My aunt was inside
what seemed like a long time
and while I waited I read
the *National Geographic*
(I could read) and carefully   15
studied the photographs:
the inside of a volcano,
black, and full of ashes;
then it was spilling over
in rivulets of fire.   20
Osa and Martin Johnson
dressed in riding breeches,
laced boots, and pith helmets.
A dead man slung on a pole
— 'Long Pig,' the caption said.   25
Babies, with pointed heads
wound round and round with string;
black, naked women with necks
wound round and round with wire
like the necks of light bulbs.   30
Their breasts were horrifying.
I read it right straight through.
I was too shy to stop.
And then I looked at the cover:
the yellow margins, the date.   35

Suddenly, from inside,
came an *oh!* of pain
— Aunt Consuelo's voice —
not very loud or long.
I wasn't at all surprised;   40
even then I knew she was
a foolish, timid woman.
I might have been embarrassed,
but wasn't. What took me
completely by surprise   45
was that it was *me*:
my voice, in my mouth.
Without thinking at all
I was my foolish aunt,
I — we — were falling, falling,   50
our eyes glued to the cover
of the *National Geographic*,
February, 1918.

I said to myself: three days
and you'll be seven years old.   55
I was saying it to stop
the sensation of falling off
the round, turning world
into cold, blue-black space.
But I felt: you are an *I*,   60
you are an *Elizabeth*,
you are one of *them*.
Why should you be one, too?
I scarcely dared to look
to see what it was I was.   65
I gave a sidelong glance
— I couldn't look any higher —
at shadowy gray knees,
trousers and skirts and boots

and different pairs of hands   70
lying under the lamps.
I knew that nothing stranger
had ever happened, that nothing
stranger could ever happen.
Why should I be my aunt,   75
or me, or anyone?
What similarities –
boots, hands, the family voice
I felt in my throat, or even
the *National Geographic*   80
and those awful hanging breasts —
held us all together
or made us all just one?
How — I didn't know any
word for it — how 'unlikely'...   85
How had I come to be here,
like them, and overhear
a cry of pain that could have
got loud and worse but hadn't?

The waiting room was bright   90
and too hot. It was sliding
beneath a big black wave,
another, and another.

Then I was back in it.
The War was on. Outside,   95
in Worcester, Massachusetts,
were night and slush and cold,
and it was still the fifth
of February, 1918.

📖 Glossary

Line 1 Worcester, Massachusetts: where Elizabeth Bishop was born on 8 February 1911.

Line 2 Consuelo: Aunt Florence in real life.

Line 9 arctics: an American expression for waterproof overshoes/galoshes.

Line 21 Osa and Martin Johnson: a well-known and popular husband and wife team of explorers and naturalists; Osa Johnson (1894–1953) and Martin Johnson (1894–1937) wrote several travel books.

Line 23 pith helmets: sun helmets made from dried pithy stemmed swamp plant.

Line 25 'Long Pig': the name given by Polynesian cannibals to a dead man to be eaten.

Line 53 February 1918: this poem, though first published in 1971, was written in 1967. She included it in a letter to her friend, the American poet Robert Lowell. The setting of the poem is precisely dated – 5 February 1918 – 'three days and you'll be seven years old' – she writes in lines 54–55. Bishop waited 49 years before she wrote about the experience.

Line 61 Elizabeth: this is the first poem in which Elizabeth Bishop names herself.

> Though it remembers and recalls a moment from 1918, Elizabeth Bishop did not write so directly about early childhood until she was in her fifties.

❓ Questions

1. What does the title suggest? Can it be interpreted in different ways?

2. Like 'First Death in Nova Scotia', 'In the Waiting Room' is a poem, also written in her fifies, where Elizabeth Bishop recalls a moment from early childhood, a very precise moment in this instance: 5 February 1918. What does the adult remember of her childhood in the opening lines of the poem?

3. Prompted by her reading of the *National Geographic*, the location of the poem shifts (at line 17) to an altogether different and unfamiliar world. Describe what the young Elizabeth Bishop reads and sees and discuss her reaction to it.

4. What does the young girl think of her aunt? Why? Consider the women in the poem – Aunt Consuelo, Osa Martin, the black, naked women, the women in the waiting room.

5. Why does Bishop write 'I — we — were falling, falling'. Why does she think that she becomes her foolish aunt? And why 'foolish'?

6. In the poem's third section, why does the speaker focus on herself?

7. In the poem as a whole, 'I' is used twenty-six times. Considering that in some of Bishop's poems the personal pronoun is never used, why is it used so often here?

8. What do you think is meant by lines 72–74: 'I knew that nothing stranger/ had ever happened, that nothing/ stranger could ever happen.'

9. Discuss this poem as an exploration of childhood and adulthood. Use the text to support your answer.

10. Of the ten poems by Elizabeth Bishop on your course, which one is your favourite? Which one do you admire most? Give reasons for your answer.

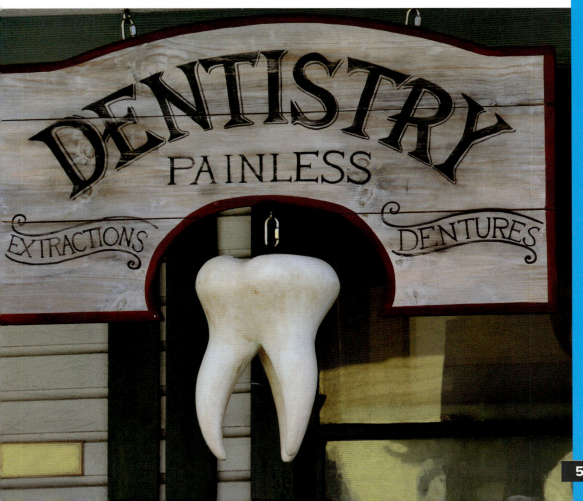

General Questions

A. 'Bishop, in her poetry, writes about the familiar and the unusual and does so in an interesting and unusual way.' Discuss this view, supporting your answer by relevant quotation from or reference to the poems by Elizabeth Bishop on your course.

B. 'The full complexity of childhood and adulthood is effectively evoked by Elizabeth Bishop in her poetry.' Discuss this view, supporting your answer by appropriate quotation from or reference to at least six of the poems by Bishop on your course.

C. 'In her poetry Elizabeth Bishop is a curious and sympathetic observer.' Discuss this view, supporting your answer by quotation from or reference to the poems by Bishop on your course.

D. 'In Elizabeth Bishop's poetry, description is never mere description; her poetry is a moral landscape, an emotional journey.' Discuss this statement, supporting your answer by relevant quotation or reference to the poems by Elizabeth Bishop on your course.

E. 'Bishop's poetry through both natural speech rhythms and formal patterns achieves an extraordinary immediacy and musical quality.' Discuss this view, supporting your answer by reference to the poems by Bishop on your course.

F. Discuss how Bishop uses images from Nature (water, fire, snow, for example) in her poetry, supporting your answer with reference to or quotation from the poems by Bishop on your course.

G. Randall Jarrell, the American poet, said of Elizabeth Bishop's work: 'all of her poems have written underneath, "I have seen it"'. Discuss what Bishop sees and explores in her poetry and how her descriptions and insights are vividly conveyed. You should refer to the poems on your course in your answer.

H. Bishop, according to Craig Raine, has 'a plain style in which the images appear like sovereigns'. Would you agree with this estimate of Elizabeth Bishop's poetry in the light of your reading the poetry by Bishop on your course? Support your answer with suitable quotation or reference to the poems.

I. Bishop herself said that 'I like painting probably better than I like poetry'. Discuss the painterly qualities of Elizabeth Bishop's work. In your answer you should refer to or quote from the poems by Bishop on your course.

J. 'Elizabeth Bishop's poems are not poems that begin with conclusions nor do they reach conclusions and yet we learn a great deal from them.' Would you agree with this statement? Support your answer by relevant quotation or reference to the poems by Bishop on your course.

K. Bishop, in her poetry, 'asks us to focus not on her but with her.' Would you agree with this statement? Support your answer with suitable quotations or reference to the poems by Bishop on your course.

Critical Commentary

The Fish

Elizabeth Bishop loved Florida and settled in Key West between 1939 and 1948. There Bishop discovered her love of fishing and, days after pulling in a sixty-pound amberjack, she began recording in her notebook descriptions which would later become part of her poem 'The Fish'. In Brett Millier's words, it is a poem of 'remarkable clarity and straightforwardness'. The form of the poem is the trimeter line interspersed at times by the dimeter. This is a form often suited to storytelling.

The fish of the poem is the enormous Caribbean jewfish which Bishop caught at Key West. Though the opening line is direct, 'I caught a tremendous fish', the adjective adds interest and excitement immediately. The fish isn't just described as 'large' or 'huge', though it is both. Instead, Bishop chooses the more powerfully subjective word 'tremendous', meaning immense and something that causes one to tremble. That first sentence is almost matter-of-fact:

> I caught a tremendous fish
> and held him beside the boat
> half out of water, with my hook
> fast in the corner of his mouth.

Yet it is 'my hook'. That detail, along with 'half out of water' (the fish is out of his element, between worlds) and 'fast', adds to the dramatic quality of the opening lines.

The focus shifts with the second sentence, line 5, 'He didn't fight', from Bishop to the fish, from fisher to the thing caught. Now we are told something about this fish and the personality which the poet attributes to it.

> He hadn't fought at all.

The fish submitted. The description of it as a 'grunting weight' is the first of many vivid pictures:

> He hung a grunting weight,
> battered and venerable
> and homely.

'Grunting', 'battered' and 'homely' (meaning, in American English, plain-looking) capture the exhausted and ugly state of the fish, but then Bishop's use of 'venerable' casts a different light on things. It means both aged looking and worthy of reverence.

Bishop is an extraordinary observer. The fish, once caught, is not just cast aside. She looks at it in great detail. Line 9 begins this thorough examination and observation of the fish:

> Here and there
> his brown skin hung in strips
> like ancient wallpaper:
> shapes like full-blown roses
> stained and lost through age.

Throughout the poem there is a very definite sense of Bishop as participant and observer: 'I caught', 'I thought', 'I looked', 'I stared and stared', but the poem is so much more than a matter-of-fact account of catching a fish. The fish intrigues her; it fascinates and frightens her, teaching her something about the fish and something about herself.

The simile in line 14, 'like full-blown roses', is a beautiful image, even if the shapes on the fish are 'stained and lost through age'. Here the fish becomes less 'homely' but, as Bishop looks more closely, a less attractive aspect of this fish is revealed:

> He was speckled with barnacles,
> fine rosettes of lime,
> and infested
> with tiny white sea-lice,
> and underneath two or three
> rags of green weed hung down.

These physical details are such that the texture (speckled, infested, rags) and the colours (lime, white, green) vividly help to create the complete picture.

The fish exists between the two elements of air and water: 'his gills were breathing in/the terrible oxygen'. The fish will die if its gills drink in the air, not water, and the gills are 'frightening': they are 'fresh and crisp with blood', they 'can cut so badly'.

In line 27, there is a shift in emphasis signalled by the phrase 'I thought'. Here Bishop imagines the insides of the fish, that aspect of the fish invisible to the fisherman or fisherwoman. By speaking now of

> the coarse white flesh
> packed in like feathers,
> the big bones and the little bones,
> the dramatic reds and blacks
> of his shiny entrails,
> and the pink swim-bladder
> like a big peony.

we have a sense of the whole fish, outside and inside. The image of the feathers, the use of 'little', the colours red, black and pink signal Bishop's sympathetic imaginative response.

The 'big peony' is a startling and beautiful image. The guts of a fish are not often viewed in this delicate, imaginative manner. And this peony image sends us back to line 14, where the fish's skin was also described in terms of flower imagery – the shapes of full-blown roses.

In some respects, the fish is familiar – his skin is compared to 'ancient wallpaper' – but the fish is also 'infested', 'coarse' and 'weapon-like'. She admires him, but she also recognises something disgusting in the fish. Yet the fish is ugly only to the careless observer; Bishop recognises that the fish is beautiful too.

When, in line 34, Bishop tells us that she 'looked into his eyes', a more immediate relationship between the poet and the fish is being established. The captor is now looking straight into the eyes of the captive. The eyes of the fish are then described in typical Bishop style: a style which seems objective at first but in fact reveals Bishop's unique and subjective eye. First, the eyes are described in terms of size, shape, colour:

> his eyes
> which were far larger than mine
> but shallower, and yellowed.

Then we are given more detailed imagery; the irises are

> backed and packed
> with tarnished tinfoil

and even this image is overlain with another image – the image of the irises

> seen through the lenses
> of old scratched isinglass.

The fish does not return her look, her stare. The eyes, we are told,

> shifted a little, but not
> to return my stare.

The fish not looking, not returning Bishop's stare, suggests the separateness, the independence, the dignity and yet the vulnerability of the fish. When the stronger captures the weak, it does not mean that the weaker one surrenders everything.

As in much of Bishop's poetry, the writing is such that, as we read through the poem, it is as if we are reading her thoughts directly as they are being formed.

The use of the dash at line 43 (she also uses the dash elsewhere in the poem at lines 24, 49 and 74) suggests a considered, explanatory addition; it indicates Bishop's attempt at getting it right. She has spoken of how the eyes shifted slightly and then we are given the further explanation or clarification:

> — It was more like the tipping
>   of an object toward the light.

'I caught' (line 1), 'I thought' (line 27) and 'I looked' (line 34) have already marked certain stages in the poem. Now, with line 45, we have a new development: Bishop tells us that

> I admired his sullen face,
> the mechanism of his jaw.

Sullen is not a quality usually or often admired, but Bishop attributes a resolute quality to the fish and senses a gloomy and unresponsive state. It is at this point that she mentions how she saw 'five pieces of fish-line', each one indicating a former struggle and unsuccessful catch. The struggle was powerful and determined, and the fish still bears the evidence to prove it:

> A green line, frayed at the end
> where he broke it, two heavier lines,
> and a fine black thread
> still crimped from the strain and snap
> when it broke and he got away.

Here the adjectives and the verbs achieve the convincing effect: frayed, broke, heavier, crimped, broke, got away — that of a long, determined struggle. This fish has had an interesting and vivid past.

Bishop is clearly impressed. She sees the hooks as victory medals, while the gut lines are like the ribbons attached to such medals and they form a five-haired beard of wisdom. The fish, personified, has survived the wars — in this instance the fight with the fisherman's hook.

Earlier in the poem (line 46), Bishop has spoken of 'the mechanism of his jaw'; in line 64 we read of the fish's aching jaw. Bishop has become more engaged with the plight of this tremendous, battered and venerable fish. There is also, of course, the sense of the fish as male, as conqueror – it has battled with the hook and won. Now it is well and truly caught, but Bishop, female, does not play conqueror, as the last line of the poem indicates.

All the details so far lead us to the poem's conclusion. The second last sentence begins with the line 'I stared and stared'. It is a moment of triumph and victory; Bishop speaks of how

> victory filled up
> the little rented boat.

Everything seems transformed. The boat is 'little' and 'rented': nothing remarkable there. The fish, however, was 'tremendous' and 'victory' seems to belong to Bishop for having caught the fish, but also to the fish itself for having survived five previous hooks.

She mentions no other person in this poem; Bishop, it would seem, is alone in the boat. One person in a little boat floating on the sea conjures up a small scene, but the feeling which she is experiencing is an expansive feeling, a feeling which begins within and spreads to embrace and include the very ordinary details of the boat. 'The 'pool of bilge', the 'rusted engine', 'the bailer', 'the sun-cracked thwarts', 'the oarlocks', 'the gunnels' are transformed. In the pool of bilge at the bottom of the boat, Bishop notices where oil had 'spread a rainbow'. And that rainbow spreads everywhere

> – until everywhere
> was rainbow, rainbow, rainbow!

The poem's final line is one of the shortest sentences in the poem. By the poem's end, we ask what has happened between line 1 ('I caught a tremendous fish') and line 76. 'And I let the fish go' is not surprising. The word 'and' suggests that everything has led to this conclusion.

Bishop's use of rhyme in the final couplet (rainbow/go; elsewhere in the poem she prefers to use internal rhymes) also adds to the mood of exultation with which the poem ends:

> – until everything
> was rainbow, rainbow, rainbow!
> And I let the fish go.

This is the moment of epiphany and revelation, a visionary moment. (An *epiphany* is an extraordinary moment of heightened awareness, insight and understanding.)

The poem not only describes the fish, but also tells us a great deal about Elizabeth Bishop. The poet Randall Jarrell admired this poem for its moral quality.

The speaker sets out to catch a fish: it is a battered creature and in the end the fish is let go. The fish has escaped the hook five other times – the 'five big hooks' have 'grown firmly in his mouth' to remind us, but this time it is literally being let off the hook. Bishop admires the fish for its individual self; as the American writer and literary critic David Kalstone observed, 'victory belongs both to the wild survivor and his human counterpart'.

Bishop's 'The Fish' can also be seen as an allegorical poem: in other words, it gives us a narrative that can be understood symbolically or at a level other than the literal or actual one. It is but one of several poems by Bishop which Andrew Motion has called 'arguifying, Metaphysical and fabling'. Between that opening and closing line, not only is there, in Craig Raine's words, an 'unhurried, methodical, humane' response to the fish but 'she pronounces a true but merciful verdict on our precarious existence'.

These closing lines can also be read as a reversal of the macho stance. American literature has memorable examples of the fisherman in search of the fish. Melville's great novel *Moby Dick* (1851) and Ernest Hemingway's *The Old Man and the Sea* (1952) reveal a man's determined and ambitious attempt to conquer. But this is not a poem about the fish that got away: 'I let the fish go'.

At The Fishhouses

There is almost something anti-poetic or non-poetic about the words 'At the Fishhouses'. But Elizabeth Bishop was to make and shape her poetry from what might be termed the very opposite of the traditional sources of poetic inspiration. 'Filling Station' and 'In the Waiting Room' are other such titles which suggest the apparently unpoetic. Fishhouses are functional buildings, reeking of fish. Fishhouses are also places linked with death in that all the fish stored and processed are dead. The fishhouses of the title are fishhouses on Cuttyhunk Island, Massachusetts, by the cold Atlantic, though the notebooks Bishop kept while at Lockeport Beach in Nova Scotia in 1946 also found their way into this poem.

The poem begins unassertively, almost apologetically:

> Although it is a cold evening
> down by one of the fishhouses
> an old man sits netting,
> his net, in the gloaming almost invisible,
> a dark purple-brown,
> and his shuttle worn and polished.

The only other person beside the poet is 'an old man'. He 'sits netting, / his net, in the gloaming almost invisible'. There are echoes of Wordsworth here, in that William Wordsworth often wrote about ordinary working people and the lives they lived against a background of 'the goings on of earth and sky'. The fisherman is a solitary figure. So too is Bishop.

The opening section of the poem describes the five fishhouses and her conversation with the old fisherman while he is waiting for a herring boat to come in. The language, though conversational, is also very musical. Within the opening lines, for example, are alliteration and internal rhyme, two of Bishop's favourite techniques. The long 'o' sound of 'although' is echoed in the word 'gloaming'; 'cold' and 'old' rhyme; the words 'brown', 'worn', 'strong', and 'run', together with 'sits', 'nets', 'purple' and 'polished', all add to this musical effect.

Feeling the cold, seeing the fisherman and smelling the codfish establish immediately a world created through the senses:

> The air smells so strong of codfish
> it makes one's nose run and one's eyes water

And again:

> The five fishhouses have steeply peaked roofs
> and narrow, cleated gangplanks slant up
> to storerooms in the gables
> for the wheelbarrows to be pushed up and down on.

These lines illustrate the music of poetry. In 'five' and 'fish. . .' the poet uses alliteration and assonance and the rhyming 'steep ly' and 'peak ed'; alliteration again with 'slant' and 'storerooms'. The 'up' of 'pushed up' echoes the 'up' at the end of the line two lines earlier and everything goes to create what seems both a very natural sounding utterance and a musical quality which is typical of Elizabeth Bishop.

The initial effect of the place on the poet is physical. Bishop, in lines 7 and 8, tells us that

> The air smells so strong of codfish
> it makes one's nose run and one's eyes water

but her use of 'one's' rather than 'my' makes it more impersonal. What the opening lines offer us is, according to Seamus Heaney, 'the slow-motion spectacle of a well-disciplined poetic imagination'. Everything is presented to us without fuss.

Line 13 announces that 'All is silver'. This is the cold opaque silver of the sea, the apparently translucent silver

> of the benches
> the lobster pots, and masts, scattered
> among the wild jagged rocks.

Such detail is characteristic of Bishop. She watches everything closely. In many of her poems, she will begin with a description (a particular place, a particular time, an object) and from description, through imagination, she moves towards understanding and insight.

What Seamus Heaney called Bishop's 'lucid awareness' is clearly at work in lines 21 and following:

> The big fish tubs are completely lined
> with layers of beautiful herring scales
> and the wheelbarrows are similarly plastered
> with creamy iridescent coats of mail,
> with small iridescent flies crawling on them.

Her eye picks out the tiny detail of the 'small iridescent flies' crawling on the silvered, rainbowed wheelbarrows. For Bishop there is a beauty here in the sensory details she describes. She uses the word 'beautiful' in line 22, and the 'creamy iridescent coats of mail' is an example of that beauty.

The poem's focus then moves, camera-like, from the minute, the flies in line 25, to the wide-angle shot captured in line 26:

> Up on the little slope behind the houses,
> set in the sparse bright sprinkle of grass,
> is an ancient wooden capstan,
> cracked, with two long bleached handles
> and some melancholy stains, like dried blood,
> where the ironwork has rusted.

The capstan, cracked and rusted, is a reminder of the work done over the years. This detail and precision is, yet again, giving us the exterior world. Bishop does not hurry us through the poem, though the poet's main preoccupation, or that which forms one of the poem's main themes (how to make sense of the world), is not yet arrived at.

Up until now, Bishop has been describing what she sees, but line 32 ('The old man accepts a Lucky Strike') marks the human encounter and conversation. Bishop enters into the poem in a more obvious way. The detail that the old man 'was a friend of my grandfather' creates a human and personal story. The final lines in this first section of 'At the Fishhouses' give the reader the factual, outward, public world:

> We talk of the decline in the population
> and of codfish and herring
> while he waits for a herring boat to come in.

And Bishop's own private observations:

> There are sequins on his vest and on his thumb.
> He has scraped the scales, the principal beauty,
> from unnumbered fish with that black old knife,
> the blade of which is almost worn away.

The old man in these four lines is described as expert at his task but one who is also coming to the end of his life. His 'blade is almost worn away'. The literary critic Bonnie Costello sees the fisherman as a divine agent. Bishop herself said of these four lines (37–40) that they came to her in a dream.

To see the fishscales as sequins is another example of Bishop's ability to bring a word with such specific connotations and associations (glittering ballgowns, glamour) and to give it a new life and appropriateness. The man, both times he is mentioned, is spoken of as old. The awareness of mortality is never explicitly stated, but, in the third section of the poem, Bishop confronts her own mortality.

Meanwhile, in the second section, lines 41–46, the picture is of the water's edge:

> Down at the water's edge, at the place
> where they haul up the boats, up the long ramp
> descending into the water, thin silver
> tree trunks are laid horizontally
> across the gray stones, down and down
> at intervals of four or five feet.

Bishop has shifted her focus from the details of the old man's hands (he is not mentioned again in the poem) and 'that black old knife' to that in-between world of land and sea:

> the place
> where they haul up the boats, up the long ramp
> descending into the water.

The phrase 'down and down' in line 45 suggests not only the angle of the tree trunks but the direction of the poem, in that Bishop, in the third and final section, goes deep beneath the surface of the moment, deep into her own consciousness and this leads her to a fuller understanding and awareness of her own aloneness and mortality.

Section 3 begins with the line:

> Cold dark deep and absolutely clear

Seamus Heaney refers to this line as 'a rhythmic heave which suggests that something other is about to happen'. Eavan Boland recognises its 'serious music', and we are reminded of its importance when the same line is repeated 13 lines later. The four adjectives present us with the chilling reality of the water of the North Atlantic, an 'element bearable to no mortal'. It is in this third section that the seal makes his appearance. In an earlier draft of this poem, Bishop speaks of seals; in the final draft of 'At the Fishhouses', the seal is solitary, just as the old man and Bishop herself are.

Bishop is drawn to this sea shore 'evening after evening', to this curious seal. In his element, the seal believes in total immersion and Bishop says that she too believes in it. Total immersion can refer to a baptism by water and this is why Bishop adds 'so I used to sing him Baptist hymns', but the phrase can also mean a state of deep absorption or involvement, a meaning which is also interesting in this context. The seal belongs to another world and a different world.

The seal appears in line 49 and disappears in 59, but it is more than a charming, distracting and delightful interlude.

> One seal particularly
> I have seen here evening after evening.
> He was curious about me. He was interested in music;
> Like me a believer in total immersion,
> so I used to sing him Baptist hymns.
> I also sang 'A Mighty Fortress Is Our God'.
> He stood up in the water and regarded me
> steadily, moving his head a little.
> Then he would disappear, then suddenly emerge
> almost in the same spot, with a sort of shrug
> as if it were against his better judgement.

Though Bishop here refers to religion and belief she finds no comfort or consolation there. God may be a fortress but one to which Bishop does not belong.

Seals belong to sea and land; they are often seen as ambiguous creatures. In the water, the seal is in its element, 'a believer in total immersion', and it allows Bishop to imagine more fully the element to which it belongs. Total immersion for Bishop is immersion of herself in knowledge, and what she imagines knowledge to be is this 'Cold, dark deep and absolutely clear' water before her.

Immediately after the seal disappears from the poem, Bishop repeats the line which began this third section:

> Cold dark deep and absolutely clear,

bringing us again to the more serious concerns of the poem, namely that, like the 'cold dark deep' water there are, in Eavan Boland's phrase, corresponding 'cold interiors of human knowledge'.

That passage in the poem from line 60 to the end marks a very different order of experience. The thinking within these lines is at a different level from the earlier part of the poem. Before Bishop is 'the clear gray icy water', like knowledge. Behind,

> ... Back, behind us,
> the dignified tall firs begin.
> Bluish, associating with their shadows,
> a million Christmas trees stand
> waiting for Christmas.

It has been suggested that the Christmas trees are behind her in more than one sense. These have been interpreted as the traces of Christianity which Bishop herself has put behind her. Here the Christmas trees are waiting not for Christ's birth, but to be cut down.

There is also the use of 'us' here, the only time Bishop uses it in the poem. The 'us' refers to Bishop, the seal and the old man, but it has been argued that she could also be including us, the readers, here.

It is only in this third section of 'At the Fishhouses' that Elizabeth Bishop uses the personal pronoun 'I'. What fascinates her and what makes her human is knowledge. She has seen the water 'over and over, the same sea' and it is

> icily free above the stones,
> above the stones and then the world.

The sea of knowledge is a familiar phrase. Bishop's sea of knowledge is cold, dark and painful.

The final section of the poem is more private and more difficult to grasp. Yet Bishop in this very passage speaks directly to the reader, using 'you' (line 71). The water is bitterly cold:

> If you should dip your hand in,
> Your wrist would ache immediately,
> your bones would begin to ache and your hand would burn
> as if the water were a transmutation of fire
> that feeds on stone and burns with a dark gray flame.
> If you tasted it, it would first taste bitter

> then briny, then surely burn your tongue.

Bishop herself makes her meaning clear. To dip into this bitterly cold water and to taste it

> is like what we imagine knowledge to be:
> dark, salt, clear, moving, utterly free.

Knowledge, the poet tells us, is 'drawn from the cold hard mouth / of the world, derived from the rocky breasts / forever'. Knowledge, in other words, hurts. The 'cold hard mouth' and 'the rocky breasts' are uncomfortable images. The source is part maternal, but Mother Nature here is cold and forbidding.

What began seemingly as an objective descriptive poem has become a personal and private poem. Yet, 'At the Fishhouses' is a poem in which the reader can enter into the experience and share the poet's understanding. When she writes 'It is like what we imagine knowledge to be', Bishop is speaking for herself, the reader and everyone.

What we know, our knowledge, is drawn from the past, but knowledge is also something which is ongoing, never static and flowing. Knowledge, as Bishop puts it in those closing lines, is

> forever, flowing and drawn, and since
> our knowledge is historical, flowing, and flown.

We have moments of insight and understanding that might enrich or unsettle us and we have witnessed one such moment in this poem. The moment is 'flowing', in that it belongs to the present, and it is 'flown', in that it becomes part of our past. As humans we are part of flux and we cannot hope to control or to stop it.

The poem ends with this heightened moment of insight. In *Elizabeth Bishop: An Oral Biography*, we learn that Bishop told her friend Frank Bidart that 'when she was writing it she hardly knew what she was writing, knew the words were right, and (at this she raised her arms as high straight above her head as she could) felt ten feet tall.'

The Bight

The poem begins with description and in fact most of the poem describes a place. Yet the poem is much more than a place-picture; it becomes a romantic meditation. The phrase 'it seems to me' (line 13) and the final line are the most personal, though in fact what Bishop chooses to describe and how she describes it reveals her personality everywhere.

The opening lines are both plain and sensuous, in that the bight is described in terms of sight, touch, smell and hearing. And though the place is neither remarkable nor beautiful, Bishop makes it interesting and almost beautiful through her choice and control of language.

The very first line – 'At low tide like this how sheer the water is' – achieves an immediacy with the phrase 'like this', and Bishop's sense of engagement or awe is expressed in the words 'how sheer the water is'. Here and elsewhere, Elizabeth Bishop often writes a line which is almost entirely composed of monosyllabic words (lines 1, 9, 16, 26, 33 are other examples in 'The Bight'). It is a spare, simple and strong style.

What is remarkable about these opening lines, and it is one of Bishop's identifying characteristics, is her ability to bring a particular place alive. Marl isn't just marl:

> White, crumbling ribs of marl protrude and glare

Details – the adjectives and verbs – give it a vivid presence.

The dry boats, the dry pilings and the water in the bight that doesn't wet anything create a very distinctive atmosphere. Bishop describes the colour of the water as 'the color of the gas flame turned as low as possible' and this accurate image is followed by the surreal when Bishop says:

> One can smell it turning to gas; if one were Baudelaire
> one could probably hear it turning to marimba music.

The use of 'one' here, not 'I', includes rather than excludes the reader, and yet the use of 'one' is more impersonal than 'I'. This imagined transformation of water 'turning to gas', 'turning to marimba music', involves the senses. Smell allows us to imagine water as gas; our sense of hearing can turn the water into vibrant jazzy sounds. As Bishop reminds us, this is a way of thinking or of viewing the world that can be found in Baudelaire's poetry. Unusual and marvellous connections are being made. Bishop herself, in lines 9 and 10, is now thinking in this way when she hears a Latin American dance music in the sounds of the dredging machine:

> The little ochre dredge at work off the end of the dock
> already plays the dry perfectly off-beat claves.

The poem is a busy one. There is a great deal of activity. Lines 11 to 19 describe the pelican and man-of-war birds. A phrase like 'humorous elbowings' catches the pelicans' movements; the man-of-war birds are also caught: they 'open their tails like scissors on the curves / or tense them like wishbones'.

The next section of the poem has sponge boats, the shark tails and the little white boats, but they are not simply listed. The sponge boats are 'frowsy', coming in 'with the obliging air of retrievers', and the words 'bristling' and 'decorated' give them energy; the shark tails are 'blue-gray' and are 'glinting like little plowshares'; and the damaged little white boats are 'like torn-open, unanswered letters'. In a letter to Robert Lowell, Bishop had written, 15 January 1948, that the harbour was a mess – boats piled up, some broken by a recent hurricane – and that it had reminded her a little of her desk. Here the image from the letter reappears in the poem, not as Bishop's untidy writing desk, but in the phrase 'old correspondences'.

'The bight is littered with old correspondences', but the personal detail of Bishop's own desk is made less personal and the word 'correspondences' also has the literary echo of Baudelaire's sonnet 'Correspondances'. The bight is not only a place that resembles a paper littered desk; it is also a place where interesting, unusual connections or correspondences can be found.

The poem ends with the sound of the dredger, first mentioned in line 9. The 'little ocher dredge' continues its digging. Bishop spoke of the pelicans crashing into the water and 'rarely coming up with anything to show for it'. The dredge comes up with something:

> Click. Click. Goes the **d**redge,
> and brings up a **d**ripping *jawful* of marl.
> All the untidy activity continues,
> *awful* but cheer*ful*.

The sounds here are spot on. First, the mechanical sharpness of the 'Click. Click.', each one given a definition of its own with those full stops. The sound contained in the phrase 'a dripping jawful of marl' is the sound of heavy wetness. And the movement of that line – 'and brings up a dripping jawful of marl' is awkward and staggered, just as the dredger's digger would be as it gouges out, scoops and lifts up the clayey, limey wet soil. Apart from rhythm and individual sounds, there is another music also, which Bishop captures in the use of alliteration, assonance and cross or slant rhyme. Look again. Listen.

> Click. Click. Goes the **d**redge,
> and brings up a **d**ripping *jawful* of marl.
> All the untidy activity continues,
> *awful* but cheer*ful*.

The second last line in the poem refers to all that is going on before her in the bight, but it could also be read as a description of life itself. Life goes on, but life can be random, chaotic, disorganised. It is a poem that she associates with her thirty-seventh birthday, and every birthday is a moment of natural reflection on the passing of time and the nature of one's life.

That famous last line, 'awful but cheerful', sums up much about Elizabeth Bishop. Towards the end of her life she herself asked that those words be inscribed on her tombstone in the Bishop family plot in Worcester, Massachusetts. The accepted and most usual meaning for 'awful' is 'very bad, terrible, unattractive', but there is also its original meaning of 'inspiring awe, solemnly impressive'. This bight and its untidy activity are not conventionally pretty. It has, of course, been the inspiration for this very poem. The first and more common interpretation of the word is probably the more valid in the context of the 'untidy activity' in the preceding line. Bishop has clearly enjoyed observing. Life does go on and it can be both 'awful' and 'cheerful'. Bishop does say 'awful but cheerful', suggesting perhaps that the birds, the 'frowsy sponge boats' and the dredger all continue their activity with good humour, as we should and must. It is perhaps the only way to go on.

The Prodigal

It is worth asking at the outset why Bishop should be drawn to such a figure as the prodigal; she often felt like an outsider, someone away from home, and, like the prodigal son of the poem, she also engaged in drinking bouts.

The structure of the poem consists of a double sonnet and the irregular but ordered rhyming scheme is as follows: abacdbcedfeggf

A different sound rhyme and a different rhyming scheme is used in stanza 2: abacdbecfedfgh. An identical rhyming scheme is used in the first six lines of each stanza. The American literary critic David Kalstone spoke of 'two nicely rhymed sonnets' and how the 'air of sanity' in the poem is what makes it frightening, 'its ease and attractiveness only just keeping down panic and fear'.

The poem, though based on the biblical story of the Prodigal Son, chooses to focus on the lowest and ugliest part of that man's life – his time minding pigs. The ugliness and unpleasantness is presented immediately in the opening line: 'The brown enormous odor' captures the colour and the impact of the stench. This is the world he knows now. It is 'too close', too close for comfort, and so close that he does not judge. Not judging in this context could mean he has lost all sense of a world other than this one. It could also mean that this man does not judge – in other words, he is not thinking whether he deserves this life or not. Later there will come a time when he will judge it wise or best to go home and ask his father for forgiveness, but Bishop is suggesting at this point that the world of the pigs is so overwhelming that he does not judge. The phrase 'he lived by' in line 1 can mean that the prodigal son lived next to this horrible smell or it could also be interpreted to mean that he lived by it in the sense that it allows him to survive. The presence of the pigs is there before us in the two details 'breathing and thick hair'.

The first part of the poem brings us within the pig shed. 'The floor was rotten; the sty / was plastered halfway up with glass-smooth dung.' The vivid ugliness of 'glass-smooth' is all the more effective in that 'glass-smooth' is more often associated with the surface of a calm, beautiful lake. That the dung is 'halfway' up the wall reminds us of its prevalence and liquid state.

Lines 5 to 8 focus on the pigs themselves, their heads, more specifically their eyes, their snouts. As everywhere in Bishop, the observations are exact: the eyes are 'light-lashed' and 'self-righteous'. Who gives the 'cheerful stare' – the pigs or the prodigal? The dash at the end of line 6 suggests that the stare belongs to the pigs' eyes and that the pigs even stare in a cheerful manner at the 'sow that always ate her young'. The 'always' is frightening. Whether it is intentional or not, line 7 does prompt the reader to consider this sow's behaviour towards its offspring and the comparison between that and the subsequent attitude of the father towards his prodigal son.

The pigs follow their carer and, even though he feels sickened by it all, something eventually ('till' – line 8) in the prodigal causes him to offer a gesture of comfort or affection:

> sickening, he leaned to scratch her head.

In line 9, we are given a sense of the prodigal's meaningless life and secret drinking bouts but something else, something other, is also introduced. Bishop reminds us that there is a world beyond the pigsty. There is the sunrise, and the morning sun transforms the ordinary and everyday. In this instance, the barnyard mud is glazed with red. Earlier in line 4 we read that the ugly smelly pigsty walls were glazed with dung; here the mud and the puddles are made beautiful by the sunrise and, seeing them, the heart seems to be reassured.

Such a moment of passing beauty sustains him in his suffering and loneliness and exile:

> And then he thought he almost might endure
> his exile yet another year or more.

The use of 'But' at the beginning of line 9 indicates hope. And Bishop also uses 'but' to begin the second section of 'The Prodigal', this time to signal a change of direction.

> But evenings the first star came to warn.

Perhaps Bishop is using 'star' here as a signal of fate or destiny. If it is spoken of in terms of warning then the prodigal is being told that he must act or make decisions. Then follows such a comforting picture of order and safety (the farmer tending to his cows and horses and seeing that they are safe for the night) that

Bishop speaks of it in terms of it being

> safe and companionable as in the Ark.

Lines 18 and 19 give only some details of the inside of the barn in lantern light:

> beneath their overhanging clouds of hay,
> with pitchforks, faint forked lightnings, catching light,
> yet these few details allow the reader of the poem to picture it clearly.

'Clouds of hay' and the words 'safe and companionable' suggest warmth and a dry place, a contrast with the wet, dung-covered pigsty where the prodigal works. Line 21 is one sentence. It returns us to the world of the pigs and gives us both their vulnerability – 'their little feet' – and their ugly side – they snored.

The farmer shuts the barn door and goes home, but Bishop, imagining the life of the prodigal, never speaks of him as having a home separate from the animals. The farmer's lantern is observed: its light 'laid on the mud' forms a moving or 'pacing aureole', and this interpretation of light on mud is similar to the earlier lines in which the early morning sun colours the mud and puddles. The lantern light becomes an aureole or halo and this too, like the glazed mud in stanza 1, sustains him.

We are given another very vivid description of the prodigal at work before the poem ends. It is as if the time spent among the pigs is so long and the drudgery so great that Bishop returns to it again to remind us of its awfulness. With

> Carrying a bucket along a slimy board,
> he felt the bats' uncertain staggering flight

we are once again in the wet and smelly dark. The prodigal's private, inner self is spoken of in terms of 'shuddering insights'. We know from the biblical story what he is thinking, what conclusions he is reaching. These insights are 'beyond his control, / touching him'. This is the disturbed, aware Prodigal Son. But Elizabeth Bishop does not give us a simple, quick ending. St. Luke says 'And when he came to himself. . .'. Bishops charts the journey towards that difficult decision with words such as 'shuddering', 'touching him' and the final sentence in the poem. Here again she uses 'But' with great effect; it wasn't an easy or sudden decision:

> But it took him a long time
> finally to make his mind up to go home.

The final word resonates particularly because the word does not hark back to an obvious rhyme and because of what it implies within the poem as a whole. The loner, outsider, exile is returning to the place where he will be forgiven and loved.

Our knowing the ending of this biblical story adds to the poem's effect. However, our knowing that Bishop's mother was confined to a hospital for the insane and that Bishop herself grew up never having a home to go to also adds to the poem's power and effect.

In a letter to Robert Lowell, dated 23 November 1955, Bishop herself said that in 'The Prodigal' the technique was like a spiritual exercise of the Jesuits – where one thinks in great detail about how the thing happened. In another letter to U. T. and Joseph Summers, dated 19 October 1967, she tells of how 'The Prodigal' suggested itself. It 'was suggested to me when one of my aunt's stepsons offered me a drink of rum, in the pigsties, at about nine in the morning, when I was visiting her in Nova Scotia'.

Filling Station

'Oh, but it is dirty!' There is no introduction, no explanation. The title sets the scene and there is an immediacy in that opening line. The 'Oh' is spontaneous, the word 'dirty' given extra force with that exclamation mark. In this, as in many of Bishop's poems, we begin with a place and Bishop's description of it but, by the end of the poem, the experience has expanded to include wider, deeper issues. It is a poem that moves towards a wonderful and, in the end, an unsurprising last line.

The place is black, glistening and disturbing because it can also be dangerous:

> oil-soaked, oil permeated
> to a disturbing, over-all
> black translucency.
> Be careful with that match!

That final line in stanza 1 – 'Be careful with that match!' – is very ordinary and everyday. It certainly isn't a line one might associate with the language of poetry, but poetry is the living, speaking voice of the time. This opening stanza combines a language that is exact ('black translucency', for example) with an equally effective the language which may seem throwaway or commonplace, but which in the context of the poem is perfectly right.

A masculine place, usually, the filling station is given a human and domestic dimension in the second stanza. Father and sons give it a family feeling, as do details later in the poem such as the wicker sofa, the dog, the doily. The word 'dirty' occurs in the first three stanzas. The place is dirty, the father dirty, the sons dirty; the dog is a 'dirty dog'.

The dirt is fascinating. Every aspect of it is noted: the father's clothes are so black they resemble an

> oil-soaked monkey suit
> that cuts him under the arms

The 'several quick and saucy' sons are 'greasy'. 'All', Bishop tells us, is 'quite thoroughly dirty'.

Stanza 3 draws us in further with the question 'Do they live in the station?'

The comic books are the only things which seem to have retained their original, 'certain color'. Bishop's humorous eye suggests that the plant is oiled, not watered; the doily is 'dim', yet the plant on the doily-covered taboret fascinates her. The doily is improbable and unexpected, totally unnecessary, it could be argued, and it is dirty:

> Why, oh why, the doily?

This question is both simple and crucial. The doily reminds us that there are such things as creativity, grace, manners; it is a gesture towards elegance. Filling stations are naturally oily and dirty, and we've already seen how the father, the sons, the furniture and the dog are filthy. The doily is not as fresh as the day it was made, but it was created to decorate and to enhance. It was also most likely embroidered and crocheted by a woman, which may be another interesting consideration. A woman brought something special to this place and it is a woman who is reminding us of this in the very act of writing the poem.

The cans of oil have also been attended to in a special way:

> Somebody
> arranges the rows of cans
> so that they softly say:
> ESSO—SO—SO—SO
> to high-strung automobiles.

Whoever embroidered the doily, whoever waters the plant, whoever arranges the oil cans, is a 'somebody' never named. There is, it would seem, always someone doing small, almost unnoticeable little acts of kindness or acts which reflect our ability as humans to care, to shape, to bring order or to create. They are not always named and they do not need to be named, but the world is a better place because of them. Andrew Motion thinks the filling station 'the small theatre for a degraded life which stubbornly refuses to give up the effort to decorate and enjoy'. No matter where we live, we try to make it home.

The oil cans so arranged say musically and comfortingly 'SO-SO-SO', which was, according to Bishop herself, a phrase used to calm and soothe horses. This little detail adds a further interesting perspective to the poem. 'High-strung' automobiles refers to the tension and busyness of the cars' occupants more than the cars themselves, but the 'so-so-so' is doubly effective in that it was once used to comfort horses and now the phrase is read by those who sit in automobiles whose power is often described in terms of horse-power. The word 'high-strung' is also applied to thoroughbred horses; Bishop is describing the cars in terms of horses.

The last line is astonishing and wonderful and totally justified.

> Somebody loves us all.

It is a short sentence, a line complete in itself and gains the power of proverb. It is a wise, true, and marvellously comforting thought with which to end, all the more effective and powerful when we see how the dirty filling station, observed closely, reveals this truth and makes possible this insight.

Questions of Travel

The poem begins with the description of a place and its climate, movement and flux. Unlike, say, the opening lines of 'At the Fishhouses', Bishop's presence is more evident:

> 'There are too many waterfalls here'

This gives both a sense of the landscape and her opinion of it. Bishop speaks of her travels in the opening section. There are clouds and mountain tops and movement. A scientist would talk about the hydrological cycle, but Bishop, a poet, sees it differently. She is clearly engaged with the 'too many waterfalls'; the water is described as 'those streaks, those mile-long, shiny, tearstains' becoming waterfalls. This is what she sees on her travels, and she even imagines more and more water falling and waterfalls:

> the pressure of so many clouds on the mountaintops
> makes them spill over the sides in soft slow-motion,
> turning to waterfalls under our very eyes.

Not only is Bishop the traveller, the 'streams and clouds' (line 10) 'keep travelling, travelling' too. It is as if the mind cannot take everything in. This first section ends with yet another example of how Elizabeth Bishop can make us see:

> the mountains look like the hulls of capsized ships,
> slime-hung and barnacled.

In section 2, Bishop's mood, her preoccupation, becomes more complex and philosophical. Should we travel? Why do we travel? What if we were to stay at home? What right have we to be here in a strange, foreign place?

Section 2 is made up of nine sentences, eight of which end with question marks, and these questions become the questions of travel. First, there is the invitation to

> Think of the long trip home.

and then the sequence of eight questions.

> Should we have stayed at home and thought of here?
> Where should we be today?
> Is it right to be watching strangers in a play
> in this strangest of theatres?
> What childishness is it that while there's a breath of life
> in our bodies, we are determined to rush
> to see the sun the other way around?
> The tiniest green hummingbird in the world?
> To stare at some inexplicable old stonework,
> inexplicable and impenetrable,
> at any view,
> instantly seen and always, always delightful?

Bishop is clearly intrigued by the whole concept of travel and is disoriented and a little uneasy about it. She wonders, in line 18, if it is childishness that causes us 'to rush / to see the sun the other way round?' (Brazil being below the Equator). Her focus has been on landscape and the natural world, but people and their work are also included. The people are 'strangers in a play'; the old stonework is 'inexplicable'. Bishop is in a place and yet feels separate and outside of it.

The American academic Brett Millier thinks that 'Questions of Travel' is concerned with 'the limitations of one's knowledge and understanding of a foreign culture'. It is a poem that admits to difference: the view may be 'inexplicable and impenetrable', yet the traveller is forever looking. To the questions

> Oh, must we dream our dreams
> and have them, too?
> And have we room
> for one more folded sunset, still quite warm?

the answers are implied but never given. The traveller did not stay at home and think or dream of here. The dream became a reality. There is a human need to see for oneself. The traveller has not grown weary of collecting sunsets. The image is that of folded, ironed clothes being packed away in a suitcase.

Bishop reinforces this viewpoint in the third section, which begins:

> But surely it would have been a pity
> not to have seen the trees along the road,
> really exaggerated in their beauty,
> not to have seen them gesturing
> like noble pantomimists, robed in pink.

Here Bishop is clearly enthralled and captivated, as a child is at the pantomime. She notices and delights in the tiniest of details, such as the clacking sounds of the petrol pump attendant's clogs:

> the sad, two-noted, wooden tune
> of disparate wooden clogs
> carelessly clacking over
> a grease-stained filling station floor.

Bishop adds in brackets the observation that the clogs are imperfectly made:

> (In another country the clogs would all be tested.
> Each pair there would have identical pitch.)

Is this in praise of Brazil? She prefers the disparate music of these clogs to the perfectly made, perfectly pitched clogs of a more precise and efficient country. Such an observation and such a response is typical of Elizabeth Bishop. She can focus on the ordinary and the inconsequential and find them interesting and engaging. She is a poet who tells of things as they are.

In this third section, Bishop continues to give reasons to justify travel. She presents us with other enjoyed aspects of her journey: the music of the fat brown bird, the ornate, church-like, wooden songbird's cage, the pounding rain and the subsequent 'sudden golden silence'.

> – A pity not to have heard
> the other, less primitive music of the fat brown bird
> who sings above the broken gasoline pump
> in a bamboo church of Jesuit baroque:
> three towers, five silver crosses.

These are the details which Bishop notes and remembers, details which most tourists wouldn't notice, let alone remember, and it isn't a mere list. In this section we are shown how Bishop ponders the connection, if any, between the making of wooden clogs and the making of wooden cages. Why do these people put their efforts into ornate impractical objects, and not bother about perfecting the practical ones? It doesn't matter that the connection between clogs and cages is pondered 'blurr'dly and inconclusively' (she playfully blurs the very word blurr'dly). The form of the cage, with its 'weak calligraphy', encapsulates the colonized history of Latin American. The traveller who views the cage is seeing history.

She reveals herself to be good-humoured, curious, open-minded and tolerant when she writes:

> – Yes a pity not to have pondered,
> blurr'dly and inconclusively,
> on what connection can exist for centuries
> between the crudest wooden footwear
> and, careful and finicky,
> the whittled fantasies of wooden cages.
> – Never to have studied history in
> the weak calligraphy of songbirds' cages.
> – And never to have had to listen to rain
> so much like politicians' speeches:
> two hours of unrelenting oratory
> and then a sudden golden silence...'

Section 3 began with Bishop saying that 'it would have been a pity' not to have witnessed or experienced what she then describes, and each time a new aspect of her travels is added to the list, the phrase 'a pity' is repeated or implied: It would have been a pity 'Not to have had to stop for gas ...' (line 34); 'A pity not to have heard' (line 42); '– Yes, a pity not to have pondered' (line 47); 'Never to have studied ...' (line 53); '– And never to have had to listen to rain ...' (line 55).

The uncertainty of line 14, 'Should we have stayed at home and thought of here?', is now answered. And it is answered also in the final eight lines of the poem when Bishop imagines 'the traveller' (all travellers?) writing in a notebook, during 'a sudden golden silence', a philosophical musing on the nature of travel. There is no 'I' in this poem. Bishop has used 'we' five times already, and she also uses 'we' in the traveller's notebook, suggesting that the questions she has asked and the conclusions she has reached are shared with all travellers.

There is still some unease and some uncertainty in the traveller's notebook entry, despite the many convincing reasons given in section three in support and in praise of travel. The reference to the seventeenth-century French philosopher Blaise Pascal is a dramatic touch. Pascal was famous for staying at home. Elizabeth Bishop, his opposite, spent her life travelling, and 'Questions of Travel', dated 1965, when Bishop was in her mid fifties, asks questions which Bishop asked her entire life. She wonders whether the impulse or the need to travel is due to a lack of imagination:

> 'Is it lack of imagination that makes us come
> to imagined places, not just stay at home?'

The imagined places, however, once visited, as we have seen from the poem, do not disappoint. This is what allows her to suggest (Bishop is never dogmatic):

> *'Or could Pascal have been not entirely right*
> *about just sitting quietly in one's room?'*

The italicised final lines, like section 2, consists of questions, and the poem 'Questions of Travel' appropriately ends with a question mark. There are eleven known drafts or versions of this poem and the statement in line 65:

> *the choice is never wide and never free*

originally read as 'the choice perhaps is not great . . . but fairly free', proving that Bishop changed her mind during the writing of this poem (like many Bishop poems it was written over a period of time). For the traveller the world seems varied and huge. Does one choose 'continent, city, country, society'? (line 63). Does one choose 'here, or there'? Is one still restricted?

> *Continent, city, country, society:*
> *the choice is never wide and never free.*
> *And here, or there... No. Should we have stayed at home,*
> *where*ever that may be?

The placing of the word 'No' is important here, and the poem suggests that the restrictions need not invalidate the experience. The question 'Should we have stayed at home?' has already been answered.

Throughout this poem, there is the implied sense of a place called home, the place from which the traveller set out and to which the traveller returns. 'The Prodigal' also explores this idea. In Bishop's case, she lost home after home (an idea she writes about in her poem 'One Art'), and her final question in 'Questions of Travel' is shadowed by her own sense of homelessness. The speaker in the poem is a traveller. Beyond the questions of travel is the ultimate question of belonging:

> *'Should we have stayed at home,*
> *wherever that may be?'*

In Bishop's case, the question suggests that she has never felt at home.

The Armadillo

On the page, the structure and shape of 'The Armadillo' are ordered: ten four-lined stanzas. The rhyming scheme in the first stanza – abab – is not strictly observed throughout, but the second and fourth lines in each stanza rhyme.

The armadillo itself does not appear until line 30, and for most of the poem Bishop describes the balloon offerings associated with the religious festival. The balloons are 'frail, illegal', dangerous, fascinating and beautiful. Their delicacy is captured in a phrase such as 'paper chambers', and the simile 'like hearts' suggests that they are an expression of love.

From her house, Bishop watches the fire balloons rising towards 'a saint / still honored in these parts'. Bishop, though living in Brazil, is the observer, not the participant. The poem traces their movement as they move skywards, 'climbing the mountain height'. The balloons are offerings, forms of prayer, and they drift heavenwards. Bishop does not dwell on their religious source and symbolism, but their beauty is captured in stanza 3:

> Once up against the sky it's hard
> to tell them from the stars –
> planets, that is – the tinted ones:
> Venus going down, or Mars,
> or the pale green one.

They have become part of the night sky, the constellations where there is even a star group known as the Southern Cross. When she uses the phrase 'steadily forsaking us' in line 18, Bishop gives us a sense of our earth bound selves. The people who released these balloons watch them drift upwards and away. If we are forsaken, we are being abandoned or left behind. We cannot go with them. But they are also dangerous if caught in a downwind and line 21 introduces this other aspect:

> Last night another big one fell.
> It splattered like an egg of fire
> against the cliff behind the house.

The human world is threatened, as is the natural world. The house and its inhabitants, the owls, the armadillo and the rabbit are all threatened, and Bishop has seen the birds and animals suffer. 'Whirling', 'stained bright pink' and 'shrieked' all suggest confusion, pain and suffering. Fire that was once contained and distant has become destructive.

The armadillo makes its brief appearance in line 30: it is frightened and alone and can protect itself from almost everything, except fire. 'Glistening' and 'rose-flecked, head down, tail down' give the reader a vivid sense of the animal's presence. It has been suggested that the armadillo, a threatened creature on the edge of the human and the natural world, resembles the artist who has to discover a means of survival.

The owls, and the rabbit which appears suddenly in line 33, are even more vulnerable creatures. The birds flee their burning nest; the 'baby' rabbit, 'so soft!', is also frightened. Bishop's use of the dash in line 35 suggests that the rabbit is or will become 'a handful of intangible ash'; its eyes are 'fixed, ignited', yet she notices with surprise that the rabbit is 'short-eared'. The balloons have now become sources of threat and violence.

The last stanza is italicised, not only for emphasis and force:

> *Too pretty, dreamlike mimicry!*
> *O falling fire and piercing cry*
> *and panic, and a weak mailed fist*
> *clenched ignorant against the sky!*

These last four lines dismiss the earlier stanzas in a way, in that Bishop says that her descriptions of the fleeing animals are 'too pretty'. What the poem has presented to the reader so far is a 'dreamlike mimicry!'

Those closing lines emphasise the horrible reality:

> *O falling fire and piercing cry*
> *and panic*

Here, it is as if Bishop is questioning language and poetry itself; is poetry capable of conveying ugly, frightening reality? The italics and the exclamation marks in the final stanza add an urgency to the moment of suffering which has already been described in stanzas 7, 8 and 9. The final idea in the poem, which is that of

> *a weak mailed fist*
> *clenched ignorant against the sky!*

suggests both defiance and helplessness. The 'mailed fist' could be taken to refer to the armadillo's coat of mail, its defensive armour. Here Bishop does not offer just the accurate, objective description of the armadillo. She has done that in lines 30 to 32. The last two lines of the poem describe the armadillo, but now from a different and sympathetic perspective – that of the armadillo itself. The animal is spoken of as clenching its weak mailed fist, but clenching it nonetheless. And it is 'clenched ignorant against the sky!' The word 'ignorant' in line 40 reminds us that the armadillo does not understand the origins of this threatening fire and, since fire is the one thing from which the armadillo's outer coat cannot protect him, we are asked perhaps to consider the objects of supposedly religious worship in another light.

The owls, the armadillo and the rabbit are all victims, but the armadillo is the most striking presence among the creatures mentioned. It is the armadillo that gives the poem its title and it is to the armadillo that Bishop, clearly moved, returns in that final stanza. These closing lines of the poem have also been interpreted as symbolic of an ignorant and victimised working class, society's underdog, and the attempt by the working classes to strike for and assert their rights.

Sestina

The first lines of the poem establish a mood. It is as if the world itself is in mourning: the September rain and the failing light suggest sorrow and dying; it is the dying of the year and the dying of the day, but what is at the heart of the stanza is the human sorrow of the grandmother holding back her tears. In Bishop's story 'In the Village', the grandmother is crying openly; in the poem, those tears are stifled.

The last word in the first line is the word 'house'. This being a sestina, the word will occur in every stanza and occur seven times in all; it is the word with which the poem ends. This house has a grandmother and child and, as Seamus Heaney points out, 'the repetition of grandmother and child and house alerts us to the significant absence from this house of a father and a mother'.

The scene in stanza 1 is part cosy and comfortable, part dark and painful. There is the grandmother sitting in the kitchen with the child. It is warm; they sit 'beside the Little Marvel Stove' and the grandmother is reading jokes from the almanac. However, the grandmother's laughter and talking hide her tears.

The speaker in 'Sestina' is the adult Bishop, but she records her own experience as if she were an observer at a play. Bishop also interprets what is going on. In stanza 2, for example, Bishop allows us to glimpse the workings of the child's mind.

There is a significant difference between the grandmother and the young girl: the grandmother thinks that her autumn tears and the rain beating on the roof were known about and recorded in the almanac. Sorrow and the autumn rain seem inevitable. This is experience. The grandmother

> thinks that her equinoctial tears
> and the rain that beats on the roof of the house
> were both foretold by the almanac...

Normality keeps returning to the poem. Lines 11, 12 and 13 are pictures of domestic ordinariness and harmony:

The iron kettle sings on the stove.
She cuts some bread and says to the child,

It's time for tea now...

But then the child transfers the unwept tears of the grandmother to the drops, falling from the kettle on to the stove. As in 'First Death in Nova Scotia', the child's mind is attempting to connect and make sense of the world. In the Nova Scotia poem, the first person is used; here Bishop stands outside or apart from the experience by writing about herself and her childhood in the third person. The two people in the poem are never given personal names.

She knows that the grandmother has held back her tears and now the child

is watching the teakettle's small hard tears
dance like mad on the hot black stove,
the way the rain must dance on the house.

To the child, it now seems as if the tears are everywhere and they are 'hard' tears; they 'dance like mad', and she imagines them dancing on the house. In these lines Bishop returns us again to the child's thinking, the child's inner world.

Line 17 switches back to the everyday and ordinary:

Tidying up, the old grandmother
hangs up the clever almanac
on its string.

This domestic busyness and organisation indicates that life must go on, even if a life is overshadowed by great sadness. The almanac was said to have foretold this sorrow, in lines 7–10. In lines 19 and 20, the almanac is seen as a sinister presence, but this time it is not the child or the grandmother who thinks it, but Bishop, the adult poet.

Birdlike, the almanac
hovers half open above the child,
hovers above the old grandmother
and her teacup full of dark brown tears.

The future that the almanac represents hovers above child and grandmother. The tea in the teacup, like the water from the kettle, is described in terms of tears. Stanzas 2, 3 and 4 associate the ordinary things of the household with tears, but end with the business of the house. The 'tidying up' in stanza 3 and the building of the fire in stanza 4:

She shivers and says she thinks the house
feels chilly, and puts more wood in the stove.

Stanza 5 begins with a sense of inevitability and even the stove seems to have become a part of that inevitability:

> *It was to be,* says the Marvel Stove.
> *I know what I know,* says the almanac.

The italicised phrases are highly charged. The ordinary, familiar domestic world is no longer ordinary and familiar. The child withdraws by drawing an imaginary house, but that house is 'rigid' or tension filled and can only be reached by a 'winding pathway'.

> With crayons the child draws a rigid house
> and a winding pathway. Then the child
> puts in a man with buttons like tears
> and shows it proudly to the grandmother.

It is hardly straining the interpretation to see the presence of the man as a father figure; Elizabeth Bishop never knew her father. She, the child, does not shed any tears in the poem, but there are tears everywhere, even in the drawing.

The child is proud of her representation of a house, but the adult, in this instance the grandmother, the grown-up Elizabeth Bishop, and the reader, sees the drawing with a different understanding.

The grandmother is busy again while the little girl looks at the sun, moon and stars on the open pages of the almanac. She imagines 'little moons' fall secretly, and the description of these as tears reveals yet again the enquiring, puzzled, yet perceptive mind of the child. Reality and fantasy merge. Those same tears fall into the child's world of the flower beds.

The closing three lines tighten up: the six words focused on in the previous stanzas were each given a line of their own. Here, in the final stanza, the ideas which those same six words represent must be brought even closer:

> *Time to plant tears,* says the almanac.
> The grandmother sings to the marvellous stove
> and the child draws another inscrutable house.

What is past is past was how the literary critic David Kalstone interpreted those italicised words. The almanac, more often associated with future events, seems to declare the time of tears is over. The grandmother pretends to be cheerful in the same spirit in which she hid her tears in stanza 1. The child draws another house. The actual house in which the child lives with her grandparents is the only home she has really known. A child instinctively draws a house; it should be a familiar, comfortable and comforting place. But this house she draws is 'another inscrutable house'.

First Death in Nova Scotia

The poem 'First Death in Nova Scotia' is told from a child's point of view. The very title suggests this. It is as if no one had ever died in Nova Scotia before now. This is the child's first experience of death, and in the poem the child attempts to understand reality and, in doing so, makes confused, extraordinary, and sometimes almost fairytale connections. The fairytale element is most clearly seen, for example, when the child-speaker in the poem imagines that the royal presences in stanza 1 invite little Arthur in the final stanza to become 'the smallest page at court'. American academic Helen Vendler says that the poem 'goes steadily, but crazily, from little Arthur in his coffin to the royal pictures to the loon to Arthur to the child-speaker to the loon to Arthur to the royal pictures. This structure, which follows the bewildered eye of the gazing child trying to put together all her information (sense data, stories of an afterlife, and the rituals of mourning) is a picture of the mind at work.'

An elegy does not usually begin in such a stark manner, but in this poem it is the young uncomprehending child who speaks. It is as if Bishop can present us immediately with a grim picture. The repetition is chilling:

> In the cold, cold parlor
> my mother laid out Arthur

Bishop's mother is seldom mentioned in her poems, and she is mentioned here in a matter-of-fact way. The little body is spoken of in line 2, but the rest of the stanza describes the furnishings in the room. The royal presences lend the moment importance and dignity.

In line 7, the attention shifts to the stuffed bird on the table beneath the pictures. The stuffed loon, like Arthur, is dead. It has been

> shot and stuffed by Uncle
> Arthur, Arthur's father.

The room is 'cold, cold', and to the child observer it is as if everything has been frozen in time: the lifeless corpse, the still photographs, the stuffed loon. The use of repetition throughout the poem reflects the mind of a child attempting to make sense of the world it is describing.

In stanza 2 the child is wholly preoccupied with the bird, the violence of its death its silence, its cold stance and, contradicting everything else, its attractiveness ('caressable' and 'much to be desired' red glass eyes). Little Arthur is forgotten. Attention has shifted to the object:

> on his white, frozen lake,
> the marble-topped table.

The bird hasn't said a word since it was shot (nor of course has little Arthur since his death, but this is implied, never stated), and there is a sense of mystery, power and separateness in Bishop's phrase 'He kept his own counsel' in line 14. The child's mind works by association: an idea in stanza 1 recurs later; a phrase, 'deep and white', used once to describe the loon's breast, is later echoed in Bishop's description of the snow; and the red of the loon's eye recurs in the red of the Maple Leaf, little Arthur's red hair and the red royal clothes.

The child's gaze is broken by her mother's words:

> 'Come,' said my mother,
> 'Come and say good-bye
> to your little cousin Arthur.'

She is lifted up to place a lily of the valley in Arthur's hand. The poem's setting is the familiar, domestic world of the parlour, but death and the coffin turn the familiar into the strange. The mother asks the child to look on death and to put 'one lily of the valley' in her dead little cousin's hand. The coffin becomes in the child's mind 'a little frosted cake' and the loon is now seen almost as predator, as something alive:

> Arthur's coffin was
> a little frosted cake,
> and the red-eyed loon eyed it
> from his white, frozen lake.

Stanza 4 focuses on little Arthur. The language also marks the simplicity of childhood grappling with a first death:

> Arthur was very small.
> He was all white, like a doll
> that hadn't been painted yet.
> Jack Frost had started to paint him
> the way he always painted
> the Maple Leaf (Forever).

She imagines first that the body is like an unpainted doll, then that Jack Frost had 'started to paint him'. The child-speaker knows how Jack Frost always 'paints' the leaves red in autumn, specifically the maple leaf, and this thought is immediately connected with her being in Canada and the maple leaf as it is mentioned in the Canadian national anthem: 'the Maple Leaf (Forever).' The reference to the hair as red strokes/brush strokes is another indication of how the child's mind can process and transfer ideas: she imagines that hair on the white body has been painted red.

The 'Forever' associated with the Maple Leaf is the forever of Canadian patriotism.

The 'forever' in the last line of the stanza is the same word but with a different meaning; this time it signifies the finality of death:

> Jack Frost had dropped the brush
> and left him white, forever.

The poem ends with an imagined royal court, but there is no trace of a Christian or religious consolation. And the child invents this world, more fairytale than paradise; the mother does not offer one.

The cold is felt throughout the poem. Words such as 'cold, cold', 'white, frozen', 'marble-topped', 'white, cold', 'lily of the valley', 'frosted cake', 'white, frozen lake', 'all white', Jack Frost', 'white, forever' and the effect of repetition turn the parlour white and cold. But the last stanza brings warmth, pomp and ceremony:

> The gracious royal couples
> were warm in red and ermine;
> their feet were well wrapped up
> in the ladies' ermine trains.

Even the white of the ermine seems warm. The gracious presences of the two couples in the two pictures are warm, comfortable, welcoming. They invite little Arthur to join them; it is they who make possible his future.

> They invited Arthur to be
> the smallest page at court.

This, in the eyes of the observing child, is how and where little Arthur will live now that he has died.

In the closing lines, however, the speaker's fears return: Arthur is in his coffin. It is winter. How can Arthur escape from his coffin in the 'cold, cold parlor' and join the faraway royal court?

> But how could Arthur go,
> clutching his tiny lily,
> with his eyes shut up so tight
> and the roads deep in snow?

The details here ('clutching', 'tiny', 'tight', 'deep') suggest vulnerability, terror and fear. The final image in the poem is of Arthur, a child all alone in the world, incapable of reaching safety and a place he could call home.

Instead of heaven as Arthur's destination or Christian consolation, it is Bishop's imagination that makes possible and gives new life to the dead little boy; she imagines him, frightened, and wonders how he will travel 'roads deep in snow'.

Death is a powerful displacer. Of course there is a danger that biographical details will colour our reading of a poem too much, but the reader, realising that this poem was written by a woman whose father had died when she was eight months old and whose mother disappeared from her life when she was five, may see how fully 'First Death in Nova Scotia' reflects Bishop's uncomprehending childhood and her attempts to come to terms with absence and death.

In the Waiting Room

The poem begins with a place, a location, in this instance Elizabeth Bishop's own birthplace; it focuses on her place in the world and the distances between the personal world and the wider world beyond. There are references to 'in' and 'outside' throughout the poem.

In February 1918, Elizabeth Bishop was but a few days from her seventh birthday and the poem is spoken in the innocent, naive, unaffected voice of a seven year old. There is a matter-of-factness about it:

> In Worcester, Massachusetts,
> I went with Aunt Consuelo
> to keep her dentist's appointment
> and sat and waited for her
> in the dentist's waiting room.

The setting consists of unglamorous places: a waiting room suggests a form of displacement. In the waiting room one is neither here nor there. The ordinary world has been left behind: it is outside the door and can only be re-entered through that same door. The fact that it is a dentist's waiting room adds another dimension: waiting often involves tension, uneasiness and it often anticipates pain, but Bishop is not attending the dentist, merely accompanying her aunt. Later in the poem, a painful cry is heard from the dentist's room. The poem also explores how childhood can sometimes view adulthood harshly.

The scene is built up gradually. Bishop begins with town, state, waiting room, then the time of year.

Elizabeth Bishop sees herself as the odd-one-out. Everyone else in the waiting room is an adult:

> The waiting room
> was full of grown-up people,
> arctics and overcoats,
> lamps and magazines.

The adults in the room are never given personalities or individuality and are described in terms of what they wear. She is so shy of them that in line 64 she says 'I scarcely dared to look'.

The child-speaker in the poem retreats into the world of the *National Geographic* and carefully studies photographs of places and people very far away. Everything she sees in the magazine is different. The volcanic landscape with its black ashes and 'rivulets of fire' is different and in sharp contrast with a New England town in winter. The people she sees are also different: first the two explorers Osa and Martin Johnson in their travellers' attire and then 'the dead man slung on the pole', black women, black babies. The women have mutilated themselves in order to be sexually attractive. That this is a form of enslavement is not fully grasped by the seven-year-old child: it is certainly not articulated in the poem, but the reader recognises Bishop's genuine revulsion on seeing what they have done. 'In the Waiting Room' records Bishop's early and growing awareness of herself and the choices that await her, especially as a woman.

The language is simple and clear. The reader is presented with no difficulty in understanding what the child describes, but what is more important and interesting is Bishop's response.

> A dead man slung on a pole
> – 'Long Pig,' the caption said.
> Babies with pointed heads
> wound round and round with string;
> black, naked women with necks
> wound round and round with wire
> like the necks of light bulbs.

The dead man or 'Long Pig' will be eaten by the Polynesian cannibals; the babies have had their heads reshaped and the women's necks have been elongated, 'their breasts were horrifying.' This is inflicted and self-inflicted violence, and the child in the waiting room finds it repulsive and yet:

> I read it right straight through.
> I was too shy to stop.

Her emotions on reading the magazine are not shared or discussed with anyone in the room, and, having read and having been horrified, she attempts to objectify the experience by closing the magazine and observing mundane details:

> And then I looked at the cover:
> the yellow margins, the date.

The child has entered into an experience and, though not unmoved, she has retreated from it.

The child's gaze is abruptly broken at line 36. There is the cry of pain from the dentist's room. The dentist is unintentionally causing Aunt Consuelo to suffer:

> Suddenly from inside,
> came an *oh!* of pain
> – Aunt Consuelo's voice –
> not very loud or long.

The attitude to the pain in the next room is not Bishop's attitude to the pain of head shaping and neck lengthening she saw a moment before in the *National Geographic*. Instead, she sees her aunt as foolish and timid; she is neither surprised nor embarrassed:

> I wasn't at all surprised;
> even then I knew she was
> a foolish, timid woman.
> I might have been embarrassed,
> but wasn't.

However, the poem takes an interesting and unexpected direction when Bishop, the seven-year-old girl sees herself as a grown woman and as foolish as her aunt.

> What took me
> completely by surprise
> was that it was me:
> my voice, in my mouth.

Her aunt's cry becomes the speaker's own cry. The woman and the girl are one. It is as if the girl has no option but to grow up to become the kind of woman she does not want to be.

The child-speaker imagines, 'without thinking at all', that 'I was my foolish aunt', and, in a surreal leap of the imagination, both the aunt 'from inside' and the girl 'in' the waiting room are falling:

> I – we – were falling, falling,
> our eyes glued to the cover
> of the *National Geographic*,
> February, 1918.

The eyes are 'glued' to reality, to the magazine, the month and year, and then the aunt is forgotten about for 21 lines. The 'I' takes over and the defining 'I' is used nine times. Like Alice, she is falling but there is no Wonderland as such. It is, however, she says at lines 72–73, the strangest thing that could ever happen.

She hangs on to hard facts: her imminent birthday in three days.

> I was saying it to stop
> the sensation of falling off
> the round, turning world
> into cold, blue-black space.

The date of the experience recorded in the poem and given in the poem itself, in the closing lines, is 5 February and the facts give way to intense feeling:

> But I felt: you are an *I*,
> You are an *Elizabeth*

What she discovers with a sharp perceptiveness is that there is only one Elizabeth Bishop, separate, unique, but that that unique individual self is also one of womankind and destined perhaps to become like the women she has been thinking about – the trapped black women, the foolish Aunt Consuelo:

> you are one of *them*.
> *Why* should you be one, too?

Here the child-speaker wants to hang on, to stay on earth, and not to tumble into space or unknown territory.

Line 64 brings a lull. The language is no longer so insistent (the 'you are', 'you are' of the previous lines) and Bishop attempts to take her bearings:

> I scarcely dared to look
> to see what it was I was.
> I gave a sidelong glance
> – I couldn't look any higher –
> at shadowy gray knees,
> trousers and skirts and boots
> and different pairs of hands
> lying under the lamps.

This return to the familiar is comforting, and yet she is still shy, uneasy, and deeply aware that this moment has somehow altered and clarified her understanding of herself, that it is a moment of such insight and understanding that it will affect the rest of her life:

> I knew that nothing stranger
> had ever happened, that nothing
> stranger could ever happen.

And this sends her back to the earlier question (line 63 – '*Why* should you be one, too?') which Bishop now repeats with a different emphasis. The question at line 63 implies that Bishop resisted becoming a certain kind of woman. Now the question opens out into a question that explores the mystery of existence, the very strangeness of being alive:

> Why should I be my aunt,
> or me, or anyone?

It then opens out further to include the questions whether and how there are connections between people so obviously different:

> What similarities –
> boots, hands, the family voice
> I felt in my throat, or even
> the *National Geographic*
> and those awful hanging breasts –
> held us all together
> or made us all just one?

The child, almost seven, has been unnerved by the black women and their 'horrifying' breasts, their 'awful hanging breasts'. This is the outside world. She is also unnerved by the aunt's cry 'from inside',

> a cry of pain that could have
> got loud and worse but hadn't?

The poem ends with Bishop feeling faint and her sense of the waiting room

> sliding
> beneath a big black wave,
> another, and another.

The fainting spell is a loss of consciousness and then she is back in the waiting room. In the short closing section of the poem, there is an intense awareness again of place, outside and inside, and the specifics of time. In the first section of the poem, outside meant winter (line 6); later outside includes Polynesian culture and, in the final reference to a world beyond the waiting room, we are told that a war is being fought.

The young Elizabeth Bishop has waited in the waiting room. The place could be read as a symbol of childhood, a time spent waiting for adulthood, but everything that is spoken of in relation to the world beyond the immediate one is frightening, strange, confusing (what the academic Brett Millier calls 'the awful otherness of the inevitable world'). Elizabeth Bishop's relationship with that world and her feeling of not belonging to it recurs in many of her poems.

Emily Dickinson
(1830–1886)

Contents	Page
The Overview	97
Biographical Notes	99
POEMS	107
Critical Commentary	129

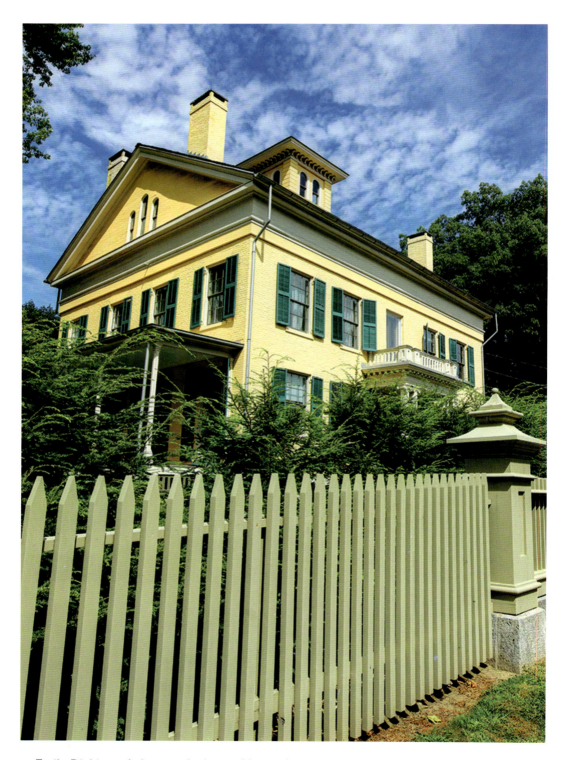

Emily Dickinson's house, Amherst, Massachusetts.

The Overview

Every true poet is unique and Dickinson's uniqueness is visually and verbally striking. She is the most instantly recognisable of poets. Her idiosyncratic genius is clearly seen in the imaginatively intense short lyrics without titles; the eccentric, unconventional punctuation; the capitalisations; the irregularities; the cryptic, puzzling images; the dash; the rhymes and half-rhymes; the hymn metre; the vigorous rhythm. Many of the lines in a Dickinson poem reach an abrupt and definite end; when she uses the run-on line, as she does in the closing stanzas of 'A narrow Fellow in the Grass', she does so effectively. It is said that, in Emily Dickinson's poetry, 'language remains itself and becomes at the same time brand new.'

These ten poems capture Dickinson's different moods, her extreme psychological states: there are moments of sudden intoxication ('I taste a liquor never brewed'), hopefulness, pain and suffering ('The Soul has Bandaged moments—'); there is a detailed exploration of the meaning of death; a delight in the world of nature ('A Bird came down the Walk') and its danger and mystery ('A narrow Fellow in the Grass').

Though Dickinson lived in Amherst for most of her life and lived in her father's house all of that time, it is characteristic that she only mentions Amherst by name in two of her 1,775 poems. Other personal details are never explicitly revealed in her poetry. It is not always possible to say if the poet is addressing another or if she is speaking to herself. In Adrienne Rich's words, Dickinson writes of 'the intense inner event, the personal and psychological'.

Many of her themes are abstract — she frequently writes about life, time, death and eternity — but her abstractions are often rendered vividly and imaginatively in her work. In 'I taste a liquor never brewed', she sees 'Seraphs swing their snowy Hats'; describing a numbed sensation, she says 'The Nerves sit ceremonious, like Tombs—'; and the poem 'I felt a Funeral, in my Brain' is typical of Emily Dickinson in its description of an interior state in such distinct, memorable, physical terms. Though short, the poems are intense. Compression is trademark. Her poems have been described as 'the drama of process'.

She is also a brilliant observer of nature. She watches a bird eat a raw worm or she sees the snake, 'a spotted shaft', and feels 'a tighter breathing'. On winter afternoons she notices 'a certain Slant of light' and finds it oppressive.

There is in her poetry an intense awareness of the private, inner self. 'Vesuvius at Home' was how she once described her domestic world, suggesting as it does an image of great emotional force and power. The poems often strike the reader as self-contained, riddling, elusive. Her tone is often confident, strong-willed and knowledgeable, as in 'I could bring You Jewels — had I a mind to'. She wrote for herself primarily; there was no audience for her work during her lifetime. In a letter she said 'Pardon my sanity in a world insane'.

Dickinson's poems on mortality ('I felt a Funeral, in my Brain' and 'I heard a Fly buzz — when I died') sometimes lead to uncertainty or despair ('And hit a World, at every plunge,/ And Finished knowing—then—' or 'And then the Windows failed—and then/ I could not see to see—'). The chilling mood is in stark contrast to a playful, delightful or happily confident note which is found in such poems as 'I taste a liquor never brewed' or 'I could bring You Jewels—had I a mind to'.

In one of these ten poems she adopts a persona: in 'A narrow Fellow in the Grass' she is remembering a time 'when as a Boy, and Barefoot' she saw a snake. 'I' is frequently used, but 'There's a certain Slant of light', 'After great pain, a formal feeling comes—' and 'The Soul has Bandaged moments—', where 'I' never occurs, achieve a different effect.

Dickinson believed that 'to shut our eyes is travel'. For her, the inner world of mind and imagination and heart were sufficient and these she explored brilliantly and honestly. 'My business,' she said in a letter, 'is circumference'. By circumference, one of her favourite words, she meant the 'comprehension of essentials'.

The interior of Emily Dickinson's home.

Biographical Notes

Emily Elizabeth Dickinson was born on 10 December 1830 in a house which her grandfather had built on Main Street, Amherst, Massachusetts. She was the second of three children born into a conventional Protestant family. Her grandfather was a lawyer, a pillar of the church and a founder of Amherst College; her father was also a lawyer. Amherst, at that time, was a small farming community of less than three thousand people.

Little is known of her childhood. When she was two and a half she stayed with her twenty-one-year-old aunt in Monson, twenty miles away, while Mrs Dickinson was recovering after the birth of her third child, Lavinia. Such details must seem trivial until one realises how little, outwardly, seems to have happened to Dickinson. In adult life, Dickinson rarely left home and her aunt, in a letter to her sister, tells of how, on that same journey, Dickinson's first, there was thunder and lightning which the little girl called 'the fire'. These are Emily Dickinson's first recorded words.

Emily Dickinson grew up in Puritan, small-town, New England and later she was to say that she viewed the world 'New Englandly' (Poem 285). Many books have argued that her childhood was bleak, but in a letter written when she was fourteen she says 'I am growing handsome very fast indeed! I expect I shall be the belle of Amherst when I reach my 17th year'. When she was sixteen she won second prize in the Bread Division at the local cattle show, and in 1858 was one of the judges. That same year she wrote 'Amherst is alive with fun this winter' and yet, when Dickinson was twenty-two, she wrote to her brother Austin, 'I wish we were children now. I wish we were *always* children, how to grow up I don't know'.

After primary school, Emily Dickinson attended Amherst Academy from 1840 to 1847, which she enjoyed very much. The Principal of the Academy remembered Emily Dickinson as 'a very bright, but rather delicate and frail looking girl; an excellent scholar, of exemplary deportment, faithful in all school duties; but somewhat shy and nervous. Her compositions were strikingly original; and in both thought and style seemed beyond her years, and always attracted much attention in the school and, I am afraid, excited not a little envy.' Another source described Emily Dickinson as one of 'the wits of the school' and named her as one of the liveliest contributors to *Forest Leaves*, the school paper, no copy of which survives.

At Amherst Academy, Dickinson's subjects included Latin, history, botany, geology and mental philosophy. A study of her poetry has revealed that the largest group of words in Dickinson's vocabulary drawn from special sources is drawn from contemporary technology or science; 328 words are technical terms generally found only in scientific or academic discourse.

In September 1847 Emily Dickinson attended Mount Holyoke Female Seminary at South Hadley, ten miles south of Amherst, but left after ten months or two terms.

The reasons for her not continuing there have been given as poor health, homesickness, her father wanting her at home, her dislike of the place and so on, but nothing definite is known. Subjects studied at Mount Holyoke included chemistry, physiology, algebra and ancient history.

Mount Holyoke was known for its missionary spirit and the young women were encouraged to become Christian and to commit themselves to Christianity in an open and public manner. Mary Lyon, who had founded the Seminary in 1837, divided the girls into three groups: 'No-hopers', 'Hopers' and 'Christians'. Emily Dickinson was classed among the 'No-hopers' and, in a letter written during her final term there, she said that she regretted the 'golden opportunity' of becoming a Christian but 'it is hard for me to give up the world'.

Back in Amherst, Dickinson dissociated herself from revivalist, religious fervour. An excerpt from a letter dated January 1850 gives us an idea of nineteen-year-old Dickinson's stance: 'Sewing Society has commenced again – and held its first meeting last week – now all the poor will be helped – the cold warmed – the warm cooled – the hungry fed – the thirsty attended to – the ragged clothed – and this suffering – tumbled down world will be helped to its feet again – which will be quite pleasant to all. I don't attend – notwithstanding my high approbation – which must puzzle the public exceedingly . . . – and my hardheartedness gets me many prayers'. Her closest friends and her sister Lavinia were answering Christ's call but Dickinson in that same letter says: 'I am standing alone in rebellion . . . I can't tell you what they have found, but they think it is something precious. I wonder if it is?'

It is at this time also that Emily Dickinson began to write poems. The very first poem in *The Complete Poems* is a poem dated 'Valentine week, 1850' when she was twenty, but it was not until her late twenties that Dickinson began to write what became her prolific output. From the beginning she was an original and her earliest work has all the characteristics of her idiomatic style and originality.

Though she rejected conventional religion, Dickinson never openly rebelled. Her biographer Richard B Sewell says that 'she was not geared to rebellion. She had been a model child, a good girl in school, a dutiful daughter. She had to find another way'. And one of those ways was undoubtedly the 1,775 poems which she wrote. In one poem (569) Dickinson writes about how much poetry and poets meant to her, more than Nature itself or God in Heaven. It begins:

> I reckon — when I count at all —
> First — Poets — Then the Sun —
> Then Summer — Then the Heaven of God —
> And then — the List is done —
>
> But, looking back — the First so seems
> To Comprehend the Whole —
> The Others look a needless Show —
> So I write — Poets — All —

Though Emily Dickinson was not part of the Revival Movement, she was deeply spiritual. When a friend died in Worcester, Massachusetts, she wrote to the minister there to enquire if 'he was willing to die, and if you think him at Home, I should love so much to know certainly, that he was today in Heaven'. The friend was Benjamin Franklin Newton, a law student in her father's office from 1847 to 1849. He was nine years older than her, an important influence who believed she would be a poet, but he died in 1853.

On 15 April 1862 Emily Dickinson, at thirty-one, wrote to Thomas Wentworth Higginson, enclosing four poems and asking 'if my Verse is alive? . . .' and 'Should you think it breathed'. Higginson was a man of letters and former Minister of the Free Church. He was a liberal thinker interested in promoting women writers. He had written an article in the *Atlantic Monthly* advising aspiring writers, and Dickinson, who by now had written three hundred poems, felt a need for criticism. Higginson, not fully understanding her work, advised her to tidy the 'irregularity' of her poems and her first printed poems have been 'tidied' up by him – he altered Dickinson's original punctuation, rhymes and vocabulary. It was not until 1955, with the publication of Thomas H Johnson's edition, that Emily Dickinson's work was restored to its original form. In that same letter to Higginson, written nine years after Newton had died, she wrote 'for several years, my lexicon – was my only companion –'.

The Dickinson family had to leave their home, known as 'The Mansion', for a clapboard house on North Pleasant Street, Amherst, where they lived from 1840–1855. By 1856 the Dickinsons, having overcome some financial difficulties, had returned to the Dickinson Homestead on Main Street, where Emily Dickinson had been born. We also know that by this time Dickinson had stopped going to church, though she remained deeply religious in her own way. A poem dated c.1862 contains the lines:

> Some keep the Sabbath going to Church —
> I keep it, staying at Home —

and in a letter written around 1884 Dickinson reveals her religious views: 'When Jesus tells us about his father, we distrust him. When he shows us his Home, we turn away, but when he confides to us that he is "acquainted with grief," we listen, for that is an Acquaintance of our own.'

•

When young, she took lessons in voice and piano, and music became a very important part of Emily Dickinson's life. She played the piano, especially late at night when the rest of the house was asleep, and the hymns which she had heard in church, hymns such as 'Our God, our help in ages past', were to become the metrical pattern for her poems.

So little is known of Emily Dickinson's adult life that the few details we do know have assumed an almost mythic quality, but it has been argued that something cataclysmic and decisive happened when she was thirty or thereabouts. On 25 April 1862 she wrote to Higginson: 'I had a terror – since September – I could tell to none – and so I sing, as the Boy does by the Burying Ground – because I am afraid . . .'

An unhappy love affair has been suggested. Benjamin Franklin Newton, Reverend Charles Wadsworth, Samuel Bowles and Thomas Wentworth Higginson were certainly important in her life, but Newton died in the early 1850s and she only met Higginson face to face twice. Here is an extract from Higginson's diary in which he describes his first meeting with Dickinson:

> a step like a pattering child's in entry . . . a little plain woman with two smooth bands of reddish hair and a face with no good feature . . . She came to me with two day-lilies, which she put in a sort of childlike way into my hand and said 'These are my introduction', in a soft, frightened, breathless childlike voice – and added under her breath, 'Forgive me if I am frightened; I never see strangers, and hardly know what to say'.

Ted Hughes writes that 'the central themes of the poems have suggested to many readers that the key event was a great and final disappointment in her love for some particular man, about this time' [early 1860s]. Three draft letters addressed to one whom she called 'Master' were found among her papers when she died. These are intense and passionate letters, but the identity of Master has never been known. The secret remains just that. What is significant is that in 1862, Dickinson wrote 366 poems; in 1863, 141 poems; and in 1864, 174 poems: more than one-third of her 1,775 poems were written during these three years when she was in her early thirties.

Philip Larkin put it like this: 'If Emily Dickinson could write 700 pages of poems and three volumes of letters without making clear the nature of her preoccupations, then we can be sure that she was determined to keep it hidden, and that her inspiration derived in part from keeping it hidden.' He concludes: 'The price she paid was that of appearing to posterity as perpetually unfinished and wilfully eccentric.'

And Dickinson herself wrote in poem number 1129:

> Tell all the Truth but tell it slant —
> Success in Circuit lies
> Too bright for our infirm Delight
> The Truth's superb surprise
> As Lightning to the Children eased
> With explanation kind
> The Truth must dazzle gradually
> Or every man be blind —

Dickinson rarely left her home in Amherst. In a letter dated 1853, when she was twenty-three, she wrote 'I do not go from home'. She read Shakespeare, the Brownings, George Eliot, the Brontes, Keats, Emerson, Ruskin, Sir Thomas Browne, the Bible, especially the Book of Revelations; she read the newspaper daily and wrote over a thousand letters. She even used letters to communicate with her brother Austin and sister-in-law, Susan Gilbert, who lived next door. Dickinson wrote more letters to Susan Gilbert Dickinson than to any other individual. Frequently her letters contained poems and her letters and poems share many stylistic similarities.

Dickinson spent ten months away from home in a boarding seminary when she was seventeen and in all she made seven trips from home during her lifetime, to Boston (for eye treatment), Washington D.C. and Philadelphia, but her life was very much lived indoors in Amherst, Massachusetts. Yet Dickinson chose to stay at home. Her niece, Martha Dickinson Bianchi, tells us that she once 'repeated to Aunt Emily what a neighbour had said – that time must pass very slowly for her, who never went anywhere – and she flashed back with Browning's line: "Time, why, Time was all I wanted!"' Once, when her niece visited her in her corner bedroom which overlooked the main street of Amherst in front and the path to her brother Austin's house to the side, Emily Dickinson pretended to lock the door with an imaginary key and said 'here's freedom'.

She always lived in her father's house. 'Probably no poet ever lived so much and so purposefully in one house; even, in one room,' says Adrienne Rich. But intellectually Dickinson was well-travelled. There are other well-known personal details: she wore white (one of her white dresses is displayed at her home in Amherst); she would lower little treats for the local children from her bedroom in a basket; when her nephew died from typhoid, aged eight, Emily Dickinson went next door for the first time in fifteen years.

Mabel Todd, who came to live in Amherst in August 1881, when she was twenty-six, wrote to her parents on 6 November 1881 and described 'a lady whom the people call the *Myth*':

> 'She is a sister of Mr Dickinson, & seems to be the climax of all the family oddity. She has not been outside of her own house in fifteen years, except once to see a new church, when she crept out at night, & viewed it by moonlight. No one who calls upon her mother & sister ever see her, but she allows little children once in a great while, & one at a time, to come in, when she gives them cake or candy, or some nicety, for she is very fond of little ones. But more often she lets down the sweetmeat by a string, out of a window, to them. She dresses wholly in white, & her mind is said to be perfectly wonderful. She writes finely, but no one ever sees her . . . No one knows the cause of her isolation, but of course there are dozens of reasons assigned.'

[Mabel Todd was the wife of a professor at Amherst College and she and Dickinson's brother Austin became lovers in 1882, a relationship which lasted until Austin's death in 1895. Austin Dickinson was fifty-two, while Mabel Loomis Todd was twenty-five. The two spouses knew of the relationship and the affair was widely known in Amherst. Dickinson, though she led a hidden life, was aware of these domestic difficulties and tensions. She was also aware of difficulties at a national level: the American Civil War was being fought, and many young men from Amherst went to war and never came home.]

After their mother's death in 1882 and towards the end of her own life, Dickinson and her sister Lavinia were living alone in their Amherst home. They were cared for by a servant and it was there that Emily Dickinson died, on 15 May 1886 of Bright's disease. The day before she died, Dickinson wrote to her cousins, the Norcross sisters, her final, short note: 'Little Cousins, – Called back. – Emily.'

Emily Dickinson had left directions for her funeral: her body was to be prepared for burial in one of her own white dresses, with a sprig of violets and a single pink orchid pinned at the throat. The coffin was also to be white and it was to be carried out the back door, around through the garden, through the open barn from front to back, and then through the grassy fields, 'three fields away', to the family plot in Amherst's West Cemetery, always in sight of the house. She was borne to her grave by six Irishmen, all of whom had worked at one time on her father's grounds.

At her funeral service which was held at the Dickinson home, Thomas Wentworth Higginson, whom she had written to twenty-four years earlier seeking advice, read Emily Bronte's poem 'Last Lines'. According to Higginson it was 'a favorite with our friend, who has put on that Immortality which she seemed never to have laid off':

> No coward soul is mine,
> No trembler in the world's storm-troubled sphere!
> I see Heaven's glories shine,
> And Faith shines equal, arming me from Fear . . .

And on her gravestone in West Cemetery, Amherst, are the words 'Called Back'.

During her lifetime, only eleven (some studies say seven, others ten) of her poems were published, anonymously, and after her death Dickinson's poems were published gradually. On going through her sister's belongings, Lavinia discovered a small box containing about 900 poems, arranged and sewn together in sixty little bundles or fascicles which make up two-thirds of Dickinson's poetry. Though it was known that Dickinson wrote poetry, no-one knew until after her death the range or the extent.

Lavinia asked Mabel Loomis Todd to prepare a selection of Dickinson's poems for publication. Todd asked Higginson to help and in 1890 they published 115 of Dickinson's poems in edited form. The book, *Poems by Emily Dickinson*, was a success. There were six printings of the book in six months. The following year, Todd and Higginson published *Poems, Second Series*, containing 166 poems. *Poems, Third Series*, edited by Todd, was published in 1896.

The first selection of 115 poems, with titles added, had certain words and punctuation altered to suit the prevailing tastes of the time. It was not until 1955, sixty-nine years after Dickinson's death, that an accurate and faithful edition of her poems was published. For example in the 1890 edition we read the following:

> There's a certain slant of light,
> On winter afternoons,
> That oppresses, like the weight
> Of cathedral tunes.

This is what Dickinson wrote:

> There's a certain Slant of light,
> Winter Afternoons —
> That oppresses, like the Heft
> Of Cathedral Tunes —

In the original, Dickinson's use of dashes, her capitalisation of certain words, her omission of the word 'on' in line two, gives the poem far greater force and focus. When printed as Dickinson intended, the poems, in Adrienne Rich's words, became 'jagged, personal, uncontrollable'. Ted Hughes has said of those Emily Dickinson dashes that they are 'an integral part of her method and style, and cannot be translated to commas, semicolons and the rest without deadening the wonderfully naked voltage of the poems'.

Ted Hughes also says of Emily Dickinson that 'There is the slow, small metre, a device for bringing each syllable into close-up, as under a microscope; there is the deep, steady focus, where all the words lie in precise and yet somehow fine relationships, so that the individual syllables are on the point of slipping into utterly new meanings, all pressing to be uncovered . . .'

Higginson, to whom Dickinson had sent four of her poems and who was one of the first to read her work, speaks of Dickinson's 'curious indifference to all conventional rules of verse' but wisely adds that 'when a thought takes one's breath away, a lesson on grammar seems an impertinence'.

●

Dickinson herself 'found ecstasy in living': the seasons, birdsong, sunset became the subject matter for her poems. And the darker aspects of life – a storm, 'a certain slant of light', our final moments, death itself – all were of interest to her. Though she wrote in a small way the big themes are all there: Life, Time, Nature and Eternity. And she uses language in a fresh and original way: 'Friday I tasted life. It was a vast morsel. A circus passed the house – still I feel the red in my mind'. She described herself as 'small, like the Wren, and my hair is bold, like the chestnut burr– and my eyes, like the Sherry in the Glass, that the Guest leaves.' Or she can capture a marvellously atmospheric image in a single line: 'The Day undressed – Herself –'

Sean Dunne described her poems as 'concise fragments from a diary, a logbook of the mind's voyages, and where Melville wrote of the sea and Whitman of the plains, she wrote of a space equally vast: her own mind.' Like Henry David Thoreau, she believed that self exploration is the only worthy kind of travel. Emily Dickinson understood the vast imaginative, intellectual world when she wrote:

> The Brain — is wider than the Sky —
>
> The Brain is deeper than the sea —

And it is worth remembering that Sewell concludes his detailed and wide-ranging biography of Dickinson with a reminder: 'The whole truth about Emily Dickinson will elude us always; she seems wilfully to have seen to that . . . There is a feeling of incompleteness, of areas still to be explored, of mysteries that still beckon.'

●

Of all poets in English, Emily Dickinson is one of the most strikingly original and eccentric. This is immediately seen in the unconventional capitalisations and the use of the dash. Although capitalisation was used earlier in English poetry, in Elizabethan printing houses capitalisation was up to the compositor and personified abstractions, the names of animals, plants, rocks, or minerals were capitalised. Later, Pope and Johnson, for example, in the eighteenth century, used capitals especially for abstractions, such as in this line from Johnson's 'A Short Song of Congratulation': 'Pomp and Pleasure, Pride and Plenty'. However, Dickinson gave the capital letter a new energy. Words which might have been considered commonplace (hats, sea, drum, walls, chill, bandaged, comb and so on) were given fresh attention and a more important role once capitalised.

The metre most often used by Dickinson was a conventional one, yet the poems sound anything but conventional because of the dash. Even if the poems were listened to and not read from the page, the dashes are felt and heard, and hearing the poem is every bit as important as seeing it on the page. Dashes are not only a striking feature of Emily Dickinson's poetry; her letters used a similar style and she often included poems in her letters. Here is part of a letter she wrote to console Mary Bowles, whose husband Samuel, whom, it has been argued, Emily Dickinson herself loved, had gone to Europe:

> Dear Mary —
> When the Best is gone — I know that other things are not of consequence — The Heart wants what it wants — or else it does not care —
> You wonder why I write — so — Because I cannot help — I like to have you know some care — so when your life gets faint for its other life — you can lean on us — We won't break, Mary. We look very small — but the Reed can carry weight . . .

Dashes were used much more frequently in the nineteenth century than they are today as Keats's or Queen Victoria's letters prove. Dashes, in Dickinson's hand, may be stately, dignified, measured; dashes can also be used for emphasis; they can suggest hesitation, the unknown.

POEMS

(The numbers given after each poem are the numbers given in *The Complete Poems of Emily Dickinson*; the first date is the conjectural date of composition; the second is the date of publication. Emily Dickinson gave none of her poems titles.)

I taste a liquor never brewed

I taste a liquor never brewed —
From Tankards scooped in Pearl —
Not all the Vats upon the Rhine
Yield such an Alcohol!

Inebriate of Air — am I —   5
And Debauchee of Dew —
Reeling - thro endless summer days —
From inns of Molten Blue —

When 'Landlords' turn the drunken Bee
Out of the Foxglove's door —   10
When Butterflies — renounce their 'drams' —
I shall but drink the more!

Till Seraphs swing their snowy Hats —
And saints — to windows run —
To see the little Tippler   15
Leaning against the — Sun —

Glossary

Line 2 Tankards: large open tub-like vessels, usually of wood, hooped with iron; a drinking vessel, formerly made of wooden staves and hooped; now, especially, a tall one-handled mug or jug, usually of pewter.

Line 2 scooped: hollowed out.

Line 3 Vats: large vessels used for the fermentation of alcohol.

Line 3 Not all the Vats upon the Rhine: a variant reading for line 3 is 'Not all the Frankfort Berries'.

Line 5 Inebriate: made drunk, exhilarated.

Line 6 Debauchee: one who has been seduced, one who over-indulges and neglects duty and allegiance.

Line 8 Molten: melted.

Line 11 renounce: reject.

Line 11 drams: a small drink of alcoholic liquor.

Line 13 Seraphs: angels of the highest of the nine orders.

Line 13 snowy Hats: haloes?

Line 15 Tippler: one who drinks often, but without getting drunk.

Line 16 Leaning against the – Sun –: a variant reading of this line is 'From Manzanilla come!', Manzanilla being in Cuba and famous for its rum.

This is one of the very few poems published during Dickinson's lifetime. The *Springfield Daily Republican* printed it on 4 May 1861, when Dickinson was thirty. It was published anonymously as 'The May-Wine'.

Questions

1. The moment captured here is special. How does Dickinson convey that it is? How would you describe Dickinson's relationship with nature?

2. How would you describe the poet's mood in the second stanza?

3. List everything you find unusual about Emily Dickinson's poetry as revealed to us in this poem. Give reasons for your answer.

4. Would you agree that the final stanza is particularly imaginative? What details suggest this?

5. How does the poem achieve its momentum of increased happiness?

6. Consider the final dash. Of the ten poems by Dickinson on your course, seven end with a dash, one with a question mark and two with a full-stop. How significant is the punctuation here?

'Hope' is the thing with feathers

'Hope' is the thing with feathers —
That perches in the soul —
And sings the tune without the words —
And never stops — at all —

And sweetest — in the Gale — is heard —   5
And sore must be the storm —
That could abash the little Bird
That kept so many warm —

I've heard it in the chillest land —
And on the strangest Sea —   10
Yet, never, in Extremity,
It asked a crumb — of Me.

Glossary

Line 7 abash: astound, defeat.

In any anthology of quotations, the entries under Hope are many and varied. Among the best known are 'Hope deferred maketh the heart sick' from the Book of Proverbs in the Bible and Alexander Pope's couplet from his Essay on Man:

> 'Hope springs eternal in the human breast:
> Man never is, but always to be, blest.'

Dickinson in a poem written c. 1877 (poem number 1392) says:

> Hope is a strange invention –
> A Patent of the Heart –
> In unremitting action
> Yet never wearing out –
>
> Of this electric Adjunct
> Not anything is known
> But its unique momentum
> Embellish all we own –

This is Dickinson in her late forties. '"Hope" is the thing with feathers –' is dated about sixteen years earlier when Dickinson was thirty-one.

Questions

1. How does Emily Dickinson give something abstract a vivid presence? Do you think the 'little Bird' metaphor and associated images are effective? Why is the metaphor of the bird appropriate? Give reasons for your answers.

2. What qualities does the poet attribute to Hope? How do the words and rhythm capture these qualities? Examine, for example, the poet's use of 'And', its place in the line and the use of the dash.

3. What is Dickinson's attitude towards Hope? Is she grateful, perplexed?

4. What is the significance of 'chillest land' and 'strangest Sea'? What do such references tell us about the nature of Hope?

5. What do you think Dickinson reveals of herself in the last two lines?

There's a certain Slant of light

There's a certain Slant of light,
Winter Afternoons —
That oppresses, like the Heft
Of Cathedral Tunes —

Heavenly Hurt, it gives us —   5
We can find no scar,
But internal difference,
Where the Meanings, are —

None may teach it — Any —
'Tis the Seal Despair —   10
An imperial affliction
Sent us of the Air —

When it comes, the Landscape listens —
Shadows — hold their breath —
When it goes, 'tis like the Distance   15
On the look of Death —

Glossary

Line 1 Slant: an oblique reflection; in American English it can also mean a gibe, a sly hit, or sarcasm. Harold Bloom interprets the phrase 'Slant of light' to mean a way of looking at the world; he sees the 'slant of light' as an image for a particular slant in Dickinson's own consciousness.

Line 3 oppresses: overwhelms with a sense of heaviness in mind or body.

Line 3 Heft: weight (American English) also means vigorously strong.

Line 9 Any: here 'Any' means anything. Shortening the word in this way is part of Dickinson's personal idiom or form of expression.

Line 10 Seal: something that authenticates or confirms, a sign or symbol.

Line 11 imperial affliction: a state of acute pain or distress caused by a supreme authority.

Line 15/16 the Distance / On the look of Death —: In Richard Ellmann's and Robert O'Clair's edition of this poem, they supply the following observation in relation to the poem's last lines: In a letter dated 1878 Dickinson wrote 'I suppose there are depths in every Consciousness, from which we cannot rescue ourselves – to which none can go with us Mortally – the Adventure of Death –'.

> Light and its effect was something that interested Dickinson. For instance, in one letter she wrote that 'November always seemed to me the Norway of the year' and she told Higginson that the 'sudden light on Orchards' was one of the things that moved her to write. Winter, it seems, was her least favourite season, and in *Emily Dickinson: An Interpretative Biography*, Thomas H Johnson says she 'devoted the fewest poems to winter'. Dickinson, however, refers to summer in at least two hundred poems.

Questions

1. A certain mood is created in the opening lines of the poem. Identify this mood and say which details convey it best. What connection does Emily Dickinson make between 'a certain Slant of light' and 'Cathedral Tunes'?

2. Why, in your opinion, does Dickinson speak of 'Heavenly Hurt'? What causes such pain and suffering? What is the distinguishing characteristic of such hurt according to Dickinson in stanza two?

3. Would you agree that there is an oppressive air and a feeling of despair expressed here? What words or phrases suggest a feeling of helplessness?

4. The poet responds to the 'certain Slant of light'; so too does the 'Landscape'. Is their response similar? How?

5. Would you consider this an optimistic or a pessimistic poem?

6. What is the effect of the final line? Is the reader prepared for this ending by what has gone before?

I felt a Funeral, in my Brain

I felt a Funeral, in my Brain,
And Mourners to and fro
Kept treading — treading — till it seemed
That Sense was breaking through —

And when they all were seated,   5
A Service, like a Drum —
Kept beating — beating — till I thought
My Mind was going numb —

And then I heard them lift a Box
And creak across my Soul   10
With those same Boots of Lead, again,
Then Space — began to toll,

As all the Heavens were a Bell,
And Being, but an Ear,
And I, and Silence, some strange Race   15
Wrecked, solitary, here —

And then a Plank in Reason, broke,
And I dropped down, and down —
And hit a World, at every plunge,
And Finished knowing — then —   20

📖 Glossary

Line 12 toll: to give out the slowly measured sounds of a bell when struck at uniform intervals, as at funerals.

Line 13 As all: as if all – another example of Dickinson's idiomatic style.

> Dickinson has been called the greatest realist of the interior that America has produced. 'I felt a funeral, in my Brain' is a poem of the interior. Here Emily Dickinson is imagining, anticipating, her own breakdown or her own funeral and death. It has also been suggested that the poem describes a fainting spell. Sewell, in his biography of Dickinson, says:
>
> *'I felt a Funeral, in my Brain' where Reason 'breaks' may be a tortured requiem on her hopes for Bowles [Samuel Bowles] both to love her and to accept her poetry; or it may commemorate a period of stagnation as a poet, when her mind, as she looked back, almost gave way under the weight of her despair; or it may refer to a mental or spiritual crisis of the sort she predicted . . . She seems as close to touching bottom here as she ever got. But there was nothing wrong with her mind when she wrote the poem.*

❓ Questions

1. Identify how each stanza focuses on particular aspects of funeral rituals. What is unusual about this particular funeral?

2. Consider the effect of repetition in stanzas one, two and five. What do these repetitions suggest?

3. How would you describe the poet's mood throughout the poem? Which words and phrases, in your opinion, best convey this mood?

4. Is the poet's tone uncertain or fatalistic or both?

5. What is the effect of the thirteen 'ands' in the poem? What is the significance of 'And' at the beginning of each line in the final stanza?

6. Do you sense a change in the poem at the beginning of stanza four? How is this change achieved?

7. Comment on the significance of the imagery of 'Bell' and 'Ear' and 'strange Race' in stanza four.

8. What is the impact of the final stanza?

A Bird came down the Walk

A Bird came down the Walk —
He did not know I saw —
He bit an Angleworm in halves
And ate the fellow, raw,

And then he drank a Dew   5
From a convenient Grass —
And then hopped sidewise to the Wall
To let a Beetle pass —

He glanced with rapid eyes
That hurried all around —   10
They looked like frightened Beads, I thought —
He stirred his Velvet Head

Like one in danger, Cautious,
I offered him a Crumb
And he unrolled his feathers   15
And rowed him softer home —

Than Oars divide the Ocean,
Too silver for a seam —
Or Butterflies, off Banks of Noon
Leap, plashless as they swim.   20

📖 Glossary

Line 3 Angleworm: any worm used as bait by anglers.

Line 20 plashless: splashless, without causing a splash.

❓ Questions

1. Is this poem different in any way from the poems by Dickinson which have gone before? Is it a difference in subject matter or in style?

2. How does Dickinson respond to the bird? Which details indicate her powers of accurate observation? Which details indicate her attitude towards the bird? What do we learn about Dickinson from this poem?

3. What does this poem suggest about the world of nature and the relationship between man/woman and nature?

4. Can you suggest why this poem ends with a full stop?

5. What is the significance of the image of the butterflies in the final stanza? What is the connection between bird and butterfly?

6. How would you describe Dickinson's mood in this poem? Does the word 'Cautious' in line 13 refer to the bird or Dickinson or could it refer to both?

After great pain, a formal feeling comes

After great pain, a formal feeling comes —
The Nerves sit ceremonious, like Tombs —
The stiff Heart questions was it He, that bore,
And Yesterday, or Centuries before?

The Feet, mechanical, go round —   5
Of Ground, or Air, or Ought —
A Wooden way
Regardless grown,
A Quartz contentment, like a stone —

This is the Hour of Lead —   10
Remembered, if outlived,
As Freezing persons, recollect the Snow —
First — Chill — then Stupor — then the letting go —

Glossary

Line 1 formal: precise, ceremonious.

Line 3 He: Christ.

Line 6 Ought: what they are obliged to do (the feet move as they are obliged to move, mechanically); Helen Vendler suggests that ought here means nothing/void; it has also been suggested that Dickinson was thinking of 'aught' here, meaning 'in any respect at all'. In Shakespeare, Milton and Pope, *ought* and *aught* occur indiscriminately.

Line 9 Quartz: the commonest rock-forming mineral.

Line 13 Stupor: a state in which one feels deadened or dazed.

'After great pain, a formal feeling comes —' is dated circa 1862; Dickinson was thirty-two or so when she wrote it. It was first published in 1929.

Questions

1. What, according to Dickinson, occurs when one has experienced great pain? Is it a physical reaction only?

2. Why does Dickinson refer to Christ here? Why is there confusion in line 4?

3. Consider the shape and structure of the poem on the page. Can you suggest why stanza two is different from the others?

4. Which details capture best a state of numbness? Is 'Quartz contentment' similar to 'Wooden way' and 'Hour of Lead'? What is the significance of 'Remembered, if outlived'?

5. How would you describe the rhythm and how is it achieved?

6. Would you consider the final two lines hopeful in any way? Give reasons for your answer. Do you think this poem expresses an unusual view of human suffering?

I heard a Fly buzz — when I died

I heard a Fly buzz — when I died —
The Stillness in the Room
Was like the Stillness in the Air —
Between the Heaves of Storm —

The Eyes around — had wrung them dry —   5
And Breaths were gathering firm
For that last Onset — when the King
Be witnessed — in the Room —

I willed my Keepsakes — Signed away
What portion of me be   10
Assignable — and then it was
There interposed a Fly —

With Blue — uncertain stumbling Buzz —
Between the light — and me —
And then the Windows failed — and then   15
I could not see to see —

📖 Glossary

Line 4 Heaves: force, great efforts.

Line 7 Onset: commencement, the action or act of beginning something; onset also means attack, assault.

Line 9 Keepsakes: things given to be kept for the sake of the giver.

Line 12 interposed: to put oneself forward or interfere in a matter.

> This poem says the impossible. *No one can speak the words 'I died'. Yet Dickinson writes of the moment of death as a moment inevitable and fascinating.*

❓ Questions

1. Why is this poem written in the past tense? Once you have registered the unusual perspective from which this poem is written, trace through each stanza how the poet builds up the details of the story being told. Consider sensory details in your response.

2. How do you interpret the fly? Is it symbolic and, if so, what could it symbolise?

3. What is the poet's sense of the other persons in the room? How does she speak of witnessing the King (line 7)? Are her perceptions different from the others in the room? Is this a conventional nineteenth-century death-bed scene?

4. Consider the capitalised words. Do they form a short-hand narrative of their own?

5. The fly is mentioned in the opening line and again in line 12 which leads into the final stanza. What is the effect of beginning and ending with the fly?

6. It has been said that in this poem Emily Dickinson 'sees only disappointment' and that the poem tells of 'the terrible attempts of a soul to prolong life.' Would you agree with this view?

7. Is the light spoken of here the same as the light in 'There's a certain Slant of light'?

8. Which other poems by Emily Dickinson on your course would you compare with this one? Give reasons for your answer.

The Soul has Bandaged moments

The Soul has Bandaged moments —
When too appalled to stir —
She feels some ghastly Fright come up
And stop to look at her —

Salute her — with long fingers —   5
Caress her freezing hair —
Sip, Goblin, from the very lips
The Lover — hovered — o'er —
Unworthy, that a thought so mean
Accost a Theme — so — fair —   10

The soul has moments of Escape —
When bursting all the doors —
She dances like a Bomb, abroad,
And swings upon the Hours,

As do the Bee — delirious borne —   15
Long Dungeoned from his Rose —
Touch Liberty — then know no more,
But Noon, and Paradise —

The Soul's retaken moments —
When, Felon led along,   20
With shackles on the plumed feet,
And staples, in the Song,

The Horror welcomes her, again,
These, are not brayed of Tongue —

📖 Glossary

Line 2 appalled: dismayed, made pale, made flat or stale, bereft of courage, etc. by sudden terror.

Line 7 Goblin: an evil or mischievous spirit; here it may mean 'goblin-like'.

Line 10 Accost: to approach or address.

Line 13 Bomb: in Dickinson's own lexicon, *Webster's American Dictionary*, 'bomb' has the alternative definition – 'the stroke upon the bell'.

Line 20 Felon: a wicked person; one guilty of a serious crime, a criminal.

Line 21 shackles: fastenings which confine the limbs and prevent free motion.

Line 21 plumed: feathered.

Line 22 staples: obstructions – the song is being held down.

Line 24 brayed: sounded harshly.

> This is one of Dickinson's longer poems. It is irregular in shape with four four-line stanzas, one six-line stanza and a final two-line stanza.
>
> Usually it is the body that is bandaged. Here, Dickinson imagines the soul as a physical and wounded entity.

❓ Questions

1. What does the word 'bandaged' suggest?

2. How does Dickinson in this poem convey a feeling of helplessness? Is helplessness the only feeling associated with the soul in this instance? If not, how would you characterise the soul as revealed to us in the poem?

3. Who might Fright (line 3) stand for in the context of the poem? Lines 7–10 are particularly difficult. Who might the Goblin and the Lover be?

4. What change takes place at line 11? Is there anything to suggest what makes such change possible? What is the effect of such words as 'dances', 'Bomb', 'abroad', 'swings'? How does the third stanza contrast with what has gone before?

5. What is the significance of the bee simile? Do you think it an appropriate image? Why?

6. There is a shift of mood again in the final two stanzas. How is this achieved? Why does Horror welcome the Soul? Comment on the word 'welcomes'. Is it similar in any way to 'Caress' in line 6?

I could bring You Jewels — had I a mind to

I could bring You Jewels — had I a mind to —
But You have enough — of those —
I could bring You Odors from St Domingo —
Colors — from Vera Cruz —

Berries of the Bahamas — have I —   5
But this little Blaze
Flickering to itself — in the Meadow —
Suits Me — more than those —

Never a Fellow matched this Topaz —
And his Emerald Swing —   10
Dower itself — for Bobadilo —
Better — Could I bring?

Glossary

Line 3 Odors: scents, fragrances.

Line 3 St Domingo: Santo Domingo in the Caribbean.

Line 4 Vera Cruz: city on the east coast of Mexico.

Line 5 Bahamas: a group of islands south-east of Florida.

Line 6 Blaze: a brilliant, splendid, clear light.

Line 11 Dower: dowry, the property which a woman brings to her husband in marriage.

Line 11 Bobadilo: braggart(?); in Ben Jonson's *Everyman in his Humour,* the character Bobadil is a swaggering boaster.

> The chapter containing the description of Jerusalem as a jewel in the biblical Book of Revelations was Dickinson's favourite chapter in the Bible. She called it the 'Gem Chapter'. Here jewels are rejected for something more precious.

Questions

1. Who might the poet be speaking to here? Is it clear from the context? How would you describe her tone? Which words and phrases capture that tone?

2. Why does the speaker reject jewels, scents and other possible gifts? Are the exotic places – St Domingo, Vera Cruz, the Bahamas – significant? How do they compare with 'the Meadow' of line 7? What does she choose instead? What does the choice tell us about the poet?

3. What does Dickinson find attractive in 'this little Blaze'?

4. Compare this poem with 'I taste a liquor never brewed' as expressions of happiness and in terms of imagery drawn from nature.

5. What is the effect of the question mark with which the poem ends?

A narrow Fellow in the Grass

A narrow Fellow in the Grass
Occasionally rides —
You may have met Him — did you not
His notice sudden is —

The Grass divides as with a Comb —   5
A spotted shaft is seen —
And then it closes at your feet
And opens further on —

He likes a Boggy Acre
A Floor too cool for Corn —   10
Yet when a Boy, and Barefoot —
I more than once at Noon
Have passed, I thought, a Whip lash
Unbraiding in the Sun
When stooping to secure it   15
It wrinkled, and was gone —

Several of Nature's People
I know, and they know me —
I feel for them a transport
Of cordiality —   20

But never met this Fellow
Attended, or alone
Without a tighter breathing
And Zero at the Bone —

Glossary

*Line 13 **Whip lash***: the lash or striking end of a whip.

*Line 14 **Unbraiding***: unwinding, unravelling.

*Line 20 **cordiality***: kindness, warm affection.

*Line 24 **Zero***: a freezing sensation.

'A narrow Fellow in the Grass' was published as 'The Snake' during Dickinson's lifetime – in *Springfield Daily Republican*, 14 February 1866.

In her poetry Dickinson sometimes adopts the voice of a persona. In 'A narrow Fellow in the Grass' the speaker is male and remembers boyhood. Dickinson has chosen to frame an eight-line stanza with two four-line stanzas.

Questions

1. Who is speaking here? What detail suggests a persona? What is revealed to us of the speaker? Consider, for example, the significance of the phrase 'Nature's People' (line 17).

2. There is a fascination with the 'narrow Fellow' for much of the poem but what feeling is expressed in the final stanza?

3. Which details do you think capture the snake best?

4. In the first three stanzas each line is self-contained and separate; in the final two stanzas Dickinson uses a run-on line. What is the effect of this?

General Questions

A. 'The poetry of Emily Dickinson is both startling and eccentric.' Discuss this view in the light of your reading the poems by Emily Dickinson on your course.

B. What would you identify as the principal preoccupations of Emily Dickinson as revealed to us in her poetry? In your answer, you should quote from or refer to the poems by Dickinson on your course.

C. Philip Larkin says of Emily Dickinson: Her epitaph might have been her own words: 'Nothing has happened but loneliness'. Discuss this view quoting from or referring to the Emily Dickinson poems on your course.

D. 'My business is circumference', says Emily Dickinson, and she defined circumference as 'the comprehension of essentials'. Discuss how she explores what is essential. In your answer you should quote from or refer to poems by Emily Dickinson on your course.

E. 'Dickinson's poetry is striking in its individual expression of happiness and suffering or death.' Discuss this statement, supporting your answer by quotation from or reference to the poems by Emily Dickinson on your course.

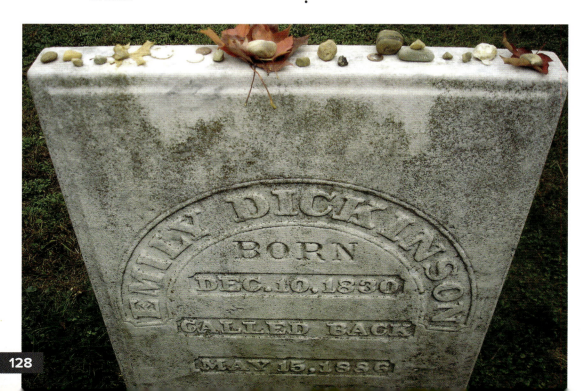

I taste a liquor never brewed

This poem begins with an intensely imagined moment. Here Dickinson speaks of a drink, unlike any ordinary drink, which she says she can taste:

> I taste a liquor never brewed —
> From Tankards scooped in Pearl —
> Not all the Vats upon the Rhine
> Yield such an Alcohol!

The moment is rare and special; the moment is hers. How special this particular drink is can be seen in line 1: liquor involves fermentation or distillation but this is a liquor which has not needed brewing. 'Tankards scooped in Pearl', line 2, is one of those lines which can be interpreted in different ways, yet labouring over this line is counterproductive. 'Tankards' can mean both large containers or drinking vessels. What is important here is the otherness or strangeness of the drink ('never brewed') and the unusual nature of the tankard. The tankard is made of pearl, or is so decorated that its surface looks as if it is hollowed out in pearl. The lustrous, beautiful pearl image makes the experience of drinking all the more special.

In line 3 Dickinson uses a negative to emphasise a positive. What she tastes is superior to what one of the world's finest, best-known wine regions can produce.

> Not all the Vats upon the Rhine
> Yield such an Alcohol!

This first stanza ends, as does stanza three, with an exclamation mark, signalling Dickinson's sustained delight.

The first stanza does not follow an exact rhyme, but Dickinson uses a regular end-rhyme in the following three stanzas: Dew / Blue; door / more; run / Sun.

[In an article published in *The Atlantic Monthly* in 1892, Thomas Bailey Aldrich set about 'correcting' the poem. His revised version of stanza one read:

> I taste a liquor never brewed
> In vats upon the Rhine:
> No tankards scooped in pearl could yield
> An alcohol like mine.

and 'in Miss Dickinson's book', he complained, 'for the most part the ideas totter and toddle, not having learned to walk'.]

The true nature of this liquor is revealed in lines 5–8:

> Inebriate of Air — am I —
> And Debauchee of Dew —
> Reeling — thro endless summer days —
> From inns of Molten Blue —

She is drunk on summer, its 'endless summer days', and that sense of a never-ending summer is captured even in her use of the dash. Stanza two is the only one to have a dash at the end of each line, suggesting the reeling, on-going sense of delight which Dickinson is celebrating.

The use of 'am I' and not the more usual 'I am' along with its place in the line give a mood of total happiness; 'am I' here is a phrase with flourish. And to describe herself as 'Debauchee' suggests a reckless sense of pleasure. She is drunk on summer air, morning dew; she is 'reeling', dizzy with excitement.

Line 8, 'From inns of Molten Blue —' suggests summer nights. When the night sky is melted or molten blue, the time is one of rest. The night-time is an inn, but once the summer days begin again Dickinson is reeling through them:

> Reeling — thro endless summer days —
> From inns of Molten Blue —

Like so many single lines from Dickinson, this yields a striking, memorable and original image.

The image of the inn is taken up in stanza three, when Dickinson speaks of nature:

> When 'Landlords' turn the drunken Bee
> Out of the Foxglove's door —

Here the bee is shown as having had enough; it is drunk and Dickinson imagines it is being told to leave the foxglove where it has been drinking its fill of nectar. Who or what the landlords are is difficult to say; it could well refer to the closing flower when the sun goes down. The inverted commas add a playful interpretation to the word. Perhaps she is referring to the stamens in the foxglove and how they prevent an already 'drunken Bee' from entering the flower. Dickinson then speaks of butterflies who, unlike the bee, realise that they have had enough to drink.

> When Butterflies — renounce their 'drams' —
> I shall but drink the more!

The bee, the butterflies and Dickinson herself have all been drinking in the experience of summer. The use of 'When' in lines 9 and 11 indicates a certain time when nature itself is satisfied. The drunken bee is told that it has had enough; the butterflies realise that they do not need more and 'renounce their "drams" —'; but Dickinson at such a moment is all the more inspired to drink on, and to experience summer to excess. 'I shall but drink the more!', with its exclamation mark, is joyfully determined in tone.

The final stanza pictures this ecstatically happy state, a state of drunken bliss. It is heavenly:

> Till Seraphs swing their snowy Hats —
> And saints — to windows run —
> To see the little Tippler
> Leaning against the — Sun —

Here is a self-portrait of Dickinson in a state of total happiness. The 'endless summer days' allow her to imagine that she is in heaven. 'When' and 'When' give way to 'Till' at the beginning of line 13. The 'Seraphs swing their snowy Hats —'. The highest order of the angels shares in Dickinson's delight. The verb 'swing' brings a music to the image, as does the alliteration on 'Seraphs', 'swing' and 'snowy'. The use of 'snowy' here also suggests hats or haloes the colours of bright clouds high in the heavens, and the excitement is shared by the saints who run to windows to see Dickinson. She is the centre of attention, the 'little Tippler', and she has achieved a heavenly state without ever mentioning death.

By stanza four, Dickinson has transported herself to a place close to heaven itself. She drinks often, is 'Inebriate of Air', has been 'Reeling – thro endless summer days –' but now in the final line of the poem she is leaning against the sun. The critic Charles R. Anderson speaks of stanza four and the 'unorthodox scene of hurrahing in heaven, with its bold metaphor converting the sun into a celestial lamp-post' and thinks that it may well be 'a comic version of spiritual intoxication as set forth in the Book of Revelation'.

The sun is the source of those 'endless summer days' and Dickinson has imagined herself growing closer to it, so close that she can lean against it. This final unique and striking image suggests ease and comfort.

The poem is exploring a heightened state. It is celebrating Dickinson's love of summer but it is also about inspiration: the inspiration of summer and the inspiration which makes possible the poem. Here Dickinson is a poet of euphoria ('I taste a liquor never brewed'); she is also a poet of great pain and suffering ('I felt a Funeral, in my Brain').

Critical Commentary

'Hope' is the thing with feathers

In the dictionary 'Hope' is defined: to entertain expectation of something desired. Dickinson offers her own understanding and definition. In '"Hope" is the thing with feathers—', Hope is a little song bird yet Dickinson refers to it throughout the poem as 'thing' and 'it'. Stanza one establishes the comparison. Hope, an abstraction, is given a strong physical presence in the bird metaphor:

> 'Hope' is the thing with feathers —
> That perches in the soul —
> And sings the tune without the words —
> And never stops — at all —

Hope is small; it 'perches in the soul', yet it is feathered and therefore capable of flying. The detail 'perches' suggests that hope has alighted or settled in the soul, its presence there permanent. Dickinson speaks of the song it sings as 'a tune without the words'. It cannot be understood on the level of language; it is beyond the verbal. The poem is made of words but tells of the song within the soul which transcends language.

Line 4 is very confident in tone. There is no end to hope; its song 'never stops':

> And never stops — at all —

Stanza one speaks of hope within, hope as something which inhabits the soul. In the second stanza, Dickinson speaks of 'the Gale', a storm that could be heard within or without. It is during such turmoil that the song of the bird is sweetest. The storm, Dickinson says, must be severe if it astounds and attempts to destroy the little bird of hope which has helped so many during other difficult times:

> And sweetest — in the Gale — is heard —
> And sore must be the storm —
> That could abash the little Bird
> That kept so many warm —

Hope, in this stanza, is portrayed as courageous. The bird will sing in the gale and its tune will be sweetest then. Sympathy for the bird is clearly felt in the line 'abash the little Bird'.

The phrase 'so many' in line 8 allows the poem to move from the individual to the many. Hope is experienced by others; many can be kept warm and can experience a warmth within, though the landscape be chill.

The final stanza turns to Dickinson and her own personal experience. Up to now she has spoken of hope in general terms. Stanza three has I and 'Me':

I've heard it in the chillest land —
And on the strangest Sea —
Yet, never, in Extremity,
It asked a crumb — of Me.

Hope is heard in times of difficulty and Dickinson represents such times in terms of landscape and seascape: 'the chillest land'; 'the strangest Sea'. Hope makes no demands. The 'never' in line 11 is absolute; Dickinson gives it extra power by placing it between two commas. In times of 'Extremity' the bird of hope never asked for so much as a crumb.

The poem is a celebration. All difficulties are overcome because of hope and Dickinson's confident belief in hope is the way she has structured her poem. The first two lines are a statement of belief and then follow four lines, each beginning with 'And', which gather momentum and emphasis through repetition and imagery. 'Gale', 'storm', 'abash' are all loud-sounding and destructive, but hope's 'sweetest' sound cannot be drowned out. The final stanza achieves a quieter sound but its tone is one of absolute conviction and gratitude.

The poem begins with an abstraction, 'Hope', and ends with the definite, unique self, 'Me'. The abstraction has been interiorised; the speaker here has learned through experience that hope is essential and that hope has proved to be a constant. [Elsewhere in her poetry, Dickinson also offers her own, unique definitions. In poem number 76, for example, she writes:

Exultation is the going
Of an inland soul to sea

In poem 709, she defines publication: 'Publication — is the Auction/ Of the Mind of Man —'; and in poem 910, experience: 'Experience is the Angled Road'.]

There's a certain Slant of light

This is both a mood poem and a meditative poem; it is also a poem in which Dickinson's meditation leads to an insight which she feels is shared by all. 'There's a certain Slant of light' explores, among other things, the relationship between man and God.

Though the poem focuses in line 1 on a slant of light, something that can often be beautiful in itself, there is a mood of heaviness and melancholy throughout the first stanza. 'Winter' and 'Afternoons' suggest the dying of the year and the dying of the day. The words 'oppresses' and 'Heft' add to this feeling of being weighed down. 'Cathedral Tunes' suggest solemnity, seriousness. Denis Donoghue thinks that 'The cathedral tunes oppress because of the sullen weight of faith which they ask the listener to receive and to lift'.

> There's a certain Slant of light,
> Winter Afternoons —
> That oppresses, like the Heft
> Of Cathedral Tunes —

The images conjured up here are neither light-hearted nor celebratory. The mood can be more fully grasped if these opening lines are read next to a poem such as 'I taste a liquor never brewed', where the words and sounds create a totally different mood. The mood here is sombre; the other is ecstatic.

In this first stanza, Dickinson uses the senses to convey the moment of perception. We see the beam or ray of winter light; it is compared to 'Cathedral Tunes' which we can imagine ourselves hearing. Light waves have become sound waves and 'oppresses' and 'Heft' are sensuous words, suggesting a heaviness which we can feel. A 'Slant of light' is not usually associated with heaviness, yet here in the context of a New England winter afternoon Dickinson has associated light with oppressiveness and dying. If it a heavenly light, it is also a light that brings about a darkened understanding of heaven and our life on earth.

The certain light of winter afternoons can cause hurt:

> Heavenly Hurt, it gives us —

and the word 'us' is interesting here. Dickinson does not use 'I' in this poem; 'us' and 'we' are the personal pronouns used. 'Us' is used twice, and by doing so Dickinson is involving and including the reader in a very direct way in the experience she is writing about. She is confident that her experience is also ours.

The hurt felt is a 'Heavenly Hurt', one whose source is heaven. This suggests that Dickinson sees heaven as a place which can cause humans pain. God is distant and this 'Heavenly Hurt' is the source of earthly pain. In Dickinson's dictionary 'slant' was also defined as a gibe which, if intended, suggests a merciless heaven. Its light mocks us. The scarless wound is a reminder to us of our mortality.

Ralph Waldo Emerson, the nineteenth-century American poet and essayist, influenced Dickinson's thinking and she heard him lecture in Amherst. Emerson believed that Nature was God's benign deputy; Dickinson differed from Emerson, in that for her God's deputy could be hostile.

The phrase 'Heavenly Hurt' is paradoxical yet, just as the Cathedral Tune can weigh upon us, it would seem that a slant of light can give us hurt. Light comes from the heavens; 'Hurt' causes pain and sadness, and 'Heavenly Hurt' perhaps suggests an intense awareness of mortality, dying. It is the hurt of knowing that we must die. Such knowledge wounds us, yet

> We can find no scar,
> But internal difference,
> Where the Meanings, are —

Knowing that life must end, just as the day and the year must end, is a profound part of our being. There is no 'scar' but there are 'internal differences'. Deep inside, one is aware of life's reality and it is the deep knowledge within that matters. That's 'Where the Meanings, are —'.

Line 9, 'None may teach it — Any' seems to mean that no human may teach anything to someone in a state of such hurt; it is a situation beyond hope.

> None may teach it — Any —
> 'Tis the Seal Despair –
> An imperial affliction
> Sent us of the Air –

Just as the 'Slant of light' comes from afar, so too does this 'Heavenly Hurt'. This third stanza is pessimistic. It speaks of the Seal of Despair and Dickinson sees this 'Seal despair' as an 'imperial affliction / Sent us of the Air —'. The 'Seal' suggests the sign of authority. The individual experiences despair and is marked by the seal of despair. Despair is a very strong and powerful word. Nowhere in the poem is there a sense of hope.

'Imperial affliction' could be read as an image of a cruel, distant, all-powerful, impersonal force. As human beings, Dickinson is suggesting that we are given moments of hurt, but such moments are also moments of insight and understanding about the human condition. Knowing the reality allows us to live with reality.

The final stanza uses a longer line than is found in the previous three:

> When it comes, the Landscape listens —
> Shadows — hold their breath —
> When it goes, 'tis like the Distance
> On the look of Death —

This line, though longer only by a syllable, slows down the rhythm and adds to the already sombre mood. There is a chilling quality in line 13:

> When it comes, the Landscape listens —

Such moments will come but it is as if we know not the day nor the hour. Similarly, the phrase 'When it goes' in line 15, suggests that we have no way of knowing when such moments occur. They come and they go, and they have a profound effect on us.

In lines 13–16, Dickinson speaks of the moment and the aftermath. It refers back to the moment which she has described in the first three stanzas and its effect but now not only the individual but the landscape is affected. When such moments occur, the very landscape 'listens'. By personifying the earth, Dickinson unites the human and our earthly home. There is a sense of tension: even the 'Shadows — hold their breath —'. If the 'Shadows — hold their breath —' the suggestion is that the shadows are frightened or uneasy. Shadows are the opposite to the slant of light. Dickinson herself sees the slant of light and therefore she is not in the light but in shadow. The landscape, the shadows, and Dickinson are all aware and affected by the certain slant of light. For Dickinson what remains from such moments is a feeling that one has looked down the distance left before our death and this gives the poem a cold and realistic seriousness. The final dash opens up before us that road to death which we must all travel. Words such as 'oppresses', 'Heft', 'scar', 'Despair', 'affliction', 'the look of Death' maintain and intensify the gloomy mood.

When the moment is over and we are left with 'internal difference', then Dickinson tells us in lines 15 and 16 that it is as if we have looked on death itself, something which each one of us has to do alone. Such moments as the one described in 'There's a certain Slant of light' are moments which signal and prepare us for death.

That said, the last two lines could also be read to mean that once the moment of oppression is over, we forget death and it becomes distant again. We were made aware of our mortality during such a moment as the one described in the first stanza. But when such moments go, death seems far away once more.

The dying of the year is inevitable and natural. Yet the winter light oppresses. Our own dying is inevitable and natural also. In the poem Dickinson begins with an observation about the season and this leads to the recognition of a change within herself, a change which serves as a learning experience.

The poem has a regular end-rhyme throughout: Afternoons / Tunes; scar / are; Despair / Air; breath / Death. Giving scar, Despair and Death a rhyme emphasises their importance. Also, the placing of certain words in the line make for special emphasis and effect. For example, 'Heavenly Hurt, it gives us —' is a more powerful expression than 'it gives us Heavenly Hurt'; the 'us' is the word which stands out here and it is 'us' or 'we', not winter or heaven, that Dickinson is primarily concerned with in the poem.

Heaven is often thought of as a place of supreme happiness and redemption, but it is not spoken about as such in this poem. There is only the phrase 'Heavenly Hurt'. Dickinson does not dwell on an after life. Her focus here is on our earthly existence, our disappointments and suffering.

I felt a Funeral, in my Brain

Critical Commentary

This poem is remarkable for several reasons: its dramatic narrative, its use of repetition and its rhythmic pattern. It is written in the past tense and records a painful and strange experience. The action of the poem takes place inside Dickinson's head and the startlingly unusual opening line immediately establishes the location of the poem:

> I felt a Funeral, in my Brain,

Here, something final, sad and public, the funeral, is interiorised. If one were to say 'I felt a jungle, a circus, a desert, a waterfall, a traffic jam, an ocean in my brain', a sensation is immediately communicated and understood; the idea is simple, vivid, original.

In Dickinson's case the moment is one of nervous tension and vulnerability:

> I felt a Funeral, in my Brain,
> And Mourners to and fro
> Kept treading — treading — till it seemed
> That Sense was breaking through —

Here it seems that she is imagining her own death, the time when mourners will come to pay their last respects. The movement of 'to and fro' and the harshness of 'treading — treading' are images of restlessness, unease.

From the opening line, Dickinson places herself at the centre of the poem: 'I felt', 'I thought', 'I heard', 'And I, and Silence', 'I dropped'; 'my Brain', 'My Mind', 'my Soul'. To feel, to think, to hear, not to hear, to drop are strong sensations and at each stage in the poem Dickinson records these sensations as if they are inevitable. The use of 'And' gives the poem an increasing momentum. 'And' is used thirteen times altogether, ten times to begin a line.

In line 4 'Sense was breaking through —'. 'Breaking through' seems to mean here breaking down or giving way. The other meaning of 'breaking through', i.e. a moment of clarification or understanding, does not seem to be supported by the context here. This is the first indication of breaking in the poem, but Dickinson continues to develop the idea, and the poem ends with the climactic breaking of reason.

Whatever the form of crisis or breakdown being described, which may or may not be Dickinson's own imagined funeral, the dominant imagery is funereal. In stanza two, the 'Mourners' introduced in line 2 are 'seated'. Their 'treading — treading' is no longer felt, but the 'Service' itself is now a 'beating — beating' sensation in her mind:

> And when they all were seated,
> A Service, like a Drum —
> Kept beating — beating — till I thought
> My Mind was going numb —

The rhyming of 'Drum' and 'numb' is particularly appropriate here; one leads to the other. The rhyming throughout is regular within the first four stanzas — fro/through (slant rhyme), Drum/numb, Soul/toll, Ear/here, but the rhyme breaks down in the final stanza mirroring the final stage of breaking: down/then.

The experience which Dickinson writes about in this poem is not fully understood by her: 'it seemed', 'I thought'. In stanza three it is as if she cannot see what is happening. She can only hear.

> And then I heard them lift a Box
> And creak across my Soul
> With those same Boots of Lead, again,
> Then Space — began to toll,

The story being told parallels that of an actual funeral. In stanza one there was the sense of an ending; the people came to mourn. Stanza two tells of a Service, and in stanza three there is the journey from place of Service to the burial ground, a space in the ground.

The 'Box' in line 9 is the coffin. The mourners lift the box and then Dickinson tells us that the mourners creak across her soul. The corpse is in the box or coffin; the body has died but the mention of the soul suggests an afterlife. The manuscript shows that Dickinson wrote 'across my Brain' first and then changed it to 'across my Soul'; brain and soul were interchangeable in the nineteenth century. When she does speak of a life after death, she speaks of it in terms of 'knowing'.

Imagining oneself in a coffin at one's own funeral is a courageous and chilling thought. The mind is still aware of what is going on, the phrase 'creak across my Soul' suggesting that the soul is being hurt.

The sounds in 'I felt a Funeral, in my Brain' are harsh and severe. The references — to treading feet, the beating, drum-like service, the creaking sound, boots of lead, the silence of the bell, dropped down, hit — all create a sense of inescapable, increasing pain.

It is in stanza three that a new and different sense of space is introduced. Up until now, Dickinson has spoken of the space within her head, the place where the mourners tread and sit, the confined space of the coffin. However, in line 12 having heard the 'Boots of Lead, again'

> Then Space — began to toll

A funeral bell is a tolling bell; when Dickinson speaks of 'Space' beginning to toll, the image is one of a space opening up. By placing a dash after 'Space', the only dash used in this stanza, Dickinson is suggesting, perhaps, a great unknown space before her. 'Toll' also suggests a mournful mood.

Having spoken of where she is now in terms of a 'Space' which 'began to toll', Dickinson in stanza four continues the bell imagery when she speaks of 'the Heavens':

> As all the Heavens were a Bell,
> And Being, but an Ear,
> And I, and Silence, some strange Race
> Wrecked, solitary, here —

The treading feet, the beating drum, the creaking sounds are now no more. The sense of hearing is vital throughout the poem. In line 15 there is absolute silence and it is a silence associated with unease. Dickinson speaks of 'all the Heavens' in terms of the image of 'a Bell', the heavens suggesting a happy life beyond death. Her sense of her own entire self-awareness is now reduced to 'an Ear'; Dickinson's 'Being' is 'but an Ear' and in a chilling description of desolation and ruin she tells us that she 'and Silence, some strange Race' are wrecked and solitary. The bell of 'all the Heavens' is not heard. [It has been pointed out that in Odilon Redon's (1840–1916) surreal painting 'Silence', painted in 1890, silence is painted as a huge ear.]

Line 15 speaks of 'I, and Silence, some strange Race'. This may be read as 'I and Silence which is a strange race' or it can also be read to mean, 'I, and Silence, (and) some strange Race'. Dickinson who has, at this stage in the poem, entered into a state of strange and silent intensity is by herself; she can hear nothing and yet she is aware of the presence of others, 'some strange Race' who are also wrecked and solitary. They have reached this space before Dickinson but both Dickinson and they are estranged from 'all the Heavens'.

The reference to 'here' in line 16 is a reference to a kind of limbo land or temporary resting place, but 'Wrecked' and 'solitary' suggest destruction and being cut off. She has arrived at this place; she hears nothing here and there is increasing isolation. Where once she had 'Mourners', now there is no one but 'Silence'.

Stanza five marks another and final stage in the journey. It has a sense of finality about it. It not only ends the poem but it describes a final frightening movement in a poem which has had a great deal of movement. This stanza has the word 'Finished' in its final line. An end has been reached. Reason breaks in this stanza; intellectual power is at an end:

> And then a Plank in Reason, broke,
> And I dropped down, and down —
> And hit a World, at every plunge,
> And Finished knowing — then —

The image here of the 'Plank in Reason' is in keeping with the imagery of the funeral throughout the poem. Reason is an abstract, but Dickinson gives that faculty a vivid immediacy in the image of the plank. A plank is often placed across the open grave; the coffin rests upon the plank before being lowered into the ground. If that plank were to break, the falling coffin would be a horrifying sight. A plank is a precarious thing over a void. If the plank breaks, you enter the void. What Dickinson describes is 'a Plank in Reason' breaking, but the subsequent image is of the speaker in the poem falling uncontrollably 'down, and down':

> And I dropped down, and down —
> And hit a World, at every plunge

The verbs 'dropped' and 'hit', the repeated 'down', the idea which 'plunge' conjures up all suggest a terrible ordeal.

The sense of the poem as story or narrative is not only suggested in the various stages of a funeral service, but the adverbs also point to the development of the narrative quality of the poem. In line 5 'when' signals a particular moment; 'then' is used in lines 9, 12 and 17, marking different stages in the poem. The final word in the poem is also 'then', this time presented as '— then —'.

When reason breaks then the end is near. 'And Finished knowing' is characteristically ambiguous and may be interpreted in two ways. Is knowing a noun or a present participle? First it could refer to the end of knowing. A moment comes when the mind is no more because reason has broken down. Second, 'Finished knowing' could be interpreted as that final moment of awareness, of knowing, of understanding. At the end of this experience, there is knowledge and insight. One finally understands what is to be — a nothing, a hell or a heaven? If Dickinson intended the second reading, that 'knowing', her knowing, is never shared with the reader. Dickinson knows something in that final moment which she has depicted as a moment of rapid downward movement. Did Dickinson intend us to think that she has reached a hellish state, hell conventionally being understood to be beneath the ground, just as heaven has traditionally been understood to be high above.

The final '— then —' is different from the other thens in the text. There is no world beyond this final then. She has 'hit a World, at every plunge' and that is her end.

Dickinson speaks of 'the Heavens' but God is invisible, uninvolved. There is no suggestion of comfort at this journey's end. The poem is communicating to us a message, as it were, from beyond the grave.

A Bird came down the Walk

Dickinson in 'A Bird came down the Walk' is the keen observer. The bird enters the world of the human, it 'came down the Walk –' and the human secretly observes the world of the bird. It has a delighted, playful tone in its opening stanza:

> A Bird came down the Walk —
> He did not know I saw —
> He bit an Angleworm in halves
> And ate the fellow, raw,

Dickinson is clearly interested in observing the bird, is pleased that she is the unobserved observer. The phrase 'the fellow' captures the playfulness of the moment. By contrast, the mention of 'raw' reminds us of reality.

The size of the bird and the even smaller worm bring the poem into a concentrated focus. When Dickinson says in line 5 that 'he drank a Dew' the focus becomes almost microscopic. The unconventional use of the indefinite article here – she doesn't say the dew – makes for minute detail and is yet another aspect of Dickinson's originality. Everything in Nature seems ordered and right. The bird finds its food and drink with ease and is also courteous and caring:

> And then he drank a Dew
> From a convenient Grass —
> And then hopped sideways to the Wall
> To let a Beetle pass —

The bird does not hop sideways on seeing the worm (that would be unnatural) and Dickinson is not concerned for the worm bitten in half and eaten. It is part of the food-chain; Nature is taking its course in this poem. Dickinson is showing us how everything fits into place. Even the grass is 'convenient'.

The poem is full of busyness. The bird eats, drinks, and in stanza three appears frightened and in danger:

> He glanced with rapid eyes
> That hurried all around —
> They looked like frightened Beads, I thought —
> He stirred his Velvet Head
>
> Like one in danger,

This is brilliantly accurate and effective: 'frightened Beads' and 'Velvet Head' are superbly precise images. It is at this point in the poem, when the bird is frightened, that Dickinson makes herself known to it. The word 'Cautious' could refer to the bird or Dickinson or both.

> Cautious,
> I offered him a Crumb

The human presence and the proffered crumb cause the bird to fly away. The bird is not described as flying away suddenly. Words such as 'unrolled' and 'rowed' and 'plashless' suggest a graceful departure, but what is interesting is that the bird does not accept Dickinson's kindness. The crumb is not an angleworm; the bird belongs to the natural world and it will return to it.

> I offered him a Crumb
> And he unrolled his feathers
> And rowed him softer home —
>
> Than Oars divide the Ocean,
> Too silver for a seam —
> Or Butterflies, off Banks of Noon
> Leap, plashless as they swim.

These closing stanzas capture the smooth, silent disappearance of the bird. Dickinson thinks of the bird as having rowed himself 'softer home' and home is significant. The 'walk' where Dickinson sees the bird is not his home but elsewhere, some other place; home for the bird is also nest and sky. The use of 'And' at the beginning of line 15, not but, suggests that the bird's going is totally natural.

Two elaborate images close the poem. A rowed boat will part the water and the water will be silver in its wake, 'Too silver for a seam —'; and butterflies swim silently above banks of flowers at noon. Dickinson uses these images to convey the silent, mysterious movement of the bird. The bird moves more softly than the rowing boat, more softly than the silent, swimming butterflies.

Nature is its own world. It has its own rhythms, its own beauty. In the first stanza of 'A Bird came down the Walk' the bird is very much present; in the final stanza the bird is absent and its absence is felt by Dickinson. That she finds images to match its departure suggests her lingering sense of the bird's absence. Dickinson belongs to one world, the bird to its world. Unlike Keats, who observed the sparrow outside his window and became that bird, Dickinson observes, is captivated and kind enough to offer the bird a crumb but also realises that he is separate. He refused to take her crumb.

If Dickinson is disappointed, she does not say so. The poem is one of celebration, delight, wonder.

After great pain, a formal feeling comes

Here Dickinson speaks of having known 'great pain' and the feelings which follow such an experience. She speaks with such confidence, knowledge and insight that one does not doubt that this is a felt experience.

Great pain is spoken of as something which does not last; the last words in the poem are 'the letting go —' but what interests Dickinson here is the numbed and gradual stages which the individual experiences in the process.

There is no 'I' in the poem; it is as if Dickinson is speaking for us all.

> After great pain, a formal feeling comes —
> The Nerves sit ceremonious, like Tombs —
> The stiff Heart questions was it He, that bore,
> And Yesterday, or Centuries before?

The word 'formal' suggests precision, excessive stiffness, ceremony, and the idea is followed through in lines 2 and 3. Human aspects are personified: the 'Nerves sit ceremonious' and the 'stiff Heart questions'. The word 'sit' in this context evokes an image of rigid, pained figures (reminiscent, perhaps, of the mourners who come and are seated in 'I felt a Funeral, in my Brain'); the image contained in 'like Tombs' is precise. After great pain, the body's strength and vigour, the Nerves, feel numb and cold. The dominant imagery throughout the poem is lifelessness and the reference to 'The Nerves', 'The stiff Heart', 'The Feet' emphasises this sense of lifelessness throughout the body. The poem moves from a mind that is numb to a numbed heart to numbed feet.

The heart is pained and tense. It asks in line 3 if it was Jesus Christ who carried the cross, the implication being that this heart is so pained that it is carrying a cross itself, is suffering just as Christ did.

The moment of pain is so intense that the heart has lost track of the everyday world and has lost all sense of time. Christ's suffering is suddenly brought very close. The heart wonders if Christ suffered his great pain yesterday or hundreds of years ago:

> The stiff Heart questions was it He, that bore,
> And Yesterday, or Centuries before?

In these lines Dickinson is also suggesting that a human being can know such great pain that it is as if that individual knows a suffering similar to Christ's.

The cause or the occasion of this great pain is never explicitly revealed to us in the poem. The reference to Christ's suffering and death suggests rejection, but what is more important than the circumstances is the fact that suffering great pain is part of the human condition.

The second stanza describes the feet, but the feet are so expressive of emotion here that we are given a sense of the body and how it copes with this great pain:

> The Feet, mechanical, go round —
> Of Ground, or Air, or Ought —
> A Wooden way
> Regardless grown,
> A Quartz contentment, like a stone —

There is movement but it is 'mechanical' and 'Wooden'. The feet touch the ground, lift again through the air and again 'go round'. The circular motion here suggests an endless, futile movement. The phrase 'A Wooden way' refers to the expressionless, spiritless, dull and inert feeling; it may also be used as an echo of Christ's wooden way, the way of the cross and his journey to Calvary. The pain and suffering of Christ was certainly linked to human pain and suffering in stanza one.

The four-line, pentameter stanza form used in the first stanza is broken down in stanza two. Dickinson shortens the line and breaks what could be line 7 into two:

> A Wooden way Regardless grown

becomes

> A Wooden way
> Regardless grown

These shorter lines create a slowing-down effect and the shortest lines in the poem are at the centre of the poem.

It is as if the 'great pain' and its subsequent feelings cause us to look inwards; our focus becomes narrow and our bodies, our sensations, almost close down. The final two lines of the poem return to the formal pentameter lines of stanza one. Pattern here becomes meaning; the stages in feeling are expressed in the very lines.

Dickinson speaks of the mechanical feet as 'Regardless grown'. They do not care anymore; they are indifferent, careless, without regard of anything, and the image of 'A Quartz contentment' in line 9 sums up the 'formal feeling'. The human being is like a stone. Quartz is not chosen at random. Dickinson said in a letter dated 1883: 'I hesitate which word to take, as I can take but few and each must be the chiefest'. So too in her poetry. Perhaps Dickinson chose Quartz because it is a common mineral and as a mineral it has been transformed by process into its present state. Similarly, human suffering, 'great pain', is known to many people and their 'Quartz' like state is as a result of having been transformed by the process of pain. The sound of the word quartz is severe and harsh, another reason, perhaps, for choosing it. The use of 'contentment' seems out of place here. The pain and the questioning heart of stanza one have given way to a cold contentment.

The first line in the third stanza is slow and monosyllabic. It has a dreadful knowing quality:

> This is the Hour of Lead —

The phrase 'Hour of Lead' is a definition of depression. It is an hour of such oppression and pain that not all survive it. Those who do survive the 'Hour of Lead' remember it as a slow and painful process:

> This is the Hour of Lead —
> Remembered, if outlived,
> As Freezing persons, recollect the Snow —
> First — Chill — then Stupor — then the letting go —

The freezing person will remember the reason for feeling frozen, just as the numbed person will remember the source or cause of the 'great pain'. Dickinson in the final line identifies three distinct yet connected stages, one leading to the other:

> First — Chill — then Stupor — then the letting go —

Chill is often the first stage or symptom of illness and the dictionary also describes it as a depressing influence upon the feelings. The second stage is a deadened, dazed state but the 'letting go', the third stage, is that ability to survive, to outlive the 'great pain' which Dickinson speaks of in the opening line. 'Letting go' of course may also be read as something negative, as losing a sense of everything, of going into a deeper state of depression.

'After great pain, a formal feeling comes —' describes mental anguish step by step. It is in many ways an impersonal poem. Dickinson never uses 'I' or 'my'. The nerves, the heart, the feet belong to no specific individual, but by the use of 'the' they belong to everyone.

Critical Commentary

I heard a Fly buzz — when I died

This poem is in the first person and, though it tells of the crucial moment of death, that moment, in stanza one, is not associated with knowledge, understanding or revelation, but with a sound:

> I heard a Fly buzz — when I died —
> The Stillness in the Room
> Was like the Stillness in the Air —
> Between the Heaves of Storm —

There are two sounds here or rather a sound and the absence of sound: the still, silent sound of the room and the buzz of the fly which is heard by the speaker at the moment of death. The buzzing fly is a distraction; it trivialises a serious and unique moment and the silence in the room is even more pronounced. That stillness is ominous. The storm will return. The fly has also been interpreted, not as a distraction, but as what John Ciardi calls 'a last dear sound from the world as the light of consciousness sank from her'. Caroline Hogue disagrees with this view; she associates the fly with decay.

Another reading of this poem argues that the fly represents death itself and that Dickinson, perhaps, is thinking of Beëlzebub, the devil, the lord of the flies?

The mood in stanza one is one of calmness and control. This is another of Dickinson's poems where the lines are written in the form of hymn metre:

> Our God, our help in ages past
>
> I heard a Fly buzz — when I died —

and that tight, formal control is maintained throughout.

The speaker is at the centre of the poem and she is, it seems, in the centre of the room. What the poem suggests is a death bed setting with family gathered round:

> The Eyes around — had wrung them dry —
> And Breaths were gathering firm

The weeping is done; the eyes of those around the speaker have wrung themselves dry and the next stage is anticipated with solemnity. Their 'Breaths were gathering firm' as they await Christ's presence in the room. This is

> that last Onset — when the King
> Be witnessed — in the Room —

'Onset' here marks the moment. Dickinson does not say if the one who has died will witness 'the King' or if His presence is witnessed only by the mourners. 'I died' in line 1 suggests, as does 'Breaths were gathering firm', that Christ the King will be witnessed by those at the bedside who believe in Him and not by the speaker. 'Onset' is ambiguous. It means both a commencement and an assault. Do the speaker and the mourners view 'the King' differently?

Having considered the King to be Christ, we owe it to the poem and to ourselves as readers to ask if 'the King' here could mean Death, our physical end, and not eternal salvation.

At a nineteenth century death-bed scene, it was usual for the family to gather round the dying person. There would be last-minute bequests and hymns sung and the person who was dying was expected to repent and thereby give witness to Christ's presence in the room. It was also believed that the last words of the dying person or a sign or gesture would indicate the destiny of the soul.

Line 9 refers to the practice of bequeathing one's precious possessions. The others in the room are spoken of impersonally, as 'Eyes' and 'Breaths', but the dying person is personal and intimate in willing her keepsakes. As Dickinson describes the moment she speaks once again of the fly, this time marking her awareness of its presence precisely:

> I willed my Keepsakes — Signed away
> What portion of me be
> Assignable — and then it was
> There interposed a Fly —

All seems ordered, lucid, calm, even wry ('What portion of me be/ Assignable'), until the fly interposes.

The fly has come between the dying person and the light. The words 'Blue – uncertain stumbling Buzz' suggest a blowfly or bluebottle (Musca vomitoria) with its large bluish body, a fly which deposits its eggs or larvae in dead flesh.

The final lines chart the dead person's final thoughts:

> There interposed a Fly —
>
> With Blue — uncertain stumbling Buzz —
> Between the light — and me —
> And then the Windows failed – and then
> I could not see to see —

The light is the light from the window, though the light of Christ or the light of Paradise may be hinted at. At any rate the fly has come

> Between the light — and me —

The fly is 'uncertain' and 'stumbling', words which introduce a sense of the chaotic and directionless into a poem which is focusing on a natural and quiet death.

A fly is tiny and can hardly be said to block out the light, but for Dickinson the fly is the first stage in the dying of the light. First the fly comes between the 'light — and me —'. The next stage is signalled clearly:

> And then the Windows failed — and then
> I could not see to see —

The poem ends in darkness; it offers no vision of immortality. The light from the windows 'failed' and the speaker's own vision has failed; 'I could not see to see —'. The repetition of 'and then' in line 15 gives the line finality, tension, drama. The dash with which the poem ends invites the reader to consider the moment and beyond the moment of death and to ask if Dickinson intended to convey a sense of things beyond death.

The poem is built around the sensory details of hearing ('I heard'), seeing ('The Eyes around'), touching ('Signed away') and ends with silence, isolation, blindness.

The Soul has Bandaged moments

The opening line is arresting. It strikes the reader immediately:

> The Soul has Bandaged moments —

and its meaning is clearly understood. At times the private, inner self (the soul suggests a spiritual self) is pained and bandaged or bound. Bandaged could imply that the soul is in a state of healing. Bandaged could also mean simply to bind or cover up.

The soul here is spoken of as female and Fright is personified:

> The Soul has Bandaged moments —
> When too appalled to stir —
> She feels some ghastly Fright come up
> And stop to look at her —

In this opening stanza the soul is at its lowest. It feels intimidated. It is frightened; Fright itself is a threatening presence. If the soul is female, does Dickinson intend us to read Fright as a male presence? Fright, however, is never referred to as 'he'.

The soul cannot move; it is 'too appalled to stir'. Dickinson never reveals to us the cause of this state of dismay, this rigidity, but in this state the soul is vulnerable, looked at; the phrase 'come up' suggests that the soul itself seems and feels small. Fright chooses to look; it stops to look at her, thereby making the soul even less powerful. Bandaged may imply that the soul cannot see, yet Fright can 'look at her'. Fright is the more powerful.

Moments is plural. Such bandaged moments occur again. The phrase 'Bandaged moments' begs the question who bandages or binds the wounded soul? Is it a sense of self-preservation?

The mood in stanza one is one of acute self-consciousness and this is intensified in the second stanza. A salutation is usually associated with a happy greeting, good wishes, respect. Here Fright's salute and Fright's 'long fingers' are eerie. Fright comes up and stops to look at the bandaged soul. Fright will:

> Salute her — with long fingers —
> Caress her freezing hair —

Even 'Caress' – to fondle or touch endearingly – becomes sinister in this context and 'freezing hair' is powerfully effective personification.

Fright stops to look, to salute, to caress, to sip. Lines 7–10 reveal, it seems, the nature and the reason for the soul's hurt:

> Sip, Goblin, from the very lips
> The Lover — hovered — o'er —
> Unworthy, that a thought so mean
> Accost a Theme — so — fair —

Goblin may be read as goblin-like, an adverb modifying 'Sip'. Fright will sip from lips the Lover did not kiss or sip.

Another way of reading 'Sip, Goblin,' is to interpret it as the soul's voice addressing Goblin, presumably Fright, and it is told to sip from the very lips which a lover had hovered over. This reading is less satisfactory in that soul is portrayed in stanza one and two as victim. It would hardly address Fright; it is 'too appalled to stir'.

Who the Lover is (line 8), we are not told. It could be a person; it could be God. The Lover hovered, was hesitant and indecisive. The Lover, it seems, is no longer loving and the soul is dismayed that Fright now sips from the lips of the bandaged soul.

> Sip, Goblin, from the very lips
> The Lover — hovered — o'er —

It seems that Dickinson is writing about unrequited love of some kind and perhaps it is this which has caused the Soul to be wounded and in need of bandaging.

Dickinson has dramatised the feeling of dismay and fear. There is the still presence of the Soul, 'too appalled to stir', and the 'ghastly' Fright whose presence is described as almost inevitable. The soul when bandaged feels 'Fright come up'. The soul has to accept Fright, a Goblin-like presence.

'Unworthy', line 9, refers to what or whom? Is Fright unworthy or does it refer to the Lover? Could it refer to 'the very lips'? A case can be made for each interpretation. At this point, one is truly aware of the difficulties of reading Emily Dickinson's poetry, so much so that some readers become exasperated, impatient, dismissive.

Richard B. Sewell suggests that 'No one of her poems . . . should be regarded as a signed and sealed position paper. It's the poetry, as Emerson put it, of portfolio . . . She'd never gone through the discipline of publication. They're the portfolio poetry of a poet who had written for herself, to herself, thinking out her life, investigating what was happening, especially inside, and coming out with an extraordinary, true, certainly realistic sense of the human psyche.'

If 'Unworthy' in line 9 refers to Fright, then lines 9 and 10 clearly express the Soul's preference for the Lover over Fright or Goblin. But 'Unworthy' can also refer to the Lover who, feeling unworthy in the soul's presence, 'hovered — o'er' and did not sip. Thinking itself unworthy, the thought of kissing the very lips becomes 'a thought so mean' could accost or address 'a Theme — so — fair —'. The theme here may be the soul or the union between the Soul and Lover.

Unworthy and fair are opposites. Fair is what is beautiful or desirable and a mean thought, a feeling of unworthiness, prevents the Lover from attaining its desire.

There is a complete mood swing in stanzas three and four. The first two stanzas presented us with the Soul in dismay; now we are given the very opposite, the Soul in bliss. No mention now of Fright, nor is there any mention of Lover.

> The soul has moments of Escape —
> When bursting all the doors —
> She dances like a Bomb, abroad,
> And swings upon the Hours,
>
> As do the Bee — delirious borne —
> Long Dungeoned from his Rose —
> Touch Liberty — then know no more,
> But Noon, and Paradise —

In contrast to what has gone before, there is extraordinary energy here: 'bursting', 'dances', 'swings', 'delirious borne' express freedom, release, frenzied excitement. The soul has escaped its confines; it is 'abroad' and flying with excitement. The soul

> dances like a Bomb, abroad,
> And swings upon the Hours

'Bomb' suggests an explosion of happiness in this context. It may also be meant as an anarchic and destructive force. The alternative definition of bomb as the sounding of a bell (cf. *glossary*) is not only appropriate but in keeping with the reference to the swinging upon the hours in the following line.

These are the 'moments of Escape', the opposite of 'Bandaged moments' of line 1, but whether in pain or joyful it is significant that Dickinson speaks of both states as existing as moments. The soul will know neither pain nor joy as a constant. The word 'moments' occurs three times in the poem (lines 1, 11, 19) but, once freed, the soul 'swings upon the Hours'. Time is viewed differently. But the poem is framed by Fright and Horror, which suggests that ultimately the moments of escape are short-lived, that a form of imprisonment, or 'Bandaged moments', is the norm.

Stanza four is a sustained image. The freed soul is likened to a bee who was 'Long Dungeoned' in the hive, then 'delirious borne' on air and seeking out 'his Rose'. The sensation is one of intense happiness:

> As do the Bee — delirious borne —
> Long Dungeoned from his Rose —
> Touch Liberty — then know no more,
> But Noon, and Paradise —

Stanzas three and four are a vivid contrast to the first two stanzas. The 'bursting all the doors', dancing, swinging soul, the image of the Rose, the brightness of noon are summery and free images and the very opposite of 'Bandaged' and 'freezing'.

Stanzas one and two are about constraint, unease and fear, stanzas three and four about release and delirium. The soul, once victim, is now shown as active, not passive. Dickinson does not say what makes possible such happiness. Just as the bee knows no more 'But Noon, and Paradise —', the soul delights in its 'Escape'; it does not dwell on how it has been set free.

Line 19, at the beginning of stanza five, signals the end of the moment of escape. 'The Soul has Bandaged moments'; 'The soul has moments of Escape'; and 'The Soul's retaken moments' (lines 1, 11, 19) mark the three separate stages of the poem. The structure is such that Dickinson ends as she began with the soul once again imprisoned:

> The Soul's retaken moments —
> When, Felon led along,
> With shackles on the plumed feet,
> And staples, in the Song,

There is no reason given as to why the soul should be retaken or recaptured and imprisoned. It is led along, as if it were a felon or criminal, and the imagery in lines 21 and 22 evokes a sympathetic response from the reader. The soul's plumed or feathered feet are bound, the soul's song hindered, prevented.

The most chilling moment of all perhaps is line 23:

> The Horror welcomes her, again,

The soul has been here before. We are given no indication why the soul is being led back to this place of horror, a place where the soul knows bandaged moments. The comma in line 23 and the word 'again' create a sense of inevitability. Soul, here, has no control, unlike those moments when she burst 'all the doors'. The word 'welcomes' is sinister and unnerving. Just as it is difficult to imagine Fright caressing the Soul, it seems totally inappropriate that Horror could welcome her.

The poem's final line reminds us that the 'Bandaged moments' of the soul are not loudly boasted about:

> These, are not brayed of Tongue —

No tongue speaks of them, loudly or quietly, but by using 'brayed' Dickinson is suggesting how impossible it is to speak of such moments. However, this is just what Dickinson herself has done in the poem.

There is a marked contrast in the poem between suffering and joy, between a feeling of imprisonment and freedom, between moments of misery and moments of ecstasy. Dickinson, in choosing not to identify the cause for these emotional states, allows for a more open interpretation. The poem may refer to depression and the release from depression, the lack of inspiration and the creative imagination, the state of fear, release from fear and the return of fear.

I could bring You Jewels — had I a mind to

There is a very definite sense of the self, the speaker in this poem. 'I' is used five times in twelve lines. The speaker is confident, self-assured. The tone throughout is knowing and controlled:

> I could bring You Jewels — had I a mind to —

The 'You' is never identified but the poem is clearly expressing praise and admiration for the 'You' whom it addresses. The speaker wishes to find something suitable to honour 'You':

> I could bring You Jewels — had I a mind to —
> But You have enough — of those —
> I could bring You Odors from St Domingo —
> Colors — from Vera Cruz —

There is poise here. Though the tone is confident, it is also relaxed. The extravagance of jewels, scents, colours, the exotic locations mentioned — St Domingo, Vera Cruz, the Bahamas — all create a world of plenty and sufficiency. 'I could bring You Jewels', 'I could bring You Odors', suggest wealth and privilege.

In stanza one, Dickinson speaks of bringing this 'You' a gift of jewels. She adds 'had I a mind to —' and then immediately qualifies the idea:

> But You have enough — of those —

What she seeks is something even more special. She mentions 'Jewels', 'Odors', 'Colors' only to dismiss them.

The listing continues into the second stanza but the tense changes. The 'I could' becomes 'have I —' but the 'Berries of the Bahamas' are also rejected. What could be got (jewels, odours, colours) and what already is to hand (berries) are not as good as what Dickinson calls 'this little Blaze':

> Berries of the Bahamas — have I —
> But this little Blaze
> Flickering to itself — in the Meadow —
> Suits Me — more than those —

In the first stanza Dickinson is contemplating possibilities and the ideas flow as freely as the lines. Slant end-rhymes, 'to, those, Domingo, Cruz', suggest a mind at leisure. In stanza two there is greater focus. Dickinson, having rejected certain options, now focuses on her preference and the lines become shorter, more concentrated, to match her thinking. What 'this little Blaze' is exactly is never revealed. It is a personal choice, more unusual than the colourful and the exotic listed earlier. It is spoken of as light, as 'Blaze' and 'Flickering'.

The choice is revealing and Dickinson intends it to be so: she states clearly that 'this little Blaze . . . Suits Me – more than those –'. Though little, it is precious and treasured and the phrase 'in the Meadow' suggests a little flower.

Once chosen, 'this little Blaze' outshines everything else. The tone in the final stanza is one of conviction, the 'Never' is absolute:

> Never a Fellow matched this Topaz —
> And his Emerald Swing —
> Dower itself — for Bobadilo —
> Better — Could I bring?

Topaz suggests a yellow, white, pale blue or pale green colour and Emerald is a brilliant bright green. These natural colours again suggest meadow flowers.

The exact rhymes of 'Swing' and 'bring' make for a flourishing confidence at the end. If her choice of gift is suitable as a dower, it enhances its value; it is a worthy gift for a woman to bring to her prospective husband. The reference to 'Bobadilo' suggests that even a swaggerer and a braggart could not be given a better gift. The poem's final question is rhetorical.

We can only imagine this perfect gift, but we are given indications of its qualities. It glows with colour; it seems to be natural and it is not difficult or inaccessible or expensive. The real wealth is in the spirit in which it is given.

Of the ten poems by Dickinson on the course, this is a poem without shadows. Like 'I taste a liquor never brewed' it is celebratory and happy, but, unlike the poem celebrating 'endless summer days', this poem focuses more on a relationship rather than the individual self.

A narrow Fellow in the Grass

Though first printed under the title of 'The Snake', Dickinson never refers to the strange creature of the poem as snake. The physical details, however, certainly suggest that it describes a snake. Line 1 refers to a 'Fellow', suggesting familiarity or friendliness, and his appearance in the grass is both occasional and sudden:

> A narrow Fellow in the Grass
> Occasionally rides —
> You may have met Him — did you not
> His notice sudden is —

Here, Dickinson is obviously addressing and involving the reader: 'You may have met Him – did you not'; and she adds her own observation as to how suddenly the 'Fellow' appears. The snake 'rides' according to Dickinson, not crawls, suggesting self-possession and confidence.

In this first stanza, there is no attempt at end-rhyme ('Grass'/'rides'/'not'/'is') and few internal rhymes ('His'/'is', line 4); whereas in the final two stanzas 'me'/'cordiality' and 'alone'/'Bone' are clear rhymes.

The elusive nature of the snake is captured in stanza two: its ability to move quietly, secretly and unpredictably. Its glimpsed, variegated body is compared to a shaft which suggests an arrow:

> The Grass divides as with a Comb —
> A spotted shaft is seen —
> And then it closes at your feet
> And opens further on —

In the poem's central stanza, Dickinson goes beyond the immediate presence of a snake in the grass by her feet to describe the general nature of the snake, its preferred habitat, its characteristics. Memory is also introduced here; the poem moves from present to past tense:

> He likes a Boggy Acre
> A Floor too cool for Corn —
> Yet when a Boy, and Barefoot —
> I more than once at Noon
> Have passed, I thought, a Whip lash
> Unbraiding in the Sun
> When stooping to secure it
> It wrinkled, and was gone —

The barefoot boy suggests innocence and simplicity and clearly the boy is fascinated by the snake. Dickinson describes the boy as he attempts to catch the unwinding, wrinkled, whip-like snake. The boy has met the snake 'more than once' but, it seems, has never managed to capture one.

The language here is effective. 'A Floor too cool for Corn' captures the coolness itself through the assonance of 'Floor' and 'Corn'. Line 8 runs on into lines 9 and 10. Dickinson uses no dash or other punctuating device to create a pause at the end of line 9. The lines seem to flow, sinewy fashion, like the snake itself.

In the fifth stanza, Dickinson speaks of the boy's/her relationship with animals and birds, or 'Nature's People' as she refers to them. It is a warm and affectionate relationship:

> Several of Nature's People
> I know, and they know me —
> I feel for them a transport
> Of cordiality —

There is a shared, a reciprocated friendship here. Just as the speaker recognises 'Nature's People', they recognise her. The phrase 'transport/ Of cordiality' emphasises the warmth of feeling. Transport suggests that the speaker feels a rapture or ecstasy.

The use of 'But' and 'never' in line 21 make a very separate distinction between 'Several of Nature's People' and this 'narrow Fellow in the Grass'. It makes no difference as to whether the speaker has met with the snake alone or with others, the sensation is always frightening and chilling:

> But never met this Fellow
> Attended, or alone
> Without a tighter breathing
> And Zero at the Bone —

Dickinson makes no reference in the poem to the serpent or snake in the Book of Genesis in the Bible, nor does she explain why she feels this way about the snake. The boy in stanza three approached the snake in order to 'secure it', yet the snake has a physical effect on the speaker, the 'tighter breathing', a cold feeling in the bones. There is both a fascination with the snake and a fear and the two feelings are brought together within the poem.

John Keats
(1795–1821)

Contents	Page
The Overview	159
Biographical Notes	161
POEMS	166
Critical Commentary	193

The Overview

All eight poems by Keats are sensuous expressions of intense feeling. 'To One Who Has Been Long in City Pent' celebrates the beauty and freedom of the open countryside, where to see the blue sky and wavy grass and to hear the nightingale's song is to know happiness. Keats writes of the intellectual and imaginative pleasures of reading in 'On First Looking into Chapman's Homer': the imagery in this sonnet is drawn from exploration and discovery. In 'When I have fears that I may cease to be', Keats writes of his 'teeming brain' and the literature he hopes to write: the image of a rich harvest conveys his understanding of the creative process. 'La Belle Dame sans Merci' is atypical of Keats in some ways: he uses the ballad form, a shorter line and a cold, harsh setting. Keats also uses the persona of the knight to tell his story. The sense of longing and the presence of beauty and death, however, are familiar Keatsian themes. The three Odes celebrate music, pictorial art and a season. Each is beautiful. The song of the nightingale and the Grecian urn are untouched by change and death. Autumn is the dying of the year, but it has its own music and beauty. It is man who must accept his own mortality. In one of his final poems, 'Bright star! Would I Were Steadfast as Thou Art', Keats admires the brilliant star but rejects it eventually. He prefers the intimacy and pleasure of a love relationship knowing, however, that to be 'Pillowed upon my fair love's ripening breast' cannot last forever.

John Keats loved the beautiful and his pleasure in the beautiful and immortal found expression in his poetry. The famous opening lines from his long poem 'Endymion' – 'A thing of beauty is a joy forever:/Its loveliness increases; it will never/Pass into nothingness. . .' – sum up Keats's philosophy. Another line, this time from one of his letters, reminds us of Keats's awareness of human powers and gifts: 'I am certain of nothing but the holiness of the heart's affections and the truth of imagination.' He is a poet who loved what life offered and he also loved to share that love with his reader. He felt that 'a poet should not preach but should whisper results to his neighbour.'

It is significant that Keats is admired and remembered primarily for his odes. The ode is essentially a poem of celebration and in his odes, the song of the nightingale, the beauty and mystery of a Grecian urn and the riches of autumn are celebrated in evocative and sensuous language. He hears the song of the nightingale, sees the figures on the urn, senses autumn and plumps the hazel shells, and in his imagination travels beyond the actual and conjures up images and moods associated with all three. Keats is a generous and enthusiastic poet. He shares with us his delight on discovering Homer in Chapman's translation; he thinks of the bees in late autumn and thinks of the season as having 'set budding more,/And still more, later flowers for the bees,/Until they think warm days will never cease. . .'

Beauty is often celebrated, however, against an awareness of transience and mortality. These eight poems by Keats also tell of suffering and death and the human condition. The song of the nightingale must fade though it will be heard by others; the urn becomes a 'Cold Pastoral' but that too will remain, a 'friend to man'. Autumn must give way to winter but, as Keats reminds us in the closing stanza, winter and spring will give way to another autumn eventually.

The sonnet, the ballad and the ode are the poetic forms used in these eight poems and, while Keats is an intensely personal poet, in the ballad 'La Belle Dame sans Merci', his narrative is apparently impersonal. Yet, even here, the preoccupation with beauty and death are typical of his work.

There is a development and progression within the poems, especially within the odes. The eager questioning and engagement with the song of the nightingale and urn give way to a very calm, placid note in 'To Autumn', a poem, unlike the other two odes, without exclamation marks. The suffering which he speaks of ('Where youth grows pale, and spectre-thin, and dies' or 'A burning forehead and a parching tongue') is absent from 'To Autumn', the final ode. The dying of the year is inevitable; Keats writes of it with great calm.

Keats has often been termed 'escapist' ('Away! away! for I will fly to thee'), but he is also a realist. He returns to reality ('to my sole self!') in 'Ode to a Nightingale'; he knows that 'old age shall this generation waste' ('Ode on a Grecian Urn'). He also knows that, though the bright star is beautiful, it is cold and distant and he would prefer the beauty of human love ('Pillowed upon my fair love's ripening breast,/To feel for ever its soft fall and swell'), if only it were 'steadfast' and 'unchangeable'.

• Keats Memorial at Guys Hospital, London where he trained as a surgeon.

Biographical Notes

John Keats was born in London on 31 October 1795 (some biographers suggest 30 October). He was the eldest of five children, one of whom died in infancy. Keats's father ran a livery stables, which allowed him to educate his children well, and when John Keats was almost eight he was sent to be educated in a small private school in Enfield, ten miles outside London, where he was known to be a lively and spirited young boy who liked boxing. Andrew Motion in his biography of Keats says that the 'few specific references he makes to the school imply that when not swimming in the new river, or playing cricket in the fields near by, he spent his time gardening . . . or catching fish.' When Keats was eight, his father fell from his horse and died; his mother remarried and she then died from tuberculosis when he was fourteen. The four Keats children had only their elderly grandmother to look after them and she appointed two guardians and trustees to look after the orphaned children, who had an income of £8,000 (a huge amount at the time) from their grandmother's estate. One guardian died; the other, Richard Abbey, did not act honourably and, as a result, the children were never to experience financial comfort.

John Keats was removed from school in 1810 and apprenticed to his grandparents' doctor in Edmonton. For the next five years, Keats trained to be a doctor, but read extensively in English poetry, especially Spenser (1522–1599). One of Keats's teachers, Charles Cowden Clarke, has given us a famous description of Keats's enthusiasm for the sixteenth-century poet; John Keats, we are told, approached Spenser's *The Faerie Queene* 'as a young horse would through a spring meadow, – ramping.' His response to Spenser's poetry was so enthusiastic and revealed Keats's remarkable empathy so well that when he came across the phrase 'sea-shouldering whales', Clarke tells us that Keats 'hoisted himself up and looked burly and dominant, as he said "What an image that is – sea-shouldering whales."' When he was eighteen, Keats began to write poetry, his first poem being an 'Imitation of Spenser'.

In the autumn of 1815, Keats's apprenticeship came to an end and he began to train as a surgeon at Guy's Hospital, London. He had moved into lodgings in Southwark and he wrote a sonnet contrasting the countryside at Edmonton, Middlesex, with the busy streets of Southwark and its 'jumbled heap/Of murky buildings.' On 5 May 1816, Keats's first published poem 'O Solitude! if I must with thee dwell' appeared and in July of that same year he passed his exams and was granted a licence to practise as a surgeon and apothecary. As his interest in poetry grew, Keats became less interested in medicine. His lecture notes on bone setting are decorated with sketches of flowers and fruits, and he told a friend that 'during the lecture, there came a sunbeam in the room, and with it a whole troop of creatures floating in the ray; and I was off with them to Oberon and Fairy-land.'

Keats could not practise until he was twenty-one, which would be in October 1816. Meanwhile, he went to Margate for two months on holiday — he had never seen the sea until then. From Margate he wrote verse letters, and back in London that October wrote 'On First Looking into Chapman's Homer'. In London, at 76 Cheapside, he shared lodgings with his two brothers George and Tom (John was 21, George 19 and Tom 17; their thirteen-year old sister, Fanny, was at boarding school) and he began to make friends with writers and painters. He continued as a dresser of wounds, but at a meeting with his guardian, Richard Abbey, Keats announced that he did not intend being a surgeon but would rely on his 'abilities as a poet'.

He published his first book of poems in March 1817 — a book that went largely unnoticed — and in May abandoned work as a dresser. He and his brothers moved to Hampstead, a green and airy suburb, thinking that the move would help Tom, who was ill.

Keats found a new publisher and, thinking that great poets wrote long poems, planned to write a four thousand line poem, 'Endymion', based on the Greek myth of the young shepherd boy Endymion who is loved by Diana or Cynthia, the moon. The story can be read as that of the poet in search of beauty. Its first line is one of Keats's most famous: 'A thing of beauty is a joy for ever'.

In April 1817, Keats travelled to the Isle of Wight, to Margate, Canterbury and Hastings, returned to Hampstead and then went to stay with a friend Benjamin Bailey in Oxford, where he worked on 'Endymion'. He finished the poem in Surrey where he had gone to escape London. From here he wrote one of his marvellous letters. Writing to Bailey, he called for 'a Life of Sensations rather than of Thoughts' and he said that 'I am certain of nothing but of the holiness of the Heart's affections and the truth of Imagination — What the imagination seizes as Beauty must be truth'. That same letter also gives us Keats's profound insight on his wish to avoid self-centredness; genius, he felt, requires a 'disinterestedness': 'I scarcely remember counting upon any Happiness — I look not for it if it be not in the present hour — nothing startles me beyond the Moment. The setting sun will always set me to rights — or if a Sparrow come before my Window I take part in its existence and pick about the Gravel.' Keats felt that Shakespeare possessed this gift in an extraordinary way. The writer William Hazlitt said of Shakespeare that he was 'the least of an egoist that it was possible to be. He was nothing in himself; but was all that others were, or that they could become'.

Keats developed this idea further in a letter to his brothers, on 21 December 1817, in which he gives us his theory of **Negative Capability**. Here is how Keats explains it: 'several things dovetailed in my mind, & at once it struck me, what quality went to form a Man of Achievement, especially in Literature, & which Shakespeare possessed so enormously — I mean Negative Capability, that is when a man is capable of being in uncertainties, Mysteries, doubts, without any irritable reaching after fact & reason'. In other words, what Keats admired was a writer's ability to create/enter into a world, an experience or an emotion for its own sake and in doing so the reader is also allowed to experience it fully.

Negative Capability is 'a power of sympathy and freedom from self-consciousness which peculiarly characterises the artist', as *The New Princeton Encyclopedia of Poetry and Poetics* puts it.

In the spring of 1818, Keats got to know Charles Wentworth Dilke and Charles Armitage Brown, who were schoolfriends and had built a double house with a shared garden called Wentworth Place in Hampstead. (Today it is the building most closely associated with Keats and is known as the Keats Museum.) That same year, 'Endymion' was published. Tom's health became worse – in January he was spitting blood; George Keats married and emigrated to the United States. Keats accompanied the newly-weds to Liverpool port in June and then set off with Charles Brown on a walking tour of the Lake District, Scotland and northern Ireland. Bad weather made the journey difficult and Keats suffered frequent colds and sore throats, though on 2 August he and Brown climbed Ben Nevis, the highest mountain in Britain. Keats's health was not good and a doctor in Inverness advised him to return to London at once. He took a boat from Cromarty to London. By then, they had already walked 642 miles.

In London, he discovered that Tom was dying and Keats nursed his nineteen-year-old brother in Well Walk in Hampstead. 'Endymion' received some very negative reviews, but Keats continued to write and began 'Hyperion' around this time. In November, the twenty-three-year old Keats met eighteen-year-old Fanny Brawne, with whom he was to fall in love. On 1 December, Tom died from tuberculosis and Keats soon afterwards went to live in Brown's half of Wentworth Place.

1818–1819 was Keats's magnificent year. In the words of Walter Jackson Bate, it was 'the most productive in the life of any poet of the past three centuries.' He wrote his great odes, poems that confirmed his place among the great English poets. In January 1819, Keats wrote 'The Eve of St Agnes'; in April, 'La Belle Dame sans Merci'; in May, 'Ode to a Nightingale' (written in a single morning), 'Ode on a Grecian Urn' and 'Ode on Melancholy'.

In June, Keats realised that he needed to make money – his guardian had never been generous and George had written from America to say that he was in financial difficulties. Keats planned to write a play – *Otho the Great* – in collaboration with Brown and to do so he went to the Isle of Wight to write. From here, he wrote love letters to Fanny Brawne, to whom he had become engaged and whose family was now renting the other half of Wentworth Place: 'I have two luxuries to brood over in my walks, your Loveliness and the hour of my death.' Brown joined him and later they moved to Winchester, where, that September, Keats wrote 'To Autumn'. He also wrote 'Bright Star! Would I Were Steadfast As Thou Art' sometime during 1819 (and revised it on board ship on his journey to Rome in early autumn 1820).

Back in London, Keats took new lodgings in Westminster, but then returned to live in Hampstead. In February 1820, his health was so bad that he was coughing up blood and his medical background taught him the worst: 'I know the colour of that blood; it is arterial blood; – I cannot be deceived in that colour; – that drop of blood is my death-warrant; — I must die.' He spent two months mostly in bed and then moved to lodgings in Kentish Town a few doors away from an old friend, Leigh Hunt. After another bad haemorrhage, he moved in with Hunt and then stayed with the Brawnes in Hampstead.

A change of climate was thought best and in September John Keats left England for Rome with his friend the artist Joseph Severn. The sea journey took three weeks; in the Bay of Naples they had to wait ten days to fulfil quarantine regulations. They went ashore on 31 October 1820 (Keats's twenty-fifth birthday) and travelled to Rome, but Keats was beyond recovery. He referred to his last months as a 'posthumous existence'. Letters sent to him from England, including letters from Fanny Brawne, remained unopened.

He died on 23 February 1821 and was buried in the Protestant Cemetery in Rome, having lived twenty-five years, three months and twenty-three days. The gravestone bears the following inscription at Keats's request: 'Here lies One Whose Name was writ in Water'. He asked that his unopened letters be buried with him. In what is probably the last letter he ever wrote — to his friend Brown, dated 30 November 1820 — he ends: 'I can scarcely bid you good-bye, even in a letter. I always make an awkward bow. God bless you! John Keats.'

Romanticism

The history of literature is often seen as a series of movements (e.g. Anglo-Saxon or Old English; Medieval or Middle English; Renaissance — Elizabethan, Jacobean, Caroline, Commonwealth; Restoration; Augustan; Romantic; Victorian; Edwardian; Georgian; Modern; Postmodern) and are often discussed as such. Of course this is a very artificial way of looking at literature or art or music. However, there are certain aspects that are characteristic of an age and which separate that age from what has gone before or what follows. If you think of the times you know best — the age in which you live — you will realise that the poem that is being written today is very different from the poem written a hundred or even twenty years ago. Similarly with novels, painting and music. Violence and uncertainty are said to be characteristic of our age. Yes they are, and though it would be a sweeping generalisation and an inaccurate picture of things if it were said of the late twentieth century, the beginning of the twenty-first, that those were the only things to be said about it, violence and uncertainty are undoubtedly striking features of the times we live in.

To understand something of Keats, it is worth knowing something of the thinking and the attitudes of the age in which he lived. Together with Wordsworth, Coleridge, Byron and Shelley, Keats is part of what is now known as the Romantic Movement in poetry. The clichéd version of Romantic is that of moonlight and roses and candlelit dinners for two. Another and more interesting aspect of what

Romantic means, what is known as the Romantic Movement, can be found in painting, music, philosophy, politics and literature, especially towards the end of the eighteenth century and the beginning of the nineteenth. If you listen to a Beethoven (1770–1827) symphony, if you look at a painting by Turner (1775–1851), his 'Rain, Steam and Speed – the Great Western Railway', for example (for which Turner, as every art historian reminds us, leaned out of the train window so as to experience authentically the rain, speed and steam), or if you read a poem by Wordsworth, Coleridge, Byron, Shelley, Blake or Keats, you are experiencing what we now call Romanticism. The Romantic Movement in England is usually thought to date from the 1780s until 1830.

There are many definitions of Romanticism. T. E. Hulme defines it as follows: 'Here is the root of all Romanticism, that man the individual is an infinite reservoir of possibility.' It was a movement that certainly celebrated the individual and, above all else, the individual imagination. John Keats 'loved the principle of beauty in all things' and in his poetry his unique imagination expresses his intense and sensuous delight in things outside himself.

Romanticism is a way of viewing the world, of viewing the self, a way of viewing the relationship between the self and the world. The following lines from Blake's 'Auguries of Innocence' are often quoted as lines that express the Romantic vision:

> To see a World in a grain of Sand
> And a Heaven in a wild Flower
> Hold Infinity in the palm of your hand
> And Eternity in an Hour.

Nature was very important to the Romantic poets, especially to Wordsworth, and many of the finest Romantic meditations take place out of doors (e.g. Wordsworth's 'Tintern Abbey' or Keats's 'Ode to a Nightingale' and 'To Autumn'). M. H. Abrams says in his *Glossary of Literary Terms* that:

To an extraordinary degree external nature — the landscape, together with its flora and fauna — became a persistent subject of poetry, and was described with an accuracy and sensuous nuance unprecedented in earlier writers. It is a mistake, however, to describe romantic poets as simply 'nature poets'. While many major poems by Wordsworth and Coleridge — and to a lesser extent by Shelley and Keats — set out from and return to an aspect or change of aspect in the landscape, the outer scene is not presented for its own sake, but only as a stimulus for the poet to engage in the most characteristic human activity, that of thinking. The most important romantic poems are in fact poems of feelingful meditation about an important human problem.

POEMS

Dates refer to the year of composition. The poems as they are printed here, are in the order in which they were written.

To One Who Has Been Long in City Pent

To one who has been long in city pent,
   'Tis very sweet to look into the fair
   And open face of heaven, to breathe a prayer
Full in the smile of the blue firmament.
Who is more happy, when, with heart's content,   5
   Fatigued he sinks into some pleasant lair
   Of wavy grass and reads a debonair
And gentle tale of love and languishment?
Returning home at evening, with an ear
   Catching the notes of Philomel, an eye   10
Watching the sailing cloudlet's bright career,
   He mourns that day so soon has glided by,
E'en like the passage of an angel's tear
   That falls through the clear ether silently.

📖 Glossary

Title: The title echoes the lines from Milton's *Paradise Lost* (Book IX, line 445–448) – 'As one who long in populous city pent,/Where houses thick and sewers annoy the Air/Forth issuing on a summer's morn to breathe/Among the pleasant villages and farms....' Coleridge also uses the phrase 'in the great city pent' in his poem 'This Lime-tree Bower my Prison'.

Line 1 pent: shut in a confined space.

Line 4 firmament: sky.

Line 6 lair: a sheltered place.

Line 7 debonair: gentle, pleasant, gracious (frequently used by Spenser).

Line 8 languishment: longing.

Line 10 Philomel: the nightingale.

Line 11 career: swift course through the sky.

Line 14 ether: upper air.

This sonnet was written in June 1816, when Keats was twenty, and one month after he had seen a poem of his in print for the very first time. In many ways, it resembles his first published poem in that it focuses on the beauty of nature and the pleasures of escaping the crowded city. He was studying medicine at Guy's Hospital at the time and living in Southwark, described by Keats himself as 'a beastly place in dirt, turnings and windings'. Here Keats is nostalgic for the countryside he knew at Edmonton in Middlesex, where he had been at school. It is significant that, in addition to the joys of nature, Keats also speaks of reading 'a gentle tale of love'. Thus the experience is a combination of natural beauty and the beauty of the imagination.

❓ Questions

1. Though Keats in this sonnet does not describe city life, what does he imply about it?

2. What is the effect of the monosyllabic first line? Why, do you think, is this the only line in the poem where almost every word is a monosyllable?

3. Which words in the opening quatrain capture a sense of release and beauty and freedom? What is the effect of the run-on line or enjambment in the poem?

4. Comment on what Keats sees as perfect happiness (lines 5–8). Why the 'gentle tale of love and languishment'? What does this tell us about Keats?

5. In the closing lines, Keats mentions the song of the nightingale, the sailing cloudlet. What is the poet's mood in these lines?

6. What is the significance of the reference to 'heaven' (line 3) and 'angel's tear' (line 13)?

7. Comment on the structure of the sonnet, paying particular attention to sentence length. Comment too on the musical qualities of the language. How is this music achieved?

On First Looking into Chapman's Homer

Much have I travelled in the realms of gold,
  And many goodly states and kingdoms seen;
  Round many western islands have I been
Which bards in fealty to Apollo hold.
Oft of one wide expanse had I been told   5
  That deep-browed Homer ruled as his demesne;
  Yet did I never breathe its pure serene
Till I heard Chapman speak out loud and bold.
Then felt I like some watcher of the skies
  When a new planet swims into his ken;   10
Or like stout Cortez when with eagle eyes
  He stared at the Pacific, and all his men
Looked at each other with a wild surmise –
  Silent, upon a peak in Darien.

📖 Glossary

Line 1 the realms of gold: here it refers to the world of literature (it also refers to the discovery of the New World – El Dorado, the golden land or city imagined by the Spanish conquerors of America).

Line 3 many western islands: Britain and Ireland.

Line 4 bards in fealty to Apollo: poets are bound to Apollo, the Greek sun-god, patron of poetry and music.

Line 6 demesne: estate, region, realm (originally pronounced to rhyme with 'serene').

Line 7 serene: clear, bright expanse of air.

Line 8 Chapman: George Chapman (1559–1634) poet, dramatist, translator of Homer's *Iliad* and *Odyssey*. Chapman's translation was published in 1614.

Lines 9/10: these lines echo a description of Herschel's discovery of the planet Uranus in a book on astronomy which Keats had been given as a school prize in 1811.

Line 11 Cortez: Hernando Cortez (1485–1547), Spanish explorer/conquistador. In 1518, he led an army of 508 men that explored Mexico. In fact, Keats is here confusing Balboa's first glimpse of the Pacific with Cortez's first glimpse of Mexico City. Balboa was the first European to get sight of the Pacific.

Line 14 Darien: the isthmus (narrow neck of land) of Darien joins together North and South America; the old name for the Isthmus of Panama.

This sonnet was written in October 1816 and was first published in the *Examiner*, 1 December 1816. Keats had spent an evening with his good friend and former teacher Charles Cowden Clarke, who had been lent a folio edition of Chapman's translation of Homer. They read aloud from the book and Clarke tells of how Keats responded to certain passages with a 'delighted stare' and 'he sometimes shouted'. When Keats returned to his lodgings at day-break he sat down and composed the sonnet and sent it to his friend Clarke, who received it at ten o'clock.

? Questions

1. This is a Petrarchan sonnet, which means that between the octet and the sestet there is a change in the rhyming scheme signalling a new idea, a development with a new emphasis and energy. This psychological break is known as the turn. The octet rhymes abbaabba, the sestet usually cdcdcd. Why is this sonnet structure particularly suitable for what Keats has to say?

2. Look at the references to time in the sonnet beginning 'Much have I travelled'. Why is the word 'Then' (line 9) so important?

3. What mood or feeling is Keats conveying in the sestet? Which details are particularly effective in creating that mood?

4. What is Keats's tone towards reading in lines 1–4? Towards his reading of Homer?

5. Why do you think Keats chose to say 'looking into' and not reading? Can you suggest why Keats uses many archaic words such as 'goodly,' 'bards,' 'fealty,' in the poem?

6. Keats first compares himself to an astronomer, a watcher of the skies, then to an explorer with his men. Consider the differences between the two types of explorers and say which you think the more effective and interesting of the two.

7. The opening line refers to movement ('travelled'); in the final line there is silence and stillness. Why is this appropriate?

When I Have Fears That I May Cease to Be

When I have fears that I may cease to be
  Before my pen has gleaned my teeming brain,
Before high-pilèd books in charact'ry,
  Hold like rich garners the full-ripened grain;
When I behold, upon the night's starred face,   5
  Huge cloudy symbols of a high romance,
And think that I may never live to trace
  Their shadows with the magic hand of chance;
And when I feel, fair creature of an hour,
  That I shall never look upon thee more,   10
Never have relish in the faery power
  Of unreflecting love; then on the shore
Of the wide world I stand alone and think
Till love and fame to nothingness do sink.

📖 Glossary

Title: The title here echoes Shakespeare's Sonnet 12, 'When I Do Count the Clock that Tells the Time', a sonnet which Keats had marked in his own edition of Shakespeare's poems.

Line 2 gleaned: gathered in or collected from.

Line 2 teeming: fruitful, full, prolific.

Line 3 charactery: writing (as used by Shakespeare e.g. 'Fairies use flowers for their charactery', *The Merry Wives of Windsor*, V (v) 77).

Line 4 garners: granaries or store houses.

Line 11 faery: the spelling is Spenserian.

Keats wrote this sonnet in January 1818. It is Shakespearean in form (though there are traces of the octet/sestet structure) and many of Keats's subsequent sonnets were Shakespearean rather than Petrarchan. Keats in a letter once said that he liked to think, if it was not too daring a thought, that Shakespeare was his presiding genius. This sonnet was not published during Keats's lifetime.

❓ Questions

1. What metaphor is used in the first quatrain of the poem for Keats's 'teeming brain'. Is the image an effective one? Give reasons for your answer.

2. The entire poem is made up of one sentence. What is the effect of this?

3. How does Keats give the reader a very strong sense of the passing of time? Comment on the effect of 'when' and 'then'.

4. What kind of writing is Keats interested in? What do you think Keats is referring to in the phrase 'the magic hand of chance'?

5. A new idea is introduced in the third quatrain. Is there any connection between this reference to young loving and what has gone before?

6. Identify Keats's mood in the opening lines of the sonnet and trace his mood throughout the poem. Does the poet's mood change? Which particular words capture this mood best?

La Belle Dame sans Merci

O what can ail thee, knight-at-arms,
   Alone and palely loitering?
The sedge has withered from the lake,
   And no birds sing.

O what can ail thee, knight-at-arms,   5
   So haggard and so woe-begone?
The squirrel's granary is full,
   And the harvest's done.

I see a lily on thy brow,
   With anguish moist and fever-dew,   10
And on thy cheeks a fading rose
   Fast withereth too.

I met a lady in the meads,
   Full beautiful – a faery's child,
Her hair was long, her foot was light   15
   And her eyes were wild.

I made a garland for her head,
   And bracelets too, and fragrant zone;
She looked at me as she did love,
   And made sweet moan.   20

I set her on my pacing steed,
   And nothing else saw all day long,
For sidelong would she bend, and sing
   A faery's song.

She found me roots of relish sweet,   25
　　And honey wild, and manna dew,
And sure in language strange she said –
　　'I love thee true'.

She took me to her elfin grot,
　　And there she wept and sighed full sore,   30
And there I shut her wild wild eyes
　　With kisses four.

And there she lullèd me asleep
　　And there I dreamed – Ah! woe betide! –
The latest dream I ever dreamt   35
　　On the cold hill side.

I saw pale kings, and princes too,
　　Pale warriors, death-pale were they all;
They cried – 'La Belle Dame sans Merci
　　Hath thee in thrall!'   40

I saw their starved lips in the gloam,
　　With horrid warning gapèd wide,
And I awoke, and found me here,
　　On the cold hill's side.

And this is why I sojourn here   45
　　Alone and palely loitering,
Though the sedge is withered from the lake,
　　And no birds sing.

Glossary

Title: There is a French medieval poem 'La Belle Dame sans Merci' by Alain Chartier, written in 1424, from which the title but not the subject matter is taken. The story of a mortal man falling in love with a beautiful woman who is not quite mortal and being destroyed by her is a familiar one. La Belle Dame does not seem sinister, though the knight's love for her has brought him to his woeful and lonely state. The critic David Perkins suggests that this woeful state 'might be attributed to the hopelessness of his love for something superhuman rather than to "la belle dame" herself'.

Line 1 ail: trouble.

Line 1 knight-at-arms: Keats revised the poem and substituted 'wretched wight' for knight-at-arms. Wight is an Old English word for man. The revised version is less medieval in its associations though all scholars think the first version best.

Line 3 sedge: grass-like plant growing in marshes or by water.

Line 13 meads: meadows.

Line 18 fragrant zone: a belt or girdle made of flowers.

Line 21 steed: horse.

Line 26 manna: miraculous substance – 'manna from heaven' – supplied as food to the Israelites in the wilderness (Exodus 16: 14–36). Here it means magical food.

Line 29 elfin: from elf – a supernatural diminutive being, sometimes malignant.

Line 29 grot: grotto or cave.

Line 32 kisses four: in his letter to his brother George, Keats imagines him asking on reading the poem 'Why four kisses?'. Keats playfully answers such a question: 'I was obliged to choose an even number that both eyes might have fair play: and to speak truly I think two a piece quite sufficient – suppose I had said seven; there would have been three and a half a piece – a very awkward affair.'

Line 35 latest: last.

Line 40 in thrall: enslaved.

Line 41 gloam: twilight.

Line 45 sojourn: dwell for a while.

1819 was Keats's *annus mirabilis*, in which he wrote most of his greatest poems. This ballad was written on 21 April 1819 and, though composed in a few hours, it has, in the words of Walter Jackson Bate, 'haunted readers and poets for a century and a half'. Keats included the poem as part of a journal-letter to his brother and sister-in-law in America. The ballad form was unusual for Keats and one of the more effective and striking things about this particular ballad is Keats's use of rhythm. In the final line of each stanza, Keats shortens the metrical line to a four beat, two stress structure.

? Questions

1. What immediate differences do you see between this poem by Keats and the three earlier poems?

2. Outline, briefly, in your own words, the central narrative of the poem.

3. How many speakers are in this ballad? Identify the different voices.

4. What atmosphere is created in the opening three stanzas? Refer to details in the text to support your answer.

5. What is the effect of the shortened fourth line in each stanza?

6. From line 13 to the end of the poem, the knight-at-arms speaks. What did he find so attractive in the lady he met? Why is he suffering? Is there a suggestion that the knight-at-arms is dying? Why does he sojourn in that particular place?

7. How do you respond to, and can you explain, the nightmare element in the poem (lines 33–38)?

8. What is the effect of the medieval allusions in the poem? Comment on the lack of detail in the poem. In your view, is this a strength or a weakness?

Ode to a Nightingale

I

My heart aches, and a drowsy numbness pains
  My sense, as though of hemlock I had drunk,
Or emptied some dull opiate to the drains
  One minute past, and Lethe-wards had sunk:
'Tis not through envy of thy happy lot,   5
  But being too happy in thine happiness, –
    That thou, light-wingèd Dryad of the trees,
      In some melodious plot
  Of beechen green, and shadows numberless,
    Singest of summer in full-throated ease.   10

II

O, for a draught of vintage! that hath been
  Cooled a long age in the deep-delvèd earth,
Tasting of Flora and the country green,
  Dance, and Provencal song, and sunburnt mirth!
O for a beaker full of the warm South,   15
  Full of the true, the blushful Hippocrene,
    With beaded bubbles winking at the brim,
      And purple-stainèd mouth;
That I might drink, and leave the world unseen,
  And with thee fade away into the forest dim: 20

III

Fade far away, dissolve, and quite forget
  What thou among the leaves hast never known,
The weariness, the fever, and the fret
  Here where men sit and hear each other groan;
Where palsy shakes a few, sad, last gray hairs,   25
  Where youth grows pale, and spectre-thin, and dies;
    Where but to think is to be full of sorrow
      And leaden-eyed despairs,
  Where Beauty cannot keep her lustrous eyes,
    Or new Love pine at them beyond to-morrow.   30

IV
Away! away! for I will fly to thee,
   Not charioted by Bacchus and his pards,
But on the viewless wings of Poesy,
   Though the dull brain perplexes and retards.
Already with thee! tender is the night,   35
   And haply the Queen-Moon is on her throne,
     Clustered around by all her starry Fays;
        But here there is no light,
   Save what from heaven is with the breezes blown
     Through verdurous glooms and winding mossy ways.   40

V
I cannot see what flowers are at my feet,
   Nor what soft incense hangs upon the boughs,
But, in embalmèd darkness, guess each sweet
   Wherewith the seasonable month endows
The grass, the thicket, and the fruit-tree wild;   45
   White hawthorn, and the pastoral eglantine;
     Fast fading violets covered up in leaves;
        And mid-May's eldest child,
   The coming musk-rose, full of dewy wine,
     The murmurous haunt of flies on summer eves.   50

VI
Darkling I listen; and, for many a time
   I have been half in love with easeful Death,
Called him soft names in many a musèd rhyme,
   To take into the air my quiet breath;
Now more than ever seems it rich to die,   55
   To cease upon the midnight with no pain,
     While thou art pouring forth thy soul abroad
        In such an ecstasy!
   Still wouldst thou sing, and I have ears in vain –
     To thy high requiem become a sod.   60

VII

Thou wast not born for death, immortal Bird!
  No hungry generations tread thee down;
The voice I hear this passing night was heard
  In ancient days by emperor and clown:
Perhaps the self-same song that found a path   65
    Through the sad heart of Ruth, when, sick for home,
      She stood in tears amid the alien corn;
        The same that oft-times hath
Charmed magic casements, opening on the foam
    Of perilous seas, in faery lands forlorn.   70

VIII

Forlorn! the very word is like a bell
  To toll me back from thee to my sole self!
Adieu! the fancy cannot cheat so well
  As she is famed to do, deceiving elf.
Adieu! adieu! thy plaintive anthem fades   75
    Past the near meadows, over the still stream,
      Up the hill-side; and now 'tis buried deep
        In the next valley-glades:
    Was it a vision, or a waking dream?
      Fled is that music: – Do I wake or sleep?   80

📖 Glossary

Line 2 hemlock: a plant that can be used as a sedative but is also poisonous.

Line 3 opiate: a drug containing opium that eases pain and induces sleep.

Line 3 to the drains: to the dregs, sediments – leaving nothing.

Line 4 Lethe-wards: towards the river Lethe, whose waters cause forgetfulness in Hades, the Underworld of Greek mythology. The souls in Hades who drank the water would forget their past existence.

Line 5 lot: fortune, destiny, condition.

Line 7 Dryad: a woodland nymph (nymph being a young and beautiful maiden).

Line 11 vintage: a wine of very high quality, usually old.

Line 12 deep-delvèd earth: in a letter written May 1819, Keats speaks of 'a little claret-wine cool out of a cellar a mile deep'.

Line 13 Flora: the Roman goddess of flowers.

Line 14 Provencal song, and sunburnt mirth: that region in southern France and the festivities and celebrations associated with the grape harvest.

Line 15: wine from the Mediterranean region.

Line 16 the blushful Hippocrene: the phrase here is an example of periphrasis (round-about expression) for wine. Hippocrene is a fountain near Mount Helicon, a place sacred to the Muses, and therefore a fountain of inspiration.

Line 25 palsy: loss of feeling and control.

Line 26 Where youth grows pale and spectre-thin and dies: Keats is writing this poem in May 1819; Tom Keats had died from tuberculosis on 1 December 1818. Spectre-thin is ghostly-thin.

Line 29 lustrous: bright, shining.

Line 30 pine: to long for.

Line 32 Bacchus: the Roman god of wine – a beautiful, young man, crowned with ivy and vine leaves and carrying a thyrsus or pine-staff, twined round with ivy and vine leaves. Bacchus is said to possess eternal youth. Often portrayed being drawn in a chariot.

Line 32 pards: leopards.

Line 33 viewless: invisible.

Line 35 tender: gentle, young.

Line 36 haply: perhaps, by chance.

Line 36 Queen-moon: Diana, Roman goddess of light, representative of chastity and hunting.

Line 37 Fays: fairies.

Line 40 verdurous: fresh-green or grass-green.

Line 42 incense: fragrant scent.

Line 43 embalmed: a balm is an aromatic substance, a fragrant and healing ointment; 'embalmed darkness' refers in this instance to a fragrant darkness. 'Embalmed' would also suggest death, an idea explored by Keats in the following stanza.

Line 44 endows: enriches.

Line 46 pastoral eglantine: the sweet briar of the countryside – 'pastoral' evokes an ideal world of pastureland and shepherds.

Line 51 Darkling: in the dark.

Line 53 mused: bemused, muddled, fuzzy.

Line 54 clown: ordinary fellow, countryman.

Line 60 requiem: the requiem sung at Keats's anticipated death.

Line 66 Ruth: in the Bible, Ruth, after her husband died, did not return to her own people but went with her mother-in-law, Naomi, to Bethlehem. There, in an alien country, she became a gleaner in the fields of Boaz. In a lecture entitled 'On Poetry in General', which Keats would have known, William Hazlitt commented that 'The story of Ruth . . . is as if all the depth of natural affection in the human race was involved in her breast'.

Line 69 casements: windows.

Line 70 faery: the spelling is Spenserian and thus summons to mind not only fairy land but the world of Spenser's poetry.

Lines 71/72 forlorn: lost, remote and far away; lonely, desolate.

Line 72 toll: summon.

Line 72 sole: lonely, solitary.

Line 73 fancy: imagination.

Line 75 plaintive: mournful.

Line 75 anthem: a song of praise or gladness; a music with religious associations (echoing the 'requiem' in line 60).

This is the first of the great odes. It was written in May 1819, and was first published in *Annals of the Fine Arts*, July 1819. This would suggest that it is a poem that explores, among other things, the nature of art and the relationship between the different art forms. Many of the odes echo and develop the thoughts in a long letter which Keats had begun to write to his brother George on 14 February but did not send until 3 May. (The printed version of this letter runs to over forty pages and includes the poem 'La Belle Dame sans Merci'). The world has often been called a 'vale of tears', but in this letter Keats prefers to call the world a 'vale of soul-making'. A soul acquires an identity; 'each one is personally itself'. Keats thinks a world of pain and trouble necessary if the intelligence is to become a soul, and he uses the image of a school to explain himself more clearly. The world is the school: the book used in school is the human heart and the soul is like the child who can read the book. The poem can of course be read without reference to the letter, but a careful reading of the poem will reveal many parallels between Keats's ideas in his letters and the ideas in his poetry. Having read the poem (and other poems by Keats), we could ask how Keats's concept of soul-making is revealed to us in the poetry.

Keats was living in Wentworth Place in Hampstead at the time and his friend Charles Brown, with whom he shared a house, has left us this account of the poem's composition: 'In the Spring of 1819 a nightingale had built her nest in my house. Keats felt a continual joy in her song; and one morning he took his chair from the breakfast-table to the grass-plot under a plum-tree, where he sat for two or three hours. When he came into the house, I perceived he had some scraps of paper in his hand, and these he was quietly thrusting behind the books. On inquiry, I found those scraps, four or five in number, contained his poetic feeling on the song of the nightingale.'

Questions

1. An ode is a poem of praise and celebration. In this instance, Keats is celebrating the song of the nightingale and everything that song suggests and symbolises. What is Keats's mood in the opening four lines of the poem? Which words in particular capture that mood?

2. Contrast plays an important part in stanza 1. Discuss how Keats creates this contrast. Look, for example, at words such as 'drowsy numbness' and 'light-winged'.

3. In the poem, Keats longs to escape harsh reality, longs 'to leave the world unseen', and he succeeds for a time. What does he long for in stanza 2? How does Keats succeed in making this so attractive? Which words and phrases are particularly effective?

4. Stanza 3 tells of what Keats has known of human suffering. Which details in particular do you find effective?

5. In the end, it is not an imagined 'draught of vintage' but 'the viewless wings of poesy' that allow him to fly away and enter into the world of the song of the nightingale. In stanzas 4 and 5, Keats describes that world. Comment on the details that you find most effective.

6. In stanza 6, Keats wishes he were dead. Why? What reasons does he give? He also changes his mind in lines 59–60. Why?

7. In stanza 7, Keats thinks of the song of the nightingale heard in other times and other places. What is the effect of stanza 7 within the poem as a whole?

8. What is Keats's mood in the poem's final stanza? Why? What is the significance of Keats telling himself and us that 'the fancy cannot cheat so well'?

9. Keats is known for his sensuousness. Discuss Keats's sensuousness in 'Ode to a Nightingale'.

10. Would you consider this a realistic poem, an escapist poem or a combination of both? Refer to the text in your answer.

Ode on a Grecian Urn

I

Thou still unravished bride of quietness,
   Thou foster-child of silence and slow time,
Sylvan historian, who canst thus express
   A flowery tale more sweetly than our rhyme:
What leaf-fringed legend haunts about thy shape   5
   Of deities or mortals, or of both,
      In Tempe or the dales of Arcady?
   What men or gods are these? What maidens loth?
What mad pursuit? What struggle to escape?
      What pipes and timbrels? What wild ecstasy?   10

II

Heard melodies are sweet, but those unheard
   Are sweeter: therefore, ye soft pipes, play on;
Not to the sensual ear, but, more endeared,
   Pipe to the spirit ditties of no tone:
Fair youth, beneath the trees, thou canst not leave   15
   Thy song, nor ever can those trees be bare;
      Bold lover, never, never canst thou kiss,
Though winning near the goal – yet, do not grieve;
      She cannot fade, though thou hast not thy bliss,
         For ever wilt thou love, and she be fair!   20

III

Ah, happy, happy boughs! that cannot shed
   Your leaves, nor ever bid the spring adieu;
And, happy melodist, unwearièd,
   For ever piping songs for ever new;
More happy love! more happy, happy love!   25
   For ever warm and still to be enjoyed,
      For ever panting, and for ever young –
All breathing human passion far above,
   That leaves a heart high-sorrowful and cloyed,
      A burning forehead, and a parching tongue.   30

IV

Who are these coming to the sacrifice?
　　To what green altar, O mysterious priest,
Lead'st thou that heifer lowing at the skies,
　　And all her silken flanks with garlands dressed?
What little town by river or sea shore,　　　　　　　　　35
　　Or mountain-built with peaceful citadel,
　　　Is emptied of this folk, this pious morn?
And, little town, thy streets for evermore
　　Will silent be; and not a soul to tell
　　　Why thou art desolate, can e'er return.　　　　　　40

V

O Attic shape! Fair attitude! with brede
　Of marble men and maidens overwrought,
With forest branches and the trodden weed;
　　Thou, silent form, dost tease us out of thought
As doth eternity: Cold Pastoral!　　　　　　　　　　45
　　When old age shall this generation waste,
　　　Thou shalt remain, in midst of other woe
　　Than ours, a friend to man, to whom thou say'st,
Beauty is truth, truth beauty, – that is all
　　　Ye know on earth, and all ye need to know.　　　50

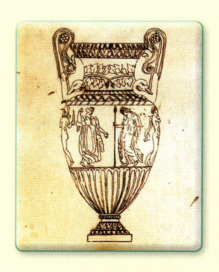

📖 Glossary

Title: Grecian in this instance means ancient Greece and an urn was a vase with a rounded body, usually with a narrowed mouth and often a foot. It contained and preserved the ashes of the cremated dead. The images on the side of the urn that Keats describes are intensely alive.

Line 1 still: the word here can be interpreted in two different ways – still (as adjective) meaning motionless, and still (as adverb) meaning 'ever' or 'as yet'.

Line 1 unravished: untouched, virginal.

Line 3 Sylvan: literally means belonging to the woods, rural.

Line 7 Tempe: is a valley in Thessaly in Greece.

Line 7 Arcady: a district in Greece associated with music and dancing. Tempe and Arcadia were associated with happiness and a beautiful landscape.

Line 8 loth: reluctant, unwilling.

Line 10 timbrels: the timbrel is an ancient Oriental tabor or tambourine.

Line 13 sensual ear: the ear of sense as distinct from the spirit/the imagination.

Line 14 spirit: inspiration, the poetic imagination, the soul.

Line 14 ditties: dit or ditt was the archaic word for poem; ditty – a little poem set to music.

Line 17 Bold: courageous, assertive.

Line 29 cloyed: wearied, surfeited.

Line 33 heifer lowing at the skies: this detail is to be found on the Elgin marbles.

Line 36 citadel: fortress, especially one guarding or dominating a city.

Line 37 pious: holy – there is to be a sacrifice.

Line 41 Attic: Grecian (Attica was that part of Greece where Athens was located).

Line 41 attitude: here it means the posture given to a figure in statues or painting.

Line 41 brede: brede is an archaic spelling of 'braid', meaning interwoven. Keats may also intend a pun on breed.

Line 42 overwrought: fashioned on the surface of the urn or here, over-excited.

Line 44 tease: entice, mock.

The Elgin marbles, which Keats had seen in the British Museum, the 'View of Delphi with a Procession', a mezzotint after Claude Lorrain, an engraving entitled 'The Sacrifice at Lystra', based on a drawing by Raphael, and a drawing of the Sosibios Vase which Keats himself had made from a book of reproductions all influenced Keats's description of the Grecian urn in this ode. The urn as described is not based on any one Grecian urn or vase; Keats uses a combination of many images from different sources. Though Keats had many painter friends he preferred sculptures or engravings to painting and this ode celebrates the sense of sight. In 'Ode to a Nightingale', Keats hears the immortal song of the bird; in 'Ode on a Grecian Urn', he looks at the immortal work of art. The images on the urn are images of moments of intensity and movement, captured forever. The poem was first published in *Annals of the Fine Arts* in January 1820.

Questions

1. What does one usually associate with the word 'urn'?

2. Keats in 'Ode to a Nightingale', 'Ode on a Grecian Urn' and 'To Autumn' has focused on three different things. Discuss the differences and the similarities among the three.

3. How does Keats begin his 'Ode on a Grecian Urn'? How does it differ from 'Ode to a Nightingale'?

4. List and discuss every description Keats gives of the urn in lines 1–3. Why does Keats think the urn can tell 'a flowery tale more sweetly' than his poem? Discuss here the different art forms and how people respond to them.

5. With lines 5–10, a dramatic change takes place within the stanza. Why and how does that come about?

6. Having entered into the life as depicted on the side of the urn, what does Keats ask? Why?

7. Why does Keats find the images on the urn so attractive? Comment on this in relation to the urn's original purpose.

8. How would you describe the rhythm throughout the ode? Your answer should refer to sound, sentence length, use of punctuation (especially the use of questions and exclamation marks) and repetition.

9. The mood is sometimes meditative, sometimes excited. Which, would you say, is the predominant mood in the poem? Give reasons for your answer and support the points you make with suitable quotation or reference.

10. In the final stanza, why does Keats compare the urn to eternity? And why does he now call the urn 'Cold pastoral!'? What similarities are there between the ending of this ode and 'Ode to a Nightingale'?

Original manuscript by Keats

To Autumn

I

Season of mists and mellow fruitfulness,
   Close bosom-friend of the maturing sun;
Conspiring with him how to load and bless
   With fruit the vines that round the thatch-eaves run;
To bend with apples the mossed cottage trees,   5
   And fill all fruit with ripeness to the core;
     To swell the gourd, and plump the hazel shells
   With a sweet kernel; to set budding more,
And still more, later flowers for the bees,
Until they think warm days will never cease,   10
     For summer has o'er-brimmed their clammy cells.

II

Who hath not seen thee oft amid thy store?
   Sometimes whoever seeks abroad may find
Thee sitting careless on a granary floor,
   Thy hair soft-lifted by the winnowing wind;   15
Or on a half-reaped furrow sound asleep,
   Drowsed with the fume of poppies, while thy hook
     Spares the next swath and all its twinèd flowers:
And sometimes like a gleaner thou dost keep
   Steady thy laden head across a brook;   20
   Or by a cider-press, with patient look,
Thou watchest the last oozings hours by hours.

III

Where are the songs of spring? Ay, where are they?
   Think not of them, thou hast thy music too –
While barréd clouds bloom the soft-dying day,   25
   And touch the stubble-plains with rosy hue;
Then in a wailful choir the small gnats mourn
   Among the river sallows, borne aloft
     Or sinking as the light wind lives or dies;

And full-grown lambs loud bleat from hilly bourn;   30
    Hedge-crickets sing; and now with treble soft
The red-breast whistles from a garden-croft;
    And gathering swallows twitter in the skies.

 Glossary

Line 1 mellow: well matured, soft and ripe.

Line 3 Conspiring: acting together towards one end (from the Latin *conspirare*: *con* – together, *spirare*, to breathe).

Line 7 gourd: a large, hard-rinded, fleshy fruit.

Line 8 kernel: the edible part of the nut.

Line 11 clammy: sticky.

Line 13 abroad: over a wide area.

Line 14 sitting careless: sitting without care or at ease.

Line 15 winnowing: separating the chaff or husks from the grain.

Line 17 poppies: associated with sleep.

Line 17 hook: scythe.

Line 18 swath: the sweep of a scythe, the band of grass or corn cut by a scythe.

Line 19 gleaner: one who gathers in handfuls after the reapers.

Line 25 barred: divided into horizontal bars.

Line 25 bloom: here, a verb.

Line 27 gnats: small flies or insects.

Line 28 sallows: willows, especially the broader leaved kinds with comparatively brittle twigs.

Line 30 bourn: boundary, domain, territory.

Line 31 Hedge-crickets: a word invented by Keats. The cricket's song in Keats's earlier poem, 'On the Grasshopper and Cricket', is associated with winter – 'On a lone winter evening, when the frost/Has wrought a silence, from the stove there shrills/The cricket's song, in warmth increasing ever'.

Line 31 treble: high-pitched.

Line 32 garden-croft: a small, cultivated piece of farm land usually adjoining a dwelling.

In the spring of 1819, Keats wrote five odes and Timothy Hilton, in his book *Keats and his World*, says that 'the odes, like so much else that he wrote, are thick with references to his current reading and his life. We can feel the weather in them, for instance, and it comes as no surprise to find that they were written in a beautiful period of spring, a spring that came early in 1819'. In 'To Autumn', Keats celebrates a beautiful September.

In a letter, dated 21 September 1819, Keats describes how he came to write the poem: 'How beautiful the season is now – How fine the air. A temperate sharpness about it. Really, without joking, chaste weather – Dian skies – I never liked stubble fields as much as now – Aye better than the chilly green of the spring. Somehow a stubble plain looks warm – in the same way that some pictures look warm – this struck me so much in my Sunday's walk that I composed upon it.' The last of the great odes, 'To Autumn', was written on 19 September 1819 in Winchester.

Questions

1. Keats is present in all of his poems, but in different ways. In some instances, there is an intense awareness of himself – 'I', 'my' and 'me'. Where is Keats in this poem?

2. The poet Shelley says that 'there is a harmony/In autumn, and a lustre in its sky,/Which through the summer is not heard nor seen.'
   Look and listen to the words, especially in the first stanza, and comment, in detail, on how Keats uses language to create the harmony and music of autumn.

3. What are the characteristics of autumn as revealed to us in this ode? Discuss how Keats personifies the season, especially in stanza 2. Why do you think autumn is viewed as female?

4. How would you describe the movement of this poem? Consider the eleven line stanza, the references to the passing of time, the sounds of the words and their arrangement on the page.

5. In stanzas 1 and 2, the emphasis is on seeing, and in the final stanza on listening. Discuss the imagery in the poem and say why Keats changes from eye to ear in the closing lines.

6. How does Keats involve the reader in this poem?

7. What is the significance of the last line? How do the sounds in words such as 'twitter' and 'skies' echo the sense? Compare these sounds with words such as 'mellow fruitfulness' in line 1.

8. Pick out some examples of accurate, effective words or phrases and discuss them within the context of the poem as a whole. You could begin with 'bosom-friend', 'load', 'plump'.

9. What is Keats's view of the passing of time, dying and death as revealed to us in this poem?

10. Is this a great poem? If your answer is no, please read it again.

Bright star! Would I were steadfast as thou art

Bright star! Would I were steadfast as thou art –
   Not in lone splendour hung aloft the night
And watching, with eternal lids apart,
   Like nature's patient, sleepless eremite,
The moving waters at their priestlike task   5
   Of pure ablution round earth's human shores,
Or gazing on the new soft-fallen mask
   Of snow upon the mountains and the moors;
No – yet still steadfast, still unchangeable,
   Pillowed upon my fair love's ripening breast,   10
To feel for ever its soft fall and swell,
   Awake for ever in a sweet unrest,
Still, still to hear her tender-taken breath,
And so live ever – or else swoon to death.

Glossary

Line 1 steadfast: constant, fixed.

Line 2 aloft: above or high up.

Line 4 eremite: hermit or recluse; this was an archaic word even in Keats's time.

Line 6 ablution: act of washing (often ceremonial and refers to the religious rites of purification).

Line 13 tender: young, youthful; also, gentle.

There is a very moving and attractive story told about this poem. It was thought that this sonnet was the last poem Keats ever wrote, though this has never been proved. Keats certainly wrote the poem in his friend Severn's copy of Shakespeare, while their ship the *Maria Crowther* waited for favourable winds off the Dorset coast during their sea journey to Italy in September 1820. That manuscript of the poem can be seen in the Keats Museum in Hampstead. However, the discovery of a copy of the poem, in a slightly different version and dated 1819, proves that it belongs to the year in which he wrote the odes.

Questions

1. Why is Keats so attracted to the star initially? Why does he then reject the star? What is Keats's idea of happiness?

2. Keats in this sonnet imagines a bright and distant star watching planet earth. What is the significance of what it sees?

3. What is the effect of 'No—' at the beginning of line 9?

4. Which starlike qualities does Keats still long for having rejected the star? Which lines in the sonnet are the most deeply human?

5. How important is repetition in this poem? Consider words such as 'steadfast', 'forever', 'still'. What is the effect?

6. The poem consists of one sentence. Identify the various stages in the poem's structure. How does the progress of thought in the poem lead to the dramatic concluding line?

General Questions

A. Keats himself said: 'I have loved the principle of beauty in all things'. Discuss this statement in the light of your reading of at least six poems by Keats on your course.

B. 'In Keats's poetry, the transient and the immortal are keenly felt.' Discuss this statement, supporting your answer with quotations from, or references to, at least six poems by Keats on your course.

C. 'How does an understanding of Keats's theory of Negative Capability relate to your understanding of the poems?' In your answer, you should quote from, or refer to, at least six poems by Keats on your course.

D. What do you understand by the term 'Keatsian'? Discuss the term in relation to at least six poems by Keats on your course.

E. In a verse letter to his friend Reynolds, Keats writes: 'It is a flaw/In happiness, to see beyond our bourn –/It forces us in summer skies to mourn:/It spoils the singing of the nightingale.' Discuss this view supporting your answer with quotations from, or references to, at least six poems by Keats on your course.

F. 'John Keats's poetry is striking for its symbolism and sensuousness.' Discuss this view supporting your answer with quotations from, or references to, at least six poems by Keats on your course.

G. 'Though familiar with sorrow and suffering Keats, in his poetry, also experiences moments of intense happiness and beauty.' Would you agree with this view? In your answer, you should quote from, or refer to, at least six poems by Keats on your course.

• Keats in 1819.

Critical Commentary

To One Who Has Been Long in City Pent

The first line of this sonnet and the comma at the end of that line encourge the reader to dwell on the reality of being cooped up or imprisoned in a city. The words in line 1 are for the most part monosyllabic and, appropriately, are lacking in music. The second part of the sentence, however, captures the sense of freedom and release that looking skywards brings. The sounds are softer and gentler ('sweet', 'breathe', 'prayer', 'smile', 'blue') and the punctuation allows for a sense of freedom, with the run-on lines and the sense of a world opening up beyond the confines of the city. The answer to the question Keats poses in the second quatrain is implied. For Keats, to be out of doors in pleasant weather, enjoying the countryside and reading 'a gentle tale of love', is perfect happiness.

One of the more striking characteristics of Keats's poetry is his sensuousness and, even in this very early poem, his sensuous response to an experience is clearly seen in such details as 'look', 'sinks', 'wavy', 'an ear/Catching the notes of Philomel', 'an eye/Watching the sailing cloudlet's bright career'.

In line 9, Keats speaks of returning home in the evening and the happiness of the experience is drawing to an end. 'Mourns' introduces a sad mood, yet the ear hears the song of the nightingale and the eye still sees small clouds in the evening sky.

The final word in the poem – 'silently' – captures the special atmosphere of the experience. Everything is still and silent – assonance and alliteration contributing to the effect, as does the image of 'an angel's tear'.

On First Looking into Chapman's Homer

This is a poem about exploration and discovery; it is also about the pleasures of reading. It speaks of astronomers and adventurers, but it is also about poetry itself. That evening in October 1816 obviously made a huge impression on the twenty-one year old Keats. The first eight lines, the octet, speaks of his reading of poetry up until now, while the sestet expresses the intense joy and excitement that Keats felt when he first read Chapman's translation of Homer. The travel imagery in the opening lines are drawn from the *Odyssey* itself, one of the great journey poems in literature.

The American academic Helen Vendler points out that when we read a passage of prose or verse, and as we make sense of it, we come up with a summary and this is a very important initial step. Here is how Vendler summarises this sonnet: 'The speaker says that he has travelled through a lot of golden terrain – had read a lot of poems – and people had told him about the Homeric domain, but he had never breathed its air till he heard Chapman speak out. Then he felt like an astronomer discovering a new planet; or like the explorer who discovered the Pacific, whose men, astonished by his gaze, guessed at his discovery.'

The structure here, that of the Petrarchan sonnet, with its very definite break between octet and sestet, highlights the power of the experience. In the octet, he uses one rhyme scheme (abbaabba), in the sestet another (cdcdcd). The use of the word 'yet' at the beginning of line 7 and 'till' at the beginning of line 8 prepares us for the dramatic elements of the final six lines.

The imagery of landscape, seascape and skyscape becomes more and more highly charged as we read through the poem: from 'states and kingdoms' to 'planet' to 'a peak in Darien'. There is a mood of quiet excitement. Leigh Hunt, a friend of Keats, called it a noble sonnet and says that the poem 'terminates with so energetic a calmness' that it marked a new development in Keats's poetic voice.

Though it is a poem about imaginary journeys, Keats gives a very vivid sense of how he feels about entering into the world of the imagination. He achieves this by means of his many references to places and to the person of Cortez. The image of astronomer differs from Cortez. One is alone, the other part of a group. When Keats read Homer for the first time it was a private experience, but he was also joining a group of people who were already familiar with the work.

In 'To One Who Has been Long in City Pent', Keats spoke of the wish to escape the city. The countryside was preferred – there he could find happiness, he could read and, by doing so, enter into an imagined world. In this sonnet, Keats is reading Homer in London and he writes the poem in his lodgings in Southwark. In this very autobiographical poem, Keats is discovering that fine poetry could be written in London. Robert Gittings in his biography of Keats says that the poem is 'an expression of his life at the exact point he had reached'.

When I Have Fears That I May Cease to Be

Keats had a very definite sense of himself as a poet from an early age: when, at a meeting with his guardian Richard Abbey, it was requested that Keats should set himself up as a surgeon, he is said to have told Abbey that he would not follow a career in medicine – 'I mean to rely upon my abilities as a poet'. He was a determined and devoted poet who had a fine sense of his own worth. Keats declared that he would be numbered among the great English poets after his death.

The imagery here has to do with autumn and harvest time. The teeming brain is like a field that must be harvested. His pen will glean that harvest and the full-ripened grain, the poems, will be stored in garners, in this instance books. This poem was written in January but it speaks of fully ripened grain. Just as the grain is gathered and used to feed and sustain, so too the poem can feed and sustain the mind.

This is the twenty-two year old Keats, who is intensely aware of the passing of time and also aware of the immortal power of poetry. The use of the word 'when' in the opening line – it is the first word in the poem – and its repetition in lines 5 and 9 emphasises this awareness in Keats of the passing of time.

In lines 5 to 8, Keats speaks of the world he wishes to capture in his writings: that distant, magical, mysterious and beautiful world of a night sky, 'the night's starred face'; not only the stars, but what they symbolise. The stars are 'cloudy' or unclear as symbols. They stand for 'high romance'. As a poet, he hopes to live to trace their shadows. The phrase 'the magic hand of chance' gives us an insight into Keats's understanding of the writing of poetry. In a letter, Keats asserted that, if poetry does not come as naturally as the leaves to the tree, it had better not come at all, suggesting that the process of composition is a spontaneous, inspired and natural thing. That is not to say that Keats did not rework or revise his poems, but in many instances he had no need to. The 'magic hand of chance' captures the mysterious act of writing poetry. It is something that Keats has already experienced and he afraid that death will come too soon, before he has written all that he wants to write.

In line 9, a different idea is introduced – Keats turns to human beauty, a beauty that must end: 'fair creature of an hour' refers, it is thought, to a young woman whom Keats had seen in Vauxhall Gardens in 1814. This biographical fact is not important. What is important is that Keats is talking about youthful beauty and how he feels that there will come a time when he will no longer look upon that beauty. What is striking is the realisation that 'I shall never look upon thee more'.

The phrase 'unreflecting love' suggests a love not troubled by reflection, meditation or analysis. Love's 'faery power' is such that the experience is one of pure happiness, one that is separate from sorrow and sadness.

From line 9, Keats speaks of the human love story, man's longing for perfect love (the reference to 'an hour' suggests that this is love's span). Keats ends with a stark and grim picture of how his thinking on transience has affected him. When he feels that he will not live to write of 'high romance' and that he himself will not experience 'unreflecting love', then he sees himself as one alone on the shore of the wide world.

Thinking is inevitable and inescapable. When Keats contemplates the brevity of life, his teeming brain, the nature of love, he feels isolated. His energetic and idealistic mood in the opening lines of the sonnet has given way to a grim reality. Earlier, Keats spoke of writing poetry and the fame that might bring; he then dwelt on the happiness of human love. But the phrase 'then on the shore. . .' marks the turning point. If he considers poetry and love in the face of time, love and fame become impossible, are unattainable: love and fame sink to nothingness.

The poem expresses a particular mood which verges almost on despair. Keats tells us that it is *when* he dwells on transience, the end of youth and beauty, that an air of gloom prevails.

La Belle Dame sans Merci

This is clearly a very different kind of poem from the previous three. It is not a sonnet and is not immediately autobiographical. As ballad, it tells a story; it is unusual, mysterious, dramatic. The setting is medieval and it is open to several interpretations. Is the beautiful woman deliberately cruel towards the knight or is it that the knight is unable to enter into her dream world and finds himself on the cold hillside? Is it a poem, like so many of Keats's poems, about the mortal and the immortal? A poem about man's love for the beautiful and sensuous and the realisation that beauty does not last? The absence of specifics in the poem allows it to be read and interpreted in many ways.

Some readers feel that this is a poem about Keats's relationship with Fanny Brawne; others see it as a poem about the relationship between the poet and his imagination (the poet Robert Graves considers this poem an account of the poet's destruction by his muse) or the poet and death.

As in many folk ballads, this ballad consists of a dialogue. The first three stanzas address the knight; the other nine are his reply. Our entering into the poem is sudden and total: immediately before us is a knight, but a directionless, ill knight, 'alone and palely loitering'. He is none of those things we usually associate with knights. The voice of the poet, the direct address, becomes the reader's voice. Keats and we, as readers, are involved in the story of this knight from the beginning.

The time of year – late autumn – adds to the atmosphere of loneliness and loss. That closing line in stanza 1 stops the stanza short. The flow that the ear expects, having heard three lines with four beats in each, has now been stopped short. The abrupt 'And no birds sing' (two beats) expresses the knight's loneliness and disappointment.

Though the natural world is dying, part of that world has achieved completion. There is an inner, hidden world – the squirrel's granary is full and the harvest has been gathered in. The world of the knight, however, is one of loss. He looks ill and he feels lost. In stanza 3, the images of the lily and the rose, usually associated with women's beauty, are used to capture the knight's condition.

When the knight tells his story, the lady of the poem, la belle dame, is introduced. The phrase 'I met' suggests something accidental, something that happened by chance, but the woman, it could be argued, has gone in search of the knight and sought him out. Everything about her is flowing and beautiful. She is associated with summer meadows and flowers; her hair is long and her foot is light. The wild eyes, however, give us a sense of her strange and haunting qualities. The language she speaks is 'strange'; she sings a fairy's song but we never hear her directly. We only have the knight's account.

The knight was clearly enchanted from the beginning. He makes her a garland of flowers, a bracelet and a belt (the fragrant zone). He felt that she looked at him 'as she did love'.

A pacing steed is usually ridden by the knight. The clichéd or familiar image is that of the knight in shining armour on horseback. In this version of events, the woman is set on the knight's pacing steed and he tells us that he gazed upon her all day long. The song she sings is enchanting.

All the while, as we read through the poem, the ballad form and its momentum, its narrative and its rhythmic pattern heighten our sense of plot. We know we are going to be told an ending and, of course, the opening three stanzas of the poem have already given us a sense of that ending.

In this poem, the woman seduces the man. She feeds him 'roots of relish sweet/ And honey wild and manna dew'. She tells him that she loves him – 'I love thee true'.

In stanza 8, the setting of the poem moves from the wide open world of meadows, and places where strange and wonderful food can be found, to a grotto or cave. Here words such as 'wept' and 'sighed' darken the once happy, infatuated mood. The knight tells of how he tried to comfort and console this beautiful woman – 'And there I shut her wild wild eyes/With kisses four.'

By stanza 11, the woman is once again controlling the knight – 'she lulled me asleep'. The waking world gives way to dream and the dream gives way to nightmare. The warning cry of 'Ah! woe betide!' suggests danger and terror.

The dream sequence is one of death-pale figures — kings and princes and, presumably, other knights. These others too have been enslaved by la belle dame and they cry out their warning: 'La belle dame sans merci/Hath thee in thrall!' Now the significance of 'sans merci' becomes clear. She is beautiful but she is without pity. Her victims are deluded. The knight speaks of 'starved lips' and open mouths crying out 'horrid warning'.

The poem ends where it began, but line 3 — 'the sedge has withered from the lake' — has become 'the sedge is withered from the lake' in line 47. The present tense as used here has an eerie effect. The knight is one who has escaped the nightmare and yet he can never escape; la belle dame haunts him. The repetition of detail from stanza 1 suggests the knight's inability to escape his aloneness. The final line 'And no birds sing' is powerfully stark and, like all negatives, it emphasises the effect by having the reader imagine its opposite. The positive that is birdsong and everything which that implies is, it would seem, no longer possible.

Ode to a Nightingale

The nightingale was a popular subject for poets. Its song is beautiful and is only heard in darkness (there are no nightingales in Ireland) and the Greek myth of Procne and Philomel, which tells of how the nightingale came to sing such a heartbreakingly beautiful song, adds to the nightingale's memorable and interesting qualities.

Keats in his letters once wrote that 'the world is full of misery and heartbreak, pain, sickness and oppression'. The opening stanza of Ode to a Nightingale certainly suggests misery and oppression:

> My heart aches and a drowsy numbness pains
> My sense, as though of hemlock I had drunk,
> Or emptied some dull opiate to the drains
> One minute past, and Lethe-wards had sunk:

This emphasis on the self — 'my heart', 'my sense' — is evident throughout the poem and, though Keats tries to escape the self and reality and enter into the world of the song of the bird, he realises in the final stanza that he is left with an intense awareness of his 'sole self'.

There is a striking contrast in the opening stanza between the mood of the poet and the world of the song of the bird. The first four lines express heaviness, heartache and pain. Keats wants to escape from the world, and the song of the bird symbolises for him a beautiful, harmonious, happy and free sense of otherness. The song seems effortless — 'full-throated ease'. Nowhere in the poem does Keats describe the actual bird; he does not see it, but he hears its song. The title is 'Ode to a Nightingale' ('a' not 'the') and the poem celebrates the song of the nightingale; the bird itself is mortal but its song is immortal, heard in every age.

The poem begins on a low note: 'drowsy numbness', 'dull opiate', 'sunk' capture a sinking, downward feeling. The sounds here are sinking sounds. However, 'light-winged', 'melodious', 'beechen green' and 'singest' provide a striking contrast. The emphasis is first on the self – 'My heart aches' – an inward, self-concerned focus. In lines 5 and 7, the phrases 'thy happy lot' and 'That thou' focus on the very different and contrasting world of the bird.

In the opening line of stanza 2, Keats has abandoned his listlessness and has entered into an extraordinarily imaginative world which has been prompted by the song of the bird. The word 'O' at the beginning of the line and Keats's use of the exclamation mark add to the energy and the tone of longing. The senses of sight and sound are evident in stanza 1. Here the sense of taste is also introduced. The drink Keats longs for is no ordinary wine. It is a drink associated with place, time and season. It is, above all else, a means of escape. The nightingale is not mentioned specifically in this stanza until the very last line, yet every line leads to the world of the nightingale's song. For Keats, the song represents the ideal.

The richness of association ('Flora', 'Provencal song', 'the warm South', 'the blushful Hippocrene'), the sensuous detail ('beaded bubbles', 'purple-stained mouth') and the sense of longing is repeated throughout ('O for a beaker full of the warm South' – 'O, for' in line 11, 'O for' in line 15). In stanza 1, Keats speaks of hemlock; in stanza 2, the 'draught of vintage' is a totally different drink. One destroys, the other brings release, happiness and freedom.

The third stanza returns to the grim reality of life, a world of pain, suffering, death. Keats may wish to escape but it is not easily done. 'The weariness, the fever, and the fret' is what Keats has known. The structure of this third stanza is such that it would seem that the imagination is failing Keats. The word 'Here' in line 24 roots unhappiness in the world of now. The following lines, each beginning with 'Where' and each listing more and more sorrow, make for a very effective rhythmic pattern:

> Where palsy shakes a few, sad, last gray hairs,
> Where youth grows pale, and spectre-thin, and dies;
> Where but to think is to be full of sorrow
> And leaden-eyed despairs,
> Where Beauty cannot keep her lustrous eyes,
> Or new Love pine at them beyond tomorrow.

Beauty and Love are what Keats is searching for. Both, he suggests in the closing lines of stanza 3, cannot exist in a world that is overshadowed by pain and death. The words Beauty and Love are capitalised, personified presences, highlighting their importance.

In stanza 4, Keats enters into the world of the imagination. The first line of the stanza

'Away! Away! for I will fly to thee'

echoes the longing of line 11, but has a greater liveliness and energy to it. The god of wine and the 'draught of vintage' are dismissed; Keats will enter into an imagined landscape. We know that he wrote the poem during a warm May morning but Keats has chosen a midnight setting for the ode. The poet tells us that, though the 'dull brain' attempts to draw him back, he flies to this magical and midnight world on the 'viewless wings of Poesy'. Line 35 answers line 31: 'Already with thee! tender is the night'. And lines 36 to 40 describe an unspoilt happiness:

And haply the Queen-Moon is on her throne,
    Clustered around by all her starry Fays;
        But here there is no light,
Save what from heaven is with the breezes blown
    Through verdurous glooms and winding mossy ways.

Keats imagines Diana, the Queen-Moon, surrounded by fairies. There is no light, but the darkness is neither frightening nor threatening. And yet there is light, Keats tells us, a magical, heavenly light. The woodland setting is green and winding and mossy – everything is soft and gentle, mysterious and wonderful. The lines 'here there is no light,/Save what from heaven is with the breezes blown' have to be imagined. This is not a scientific description, but a sensuous, imaginative one. There is darkness, yet there is some light. The closing two lines of stanza 4 are not slowed or hindered by punctuation: line 39 flows into line 40, creating a sense of release and relaxation.

In stanza 3, 'Here' referred to the world of suffering. In stanza 4, the same word 'here' (in line 38, 'But here there is no light') refers to a world far removed, a world that the human being can enter into by means of the imagination.

The ode celebrates the song of the bird, more importantly it celebrates the imagination. Keats is at the centre of the poem. The pronoun 'I' is used in every stanza except stanza 3.

Keats uses the five senses (sight, sound, taste, touch and smell) in the ode, but stanza 5 begins with Keats telling us that 'I cannot see what flowers are at my feet'. He then guesses each scent and lists the different fragrances:

The grass, the thicket, and the fruit-tree wild;
    White hawthorn, and the pastoral eglantine;
        Fast fading violets covered up in leaves;
            And mid-May's eldest child,
    The coming musk-rose, full of dewy wine. . .

The stanza is made up of one long, flowing sentence, and the language, enhanced by alliteration, assonance, onomatopoeia, achieves a beautiful and musical quality. He smells the musk-rose, tastes the dewy wine, hears 'The murmurous haunt of flies on summer eves'.

The word 'embalmed' in line 43 refers to fragrance, but it also suggests death, an idea that Keats returns to in stanza 6. He has already spoken of death in stanza 3. Keats tells us here that he has viewed death as 'easeful'; he has been 'half in love' with death. Here death becomes a means of achieving total happiness. His happiness is so complete that if he were to die, the happiness of the moment would last forever: 'Now more than ever seems it rich to die'. But the 'half in love' is significant. He does not trust it totally, though he describes the imagined sense of release that death would bring – 'To cease upon the midnight with no pain'. Keats, in his use of the phrase 'quiet breath', suggests that he wishes to slip away, to 'cease upon the midnight with no pain'. In contrast, the song of the bird is full, ecstatic. It is pouring forth its soul. If he were allowed to 'leave the world unseen', he would not be united with the bird; the very opposite in fact would occur. By the end of the stanza, he realises that death is not the answer; the nightingale will continue to sing its song and Keats will no longer hear it: 'Still wouldst thou sing, and I have ears in vain –/To thy high requiem become a sod.'

In the seventh stanza, Keats admits to himself that he is mortal, whereas the song of the bird is not. The second half of stanza 4 and all of stanza 5 are at the centre of this poem. Those lines are untouched by sorrow or mortality, except for the phrase 'Fast fading violets', though even this is balanced with 'the coming musk-rose'. However, Keats is enough of a realist to know that the moment that the nightingale's song has made possible cannot last forever. He resents death. F. R. Leavis has described the feeling in lines 61 and 62 as a feeling of 'strong revulsion'. In this seventh stanza, Keats introduces a wonderful temporal perspective into the poem. The actual moment that Keats himself has just imagined and experienced has been experienced by unknown, great ('emperor') and ordinary people ('clown'), and Keats then names a particular person, Ruth. This sense of other places and of other times is a generous and consoling aspect of the poem. Keats is saying that we, though mortal, can all have such moments, which allow us to understand ourselves more fully and to experience a beauty that is all the more precious and valuable because it is shortlived. Such moments allow us to glimpse 'the foam/Of perilous seas, in faery lands forlorn.'

'Ode to a Nightingale' is structured in terms of a journey from the reality of the here and now to the world of imagined perfection and the return to the mortal self. But the experience captured in the poem can never be lost. This poem, like so many works of art, reminds us that, though the artist is mortal, the work of art achieves an immortality. Thus the song of the nightingale can be heard in every age and, once the poem has been made, it too lives in every age. We, the readers of this poem, are mortal too, but we are allowed to enter into the world of immortality when we read the poem, just as Keats did when he shaped and structured it.

In line 70, the word 'forlorn' means far away. The word 'Forlorn!' with which stanza 8 begins strikes a different note. Here it means abandoned, forsaken and lonely. It is the brain, which in line 34 almost prevented him from entering into the world of the imagination, that causes him to return from 'thee to my sole self!' It has been said that the word 'forlorn' has its feet in two worlds, the world of the imagination and the woe of reality. The image of the bell tolling in lines 71–72 suggests the image of death and funeral and echoes the religious imagery of requiem in line 60. This final stanza contains the realisation that the fancy (the imagination) cannot cheat so well. In other words, he feels let down by the imagination because he has had to return to his 'sole self', a self that knows only too well that the song of the bird must fade away.

It is of course significant that the nightingale's song, the plaintive anthem, fades. It does not die nor does it stop. Keats knows that it will be heard again, 'Past the near meadows, over the still stream,/Up the hill-side; and now 'tis buried deep/In the next valley-glades'. Keats describes the song as plaintive, meaning sorrowful or mournful. The emotion is an appropriate one. There is something heartbreakingly beautiful about something that is beautiful but which is also something that must fade away. The magical and beautiful experience is over. He wonders if it was 'a vision or a waking dream?' A vision and dream are closely linked in that both are often associated with the ideal. The word 'waking' in the second last line of the ode reminds us that Keats is back where he began, but of course he has had an extraordinary experience and he has captured it forever in the poem.

Ode on a Grecian Urn

This is titled 'Ode on a Grecian Urn' not 'to' as in the nightingale ode. Stanza 1 begins in a very quiet, meditative mood. The sounds are soft ('still', 'unravished', 'quietness') and the rhythm is slow, capturing a tone of reverence. The word still is interesting because it is ambiguous. Both meanings – 'still' meaning motionless and 'still' meaning 'yet' – add to the mystery of the urn. The artist who created this urn, its maker or 'parent', has long since died, but Keats imagines that the urn has had foster parents, 'silence and slow time' (line 2).

The phrase 'Sylvan historian' in line 3 suggests the urn is a story-teller and it also records the past. The story it tells is a country tale. The urn does not speak; it communicates through images, yet Keats in lines 3 and 4 feels that the urn is capable of telling a story more beautifully than the poet and the poem: the urn can 'thus express/A flowery tale more sweetly than our rhyme'.

With line 5, there is a change of mood. Keats is no longer speaking of the urn as an object that he has spoken about as distant and separate. He has entered into the world of the story as depicted on the sides of the urn. The sentences quicken, becoming shorter, and there are seven question marks, capturing Keats's involvement and his excitement, in the last four lines of stanza 1.

The urn is still, quiet, silent, and yet it is also a warm-blooded, life-filled, energetic, mad, ecstatic presence. In line 6, Keats wonders if the people depicted on the side of the urn are gods or men – 'deities or mortals'. He wonders are they both. The stanza has changed dramatically from a mood of quiet contemplation to that of an excited and stimulated imagination. Keats is not merely describing what he sees on the side of a Grecian urn: he is inventing narratives (the legend that 'haunts about thy shape') and he is involving himself in the stories. He wants to know more and he marvels at the energy and the excitement of it all: 'What men or gods are these?' (line 8), 'What wild ecstasy?' (line 10).

The questioning, with which the stanza ends, subsides and Keats asks no questions in stanzas 2 and 3.

The pipes and timbrels depicted on the urn can be seen but not heard. Keats has imagined the sounds that they make and stanza 2 begins with a reference to the imagined sound which is ideal, perfect. This is why 'Heard melodies are sweet, but those unheard/Are sweeter'. The pipes, though carved in hard marble, have become 'soft', that is soft sounding, because Keats has imagined the pipes playing their music. Keats says to the pipes to play on, but not to play to the ear which is the instrument of the sense of hearing. Play instead to the spirit, and play a music that cannot be heard. That music is even sweeter.

In this second stanza, Keats, having asked for an imagined, ideal and beautiful music, now looks at the images on the side of the urn again and this time in more detail. Stanza 1 gives us a sense of groups – 'deities or mortals', 'men or gods', 'maidens'. He focuses on particular images. First, that of a 'fair youth, beneath the trees' who will sing forever and, second, the image of two young lovers who will love forever. Human love is subject to change, growing old and dying. The love depicted here is forever beautiful and forever young. The use of negatives 'not leave/Thy song', 'Never, never canst thou kiss', 'thou hast not thy bliss', captures the moment's shortcomings. It is a moment frozen in time and there is the happiness of the song and the spring and the anticipation of the kiss. Keats, however, tells the 'bold lover' 'do not grieve'. That special moment will not change. In the real world, Keats knows that 'youth grows pale and spectre thin and dies'. Also, in 'Ode to a Nightingale', Keats speaks of a world where 'Beauty cannot keep her lustrous eyes,/Or new Love pine at them beyond to-morrow'. In the world of the work of art, by contrast, 'She cannot fade. . ./For ever wilt thou love, and she be fair!' After the 'never, never' of line 7, 'yet' in line 8 serves as a turning point. Keats celebrates the immortality of the work of art.

'Happy' is used six times in the first five lines of stanza 3 and the 'Ah' which leads us into the stanza signals Keats's total delight in his vividly imagined eternal spring, eternal music, eternal love, eternal youth. Keats is the outsider, as is the reader. We are outside this intensely happy experience. As human beings, we know that happiness is shortlived, yet the work of art can hold a happy moment forever.

'Happy' is a key-word here. So too is 'for ever'. The 'nor ever' and 'never, never' of the earlier stanza (lines 16, 17) is echoed in the line 'nor ever bid the spring adieu', but the five 'for evers' in lines 24, 26, 27 give a vibrant sense of the now becoming eternal. The repetition, especially in the line 'More happy love! more happy, happy love!', and the exclamation marks heighten the mood. The adjective 'warm' and the verb 'panting' give the scene a powerful, physical touch.

The closing lines of the third stanza acknowledge and accept the mortal, the reality. Keats was twenty-three when he wrote the ode. He knew love (the previous December he had become engaged to Fanny Brawne) and he knew death, having nursed Tom in his final illness, and he returns to a world very different to the world which he has entered into elsewhere in the ode. The phrases 'a heart high-sorrowful and cloy'd', 'a burning forehead', 'a parching tongue' are similar to those lines from 'Ode to a Nightingale' where Keats gives us a vivid sense of his experience of suffering.

The urn is separate, untouched, unmoved by such suffering, but it is Keats's humanity that draws him back, that causes him to return to the real world. We have seen this happen in the nightingale ode. Throughout that poem, there are words and phrases that remind the reader of reality. Less so in the 'Ode on a Grecian Urn', but it is certainly there. The melodist, the music-maker of line 23, is 'unwearied' because he is part of the ideal world; in the real world, Keats knows 'A burning forehead and a parching tongue'. Keats, however, is also saying here that the urn does not know real love, real breathing human passion. The urn, we are told in line 28, is 'far above', at a distance from 'All breathing human passion'. It does not know the disappointment, the anguish, the suffering and the pain that real love may sometimes lead to. Keats, by returning to the world which we know as humans, is recognising and accepting that world with all its limitations. It is not the frozen, perfect moment in time; it is a living, breathing experience which we, because we are human, come to accept. At the beginning of stanza 2, Keats has said that the imagined is better than the real. Similarly, ideal love is above lived love because human love leaves 'a heart high – sorrowful and cloy'd'.

In the fourth stanza, Keats returns to particular details on the side of the urn. He is curious, drawn in. If you were to read the ode omitting stanza 3, there would be no sense of disconnectedness or disjointedness, but you would not have Keats's deep and interesting philosophical reflection on the nature of art and of existence.

The moment that Keats focuses on in stanza 4 is only a moment. There is a priest, a heifer, a procession of people, a ritual. It has no beginning or ending, but Keats, with his extraordinarily sympathetic imagination, wonders where they are going and from where have they come: 'To what green altar, O mysterious priest,/ Lead'st thou that heifer lowing at the skies, And all her silken flanks with garlands dressed?' The image, like all other images on the urn, is carved in marble, but Keats's choice of word here gives the image a living, breathing, flowing presence: 'green', 'lowing', 'silken'. This third scene is one which is most remote from Keats's own world and Keats goes beyond what is portrayed before him. He feels sorry for the 'little town by river or sea shore,/Or mountain-built with peaceful citadel,/

Is emptied of this folk, this pious morn?' Keats is empathising with the place, now something inanimate without its people, just as he has already empathised with the urn by entering into the world that was carved on its side.

The little town will be desolate, but Keats then gives us an even more interesting idea. This little town will never know the reason for its loneliness, why its streets 'for evermore/Will silent be'. This is a different form of 'forever'. It is not the intensely happy and excited forever of stanza 3. The people of the town have wandered into the work of art; there they will remain for ever. They have disappeared from the town and are forever captured on the urn. In one way, the desolate town is similar to human beings who can witness the happiness of the young lovers in art but can never know that immortal love for themselves.

The stillness in the closing lines of stanza 4 is in marked contrast to the frenzy of earlier sections. The very sounds in lines 35 to 40 and the rhythm create a haunting silence. Keats displays a tender concern for the town's loneliness.

With the first line of the final stanza, Keats steps back and looks at the urn as a whole. The tone here is typical of the ode: 'O Attic shape! Fair attitude!'; it is a tone of praise, awe and admiration, but the word 'shape' is strikingly impersonal, considering that the urn was viewed by Keats in line 3 of stanza 1 as a 'sylvan historian'. Keats has distanced himself from the particular when he speaks of 'marble men and maidens overwrought'. Yet again, however, in line 43, the single detail of the 'trodden weed' somehow alters the still marble form; it becomes a living tableau. But Keats continues to draw himself away. The very first words in the poem are 'Thou still unravished bride of quietness' and line 44, 'Thou, silent form, dost tease us out of thought', is similar in its effect. Both lines are regarding the urn as a whole object, not as a series of intricate, lively scenes. The urn is as mysterious as eternity. It has drawn Keats into its mystery. The word 'tease' means entice. In other words, it has drawn an imaginative response from Keats, not a rational one. 'Tease' can also mean 'to mock' and the urn, as a 'foster-child of silence and slow time', does present us with mystery: the mystery of death (the ashes within the urn), the mystery of the work of art that lives in every age (the images on the urn), the mystery of the artist who has lived and died.

The phrase 'Cold Pastoral!' is dismissive, but it does not come as a shock or surprise. Keats in lines 29 and 30 has already recognised the inevitable distance between the work of art and the human being. Keats knows that 'old age shall this generation waste'. He and all others will die, but the urn will remain for others to look on and to experience.

The word 'Cold' is perfectly appropriate: the urn is made of marble and was originally intended to contain the ashes of the dead; the figures on the urn are still, unmoving. Yet so many details from the text up to now suggest warmth and a living presence. Keats cannot stay within the imaginative world that has been prompted by his viewing of the urn. Both 'Ode to a Nightingale' and 'Ode on a Grecian Urn' acknowledge and reveal beauty and, inevitably, recognise that the human being cannot dwell with beauty forever.

Critical Commentary

The phrase that Keats now uses to describe the urn is 'a friend to man'. It is a friend because it tells a story that enhances life; yet it also, because of its very purpose, reminds us of death. It is immortal and the different stories that are depicted on its side – an ideal rural paradise, music and song, passionate young love, ritual and ceremony – are things which we as humans value.

The final two lines of this particular ode have puzzled readers for generations. The 'sylvan historian', the urn, says to man: 'Beauty is truth, truth beauty'. The urn itself is beautiful and it contains a truth, a truth that even when it involves sorrow can be beautiful. But the two ideas contained in the 'Beauty is truth, truth beauty' can be read as separate statements, one an aesthetic judgement, the other a moral one: if something is beautiful it contains a truth; whatever is true is beautiful. Who is speaking these last two lines? There is no original manuscript in existence for this poem and the first printed version in 1820 was as follows:

> 'Beauty is truth, truth beauty,' – that is all
> Ye know on earth, and all ye need to know.

If this is how Keats intended the poem to be read it means that the words 'Beauty is truth, truth beauty' are spoken by the urn and addressed to man, and Keats himself perhaps is addressing his fellow man in ' – that is all/Ye know on earth, and all ye need to know.' The 'Ye' here is not in keeping, however, with Keats's own sense of 'ours' when he speaks of mankind's suffering. Robert Gittings in his edition of Keats's *Complete Poems* says that the following interpretations are possible: 1. Both lines are spoken by the urn, and addressed to man; 2. the lines are spoken by the poet to the urn; 3. the lines are spoken by the poet to the figures on the urn; 4. 'Beauty is truth, truth beauty' is spoken by the urn, and the remainder is the poet speaking to his readers; 5. 'Beauty is truth, truth beauty' is spoken by the urn and the poet then addresses the urn, not mankind. There was another printed version of the poem in 1820 and four contemporary transcripts of the text. All five omitted the inverted commas here.

The reading which argues that the urn speaks the words 'Beauty is truth, truth beauty' is certainly a valid one. Keats does say immediately before that line when he is addressing the urn 'Thou shalt remain . . . a friend to man, to whom thou say'st'. This is significant in that the urn did not communicate in words but in images up to now. It was also described as a 'silent form'. When it speaks it says two things and they are both true.

The preferred interpretation of these lines is as follows: In both lines, the urn is speaking to men. The urn is immortal and it is a friend to mortal man. Keats gives the urn these words which remind all of us, including Keats, that the urn itself, an object from ancient Greece, captures beauty and truth. The nineteenth-century critic Matthew Arnold says of these lines:

For to see things in their beauty is to see things in their truth, and Keats knew it. 'What the Imagination seizes as Beauty must be Truth,' he says in prose; and in immortal verse, he has said the same thing – 'Beauty is truth, truth beauty, – that is all/Ye know on earth, and all ye need to know.' No, it is not all; but it is true, deeply true, and we have deep need to know it.

T. S. Eliot felt that the line 'Beauty is truth, truth beauty' is 'a serious blemish on a beautiful poem, and the reason must be either that I fail to understand it, or that it is a statement which is untrue'. Another critic, Arthur Quiller-Couch, thought the last two lines of the ode 'a vague observation – to anyone whom life had taught to face facts'. You will have your own opinion, and it is impossible to say which one is the definitive interpretation.

The ode finishes on an extraordinary still note. The words with which the poem ends are the words which the urn has 'spoken' and will 'speak' in every generation, words which remind us of the power and importance of the work of art. Keats, both in the nightingale ode and in 'Ode on a Grecian Urn', though creating beautiful worlds, always returns to reality. The 'hungry generation' in 'Ode to a Nightingale' and 'this generation waste' in 'Ode on a Grecian Urn' reveal a mind that can recognise reality. That Keats can create for us worlds other than the real and the transient is part of his greatness as a poet.

On a lighter note, here is a spoof version of Keats's 'Ode on a Grecian Urn':

> Round Vase
> Gods chase
> What say?
> What play?
> Don't know.
> Nice though.

To Autumn

The nightingale is female and the Grecian urn is an 'unravished bride'. In 'To Autumn', Keats once again focuses on a female presence. Each of the other odes had ten-line stanzas. Keats introduces a variation here – there is an extra line which is appropriate in a poem which celebrates the lingering season.

In the earlier odes, Keats is very much a presence within the poem, as can be seen from the use of 'I', 'my', 'me' ('I' is used nine times in 'Ode to a Nightingale'). In 'To Autumn', it is as if he has allowed the season itself to speak and has absented himself; there is no personal pronoun, and yet, of course, Keats is everywhere in the poem. It is his sensibility, his imagination and his sensuous evocation of the season which make the poem possible. The achievement of 'To Autumn' is most clearly seen when it is read as the final ode in a sequence.

Sensuousness is one of Keats's hallmarks as a poet and it has been pointed out by the literary critic Douglas Bush that the three stanzas of 'To Autumn' contain sensuous imagery with a different emphasis in each stanza. The first is mainly to do with touch, the second with the visual, and in the final stanza the world of the poem is conveyed through the ear.

The opening line of 'To Autumn', 'Season of mists and mellow fruitfulness', differs considerably from the opening lines in the other two odes. In 'Ode to a Nightingale', the focus is on the suffering self: 'My heart aches'; in 'Ode on a Grecian Urn', it is on the otherness of the urn, its separateness: 'Thou still unravished bride…'; in 'Ode on Melancholy', Keats is urging himself, another, the reader, not to commit suicide: 'No, no, go not to Lethe'. Here, in 'To Autumn', there is a wonderful sense of having entered into, having become part of, the season itself. That opening line offers a sense of completion: it sums up the qualities of the season, its landscape and its produce: 'Season of mists and mellow fruitfulness'.

The first eleven lines of the poem speak of ripeness and fulfilment. Everything is in harmony: the season itself and the sun are bosom-friends. Keats speaks of how the fruit trees are loaded and blessed by the autumn sun. Autumn is the season closest to winter and is often associated with the beginning of the year's end, but for Keats the sun is 'to set budding more,/And still more, later flowers for the bees'. The mood is one of excess; in this first stanza, there is no suggestion that it will ever fade away. The phrase 'budding more', followed by 'and still more', suggests an endless pleasure. The bees are deceived. Keats tells us that they 'think warm days will never cease'. The verbs 'load', 'bless', 'bend', 'fill' 'swell', 'plump', 'o'er-brimmed' all create the sense of an ongoing, enriching process. There is a great deal of quiet activity. The first stanza consists of one sentence, a sentence which, as we read it, records the fullness of autumn. Keats knows, and we know, that autumn will end but it is as if he is saying that there is no need to go into that.

In the second stanza, autumn is personified as 'sitting careless on a granary floor' or 'on a half-reaped furrow sound asleep'. The harvest is not done and autumn itself, though described as harvester and reaper, is lingering. She is neither harvesting nor reaping. There is very little movement. Autumn's scythe (hook) spares the next swath. It is autumn, a time of change leading to inevitable decay, but here autumn sits still.

The image of autumn as gleaner who 'dost keep/Steady thy laden head across a brook' and the image of autumn as patient watcher by the cider-press are also images of silence and stillness. The phrase 'last oozings' refers both to something almost over and to very, very slow movement, the pressing of the apples into cider. These are the apples that weighed down the 'mossed cottage trees' in line 5. But there is no hurry. Keats never once laments the fact that autumn will soon give way to winter. In the nightingale and Grecian urn odes, he was intensely aware of happiness and its opposite. Here, it is the beauty and music and harmony of autumn which holds him. 'To Autumn' is a poem where Keats's theory of Negative Capability is demonstrated fully.

Keats does not look ahead to winter. Instead, he goes back to spring, autumn's origin. Stanza 3 introduces this idea. The first line of the third stanza, contains two questions. But these questions do not trouble Keats: 'Where are the songs of Spring?' he asks, only to let them be: 'Ay, where are they?' There is no need to think of the songs of spring. Four months earlier, in May, he did think of the song of the nightingale, a song of spring, but that was another occasion and he celebrated it in a separate poem.

In line 24, he turns to autumn and listens to its music. The poem's movement is from visual to aural. Autumn is not spring, but he knows that 'thou hast thy music too'. The closing lines of the poem are a symphony of autumn's music: 'the wailful choir' of the gnats; the sound of 'the light wind' as it 'lives or dies'; the 'loud bleat' of the full-grown lambs; the song of the hedge-crickets; the 'treble soft' of the red-breast; the twitter of the 'gathering swallows'. The music is sad: 'wailful' and 'mourn' in line 27 tell us that. The gnats mourn the end of the year and they mourn their own brief lives. Their music rises and falls. The phrase 'sinking as the light wind lives or dies' is of a very different texture to the abundance and excess of the first stanza, only 20 lines before. Yet the final music in the poem is not wailful or mourning; it is the music of song and treble soft. The swallows are gathering either because it is the day's end or for migration. The music of the song of the nightingale allowed Keats to forget suffering and death momentarily. Keats listens with a very attentive ear to the music of autumn and the music itself is not a means of escape. In thirty-three lines, Keats has captured the essence of autumn. It charts the dying of an autumn day ('the soft-dying day') and the dying of the year.

The autumn of the final stanza is different from the autumn of the opening lines. In stanza 3, the harvest's done: 'the next swath and all its twined flowers' have become 'the stubble-plains' touched with 'rosy-hue'. Change has come about, imperceptibly, inevitably: 'while', line 25, leads to 'then', line 27, until 'now' is reached in line 31. Yet Keats even gives the dying day a sense of new beginnings. The 'barred clouds bloom the soft-dying day'. He also, in line 30, speaks of 'full-grown lambs' which bring us back to spring and the beginning of the year.

The structure of the poem allows the imagery to speak for itself. It is, of course, how Keats viewed that particular autumn, September 1819, but those very images draw the reader in. Autumn reveals itself. It is as if there is no intermediary. The poem, according to the poet Sean Lysaght, embodies the truth that the poet 'does not have to parade his/her own private emotions to write effectively. At this late stage in his career, with the knowledge that he is soon going to die, Keats transcends the psychological drama of the Odes by writing a poem descriptive of the dying year. His art achieves great serenity here; at the same time it communicates the full pathos of his personal situation.'

The season of spring in 'Ode on a Grecian Urn' did not end because it is part of the work of art. The 'happy boughs' never shed their leaves. Here the spring which he mentions in the final stanza has given way to summer and autumn, and winter must follow. Of all the odes, the subject matter of 'To Autumn' – the season itself – is the most familiar and the most immediate. It is a poem that speaks to everyone who knows the seasons and, if you consider Keats's own belief that there are four seasons in the mind of man, this poem takes on an added poignancy. He wrote it when he was twenty-three. He would be twenty-four that October and two years later he was dead.

Sensuousness is one of the striking qualities in Keats's work. So too is his love for the beautiful, which is often expressed against the overshadowing reality of suffering and death. Matthew Arnold, in an essay published in 1888, said: 'The thing to be seized is that Keats had flint and iron in him . . . indeed nothing is more remarkable in Keats than his clear-sightedness, his lucidity.' Here Arnold is recognising that, though Keats is sensuous and passionate, he also views the world honestly. Keats knows that moments of intense pleasure and happiness do not last.

Bright Star! Would I Were Steadfast as Thou Art

What strikes the reader immediately in this sonnet is the contrast and the distance between the high, bright star and the human being on earth. The first two words, 'Bright star!', and that exclamation mark, focus on the far away. In the first line, Keats expresses a longing to be steadfast like the star. But, having highlighted this particular quality, Keats immediately expresses some reservations. The word 'not' at the beginning of line 2 indicates his reservation. Though the steadfastness is a quality that he admires, he does not want to experience the star's loneliness and its sense of distance, its sense of being separate and apart.

Keats's fine imaginative powers are clearly seen in the first eight lines of this Shakespearean sonnet. This poem is charged with imagery. The star is splendid, brilliant and magnificent, but it is detached and alone. Keats wants to be and does not want to be like the star. It is hermit-like in its loneliness. The phrases 'watching, with eternal lids apart' and 'sleepless' give the star a human quality, but it is an unattractive human quality. Though what the star sees is beautiful – the cleansing tides and the new-fallen snow – it knows no ease or rest. Planet Earth in this poem is beautiful. 'The moving waters' and 'the new soft-fallen mask/Of snow upon the mountains and the moors' create a sense of varied landscape (seashore, steep slopes and level land), and the sounds here, moving waters, snowfall, are quiet and gentle. Everything associated with Earth in the poem is in a state of flux. The tides rise and fall and the image of cleansing waters suggests flux, change, renewal; the snow falls, but it is only a 'mask', without steadfastness.

At the beginning of the third quatrain, Keats emphasises again that the star is being rejected: 'No' in line 9 echoes the 'Not' of line 2. The star is steadfast; it looks upon a cold beauty (the night, the water, the snow-covered landscape) and the poem, consisting of a single sentence, moves towards the warm, living, transient world of human love. Keats longs for the 'still steadfast, still unchangeable', but prefers the sweet unrest of love to the cold and lonely unchanging world of the bright star. In this, it resembles 'Ode to a Nightingale' and 'Ode to a Grecian Urn' especially. Both odes express a longing for otherness, but in both Keats accepts that it is impossible to dwell in an ideal world permanently.

The song of the nightingale and the world depicted on the side of the urn were at a remove from reality. In 'Bright Star', Keats chooses the world of 'breathing human passion': in lines 10 and 11 he describes the soft, warm, gentle intimacy between lovers: 'Pillowed upon my fair love's ripening breast,/To feel for ever its soft fall and swell'. The phrase 'fall and swell' describes movement, movement of the tide in line 5, the movement of the human breath. And 'ripening' also suggests maturing, changing. It is this which Keats ultimately prefers. The warmth of this shared experience is all the more effective when contrasted with the cold isolation of the bright star.

The moment of human love is cherished by Keats. He wants the sensuous experience (the sensuousness of 'pillowed', ripening', 'soft fall and swell') to last forever. Sleep would deny him that pleasure: Keats longs to remain 'awake for ever in a sweet unrest', and it is unrest because he knows that human love cannot remain unchanged. It is not steadfast and unchangeable like the star.

If it were possible to hear his love's 'tender-taken breath' forever (and the repetition of still at the beginning of line 13 emphasises his desire), 'Still, still to hear her tender-taken breath' would be to 'live ever'. Elsewhere in Keats's poetry, we have seen that he knows that the beautiful moment cannot be held forever. It must end and, when it cannot last, then the only other choice is to 'swoon to death'.

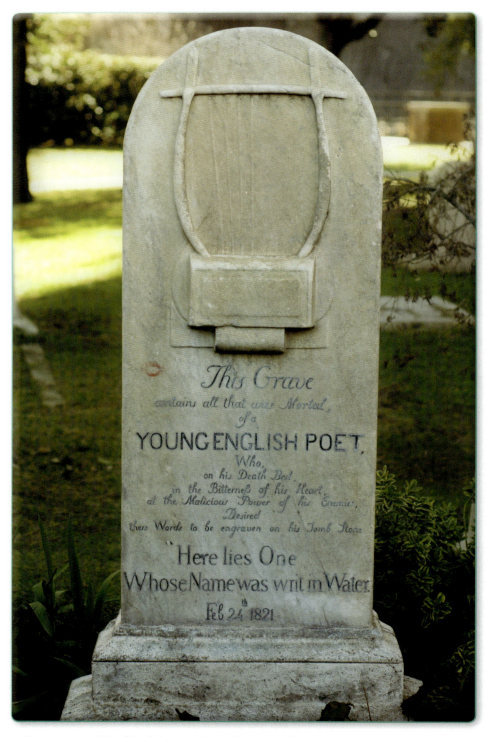

- The grave of the English poet John Keats in Rome.

Brendan Kennelly
(Born 1936)

Contents	Page

The Overview

Brendan Kennelly in his preface to *Selected Poems* (1972) wrote that his poems 'fall naturally into three divisions: poems about the countryside; poems about the city; and poems which, broadly speaking, make an attempt to express some kind of personal philosophy' and that poetry, for him, is 'basically a celebration of human inadequacy and failure.' He has reached a wide audience and his books, unusually for volumes of poetry, have appeared on bestseller lists. Kennelly himself has spoken of how again and again people stop him in the street to thank him for writing a particular poem that was a great help to them at a particularly difficult time.

'His poems shine with the wisdom of somebody who has thought deeply about the paradoxical strangeness and familiarity and wonder of life,' says Sr. Stanislaus Kennedy, and the critic Richard Pine identifies among Kennelly's themes, violence, greed, dishonesty, simple virtues, innocence, inborn dignity and sham respectability.

The thirteen poems by Brendan Kennelly prescribed for the Leaving Certificate course include two translations from Irish and his writing at times speaks in the voice of someone other than the poet: the voice of a three-year-old child, Oliver Cromwell, a woman whose husband has been murdered, a saint. These poems capture and explore what the writer Patrick Kavanagh calls 'the newness that was in every stale thing', city life, relationships, memory, grief, intense happiness, loneliness and an unusual idea of heaven.

'Begin' is a poem filled with gratitude. It recognises the realities of life, its challenges and disappointments, but the poem is on the side of life and the rhythm and repetition make for an upbeat, optimistic voice. In 'Bread', the speaker traces the making of a loaf of bread from wheat field to oven; 'Dear Autumn Girl' links a season and a young woman and praises both. 'Poem from a Three Year Old' asks complex, unanswerable questions in a poem that reminds us of the mystery of life. Two very different family-relationship poems, one set in the seventeenth century, the other in the twentieth, are found in 'Oliver to His Brother' and 'I See You Dancing Father'. Oliver Cromwell, a figure from the history books, speaks in a brother-to-brother poem; Kennelly's father features in a son-to-father poem. One refers to Cromwell's children, but also to public, brutal deeds; the other is a private tender love poem by a son observing his ageing father.

'A Cry for Art O'Leary', one of the finest poems in the Irish language, is given renewed life in Kennelly's translation. This poem is based on a true story in which a young woman passionately mourns her murdered husband, who was killed in May 1773. It paints a picture of a political world, of injustice and this newly widowed young woman calls for revenge. A different voice, that of Judas – Judas Iscariot, one of the twelve disciples who also betrayed Jesus – speaks in 'Things I Might Do'. It is a troubled voice, unlike the voice in 'A Great Day', a wedding-day poem, in which the poet captures the special occasion as two young people set out on their journey together. By contrast, 'Fragments' looks at a married couple from the man's perspective, a poem that expresses disappointment and sadness at how life has turned out. 'The soul's loneliness' explores the body's awareness of itself in the light of its housing the soul, while in 'St Brigid's Prayer', in this translation of a tenth-century poem, a playful voice paints a surreal and very happy picture of life in Heaven.

'Voice has always been a central concern of Brendan Kennelly's poetry. In over thirty books...he has given a voice to outsiders, rebels, vagabonds and charlatans,' says the poet Paul Perry, and in his collection *Reservoir* Kennelly tells us that the voice in each poem in the book is the voice of each poem's title, so we have Shame, Mercy, Loneliness, Flesh.

Brendan Kennelly believes that 'we should have the courage to be faithful to our relatively few moments of intensity', but whether those moments are happy or sad he faces both, and when Kennelly was once asked what was the lowest point in his life, he replied, 'I don't think like that. I like that old Kerry saying: "Once you get up in the morning and stick your old leg out, you should be grateful."'

For Kennelly, 'Words are wild creatures.' He has said in an interview with Richard Pine: 'One of my favourite pastimes is reading the *Oxford English Dictionary* and I'll take a word and trace its joyous history. It reminds me of my own life, and the struggle of a word to survive its own stages, to stay alive, to serve a young boy or girl who's encountering that word for the first time, and behind it are centuries of experience, and it's in the mouth of that child, and that's joy to me, the word as survivor.' Kennelly has also suggested that in his poetry he wants 'to step beyond the mere self and create space for those voices that wander not only through our minds but through the air about us, deep in our receptive beings.'

In the same interview, Kennelly remarked: 'At some level, I suffer from what every poet suffers from – I'd like to become a poem, to become coherent and accomplished and singing, as it were, and communicate and touch, an object that is there, fixed and changing, according as people consider you and experience you.' In his introduction to *Breathing Spaces* (1992), he wrote: 'There are few states as secure as living in the clichés and labels of religion and history. Ireland is, above all, the Land of Label, a green kingdom of clichés. To write poetry in Ireland is to declare war on labels and clichés. Needless to say, I find I have more than enough in my own heart and head, not to mention my language. But I try to fight them, to fight their muggy, cloying, complacent, sticky, distorting, stultifying, murderous and utterly reassuring embrace. And I've tried to do this from the beginning.' In his preface to *Selected Poems*, Kennelly says, 'I believe that each of us is blind in a great number of ways; and that saves us. I believe that occasionally we see things in our blindness; and that elevates us.'

In *Ireland's Writers*, A. Norman Jeffares says that 'Kennelly has developed a very personal kind of poetry in which his thought flows freely, kindness keeps breaking out and an understanding of the difference in individual human beings. His written poetry has all the spontaneity of oral tradition but is searching in its investigations.'

At Kennelly's eightieth birthday celebration, held in the Abbey Theatre on Sunday 23 October 2016, President Michael D. Higgins spoke of the poet's 'immense' influence on Irish arts and society and said: 'Brendan is a just a splendid, wonderful person who belongs to the world and will always belong to the world.'

Biographical Notes

'I am come of Kerry clay and rock', says Brendan Kennelly and he always remembers those lines from the poet and playwright Sigerson Clifford (1913–85) who, though Cork-born, grew up in Kerry and had Kerry parents: 'I am Kerry like my mother before me,/ And my mother's mother and her man./ Now I sit on an office stool remembering,/ And the memory of them like a fan/ Soothes the embers into flame./ I am Kerry and proud of my name.'

Brendan Kennelly, poet, novelist, dramatist, anthologist, teacher, cultural commentator, was born in Ballylongford, County Kerry on 17 April 1936. One of eight children, his father was a publican and garage owner; his mother was a nurse. Kennelly grew up in a largely rural community and when the locals gathered in Kennelly's pub of an evening, songs were sung, stories were told and poems were recited. Terence Brown and Michael Longley in their foreword to *The Essential Brendan Kennelly* (2011) describe Kennelly's Ballylongford as a place that 'would resurface memorably in many of his poems', a place 'recalled in his work as the primal place of familial relationships, of a local community with its legends and lore, its gossip, stories, songs and ballads, and as a setting close to the natural world with its splendours and casual brutalities, yet open to history and the great world beyond.'

Football was another Ballylongford passion, while politics and religion played a huge part in shaping that part of north Kerry. During the war of independence (1919–21), Ballylongford's republicans fought against the British and the village was burned by the Black and Tans; during the subsequent civil war, the town's anti-Treaty (republicans) and those pro-Treaty (Free Staters) were at odds, but still managed to play together on the county team.

In an interview with Richard Pine in 1993 (and reprinted under the title 'The Roaring Storm of Your Words' in *Dark Fathers Into Light*), Brendan Kennelly spoke of himself as labelled as 'a member of a large family – "one of the Kennellys" – you are Kerry, Catholic, Republican, Irish-speaking, and wild and cute.' And he added, 'All these things *might* be true, but somehow or other I resisted, or resented, people beating you with labels and *assuming* all that to be true about you...I fought against it unconsciously at first, by following the irrational call of writing, and then later by deliberately disrupting the idea of the "great character" in myself – which, again, you could argue, is there – by choosing characters to write about, in an aesthetic sense, to write *through*, who were outside my culture or offensive to it – so that my identity became clearer to me, if that is possible, by identifying with opponents, scapegoats or legendarily offensive people.'

Kennelly was educated at the local national school, St. Ita's in Tarbet, and then at Trinity College, Dublin where he was awarded a double-first B.A. degree in English and French. He has said that 'behind everything I write is the story/ballad culture of my youth.' Kennelly married the American academic Peggy O'Brien and they had a daughter, but the marriage broke down and O'Brien returned to the United States. He gave up alcohol in 1986 when he was fifty.

Brendan Kennelly was an inspiring and charismatic lecturer and students from other disciplines would often attend his literature classes. The large lecture hall had a movement-sensitive lighting system which meant that the lights would go out if no movement were detected in the room and during Kennelly's lectures the packed lecture hall would frequently go dark because everyone his audience was so rapt with attention. Kennelly was also a very popular contributor to radio and television programmes. In 1991–92, Kennelly advertised a certain brand of car on TV and radio. That Kennelly himself cannot drive reminds us of his good-humoured, mischievous nature.

Kennelly has written novels, translated plays, edited anthologies and has published over forty volumes of poetry including *Let Fall No Burning Leaf* (1963), *The Boats are Home* (1980), *The Book of Judas* (1991), *Poetry My Arse* (1995), *The Man Made of Rain* (1998). *The Essential Brendan Kennelly: Selected Poems*, edited by Terence Brown and Michael Longley, and from which all poems on the Leaving Certificate course have been taken, was published in 2011, to mark and celebrate Brendan Kennelly's seventh-fifth birthday. In 2016, Brendan Kennelly returned to live in his native Kerry.

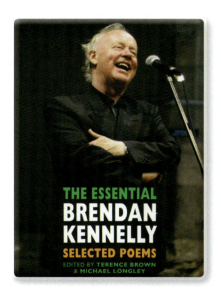

POEMS

The poems, and in the order that they are printed here,
are from *The Essential Brendan Kennelly: Selected Poems* (2011),
edited by Terence Brown and Michael Longley.

Begin

Begin again to the summoning birds
to the sight of light at the window,
begin to the roar of morning traffic
all along Pembroke Road.
Every beginning is a promise   5
born in light and dying in dark
determination and exaltation of springtime
flowering the way to work.
Begin to the pageant of queuing girls
the arrogant loneliness of swans in the canal   10
bridges linking the past and future
old friends passing though with us still.
Begin to the loneliness that cannot end
since it perhaps is what makes us begin,
begin to wonder at unknown faces   15
at crying birds in the sudden rain
at branches stark in the willing sunlight
at seagulls foraging for bread
at couples sharing a sunny secret
alone together while making good.   20
Though we live in a world that dreams of ending
that always seems about to give in
something that will not acknowledge conclusion
insists that we forever begin.

 # Glossary

Line 4 Pembroke Road: in Dublin 4.

Line 7 exaltation: rapturous emotion, elation; the collective noun 'an exaltation of larks' sums the feeling up.

Line 9 pageant: brilliant spectacle.

Line 10 arrogant: proud, haughty

'I wrote this after a heart operation. It came into my mind as I lay there – and I felt grateful to Maurice Nelligan [heart specialist] who had given me a new start to my life. In Christianity, there's the resurrection, prayers, starting out, starting to live again. The poem seemed to write me. It was written before I left the hospital.' (Brendan Kennelly, RTE Radio 1, 9 October 2016)

In 1997, on *The Late Late Show*, Gay Byrne phoned a woman to tell her she was in with a chance of winning a big prize only to be told by a mother that her daughter, who had entered the competition, had died between posting the entry and the phone call. It was probably the most difficult moment in Byrne's broadcasting career. He handled the situation with sensitivity and Brendan Kennelly's contribution that evening helped to bring some comfort to a heart-breaking, heart-stopping moment. He recited his poem 'Begin' (from *Good Souls to Survive*, 1967).

The Dublin poet Paula Meehan in an eightieth birthday tribute to Brendan Kennelly wrote: 'Your much-loved poem "Begin" is one of the poems I've heard most often at funerals over the years. Once someone close to me left it with their suicide note. I knew that it was left to console us, long after.'

Kennelly himself, in a 1993 interview with Richard Pine, said of the poem: 'I have heard that [the] four [last] lines have helped a lot of people, even though it was a poem specifically about Pembroke Road, about that bridge [Baggot Street Bridge]: it's Kavanagh territory, but I myself lived in Raglan Road. It's the most normal thing in the world, this strange life-giving quality of Dublin, co-existing with the crushing narcissism and the assassins among us and the begrudgery, the knockery, the refusal to let hope live, as if up from the very streets themselves came the opposite of all that. *That* quality, that is sacramental to me. And it's also the most "romantic". I like the outrageously irrational assertion of hope where there doesn't seem to be much. If I didn't do that, I wouldn't live, if I didn't fly in the face of myself, in the face of my own depression, if I were not a rebel against myself.'

? Questions

1. The mood is forward-looking, upbeat and optimistic from the poem's opening line. Is that mood sustained throughout the poem?

2. List the images as they occur and discuss what they contribute to the overall effect of the poem. If it were filmed, do you think the poem would be visually effective? Why or why not? Explain your answer. Does the poem contain something that the film couldn't capture?

3. Halfway through the poem we read, 'Begin to the loneliness that cannot end.' What does such a line tell us about the speaker?

4. Kennelly has been praised for his 'buoyant' poetry. This is one such poem, but, in your opinion, is it an escapist or a realistic poem?

5. The poem's first and final words are the same. Explore how repetition and rhythm work throughout the poem.

6. This is one of Kennelly's most popular poems. Can you suggest reasons why?

Bread

Someone else cut off my head
In a golden field.
Now I am re-created

By her fingers. This
Moulding is more delicate   5
Than a first kiss,

More deliberate than her own
Rising up
And lying down,

I am fine   10
As anything in
This legendary garden

Yet I am nothing till
She runs her fingers through me
And shapes me with her skill.   15

The form that I shall bear
Grows round and white.
It seems I comfort her

Even as she slits my face
And stabs my chest.   20
Her feeling for perfection is

Absolute.
So I am glad to go through fire
And come out

Shaped like her dream.   25
In my way
I am all that can happen to men.
I came to life at her finger-ends.
I will go back into her again.

📖 Glossary

Line 5 moulding: shaping.

Line 12 legendary: remarkable, special, famous; a reference, perhaps, to the Garden of Eden.

? Questions

1. This poem records the story of a loaf of bread from 'a golden field' to its being eaten by the woman who made and baked it, from the bread's point of view. Did this poem make you think differently about something as familiar and everyday as bread?

2. Though bread is eaten every day, this poem was written in 1971. How can you tell? Which details belong to long ago?

3. How would you describe the flow of the poem, its rhythm?

4. The relationship between the woman and the bread is crucial. Trace how the speaker captures that relationship through the poem. Comment on 'Her feeling for perfection is/ Absolute'.

5. 'Someone else cut off my head'; 'This/ Moulding is more delicate/ Than a first kiss'; 'she slits my face/ And stabs my chest.' Explore these contrasting aspects and their effect.

6. In the closing lines, a new idea is introduced, a new comparison is made between men and bread: 'I am all that can happen to men'. What is being explored and suggested here? Consider how the wheat comes from the earth, how man, if buried, returns to the earth.

'Dear Autumn Girl'
(from *Love Cry*)

Dear Autumn girl, these helter-skelter days
When mad leaf-argosies drive at my head,
I try but fail to give you proper praise
For the excitement you've created
In my world: an islander at sea,   5
A girl with child, a fool, a simple king,
Garrulous masters of true mockery –
My hugest world becomes the littlest thing

Whenever you walk smiling through a room
And your flung golden hair is still wet   10
Ready for September's homaged rays;
I see what is, I wonder what's to come,
I bless what you remember or forget
And recognise the poverty of praise.

📖 Glossary

Line 1 helter-skelter: disordered, commotion-filled.

Line 2 mad leaf-argosies: swirling leaves shaped like large sailing vessels.

Line 7 garrulous: talkative, chattering.

Line 11 homaged: praising, reverential.

Line 14 the poverty of praise: the inadequacy of praise.

❓ Questions

1. Is the 'Dear Autumn Girl' an actual girl, or is the poet addressing something else? Where in the poem is this made clear?

2. How would you describe the speaker as revealed to us here?

3. The poem runs without a full-stop. Why do you think the poet chose to do this?

4. The poem takes the form of a Petrarchan sonnet with an octet and a sestet. Does a change occur between the first section and the second?

5. Lines 5 and 6 contain some mysterious phrases: 'an islander at sea,/ A girl with child, a fool, a simple king'. How would you interpret these?

6. Comment on the words 'hugest' and 'littlest' in line 8. What is the speaker telling us here?

7. The poem is from a sonnet sequence called *Love Cry*. What is meant by those words? Why is 'Love Cry' an appropriate title in this instance?

Poem from a Three Year Old

And will the flowers die?

And will the people die?

And every day do you grow old, do I
grow old, no I'm not old, do
flowers grow old?   5

Old things – do you throw them out?

Do you throw old people out?

And how you know a flower that's old?

The petals fall, the petals fall from flowers,
and do the petals fall from people too,   10
every day more petals fall until the
floor where I would like to play I
want to play is covered with old
flowers and people all the same
together lying there with petals fallen   15
on the dirty floor I want to play
the floor you come and sweep
with the huge broom.

The dirt you sweep, what happens that,
what happens all the dirt you sweep   20
from flowers and people, what
happens all the dirt? Is all the
dirt what's left of flowers and
people, all the dirt there in a
heap under the huge broom that   25
sweeps everything away?

Why you work so hard, why brush
and sweep to make a heap of dirt?
And who will bring new flowers?
And who will bring new people? Who will   30
bring new flowers to put in water
where no petals fall on to the
floor where I would like to
play? Who will bring new flowers
that will not hang their heads   35
like tired old people wanting sleep?
Who will bring new flowers that
do not split and shrivel every
day? And if we have new flowers,
will we have new people too to   40
keep the flowers alive and give
them water?

And will the new young flowers die?

And will the new young people die?

And why?   45

Glossary

Line 38 shrivel: wither, dry up.

In this poem, Kennelly speaks in the voice of a child. Appropriately, there isn't a difficult word in the poem.

? Questions

1. 'And…And…And…' How would you describe the tone of voice in this poem? Questioning? Insistent? Unintentionally humorous? Perplexed? Or a mixture of all these? Explain your answer.

2. Would you agree that though the language is simple, this is not a simple poem?

3. Explore how the comparison between people and flowers work?

4. The poem is framed by a series of questions. Are any answers found?

5. In the poem's three main sections (lines 9–42), the language imitates the workings of a three-year-old's mind. Which phrases, in your opinion, best capture this?

6. Is this a disturbing or a consoling poem? Explain your answer.

Oliver to His Brother

Loving brother, I am glad to hear of your welfare
And that our children have so much leisure
They can travel far to eat cherries.
This is most excusable in my daughter
Who loves that fruit and whom I bless.   5
Tell her I expect she writes often to me
And that she be kept in some exercise.
Cherries and exercise go well together.
I have delivered my son up to you.
I hope you counsel him; he will need it;   10
I choose to believe he believes what you say.
I send my affection to all your family.
Let sons and daughters be serious; the age requires it.
I have things to do, all in my own way.
For example, I take not kindly to rebels.   15
Today, in Burford Churchyard, Cornet Thompson
Was led to the place of execution.
He asked for prayers, got them, died well.
After him, a Corporal, brought to the same place
Set his back against the wall and died.   20
A third chose to look death in the face,
Stood straight, showed no fear, chilled into his pride.
Men die their different ways
And girls eat cherries
In the Christblessed fields of England.   25
Some weep. Some have cause. Let weep who will.
Whole floods of brine are at their beck and call.
I have work to do in Ireland.

📖 Glossary

Title Oliver: Oliver Cromwell (1599–1658). English puritan, soldier and politician, who was one of the signatories on the death warrant of Charles I, executed on 30 January 1648. He massacred the Catholic garrisons at Drogheda and Wexford. An entry for Cromwell in *Brewer's Dictionary of Irish Phrase & Fable* reads as follows: 'One of the great hate-figures of Irish history, because of the massacres of the civilian population committed by his soldiers, and because of his open detestation of Catholicism, the religion of the majority of Irish people in the seventeenth century – as now. The Cromwellian Settlement is credited with robbing the people of Ireland of their land.'

Line 10 counsel: advise.

Line 16 Burford Churchyard: in Oxfordshire.

Line 16 Cornet Thompson: one of a number of soldiers in the New English Model Army who took part in the Banbury mutiny in May 1649 and was imprisoned afterwards in Burford Church; Cornet James Thompson was a leading participant. Ordered by Oliver Cromwell to be executed, he was shot on 17 May 1649 along with two others. The mutineers were members of the Levellers' movement, which demanded greater democracy, equality and religious toleration. Cornet Thompson's brother, Captain William Thompson, was the leader of the mutiny but was killed in action by Cromwell's troops.

Line 19 corporal: Corporal Perkins, another of the Banbury mutineers executed in Burford churchyard on 17 May 1649.

Line 21 a third: The third Leveller executed was John Church.

'Oliver to His Brother' is from *Cromwell*, a book-length sequence of poems containing 254 poems in all. It was first published in 1983. In a short essay titled 'Voices' from 2000, Kennelly says that he was interested in letting voices be heard, 'especially the voices of those whom my culture would dismiss or damn forever to arid silence. I'm thinking of Cromwell, for example, about whom it is a sin (or was when I was growing up) to say a good word, or even to begin to try to understand as a complex human being.'

Plaque in Burford in memory of the mutineers.

The poem is inspired by a letter sent from Oliver Cromwell to his brother, Richard Mayor, Bristol on 19th July 1645. Here is an extract:

Loving Brother,

... I am very glad to hear of your welfare, and that our children have so good leisure to make a journey to eat cherries: - it's very excusable in my Daughter; I hope she may have a very good pretence for it! I assure you, Sir, I wish her very well; and I believe she knows it. I pray you tell her from me, I expect she writes often to me; by which I shall understand how all your Family doth, and she will be kept in some exercise. I have delivered my Son up to you; and I hope you will counsel him: he will need it; and indeed I believe he likes well what you say, and will be advised by you. I wish he may be serious; the times require it.

I hope my Sister is in health; to whom I desire my very hearty affections and service may be presented; as also to my Cousin Ann, to whom I wish a good husband. I desire my affections may be presented to all your Family, to which I wish a blessing from the Lord. I hope I shall have your prayers in the Business to which I am called...

? Questions

1. The poem is in the form of a letter from a man to his brother written in the first half of the seventeenth century. When is the reader first aware of this? In your opinion, which details best convey another age and time?

2. List Oliver's concerns in his letter to his brother. Were you surprised by anything he says? Why? Why not?

3. Cromwell is a hate-figure in Irish history. Does this poem invite us to reassess Cromwell's reputation? Does it succeed in humanising Cromwell?

4. 'Let sons and daughters be serious; the age requires it.' How does that line fit within the poem as a whole?

5. How would you describe the poem's structure? As you read through the poem, does he focus on different things?

6. 'I take not kindly to rebels.' Discuss this line within the context of what you know about Oliver Cromwell.

7. How would you describe the tone of line 16?

8. This 'letter' can be dated precisely: 17 May 1649, the day Cornet James Thompson was executed. How does the speaker view what has happened?

9. Cherries are mentioned and the fields of England are 'Christblessed'. Comment on such details in the context of the poem as a whole.

10. The final line introduces a new topic. What is the effect of this?

I See You Dancing, Father

No sooner downstairs after a night's rest
And in the door
Than you started to dance a step
In the middle of the kitchen floor.

And as you danced   5
You whistled.
You made your own music
Always in tune with yourself.

Well, nearly always, anyway.
You're buried now   10
In Lislaughtin Abbey
And whenever I think of you

I go back beyond the old man
Mind and body broken
To find the unbroken man.   15
It is the moment before the dance begins,

Your lips are enjoying themselves
Whistling an air.
Whatever happens or cannot happen
In the time I have to spare   20
I see you dancing, father.

📖 Glossary

Line 11 Lislaughtin Abbey: a ruined medieval Franciscan Abbey near Ballylongford, north County Kerry, raided during the Cromwellian invasion of Ireland.

Kennelly, remembering his father in a radio interview with Miriam O'Callaghan on 9 October 2016, said: 'Every morning he'd come into the kitchen and he'd be dancing. And he'd sing. His song was "When You Were Sweet Sixteen".'

? Questions

1. The poem's title is also the poem's final line. Comment on this in the light of the speaker remembering his father as an 'old man/ Mind and body broken'.

2. How is the father figure portrayed in the first two stanzas? How would you describe the mood in these lines?

3. What happens at line 9? Comment on the contrast between stanzas 1 and 2 and what follows.

4. The father's physical and mental qualities are celebrated, but comment on how a darker aspect of the father's life is also mentioned.

5. The father dances alone, whistles alone. What does the speaker say about this image in the final two lines?

6. What do you understand by line 16: 'It is the moment before the dance begins'? Why does the speaker return to this moment? Why is this moment special?

7. Do you think this a happy or a sad poem? Give reasons for your answer. Why does the speaker choose 'In the time I have to spare' to 'see you dancing, father'?

A Cry for Art O'Leary
(from the Irish of Eibhlín Dubh Ní Chonaill)

My love
The first time I saw you
From the top of the market
My eyes covered you
My heart went out to you   5
I left my friends for you
Threw away my home for you

What else could I do?

You got the best rooms for me
All in order for me   10
Ovens burning for me
Fresh trout caught for me
Choice meat for me

In the best of beds I stretched
Till milking-time hummed for me   15

You made the whole world
Pleasing to me

White rider of love!

I love your silver-hilted sword
How your beaver hat became you   20
With its band of gold
Your friendly homespun suit
Revealed your body
Your pin of glinting silver
Glittered in your shirt   25

On your horse in style
You were sensitive pale-faced
Having journeyed overseas
The English respected you
Bowing to the ground   30
Not because they loved you
But true to their hearts' hate

They're the ones who killed you
Darling of my heart

My lover   35
My love's creature
Pride of Immokelly
To me you were not dead
Till your great mare came to me
Her bridle dragging ground   40
Her head with your startling blood
Your blood upon the saddle
You rode in your prime
I didn't wait to clean it
I leaped across my bed   45
I leaped then to the gate
I leaped upon your mare
I clapped my hands in frenzy
I followed every sign
With all the skill I knew   50
Until I found you lying
Dead near a furze bush
Without pope or bishop
Or cleric or priest
To say a prayer for you   55

Only a crooked wasted hag
Throwing her cloak across you

I could do nothing then
In the sight of God
But go on my knees   60
And kiss your face
And drink your free blood

My man!
Going out the gate
You turned back again   65
Kissed the two children
Threw a kiss at me
Saying 'Eileen, woman, try
To get this house in order,
Do your best for us.   70
I must be going now
I'll not be home again.'
I thought that you were joking
You my laughing man

My man!   75
My Art O'Leary
Up on your horse now
Ride out to Macroom
And then to Inchigeela
Take a bottle of wine   80
Like your people before you
Rise up
My Art O'Leary
Of the sword of love

Put on your clothes   85
Your black beaver
Your black gloves
Take down your whip
Your mare is waiting

Go east by the thin road   90
Every bush will salute you
Every stream will speak to you
Men and women acknowledge you

They know a great man
When they set eyes on him   95

God's curse on you, Morris,
God's curse on your treachery
You swept my man from me
The man of my children
Two children play in the house   100
A third lives in me

He won't come alive from me

My heart's wound
Why was I not with you
When you were shot   105
That I might take the bullet
In my own body?
Then you'd have gone free
Rider of the grey eye
And followed them   110
Who'd murdered me

My man!
I look at you now
All I know of a hero
True man with true heart   115
Stuck in a coffin
You fished the clean steams
Drank nightlong in halls
Among frank-breasted women

I miss you   120

My man!
I am crying for you
In far Derrynane
In yellow-appled Carren
Where many a horseman   125
And vigilant woman
Would be quick to join
In crying for you
Art O'Leary
My laughing man   130

O crying women
Long live your crying
Till Art O'Leary
Goes back to school
On a fateful day   135
Not for books and music

But for stones and clay

My man!
The corn is stacked
The cows are milking   140
My heart is a lump of grief
I will never be healed
Till Art O'Leary
Comes back to me

I am a locked trunk   145
The key is lost
I must wait till rust
Devours the screw

O my best friend
Art O'Leary   150
Son of Conor
Son of Cadach
Son of Lewis
East from wooded glens
West from girlish hills   155
Where rowanberries grow
Yellow nuts budge from branches
Apples laugh like small suns
As once they laughed
Throughout my girlhood   160
It is no cause for wonder
If bonfires lit O'Leary country
Close to Ballingeary
Or holy Gougane Barra
After the clean-gripping rider   165
The robust hunter
Panting towards the kill
Your own hounds lagged behind you
O horseman of the summoning eyes
What happened you last night?   170
My only whole belief
Was that you could not die
For I was your protection

My heart! My grief!

My man! My darling!

In Cork   175
I had this vision
Lying in my bed:
A glen of withered trees
A home heart-broken
Strangled hunting-hounds   180
Choked birds

And you
Dying on a hillside
Art O'Leary
My one man   185
Your blood running crazily
Over earth and stone

Jesus Christ knows well
I'll wear no cap
No mourning dress   190
No solemn shoes
No bridle on my horse
No grief-signs in my house
But test instead
The wisdom of the law   195
I'll cross the sea
To speak to the King
If he ignores me
I'll come back home
To find the man   200
Who murdered my man

Morris, because of you
My man is dead

Is there a man in Ireland
To put a bullet through your head   205

Women, white women of the mill
I give my love to you
For the poetry you made
For Art O'Leary
Rider of the brown mare   210
Deep women-rhythms of blood

The fiercest and the sweetest
Since time began
Singing of this cry I womanmake
For my man

📖 Glossary

Line 20 beaver hat: a fashionable hat made from beaver fur.

Line 39 mare: female horse.

Line 48 frenzy: mental derangement; delirious agitation.

Line 78 Macroom: a town on the River Sullane in Co. Cork; Má Chromtha (Sloping Field).

Line 79 Inchigeela: a place on the River Lee.

Line 96 Morris: Abraham Morris, the Protestant high sheriff.

Line 97 treachery: deceitfulness; untrustworthiness.

Line 101 A third lives in me: she is pregnant with her third child.

Line 123 Derrynane: Co Kerry where Eibhlín Dubh Ní Chonaill was born.

Line 126 vigilant: watchful; on the lookout for.

Line 135 fateful: decisive, pivotal, crucial; a fateful day is a day of far-reaching and often disastrous consequences.

Line 163 Ballingeary: near the western end of Lough Allua in Co. Cork.

Line 164 Gougane Barra: where the River Lee rises; St. Finbarr founded a monastery there in the seventh century.

Line 166 robust: healthy, strong.

Line 168 lagged: went too slowly; could not keep up.

Line 198 the King: in 1773, King George III was monarch of Great Britain and Ireland.

This poem was composed by Eibhlín Dubh Ní Chonaill (c.1743–c.1800) in Irish – *Caoineadh Airt Uí Laoghaire* – following her husband's murder in May 1773. One of twenty-two children, she was born in Derrynane, Co. Kerry (Daniel O'Connell was her nephew). At fifteen, she was married to an old man and he died months later. She then fell in love with and married, against her family's wishes, Colonel Art Ó Laoghaire of the Hungarian Army who had returned from the continental wars. They settled at Rathleigh near Macroom, Ó Laoghaire's home place, but Ó Laoghaire fell foul of the high sheriff Abraham Morris. In 1773, Ó Laoghaire's mare had beaten Morris's horse at Macroom races and Morris allegedly demanded of Ó Laoghaire his mare for £5, something he was entitled to do, as a Protestant, under the old and largely inactive anti-Catholic Penal Laws enacted between 1695 and 1709.

Ó'Laoghaire, a proud man and an experienced army officer, refused and went on the run, with a price of 20 guineas on his head; he was hunted down by Morris and his soldiers and killed at Carrignanimma on 4 May 1773. He was twenty-six. According to legend Ó'Laoghaire's bloodied mare galloped home and Eibhlín mounted her and then rode to where her dead husband lay. She drank his blood.

This famous poem is a keen or lament and is considered to be one of the most beautiful love poems in the Irish language – a language that is 'formal, incantatory, traditional and impassioned'. It has been suggested that his widow did not actually compose the poem. It belonged to the oral tradition, was not written down until the nineteenth century and has been translated many times, including by Frank O'Connor, Thomas Kinsella and Eilís Dillon.

The poem's opening line 'Mo ghrá go daingean tu!' has been translated as 'My steadfast love!' Kennelly opts for 'My love'.

? Questions

1. A keen has been described as a formal lamentation over the dead at a wake or at the graveside. Keening was observed in parts of rural Ireland until the beginning of the twentieth century. What would you consider the effect of a public mourning ritual as opposed to grieving in private?

2. Having read the poem through, how would you sum up the poem's structure? It begins with the speaker remembering the first time she saw Art O'Leary. Does the poem follow a straightforward structure?

3. In the opening section (lines 1–7), how is the sense of the speaker's infatuation with and love for Art O'Leary conveyed?

4. Comment on line 8. Why do you think it is on its own? What does it tell us about the speaker?

5. Lines 9–32 paint a picture of their life together as husband and wife. Which details, in your opinion, best convey their life together?

6. Comment on the different moods within the poem. When is the speaker most happy, most sad, most angry?

7. Repetition is a key aspect of the keen. Explore how repetition is used in this version and comment on its effect.

8. Why are genealogy and place names so important here?

9. Her husband has been killed but, in remembering and honouring him, Eibhlín Dubh Ní Chonaill brings him back to life. What kind of a person is Art O'Leary as portrayed by his wife?

10. Do you think they were well suited as a couple? Give reasons for your answer.

11. Towards the end of the poem (at line 176), she speaks of having had a vision. What does that contribute to the situation?

12. At line 190, she speaks of Jesus Christ in an interesting way. Tease out this reference and explore its significance.

13. Though this poem laments her husband's death, she also *refuses* to mourn (lines 190 forward). Why is this?

14. Who is she addressing in the closing lines of the poem? Is this an appropriate ending do you think? Give reasons for your answer.

15. What is your overall impression of this poem? It has been translated from Irish and though it dates from the eighteenth century, do you think it has a timeless quality? Why? Why not?

Things I Might Do

I thought of things I might do with my heart.
Should I make it into a month like October,
A chalice for the sad madness of leaves
That I might raise in homage to the year's end?

Should I make it into a small white church in   5
A country-place where bells are childhood prayers?
Or a backroom of a brothel in Dublin
Where the trade of somethinglikelove endures?

Should I make it a judge to judge itself?
Or a caring face in a memory-storm?   10
Or a bed

For Judas dreaming of the tree:
       'There now, there now, rest as best you can,
       Darling, rest your treacherous head
       And when you've rested, come home to me.'   15

📖 Glossary

Line 3 chalice: goblet, drinking cup; the chalice is also central to the Catholic mass.

Line 4 homage: praise, reverence.

Line 12 the tree: a reference, perhaps, to the tree Judas Iscariot hanged himself on. ('And he cast down the pieces of silver in the temple, and departed, and went and hanged himself', Matthew 27:5).

This is from Kennelly's book-length poem *The Book of Judas* (1991) and gives voice to Judas Iscariot, one of Jesus' twelve disciples who also betrayed him. The author John McDonagh in *Brendan Kennelly: A Host of Ghosts* says that, 'In virtually all areas of the Western world, the name of Judas carries connotations of the deepest and most hurtful betrayal, a figure who was chosen to share in the most intense of relationships but who apparently chose to sell that commitment for a handful of silver.'

Bono called *The Book of Judas* 'an epic achievement and as over the top as the subject deserves.' In 584 poems, Judas, in what Kennelly himself calls the 'Judasvoice', gives his take on Christianity, but the book also spans centuries during which Judas has conversations with diverse individuals such as Adolf Hitler, Marilyn Monroe and James Joyce. At one stage, Judas asks Jesus why 'You haven't even/ A single woman among your twelve apostles?'; he also hosts a TV chat show and interviews God.

'Things I Might Do' is from section IX in *The Book of Judas* called 'I know I've arrived, can you tell me why I'm here?'

❓ Questions

1. Who is speaking here? How would you describe the voice? Direct, questioning, revealing? How did you respond? Did the poem make you think about Judas in a different way? Why?

2. How would you describe the mood in the opening line? Why do you think the emphasis is on the heart?

3. Why is October relevant here? What does the speaker associate it with?

4. Comment on the contrasting images of church and brothel in stanza 2. What do these images tell us about the speaker?

5. Consider the shape of the poem on the page. Why do you think Brendan Kennelly arranged it in this way?

6. Does knowing how Judas died colour your reading of the closing lines? Explain your response.

7. In his preface to *The Book of Judas*, Kennelly says: 'The damned soul has a special perspective on us all, but how can we believe him, how can we believe one who is a liar and traitor by instinct?' and 'The Judasvoice is odd and ordinary, freakish and free, severed and pertinent.' Comment on these remarks in the light of your reading of 'Things I Might Do'.

8. In your opinion, does this poem contain what is ugly and what is beautiful? Explain.

A Great Day

She was all in white.

Snow
Suggests itself as metaphor

But since this has been so often said
I may be justified in considering it dead.   5
Something about snow is not quite right.

Therefore, she was all in white.

He was most elegant too
All dickied up in dignified blue.

They came together, as is habitual   10
In that part of the world,
Through a grave ritual,

Listening
With at least a modicum of wonder –
What God has joined together   15
Let no man put asunder.

Man in woman, woman in man.
Soon afterwards, the fun began.

It was a great day –
Long hours of Dionysiac festivity.   20

Songs poured out like wine.
Praises flowed as they had never done.

The people there
Seemed to see each other in a new way.
This added to the distinction of the day.   25

And all the time she was all in white
Enjoying every song and speech
Enjoying every sip and every bite.

Such whiteness seems both beautiful and true
He thought, all dickied up in dignified blue.   30

He looks so good in blue
(This warmed her mind)
Blue suits him
Down to the ground.

At the table where they sat   35
Things seemed to fit.

And the loud crowd sang and danced
The whole day long, the whole night long.
There could never be anything but dance and song.

I must change, she whispered,   40
I must change my dress.

He never saw the white dress again.

In the train, the trees wore their rainy veils
With a reticent air.

It's good to get away, she whispered,   45
Touching her beautiful hair.

She closed her eyes, the trees were silent guests,
A tide of thoughts flowed in her head,
In his head.

'Darling, it was a great day,' she said.   46

📖 Glossary

Line 3 metaphor: an imagined comparison.

Line 9 dickied up: a slang term meaning 'fashionably and well dressed'.

Line 10 habitual: customary, the habit.

Line 12 grave ritual: serious religious ceremony.

Line 14 modicum: small quantity.

Line 20 Dionysiac: celebratory, alcoholic; Dionysus was the Greek god of wine.

Line 25 distinction: specialness, importance, significance.

Line 44 reticent: shy, retiring.

? Questions

1. Having read the poem, do you think the poet has described and captured a great day? Give reasons for your answer.

2. The poem is written in twenty-two short sections. Trace the poem's structure, examining how it begins and ends with the bride.

3. There are many contrasting and different images in the poem. Consider these and their effect. Are they important in creating mood? Explain. Comment on the colours white and blue.

4. The poem focuses on the public and the private. Explain how the bracketed line – '(This warmed her mind)' – works within the poem as a whole.

5. How would you describe the newly-weds in the closing lines of the poem? Has a change occurred? Explain.

6. Does this poem match your idea or experience of a wedding celebration? Why? Why not?

Fragments

What had he to say to her now?
Where was the woman he believed he had known
In a street, out walking, by the sea,
In bed, working, dancing, loving the sun

And saying so, always for the first time?   5
Who was this stranger with the graven face?
What led to the dreaming-up of a home?
And what was he, at sixty? Who was

That man lifting the blackthorn stick
With the knobbed top from its place   10
At the side of the fire, quietly dying?

He listened to his own steps in the walk
Past the reedy mud where plover rose
And scattered, black fragments, crying.

Glossary

Line 6 graven: strongly fixed.

Line 13 plover: wading bird.

This poem is a sonnet but, unlike a one-stanza, fourteen-line poem, it is divided into four sections. Fragments, perhaps.

? Questions

1. The poem describes a 'his and her' situation. How easy is it to piece that situation together? Does the poet make it clear?

2. The poem is told from a man's point of view, a man who is aware of ageing and changing. How would you describe the man's outlook as revealed in the poem?

3. How would you describe the rhythm here? Does it suit the theme of the poem?

4. Comment on the opening line with its eight simple and monosyllabic words?

5. Look at the imagery and say how it changes between stanza 1 and stanza 4.

6. Who is asking the question, 'Who was/ That man lifting the blackthorn stick'?

7. What does it tell us about the man's situation?

8. Is this poem interesting to a young person? Why? Why not?

The soul's loneliness

it's nothing to go on about
but when I hear it
in the ticking of the clock

beside the books and photographs
or see it in the shine   5
of an Eason's plastic bag at midnight

or touch it in the tree I call
Christ there outside my window
swaying in the day's afterglow

I shiver a little at the strangeness   10
of my flesh, the smell of sweat,
the child's poem I'll never forget

and find my eyes searching the floor
for a definition of grace
or a trace of yourself I've never noticed before.   15

📖 Glossary

Line 6 Eason's: well-known shop that sells newspapers, magazines, books, stationery.

Line 14 grace: a special God-given quality (within a Christian context).

'The soul's loneliness' is from Kennelly's collection, *Poetry My Arse* (1995).

? Questions

1. How does the speaker respond to loneliness? What creates a sense of loneliness in the speaker? Do you identify with him?

2. In the opening line, the speaker resists self-pity. How does he follow on from this?

3. A change occurs at line 10. What happens here and how is it different from the first three stanzas?

4. Why is grace important? What do you understand by the phrase 'a trace of yourself'?

Saint Brigid's Prayer
(from the Irish)

I'd like to give a lake of beer to God.
　I'd love the Heavenly
Host to be tippling there
　for all eternity.

I'd love the men of Heaven to live with me,　　　　5
　to dance and sing.
If they wanted, I'd put at their disposal
　vats of suffering.

White cups of love I'd give them
　with a heart and a half;　　　　10
sweet pitchers of mercy I'd offer
　to every man.

I'd make Heaven a cheerful spot
　because the happy heart is true.
I'd make the men contented for their own sake.　　　　15
　I'd like Jesus to love me too.

I'd like the people of Heaven to gather
　from all the parishes around.
I'd give a special welcome to the women,
　the three Marys of great renown.　　　　20

I'd sit with the men, the women and God
　there by the lake of beer.
We'd be drinking good health forever
　and every drop would be a prayer.

Glossary

Title Saint Brigid's: Brigid, a Christian saint, according to tradition, was born circa 450 at Faughart, near Dundalk, County Louth. She founded a double abbey in Kildare. It was the first Irish convent and a perpetual flame was kept burning there in her honour until the Reformation. In *Vita Sanctae Brigitae*, Cogitosus's life of St. Brigid from c.650, the story is told that St Brigid was asked by lepers for beer. She had none but on seeing that there were baths of water nearby, Brigid blessed the water and it was turned into beer.

The poem which Brendan Kennelly translated dates from the tenth century.

Lines 2–3 Heavenly/Host: guests in heaven.

Line 3 tippling: regularly drinking.

Line 8 vats: large tubs or tanks to hold liquid.

Line 11 pitchers: large jugs.

Line 20 three Marys: the three Marys present at the Crucifixion – Mary Cleophas, Mary Magdalene and Mary, the mother of God (*cf.* John 29:27).

Questions

1. This poem, in the voice of a woman who lived in the fifth century, addresses God and the people of Heaven. Did the prayer's request surprise you?

2. Is this a light-hearted or a serious prayer or is it both? Would you know that it is an Irish prayer? Why? Why not?

3. The poem paints a picture of happiness as envisioned by Brigid. What kind of a woman is Brigid as portrayed here?

4. The poet uses regular end-rhymes frequently. What is the effect of this?

5. Consider the way men and women are spoken of in the poem and comment on this.

6. In his introduction to his book *Breathing Spaces*, Kennelly writes: 'If there's such a thing as wisdom, it wears a distinctive grin'. Is this relevant here? Explain your answer.

General Questions

A. 'Kennelly, in his poetry, combines an urgent utterance with a compellingly personal voice.' Discuss this statement, supporting your answer with reference to the poetry of Brendan Kennelly on your course.

B. 'Kennelly explores contrasting aspects of life in poems of direct emotional intensity.' Discuss this statement, supporting your answer with reference to the poetry of Brendan Kennelly on your course.

C. 'Kennelly speaks to many and for many in his engaging poetry.' Discuss this statement, supporting your answer with reference to the poetry of Brendan Kennelly on your course.

D. 'Brendan Kennelly's poetry is deceptive. It seems simple yet it deals with many of life's complexities.' Discuss this statement, supporting your answer with reference to the poetry of Brendan Kennelly on your course.

E. 'People and language are at the heart of Kennelly's poetry.' Would you agree with this estimation of Kennelly's work? Support your discussion with reference to, or quotations from, the poems by Kennelly on your course.

F. 'Kennelly's poetry is accessible, wide-ranging and challenging.' Discuss this statement, supporting your answer with reference to the poems by Brendan Kennelly on your course.

Critical Commentary

Begin

This poem has a spring in its step. It was written, says Kennelly, after a serious illness, with the sense of beginning again, the thrill of it, the beauty of it, the 'promise of it'; it celebrates the ordinary and the everyday; it reminds us that every day is special and that the ordinary is extraordinary. A new day brings new possibilities and new opportunities, and though the setting is urban it reminds us that nature is a life-force in busy city lives. The title is repeated seven times in the poem; the word 'begin' opens and ends the poem, and its frequent use gives the poem momentum and flow.

It is a poem filled with sound and light and movement. In the very first line, birdsong announces a brand new day. First, we hear and then in line 2 we see the daylight.

> Begin again to the summoning birds
> to the sight of light at the window

These two lines bring us to our senses.

The very different, contrasting sound of 'the roar of morning traffic/ all along Pembroke Road' is also viewed as a positive. It is part of a new morning's activity and the speaker willing embraces all aspects of life, even traffic because his optimistic outlook is such that

> Every beginning is a promise

But this poem, though it celebrates 'sweetness and light' – the birds' chorus at dawn, introduces a different note at line 6 when every beginning is spoken of in terms of being 'born in light and dying in dark'.

The poem is one of celebration and exuberance, but a contrasting mood is introduced and it gives the poem a more realistic atmosphere. The poem lists beautiful things such as springtime, girls and swans, but it also acknowledges loneliness, death, and a world of rain and stark branches. The 'determination and exaltation of springtime' inspire and the word 'flowering' in line 8 – 'flowering the way to work' – is an inventive and unusual description of how an everyday activity such as going to work can be transformed into something special if your outlook is positive.

The 'determination...of springtime' becomes an image for how humans respond to life and the poem not only moves from a particular room on a particular morning to the street and the canal, but also explores the idea of time past, time present and time future. Spring each year is part of the passing of time and when the speaker refers to

> bridges linking the past and future
> old friends passing though with us still

the poem, at this point, opens up a longer sense of time. The canal bridges have been crossed for generations and the bridge is liked to the passing of time. When the speaker refers to 'old friends passing', he acknowledges the reality of death, but also reminds us that memory plays an important part; it allows those old friends to live on.

Loneliness and death are inevitable, and when the speaker identifies 'the loneliness that cannot end' it is seen as a positive, in that endless loneliness perhaps prompts us to keep going, to begin again. The word 'perhaps' offers possibility; it is a welcoming tone and there follows a series of images not as attractive as the earlier ones, images of 'crying birds in the sudden rain', 'branches stark in the willing sunlight', 'seagulls foraging for bread'.

The poem features 'the pageant of queuing girls', 'old friends' – people we see and remember; the speaker then invites us to 'wonder at unknown faces' and to see the possibility in 'crying birds', 'sudden rain', 'seagulls foraging'. The use of 'at' five times in lines 15–19 impresses upon the reader the need to consider these and the sense of wonder they bring.

An image of 'couples sharing a sunny secret/ alone together while making good' paints a picture of happy intimacy and, yet, the phrase 'alone together' might suggest that even couples must come to terms with being alone.

Looking at lines 1–20, we see that five of these lines start with 'begin' and at line 21 the word 'though' echoes an idea explored earlier – though life is overshadowed by loneliness and death – the word 'though' here strengthens the speaker's resolve to make the most of things.

> Though we live in a world that dreams of ending
> that always seems about to give in
> something that will not acknowledge conclusion
> insists that we forever begin.

Words such as 'ending' and 'give in' suggest something negative, but the poem ends with a recognition and belief that 'something' gives us the energy and the hope to keep going. That something is never named. It could be the spirit, the soul, an optimistic nature, but whatever it is it makes possible a future. The poem, as a result, ends on an upbeat and positive note.

The poem's musical qualities are captured in the repetition, the run-on line, the many words ending in '-ing', alliteration ('sharing a sunny secret') and internal rhyme ('sight of light').

In John McDonagh's anthology *A Fine Statement: An Irish Poets' Anthology*, Kennelly says of 'Begin': 'I know it has helped people in sickness, in marriage break-ups, in deep personal problematic, even tragic, situations. It is a poem rewritten from many years ago. This rewriting came after a heart operation (which also produced *The Man Made of Rain*). To be quite frank and honest, if a poem of mine helps others (as this 'Begin' strangely helped me), I simply love to make that poem available to people in need. And I think there is a fundamental, essential, enduring truth in the lines.'

Bread

This poem, says Kennelly, is in 'the voice of bread, an old tradition in Ireland and Wales and England, where the poet gives an object its voice. A woman is making bread and the bread is talking.'

This cyclical poem begins in a golden field where the wheat is harvested. It is then milled, becomes flour, becomes a loaf of bread, and the poem focuses mainly on the vital, sensuous relationship between the speaker and the woman who creates that loaf.

The poem, arranged in eight three-line stanzas and a concluding five-line one, is in the first person. The word 'I' is used nine times and the speaker tells a story that belongs to a time when women baked bread in their own kitchens. The phrase 'our daily bread' is known to Christians everywhere and the regular baking of bread was a familiar and necessary ritual.

The opening line – 'Someone else cut off my head' – is impersonal and violent. That person, the worker in the field, is just a 'someone', but the cutting of wheat is necessary. Without that violent act, the re-creation mentioned in line 3 could not happen.

The poem describes in sensuous detail the art of bread-making. Description of how the dough is kneaded is, we are told, 'more delicate/ Than a first kiss' and the image of the woman's 'own/ Rising up/ And lying down' is an image of the rhythm of the day. The bread tells of how it is nothing without the woman. It is she who gives birth to the loaf.

The speaker is confident when saying, 'I am fine/ As anything in/ This legendary garden'.

> Yet I am nothing till
> She runs her fingers through me
> And shapes me with her skill.

The poem contains many gestures, some gentle and elegant, some violent – 'moulding', 'runs her fingers through me', 'shapes me', 'slits my face', 'stabs my chest' – and these contrasting movements are necessary in the creation of the loaf.

The bread speaks of its awareness of the bread maker – 'It seems I comfort her' – and the poem paints a sensitive portrait of this woman. Slit and stab are ugly actions in themselves, but without these gestures the bread would not rise well. It is a paradox that such apparently violent gestures can lead to such goodness.

The woman is viewed as an artist: 'Her feeling for perfection is/ Absolute' and the feeling within the speaker is one of respect. The bread tells us that it is glad and willing 'to go through fire/ And come out// Shaped like her dream'. The round, white bread will go into the oven; it goes through fire and comes out, so that the woman's dream is achieved.

The final three lines – each beginning with 'I' – take the form of three confident statements and become a meditation on the relationship not only between a bread maker and bread but on the relationship between man and woman. Women, in giving birth, create men, but it could be argued that the poem is also suggesting that men need women if they are to come to life.

> In my way
> I am all that can happen to men.
> I came to life at her finger-ends.
> I will go back into her again.

The relationship between the two is intimate, sensuous and vital.

'Dear Autumn Girl'

This sonnet, a poem of praise, conjures up a sense of excitement within and without. There is the world of swirling leaves in autumn and a world that contains 'A girl with child, a fool, a simple king'. And though it praises this 'Dear Autumn girl', the speaker also recognises how praise sometimes can never be expressed adequately.

Who is the autumn girl? What is the speaker's relationship with her? These details are never revealed in the poem and they are less important than the sensation felt by the speaker when he thinks of this girl who he associates with a season.

In the opening lines, 'these helter-skelter days' and 'mad leaf-argosies' describe windy days and swirling leaves, but they could also be read as descriptions of an excitement and commotion within the speaker, what he is experiencing in his head and in his heart: 'these helter-skelter days...drive at my head'.

The opening words 'Dear Autumn girl' are an affectionate address, but by line 3 the speaker admits that he will try:

> but fail to give you proper praise
> For the excitement you've created
> In my world

The tone here is open and honest and grateful, and the speaker then offers the reader a description of his world. His world is that of 'an islander at sea' and also includes 'A girl with child, a fool, a simple king'. Such images suggest an isolated figure, a pregnant girl, and a world containing foolishness ('a fool') and wisdom ('a simple king': could that 'simple king' be Jesus Christ?). That this world also contains 'Garrulous masters of true mockery' adds another dimension: harsh, relentless mocking voices.

The octet's concluding line – 'My hugest world becomes the littlest thing' – conveys a sense of large becoming small and suggests that the speaker's focus here is on 'littlest' rather than 'hugest'. 'Littlest' in this instance could be preferred. Has the 'Dear Autumn Girl' changed how the speaker views the world?

The sestet begins with a flowing, happy, free image of the autumn girl:

> Whenever you walk smiling through a room
> And your flung golden hair is still wet
> Ready for September's homaged rays;

Her golden hair compares with September sunshine and the speaker then reflects on the passing of time. If the girl is viewed as an 'Autumn Girl', she is part of life's cycle.

Line 12 introduces an uncertain note. What will the future bring?

> I see what is, I wonder what's to come

But the poem ends with a mood of generous acceptance. The speaker expresses an unconditional love for this girl. He accepts her for what she is – 'I bless what you remember or forget' – and the poem's final line in which he recognises 'the poverty of praise' echoes line 3 – 'I try but fail to give you proper praise' – in conceding that this poem of praise will never succeed in praising her sufficiently.

Poem from a Three Year Old

Brendan Kennelly, writing in *A Fine Statement: An Irish Poets' Anthology* (edited by John McDonagh), says of this poem: 'Here is the true beauty of childhood, or a good part of it, anyway: passionately asking questions and at the same time wanting to have fun, to play, to shake off the darkness of asking questions about death. Having fun, asking questions. After forty-two years as a teacher, I think these two elements are at the heart of education. I love learning from children.'

On the page, this looks like a poem that begins and ends with fragments. The opening lines are mainly one-line questions and it also ends with these, but at the heart of the poem are three stanzas that explore ageing and mortality using simple but memorable images of flowers and sweeping.

Viewing the world from a three-year-old's point of view allows for direct questions, simple language and complex ideas. Many of the questions asked here would not be asked by adults – the questions are too blunt and unsettling – but in the Christian Old Testament (Psalms 8:2), we find that 'God ordains strength out of the mouths of babes'. In other words, a child can say something both surprising and wise.

The poem begins simply: 'And will the flowers die?' And the reader immediately supplies the answer. By line 2, the question has become more serious: 'And will the people die?' Again, the reader knows the answer and the subject matter has become very weighty.

With lines 3–5, the rhythm quickens and imitates the workings of the three-year-old's mind.

> And every day do you grow old, do I
> Grow old, no I'm not old, do
> flowers grow old?

Kennelly has listened carefully to the rhythms and repetition and vocabulary of this three-year-old and the shift from line 6 to line 7 startles: 'Old things – do you throw them out?// Do you throw old people out?' And line 8 returns to the idea contained in the poem's opening line – 'And how you know a flower that's old?'

The poem's three main stanzas bring together dying flowers and dying people and a new image is introduced, the image of sweeping up with a big broom. The lines flow easily here. There is little or no punctuation and rarely at the end of a line. Words, many of them monosyllabic, are frequently repeated and the music created through alliteration and assonance.

The speaker's tone is gentle and questioning at first, but then the voice becomes a little sulky when the child is prevented from playing and the poem paints a somewhat exaggerated, surreal picture of old flowers and people:

> together lying there with petals fallen
> on the dirty floor I want to play
> the floor you come and sweep
> with the huge broom.

The poem begins and ends with queries, but the questioning does not let up throughout. A child never stops asking questions and the poem captures that.

The voice focuses on 'The dirt you sweep' and asks:

> what happens that,
> what happens all the dirt you sweep
> from flowers and people, what
> happens all the dirt?

This creates a darker mood within the poem. And 'the huge broom that/ sweeps everything away' could be interpreted as death.

But a new direction is seen in the third main stanza (lines 27–42) beginning 'Why you work so hard, why brush/ and sweep to make a heap of dirt?' In this section, the voice dwells not on the present but on the future; this is achieved through the word 'new', which occurs seven times. New flowers and new people mean continuity, tomorrow, a feeling that life goes on. Yes, there is dying, but there is also hope.

Lines such as 'new flowers/ that will not hang their heads/ like tired old people wanting sleep?' brings together old age and new life and offers a realistic account of birth, ageing and death. The final lines cast a shadow. They ask sad questions and there is no answer to the poem's final question:

> And will the new young flowers die?
>
> And will the new young people die?
>
> And why?

A question without answers ensures that the poem ends on a mysterious note.

Oliver to his Brother

Among these prescribed poems by Brendan Kennelly, you'll find poems in very different voices: a loaf of bread speaks; you'll hear the voice of a three-year-old; and there is a woman from the eighteenth century, whose husband has been murdered. 'Oliver to his Brother' takes the form of a letter written by a man hundreds of years ago to his brother. It talks of familiar things – family, work – but once the 'Oliver' of the title is identified as Oliver Cromwell, the poem takes on a new resonance and significance.

It opens with an affectionate greeting and acknowledges his brother's letter which clearly contained an account of their children; we learn that Oliver Cromwell's daughter and son are being looked after by this brother. Lines 1–12 focus on the domestic and they express delight in the freedom and ease these children enjoy: they have 'so much leisure/ They can travel far to eat cherries'. That speaker also reminds his brother that he expects his daughter to 'be kept in some exercise' and to write 'often to me'; this introduces a note of duty, of doing what is right. When Oliver Cromwell speaks of his son, he hopes that 'you counsel him; he will need it;/ I choose to believe he believes what you say.' This section ends with 'I send my affection to all your family'. The language here is formal – 'This is most excusable in my daughter' and 'I have delivered my son up to you' – and the tone is one of gentle concern, gratitude and hope.

At line 13 – 'Let sons and daughters be serious; the age requires it' – the poem's focus changes. The speaker now considers the bigger picture, the world of politics, law and order and Cromwell's own part in it: 'I have things to do, all in my own way.' Within the context of what we know about this figure from history, such a line becomes a line steeped in complex acts and deeds. It is a confident and chilling line.

When the letter gives, in lines 15–23, an account of 'today', we read a matter-of-fact account:

> For example, I take not kindly to rebels.
> Today, in Burford Churchyard, Cornet Thompson
> Was led to the place of execution.
> He asked for prayers, got them, died well.
> After him, a Corporal, brought to the same place
> Set his back against the wall and died.
> A third chose to look death in the face,
> Stood straight, showed no fear, chilled into his pride.
> Men die their different ways

Reporting what happened 'today' roots the poem in history. The brutal event on 17 May 1649 is brought vividly alive.

Using understatement, the speaker first expresses his viewpoint – 'I take not kindly to rebels' – and then tells of how three men were executed earlier on the very day that the letter is being written. He names the place and the language is stark. A line such as 'He asked for prayers, got them, died well' is factual, though 'died well' contains a judgement. Plain, monosyllabic words become clinical in lines such as, 'a Corporal, brought to the same place/ Set his back against the wall and died./ A third chose to look death in the face,/ Stood straight, showed no fear, chilled into his pride.'

The speaker, having watched these men face death, concludes 'Men die their different ways'. And then the poem returns to where it began when it mentions girls eating cherries: 'And girls eat cherries/ In the Christblessed fields of England.' A more dramatic contrast would be difficult to imagine following the churchyard executions. The reader is now invited to consider again young life, young pleasures, and a country supposedly favoured by Christ.

The concluding lines offer a sweeping image of England:

> Some weep. Some have cause. Let weep who will.
> Whole floods of brine are at their beck and call.

A weeping nation is pictured. The tone of voice here is that of someone at a distance. The speaker believes he is doing what is right in God's eyes. The poem's final sentence looks to a new chapter in the history books. It is the speaker's conviction that what he has to do in Ireland is justified and the placing of 'Ireland' as the poem's final word prompts readers, especially Irish readers, to consider Cromwell's time in Ireland beyond the particular date that the poem records. Oppression and slaughter are termed 'work'.

Kennelly in an essay titled 'Voices' (2000) speaks of his 'attempts to let voices be heard, especially the voices of those whom my cultures would dismiss or damn forever to arid silence', and speaking of Cromwell he says, 'This giving-a-voice in poetry is like giving such a man a licence to exist. To be, where previously his name was a spit in the street, a black, horrible curse in the night, a maligned monster in a nowhere desert.'

'Oliver to his Brother' is an excerpt from *Cromwell*, Kennelly's book-length poem published in 1983, which the academic A. Norman Jeffares described as 'the result of scholarly enquiry into the history of the man, that contradictory figure, at once civilised, a lover of his family, of mathematics and music, yet one whose exploits make his name "eternally hated in Ireland".'

Oliver Cromwell (1599–1658)

I See You Dancing, Father

This is a very personal memory poem. The poem's title and final line frame a happy, joyful moment, but the poem also acknowledges that the father who danced in the early morning had his difficulties and is now dead.

The two opening stanzas summon up a domestic scene: a man happy in his own home. It is a celebration of the new day; the mood is upbeat and freeing:

> No sooner downstairs after a night's rest
> And in the door
> Than you started to dance a step
> In the middle of the kitchen floor.
>
> And as you danced
> You whistled.
> You made your own music
> Always in tune with yourself.

The rhyming 'door' and 'floor' and the light and tripping rhythm in lines 3 and 4 are musical. Whistling, actual music, mirrors an inner music and these lines create their own harmony.

The mood changes in stanza 3 and the rhythm slows. Stanzas 1 and 2 were four-line, flowing sentences. That flow is checked when the speaker says:

> Well, nearly always, anyway.

Two commas and a full-stop bring a seriousness to the poem's movement. A happy memory gives way to sad reality:

> You're buried now
> In Lislaughtin Abbey

The past contains two contrasting pictures of the speaker's father: a dancing father and the father as an 'old man/ Mind and body broken'. It is the image of the unbroken man that the speaker returns to, back in time, beyond the broken one, and that we learn is 'the moment before the dance begins'.

The past tense – 'started', 'danced', 'whistled', 'made' – gives way to another past tense – 'buried', but the present tense dominates the closing stanza.

> Your lips are enjoying themselves
> Whistling an air.

The use of the present participle here (form of a verb ending in '-ing') – 'enjoying', 'whistling' – bring that past moment into the present and the closing lines look to the future and a continuous present:

> Whatever happens or cannot happen
> In the time I have to spare
> I see you dancing, father.

The speaker knows that he has only a finite time left to live, and that life and death cannot be predicted, but he also knows that those remaining years will be enriched and happier because he sees in his mind's eye his dancing father.

A Cry for Art O'Leary

This is a long passionate love cry in the voice of Eibhlín Dubh Ní Chonaill. Though over 200 lines long (the original is much longer), the dramatic narrative, the use of the short line, and this intense, passionate and emotional poem draws the reader in. The opening stanza captures a love-at-first-sight moment. The setting is particular. The 'top of the market' – *ceann tí an mhargaidh* – poet Nuala Ní Dhomhnaill says 'is still a noted landmark in the middle of Macroom and every time I pass it, I start murmuring parts of this great poem to myself. More to the point, the site of such nuptial bliss described by Eibhlín Dubh, is still extant in Art Ó Laoghaire's house in Rathleigh, near Macroom.'

A phrase such as 'My eyes covered you' captures the speaker's immediate and infatuated response to the man who she would leave all for:

> My love
> The first time I saw you
> From the top of the market
> My eyes covered you
> My heart went out to you
> I left my friends for you
> Threw away my home for you

Five of the stanza's seven lines appropriately end with 'you', for it is 'you' who is the object of the speaker's desire.

However, at the outset, it might be useful to consider the poem's structure. To facilitate discussion, it can be divided into the following sections:

Lines 1–32: The speaker remembers her lover/husband, how they met, all he did for her, why she loved him, his stylish presence and how he earned his enemies' respect.

Lines 33–74: His murder and how she learned of his death. Her rushing to his side, how she kisses his body, drinks his blood and remembers the last time she saw him alive.

Lines 75–95: The speaker summons her dead husband to come back to life and paints a noble picture of him on horseback.

Line 96–102: The speaker curses her husband's murderer and speaks of her two children and one yet unborn whom she fears for.

Line 103–11: Her regret that she was not with her husband when he was shot and how she wished she had been killed instead.

Lines 112–48: Her own grief and heartbreak and how others would grieve, too. Life goes on, but the speaker says that she will never be healed.

Lines 149–75: The speaker describes Art O'Leary's distinguished family background and how she thought that she would always protect him.

Lines 176–88: The speaker's strange vision of a desolate landscape, her dying husband, his spreading blood.

Lines 189–216: The speaker's belief that Jesus Christ is on her side, her decision not to mourn her husband in a conventional way; her determination to seek justice, revenge; she acknowledges the power of poetry in remembering Art O'Leary.

Section 1 (lines 1–32) conjures up happy, domestic images of their young, married life. All was done 'for me' – good rooms, fresh trout, choice meat, best beds.

> You made the whole world
> Pleasing to me
>
> White rider of love!

Her portrait of her husband on horseback, with his silver-hilted sword, beaver hat, friendly homespun suit, a pin of glinting silver glittering in his shirt cuts a dashing, stylish figure. His travel overseas and his military background add other interesting dimensions. That single line, 'White rider of love!', is an intense, passionate utterance.

Section 2 (lines 33–74) remembers the dreadful day of her husband's murder and how she learned of it when his riderless horse returned home. Details such as

'Her bridle dragging ground/Her head with your startling blood/Your blood upon the saddle/You rode in your prime' create a poignant picture, while the urgency in the repeated pronoun and the verb 'leaped' give the moment drama.

> I didn't wait to clean it
> I leaped across my bed
> I leaped then to the gate
> I leaped upon your mare

The speaker comes across as a strikingly fearless individual. She goes alone and immediately to find her husband. That she 'drinks' his 'free blood' is an intimate act with religious connotations.

This mentions her memory of his 'Going out the gate' that morning, his kissing his family goodbye and saying 'I'll not be home again', which she thought a joke. That she calls him 'my laughing man' suggests that he was happy, good-humoured, easy in himself, but now she realises that he will not come home again.

Section 3 (lines 75–95) brings her husband back to life. The speaker addresses 'My Art O'Leary/ Up on your horse now'. The words 'Rise up' suggest resurrection and the physical description of her well-dressed husband riding through Macroom and Inchigeela emphasises the strong connection between O'Leary and his homeplace. The exaggerated details in 'Every bush will salute you/ Every stream will speak to you' are understandable in context and she knows that 'Men and women acknowledge you// They know a great man/ When they set eyes on him.'

Section 4 (lines 96–102) shifts from praise to cursing. It imagines her husband in his prime and is filled with hatred for his murderer. The use of the word 'swept' (in 'You swept my man from me') highlights the suddenness of his death. That she has two young children and is pregnant with a third, whom she believes 'won't come alive from me', earns the reader's sympathy.

Section 5 (lines 103–11) expresses her deep love for her husband, a love so great that she wishes that she were with him 'When you were shot/ That I might take the bullet'. Her feisty nature is also seen is her imagining how if she had died instead of him:

> Then you'd have gone free
> Rider of the grey eye
> And followed them
> Who'd murdered me

Section 6 (lines 112–48) focuses on the contrast between the vibrant Art O'Leary when he lived and the dead man in his coffin: he once 'fished the clean steams/ Drank nightlong in halls/ Among frank-breasted women', while line 120 – 'I miss you' – on its own, is simple, direct and powerful. She knows that life does go on: 'The corn is stacked/ The cows are milking' but 'My heart is a lump of grief'.

Section 7 (lines 149–75) tells of Art O'Leary's family background. The O'Learys lived close to and in tune with nature and, picturing a happier time in the past, the speaker tells us that Art was a 'robust hunter' and so accomplished that 'Your own hounds lagged behind you'. That picture is shattered when the new reality intrudes: 'My only whole belief/ Was that you could not die/ For I was your protection'. And, once again, using single, standalone lines, this section ends with intensity.

> My heart! My grief!
>
> My man! My darling!

The poet's use of the exclamation mark and the repeated 'My' convey deep anguish.

Section 8 (lines 176–88) contains a 'vision' that is more nightmare. The speaker – 'Lying in my bed' – sees a bare and withered landscape. The hunting hounds, mentioned earlier (line 168), are now strangled and the birds are choked and Art O'Leary is seen:

> Dying on a hillside
> Art O'Leary
> My one man
> Your blood running crazily
> Over earth and stone

Here, the speaker is haunted by his death and it is as if everything in the natural world has died too.

Section 9 (lines 189–216) concludes this version of the eighteenth-century Irish poem. Like Kennelly's 'Oliver to his Brother', the events can be dated specifically, in this instance to 4 May 1773, but the poem goes beyond historical fact and becomes a deeply personal love poem within an historical context. The poem celebrates a woman's great love for her husband and hero; 'My man' is repeated again and again throughout the poem. Five stanzas begin with those words and 'my man' are also the poem's final words.

Line 189 speaks of Jesus Christ and how he is understanding of her plight. She will wear neither mourning cap, nor mourning dress, there will be 'No grief-signs in my house'. The tone here is defiant. The speaker will concentrate her energies on finding justice. She will 'test instead/ The wisdom of the law'. She will go to nay lengths:

> 'I'll cross the sea/ To speak to the King' and if that does not work –
> 'If he ignores me' – 'I'll come back home/ To find the man/
> Who murdered my man.'

Nuala Ní Dhomhnaill in her Ireland Chair of Poetry lecture said of the original 'Ag Caoineadh Airt Uí Laoghaire': 'On 4 May 1773, Art Ó Laoghaire, a young hot-blooded captain in the Hungarian Hussars, back from service on the continent and outlawed because of a bitter quarrel with Abraham Morris, the High Sheriff of Cork, was shot at Carraig an Ime, County Cork. The quarrel was over a horse, which Morris, according to the penal laws in force at the time, wanted to buy from Ó Laoghaire for five pounds. This was the maximum value of a horse that a Catholic could own, according to the law. The event was to everyone except the immediate victims, a more-or-less minor episode in a time of more serious injustices. We would probably not know anything much about it, were it not for the fact that it became the occasion of one of the great laments and also love poems of all time – 'Ag Caoineadh Airt Uí Laoghaire', the 'Lament for Art O'Leary', composed by his young widow. Eibhlín Dubh Ní Chonaill...whether it was written at all, or was composed basically as an oral performance; whether, indeed, it was actually composed by Eibhlín Dubh herself – these are all moot points, and a source of major contention to many great scholars at the moment, and I will not deem to point my toe where angels fear to tread. But it does exist...[and is a work with] vivacity, intense grief, and remarkable immediacy and verve.'

Things I Might Do

This is but one poem from the 584-poem sequence in a 440-page book called *The Book of Judas* (1991). Many of the poems are from Judas's point of view.

The unnamed speaker in stanza 1 is in an uncertain mood. The heart, a familiar symbol for one's emotional life, is troubling the speaker. The first-person voice wonders if his heart might become October-like; he remarks that he might 'make it into a month like October'. This month is associated with the dying of the year; this could suggest that the speaker's heart is ready to die.

> I thought of things I might do with my heart.
> Should I make it into a month like October,
> A chalice for the sad madness of leaves
> That I might raise in homage to the year's end?

In a surreal imagining, the heart becomes a chalice to contain the 'sad madness of leaves'. In a poem that features Judas, the image of the chalice could perhaps echo the cup used at the Last Supper before Judas betrayed Jesus Christ. And yet the speaker tells us that he might honour 'the year's end' because he has lived to see it.

Stanza 1 ended with a question and stanza 2 begins with one. Here the speaker wonders if the heart could become a quiet, prayerful place:

> Should I make it into a small white church in
> A country-place where bells are childhood prayers?

Here the speaker is remembering time past – childhood – a time that could be interpreted from images such as 'white church', 'bells', an innocent and holy place.

Stanza 2 then offers a dramatic contrast and the questioning continues. Will the speaker turn the heart into a month, a chalice, a church?

> Or a backroom of a brothel in Dublin
> Where the trade of something like love endures?

This shift of focus from church to brothel, from a place of prayer to a place of sordid sex, reminds the reader of the heart's complexities. The title of the poem ('Things I Might Do') offers possibilities and now, even though the speaker has listed them, the reader is still unsure what the speaker will do.

Another option is presented at line 9: 'Should I make it a judge to judge itself?' Similarly, line 10 contains another example of things I might do: 'Or a caring face in a memory-storm?' If the heart were to become such a caring face in a memory-storm, who might it be remembering?

The final suggestion is a bed for Judas and the deliberate line-break not only indicates a break in the flow but perhaps the final and best choice among the many things listed already:

> Or a bed
>
> For Judas dreaming of the tree

If the speaker's heart becomes a bed for Judas, then Judas might find rest there.

The closing lines, in inverted commas, introduce another speaking voice in the poem. It is never made clear who is speaking these comforting, soothing lines:

> 'There now, there now, rest as best you can,
> Darling, rest your treacherous head
> And when you've rested, come home to me.'

The voice is gentle. Kennelly, elsewhere, has said that 'Nature caresses us. Like our mother', and perhaps it is Mother Nature speaking to Judas. Or perhaps it is the tree? And is this the tree on which Judas hanged himself? Perhaps it is Christ speaking? It is not entirely clear and remains open to interpretation.

That voice in the closing lines uses terms such as of 'Darling' and 'treacherous' contradictory words indicative of the speaker's loving, forgiving nature and that Judas is recognised for his act of betrayal.

The poem, perhaps, could be read as a poem in which Judas speaks of his confusion, his longing and his search for release and comfort. The closing lines appear to offer comfort and release.

A Great Day

Some events are momentous. You'll never forget the year you did your Leaving Certificate and you'll never forget the year you marry (should you decide to). 'A Great Day' presents us with a series of snapshots from a wedding day and the poem's title leaves us in no doubt that this is an important and happy occasion. The title is taken from the bride's quoted words in the closing line.

The wedding is a conventional one: a church wedding, the bride wears white, the groom wears a dignified blue; there are a large number of guests, food, drink and song. But the poem goes beyond description and explores how such a significant day changes those who were part of that special event.

The poem begins with a familiar image: 'She was all in white.' But the poem then moves from the picture of a bride, as we might imagine her, to the speaker's thoughts on the nature of language. A snow metaphor to capture the bride's dress is rejected because it is too jaded and clichéd: 'Snow/ Suggests itself as metaphor// But since this has been so often said/ I may be justified in considering it dead./ Something about snow is not quite right.' Perhaps snow is also rejected for its wintry, cold associations. The speaker, therefore, rejects metaphor for the plain, simple statement:

> Therefore, she was all in white.

The location is never specified, but the brief glimpse we are given of the lead-up to the wedding day suggests a traditional courtship, a solemn and serious ceremony. We are told that:

> They came together, as is habitual
> In that part of the world,
> Through a grave ritual,
>
> Listening
> With at least a modicum of wonder –
> What God has joined together
> Let no man put asunder.

The speaker, while witnessing the union, tells us that he listens with 'at least a modicum of wonder'. This muted response reveals something interesting about the speaker. He is not in total awe of the moment, but he still finds that there is something wonderful when man and woman are united in marriage.

The couplet 'Man in woman, woman in man./ Soon afterwards, the fun began' marks the end of the serious religious ceremony and the beginning of the wedding reception. In a fifty-line poem, at line 20 we read the line 'It was a great day' and those words close the poem.

The second part of the poem focuses on 'Long hours of Dionysiac festivity'.

Songs poured, praises flowed and even more important, something changed inside people:

> The people there
> Seemed to see each other in a new way.
> This added to the distinction of the day.

The married couple has created a positive atmosphere and there are jaunty details in how the speaker lists aspects of the wedding – song, speech, sip, bite and the white dress, the blue suit.

> Such whiteness seems both beautiful and true
> He thought, all dickied up in dignified blue.

Here the rhythm matches the couple's harmony and this is continued when the speaker enters the woman's mind and presents us with her thoughts. Even the pun in 'Down to the ground' adds to the easy, relaxed mood of the day.

> He looks so good in blue
> (This warmed her mind)
> Blue suits him
> Down to the ground.

If this poem were filmed, it would involve close-ups and wide-angle shots and in its closing section images of the guests, a 'loud crowd' singing and dancing:

> The whole day long, the whole night long

This contrasts with more intimate shots of the bride whispering to her husband. The final lines bring us to the train, which carries the married couple into the future. The white dress is no more and in one of the few stand-alone lines in the poem we read that 'He never saw the white dress again'.

Rain and reticence are mentioned in relation to their first journey together as man and wife, and there is a sense of relief. Their future is before them, the trees are 'silent guests' in contrast to the loud roaring of the wedding. They are together:

> A tide of thoughts flowed in her head,
> In his head

And though we hear the bride's voice earlier in the poem, her words in that final line are placed within inverted commas for special emphasis.

> 'Darling, it was a great day,' she said.

The poem charts 'a whole day long, the whole night long' and leaves us with a sense of a man and woman well-suited and united, each with their own thoughts, but thoughts that are in harmony with each other. The phrase 'A tide of thoughts flowed' conjures up an image of timelessness.

Fragments

This poem comes immediately after 'A Great Day' in *The Essential Brendan Kennelly: Selected Poems* and offers a contrasting view of a couple's relationship.

The title suggests something broken and shattered; the poem portrays a sixty-year-old man contemplating his relationship with 'the woman he believed he had known'. We are not given hard facts – their names, where they live – or why their relationship has come to this. What we are given is a portrait of loneliness, confusion, old age, sadness. The poem is told in the third voice not first – 'he' not 'I' – and avoids self-pity; the speaker describes the situation with sympathetic engagement.

The bleak question in line 1 – 'What had he to say to her now?' – is never answered, but the poem reveals an estrangement. Their relationship had ended. Stanza 1 contains several happy images of times spent together, but they belong to the past. Lines such as

> In a street, out walking, by the sea,
> In bed, working, dancing, loving the sun

conjure up a loving companionable togetherness. The sense of freshness and newness is captured in the line, 'And saying so, always for the first time?'

The speaker tells us that this man believed he had known and understood this woman then. He remembers their shared life, how familiar, repeated things never became jaded. But all of that has changed. She has become 'this stranger with the graven face.'

Some details in the poem mention different places and how 'the dreaming-up of a home' was once a shared dream. However, each line in stanza 2 asks a question. There is now 'this stranger with the graven face' and 'Who was/ That man...At the side of the fire, quietly dying?'

The man is shown alone within a domestic setting ('At the side of the fire') – he is alone and asks 'what was he, at sixty?', and when he goes for a walk, he walks alone.

The poem, with its two four-line stanzas and two three-line stanzas, is a broken sonnet. The first three stanzas are linked with their run-on lines (line 4 leads to line 5; line 8 leads to line 9), but the final stanza which paints a picture of loss and loneliness is all the more lonely for being on its own.

> He listened to his own steps in the walk
> Past the reedy mud where plover rose
> And scattered, black fragments, crying.

That final stanza echoes with his own steps. The outer world, the landscape with its 'reedy mud' and 'scattered, black fragments' of plover, expresses an inner emotional one. Placing 'crying' as the poem's final word not only leaves the reader with a feeling of sadness and sorrow but becomes one of the dominant moods in the poem.

The soul's loneliness

The title becomes the poem's first line and so 'soul' and 'loneliness' are not given capital letters. This is appropriate in this instance in that it is a poem that doesn't dwell on the exuberant, celebrating soul but a soul that knows aloneness, isolation and loneliness.

The speaker recognises this feeling and the mood is one of acceptance: 'it's nothing to go on about.' But the poem then presents us with moments that emphasise the speaker's awareness of being lonely. These are ordinary moments – 'the ticking of the clock', 'the shine/ of an Eason's plastic bag at midnight', or 'in the tree I call/ Christ there outside my window' – but the clock, plastic bag and tree heighten a loneliness within him. The reference to books and photographs suggests a rich intellectual life, a world of family and friends, but loneliness cannot always be kept at bay.

The speaker hears, sees and touches this loneliness – it is a palpable, unmistakable thing. Details such as 'midnight' and 'the day's afterglow' add to the atmosphere, while the tree 'I call Christ' suggests a spiritual dimension and belief.

The first three stanzas present us with lonely situations. The concluding two stanzas, with their end-rhymes, focus on the speaker's physical self

> I shiver a little at the strangeness
> of my flesh, the smell of sweat,
> the child's poem I'll never forget

Here we are given a sense of the speaker's awareness of his flesh, sweat and by implication his mortality. Memory, however, redeems the moment. There is 'the child's poem I'll never forget'. A poem by a child symbolises creativity, imagination, potential and possibility. That the speaker, aware of his loneliness, will never forget this poem introduces a positive note.

That memory of 'the child's poem' also prompts the speaker to search for grace. He looks for goodness and forgiveness, and the poem's closing line suggests that the speaker also searches for 'a trace of yourself I've never noticed before'. The poem reaches out beyond 'the soul's loneliness' and the speaker wants to connect with this unnamed other person who is both absent and present. That 'trace of yourself I've never noticed before' allows the poem to end on a quietly optimistic note. The words 'a trace of yourself' could also refer to the speaker himself and his awareness of an aspect of himself that is redemptive.

Saint Brigid's Prayer *(from the Irish)*

Brendan Kennelly's poetry contains many voices. In 'Saint Brigid's Prayer', Brigid, a fifth-century Irish saint, speaks of her vision of Heaven, a place usually portrayed as populated by fluffy clouds, harp-playing angels and a host of individuals wearing white.

The poem sounds an upbeat, surprising note at the outset and that mood is sustained though the six stanzas. From the opening line, we know that this is an unconventional prayer. St. Brigid would:

> like to give a lake of beer to God.

Beer-drinking is something that most of us would not associate with Heaven and 'tippling there/ for all eternity' also pokes fun at our assumptions regarding Heaven.

The speaker paints a happy picture of Heaven that involves drinking, dancing and singing, and the regular end rhymes add to that sense of harmony. Saint Brigid is clear in what she prays for – 'I'd like...I'd love... I'd make...I'd make...I'd like...I'd give...I'd sit' – and the poem's final sentence is inclusive: 'We'd be drinking good health forever/ and every drop would be a prayer'.

Saint Brigid, a giving individual, would like 'the men of Heaven to live with me,/ to dance and sing'; she would 'like Jesus to love me too'. It is a social place. Her list of what she would give to God and 'the men of Heaven' includes the contrasting 'vats of suffering' and 'sweet pitchers of mercy'. These details introduce a realistic note. Heaven, as envisaged by Brigid, is not only the lake of beer but a place where suffering and mercy are remembered.

> If they wanted, I'd put at their disposal
> vats of suffering.

And:

> sweet pitchers of mercy I'd offer
> to every man.

Above all, Brigid wants to make 'Heaven a cheerful spot/ because the happy heart is true./ I'd make the men contented for their own sake./ I'd like Jesus to love me too'.

The first four stanzas speak of God, men and Jesus, and women are introduced in stanza 5: 'I'd like the people of Heaven to gather/ from all the parishes around./ I'd give a special welcome to the women,/ the three Marys of great renown.' The phrase 'all the parishes around' is one familiar to Irish ears and we are presented with a Heavenly scene that brings people together: 'the men, the women and God'.

That strange wish – 'to give a lake of beer to God' – mentioned in line 1 is found again in the closing lines, and prayer and beer come together in the final line where Brigid's wish, while 'We'd be drinking good health forever', is that 'every drop would be a prayer'. The idea of 'drinking good health forever' is more wishful thinking than practical, but Heaven is a different place and Saint Brigid's version of it is certainly different.

D.H. Lawrence
(1885–1930)

Contents	Page

The Overview

These eleven poems by D.H. Lawrence cover over twenty years. *The Collected Poems of D.H. Lawrence* was first published in two volumes in 1928 (and in a single volume the following year). The poems 'Call into Death', 'Piano', 'The Mosquito', 'Snake' and 'Humming-Bird' are from Volume I; 'Intimates', 'Delight of Being Alone', 'Absolute Reverence', 'What Have They Done to You?', 'Trailing Clouds' and 'Bavarian Gentians' are from Volume II.

Lawrence wrote in a preface to *Collected Poems*, dated 12 May 1928, that 'The crisis of Volume I is the death of the mother, with the long haunting of death in life, which continues to the end, through all the last poems.' Death and loss feature in 'Call into Death', while in 'Piano' a son remembers his childhood and his mother playing a piano and singing on Sunday evenings. The setting for those very early poems is English, but 'The Mosquito' and 'Snake' are set in Italy and 'Humming-Bird' was completed in New Mexico in the United States. 'Intimates' enacts a little drama between unhappy lovers; in 'Delight of Being Alone', Lawrence celebrates solitude; and 'Absolute Reverence' is a celebration of the mystery of our origins. In 'What Have They Done to You?', an urgent voice addresses and urges the working class not to be enslaved by a system. 'Trailing Clouds' captures the thoughts and sensations of a man holding a vulnerable, weeping baby at the beginning of its life. It was written about his landlady's baby in London in 1909. 'Bavarian Gentians' is about last things and the approaching darkness of death. In the *Collected Poems*, a poem called 'Glory of Darkness' preceded 'Bavarian Gentians' and it was followed by 'Ship of Death'.

Though you are encountering D.H. Lawrence through words on a page, there is something so extraordinarily alive and immediate in the writing that the energy of the man always shines through. Lawrence is always very present in his work; he speaks with a refreshing directness and intensity: 'My great religion is a belief in the blood, the flesh, as being wiser than the intellect...what our blood feels and believes and says, is always true. The intellect is only a bit and a bridle...I conceive a man's body as a kind of flame, like a candle flame forever upright and yet flowing: and the intellect is just the light that is shed on the things around. And I am not so much concerned with the things around – which is really mind – but with the mystery of the flame forever flowing...' (Lawrence, in a letter dated 17 January 1913).

Richard Aldington in his introduction to *Last Poems and More Pansies* (1932) praises Lawrence's work: 'how fluid, how personal, how imperfect, a series of inconclusive adventures only related because they all happened to the same man. There is nothing static about this – everything flows...Lawrence's writing was not something outside himself, it was part of himself, it came out of his life and in turn fed his life. He adventured into himself in order to write, and by writing discovered himself.'

In a letter dated 17 July 1908, Lawrence wrote: 'my verses are tolerable – rather pretty, but not suave; there is some blood in them. Poetry nowadays seems to be a sort of plaster-cast craze, scraps sweetly moulded in easy Plaster of Paris sentiment. Nobody chips verses earnestly out of the living rock of his own feeling...Before everything I like sincerity, and a quickening spontaneous emotion.'

In a preface to *New Poems* (American edition, 1918), Lawrence identifies two kinds of poetry: a poetry that is perfect and complete and formal in structure and 'another kind of poetry: the poetry of that which is at hand: the immediate present' and Lawrence believed that, 'In the immediate present there is no perfection, no consummation, nothing finished...Life, the ever-present, knows no finality, no finished crystallisation...Give me nothing fixed, set, static.' In other words, Lawrence believed in the poetry of now and he thought that free verse was the best and most effective way of expressing himself in his poetry. 'It seems to me that no poetry, not even the best, should be judged as if it existed in the absolute, in the vacuum of the absolute. Even the best poetry, when it is at all personal, needs the penumbra of its own time and place and circumstance to make it full and whole.' (D.H. Lawrence in 1928, in the preface to *Collected Poems*.)

Lawrence believed that his novels and poems were 'pure passionate experience' and in 1919 wrote: 'in free verse we look for the insurgent naked throb of the instant moment...It is the instant; the quick; the very jetting source of all will-be and has-been. The utterance is like a spasm, naked contact with all influences at once. It does not want to get anywhere. It just takes place.'

This urgency means that D.H. Lawrence, as the British writer James Reeves puts it, 'can seldom have conceived a poem as a whole before he sat down to write it. It grew under his pen.' Poet and novelist Elaine Feinstein says that Lawrence is one of those poets who 'always renew my alertness to the world around me.'

D.H. Lawrence (right) with his wife Frieda and John Middleton Murray in 1914.

Biographical Notes

David Herbert Lawrence, novelist, poet, essayist, travel writer and playwright, was born, the son of a miner and the fourth of five children – three boys, two girls – in Eastwood, Nottinghamshire, in England on 11 September 1885. In his novel *The White Peacock*, Lawrence writes 'I was born in September, and love it best of all the months. There is no heat, no hurry, no thirst and weariness in corn harvest as there is in hay...The mornings come slowly. The earth is like a woman...she does not leap up with a laugh for the first fresh kiss of dawn, but slowly, quietly, unexpectedly lies watching the waking of each new day.'

D.H. Lawrence's father, Arthur, who began working in the colliery aged ten, 'hated books, hated the sight of anyone reading or writing.' However, his mother, Lydia Beardsall, was intelligent, quick-witted, ambitious and was, by age thirteen, a pupil-teacher. It was she who encouraged her son. Arthur and Lydia had met at a Christmas party, they married a year later and it was seen as 'marrying beneath her'.

Lawrence (between his parents) as a young boy.

Of the five Beardsall daughters, Lydia was the only one to marry into the working class. Her marriage to a handsome, muscular, non-intellectual was not a happy one and John Worthen in his biography, *D.H. Lawrence: The Life of an Outsider*, says that 'many of Lawrence's problems and the sources of his unhappiness, as well as his creativity, were acted out from the start in the troubled marriage of Lydia and Arthur...the terrible conflicts of opposites: intellectual and physical, controlled and passionate, strict and carefree, genteel-minded and working class.' Lydia Lawrence, a great reader, wanted her sons to become 'respectable', at least clerks, and not go down the mines.

Though Lawrence started school aged three years and four months, his delicate health meant irregular school attendance. He also disliked school when he was there, kept to himself, was lonely and was nicknamed 'Mardy', a mother's boy. But at home he was different; he was lively and creative, and his sister Ada said that, 'It seemed inevitable that Bert should spend his life creating things.' Aged twelve, Lawrence won a scholarship to Nottingham High School, but as a miner's son among middle-class children he felt different and left before his sixteenth birthday without having achieved much academic success. Later, Lawrence, aged twenty-four, would say that 'my youth was the most acute and painful time I shall ever see, I'll bet.'

He began work in the autumn of 1901 as a warehouse clerk at a surgical goods factory in Nottingham and in *Sons and Lovers* his description of Paul Morel's working day mirrored his own. That same autumn, his older brother Ernest died of the inflammatory disease erysipelas. Around the same time, Lawrence contracted pneumonia. Lydia nursed him back to health and, having recovered, he trained to become a pupil-teacher at seventeen at the British Schools in Eastwood. It was during this time that the affection between Lydia and her third son David would reach a new intensity, so much so that when Lydia Lawrence died in 1910, in a letter he wrote: 'We have loved each other, almost with a husband and wife love, as well as filial and maternal. We knew each other by instinct.' Again, this is a relationship fully explored in *Sons and Lovers* published in 1913.

In the classroom, Lawrence found himself teaching working-class boys like the very boys who mocked him when he himself was in school. His poem 'Last Lesson of the Afternoon' begins 'When will the bell ring. And end this weariness?/ How long have they tugged the leash, and strained apart,/ My pack of unruly hounds!' and he discovered that he had 'to fight bitterly for my authority'. He taught for nine years. During that time, Lawrence became friendly with the large Chambers family who lived on a farm. He became very much part of the household, cooking and washing, and it was where he also began to paint. His mother and sisters resented his frequent visits, but he continued going and Jessie Chambers and he became close through their deep love of reading. Meeting frequently at the library, he would walk her the three miles home, talking books: novels but also poetry. In spring 1905, D.H. Lawrence also began to write. He later remarked that one Sunday afternoon 'I "composed" my first two "poems".' And his signature, from this time on, was the professional looking 'D.H. Lawrence' or 'DHL', though, at first, he kept his writing secret from everyone except Jessie. It was thought that

Jessie and Lawrence would marry, but she was far more interested in him than he was in her; in 1905, when Lawrence was twenty, he told Jessie that he could not love her as a husband should love his wife and their relationship changed forever. Lawrence now, just before he attended Nottingham University where he would study for his teacher's certificate and be disappointed ('I might as well be taught by gramophones as by those men, for all the interest or sincerity they felt'), turned to writing a novel, even writing parts of it during lectures; this eventually became *The White Peacock*. He also began writing short stories. At university, he was a founder member of a socialist group – 'lost forever my sincere boyish reverence for men in position' – and became increasingly disillusioned with organised religion, rejecting the idea of a personal God, and instead thought it better 'to establish one's own religion in one's heart.'

He eventually found a job in October 1908 in a boys' school in Croydon, thirty minutes by train from London. It was his first time away from home and he was glad to get away and yet he returned again and again to the midlands in his writing. But the teaching proved challenging: 'Think of a quivering greyhound set to mind a herd of pigs and you see me teaching', he wrote in a letter. In time, however, he mastered things and when an inspector visited Lawrence's classroom unannounced one day he discovered curious sounds beneath a blackboard in a far corner. The class were reading Shakespeare's *The Tempest* and the boys were singing a song from the play, 'Full fathom five thy father lies'. Lawrence rushed towards the visitor saying 'Hush! Hush! Don't you hear? The sea chorus from *The Tempest.*'

However, writing took over from teaching. In 1909, Lawrence had some poems published in *The English Review* and his first novel was also accepted for publication; that same year he met H.G. Wells, Ezra Pound and W.B. Yeats. He also renewed his relationship with Jessie Chambers; they now became physically intimate, but Lawrence ended their relationship early in 1910. Soon afterwards, his mother became very ill with cancer and she died in December that same year. 'I have died, a bit of me,' wrote Lawrence to Louie Burrows, a teacher whom he had known since college, whom he had proposed to and who accepted just days before his mother's death.

In January, Lawrence's first novel, *The White Peacock*, was published. He was earning £95 a year; Louie earned £90. They were supposedly saving to get married, but Lawrence was also involved with other women at this time. The year 1911 was later described by Lawrence as 'ghastly' and 'dreadful'; he began to drink, claiming that 'a drinking bout' was 'better than a bout of ferocious blues'. Back in the classroom, he found in August 1911 that teaching 'wearies me to death'. Though still involved with Louie Burrows, he began an affair with Alice Dax, a married woman. In November, Lawrence developed double pneumonia, was very ill, survived, but never returned to teaching. He hoped at this point to earn his living from his writing. In January 1912, he broke off his engagement to Louie: 'I ask you to dismiss me. I am afraid we are not well suited.' They met for the last time in February and never saw each other again.

He worked hard at *Sons and Lovers*, wrote short stories, and planned to go to Germany once he had submitted his novel. He contacted Professor Ernest Weekley who had taught him at Nottingham University for advice. Weekley invited him to lunch and when he met Frieda, his German-born wife and mother of the three Weekley children, his life changed. He was 27; she was 33. Frieda was unconventional. Though married, she had had love affairs, but did not abandon her husband for Lawrence immediately. Sexually liberated and carefree, Lawrence thought her 'the woman of a lifetime'. They became lovers, spent time in Germany together, where he wrote her poems and then they travelled to Italy. In Gargnano, Lawrence worked and re-worked *Sons and Lovers*. It was a happy time, but in choosing Lawrence, Frieda had to give up her children, which was heartbreaking for her and the Weekley children caused huge tensions in their relationship. They went back to Germany, where they still quarrelled about the children. They returned to England but Frieda, denied access to her children, eventually set off for Germany and Italy, this time settling in a little fishing village on the gulf of Spezia. Once her divorce was granted, Lawrence and Frieda were married in London on 13 July 1914, though nobody from Lawrence's family attended. However, Lawrence, now with lucrative book contracts, enjoyed an expanding literary circle. While on a walking tour of the Lake District with three male friends, news came in early August that war had been declared and Lawrence's 'old great belief in the oneness and wholeness of humanity' was 'torn clean across, for ever'.

When *The Rainbow* was published the following year (1915), it met with a hostile reception, with one reviewer commenting that it was 'a greater menace to our public health than any of the epidemic diseases'. Libraries did not buy it and the police confiscated all undistributed copies from the publisher. Plans were made to go and live in Florida and establish a commune. Nothing came of it but a friend lent Lawrence and Frieda a house on the Cornish coast and on 31 December 1915 they headed west, once again uncertain of their future. They survived on what friends and family gave them, money from the Royal Literary Fund, some earnings from his writing. Their marriage was stormy, then calm, then stormy. When they quarrelled, they hit each other. Lawrence was ill again, but finished *Women in Love* in October. The novel was rejected by several publishers and he revised it significantly before it was eventually published in 1921.

As the war worsened, the Lawrences were viewed with suspicion; she was German; he hadn't been conscripted; were they spies? The police searched their house and, though no evidence of wrongdoing was found, they were told to leave Cornwall. Back in London, they were put under police surveillance and for the next two years stayed in numerous places lent to them by friends until eventually his sister provided them with a cottage in the midlands. In 1912 they had left the midlands; now, in 1918, they were back where they had started and Lawrence's father met Frieda at Mountain Cottage for the first time. Called up for a third time to fight, Lawrence was deemed unfit for service but was disgusted by the medical examination and vowed that, 'They shall *not* touch me again'. In the spring of 1919, he almost died of a flu that killed millions across Europe. In October, Frieda left England for Germany, Lawrence following in November. In the ten and a half years that remained, Lawrence would only return to England three times for ten weeks in total. He led what the critic and academic Edna Longley calls 'a nomadic life: always seeking a utopian alternative to the restrictions and repression of England.'

For a while, Italy became their home. They stayed in several places, including Capri, and settled in Sicily. In Taormina, they rented the top half of Fontana Vecchia, a house outside the town; the owners, an Italian family, lived downstairs. They settled there in March 1920 and loved it — 'the sun rose with a splendour like trumpets every morning.' It was here that Lawrence wrote some of his finest poetry about the natural world, including 'Snake'. To escape the intense summer heat, Frieda visited family in Germany, while Lawrence visited northern Italy where he had an affair with an old acquaintance, Rosalind Baynes, mother of three children. During this time, he wrote many poems including what his biographer John Worthen calls the sexually outrageous 'Figs'; the poems were gathered together in *Birds, Beasts and Flowers*.

Increasingly disillusioned with England's response to his books, Lawrence turned to the United States when a wealthy woman admirer of his work invited the Lawrences to Taos in New Mexico and offered them a house to live in. Between 1920 and 1922, Lawrence had written eight books — two novels, a collection of short stories, two books on psychoanalysis, a book of three novellas, a travel book and a volume of poems. But first, Lawrence and Frieda travelled to Ceylon (now Sri Lanka) at the invitation of an American couple. Then they would go to New Mexico. Lawrence was thirty-six. He was putting Europe behind him.

The plan was to stay in Ceylon for a year, but they left after just six weeks and travelled to Perth, Australia on the invitation of Australians they had met on the boat to Ceylon. They spent three months in Australia where he wrote *Kangaroo* and then sailed for San Francisco arriving in September 1922. From there they travelled onward to Taos where they arrived on 11 September 1922, Lawrence's thirty-seventh birthday. Though he disliked it at first, he came to love New Mexico. They later travelled to Mexico where Lawrence began writing *The Plumed Serpent*.

Next to New York. The plan was for both to return to Europe but they had a blazing row, partly because Frieda wanted to see her children, and so she sailed alone and Lawrence travelled to Chicago, the west coast and then to Mexico where he was miserable for three months. In November, he sailed for England and when he arrived felt that he did not belong there any more. In January, Lawrence and Frieda went to Paris, then Germany, then England again, but Europe was 'weary and wearying' and, accompanied by the artist Dorothy Brett, they sailed back to the United States in March 1924. Lawrence had often spoken of forming an idealistic commune where like-minded people would live together. While in London, he invited friends to join Frieda and him in New Mexico. Only Brett agreed to join them in Taos where Mabel Luhan, an old friend, signed over a rundown ranch on Lobo mountain to Frieda which Lawrence himself set about restoring with Native American workmen. It was the first time in their lives that the Lawrences owned a home. He was 39; she was 45. By way of thanks, Lawrence presented Mabel with the manuscript of *Sons and Lovers*. (Later, she had a breakdown, sought therapy and handed over the manuscript by way of paying her analyst's bills.)

It was a life without creature comforts; rats and ants were a problem, and the nearest shop was half a day away on horseback. Nonetheless, Lawrence liked having 'big, unbroken spaces round me.' He was always writing, but in August 1924 he fell ill, spat up blood, signalling the tuberculosis that would kill him five years later. In September, his father died. By the following month, Frieda, Brett and Lawrence were in Mexico. They stayed in Oaxaca where he continued working on *The Plumed Serpent*, writing two or three thousand words a day and collapsed when he finished it and almost died. In Mexico city, they were told by a doctor that Lawrence had a year or two to live. He was very weak, wore rouge to hide his tuberculosis and had difficulty entering the United States.

He eventually recovered, began writing again (a play, essays) and in September they sailed once more for Europe – for the last time. He was forty. London, then the midlands, then Germany and Spotorno on the Italian Riviera where they rented a villa for four months. Lawrence's sister visited; Frieda's daughters did. Frieda had an affair with an Italian and continued to do so for years. Lawrence travelled to Capri where he met up with Dorothy Brett and, in Ravello, they had, what biographer John Worthen calls, 'some kind of miserable sexual relationship.' Brett left Lawrence in Ravello, returned to New Mexico, they corresponded but she never saw him again. Lawrence returned to Spotorno and travelled to Florence with Frieda and her daughters where they rented a villa, an hour away, for six months. It became their base for two years. There were more visits to Germany, London, Scotland and, back in Italy, he began his best-known and notorious novel, *Lady Chatterley's Lover*. He paid more attention also at this time to painting and wrote essays on the Etruscans. More illness followed and the Lawrences, once he recovered, went to Frieda's sister in Austria. Next Bavaria, then they returned to Italy. He now rewrote his 140,000-word novel, *Lady Chatterley*. This, the third version, he shortened and decided to publish himself in 1928; he advertised it and had 1,000 copies printed by a small Italian printing house. Yet another move, on this occasion to Switzerland for his health where he described himself as follows: 'Here I am, forty-two, with rather bad health; and a wife who is by no means the soul of patience...a stray individual with not much health, and not much money'. But *Chatterley* became a bestseller, Lawrence became a household name and it made him more money than he had made from all of his other works up until now. He invested his earnings in stocks and shares. He was also invited to write for newspapers and they paid very well. *Lady Chatterley* wasn't published in England until 1960 and Penguin Books was prosecuted for publishing it because of its sexual scandal and four-letter words. At the obscenity trial, the out-of-touch chief prosecutor is remembered for asking the jury if *Lady Chatterley's Lover* were a book 'you would even wish your wife or servants to read'. He failed to convince the jury and the publishers were acquitted.

From Switzerland, the Lawrences moved to the island of Port Cros on the French Riviera near Toulon. Here he was ill, confined to bed, and he wrote poems that would form his book called *Pensées* which he later retitled *Pansies*. Christmas 1928 and Lawrence was talking about returning to New Mexico. From Port Cros they moved to a hotel in Bandol for five months. In January, a package that Lawrence posted to his London agent containing the typescript of *Pansies* was seized by English postal authorities. The Home Secretary pronounced the work 'indecent' and Lawrence was given two months to answer the indecency charge. This he either refused or simply failed to do. An unexpurgated edition appeared later.

Lawrence travelled to Paris to arrange another printing of *Chatterley*, was ill again and they travelled south this time to Mallorca. They stayed two months – 'it is certainly good for my health'. An exhibition of Lawrence's paintings opened in London. He was too ill to travel but Frieda went. Lawrence, however, remained a target for the English authorities: the London art gallery was raided by police and the supposedly 'obscene' paintings were confiscated. Then staying in Florence with friends, Lawrence was outraged when he heard about this police action. Frieda returned and they both went onwards to Germany for Frieda's mother's seventy-fifth birthday. They accepted an invitation from a doctor-writer friend to visit Rottach-am-Tegernsee in the Bavarian Alps. Here Lawrence wrote one of his finest poems, 'Bavarian Gentians'. The couple returned to Bandol, rented a chalet-bungalow – 'wonderfully in the air and light' – and Lawrence felt better. Here he corrected proofs of his poetry collection *Nettles* and composed his last poems. In the end, in February 1930, Lawrence agreed to go to a mountain sanatorium in Vence where he had a view of the Mediterranean from his balcony. Jo Davidson, an American sculptor, visited and made a clay model of Lawrence's head. Lawrence's hatred of the institution meant that he and Frieda decided to rent the nearby Villa Robermond. They moved there on 1 March and it was where he died, aged forty-four, on 2 March; he was buried in Vence. In 1935, Lawrence's body was exhumed, cremated and supposedly brought to America to the ranch at Taos. This was overseen by Frieda's lover, later her husband, Angelo Ravagli, but Ravagli confessed, after Frieda's death in 1956, that he 'threw away the D.H. cinders' in France and filled the beautiful vase that Frieda had given him with ashes when he arrived in the United States. Is this true? Who knows? They are all dead now. Those ashes were sealed in a block of concrete in a shrine that Ravagli himself built on a hill just above the ranch and it was here that Frieda was also buried.

Lawrence produced a huge body of work, often writing 3,000 words a day. His first published work was a group of poems in *The English Review* in 1910.

Love Poems and Others, Lawrence's first volume of poetry, was published in 1913; another, *Amores*, was published in July 1916. *Look! We Have Come Through!* followed in November 1917 and *Bay* was published in 1919. Other collections include *Birds, Beasts and Flowers* (1923), and *Pansies and Nettles*. A *Collected Poems* was published in 1928. Although best-known for his novels, Lawrence's poetry, says Edna Longley, 'may be his finest achievement.'

POEMS

D.H. Lawrence wrote almost 800 poems. The eleven poems here are taken from *Collected Poems, Volumes I–II*, edited by Vivian de Sola Pinto and Warren Roberts. They are printed in the order in which they appear in the *Collected Poems*.

Call into Death

Since I lost you, my darling, the sky has come near,
And I am of it, the small sharp stars are quite near,
The white moon going among them like a white bird
     among snow-berries,
And the sound of her gently rustling in heaven like a
     bird I hear.

And I am willing to come to you now, my dear,   5
As a pigeon lets itself off from a cathedral dome
To be lost in the haze of the sky; I would like to come
And be lost out of sight with you, like a melting foam.

For I am tired, my dear, and if I could lift my feet,
My tenacious feet, from off the dome of the earth   10
To fall like a breath within the breathing wind
Where you are lost, what rest, my love, what rest!

📖 Glossary

Title: originally called 'Elegy', it was first published in 1916.

Line 10 tenacious feet: feet keeping firm hold.

❓ Questions

1. The speaker here is mourning a loved one. There are few biographical details and yet the feeling contained within the poem and the feelings communicated to the reader are powerful. In your opinion, how does the poet achieve this?

2. Why is the sky so important? Trace how the speaker refers to sky, stars, moon in stanza 1? Comment on the image of the white bird.

3. In stanza 1, the speaker uses the simile 'like a white bird' for the moon; in stanza 2, the image 'As a pigeon' is used to describe his longing.

4. 'I' occurs seven times in this twelve-line poem. What other words create a very personal and intimate tone?

5. In 'Call into Death', the structure and rhymes are conventional. Look at how each first word in each stanza moves the poem forward. Comment on the music created through rhythm and rhyme.

6. This poem could be described as a death wish. Would you agree? Do you think it is a gloomy poem? Why or why not? Explain your answer.

7. Comment on the speaker's frequent use of 'my' and the terms of endearment used throughout the poem.

8. Consider the use of the word 'lost' in the closing line and the repeated use of 'rest'. What is the effect of this?

9. The mourned one is never identified. Does this detract from or enhance your response to the poem? Give reasons for your answer.

Piano

Softly, in the dusk, a woman is singing to me;
Taking me back down the vista of years, till I see
A child sitting under the piano in the boom of the tingling
    strings
And pressing the small poised feet of a mother who smiles
    as she sings.

In spite of myself, the insidious mastery of song   5
Betrays me back, till the heart of me weeps to belong
To the old Sunday evenings at home with winter outside
And hymns in the cosy parlour, the tinkling piano our
    guide.

So now it is vain for the singer to burst into clamour
With the great black piano appassionato. The glamour   10
Of childish days is upon me, my manhood is cast
Down in the flood of remembrance, I weep like a child for
    the past.

Glossary

Line 2 vista: long succession of remembered events.

Line 5 insidious: underhand, seductive.

Line 9 clamour: loud continuous noise.

Line 10 appassionato: played with passion

D.H. Lawrence began working on 'Piano' when he was twenty-one and finished it, about 1911, when he was twenty-six.

? Questions

1. In this poem, why does the present give way to the past?

2. Describe in your own words the scene the speaker journeys back to in time. Do you find it a comforting, attractive scene? Give reasons for your answer. How would you describe the relationship between the speaker and his mother?

3. Why does the speaker resist returning to his childhood? Why does he not succeed?

4. Music is a powerful prompter of memories, according to the speaker. Would you agree?

5. How would you describe the speaker's tone in the final stanza? Comment on the word 'glamour'.

6. Why do you think D.H. Lawrence uses such long lines here?

7. Comment on the poem's final sentence. Do you think the speaker prefers childhood to adulthood? Give reasons for your answer.

8. Write a note on the word you find most interesting in the poem and explain your choice.

The Mosquito

When did you start your tricks,
Monsieur?

What do you stand on such high legs for?
Why this length of shredded shank,
You exaltation?   5

It is so that you shall lift your centre of gravity upwards
And weigh no more than air as you alight upon me,
Stand upon me weightless, you phantom?

I heard a woman call you the Winged Victory
In sluggish Venice.   10
You turn your head towards your tail, and smile.

How can you put so much devilry
Into that translucent phantom shred
Of a frail corpus?

Queer, with your thin wings and your streaming legs,   15
How you sail like a heron, or a dull clot of air,
A nothingness.

Yet what an aura surrounds you;
Your evil little aura, prowling, and casting numbness on
        my mind.
That is your trick, your bit of filthy magic: 20
Invisibility, and the anaesthetic power
To deaden my attention in your direction.

But I know your game now, streaky sorcerer.
Queer, how you stalk and prowl the air
In circles and evasions, enveloping me,   25
Ghoul on wings
Winged Victory.

Settle, and stand on long thin shanks
Eyeing me sideways, and cunningly conscious that I am
     aware,
You speck.   30

I hate the way you lurch off sideways into the air
Having read my thoughts against you.

Come then, let us play at unawares,
And see who wins in this sly game of bluff.
Man or mosquito.   35

You don't know that I exist, and I don't know that you
     exist.
Now then!

It is your trump,
It is your hateful little trump,
You pointed fiend,   40
Which shakes my sudden blood to hatred of you:
It is your small, high, hateful bugle in my ear.

Why do you do it?
Surely it is bad policy.
They say you can't help it.   45

If that is so, then I believe a little in Providence protect-
     ing the innocent.
But it sounds so amazingly like a slogan,
A yell of triumph as you snatch my scalp.

Blood, red blood,
Super-magical   50
Forbidden liquor.

I behold you stand
For a second enspasmed in oblivion.
Obscenely ecstasied
Sucking live blood,   55
My blood.

Such silence, such suspended transport,
Such gorging,
Such obscenity of trespass.

You stagger   60
As well as you may.
Only your accursed hairy frailty,
Your own imponderable weightlessness
Saves you, wafts you away on the very draught my anger
        makes in its snatching.

Away with a paean of derision,   65
You winged blood-drop.

Can I not overtake you?
Are you one too many for me,
Winged Victory?
Am I not mosquito enough to out-mosquito you?   70

Queer what a big stain my sucked blood makes
Beside the infinitesimal faint smear of you!
Queer, what a dim dark smudge you have disappeared
        into!

Siracusa

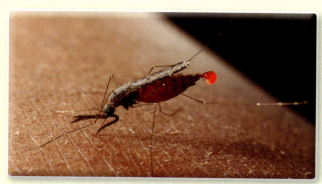

Glossary

Title Mosquito: a biting insect; the female of the species punctures the skin of humans and other animals with a long proboscis or elongated mouth to suck their blood and transmits diseases such as malaria. The title is sometimes printed without the definite article.

Line 2 Monsieur: though written in Italy, Lawrence chooses to address the mosquito in French.

Line 4 shank: leg.

Line 5 exaltation: rapturous emotion, literally – a lifting or raising up.

Line 8 phantom: ghost.

Line 9 Winged Victory: a Parian marble statue from the second century BC, now in the Louvre, depicting the Greek goddess Nike or Victory, a winged, triumphant (now headless figure) in flowing robes.

Line 10 sluggish Venice: slow-moving, and Venice because its waterways suit mosquitos.

Line 13 translucent: semi-transparent.

Line 14 corpus: body.

Line 15 queer: strange, odd.

Line 16 clot: lump.

Line 18 aura: a special atmosphere from a person or creature.

Line 21 anaesthetic power: deadening power, an ability to produce partial or complete lack of feeling/sensation.

Line 23 sorcerer: wizard, enchanter.

Line 26 Ghoul: a spirit preying on corpses.

Line 38 trump: advantage, especially involving a surprise; winning trick.

Line 40 fiend: devil.

Line 42 bugle: brass instrument; here, a sense of the mosquito's piercing sound.

Line 46 Providence: a sense of what is best to come.

Line 47 slogan: short, catchy cry.

Line 53 enspasmed: a word coined by Lawrence presumably from 'spasm' to convey a state of extreme bliss.

Line 53 oblivion: forgetfulness; the state of being forgotten.

Line 54 obscenely ecstasied: disgustingly delighted/rapturous.

Line 56 suspended transport: heightened joy.

Line 58 gorging: greedy feeding.

Line 59 trespass: unlawful intrusion.

Line 63 imponderable: cannot be estimated.

Line 64 wafts you: sweeps you lightly away.

Line 65 paean of derision: triumphant song of mockery, ridicule.

Line 70 out-mosquito: get the better/conquer.

Line 72 infinitesimal: very small.

> 'The Mosquito' was written in Syracuse in Sicily and is from Lawrence's collection *Birds, Beast and Flowers* (1923). Many of Lawrence's early poems were rhyming poems, but 'The Mosquito', written when he was thirty-two, is in free verse.

? Questions

1. What is your impression of the mosquito, as revealed in the opening lines of the poem?

2. The speaker asks several questions of the mosquito at the outset. What is the effect of this? Consider too, the questions in the poem's closing section and the exclamation marks.

3. He calls the mosquito 'Monsieur'; a woman in Venice called the mosquito 'the Winged Victory' (line 9). What do these descriptions add to your understanding of the insect?

4. The speaker describes the mosquito as 'evil' and 'filthy'. Which details best capture those qualities do you think?

5. In line 3, the mosquito stands on its high legs. At what stage in the poem does the mosquito fly?

6. The mosquito is called many things and described in many different ways. In line 17, it is a 'nothingness'. Yet in line 18 the mosquito has an 'aura'. Is this a contradiction? What kind of aura is the mosquito surrounded by?

7. Identify the different tones in the poem. How does the speaker create these tones? Which words capture the tone best?

8. When does the mosquito become aware of the speaker? Does the speaker think that he can get the better of the mosquito?

9. This is a poem in free verse – in other words, it does not follow a regular stanza structure and does not contain a regular rhyming scheme. 'The Mosquito,' says Michael Schmidt, 'erratically alternates long and short lines, attacks and retires.' Why might this technique suit this particular poem?

10. How would you sum up the relationship between the speaker and Monsieur Mosquito? Is Lawrence entertained, disgusted, bewildered? A mixture of these? Is he ever fond of the mosquito?

11. What do you think is meant by 'Am I not mosquito enough to out-mosquito you?' at line 70?

12. Comment on the difference between the opening and the closing line of the poem.

Snake

A snake came to my water-trough
On a hot, hot day, and I in pyjamas for the heat,
To drink there.

In the deep, strange-scented shade of the great dark carob-tree
I came down the steps with my pitcher   5
And must wait, must stand and wait, for there he was at
      the trough before me.

He reached down from a fissure in the earth-wall in the gloom
And trailed his yellow-brown slackness soft-bellied down,
    over the edge of the stone trough
And rested his throat upon the stone bottom,
And where the water had dripped from the tap, in a small
    clearness,   10
He sipped with his straight mouth,
Softly drank through his straight gums, into his slack long
    body,
Silently.

Someone was before me at my water-trough,   15
And I, like a second comer, waiting.

He lifted his head from his drinking, as cattle do,
And looked at me vaguely, as drinking cattle do,
And flickered his two-forked tongue from his lips, and
    mused a moment,
And stooped and drank a little more,   20
Being earth-brown, earth-golden from the burning bowels
    of the earth
Of the day of Sicilian July, with Etna smoking.

The voice of my education said to me
He must be killed,
For in Sicily the black, black snakes are innocent, the gold
     are venomous.   25

And voices in me said, If you were a man
You would take a stick and break him now, and finish
     him off.

But must I confess how I liked him,
How glad I was he had come like a guest in quiet, to drink
     at my water-trough
And depart peaceful, pacified and thankless,   30
Into the burning bowels of this earth?

Was it cowardice, that I dared not kill him?
Was it perversity, that I longed to talk to him?
Was it humility, to feel so honoured?
I felt so honoured.   35

And yet those voices:
If you were not afraid, you would kill him!

And truly I was afraid, I was most afraid,
But even so, honoured still more
That he should seek my hospitality   40
From out the dark door of the secret earth.

He drank enough
And lifted his head, dreamily, as one who has drunken,
And flickered his tongue like a forked night on the air, so
     black;
Seeming to lick his lips,   45
And looked around like a god, unseeing, into the air,
And slowly turned his head,

And slowly, very slowly, as if thrice adream,
Proceeded to draw his slow length curving round
And climb again the broken bank of my wall-face.   50

And as he put his head into that dreadful hole,
And as he slowly drew up, snake-easing his shoulders, and
    entered farther,
A sort of horror, a sort of protest against his withdrawing
    into that horrid black hole,
Deliberately going into the blackness, and slowly drawing
    himself after,
Overcame me now his back was turned.   55

I looked round, I put down my pitcher,
I picked up a clumsy log
And threw it at the water-trough with a clatter.

I think it did not hit him,
But suddenly that part of him that was left behind convulsed
    in undignified haste,   60
Writhed like lightning, and was gone
Into the black hole, the earth-lipped fissure in the wall-front,
At which, in the intense still noon, I stared with fascination.

And immediately I regretted it.
I thought how paltry, how vulgar, what a mean act!   65
I despised myself and the voices of my accursed human
    education.

And I thought of the albatross,
And I wished he would come back, my snake.

For he seemed to me like a king,
Like a king in exile, uncrowned in the underworld,   70
Now due to be crowned again.

And so, I missed my chance with one of the lords
Of life
And I have something to expiate;
A pettiness.   75

Taormina

📖 Glossary

Line 1 water-trough: long narrow open stone container for water.

Line 2 pyjamas: Lawrence wrote of his time in Taormina – 'I live in pyjamas, barefoot all day...or when I must put my suit of pyjamas in the tub, behold me *in puris naturabilis* [naked], performing the menial labours of the day'.

Line 4 carob-tree: Mediterranean evergreen tree.

Line 5 pitcher: large usually earthenware vessel.

Line 7 fissure: long, narrow opening.

Line 21 bowels: depths.

Line 22 Etna: the highest active volcano in Europe.

Line 25 venomous: poisonous.

Line 30 pacified: calmed.

Line 40 hospitality: friendly and kind response/reception.

Line 44 forked night: two-pronged darkness.

Line 48 thrice adream: in a very deep sleep dream.

Line 60 convulsed: shaking violently.

Line 61 Writhed: twisted and shrunk in pain.

Line 65 paltry: small, worthless.

Line 67 albatross: in Samuel Taylor Coleridge's poem 'The Rime of the Ancient Mariner', the mariner kills an albatross for no reason. The ship is cursed; the dead albatross was hung around the sailor's neck.

Line 74 expiate: make amends for.

Line 75 pettiness: something small and contemptible.

D.H. Lawrence wrote this poem while he was living in Sicily in a rented house high up overlooking the straits of Messina and the Ionian Sea. 'Here one feels as if one had lived for a hundred thousand years,' Lawrence wrote in a letter. In his biography *D.H. Lawrence: the Life of an Outsider* (2005), John Worthen mentions how Lawrence's landlord remembered how the writer's short journey to the well with a big terracotta jug would sometimes take him 'several hours'. He would 'loiter along the way and then relax on the little wall surrounding the reservoir, watching the other people come and go.'

In a note to the poem, titled 'Reptiles', Lawrence wrote: 'when Fire in its downward path chanced to mingle with the dark breath of the earth, the serpent slid forth, lay revealed. But he was moist and cold, the sun in him darted uneasy, held down by moist earth, never could he rise on his feet. And this is what put poison in his mouth. For the sun in him would fain rise halfway, and move on feet. But moist earth weighs him down, though he dart and twist, still he must go with his belly on the ground.'

? Questions

1. 'The setting is a dry place of intense heat. Explore how D.H. Lawrence captures the sense of place, weather and atmosphere. Which details capture the place best in your opinion?

2. R.P. Hewett says that Lawrence 'abandoned most of the conventions of traditional poetry, and devised for himself a free flowing verse, spontaneous, powerful, and expressing (and playing directly on) the emotions, yet always reflecting the play of a flexible and profound intelligence.' Consider the different aspects of this statement and explore how accurate this viewpoint is in relation to 'Snake'.

3. This poem is both a portrait of the snake and the speaker. Which words best sum up both? How can you tell that the speaker is fascinated by the snake?

4. How would you describe the poem's rhythm? How is this rhythm created within the poem?

5. According to Edna Longley, there is 'an anthropomorphic element' in Lawrence's animal poems. In other words, an animal is given a human form or personality. Look, for example, at how often Lawrence uses 'he', 'his', 'him'. Discuss this view and say whether you think such an approach is interesting and effective.

6. What does this poem say about man sharing the earth with other living things? Consider how the speaker responds to the snake and whether the speaker feels he is superior.

7. In the biblical Book of Genesis, how is the snake portrayed? Is there any suggestion here that Lawrence is thinking of that snake?

8. The first-person is used a lot in this poem: the word 'I' appears twenty-three times. What is the effect of the use of 'my' and 'I' in the poem? Explore how it is 'my water-trough' in line 1 and 'my snake' in line 68.

9. In the closing lines, the speaker says that the snake 'seemed to me again like a king.' Why 'again'? When did the snake first strike the speaker as king-like?

10. Instinct versus education? Which one wins in this instance? Explain your answer.

Humming-Bird

I can imagine, in some otherworld
Primeval-dumb, far back
In that most awful stillness, that only gasped and hummed,
Humming-birds raced down the avenues.

Before anything had a soul,   5
While life was a heave of Matter, half inanimate,
This little bit chipped off in brilliance
And went whizzing through the slow, vast, succulent
      stems.

I believe there were no flowers then,
In the world where the humming-bird flashed ahead of
      creation.   10
I believe he pierced the slow vegetable veins with his long
      beak.

Probably he was big,
As mosses, and little lizards, they say, were once big.
Probably he was a jabbing, terrifying monster.

We look at him through the wrong end of the long tele-
      scope of Time,   15
Luckily for us.

Española

Glossary

Title Humming-Bird: one of the smallest of birds and so called because of the humming sound created by their beating wings which flap at a rate of fifty times per second while the bird hovers in mid-air; it also flies at speeds of 15 metres per second. This poem is from Lawrence's collection *Birds, Beasts and Flowers*, but 'Humming-Bird' is the only poem in the collection that describes a creature that Lawrence had never seen. He had read about humming birds and believed, according to Keith Sagar's book *Life into Art*, that the humming bird was 'the first jewel-like entity thrown off by hitherto undifferentiated matter, the first isolated arrogant soul.'

Line 2 Primeval-dumb: primeval refers to an ancient, primitive time, the first age of the world; dumb because it is a pre-speech era.

Line 8 succulent: juicy, thick and fleshy.

Line 14 jabbing: stabbing, thrusting.

Española: a village near Taos in New Mexico. 'Humming-Bird' was written in Italy before Lawrence had seen an actual humming bird but he added *Española* later, a place where, two years later, he frequently saw humming birds.

'Humming-Bird' was first published in *New Republic* on 11 May 1921 when D.H. Lawrence was thirty-five.

Questions

1. This poem imagines 'some otherworld' a very long time ago. In your opinion, which details best capture that sense of another world?

2. Based on your reading of this poem, how would you describe the speaker as revealed to us here? Give reasons for your answer.

3. Why is Lawrence drawn to this particular bird? How well is the brilliance of the humming bird captured in your opinion? Which details describe the bird best?

4. How does this poem view the humming bird in relation to the whole of creation?

5. Are there elements in this poem that are surreal, that belong in the realm of science-fiction?

6. Comment on the poem's final line.

Intimates

Don't you care for my love? she said bitterly.

I handed her the mirror, and said:
Please address these questions to the proper person!
Please make all requests to head-quarters!
In all matters of emotional importance   5
please approach the supreme authority direct! –
So I handed her the mirror.

And she would have broken it over my head,
but she caught sight of her own reflection
and that held her spellbound for two seconds   10
while I fled.

Glossary

Title Intimates: people who are very physically close and familiar.

Line 6 supreme authority: the absolute expert.

Questions

1. This poem is a portrait of an unhappy relationship told from one point of view. Identify the source of the unhappiness. Could this view be biased?

2. How would you describe the language spoken by her and him? What tone of voice is used in line 1? How does it differ from the tone in lines 3–6?

3. 'Intimates' was written many decades ago. Would you know that? Could it be written today? Give reasons for your answer.

4. Is there such a thing as a typical D.H. Lawrence poem? Is this one of them? Why not?

5. 'Intimates' enacts a little drama between two people. Which person are you most interested in? Who are you most sympathetic towards?

6. Would you agree that lines 8–11 contain a certain kind of humour? Comment on this and its effect.

D.H. Lawrence's birthplace in Eastwood. It now houses a museum in his memory.

Delight of Being Alone

I know no greater delight than the sheer delight of being alone.
It makes me realise the delicious pleasure of the moon
that she has in travelling by herself: throughout time,
or the splendid growing of an ash-tree
alone, on a hill-side in the north, humming in the wind.

D.H. Lawrence wrote this poem when he was ill and dying. It was unpublished during his lifetime. It was first published in 1932.

? Questions

1. The American poet Marianne Moore says that 'the cure for loneliness is solitude'. Why does the speaker here enjoy being alone? Are you convinced?

2. Why do you think the moon and the ash-tree matter to and appeal to the poet?

3. Has this poem made you think about things differently? Why?

4. How would you describe the tone in the opening line? Assured? Confident? Self-important?

Absolute Reverence

I feel absolute reverence to nobody and to nothing human
neither to persons nor things nor ideas, ideals nor religions
      nor institutions,
to these things I feel only respect, and a tinge of reverence
when I see the fluttering of pure life in them.

But to something unseen, unknown, creative   5
from which I feel I am a derivative
I feel absolute reverence. Say no more!

📖 Glossary

Line 3 tinge: a tiny bit.
Line 6 derivative: not original, something derived from another source.

❓ Questions

1. This poem presents the reader with a self-portrait. How would you describe the speaker as revealed here?

2. Do you think that the speaker presents an appealing and attractive argument? Why? Why not?

3. What does this poem say about the individual and the rest of the world?

4. Could this poem be read as a 'companion poem' to 'Delight of Being Alone'. Why? Explain your answer.

5. Who might disapprove of the thoughts and the ideas contained within this poem? Is it a poem ahead of its time? Do you think it is a suitable and necessary poem and one that should be read by teenagers in class? Give reasons for your answers.

6. Identify the different tones in the poem.

7. In line 6, the speaker praises a certain kind of derivativeness. Explain how this can be. Consider this poem as a celebration of uniqueness.

What Have They Done to You?

What have they done to you, men of the masses, creeping
      back and forth to work?

What have they done to you, the saviours of the people, oh
      what have they saved you from, while they pocketed
      the money?

Alas, they have saved you from yourself, from your own
      frail dangers
and devoured you with the machine, the vast maw of iron.

They saved you from squalid cottages and poverty of hand
      to mouth   5
and embedded you in the workmen's dwellings, where your
      wage is the dole of work, and the dole is your
      wage of nullity.

They took away, oh they took away your man's native
      instincts and intuitions
and gave a board-school education, newspapers, and the
      cinema.

They stole your body from you and left you an animated
      carcass
to work with and nothing else: 10
unless goggling eyes, to goggle at the film
and a board-school brain, stuffed up with the ha'penny
      press.

Your instincts gone, your intuition gone, your passions dead
Oh carcass with a board-school mind and a ha'penny news-
      paper intelligence,
what have they done to you, what have they done to you,
      Oh what have they done to you?   15

Oh look at my fellow-men, oh look at them
the masses! Oh, what has been done to them!

📖 Glossary

Line 1 men of the masses: men without any individuality, one of the mob.

Line 2 saviours: those who help people avoid destruction. The word is used ironically here.

Line 4 maw: stomach.

Line 5 squalid: dirty, filthy.

Line 6 embedded you: fixed you firmly.

Line 6 dole of work: portion, charitable distribution.

Line 6 the dole is your wage of nullity: the benefit is your payment of mere nothing.

Line 7 instincts and intuitions: natural responses and immediate understanding; without reasoning.

Line 8 board-school education: regulated.

Line 9 an animated carcass: a lively dead body.

Line 11 goggling: wide-eyed, staring.

Line 12 ha'penny press: cheap, popular newspapers.

There are two versions of this poem. The other, an earlier version, is twelve lines long:

What Have They Done to You – ?
What have they done to you, men of the masses,
creeping back and forth to work?
What have they done to you, the saviours of the people?
Oh what have they saved you from?
Alas, they have saved you from yourself,
from your own body, saved you from living your own
    life.
And given you this jig-jig-jig
tick-tick-ticking of machines,
this life which is no-man's-life.
Oh a no-man's life in a no-man's-life in a no-man's-land
this is what they've given you
in place of your own life.

❓ Questions

1. Who is being addressed in this poem? Do you feel that the poet is speaking directly to you? Do you think this particular poem has an 'out-of-date' feeling? Give reasons for your answers in each case.

2. Comment on how 'you' is used in the poem. What is the effect of this?

3. The 'you' in 'What have they done to you' in line 1 has become 'them' in the final two lines. Why do you think the speaker does this?

4. Consider the first word in each of the eight stanzas. How do these words contribute to the different tones in the poem?

5. What kind of picture is painted of the lives of the 'men of the masses' here? Which details do you think particularly effective?

6. This poem addresses social and political issues. Do you think such a poem can make a difference?

7. What does this poem contribute to our understanding of D.H. Lawrence?

'Trailing Clouds'

As a drenched, drowned bee
Hangs numb and heavy from the bending flower,
    So clings to me,
My baby, her brown hair brushed with wet tears
    And laid laughterless on her cheek,   5
Her soft white legs hanging heavily over my arm
    Swinging to my lullaby.
My sleeping baby hangs upon my life
    As a silent bee at the end of a shower
    Draws down the burdened flower.   10
She who has always seemed so light
    Sways on my arm like sorrowful, storm-heavy boughs,
Even her floating hair sinks like storm-bruised young leaves
Reaching downwards:
    As the wings of a drenched, drowned bee   15
    Are a heaviness, and a weariness.

📖 Glossary

Title 'Trailing Clouds': the use of quotation marks suggests the following lines from William Wordsworth's 1807 poem 'Ode (Intimations of Immortality from Recollections of Early Childhood)': 'Our birth is but a sleep and a forgetting:/ The Soul that rises with us, our life's Star,/ Hath had elsewhere its setting,/ And cometh from afar;/ Not in entire forgetfulness,/ And not in utter nakedness,/ But trailing clouds of glory do we come/ From God, who is our home'.

Line 7 Swinging to my lullaby: in the earlier version of this poem ('A Baby Asleep After Pain'), lines 7–8 read, 'Swing to my walking movements weak/ With after-pain' and line 9 reads 'Like a burden she hangs on me'.

> This is Part II of Lawrence's poem 'Baby-Movements'; Part I, a happier poem, is called 'Running Barefoot'. An earlier version of this poem is called 'A Baby Asleep After Pain'.
>
> The text here is from *The English Review*, November 1909. Lawrence was twenty-four. The baby in question is Hilda Mary, the baby daughter of Mrs Jones, his landlady in Croydon, where he worked as a teacher. In a letter, Lawrence described Hilda Mary: 'We have the jolliest fat baby, eight months old. You cannot tell how fond I am of her; her fine hazel eyes laugh at me so brightly, and her soft fingers wandering over my face and grasping my cheeks speak to me so cunningly...'

❓ Questions

1. This poem captures a relationship between adult and baby. How would you describe that relationship? Were you surprised by what you read?

2. Look at the many sensuous details in the poem. What is their effect in the overall context of the poem?

3. The speaker sings a lullaby. How would you describe the baby being sung to? Which details capture the baby best?

4. Which sounds dominate the poem? Identify them.

5. Consider the title in the light of the lines from Wordsworth's poem (see Glossary). Do you read the poem now in a different light? In your opinion, is this poem more optimistic than pessimistic?

6. D.H. Lawrence never fathered a child, but he was very fond of children. Do you think he captured well the relationship between him and 'My baby' in this poem?

Bavarian Gentians

Not every man has gentians in his house
In soft September, at slow, sad Michaelmas.

Bavarian gentians, tall and dark, but dark
darkening the daytime torch-like with the smoking blueness
      of Pluto's gloom,
ribbed hellish flowers erect, with the blaze of darkness spread blue,   5
blown flat into points, by the heavy white draught of the day.

Torch-flowers of the blue-smoking darkness, Pluto's dark-blue blaze
black lamps from the halls of Dis, smoking dark blue
giving off darkness, blue darkness, upon Demeter's yellow-pale day
whom have you come for, here in the white-cast day?   10

Reach me a gentian, give me a torch!
let me guide myself with the blue, forked torch of a flower
down the darker and darker stairs, where blue is darkened on blueness
down the way Persephone goes, just now, in first-frosted September
to the sightless realm where darkness is married to dark   15
and Persephone herself is but a voice, as a bride,
a gloom invisible enfolded in the deeper dark
of the arms of Pluto as he ravishes her once again
and pierces her once more with his passion of the utter dark
among the splendour of black-blue torches, shedding fathomless
      darkness on the nuptials.   20

Give me a flower on a tall stem, and three dark flames,
for I will go to the wedding, and be wedding-guest
at the marriage of the living dark.

📖 Glossary

Title Bavarian Gentians: Bavaria is a region in southern Germany; gentians are blue flowers usually found in mountain regions.

Line 2 Michaelmas: pronounced 'mikelmas', this is the Feast of St. Michael, 29 September; in universities, Michaelmas term is the first term of the academic year, beginning in September.

Line 4 Pluto's gloom: in Greek myth, Pluto is the god of the Underworld or Hades. He abducted Persephone and carried her off to his dark kingdom at the dying of the year. Ceres, Persephone's mother and goddess of the harvest, was heartbroken and wandered the earth in search of her daughter. While she did so, nothing grew on earth. Eventually, Pluto was persuaded to release Persephone for six months each year and when Persephone returns to earth to join her mother, the world celebrates with spring. When Persephone returns to Hades each year, winter approaches. Pluto is also known as Dis, Persephone as Proserpine, Ceres as Demeter.

Line 5 ribbed: curved.

Line 6 draught: breeze.

Line 9 Demeter's yellow-pale day: here Lawrence is contrasting the dark blue of Pluto's Underworld with the world where Demeter/Ceres dwells.

Line 10 white-cast: bright.

Line 18 ravishes: rapes.

Line 20 nuptials: wedding.

Line 22 I will go to the wedding: John Worthen, Lawrence's biographer, writes: 'At the end of the journey will be Persephone, the bride kept underground by Pluto. Lawrence gave the old myth magnificent new energy; his vivid imagination now attuned to the ideas of loss and ending.'

In 1929, D.H. Lawrence spent some time in Rottach-am-Tegernsee in the Bavarian Alps. He was very ill at the time, he died the following year, and in his biography, *D.H. Lawrence: The Life of an Outsider*, John Worthen tells of how Lawrence lay in a bare room in the village inn where next to him stood a great bush of pale blue autumn gentians and they inspired his poem 'Bavarian Gentians'.

In April 1927, he visited some Etruscan tombs and Christopher Hassall suggests that 'the physical act of entering these tombs...had become for Lawrence a symbol of death with that noble lack of bitterness or protest which is so lovely an element in his last poems.'

There are two versions of this poem. This twenty-three-line version is a variant and early draft included in Appendix III of the Vivian de Sola Pinto and Warren Roberts edition. The nineteen-line version, first published in 1932, that follows is the preferred version in Enda Longley's *The Bloodaxe Book of 20th Century Poetry*, *The Norton Anthology of Modern Poetry*, *The School Bag* edited by Seamus Heaney and Ted Hughes, and Paul Keegan's *The New Penguin Book of English Verse*. If you have an idle moment on a wet Thursday afternoon, compare and contrast!

Bavarian Gentians
Not every man has gentians in his house
in Soft September, at slow, sad Michaelmas.

Bavarian gentians, big and dark, only dark
darkening the day-time, torch-like with the smoking blueness of
    Pluto's gloom,
ribbed and torch-like, with their blaze of darkness spread blue   5
down flattening into points, flattened under the sweep of white day
torch-flower of the blue-smoking darkness, Pluto's dark-blue daze,
black lamps from the halls of Dis, burning dark blue,
giving off darkness, blue darkness, as Demeter's pale lamps give
      off light,
lead me then, lead the way.   10

Reach me a gentian, give me a torch!
let me guide myself with the blue, forked torch of this flower
down the darker and darker stairs, where blue is darkened on blueness
even where Persephone goes, just now, from the frosted September
to the sightless realm where darkness is awake upon the dark   15
and Persephone herself is but a voice
or a darkness invisible enfolded in the deeper dark
of the arms Plutonic, and pierced with the passion of dense gloom,
among the splendour of torches of darkness, shedding darkness on the
      lost bride and her groom.

? Questions

1. How would you describe the mood in the poem's opening two lines?

2. This poem contains beautiful music. Discuss this statement by exploring how rhyme, rhythm, cadence, repetition, alliteration and assonance contribute to the music of the poem.

3. Why is Lawrence reminded of the story of Persephone and Pluto when he contemplates the gentians in September?

4. Consider the colours in this poem and comment on their effect. Discuss the contrast between darkness and light.

5. How important, in your opinion, is the mythological drama of Pluto, Persephone and Demeter within the context of the poem as a whole?

6. This poem was written when D.H. Lawrence knew that he was dying. Does this distract from or enhance your understanding and appreciation of the poem?

7. The poem begins in a room and an imaginary journey down into the Underworld. What is it about the Bavarian gentians that allow the speaker to make that journey?

8. Sensuousness is a striking feature of the poem. Pick out those sensuous details and comment on their effect. Consider, for example, how the flowers become torches that light the way to the Underworld.

9. How do you interpret the poem's final stanza? What does the marriage of Pluto and Persephone signify? Why does he see himself as a wedding-guest at such a wedding?

10. What is the significance of 'first-frosted September'?

11. Trace how light and darkness, sight and sightlessness occur within the poem. Comment on the poem's final words 'the living dark'.

12. Many would consider this to be one of D.H. Lawrence's great poems and, of the eleven on your course, the greatest. Would you agree with this view? Give reasons for your answer.

D.H. Lawrence in Mexico in 1925.

General Questions

A. D.H. Lawrence has 'a vivid awareness of and insight to the physical world, the world of things'. How true is this statement of the Lawrence poems you have studied? Support your discussion by reference to, or quotation from, the poems by Lawrence you have studied.

B. In Lawrence's poetry, there is a 'brutal honesty of observation'. To what extent do you agree with this statement? Support your answer with suitable reference to the poems by D.H. Lawrence on your course.

C. In his poetry, D.H. Lawrence 'alerts us to the world around us in language that is alive and urgent'. Would you agree with this view? Support the points you make by reference to, or quotation from, the poems by Lawrence on your course.

D. 'Lawrence's poetry is not the poetry of a detached observer, he speaks with a passionate and honest voice.' Write your response to this statement, supporting your points with the aid of suitable reference to the poems by D.H. Lawrence that you have studied.

E. Lawrence's poetry has 'the greatest delicacy, the finest intelligence and the most complete honesty'. To what extent do you agree with this statement? Support your answer with suitable reference to the poems by D.H. Lawrence on your course.

F. 'Lawrence uses different voices to explore unique and memorable worlds in his poetry.' Discuss this statement, supporting your answer with reference to the poetry of D.H. Lawrence on your course.

G. 'Lawrence pays little attention to traditional forms and has a special gift for conveying sensuous experience.' Would you agree with this view? Support the points you make by reference to, or quotation from, the poems by Lawrence on your course.

Critical Commentary

Call into Death

This poem addresses and mourns a loved one. The relationship is never made clear. Is this a man addressing his lover? Could it be a son mourning his mother? This is never clearly stated, but Lawrence himself believed that a poem can only be understood within a biographical context and this poem, first published in *Amores* in 1916, six years after his mother's death and originally called 'Elegy', would seem to focus on his dead mother. Theirs was a very close relationship:

> Since I lost you, my darling, the sky has come near.

The world has changed; it is different now. The sky hasn't fallen, but it 'has come near'. The tone in that opening line is both tender and sad. The speaker still feels a very strong connection with the person he mourns and the phrases 'my darling' and the repeated 'my dear' express a deep love.

'And I am of it' refers to the near sky; the speaker feels part of it. A low sky is a negative image, but here it allows the speaker feel closer to her, whom he misses.

The opening line uses an image of a low sky to capture the speaker's feelings and then through beautiful images of stars and the moon in the night sky, the speaker's deeper feelings are conveyed: 'the small sharp stars' and '[t]he white moon going among them like a white bird/ among snow-berries' are beautiful to imagine and similar in their whiteness, though the word 'sharp' might suggest the loneliness he is feeling. But the final line in the first stanza describes how he imagines his lost loved one:

> And the sound of her gently rustling in heaven like a
> bird I hear.

Heaven is usually associated with a place up above beyond the sky. The speaker imagines that she is there and words such as 'gently rustling' paint a soft picture. The moon was compared to a white bird and her presence in heaven is 'like a bird I hear'. These bird similes suggest something pure and small and delicate.

The poem as a whole has a gentle rhythm. The word 'Since' with which the poem opens creates a timeframe. His darling died in the past, she has been called into death and the present time is now filled with loneliness and longing. The use of 'And' at the beginning of lines 2, 4, 5, 8 and the use of 'For' at the beginning of stanza 3 signal his awareness of past, present and future. The end rhymes 'near/near/hear' create their own music but Lawrence does not use a perfectly regular end rhyme – in stanza 1 'snow-berries' breaks the pattern for example.

The imagery in stanza 2 matches the speaker's longing to escape his sorrow. Once again a bird image is used to suggest his desire to be with his 'dear', to disappear and melt into each other.

> And I am willing to come to you now, my dear,
> As a pigeon lets itself off from a cathedral dome
> To be lost in the haze of the sky; I would like to come
> And be lost out of sight with you, like a melting foam.

The repeated 'lost' captures this desire and the use of 'I' ('I am willing . . . I would like') intensifies the feeling just as the repeated 'you' does.

The mood in the final stanza is one of tiredness and resignation. He wishes he could rise up 'off the dome of the earth' and if he could he imagines that he and she could become one 'within the breathing wind'. The poem's closing words are intense: 'what rest, my love, what rest!' The repetition and exclamation mark add to the intensity and the idea of being lost, which occurs twice in stanza 2, recurs here in the final line. In lines 7 and 8, to be lost meant that he had found his darling, his dear; and '[w]here you are lost' also means that he is united with his loved one.

Piano

If you were asked to find a piano tune to match this particular poem, what type of music would you look for? A jig or a nocturne? The answer is in the poem's first word and in the time of day referred to. The music is soft, the time of day is of fading light and shadows. 'Piano' is a memory poem and the memories are very personal. The adult poet is remembering his mother and the scene is brought alive in the poet's imagination.

A poem about music is often a musical poem and in this instance the very regular end-rhymes (aabb, ccdd, eeff), the long leisurely lines and the rhythm all add to the effect. The poem begins in the present:

> Softly, in the dusk, a woman is singing to me

But the moment summons up a moment from long ago and the song and its music take him back 'down the vista of the years'. When the speaker journeys back in his imagination, he sees:

> A child sitting under the piano, in the boom of the tingling strings.
> And pressing the small, poised feet of a mother who smiles as she sings.

The poem's first stanza is one sentence, a sentence that begins slowly (line 1 contains two commas and a colon) and opens up to become a flowing and musical line. The image of the mother and child is one of the most familiar and powerful in painting and Lawrence, here, creates a very intimate and harmonious picture. The child is involved in the music making in that he presses the mother's feet poised above the pedals and the mother not only accompanies the music with song but she 'smiles as she sings'. The speaker says 'a' child, 'a' mother, not 'my' mother, and this distancing may suggest how time itself has distanced the memory for him.

A different note is introduced in the second stanza. The music is 'insidious'; he speaks of feeling betrayed and the heart of him weeps. Here the speaker admits to a feeling of intense longing to return.

> To the old Sunday evenings at home, with winter outside
> And hymns in the cosy parlour, the tinkling piano our guide.

These lines capture a sense of the long ago: 'old Sunday evenings' 'winter', 'hymns', 'cosy', 'tinkling', 'guide' all suggest comfort, safety, security. Here Lawrence is returning in his imagination to his childhood and, when one realises that the Greek word for 'return' is *nostos* and *algos* means 'suffering', the mood could truly be described as nostalgic. There is sadness and suffering in the poem and a yearning to return to a moment of happiness.

'Piano' begins with a reference to 'a woman' who 'is singing to me'. This woman and her song reminds him of another woman, his mother, and her singing. Stanza 3 returns to the present and the 'great black piano' suggests a grand piano a concert platform, a public recital. But Lawrence tells us, though he is listening to an accomplished singer, accompanied by piano, his heart and mind are elsewhere. He is lost in memory and:

> So now it is vain for the singer to burst into clamour
> With the great black piano appassionato

His childhood days are more attractive to him – 'The glamour/ Of childhood days is upon me' – and when he says that his 'manhood is cast/ Down' he is admitting that memory has somehow unmanned him, that he feels he has lost his manly qualities, and he weeps.

Every word in the poem's final sentence – 'I weep like a child for the past' – is simple, but the emotion it contains is deep and complex. His longing to escape to this world is intense and the poem, understandably, focuses more on the past than the present.

The Mosquito

This is a long poem, written in free verse, but its central idea is easily grasped. It begins with a question, ends with an exclamation mark and addresses the mosquito in a voice that is intrigued, fascinated and annoyed by this creature, a creature that is difficult to like. Because the poem is divided into twenty-two short sections, the reader, reading through the poem and looking at the layout on the page, senses the speaker's mind at work as he questions, comments and responds to this insect. Each section, as it were, captures the speaker's mind as it moves from one idea to the next and the words that begin the different sections frequently suggest the speaker's immediate engagement with the subject-matter, words such as 'When', 'What', 'How', 'Yet', 'But', 'You'. That two sections (section 6 and 22) begin with 'Queer' reminds us of Lawrence's fascination with the mosquito.

The opening lines – 'When did you start your tricks,/ Monsieur?// What do you stand on such high legs for?' – convey the speaker's disapproval. And yet the use of 'tricks' and 'Monsieur' convey a sense of class and sophistication.

The poem contradicts itself in that, in its portrait of the mosquito, it contains words of praise and condemnation. The speaker recognises qualities in the mosquito that are somehow admirable and then he dismisses the creature as horrible and ugly.

> Why this length of shredded shank,
> You exaltation?

This technique allows for a dynamic within the poem and this makes it difficult to sum up how the speaker thinks and feels about this insect. The mosquito is a 'shredded shank', a 'phantom', a 'nothingness', a 'streaky sorcerer', a 'Ghoul on wings', a 'speck', a 'winged blood-drop', and the poem focuses on all of these aspects in turn.

Though the mosquito is tiny and weighs 'no more than air as you alight upon me', it is a very definite presence and at times seems to dominate the relationship with the speaker.

Section 4 introduces another voice, the voice of a woman who called the mosquito 'the Winged Victory/ In sluggish Venice'. Such a grand image of triumph, that of 'Winged Victory', and spoken by another adds to the mosquito's power.

This speaker is not alone in recognising the mosquito's presence — both a woman in Venice and Lawrence in Siracusa are aware of its uniqueness. The 'Winged Victory' referred to here is the classical sculpture in the Louvre in Paris and celebrates the triumphal goddess Nike. But the statue has no head and no arms and as such could resemble the mosquito's body except that the mosquito has the advantage of having a head, a head that smiles. The insect is personified and the sinister detail in line 11 – 'You turn your head towards your tail, and smile' – reveals the speaker's imaginative response: a smiling mosquito. He goes on to ask:

> How can you put so much devilry
> Into that translucent phantom shred
> Of a frail corpus?

Devilry suggests evil and what perplexes the viewer is how the mosquito's tiny body can contain such wickedness, that something that looks so insignificant, so see-through, can be dangerous.

The mosquito is never given a voice and yet its movements and actions suggest a dialogue of sorts between man and insect. The mosquito seems to have the advantage for much of the poem; it is only in the closing lines that the insect is squashed and killed, and the speaker sees the mosquito – blood-filled with sucked human blood – as somehow being truly conquered. It has not only been reduced to an 'infinitesimal faint smear of you', but it has disappeared into the 'big stain'.

There are some striking descriptions of Monsieur Mosquito before it meets its end that are graceful, even elegant: 'with your thin wings and your streaming legs, How you sail like a heron, or a dull clot of air,/ A nothingness.'

A phrase such as 'an aura surrounds you' conveys the speaker's fascinated response, but it is an 'evil little aura, prowling, and casting numbness on/ my mind.' And though the words magic and trick are used, it is a 'filthy magic'. There is disgust and there is anger in the speaker's tone and, although the mosquito seems an invisible, infuriating presence, by stanza 8 the speaker feels he is gaining an understanding and control of the situation:

> But I know your game now, streaky sorcerer.
> Queer, how you stalk and prowl the air
> In circles and evasions, enveloping me,
> Ghoul on wings
> Winged Victory.

Sentences such as 'I hate the way you lurch off sideways into the air' are not only straightforward but brilliantly accurate, as anyone who has ever met with a mosquito will know. Descriptions such as 'Settle, and stand on long thin shanks' or 'Eyeing me sideways, and cunningly conscious that I am aware' not only bring vividly alive the experience of seeing this 'speck,' but the use of alliteration ('Settle/stand/shanks'; 'cunningly conscious') reminds us of Lawrence's skill as a poet.

The poem began with a casual question, but as one reads through the poem the mosquito is seen close-up and the speaker becomes more direct, as in stanza 10:

> I hate the way you lurch off sideways into the air
> Having read my thoughts against you

This leads to a playful challenge:

> Come then, let us play at unawares,
> And see who wins in this sly game of bluff.
> Man or mosquito.

But that challenge gives way to hatred again:

> It is your trump,
> It is your **hateful** little trump,
> You pointed fiend,
> Which shakes my sudden blood to **hatred** of you:
> It is your small, high, **hateful** bugle in my ear.

Here 'fiend' echoes 'devilry' in stanza 5 and the choice of 'bugle' conveys the piercing mosquito sound.

A question such as 'Why do you do it?' in stanza 14 suggests fascination and perplexity, and the next line is even gentler in tone: 'Surely it is bad policy.' When the speaker says, 'They say you can't help it', he is at his most sympathetic.

Ironically, immediately following this is the moment when the insect gains advantage and there is 'A yell of triumph as you snatch my scalp.' In the poem's shortest lines, we find a succinct account of the mosquito's achievement:

> Blood, red blood,
> Super-magical
> Forbidden liquor.
> I behold you stand
>
> For a second enspasmed in oblivion.
> Obscenely ecstasied
> Sucking live blood,
> My blood.

This is the poem's climax for the insect; the climax for the speaker is in the closing lines.

The repeated 'Such' is effective and emphatic:

> Such silence, such suspended transport,
> Such gorging,
> Such obscenity of trespass

As is every idea here: the mosquito, having gorged, is now heavy with blood, that it has attacked the speaker's scalp is seen as an obscene trespass.

And then more physical description, 'You stagger'; 'your accursed hairy frailty, Your own imponderable weightlessness', until the speaker says, 'Away with a paean of derision,/ You winged blood-drop.' In other words, it is time for action; the time for mockery and hatred is over. Now the speaker hopes to match his attacker at its own game:

> Can I not overtake you?
> Are you one too many for me,
> Winged Victory?
> Am I not mosquito enough to out-mosquito you?

The end comes quickly. There is no description of the mosquito being chased and hunted, but the final stanza tells us that the mosquito has been conquered and destroyed, and the mood in the closing lines is one of fascination and satisfaction.

> Queer what a big stain my sucked blood makes
> Beside the infinitesimal faint smear of you!
> Queer, what a dim dark smudge you have disappeared
> into!

The poem's opening sentence ended with a question mark; the final sentence ends with an exclamation.

'The Mosquito', like 'Snake' and 'Humming-Bird', is from Lawrence's collection entitled *Birds, Beasts and Flowers*.

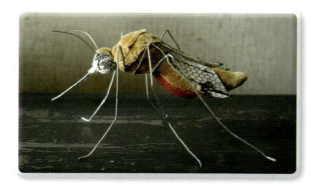

Snake

The title brings with it both dictionary definition – 'predatory reptile with a long slender limbless supple body, many kinds of which have a venomous bite' – and such associations as the serpent in the Garden of Eden where Satan takes the form of a snake to undo Adam and Eve's happiness.

The Sicilian setting, on 'a hot, hot day', sets the mood and the rhythm is suitably slow. Though it works as a narrative poem, recounting as it does the encounter between the speaker and the snake, it is also a meditation on the mystery of existence. In addition, the poem explores how we are shaped, conditioned and influenced by education and society, by the cultural context which we inherit at birth.

The opening lines are evocative but the structure is also unusual and effective. The sentence begins and ends with the snake and the speaker announces his presence in the words 'and I in pyjamas for the heat'.

> A snake came to my water-trough
> On a hot, hot day, and I in pyjamas for the heat,
> To drink there.

The word 'my' suggests that it is the man's world, not the snake's. The detail 'pyjamas' adds a languid atmosphere.

The poem uses long lines, many of them run-on lines and this suits the subject matter. It is as if the poem itself snakes its way along the page. Throughout the poem the speaker uses 'he' and 'I' and the poem paints a very clear picture of the snake's movements – how it 'reached down', 'trailed', 'rested', 'sipped', 'lifted his head', 'flickered his two-forked tongue', 'stooped'.

The speaker arrives at the water-trough, discovers that the snake is there before him and realises that he 'must wait, must stand and wait, for there he was at/ the trough before me'. Some have interpreted this as an admission of inferiority, that the speaker has to give way to the snake, a superior being. Stanza 3 is a brilliant description of the snake as it moves and drinks: 'He trailed his yellow-brown slackness soft-bellied down,/ over the edge of the stone trough...He sipped with his straight mouth,

Softly drank through his straight gums, into his slack long body', and the placing of the word 'Silently' on its own at the end of the stanza creates a sense of drama and anticipation.

The speaker knows that he must wait his turn: 'Someone was before me at my water-trough,/ And I, like a second comer, waiting.' Repetition adds a dignified quality to the snake: 'He lifted his head from his drinking, as cattle do,/ And looked at me vaguely, as drinking cattle do. The snake is portrayed as calm, in control and mysterious – it is 'earth-brown, earth-golden from the burning bowels/ of the earth'. When the speaker mentions how on this 'day of Sicilian July', Mount Etna is 'smoking', we are reminded of the power of the natural world.

But another world intrudes with a determined voice at stanza 6. Initially, the speaker stood back and acknowledged the snake. Now he wants to control and destroy it.

> The voice of my education said to me
> He must be killed,
> For in Sicily the black, black snakes are innocent, the gold
>   are venomous.

The language here is functional and impersonal. The sensuous detail in earlier stanzas has given way to textbook information. The speaker distances himself from the creature so vividly evoked in the previous stanzas and resorts to a macho stance:

> And voices in me said, If you were a man
> You would take a stick and break him now, and finish
>   him off.

These lines are brutal. Twenty-one of the twenty-three words above are monosyllabic and yet the use of 'but' immediately afterwards (at line 27) returns to focus on the snake's special qualities:

> But must I confess how I liked him,
> How glad I was he had come like a guest in quiet, to drink
>   at my water-trough
> And depart peaceful, pacified and thankless,
> Into the burning bowels of this earth?

Here, the speaker admits not only that he is glad of his encounter with the snake but he knows that it will depart peacefully and return to the 'bowels of the earth'. He questions his feelings ('cowardice'; 'perversity'; 'humility') and realises that what he feels most is a feeling of having been honoured: 'I felt so honoured.'

And yet those inner voices return and within the speaker there is conflict between what is instinctive and what is learned:

> And yet those voices:
> *If you were not afraid, you would kill him!*

The italicised line is the voice that preys on his manhood, asking what kind of a man would not want to conquer and kill this snake, the speaker's sensitive nature is revealed: 'And truly I was afraid, I was most afraid,/ But even so, honoured still more/ That he should seek my hospitality/From out the dark door of the secret earth.'

The snake is seen in the bright, harsh light of midday, but these references to its dark, secret home connects the snake with a world of ancient mystery. Once it has drunk enough, the snake 'lifted his head, dreamily, as one who has drunken,/ And flickered his tongue like a forked night on the air, so black;/ Seeming to lick his lips'. A word such as 'dreamily' contains an attractive quality, the image of the forked tongue is not but it is at this point in the poem that snake is likened to a god. That simile gives the snake a dignity, presence and power. It returns to the earth 'slowly, very slowly' and over two stanzas, Lawrence describes the snake curving, climbing and returning to 'that dreadful hole', 'that horrid black hole', 'the blackness'. Once again, the description is simple and brilliant: 'he slowly drew up, snake-easing his shoulders, and entered farther'. But the drama of his going is followed by another dramatic moment: 'A sort of horror...Overcame me now his back was turned.'

The snake's going is seen as a slight, an insult and the speaker succumbs to his worst instincts:

> A sort of horror, a sort of protest against his withdrawing
>   into that horrid black hole,
> Deliberately going into the blackness, and slowly drawing
>   himself after,
> Overcame me

The 'clumsy log' and the clattering sound it makes contrasts with the dignified, calm, slow motions of the snake. Now 'suddenly that part of him that was left behind convulsed in undignified haste,/ Writhed like lightning, and was gone/ Into the black hole, the earth-lipped fissure in the wall-front,/ At which, in the intense still noon, I stared with fascination.'

Everything has been shattered: the silence, the pace, the speaker's admiring, fascinated tone. Words and phrases such as 'convulsed', 'undignified haste', 'Writhed like lightning', convey a sense of disorder and chaos. The speaker regrets his act 'immediately' and the poem ends with the speaker's guilt. This god-like creature did not deserve to be treated in this 'paltry', 'vulgar', 'mean' way and 'my accursed human education' is blamed. The snake is now referred to as 'my snake' and spoken of as a 'king'. Earlier in the poem, the snake was 'earth-golden' and the literary allusion to Coleridge's albatross opens up the poem to another ignorant man's response to an innocent creature.

The use of the 'king' image and the snake as 'one of the lords of life' grants the snake great status, yet that snake is 'Like a king in exile, uncrowned in the underworld'. The speaker had an opportunity to honour it properly and failed. The snake belongs in this place, Taormina, in Sicily, and the speaker is only a visitor; yet, the visitor thinks he is entitled to banish the snake.

He sends it back to an underworld and admits that it should be allowed live in this world – it is 'Now due to be crowned again'. The snake is one of the lords of life and the Irish academic Augustine Martin has written regarding 'due be crowned again' that 'the poet, because he is a poet, recognises the snake to be one of the lords of life. Because of a pettiness in his nature, he refuses to grant him the honour due to a king come back from exile'. But this speaker 'missed my chance' and the mood with which the poem ends is one of regret and a feeling of being small-minded and ungenerous: 'And I have something to expiate;/ A pettiness.'

Michael Schmidt (in *Lives of the Poets*) says that in 'Snake' the speaker 'finds himself guilty of the Fall, attempting to kill a dark angel that inspires terror and fascination, the serpent visiting the water trough defining in its movement, shading and self-contained purpose another world...he attacks, laments. The snake, as an image, hovers between reptilian, human and divine. For an instant, its drinking reminds him of a cow drinking, but it ascends in his observation by stages to being god-like...As he hurls a log, the snake reverts to being merely a snake, the man becomes that limited creature, that fallen angel.'

(Poems are interpreted in many ways, sometimes wrongheadedly. A very careful reading of the text is essential. Everything should be based on that. 'Snake', it has been argued, is a poem about D.H. Lawrence's working-class hatred of and opposition to the upper class as symbolised by the snake. Do you think this is a valid reading of the poem?)

Humming-Bird

The humming-bird is among the smallest of birds, but this poem opens up a huge vista. It looks back through time and envisages a place long before humans existed. It is 'some otherworld', a world 'Primeval-dumb, far back'. Lawrence, living in the twentieth century, wrote this poem about a humming-bird, a bird that clearly fascinates him, and in one great imaginative leap he travels back to a time of 'awful stillness', a time 'that only gasped and hummed' and 'Humming-birds raced down the avenues'. The use of 'avenues' here conjures up a wide elegant road or pathway; the verb 'raced' adds excitement.

The speaker imagines what it was like:

> Before anything had a soul,
> While life was a heave of Matter, half inanimate

We are brought back to the beginnings of creation. 'Before anything had a soul' would suggest that the spiritual life had not yet begun, not even flowers had been created but the humming-bird was making its dazzling, whizzing presence felt. All other life is seen as dull, inert: 'a heave of Matter, half inanimate'. The bird is described as 'This little bit chipped off in brilliance'. It is as if the humming-bird is part of the very excitement of the beginning of life, a brilliant chip, an indictor of what is yet to come.

The poem brings us back to a time before flowers, way back in geological time: 'I believe there were no flowers then,/ In the world where the humming-bird flashed ahead of creation.' But there are 'slow, vast, succulent stems' and the contrast between 'flashed' and 'whizzing' and the 'slow' stems creates a dramatic picture.

The speaker can only guess – 'I believe', 'Probably' – what the world was like then, but he imagines that the humming-bird 'pierced the slow vegetable veins with his long beak.' The humming-bird is active and determined, and the speaker says:

> Probably he was big,
> As mosses, and little lizards, they say, were once big.
> Probably he was a jabbing, terrifying monster.

The tone here is casual, but this idea of the humming-bird, which we only know now as a very small bird, as a 'monster' turns everything upside down. But, according to the poem, mosses and lizards were once huge.

Repetition – as in 'I believe...I believe' and 'Probably he was...Probably he was' – draws in the reader and though the poem is in free verse (which means there is no regular rhyme or regularly-shaped stanzas), the poetry is in the vivid language and the unusual ideas.

a poem in praise of the humming-bird, but it ends with an image of the bird as ʼing, terrifying monster'. In doing so, it invites us to think about the long, slow from the primeval to now. The speaker, in this thinking-outside-the-box as imagined a terrifying creature that existed at the beginning of time. The final lines

> We look at him through the wrong end of the long tele-
>   scope of Time,
> Luckily for us.

contain humour and those final three words, 'Luckily for us', are colloquial, almost throwaway. The long line – 'We look at him through the wrong end of the long telescope of Time' – mirrors the very idea it contains. The humming-bird today is small. The original humming-bird as imagined in this poem is a monster; we don't see them as they really were, time has diminished them and for that the speaker is grateful.

Emily Dickinson also wrote a poem celebrating the humming-bird. It is worth a look:

A Route of Evanescence

With a revolving Wheel –
A resonance of Emerald –
A rush of Cochineal –
And every Blossom on the Bush
Adjusts its tumbled Head –
The mail from Tunis, probably,
An easy Morning's Ride –

Intimates

The title suggests a close, personal, loving relationship. In the context of the poem as a whole, the title is ironic. This him-and-her poem enacts a little drama, but everything is seen from the male perspective and in the breakdown of their relationship she is the one who is blamed.

The woman is heard only once. She speaks the harsh, complaining, bitter opening line. The strong sounding 'Don't' is negative; the line is on its own.

In the other two stanzas, the man speaks. He plans to separate himself from her. On the page, his thoughts are separated from hers. His argument is clearly structured.

The poem's second section begins and ends with a gesture – 'I handed her the mirror'/ 'So I handed her the mirror' – and in between the speaker, in cold, impersonal, formal language, tells us what he said to the woman. The entire poem is addressed to the reader (or could it be addressed to a psychiatrist?). Three lines begin with 'please' and though the tone is both distant and confident, repetition and alliteration make the words flow smoothly.

I handed her the mirror, and said:
Please address these questions to the *proper person*!
Please make all requests to head-quarters!
In all matters of emotional importance
please approach the supreme *authority* direct! –
So I handed her the mirror.

The argument, as he sees it, is clear. The tone is sarcastic. Link-words such as 'So', 'And', 'but', 'while' in the closing lines strengthen his case; the rhyming 'head' and 'fled' in the final section gives the man the advantage. The woman is portrayed as shallow and though she asks if he cared for her love, at the outset, the poem shows that she, Narcissus-like, is really in love with herself. To her question the speaker responds not with words but with a gesture. There is no dialogue.

The image of the woman, held spellbound by her reflection is insulting, belittling and humorous. The speaker accepts no blame whatsoever for the situation that he and she find themselves in. The poem could also work if the pronouns were changed and it was the man who asked the question: '"Don't you care for my love?" he said bitterly'. But in this instance it is a man's world. He is the one that gets away.

Delight of Being Alone

Solitude. Loneliness. Being alone. Being lonely. They mean different things. No one would choose to be lonely, but, as this poem reminds us, being alone does not mean lonely. In a poem called 'Loneliness', D.H. Lawrence says: 'I never know what people mean when they complain of loneliness. / To be alone is one of life's greatest delights...'. Clearly, being alone in this instance does not mean being lonely. What he doesn't dwell on is that one also knows that one can feel lonely in a crowd.

Line 1 of 'Delight of Being Alone' is a statement:

> I know no greater delight than the sheer delight of being alone.

Its confident tone, the emphatic phrase 'no greater delight' is to convince the reader and the repeated 'delight' and the adjective 'sheer' strengthen the sentence.

The poem's second and final sentence presents us with two beautiful images from nature: the moon and a tree, solitary images. There is no doubt in his mind that the moon experiences a 'delicious pleasure...travelling by herself'; the tree is not only 'splendid' growing away on its own but it is 'humming in the wind'. Two self-contained images, the moon in the night sky and the ash-tree on a hillside in the north, belong to nature poetry, but this poem goes beyond descriptions of the natural world and also reveals the speaker's own philosophy of life. He identifies with the moon and ash-tree and they are personified. They are alone but not lonely and he himself delights in that state. The word 'alone' occurs in the title, at the end of line 1 and at the beginning of the poem's final line, but it is repeated not in sorrow but delight.

Absolute Reverence

D.H. Lawrence was very much his own man. He lived a full life and often flouted society's rules. This seven-line poem is a manifesto of sorts and sums up his attitudes and beliefs. In the poem's first section, he makes it very clear what he thinks about a number of things. It is a very strong statement and the list is punctuated by 'neither...nor...nor...nor' for emphasis. There is no doubting his self-belief and confidence here.

> I feel absolute reverence to nobody and to nothing human
> neither to persons nor things nor ideas, ideals nor religions
>   nor institutions,
> to these things I feel only respect, and a tinge of reverence
> when I see the fluttering of pure life in them.

The speaker respects ideas, ideals, religions and institutions, but is wary of them. Respect yes and when he sees 'the fluttering of pure life in them', he feels 'a tinge of reverence'. Both 'tinge' and 'fluttering' are very effective here.

The conjunction 'But' at the beginning of the second section brings the poem in another direction. Having told us what he cannot fully revere, he will now reveal what earns his 'absolute reverence'. Reverence has spiritual connotations and is much stronger than respect. That is why in the poem's second section the speaker focuses on 'something unseen, unknown, creative', something metaphysical. He does not name God, he does not mention Creation, but he admits that he himself is part of this great energy and force: 'I feel I am a derivative'. By doing so, he is expressing absolute reverence for this presence and by implication for himself. The final sentence, 'Say no more!', is at once jokey, casual and quietly confident. It is a tone that suggests he enjoys his conclusion.

What Have They Done to You?

The poem begins and ends with questions. Throughout, the speaker is preoccupied with addressing injustice on behalf of the working class. Industrialisation, the poem argues, has 'devoured' the masses and those in control have destroyed 'man's native instincts and intuitions'.

Even the first word in each of the eight stanzas – 'What'; 'What'; 'Alas'; 'They'; 'They'; 'They'; 'Your'; 'Oh' – captures the speaker's anger and passion. This poem argues that the ordinary man no longer has any dignity. In the opening line, 'creeping' is used to describe crowds of men going to and from work and portrays man as something low, inelegant and oppressed.

Here, the speaker is on the side of the 'men of the masses' and the repeated question at the beginning of line 2 – 'What have they done to you?' – emphasises his concern. Initially, he addresses these ordinary men and tells them how they have been belittled, what they have become.

In the second section, he identifies how this situation has come about. Others have grown rich at the expense of these workers and in an ironic phrase he calls these others 'the saviours of the people'.

The poem then lists and explores the various ways in which the men of the masses have been conditioned and changed. Not only industrialisation and the machine but workmen's dwellings, board-school education, newspapers and the cinema are all condemned. The use of 'devoured' is a powerful means of describing how mechanisation destroys.

The word 'Alas' expresses the speaker's regret that the 'men of the masses' are no longer in charge of their own lives. To have been saved from yourself suggests that some danger has been avoided, but the speaker thinks that what the 'saviours' have done is worse:

> Alas, they have saved you from yourself, from your own
>   frail dangers
> and devoured you with the machine, the vast maw of iron.

'Frail dangers' and 'squalid cottages' are preferable, according to the speaker, and better than systems that take away your individuality. Even newspapers and the cinema are criticised because they destroy your soul. They steal your body and leave you:

>   an animated carcass
> to work with and nothing else:
> unless goggling eyes, to goggle at the film
> and a board-school brain, stuffed up with the ha'penny press.

What the speaker values most is his fellow man's 'native instincts and intuitions'. Certain kinds of work and education destroy. Work is referred to as 'the dole of work, and the dole is your wage of nullity'. One meaning of the word 'dole' is 'a person's lot or destiny' and if this meaning is intended here, then work is seen as something negative, a 'nullity' – a thing of no importance or worth, a nothingness.

The dominant tone is urgent, concerned, angry, but line 7,

> 'They took away, oh they took away'

and the use of 'oh', and using the same words on both sides of that 'oh', captures the speaker's regret.

There is no doubting the speaker's sincerity. It is a lively defence of what he values. It is an intense outburst. What he doesn't want to see is man reduced to 'an animated carcass' and the closing lines of the poem sum up not only what he has touched on already but the title of the poem; the opening line of the poem is repeated again, three times:

> Your instincts gone, your intuition gone, your passions dead
> Oh carcass with a board-school mind and a ha'penny news-
>   paper intelligence,
> what have they done to you, what have they done to you,
> Oh what have they done to you?

Repetition here – your/your, gone/gone and the use of 'dead', that word 'carcass' again – creates a strong rhythm and rhetoric. 'Oh' occurs in line 2 and 7, and five times in the final five lines. This adds momentum to the poem's powerful and passionate message. In the final couplet, the word 'you', which has been used all along, becomes 'them'. It is as if, having spoken directly to his fellow men, he now stands back and takes a look at them and calls on the reader to:

> Oh look at my fellow-men, oh look at them
> the masses! Oh, what has been done to them!

It is an invitation to explore the importance of our 'native instincts and intuitions' and to consider how these are suffocated and diminished, destroyed by outside, man-made forces.

'Trailing Clouds'

This is one of two poems called 'Baby Movements II' and captures the speaker's response to holding a baby in his arms. Everyone has seen how people respond when they see a little baby, or how the atmosphere changes when a baby is brought into a room. It brings out the best in people. A baby is also vulnerable; it needs to be protected and cherished, and those ideas are also explored here.

This poem, just three sentences long, illustrates what Aldous Huxley said of D.H. Lawrence, that he was 'a being, somehow, of another order, more sensitive, more highly conscious, more capable of feeling than even the most gifted of common men.'

The poem opens with an unusual simile. The baby is compared to a 'drenched, drowned bee' hanging on a bending flower. The bee clings to the flower just as the baby clings to the speaker. It is a poem that plays on our senses; we see, feel, touch, hear the details in the poem and sensuous words – drenched, drowned, numb, brushed – create these tactile elements.

The speaker cares for this baby, it is 'My baby' and this baby has been crying – 'her brown hair' is 'brushed with wet tears' and is 'laid laughterless on her cheek'. The speaker has sung a lullaby and the bee and flower image is used again to paint a picture of a baby depending on someone to care for it. The speaker's dedication is clear. He speaks of 'My baby', 'My sleeping baby', and there is an anxiety in how he refers to this baby as swaying 'on my arm like sorrowful, storm-heavy boughs.'

Unusually, for D.H. Lawrence, there are end rhymes – 'bee/me', 'shower/flower' – but the vivid pictures, the run-on lines, alliteration and assonance, and the intense feelings captured in the poem make it memorable. The 's' sounds create a softness as in:

> Her soft white legs hanging heavily over my arm
> Swinging to my lullaby.
> My sleeping baby hangs upon my life
> As a silent bee at the end of a shower
> Draws down the burdened flower.
> She who has always seemed so light
> Sways on my arm like sorrowful, storm-heavy boughs,
> Even her floating hair sinks like storm-bruised young leaves

But sorrow is one of the dominant feelings in the poem, a sorrow born out of the speaker's love for this baby. The 'drenched, drowned bee' image in line 1 and line 15, the wet tears, the simile 'like sorrowful, storm-heavy boughs', the realisation that 'She who always seemed so light' is associated with 'a heaviness, and a weariness', collectively bring a realistic touch to the poem. The poem was originally called 'A Baby Asleep After Pain'. The images, though drawn from the natural world – bee, flower, shower, boughs, leaves – are described in such a way that they create a wish to protect this baby from life's sorrows.

Bavarian Gentians

From the opening two lines – just read them aloud – you realise that this poem has a slow, sad, seductive, beautiful music. The alliteration, the half-rhyme, the rhythm, the punctuation all contribute to this:

> Not every man has gentians in his house
> In soft September, at slow, sad Michaelmas.

Written not long before he died, Lawrence in 'Bavarian Gentians' confronts his mortality. Written in free verse, the poem tells of how these deep-blue, trumpet-shaped flowers will guide the speaker on his journey towards darkness and death. This darkness is not seen as something frightening.

The voice, calm and gentle as it describes the 'tall and dark' gentians, recognises a link between the gentians and the underworld. The Bavarian gentians are 'dark, darkening the daytime torch-like with the smoking blueness/ of Pluto's gloom'. The flowers have become, in the speaker's imagination, ways of guiding and lighting his way into the darkness, from one world into the next.

September marks the dying of the year and that time of year in Greek myth when Persephone has to return to her gloomy husband in the underworld. The celebration of Michael the Archangel belongs to the Christian calendar. It belongs to the world above ground and this Christian references – 'Michaelmas' – is mentioned once in the poem. The Greek myth of Pluto/Dis and Persephone/ Demeter is mentioned again and again and it is this underworld that the speaker imagines journeying to in the poem.

The darkness of Pluto's realm is sensuously evoked, especially through the colour blue and the idea of smoke, and both are combined in a phrase such as 'blue-smoking'. Repetition of 'dark', 'blue' and 'smoking' create an otherworldly atmosphere:

> Bavarian gentians, tall and **dark**, but **dark**
> ribbed hellish flowers erect, with the blaze of **darkness** spread **blue**,
> blown flat into points, by the heavy white draught of the day.

> Torch-flowers of the **blue-smoking darkness**, Pluto's **dark-blue** blaze
> black lamps from the halls of Dis, **smoking dark blue**
> giving off **darkness**, **blue darkness**, upon Demeter's yellow-pale day
> whom have you come for, here in the white-cast day?

Both of these stanzas end with references to the 'white' day, the 'heavy white draught of the day', the 'yellow-pale day' and the 'white-cast day', a striking contrast with the dark smoky blues of Pluto's kingdom. In line 10, the world 'here' is described in terms of this bright, white light, but into this world comes the black lamps from the halls of Dis. The light of day is usually something positive, but not in this context.

The underworld seems more attractive and the poem conjures up a huge dark world with downward-leading stairs and halls. The speaker believes that the Bavarian gentians will serve as torches and light his way to Pluto's world.

At line 11 – 'Reach me a gentian, give me a torch!' – the tone is more urgent. It is an order. The poem then begins to move downwards. He will guide himself with the aid of the gentian torch 'down the darker and darker stairs'. Here, the speaker enters the darkness and though he has chosen to enter the underworld, what happens there, in terms of the Greek myth, is disturbing. It is the journey that Persephone is compelled to make in 'first-frosted September'; the speaker goes

> down the way Persephone goes, just now, in first-frosted September
> to the sightless realm where darkness is married to dark

and the words 'just now' give the moment an immediacy. Pluto and Persephone are married; they are bride and groom, and spoken of as 'darkness...married to dark'. In the opening line, the setting was a house, a particular place where the Bavarian gentians blazed blue. In the poem's fourth stanza, we are in 'the sightless realm', where things cannot be seen, where things can be felt, sounds can be heard – 'Persephone herself is but a voice'. Pluto symbolises male dominance and the image of

> a gloom invisible enfolded in the deeper dark

and of Persephone in

> the arms of Pluto as he ravishes her once again
> and pierces her once more with his passion of the utter dark

This paints a disturbing picture. Not only does this poem explore Christian/Pagan, light/darkness themes, male desire, sex, male dominance, but it has also been read as Lawrence's desire and primal instincts.

The Bavarian gentian flowers symbolise life and beauty, but they become symbols of darkness and the primal. Critics have argued that the flowers have sexual connotations – they are 'ribbed hellish flowers erect'. And in the closing stanza, the gentian is 'a flower on a tall stem' and the Pluto/Persephone relationship is portrayed as a sexual one.

Re-reading this poem is an enriching and rewarding experience, but it is a poem that remains mysterious and powerful. Is the speaker on Persephone's side? Is he identifying and sympathising with this figure who was abducted by the king of the underworld and imprisoned there for half of the year? Is the underworld the realm of the dead? Does death, as portrayed here, contain life? The Christian message says that death leads to eternal life.

The poem embraces the dark and when it speaks of 'the splendour of black-blue torches' it seems to accept the underworld, even if those very torches are 'shedding fathomless darkness on the nuptials'. The 'darker and darker stairs' have led to a darkness that is fathomless, yet 'living'.

In the final stanza, the mood echoes the earlier line – 'Reach me a gentian, give me a torch!' – in its determination:

> Give me a flower on a tall stem, and three dark flames,
> for I will go to the wedding, and be wedding-guest
> at the marriage of the living dark.

Here, 'the living dark' and the words 'wedding' and 'marriage' suggest new beginnings and the tone is forward-looking: 'Give me a flower' and 'I will go to the wedding'. The wedding in this instance is one shrouded in darkness and the union between Pluto and Persephone is a troubled one; their world is one of endless darkness. As a wedding-guest, the speaker will witness the union and share this darkness. Persephone, as a bride, is 'a gloom invisible enfolded in the deeper dark' and this is the world that the speaker embraces.

Adrienne Rich
(1929–2012)

Contents	Page

The Overview

Adrienne Rich, poet and political activist, has been a striking and important presence for several decades and Michael Schmidt in *Lives of the Poets* sees her in the context of the 1960s and Black Power, the rise of feminism and the gay movement and Vietnam. 'It is necessary to see her in these contexts,' he argues, 'because they provide occasions first for her formal strategies and tentativeness, then for the emerging assurance that has made her a figure central to the American women's movement and to the liberalisation of American poetry.' But she is important for more than her political activism. Her poetry is a powerful response to the time but it is also a poetry which is acutely aware of a poetic tradition.

●

The ten poems prescribed here focus on themes central to Rich's work: power, gender, sexuality, the private, the political. 'Storm Warnings' is a poem that looks at change and its implications; 'Aunt Jennifer's Tigers' explores male power and authority within a domestic setting; a similar theme is found in 'The Uncle Speaks in the Drawing Room'. The role of the female, expected and otherwise, is a central idea in 'Living in Sin' and 'The Roofwalker' with its powerful image becomes an image of the unfulfilled speaker's sense of a life that is dangerous and different and longed for. 'Our Whole Life' reviews a relationship and admits that the situation is dishonest and hopeless but this poem is, in Adrienne Rich's words, 'concerned with an entire society facing its self-delusions'.

The tension between a man and a woman is also found in 'Trying to Talk with a Man' and the speaker feels 'helpless'. A more assertive voice speaks in 'Diving Into the Wreck', in which the central image of a woman exploring wreckage and returning to the surface with a new understanding becomes an image of a woman surviving her past. 'From a Survivor', written in 1972, addresses her dead husband, 'wastefully dead', and acknowledges with tenderness and regret – 'Like everybody else, we thought of ourselves as special' – the mystery, complexities and strangeness of human relationships. And in 'Power' Rich celebrates an extraordinary, selfless woman, Marie Curie, who dedicated herself to scientific knowledge and discovery with courage and determination.

●

Change is central to Adrienne Rich's life and work. 'What does not change is the will to change' writes Charles Olson in his poem 'The Kingfishers' and, quoting Olson, *The Will to Change* became the title of Rich's 1971 collection. Her poetry is a record of private and public, of the personal and the political and at the heart of her work is the need for and the courage for change.

Her changing life is reflected in her poetry both thematically and stylistically: her poetry became more urgent and less formal, less conventional. In her Foreword to *Collected Early Poems 1950–1970*, Rich notes that 'The word "change" occurs in the titles of both the first and the last books in this collection and in the first and last poems'.

In January 1984, when Adrienne Rich wrote a Foreword to *The Fact of a Doorframe Poems Selected and New 1950–1984*, which included the ten poems here, she said that 'The poems in this book were written by a woman growing up and living in the fatherland of the United States of North America. One task for the nineteen- or twenty-year-old poet who wrote the earliest poems here was to learn that she was neither unique nor universal, but a person in history, a woman and not a man, a white and also Jewish inheritor of a particular Western consciousness, from the making of which most women have been excluded'.

●

In a 1991 interview with David Montenegro in which she discussed how the language of poetry contains a kind of code, Rich admits that for her, from the beginning, 'poems were a way of talking about what I couldn't talk about any other way' and that 'I learned while very young that you could be fairly encoded in poems, and get away with it. Then I began to want to do away with the encoding, or to break the given codes and maybe find another code. But it was a place of a certain degree of control, in which to explore things, in which to start testing the waters'.

In a Foreword to *Collected Early Poems 1950–1970,* Rich says: 'My generation of North Americans had learned, at sixteen, about the death camps and the possibility of total human self-extinction through nuclear war. Still, at twenty, I implicitly dissociated poetry from politics. At college in the late 1940s, I sat in classes with World War II vets on the G.I. Bill of Rights; I knew women who campaigned for Henry Wallace's Progressive party, picketed a local garment factory, founded a college NAACP chapter, were recent refugees from Nazism. I had no political ideas of my own, only the era's vague and hallucinatory anti-Communism and the encroaching privatism in the 1950s. Drenched in invisible assumptions of my class and race, unable to fathom the pervasive ideology of gender, I felt 'politics' as distant, vaguely sinister, the province of powerful older men or of people I saw as fanatics. It was in poetry that I sought a grasp on the world and the interior events, 'ideas of order', even power.

I was like someone walking through a fogged-in city, compelled on an errand she cannot describe, carrying maps she cannot use except in neighborhoods already familiar. But the errand lies outside those neighborhoods. I was someone holding one end of a powerful connector, useless without the other end'.

Reviewing *Diving into the Wreck* in the *New York Times* Book Review, 10 December 1973, Margaret Atwood said that 'When I first heard the author read from it, I felt as though the top of my head was being attacked, sometimes with an ice pick, sometimes with a blunter instrument: a hatchet or a hammer. The predominant emotions seemed to be anger and hatred, and these are certainly present; but when I read the poems later, they evoked a far more subtle reaction. *Diving into the Wreck* is one of those rare books that forces you to decide not just what you think about yourself. It is a book that takes risks, and it forces the reader to take them also.'

'I never had much belief in the idea of the poet as someone of special sensitivity or spiritual insight, who rightfully lives above and off from the ordinary general life,' says Adrienne Rich and her poetry is very much an including experience. Her passionate interest in her fellow human being and her belief in the power of the poem are both wonderfully captured in her poem 'In A Classroom' from 1986:

In A Classroom

Talking of poetry, hauling the books
arm-full to the table where the heads
talking of consonants, elision,
caught in the how, oblivious of why:
I look in your face, Jude,
neither frowning nor nodding,
opaque in the slant of dust-motes over the table:
a presence like a stone, if a stone were thinking
What I cannot say, is me. For that I came.

Here we are also reminded of the importance of the making of the poem, the 'how'; and that an awareness of the technical aspects of the work such as 'consonants, elision' are vital.

●

The Harper American Literature Anthology [Volume 2] says that Adrienne Rich resembles the Victorians in 'her earnestness, her direct gaze at social conditions, and her tone of public moral assertion' and that her poetry 'lacks suppleness, play, wit, and humour; she is always serious'.

These last descriptions are intended as negative and yet Adrienne Rich's poetry speaks to hundreds of thousands of readers. Why this is so is best understood when we read Rich's own account of her sense of relationship with her reader: 'In writing poetry I have known both the keen happiness and the worst fear – that the walls cannot be broken down, that these words will fail to enter another soul. Over the years it has seemed to me just that – the desire to be heard, to resound in another's soul – that is the impulse behind writing poems, for me. Increasingly this has meant hearing and listening to others, taking into myself the language of experience different from my own – whether in written words, or in the rush and ebb of broken but stubborn conversations. I have changed, my poems have changed, through this process, and it continues.'

Her poetry has charted change both private and public. It is no coincidence that Adrienne Rich is thought to have coined the term 're-visioning' – which recasts the past and reworks received opinion and received stories and in turn her poetry has changed the way people live and think about their lives.

●

As an American she has seen her country, the most powerful in the world, exert its power. And she is outspoken. Writing of the Persian Gulf War, in 'What Is Found There', she says that 'War comes at the end of the twentieth century as absolute failure of imagination, scientific and political. That a war can be represented as helping a people to "feel good" about themselves, their country, is a measure of that failure.' All the more reason then that poetry plays its part. In that same book she writes: 'Poetry becomes more necessary than ever: it keeps the underground aquifers flowing; it is the liquid voice that can break through stone'.

She was undoubtedly serious, determined and sane: 'I intend to go on making poetry. I intend to go on trying to be part of what I think of as an underground stream – of voices resisting the voices that tell us we are nothing, that we are worthless, or that we all hate each other, or should hate each other. I think that there is a real culture of resistance here [United States, 1995] – of artists' and of other kinds of voices – that will continue, however bad things get in this country. I want to make myself part of that and do my work as well as I can. I want to love those I love as well as I can, and I want to love life as well as I can'.

The poems deal with many issues and work best when, in Margaret Atwood's words, 'they resist the temptation to sloganize, when they don't preach at me'.

In her poem 'Delta' dated 1987, Adrienne Rich writes:

> If you think you can grasp me, think again:
> my story flows in more than one direction
> a delta springing from the riverbed
> with its five fingers spread

and the poem, flowing in many directions, needs its readers: 'I believe that a poem isn't completed until there's a reader at the other end of it. It just can't be produced, it also has to be received.'

Biographical Notes

Adrienne [pronounced AHdrienne] Rich was born 'white and middle-class' on 16 May 1929 in Baltimore, Maryland. Encouraged by her father, she began writing poetry as a child and she also read from her father's 'very Victorian, pre-Raphaelite' library. As a girl growing up, she read Keats, Tennyson, Arnold, Blake, Rossetti, Swinburne, Carlyle and Pater. Such was her father's encouragement to read and write that 'for twenty years I wrote for a particular man, who criticised me and praised me and made me feel "special" . . . I tried for a long time to please him, or rather, not to displease him'. Her grandmother and mother, Rich said, were 'frustrated artists and intellectuals, a lost writer and a lost composer between them'.

Speaking of her early years, Rich herself said in 1983: 'I was born at the brink of the Great Depression; I reached sixteen the year of Nagasaki and Hiroshima. The daughter of a Jewish father and a Protestant mother, I learned about the Holocaust first from the newsreels of the liberation of the death camps. I was a young white woman who had never known hunger or homelessness, growing up in the suburbs of a deeply segregated city in which neighbours were also dictated along religious lines: Christian and Jewish. I lived sixteen years of my life secure in the belief that though cities could be bombed and civilian populations killed, the earth stood in its old indestructible way. The process through which nuclear annihilation was to become a part of all human calculation had already begun, but we did not live with that knowledge during the first sixteen years of my life.'

In 1951, Rich graduated from Radcliffe College, part of Harvard University, in Cambridge, Massachusetts. As an undergraduate, Rich read male poets – Frost, Dylan Thomas, Donne, Auden, MacNeice, Stevens, Yeats and at first she saw those male poets as her models. That same year she published her first collection, *A Change of World*, which had been chosen by W. H. Auden for the Yale Younger Poets Award. In a Foreword to the book, Auden said that the twenty-one-year-old 'Miss Rich' displayed 'a modesty not so common at that age, which disclaims any extraordinary vision, and a love for her medium, a determination to ensure that whatever she writes shall, at least, not be shoddily made'. But most famously, Auden said that the poems in Rich's first collection 'are neatly and modestly dressed, speak quietly but do not mumble, respect their elders but are not cowed by them, and do not tell fibs'.

In 1952–1953 Adrienne Rich travelled to Continental Europe and England on a Guggenheim Fellowship and in 1953 she married Alfred H. Conrad, an economist at Harvard. Later, writing of this time, Rich said: 'My husband spoke eagerly of the children we would have; my parents-in-law awaited the birth of their grandchild. I had no idea of what I wanted, what I could or could not choose'.

They lived in Cambridge from 1953 to 1966 and in the 1950s had three children. In 1955, Rich published her second collection *The Diamond Cutters and Other Poems*, which won the Ridgely Torrence Memorial Award of the Poetry Society of America. In 1960 she was honoured with the National Institute of Arts and Letters Award and the Phi Beta Kappa poet at William and Mary College. In 1961–1962 she and her family spent a year in the Netherlands on a Guggenheim Fellowship.

Wife, mother, prize-winning poet, Adrienne Rich, in the words of Richard Ellmann and Robert O'Clair, 'seemed to have everything a woman was supposed to want in the American Fifties'. And in her 'When We Dead Awaken' (1971) essay, Rich said that to think otherwise about that 1950s life 'could only mean that I was ungrateful, insatiable, perhaps a monster'. Yet the 1950s and early 1960s were in Ellmann and O'Clair's words 'desperate years for her'. It was a time in Rich's life when 'I think I began at this point to feel that politics was not something "out there" but something "in here" and of the essence of my condition'.

In 1963, her breakthrough collection, *Snapshots of a Daughter-in-Law* was published, with its themes of rebellion and disaffection, and in 1966 the family moved to New York City. She and her husband became radically political, especially in relation to the Vietnam War. She was teaching inner-city minority young people in an Open Admissions programme at City College, New York and this brought her into contact with young writers from different social and ethnic backgrounds. Her next three poetry collections, *Necessities of Life* (1966), *Leaflets* (1969) and *The Will to Change* (1971), in their very titles signalled a strong political awareness.

Married for seventeen years, Rich left her husband in 1970. He died that same year. In 1973, *Diving Into the Wreck* was published and won the National Book Award the following year. Rich, however, rejected the award as an individual but accepted it 'in the name of all women'. Audre Lorde and Alice Walker, the two other nominees, together with Adrienne Rich wrote the following statement: 'We . . . together accept this award in the name of all the women whose voices have gone and still go unheard in a patriarchal world, and in the name of those who, like us, have been tolerated as token women in this culture, often at great cost and in great pain . . . We symbolically join here in refusing the terms of patriarchal competition and declaring that we will share this prize among us, to be used as best we can for women . . . We dedicate this occasion to the struggle for self-determination for all women, of every colour, identification or derived class . . . the women who will understand what we are doing here and those who will not understand yet; the silent women whose voices have been denied us, the articulate women who have given us strength to do our work.'

Over the last forty years, Adrienne Rich published more than sixteen volumes of poetry and four books of non-fiction prose. She writes of being white, Jewish, radical and lesbian in America; she writes 'in full knowledge that the majority of the world's illiterates are women, that I live in a technologically advanced country where 40 per cent of the people can barely read and 20 per cent are functionally illiterate'. As a writer, Rich sees her work 'as part of something larger than my own life or the history of literature' and 'I feel a responsibility to keep searching for teachers who can help me widen and deepen the sources and examine the ego that speaks in my poems – not for "political correctness", but for ignorance, solipsism, laziness, dishonesty, automatic writing.'

In 1986, Rich wrote 'I had been looking for the Women's Liberation Movement since the 1950s. I came into it in 1970 . . . I identified myself as a radical feminist, and soon after – not as a political act but out of powerful and unmistakable feelings – as a lesbian'.

In an Interview with Bill Moyers in *The Language of Life*, *A Festival of Poets*, Adrienne Rich says: 'I believe that poetry asks us to consider the quality of life. Poetry reflects on the quality of life, on us as we are in process on this earth, in our lives, in our relationships, in our communities. It embodies what makes it possible for us to continue as human under the barrage of brute violence, numbing indifference, trivialization, and shallowness that we endure, not to speak of what has come to seem in public life like a total loss on the part of politicians of any desire even to appear consistent, or to appear to adhere to principle.'

Her works have been translated into Dutch, French, German, Greek, Hebrew, Italian, Japanese, Spanish, Swedish and Ukrainian and her many honours and awards include the Brandeis Creative Arts Commission Medal for Poetry, the Elmer Holmes Bobst Award in Poetry from New York University and the Fund for Human Dignity Award from the National Gay Task Force. She was a member of New Jewish Agenda, a national organisation of progressive Jews which disbanded in the 1980s and was a founding editor of the Jewish feminist journal *Bridges*.

Her most recent books of poetry are *Telephone Ringing in the Labyrinth: Poems 2004–2006* and *The School Among the Ruins: 2000–2004*. A selection of her essays, *Arts of the Possible: Essays and Conversations*, appeared in 2001. She edited Muriel Rukeyser's *Selected Poems for the Library of America*. *A Human Eye: Essays on Art in Society* appeared in April 2009. She is a recipient of the National Book Foundation's 2006 Medal for Distinguished Contribution to American Letters, among other honours.

Adrienne Rich lived in California since 1984 where she taught English and feminist studies at Stanford University until 1992. She died on 27 March 2012.

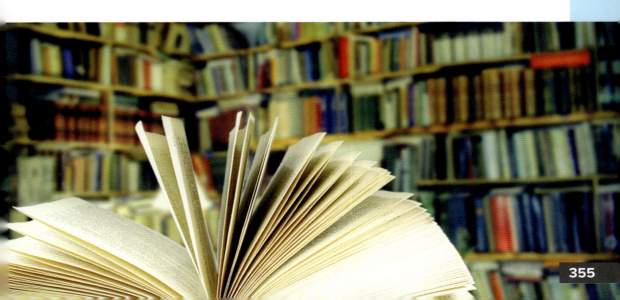

POEMS

The poems, as they are printed here, are in the order in which they are printed in *Collected Early Poems 1950–1970* and *The Fact of a Doorframe Poems Selected and New Poems 1950–1984*. Rich began dating her poems in 1954, as if, in Richard Ellmann and Robert O'Clair's words, 'to underline their provisional or journal-entry nature'. Rich herself said that she began dating poems in 1954 because she 'felt embarked on a process that was precarious and exploratory; I needed to allow the poems to acknowledge their moment'.

Storm Warnings

The glass has been falling all the afternoon,
And knowing better than the instrument
What winds are walking overhead, what zone
Of gray unrest is moving across the land,
I leave the book upon a pillowed chair   5
And walk from window to closed window, watching
Boughs strain against the sky

And think again, as often when the air
Moves inward toward a silent core of waiting,
How with a single purpose time has traveled   10
By secret currents of the undiscerned
Into this polar realm. Weather abroad
And weather in the heart alike come on
Regardless of prediction.

Between foreseeing and averting change   15
Lies all the mastery of elements
Which clocks and weatherglasses cannot alter.
Time in the hand is not control of time,
Nor shattered fragments of an instrument
A proof against the wind; the wind will rise,   20
We can only close the shutters.

I draw the curtains as the sky goes black
And set a match to candles sheathed in glass
Against the keyhole draught, the insistent whine
Of weather through the unsealed aperture.   25
This is our sole defense against the season;
These are the things that we have learned to do
Who live in troubled regions.

Glossary

Line 1 glass: weather glass or barometer – an instrument for measuring atmospheric pressure.

Line 9 core: centre/central region.

Line 11 undiscerned: unnoticed, not perceived by mind or body.

Line 12 polar realm: cold kingdom.

Line 15 averting: preventing.

Line 23 sheathed: protected by, enclosed.

Line 25 aperture: opening, gap.

'Storm Warnings' was written in 1949 when Adrienne Rich was twenty. Writing in the Foreword to *Collected Early Poems 1950–1970*, Rich says: 'Storm Warnings' is a poem about powerlessness — about a force so much greater than our human powers that while it can be measured and even predicted, it is beyond human control.' All 'we' can do is create an interior space against the storm, an enclave of self-protection, though the winds of change still penetrate keyholes and 'unsealed apertures'. Nothing in the scene of this poem suggests that it was written in the early days of the Cold War, within a twenty year old's earshot of World War II, at the end of the decade of the Warsaw Ghetto and Auschwitz, Hiroshima and Nagasaki, in a climate of public fatalism about World War III. The poet assumes that change is to be averted if it can be, defended against if it must come . . . 'Change' here means unpredictability, unrest, menace — not something 'we' might desire and even help bring to pass.

? Questions

1. How would you describe the atmosphere in the opening lines? Which details, in your opinion, best capture that atmosphere?

2. The poet says that she knows better than the instrument that a storm is on the way. What does that tell us about the poet?

3. How do you interpret the words 'a silent core of waiting'?

4. The poet describes where she is at as 'this polar realm'. What does this tell us about the speaker?

5. What connection does the speaker in the poem make between 'Weather abroad/ And weather in the heart'?

6. Do you think that there is a feeling of helplessness in the third stanza? Give reasons for your answer.

7. The setting of the poem is that of a room with a woman in it and her awareness of a gathering storm. Could this be read as a metaphor? Explain.

8. How does the speaker react to the situation that she finds herself in? Is it a head or a heart response or a mixture of both do you think?

9. Comment on the image of the guarded candle flames 'sheathed in glass/ Against the keyhole draught'. What feeling does it create?

10. How would you describe the speaker's attitude towards the drawing of the curtains, the lighting of candles? Empowered? Threatened? Defenceless? Resigned?

11. Examine how this poem explores the tensions between the individual and the wider world. Who do you think the speaker is referring to when she says 'we' in line 27?

12. 'Storm Warnings' is both an atmospheric piece of writing and an interesting personal statement. Discuss this view. Which aspect of the poem appealed to you most?

13. Commenting on this poem, W.H. Auden said that the emotions that motivated 'Storm Warnings' were feelings of 'historical apprehension'. What do you think he meant by this? Would you agree that such emotions are found in the poem?

14. The word 'change' is in the title of the collection from which 'Storm Warnings' [A Change of World] is taken. It also occurs in 'Storm Warnings', the opening poem in the collection. Why is change an important idea here?

15. It has been said that Rich in her poetry has chosen to write about people 'Who live in troubled regions'. Discuss this in relation to the poems by Rich on your course.

16. Would you agree that this is a well-crafted poem? Identify aspects which make it so. How does the formal structure contribute to the poem's theme?

Aunt Jennifer's Tigers

Aunt Jennifer's tigers prance across a screen,
Bright topaz denizens of a world of green.
They do not fear the men beneath the tree;
They pace in sleek chivalric certainty.

Aunt Jennifer's fingers fluttering through her wool   5
Find even the ivory needle hard to pull.
The massive weight of Uncle's wedding band
Sits heavily upon Aunt Jennifer's hand.

When Aunt is dead, her terrified hands will lie
Still ringed with ordeals she was mastered by.   10
The tigers in the panel that she made
Will go on prancing, proud and unafraid.

Glossary

Line 1 prance: bound, spring forward from hind legs.

Line 1 screen: an ornamental panel placed before an empty firegrate or used to keep off the heat from a fire. Not very common nowadays.

Line 2 topaz: the golden, yellow colour of the precious stone.

Line 2 denizens: inhabitants.

Line 4 sleek: smooth, glossy.

Line 4 chivalric: brave, gallant, like knights.

Line 6 ivory: made of animal tusk.

Line 10 ordeals: difficult experiences, severe trials, endurances.

> Rich, in her essay 'When We Dead Awaken' (1971), says: "Looking back at poems I wrote before I was twenty-one, I'm startled because beneath the conscious craft are glimpses of the split I even then experienced between the girl who wrote poems, who defined herself writing poems, and the girl who was to define herself by her relationships with men. 'Aunt Jennifer's Tigers' (1951), written while I was a student, looks with deliberate detachment at this split."

? Questions

1. Having read through the text, how would you act out this poem? How could a class group create an effective tableau of the situation within the poem?

2. Draw your version of the panel or screen that Aunt Jennifer is embroidering. What does the image tell us about the relationship between men and animals?

3. The poem is a series of descriptions, statements, imaginings. Which of these is the most powerful in your opinion?

4. Comment on 'fluttering' and 'massive'.

5. What does the regular rhyme contribute to the overall effect? Does the poem's formal structure match its theme? Explain.

6. What is the effect of the rhythm and rhyme here?

7. Is this, in your opinion, an out-of-date poem for today's teenage reader? Give reasons for your answer.

8. Why do you think Adrienne Rich ends her poem with a reference to the tigers 'prancing, proud and unafraid'?

The Uncle Speaks in the Drawing Room

I have seen the mob of late
Standing sullen in the square,
Gazing with a sullen stare
At window, balcony, and gate.
Some have talked in bitter tones,   5
Some have held and fingered stones.

These are follies that subside.
Let us consider, none the less,
Certain frailties of glass
Which, it cannot be denied,   10
Lead in times like these to fear
For crystal vase and chandelier.

Not that missiles will be cast;
None as yet dare lift an arm.
But the scene recalls a storm   15
When our grandsire stood aghast
To see his antique ruby bowl
Shivered in a thunder-roll.

Let us only bear in mind
How these treasures handed down   20
From a calmer age passed on
Are in the keeping of our kind.
We stand between the dead glass-blowers
And murmurings of missile-throwers.

Glossary

Title Drawing Room: an elegant and beautifully furnished room; originally 'withdrawing-room' – a room to which the company withdraws after dinner; also the room to which ladies withdraw from the dining-room after dinner.

Line 1 mob: the rabble, the vulgar, the common people; a disorderly crowd, a riotous assembly [from Latin mobile vulgus = excitable/mobile crowd].

Line 2 sullen: angry, silent.

Line 7 follies: foolish behaviour.

Line 13 missiles: weapons/objects that can be thrown or fired.

Line 16 grandsire: grandsire is an old-fashioned word for grandfather (sire means a senior or elder).

Line 16 aghast: terrified, frightened.

Line 22 in the keeping of our kind: in the custody and safe-keeping of people like us.

Questions

1. What is the effect of 'The Uncle' as opposed to 'Uncle' or 'My Uncle' in the title? Comment on 'Speaks' as opposed to, say, 'shouts'. What do the words 'Drawing Room' suggest?

2. The poet here is speaking in the voice of The Uncle. Which words in stanza one best sum up the mob in the square? What image do the words 'window, balcony, and gate' summon up?

3. Consider the effect of the drumbeat rhyme and rhythm in the opening lines. How do they suit what is being said?

4. The Uncle is confident ('These are follies that subside' – line 7) that the mob is not a realistic or serious threat. Who is he addressing when he says 'Let us consider'? What, do you think, has created that confidence?

5. He fears for 'crystal vase and chandelier'. What do these precious objects symbolise?

6. How would you describe the Uncle's tone? Smug? Superior? How do you respond to line 22: 'the keeping of our kind'?

7. What does this poem say about the relationship between the privileged classes and the ordinary people?

8. Does this read like a poem from the 1950s? Why? Why not?

9. What does this poem say about the past, the present, the future? What does this poem say about women?

10. This poem was written by an American woman in the world's supposedly greatest democracy. Why do you think Adrienne Rich wrote such a poem? Does it make you angry? Does it sadden you? Do you think it is a political poem? Give reasons for your answers.

Living in Sin

She had thought the studio would keep itself;
no dust upon the furniture of love.
Half heresy, to wish the taps less vocal,
the panes relieved of grime. A plate of pears,
a piano with a Persian shawl, a cat   5
stalking the picturesque amusing mouse
had risen at his urging.
Not that at five each separate stair would writhe
under the milkman's tramp; that morning light
so coldly would delineate the scraps   10
of last night's cheese and three sepulchral bottles;
that on the kitchen shelf among the saucers
a pair of beetle-eyes would fix her own—
envoy from some village in the moldings . . .
Meanwhile, he, with a yawn,   15
sounded a dozen notes upon the keyboard,
declared it out of tune, shrugged at the mirror,
rubbed at his beard, went out for cigarettes;
while she, jeered by the minor demons,
pulled back the sheets and made the bed and found   20
a towel to dust the table-top,
and let the coffee-pot boil over on the stove.
By evening she was back in love again,
though not so wholly but throughout the night
she woke sometimes to feel the daylight coming   25
like a relentless milkman up the stairs.

📖 Glossary

Line 1 studio: an artist's workplace, here a studio (one-room) apartment – where he lives and works.

Line 3 heresy: opposite to accepted beliefs.

Line 6 picturesque: worthy of being a picture.

Line 8 writhe: twist or squirm in extreme pain.

Line 10 delineate: show, outline (an art term).

Line 11 sepulchral: gloomy, dismal.

Line 14 moldings: strip of wood or plaster used for decoration.

Line 19 demons: evil spirits, devils.

Line 26 relentless: never-ending, persistent, merciless.

> Unlike the previous three poems in this selection, 'Living in Sin' uses a different format. In her early work Rich chose a formal structure – stanza and rhyme. She began to abandon formalism but said that formalism was once necessary: 'Like asbestos gloves, it allowed me to handle materials I couldn't pick up barehanded'. Reading through the ten Rich poems here [from 1949 to 1974], there is a change in the way that the poem is arranged on the page.

❓ Questions

1. The phrase 'Living in sin' is rarely heard or used now. What does it refer to in the poem? What does it tell us about people's attitudes at the time the poem was written?

2. The poem opens with a realisation. How would you describe the speaker's understanding of the situation (lines 1–2) that she finds herself in?

3. Why are morning and evening associated with different thoughts and feelings in the speaker?

4. How is the man portrayed in the poem? List those details which give us a sense of his personality. Do you find him interesting? Why do you think the woman found him interesting? How would you describe the relationship between the He and She of the poem?

5. There is dust on the actual furniture and on 'the furniture of love'; the speaker imagines that the beetle on the kitchen shelf belongs to a 'village' of beetles. How relevant are the grubby, grotty surroundings in the poem?

6. The man is an artist. The woman is his lover. She is also the person who cleans and tidies. What might Rich be suggesting here about gender roles? What do you understand by the words 'minor demons' (line 19)?

7. What mood dominates the closing lines of the poem? Pick out the details that best help to create that mood.

8. Comment on art in relation to this poem: the painting which the man makes and the poem which Adrienne Rich writes.

9. The critic Margaret Dickie says that Rich has never been able to write 'love' without writing 'politics'. Would you agree with this view in relation to this poem?

10. Comment of the shape of the poem on the page. Why do you think Rich chose this form instead of separate stanzas, regular rhyme as in earlier poems such as 'Aunt Jennifer's Tigers' and 'The Uncle Speaks in the Drawing Room'?

The Roofwalker

– for Denise Levertov

Over the half-finished houses
night comes. The builders
stand on the roof. It is
quiet after the hammers,
the pulleys hang slack.   5
Giants, the roofwalkers,
on a listing deck, the wave
of darkness about to break
on their heads. The sky
is a torn sail where figures   10
pass magnified, shadows
on a burning deck.

I feel like them up there:
exposed, larger than life,
and due to break my neck.   15

Was it worth while to lay—
with infinite exertion—
a roof I can't live under?
—All those blueprints,
closings of gaps,   20
measurings, calculations?
A life I didn't choose
chose me: even
my tools are the wrong ones
for what I have to do.   25
I'm naked, ignorant,
a naked man fleeing
across the roofs
who could with a shade of difference

be sitting in the lamplight   30
against the cream wallpaper
reading—not with indifference—
about a naked man
fleeing across the roofs.

1961

📖 Glossary

Dedicatee: Denise Levertov (1923–1997), poet and anti-war activist.

Line 5 pulleys: grooved wheel and rope devices used for hoisting material.

Line 7 listing: leaning.

Line 7 deck: echoing/remembering, perhaps, the once well-known opening lines from Felicia Hemans's (1793–1835) poem 'Casabianca' – The boy stood on the burning deck/ Whence all but he had fled . . . Her poetry was especially popular in America.

Line 17 infinite exertion: endless effort.

Line 19 blueprints: detailed plans of work to be done; white upon blue photographic prints representing the final stage of engineering or other plans.

❓ Questions

1. Why is the speaker drawn to the roofwalker as an image for her own situation?

2. Comment on details such as 'half-finished', 'the wave of darkness', 'a burning deck'. How significant are they, in your opinion?

3. How would you describe the speaker's mood in lines 13–15?

4. The half-finished houses will one day become homes where families – Mom and Dad and children – will live. Relate this to the idea in lines 22–25: 'A life I didn't choose/ chose me: even/ my tools are the wrong ones/ for what I have to do.'

5. The poem ends with the idea of choice. Explore how and why this is a central idea in the poem.

6. Comment on the poem's final image.

7. How does this poem explore gender issues?

8. Examine how Rich makes and shapes this poem. Consider, for example, the run-on line and the absence of end-rhyme.

Our Whole Life

Our whole life a translation
the permissible fibs

and now a knot of lies
eating at itself to get undone

Words bitten thru words   5

meanings burnt-off like paint
under the blowtorch

All those dead letters
rendered into the oppressor's language

Trying to tell the doctor where it hurts   10
like the Algerian
who walked from his village, burning

his whole body a cloud of pain
and there are no words for this

except himself   15

1969

Glossary

Line 1 translation: interpreted by another?

Line 2 permissible fibs: acceptable lies – Rich here is suggesting that she and others are living a lie?

Line 7 blowtorch: (blowlamp) – instrument that produces powerful, hot flame used to remove paint.

Lines 8/9 dead letters/rendered: letters which form words and which have been taken over and thereby murdered/killed by the oppressor? Or, letters which were written and sent but never delivered, read and responded to?

Line 9 oppressor's language: the words used/spoken by those who rule with cruelty/tyranny.

Line 11 Algerian: a North African whose body has been set alight as a result of political unrest/protest? Many nations controlled Algeria. In 1830 France invaded Algeria and occupied the country until the Algerian rebellion of 1954. The country won its independence in 1962. [Adrienne Rich has said that 'My politics is in my body.']

? Questions

1. Why does the speaker feel excluded? Who is being referred to when she says 'Our whole life'?

2. What, according to the speaker, happens when 'a knot of lies' is the reality?

3. How does the poem create a sense of helplessness? Which words, images, feelings create this sense?

4. In some poems by Adrienne Rich there is a strong narrative or storyline. What technique is the poet using in 'Our Whole Life'? Do you think it is effective?

5. The image of a man 'burning his whole body' suggests desperation, courage, the extreme. Adrienne Rich herself said that 'My politics is in my body'. Discuss this idea in relation to the closing lines of the poem.

6. Is this a typical Adrienne Rich poem? Which other poems by Rich on your course does it resemble? Explain.

Trying to Talk with a Man

Out in this desert we are testing bombs,

that's why we came here.

Sometimes I feel an underground river
forcing its way between deformed cliffs
an acute angle of understanding   5
moving itself like a locus of the sun
into this condemned scenery.

What we've had to give up to get here—
whole LP collections, films we starred in
playing in the neighborhoods, bakery windows   10
full of dry, chocolate-filled Jewish cookies,
the language of love-letters, of suicide notes,
afternoons on the riverbank
pretending to be children

Coming out to this desert   15
we meant to change the face of
driving among dull green succulents
walking at noon in the ghost town
surrounded by a silence

that sounds like the silence of the place   20
except that it came with us
and is familiar
and everything we were saying until now
was an effort to blot it out—
coming out here we are up against it   25

Out here I feel more helpless
with you than without you

You mention the danger
and list the equipment
we talk of people caring for each other   30
in emergencies—laceration, thirst—
but you look at me like an emergency

Your dry heat feels like power
you eyes are stars of a different magnitude
they reflect lights that spell out: EXIT   35
when you get up and pace the floor

talking of the danger
as if it were not ourselves
as if we were testing anything else.

1971

 ## Glossary

Line 1 desert: Margaret Atwood, commenting on this poem, says the poem occurs in a desert, a desert which is not only deprivation and sterility, the place where everything except the essentials has been discarded, but also the place where bombs are tested. The "I" and the "You" have given up all the frivolities of their previous lives, "suicide notes" as well as "love-letters," in order to undertake the risk of changing the desert; but it becomes clear that the "scenery" is already "condemned," that the bombs are not external threats but internal ones. The poet realises that they are deceiving themselves, "talking of the danger/ as if it were not ourselves/ as if we were testing anything else."

Line 4 deformed: misshaped.

Line 5 acute: sharp.

Line 6 locus: in Adrienne Rich's *Poetry* [Norton Critical Edition (1975)] locus is glossed as follows. 'In geometry, the set or configuration of all points satisfying specified geometric conditions'.

Line 9 LP collections: long-playing vinyl music records – from a pre tape, CD and iPod era.

Line 17 succulents: thick, fleshy plants.

Line 31 laceration: torn, mangled flesh.

? Questions

1. What does the title, 'Trying to Talk with a Man', imply? If the title read 'Trying to Talk to a Man', how different would that have been? In your opinion, have relations between men and women changed since 1971, when this poem was written? Why?

2. Who, do you think, is the 'we' of the opening line? Why do you think the first two lines of the poem are on their own?

3. The speaker in lines 3–7 uses an image to convey her situation. What mood is created here through imagery? Which words best capture that mood?

4. There is a striking contrast between the 'condemned scenery' of the desert and the world which 'we've had to give up to get here'. How would you describe the world that they had to give up?

5. The man and woman in this poem came to the desert for a specific reason. What is meant by 'testing bombs'? Are these actual bombs or an image of their relationship? Discuss.

6. Comment on the silence – 'the silence of the place' and the silence that 'came with us'.

7. In lines 26/27 the speaker says 'Out here I feel more helpless/ with you than without you'. Why do you think the speaker feels this way? Were you surprised by the admission?

8. How does the man respond to the private and emotional situation? Why do you think he speaks of 'the danger' and lists 'the equipment'?

9. Why do you think Rich uses punctuation the way she does in this poem?

10. Does this poem offer a convincing portrait of a relationship in your opinion? How would you imagine the poem from the man's point of view?

11. In your opinion, does the title and the poem itself offer a negative, hopeless, pessimistic view?

Diving Into the Wreck

First having read the book of myths,
and loaded the camera
and checked the edge of the knife-blade,
I put on
the body-armor of black rubber   5
the absurd flippers
the grave and the awkward mask.
I am having to do this
not like Cousteau with his
assiduous team   10
aboard the sun-flooded schooner
but here alone.

There is a ladder.
The ladder is always there
hanging innocently   15
close to the side of the schooner.
We know what it is for,
we who have used it.
Otherwise
it's a piece of maritime floss   20
some sundry equipment.

I go down.
Rung after rung and still
the oxygen immerses me
the blue light   25
the clear atoms
of our human air.
I go down.
My flippers cripple me,
I crawl like an insect down the ladder   30
and there is no one
to tell me when the ocean
will begin.

First the air is blue and then
it is bluer and then green and then 35
black I am blacking out and yet
my mask is powerful
it pumps my blood with power
the sea is another story
the sea is not a question of power 40
I have to learn alone
to turn my body without force
in the deep element.

And now: it is easy to forget
what I came for 45
among so many who have always
lived here
swaying their crenellated fans
between the reefs
and besides 50
you breathe differently down here.

I came to explore the wreck.
The words are purposes.
The words are maps.
I came to see the damage that was done 55
and the treasures that prevail.
I stroke the beam of my lamp
slowly along the flank
of something more permanent
than fish or weed 60

the thing I came for:
the wreck and not the story of the wreck
the thing itself and not the myth
the drowned face always staring
toward the sun 65

the evidence of damage
worn by salt and sway into this threadbare beauty
the ribs of the disaster
curving their assertion
among the tentative haunters.   70

This is the place.
And I am here, the mermaid whose dark hair
streams black, the merman in his armored body
We circle silently
about the wreck   75
we dive into the hold.
I am she: I am he

whose drowned face sleeps with open eyes
whose breasts still bear the stress
whose silver, copper, vermeil cargo lies   80
obscurely inside barrels
half-wedged and left to rot
we are the half-destroyed instruments
that once held to a course
the water-eaten log   85
the fouled compass

We are, I am, you are
by cowardice or courage
the one who find our way
back to this scene   90
carrying a knife, a camera
a book of myths
in which
our names do not appear.

1972

Glossary

Title: The wreck she is diving into,' says Margaret Atwood, 'is the wreck of obsolete myths, particularly myths about men and women. She is journeying to something that is already in the past, in order to discover for herself the reality behind the myth, "the wreck and not the story of the wreck/ the thing itself and not the myth." What she finds is part treasure and part corpse, and she also finds that she herself is part of it, a "half-destroyed instrument." As explorer, she is detached; she carries a knife to cut her way in, cut structures apart; a camera to record; and the book of myths itself, a book which has hitherto had no place for explorers like herself.'

Line 1 the book of myths: in this instance the stories and legends about the relationships between men and women.

Line 9 Cousteau: Jacques Yves Cousteau (b. 1910), French naval officer and underwater explorer who, in 1950, made the first underwater film. Best known for *The Undersea World of Jacques Cousteau* (1968–1976).

Line 10 assiduous: diligent, hard-working, persevering.

Line 11 schooner: swift-sailing vessel, usually with two masts.

Line 20 maritime floss: floss can be a cottony fibre and maritime relates to the sea. Here Rich is speaking of the ladder as a means of going down into the depths. But for those who have not gone down, it is just a piece of unimportant, insignificant substance.

Line 21 sundry equipment: unimportant tool, apparatus.

Line 48 crenellated fans: a reference to the swaying, indented, irregularly shaped, fan-shaped sea plants which Rich imagines as fans in the hands of those who live in the wreck.

Line 56 prevail: triumph, dominate, succeed.

Line 58 flank: side.

Line 64 the drowned face: a reference to the ornamental/decorative female figurehead which once formed the prow of old sailing ships.

Line 67 threadbare: worn, faded.

Line 69 assertion: declaration, claim.

Line 70 tentative: uncertain.

Line 70 haunters: the word suggests that those who dive into the wreck are frequent divers.

Line 80 vermeil: metal, as silver or bronze, which has been gilded; bright red, scarlet.

Questions

1. What does the title of this poem suggest? Is this an actual or a metaphorical journey?

2. What do we learn about the speaker in the opening lines (1–12)?

3. She dives alone but speaks of others who have also dived into the wreck. What does this tell us about the speaker's understanding of herself and others in relation to the wreck on the ocean floor?

4. The word 'down' is repeated ['I go down . . . I go down . . . I crawl like an insect down the ladder'] and she uses the image of an insect. Comment on the effect of this.

5. Re-read the first four stanzas. Is the speaker well-prepared for this dive? Which details suggest this? How does she feel as she descends?

6. At line 44 [And now . . .] the poem shifts from journeying to being there. What does the speaker say about being in the wreck? Why do you think 'so many . . . have always lived here'?

7. The speaker says 'it is easy to forget/ what I came for'. How would you sum up what the speaker came for? Why do you think it was easy for her to forget why she came?

8. How would you describe the atmosphere of the underwater world? Is 'the evidence of damage' physical? Is there evidence of emotional, psychological damage?

9. 'This is the place./ And I am here' (lines 71/72). Who are the mermaid and the merman? What can you tell about them from how they are described?

10. 'I' is used in eight of the ten sections of the poem and is used sixteen times in all. Comment on the poet's use of 'I', 'we' and 'you'. Who is the speaker referring to when she says 'we' and 'you'?

11. How does the past play a significant part in the experience explored in the poem 'Diving into the Wreck'? Comment on the link between past and present.

12. Why did the speaker dive into the wreck? Did she find what she sought there? How did she respond to the experience?

13. In line 88 the speaker says that 'cowardice or courage' played an important part. Why the contradiction? Which do you think was the one that made the journey possible?

14. In the poem's closing lines, the poet speaks of 'half-destroyed instruments that once held to a course'. Who or what is she referring to here?

15. Ruth Whitman, reviewing Rich's *Poems Selected and New* in *Harvard Magazine* July–August 1975, said of 'Diving into the Wreck': it is 'one of the great poems of our time'. Would you agree or disagree with this view? What, in your opinion, makes a poem 'great'? Does this poem match your criteria? Give reasons for your answer.

From a Survivor

The pact that we made was the ordinary pact
of men & women in those days

I don't know who we thought we were
that our personalities
could resist the failures of the race   5

Lucky or unlucky, we didn't know
the race had failures of that order
and that we were going to share them

Like everybody else, we thought of ourselves as special

Your body is as vivid to me   10
as it ever was: even more

since my feeling for it is clearer:
I know what it could and could not do

it is no longer
the body of a god   15
or anything with power over my life

Next year it would have been 20 years
and you are wastefully dead
who might have made the leap
we talked, too late, of making   20

which I live now
not as a leap
but a succession of brief amazing movements

each one making possible the next

1972

Glossary

Line 1 pact: agreement.

Line 17 Next year it would have been 20 years: a reference to the nineteen years Adrienne Rich and Alfred Conrad spent together.

Line 18 wastefully dead: here wastefully expresses the woman's belief that her husband's death achieved nothing, that it was a waste.

Questions

1. The poem focuses on and explores the speaker's marriage, its beginning, its ending. What does the word 'survivor' suggest in this context?

2. Looking back, what did marriage mean at the time of their wedding? Why was it viewed as an 'ordinary pact'?

3. Rich rarely uses the ampersand [&]. Why do you think she deliberately uses '&' between the words 'men' and 'women' in line 2? What does it suggest?

4. Why do you think the poet chose to arrange the poem on the page the way she did? Consider especially the two lines that are on their own.

5. Why did Rich not place a full stop at the end of the final line?

6. How would you describe the speaker's mood in this poem?

7. Is this a realistic poem, in your opinion? An optimistic poem? A pessimistic one? Give reasons for your answer.

8. Explore the significance of the speaker's reference to 'the race', 'the body of a god'.

9. How would you describe the speaker's understanding of her dead husband, her feelings for her dead husband? What does she wish for him?

10. The speaker describes her life now as 'a succession of brief amazing movements'. Comment on this.

Power

Living   in the earth-deposits   of our history

Today a backhoe divulged   out of a crumbling flank of earth
one bottle   amber   perfect   a hundred-year-old
cure for fever   or melancholy   a tonic
for living on this earth   in the winters of this climate   5

Today I was reading about Marie Curie:
she must have known she suffered   from radiation sickness
her body bombarded for years   by the element
she had purified
It seems she denied to the end   10
the source of the cataracts on her eyes
the cracked and suppurating skin   of her finger-ends
till she could no longer hold   a test-tube or a pencil

She died   a famous woman   denying
her wounds   15
denying
her wounds   came from the same source as her power

1974

Glossary

Line 2 backhoe: a heavy mechanised digger – a JCB.

Line 2 flank: side.

Line 4 melancholy: sad, gloomy state.

Line 6 Marie Curie: Polish-born French physicist (1867–1934) who with her husband Pierre Curie worked on magnetism and radioactivity (a term she invented in 1898); they were jointly awarded the Nobel Prize for Physics in 1903 with Antoine Henri Becquerel. In 1911 Marie Curie received the Nobel Prize for Chemistry. She died of leukaemia, probably caused by her long exposure to radioactivity.

Line 7 radiation sickness: an illness caused by excessive absorption of radiation in the body. Symptoms include internal bleeding and a decrease in blood cells.

Line 8 bombarded: attacked.

Line 11 cataracts: an opaque condition of the lens of the eye which allows no light through.

Line 12 suppurating: oozing thick yellowish fluid, pus.

? Questions

1. The speaker refers to 'earth-deposits'. What does the speaker mean by this? How do you think the bottle, unopened, unused ended up in the earth?

2. How is the present portrayed by the speaker? How do you interpret 'the winters of this climate'?

3. Why do you think Adrienne Rich was drawn to Marie Curie?

4. Identify different kinds of power. What type of power is being explored here? Explain 'denying/ her wounds   came   from the same source as her power'. What caused Curie's illness? Why did Curie allow her illness to continue?

5. Compare and contrast Aunt Jennifer and Marie Curie.

6. Comment on the way Rich has deliberately spaced and paced certain lines. How does that affect your reading of the poem?

7. Is Marie Curie a victim of her success? How does the speaker feel about Curie? Which details in the poem best express the speaker's viewpoint?

8. Rich has said [in 1964] that 'In my earlier poems I told you, as precisely and eloquently as I knew how, about something; in the more recent poems something is happening, something has happened to me and, if I have been a good parent to the poem, something will happen to you who read it.' Discuss this statement in the light of your reading of the poems by Adrienne Rich on your course.

General Questions

A. Write an essay on the impact the poetry of Adrienne Rich has had on you. Support the points you make by reference to the poetry of Adrienne Rich on your course.

B. Write an article for a school magazine introducing the poetry of Adrienne Rich to Leaving Certificate students. Tell them what she wrote about and explain what you liked in her writing, suggesting some poems that you think they would enjoy reading. Support the points you make by reference to the poetry by Adrienne Rich on your course.

C. 'Adrienne Rich is both a personal and a political poet.' Discuss this view, supporting your answer by quotation from or reference to the poems by Rich on your course.

D. 'Rich, in her poetry, creates memorable and powerful images.' Would you agree with this view? You should support the points you make with relevant quotation from or reference to the poems by Adrienne Rich on your course.

E. 'The poetry of Adrienne Rich explores a woman's difficulty in maintaining an identity.' Discuss this view and in your response refer to the poetry of Adrienne Rich on your course.

F. 'I enjoy (or do not enjoy) the poetry of Adrienne Rich.' Respond to this statement referring to the poetry of Adrienne Rich on your course.

G. 'There are many reasons why the poetry of Adrienne Rich is worth reading.' In response to the above statement write an essay on the poetry of Adrienne Rich. Your essay should focus clearly on the reasons why you think Rich's poetry is worth reading and should refer to the poems by Rich on your course.

H. 'Though Adrienne Rich is a woman poet who writes about the world from a woman's point of view, she is a poet who deserves to be read by men and women.' Write a personal response to this statement and in your answer refer to the poems by Rich on your course.

Critical Commentary

Storm Warnings

This poem, with its dramatic title, was written when Rich was twenty years old.

The title is both actual and metaphorical. There is a storm coming but the speaker also senses change of another kind, change that the speaker is aware of.

Though the poem is about change and disorder, it is well-organised and shaped on the page. Four seven-line stanzas, many of the lines iambic pentameter, the final line in each stanza being shorter than the others, Rich's use of repetition and occasional rhyme all reveal the careful and skilful writing of the poem.

In stanza one the barometer is but one indicator of the approaching storm. The speaker knows 'better than the instrument/ What winds are walking overhead' and the image that emerges of the speaker is of someone who belongs to a comfortable, civilised, protected world. The 'book', the 'pillowed chair', the 'walk from window to closed window' suggest privilege, comfort, an elegant drawing room. The long opening sentence runs through twelve lines and from stanza one into stanza two, a technique which could suggest the impending, unstoppable energy of the oncoming storm.

The speaker reflects on the changing weather not only in terms of 'watching/ Boughs strain against the sky' but attributes to this change something even more interesting. For the speaker the storm connects one world and another. As it moves 'inward toward a silent core of waiting', the world of the speaker is portrayed as a world anticipating, even welcoming change. And yet the speaker's natural impulse is to guard against it. Albert Gelpi in his essay 'Adrienne Rich: The Poetics of Change' says that Rich 'seeks shelter as self-preservation' and in 'Storm Warnings' the speaker 'prepares against the threats within and without by sealing off a comfortable, weather-proof sanctuary. The only exposure is the keyhole that locks the door.'

The actual weather reflects an interior state: 'Weather abroad / And weather in the heart' are known to the speaker and both external and internal storms cannot be prevented or avoided, nor can they be easily ordered, predicted or controlled. 'I', though it is only used twice, is a strong presence in the poem: 'I leave the book . . .'; 'I draw the curtains'. The restlessness of walking 'from window to closed window' leads to the speaker's attempts to protect herself against the elements. The drawing of the curtains and the lighting of candles suggest an attempt at comfort. And yet the speaker concludes in stanza four that the storm creates an 'insistent whine/ Of weather' through a keyhole draught. There is no locking it out. The lighting of candles may seem an old-fashioned detail in a poem written in 1949 but the lighting of candles in this context becomes a powerful symbol of hope and their delicate flames must be protected – they are 'sheathed in glass'. It is a small but vital gesture and the candles within the room and the woman who lit them while the storm rages outside become images of resilience.

The mood of unease, the feeling of premonition in the opening stanza changes through the poem. In stanza one 'the winds are walking overhead' and by stanza four 'the sky goes black'. The use of the present tense gives the poem an immediacy and the disturbance, the darkness, once again, become images of the poet's inner world.

Rich herself has said [in the Foreword to *Collected Early Poems 1950–1970*] that 'Storm Warnings' is about powerlessness and the need 'to create an interior space against the storm, an enclave of self-protection'. The poem ends not with the storm abating but focuses on the speaker's strong awareness of how there is a need to summon up inner resources and a keen awareness that she lives 'in troubled regions'.

Rich has said [in that same Foreword] that change in this instance means 'unpredictability, unrest, menace' and yet the mood in those closing lines reveals a clear-sightedness, strength and determination. The storm may be inevitable and unavoidable but awareness is essential. The final lines use 'we', not 'I'. The poet includes others and in doing so includes the reader. The effect is empowering and reassuring.

W.H. Auden said that 'Storm Warnings' was motivated by feelings of 'historical apprehension' and the poem, if interpreted in this way, could be seen as a reference to political unrest. A poem which tells of a woman in a room and her awareness of a gathering storm can be read at many different, interesting levels.

Aunt Jennifer's Tigers

Rich was twenty-one when this poem was published in her first collection, *A Change of World*. On the page, this poem looks neat, formal and well-organised. There are three four-line stanzas, several of the lines are written in iambic pentameter and there is a regular end-rhyme (aabb, ccdd, eeff). The poem may seem conventional but there is a feminist quality to the poem which makes it powerful and memorable and prompts important questions about gender issues. 'Aunt Jennifer's Tigers' focuses on a familiar theme, that of marriage, in this instance the speaker's aunt and uncle, but the relationship at the heart of the poem is unequal. The woman, Aunt Jennifer, is oppressed by her dominating husband. Though the aunt and uncle are fictional, this does not diminish the power or the impact of the poem.

The title suggests something powerful, exotic, unusual. The tigers in this instance belong to an embroidered image which Aunt Jennifer is working on. Aunt Jennifer's choice of image, in this context, is interesting. She is creating strong, fearless, untamed creatures the very opposite of her own life.

The poem's opening lines are powerful and are filled with movement and colour. Everything would suggest confidence, energy. The verbs 'prance' and 'pace' with the alliterative echo; the colours 'topaz' and 'green' create an upbeat feeling. That these wild animals do not fear 'men' adds to their powerful presence. The use of 'Bright' brings the embroidered panel alive. Aunt Jennifer has created these creatures; it is a striking creative act.

In the second stanza the mood changes. The energy ebbs. The speaker tells us that Aunt Jennifer's fingers are 'fluttering through her wool' which suggests nervousness, unease. The making of the panel, vividly described in stanza one, is difficult and the poet speaks of the 'massive weight of Uncle's wedding band'. The wife is engaged in making a decorative, embroidered panel but her husband's presence, their marriage, 'Sits heavily' upon Aunt Jennifer. The never-ending circle of the wedding ring usually symbolises eternity, union but in this instance the speaker sees it as a massive, heavy presence. Aunt Jennifer is trapped in a marriage and it is as if the tapestry she weaves is her only means of speaking.

The poem begins in the present tense but in the final stanza the poet focuses on the future. Here the speaker imagines a time when Aunt Jennifer is dead. The words 'terrified', 'ordeals', 'mastered' capture the attitude of the niece as she contemplates her aunt's life. The image of the wedding ring recurs in the image of the aunt's life 'ringed with ordeals'. It's an unattractive portrait of a marriage – the husband is controlling. Even in death Aunt Jennifer is terrified. And yet the poem's final image is one of freedom, escape, fearlessness. The brave, gallant tigers 'Will go on prancing, proud and unafraid'. The final two lines, perfect iambic pentameters, are charged with energy and convey a feeling of defiance. Aunt Jennifer, though she was cowed into submission, succeeded in creating an image of assertion. The hands that fluttered and found 'even the ivory needle hard to pull' paradoxically made possible the very opposite: an image of certain power and pride.

The poem offers a glimpse of Aunt Jennifer's life. The speaker expresses an opinion but does not pass judgement. It could be argued that the male/female divide is depicted in a simplistic manner – the man is a bully; the woman is a victim – and yet it prompts important questions about the nature of relationships, marriage, self-assertion and creativity. 'Aunt Jennifer's Tigers' is also a very fine illustration of the power of symbol.

The Uncle Speaks in the Drawing Room

Rich here uses a male persona and like 'Storm Warnings' the poem speaks of unrest, threat. In this instance, however, the disturbance is explicitly political. It refers to people power and their disquiet. That the title refers to uncle as 'The Uncle', not 'My Uncle' or 'An Uncle' gives the poem a particular tone. The setting of 'the Drawing Room' also creates an atmosphere of order, elegance, privilege. There is an interior world and an outer world. The aunt and uncle in 'Aunt Jennifer's Tigers' were not real people; the same may be true of this particular uncle but he stands for a way of viewing the world that is strikingly memorable.

One of the most notable aspects of this poem is picked up by the ear on a first reading. The regular rhyme scheme [abbacc] and the seven-syllable line used throughout establishes an authoritative and confident tone of voice. The speaker is a commanding presence. He speaks from his drawing room in a house with 'balcony, and gate' which suggests an impressive, wealthy structure.

The people outside the gate are referred to by the Uncle as 'the mob'. They are a 'sullen' presence and their discontent and silent anger are associated with their 'gazing' at this house. We are never told much about the Uncle's life or profession. He is wealthy and he has inherited wealth but if he is political or not we are never told. But this is a poem that is preoccupied with politics. It looks at privilege, inheritance, inequality but all from the Uncle's perspective.

The opening stanza contains an atmosphere of menace. The reader hears in the Uncle's voice a tone of distaste. The word 'mob' and the repeated use of 'sullen' ['I have seen the mob of late/ Standing sullen in the square,/ Gazing with a sullen stare'] convey a superior attitude. The closing two lines in stanza one summon up an image of a disgruntled group. There is nothing to suggest that these people are not justified in their protest.

Stanza two refers to these people's actions as 'follies'. The Uncle is not too troubled by these people beyond the gate; he feels that their sullen presence will fade away. To refer to their behaviour as foolish ['follies'] is unsympathetic, patronising, condescending. Lines 8–12 ['Let us consider . . . chandelier'] are preoccupied with the speaker's concerns for his opulent possessions. The contrast between the world of the gated house and the public square is sharpened by such details as 'fingered stones' and 'crystal vase and chandelier'.

The third stanza begins with a smug tone. The Uncle is confident that no missiles will be thrown and yet he offers an historical perspective when an earlier 'storm' resulted in an ancestor's 'antique ruby bowl' being 'Shivered in a thunder-roll'. That upheaval is spoken of in terms of a storm but it could also perhaps refer to a political riot or upheaval?

The irony here is very effective. The Uncle speaks as if the reader will agree with his view of things. He presumes that he is speaking to like-minded people. The use of 'us' [line 19] and 'We' [line 23] would suggest this. The Uncle's main concern is his material wealth and possessions. The earlier age is viewed as 'calmer' but he feels that it is his duty to ensure that the divide between privileged and underprivileged be maintained. The poem's final line is an interesting image of the world since c. 1950 when this poem was written. The Uncle does not welcome change. It suits him to be conservative.

Living in Sin

This poem is from Rich's 1955 volume *The Diamond Cutters and Other Poems*. In it Rich uses a different technique. This poem is not arranged in regular stanzas; instead it is written in free verse, a type of poetry that does not use rhyme or regular line length but depends on rhythm and repetition for effect.

The freedom of free verse allows Rich to create on the page a different kind of poem from 'Storm Warnings', 'Aunt Jennifer's Tigers' and 'The Uncle Speaks in the Drawing Room'. Not only does it look different but a more intimate connection between the poet and reader is established. The fluid line, the flow of the poem invite the reader to share the woman's private world.

The title 'Living in Sin' is still a well-known phrase, though it is rarely heard today; it meant much more in the early 1950s when the poem was written than it does now. 'Living in sin' was how church and society viewed young lovers who lived together without being married. It was seen as a disgrace by those who thought themselves morally superior and it took great courage for a man and woman to go against this attitude. Rich's use of the title prompts the reader not only to question its meaning, but also to explore why such a term should exist and how such a moral climate affects young people.

The poet uses the third person to describe a woman's situation. Everything is told from her point of view and throughout there is an important connection between past and present: between what the woman thought would happen and what actually happened. There was a time when the speaker looked on her relationship in glowing terms. Practical matters such as housework did not occur to her. They would share their love for each other and live together in a small apartment: 'She had thought the studio would keep itself;/ no dust upon the furniture of love.'

The speaker realises that it is 'Half heresy' to view household chores as something she has no interest in. This woman is not comfortable with her assigned role as housekeeper. She was expected to play housewife by society at large but her partner also seems to take it for granted that the woman's role is primarily a domestic one. The use of the word 'heresy', with its religious connotations, is interesting here. It suggests that her experience of love should be almost religious and yet this speaker opposes an established doctrine.

The poem expresses her dissatisfaction with her situation. It begins with references to the place where she and her male partner live but gradually she explores her growing unhappiness with her lover. The place is small, confined. It would seem that he is an artist; she seems to have no occupation other than homemaker and partner and these are no longer enough. The sharp contrast between the 'dust' and 'grime' and the 'plate of pears,/ a piano with a Persian shawl' highlights the difference between his world and hers. He is painting still-life pictures; she sees herself now in terms of cleaning and providing.

The studio apartment is less than glamorous, especially in the early morning light. It looks cold, lifeless at five o'clock. Lovers at dawn is a familiar subject in literature and is often associated with parting and intense expressions of undying love as in *Romeo and Juliet*. Rich rewrites that scenario. In this instance the woman is awake and listening to the sound of the milkman's steps on 'each separate stair'; 'the scraps of last night's cheese' image sums up their life.

The speaker refers to 'a pair of beetle-eyes' returning her stare. It is an original detail with a touch of black humour and she imagines that beetle living in its own space, 'some village in the moldings'.

Line 14 peters out. The poet uses ' . . . ' to indicate, in this instance perhaps, a mood of resignation. The word 'Meanwhile' which begins line 15 shifts the focus of the poem to the man. In lines 15–18 he is portrayed as easy-going, relaxed, casual: he yawns, plays 'a dozen notes upon the keyboard', shrugs at his image in the mirror, rubs his beard and goes out to buy cigarettes.

The woman's plight is emphasised in the contrasting lines 19–22. She feels 'jeered'. She makes the bed, dusts and lets 'the coffee-pot boil over on the stove'.

The line 'By evening she was back in love again' captures the complexities of a love relationship and because of this 'Living in Sin' is a realistic, convincing, necessary love poem. It alerts the reader to the romantic and realistic view; the love she feels for her partner is waning. She is back in love again but 'not so wholly'. The poem's structure is that of dawn to dusk, a life-in-a-day poem and the final image returns to that of the unsettled sleep and an unattractive description of dawn leaving the reader with a bleak picture of a once-loving relationship grown cold. That it ends with a new beginning but a beginning that is unattractive suggests that love will not survive in this particular world.

The Roofwalker

The image of a roofwalker is interesting in many ways. A figure is walking 'on top of the world'; someone is building a house or home; an individual is taking risks. At one level, a roofwalker is a male construction worker on a building site but in this Rich poem it becomes so much more.

The poem's opening line is atmospheric. The houses are 'half-finished' and the day is ended. That beautiful word 'crepuscular' could be used to describe dusk, the coming on of night. The speaker captures an in-between moment: the day's work is done and the contrasting silence on the building site is striking. There is an easy feel to such lines as: 'The builders/ stand on the roof. It is/ quiet after the hammers,/ the pulleys hang slack.'

Poets have an original way of looking at the world. Here the poet's imagination sees the rooftops as a ship, the encroaching darkness is a 'wave of darkness' and the sky becomes a 'torn sail'. The men on the rooftops are 'magnified'; they are 'Giants' and the words 'burning deck' suggest danger, adventure, courage, echoing, as they do, an earlier poem by Felicia Heman (1793–1835) in which a boy stood on a burning deck alone, the others on board having fled.

Being a roofwalker is dangerous. In the poem's middle section the speaker identifies with the roofwalker. Lines 13–15 introduce the pronoun 'I' and the poem becomes more personal, confessional, intimate: 'I feel like them up there:/ exposed, larger than life,/ and due to break my neck.'

Beyond the obvious image of male workers and the speaker's identifying with them is the image of males in general and male writers in particular who have dominated for centuries. Man not woman has played the dominant role and the poet recognises the risks in joining them. 'The Roofwalker' has been described by Albert Gelpi as 'a redefinition of psychological and poetic perspective' and the speaker knows that she must take risks, she will face danger, she will expose herself. She may break her neck.

The poem's third section begins with a question. The image of the roof recurs but now the poet refers to living beneath the roof, not walking on it. In the poem's final section she admits that she cannot live beneath this roof. The roof becomes an image of the man-made, the work they have done, the poems they have written and Rich will find her own voice, will write her own poem. The writing life is difficult; it involves truth, it involves exposure. She knows of others who have written but she did not choose to be a writer, it chose her: 'A life I didn't choose/ chose me'. She feels 'naked, ignorant', inadequate.

The poet is young, is aware of the houses of literature built by men. They have had the tools but the speaker here says 'even/ my tools are the wrong ones/ for what I have to do.'

Though she feels ill-equipped, there is also an admirable sense of purpose. She could stay at home, as it were, and read about courage and commitment – 'a naked man fleeing/ across the roofs' or become that person who will take risks and express herself. The use of 'difference' and 'indifference' here highlights her understanding of male and female worlds.

The speaker in the poem is unfulfilled but is keenly aware of the need to find expression in a male-dominated world, whatever the risk. The poem is written in free verse which allows for a more direct and immediate voice. The question asked in lines 16–18 is not answered directly but in raising the issue the speaker and reader take on board the complex situation of woman as outsider, someone who has been excluded. That very fact prompts the necessary and obvious answer.

The poem contains a simple but powerful image, an image that remains with the reader capturing as it does the complex relationship between men and women, power and inequality. She quietly asserts the woman's role and explores how women are disadvantaged as possible roofwalkers. Different tools are needed. Rich herself discovered and used those tools.

Our Whole Life

The three familiar, monosyllabic words, our whole life, contain a huge idea. 'Our Whole Life' is both title and opening words of the poem, thus giving them even greater power. But any suggestion of a big, romantic idea is quashed in the opening lines. The speaker begins with a conclusion. She has reached an understanding of her whole life, its lies and pains and silences and with admirable honesty confesses that her life is empty.

The 'Our' could refer to the speaker's understanding of herself in relation to one other person – partner, lover perhaps who is never identified; the poem focuses on her acceptance of a situation, her disillusionment, her deep understanding of a complex, difficult situation. However, the poem, as its title implies, goes beyond the idea of a relationship.

At first, however, the poem seems to dwell on a personal relationship. That relationship is also seen within a wider context. Indeed the poem may be read not as a poem that focuses on one relationship but on a whole way of life. More than a relationship between two people is implied here. 'Our whole life a translation' suggests a whole society, a society where life is lived at a remove. It is a life that is not authentic, a life that is lost in translation: there has been a failure to communicate, to understand or to be understood. If a person or persons are living a life that is determined by 'permissible fibs', then that life is a lie and the poet addresses such a situation in this poem. The speaker uses a kind of short-hand, a summary of her situation. Line 1, 'Our whole life a translation', has dropped the verb and this gives the line an urgency. Line 2, 'the permissible fibs', highlights another aspect of her life and this direct, open expression of the speaker's realisation that life, as the speaker now knows it, is somehow false.

The image of 'a knot of lies' and the use of 'and now' create a greater sense of urgency. Language has become tangled, untruthful and details such as 'bitten', 'meanings burnt-off', heighten this image.

The poem shifts its focus from the personal to the political at lines 8 and 9. 'All those dead letters/ rendered into the oppressor's language' summon up a picture of an oppressor, someone who has abused, distorted or melted down language. A translation. The speaker is acutely aware of being overpowered, helpless and the closing lines of the poem present the reader with a searing image of an Algerian walking from his village, 'burning/ his whole body a cloud of pain'. That it is a North African man whose country has known invasion and a colonial presence, that he lives in a village, that 'his whole body is a cloud of pain' are significant details. But the most important detail is found in the poem's final two lines: 'and there are no words for this/ except himself' suggest that some situations go beyond and need to go beyond language, that the body can express something profound in its very being. This could be skin colour, sexual orientation, political conviction. Rich herself has said that 'My politics is in my body' and this belief is reflected in the poem.

The image of the burning man echoes an earlier image of burning. In one instance words need to be bitten and burnt through towards meaning; the burning body is another image of extremity.

Adrienne Rich says that this poem is 'concerned with an entire society facing its self-delusions'. It looks at a whole life and can be read as an indictment of enforced, allowed, accepted oppressions and dishonesties.

There is no punctuation, the language is succinct and 'Our Whole Life' does not end with a full stop. The poet has chosen to leave this poem open-ended. The situation as described here has not ended. The lay-out of the poem on the page also plays a part. Each idea is so potent that the poet uses spacing and single-line sections for emphasis.

Trying to Talk with a Man

The opening line of this poem is immediately arresting and the use of 'we' is intriguing: 'Out in this desert we are testing bombs'. 'We' here could refer to the American nation, its military. Line 1 refers to the speaker's country, the 'we' of line 2 could also refer on a more personal level to the speaker and her partner. That lines 1 and 2 are on their own and are the only lines in the poem on their own also creates a powerful impact. The use of the full-stop, ending line 2, is particularly effective especially when one considers the number of full-stops in the poem as a whole. Though highly dramatic in their subject matter, the tone in these opening lines is almost matter-of-fact.

The setting is a desert where controlled nuclear explosions are taking place and the poem's title suggests gender conflict. The 'we' of line 2 gives way to the 'I' voice and an image that conveys a stifled individual, a person labouring to express herself. This image of an underground river 'forcing its way between deformed cliffs' suggests rigid restrictions, oppression, imprisonment. A river in a desert landscape is naturally a vibrant, nourishing source but that river is 'underground'; her feelings therefore, the image suggests, are hidden, confined, trapped.

The fourth section [lines 8–14] looks to their life together as man and woman, the experiences they have shared. The speaker lists various aspects of their relationship: music, food, her Jewishness, the intensity and extremities of their feelings during that time. The details of 'love-letters' and 'suicide notes' suggest an intensely happy and at once troubled relationship. These lines in the poem are not transparent or easily grasped but then they refer to a very private and complex experience in the life of the speaker. The reader can sense in the short-hand style a strong confessional urgency and a feeling of lived experience.

Being in the desert for the speaker means silence. The silence, significantly 'came with us/ and is familiar'. Being in the desert allows them to confront the reality of their relationship. It is a desert where bombs are being tested and the poem has shifted its focus from public to private, from military to personal so that the main thrust of 'Trying to Talk with a Man' is the speaker's attempt to confront her own relationship. That the title reads 'a Man' could also suggest that the speaker is thinking of 'a man' in particular and every man in general.

The speaker's partner speaks of nuclear testing. He focuses on the general whereas she looks to the two of them and realises that 'Out here I feel more helpless/ with you than without you'. He turns to the dangers of testing weapons; he steers clear of testing their own one-to-one relationship.

The coming to this desert is a metaphor for a relationship that is perhaps about to explode. It is certainly being tested. The poem speaks of a collapsing relationship or marriage. A huge change is occurring in the lives of the speaker and her partner and the poem assesses and evaluates their relationship.

The poem's ending signals the end of their relationship. In his eyes she reads the word 'EXIT'. She has to leave this relationship. It has been tried, tested. It has failed. The mood in the closing lines is one of honest acceptance. He paces the floor but cannot confront what is really happening here. The speaker courageously admits that their relationship is over. The man seems unable to come to terms with this. Men are portrayed as inadequate, insensitive, ill-equipped to deal with emotions. His emotions are repressed. He looks at her 'like an emergency' and paces the floor. Talking might have solved the problem but the title suggests it is not possible to talk with a man and certainly not this man. The men in the military are the ones who make the bombs and the speaker's man is the one who fails to recognise or chooses to ignore the seriousness of their personal situation.

Diving Into the Wreck

In Adrienne Rich's work, titles are often so powerful that they become in themselves mini-poems. This is certainly true of one of Rich's best-known poems 'Diving into the Wreck'. The poem is dated 1972. Rich was then forty-three and was identifying strongly with the radical feminist movement. In this poem the speaker explores her own inheritance and past, but it also speaks for all women who have been disempowered, sidelined and written out of history. This poem is her story. 'Diving into the Wreck' could also be read as a journey into the subconscious.

The poem, in free verse and in nine sections of different lengths, describes a woman going down into the ocean depths. However, as with many Rich poems, an image becomes a potent symbol and the poem goes far beyond the narrative to explore essential concerns.

The first section portrays a woman preparing for a dark and difficult journey. That she is alone makes her both vulnerable and courageous. Her preparations are thorough. But before she mentions the practical aspects such as camera, knife, wetsuit, flippers, oxygen mask, she first speaks of a mental, emotional, imaginative preparation. One usually dives to explore or to plunder; in this instance it is to explore.

Line 1 tells us that the speaker has read 'the book of myths'. This was the most important of all: 'First having read the book of myths . . .' It was this reading experience that has prompted the speaker to undertake the dive and the book of myths, according to Margaret Atwood, is a book of 'obsolete myths, particularly myths about men and women'.

The poet has clearly reached a point in her life where she is questioning, challenging assumptions and situations that she is uncomfortable with. She is prepared to go deeper in search of the truth and the image of diving into the wreck already signals that what she will find there is something broken. That she is making this journey on her own is hugely significant: 'I am having to do this/ not like Cousteau with his/ assiduous team/ aboard the sun-flooded schooner/ but here alone'. Cousteau represents the male adventurer and he was part of a team. The woman's journey is undertaken alone and the journey is not so much an adventure, but rather something necessary and essential.

'I' is used sixteen times and phrases such as 'I go down', 'I go down', 'I crawl', 'I have to learn alone', 'I am she: I am he . . .' are crucial. Each one registers the speaker's position, her strong awareness of the nature of the journey and what it involves. Details can be read at a factual level but details also resonate with symbolic significance. For example the speaker tells us: 'There is a ladder./ The ladder is always there/ hanging innocently/ close to the side of the schooner./ We know what it is for,/ we who have used it./ Otherwise/ it's a piece of maritime floss/ some sundry equipment.' Here the ladder becomes something more than a climbing instrument. It is a means of entry, a way into the dark. There is also a strong sense of others having made this same journey. She is alone but she knows that others have gone down into the depths too.

The journey is a difficult and painful one – 'My flippers cripple me', 'I am blacking out' and though others have made this journey 'I have to learn alone/ to turn my body without force/ in the deep element'. The insect image at line 30 ['I crawl like an insect down the ladder'] suggests someone small, vulnerable, undignified. Changing colours – from blue, to green, to black – describe the speaker's sense of descending and this painterly technique offers strikingly visual pictures. The 'blacking out' suggests danger, terror but 'my mask is powerful/ it pumps my blood with power'. She is willing to face danger in her search for truth and understanding.

The ocean contains the wreck and the speaker has come to explore the wreck. A vast, dark, mysterious area such as an ocean can be read as a symbol of a place within, a place where the past and memories are stored, the unconscious.

In her essay 'This Woman's Movement', Nancy Milford says that in 'Diving into the Wreck' Rich 'enters more deeply than ever before into female fantasy; and these are primal waters, life-giving and secretive in the special sense of not being wholly revealed. The female element . . .' She came to explore the wreck. And what is the wreckage; is it of marriage, or of sex, or of the selfhood within each? Is it the female body, her own? The question is never answered explicitly and the poem is all the more effective because of that. It allows the reader to journey with the speaker and interpret the journey in her or his own way. Adrienne Rich has said that: 'We go to poetry because we believe it has something to do with us. We also go to poetry to receive the experience of the not me, enter a field of vision we could not otherwise comprehend.' Whether we identify or not with the speaker in 'Diving into the Wreck', the poem takes us on a powerful journey.

The pictures which the poet paints are haunting, private and beautiful. The use of the present tense creates an immediate link between speaker and reader. The poem though it tells of a difficult, confusing and painful experience is also, like many of Adrienne Rich's poems, empowering and liberating.

The key moment occurs at lines 55 and thereabouts, the poem's central section. The diver trains the beams of her lamp and they illuminate 'the thing itself', the actual wreck.

The poem's rhythm and the use of repetition in these lines [52–65] are very effective in creating a beautiful, quiet mood. The mind is calm as it observes the wreck. The description of the 'drowned face always staring/ toward the sun' is moving and evocative. It not only describes the figurehead on the ship's prow but captures the power and thrust of the ship as it sailed. Its energy is no more, the ship is now wrecked on the ocean floor and this is what is found there. 'Diving into the Wreck' is a wonderful example of what Eavan Boland has called Rich's ability to create 'a private kingdom of music and perception'.

The speaker is interested in discovering the truth, 'the wreck and not the story of the wreck/ the thing itself and not the myth'. A central image is that of the mermaid and merman, creatures from myth, circling silently 'about the wreck' and then the dramatic detail: 'we dive into the hold'. She becomes the mermaid, she encounters the merman and she and he merge; the female and male become one: 'we dive into the hold./ I am she: I am he'. This merging of the human speaker with the mythical merman and mermaid is not only an interesting surreal touch but it is the moment when truth meets myth. It also allows us to contemplate how each one of us embody male and female qualities. The deliberately grammatical awkwardness of 'one' in 'We are, I am, you are/ by cowardice or courage/ the one who find our way . . . ' [conventionally, it should read 'ones'] emphasises the need for us to make this journey alone.

In the second-last stanza, the speaker, now androgynous, identifies with the wreck itself. The 'she' and the 'he' have become 'we' and the speaker, now mermaid and merman 'are the half-destroyed instruments/ that once held to a course'. The diver identifies with, has become the wreck. There is no doubt that this is a mysterious and complex passage but it mirrors the complex and mysterious exploration of the unconscious. Claire Keyes argues [in her study *The Aesthetics of Power: The Poetry of Adrienne Rich*] that "A man who is 'half-destroyed' has denied the woman in him; a woman, just the opposite. Both 'once held to a course'; both, however, must become whole again so that they can function properly. We are, as in Rich's poem, 'instruments'. Referring at the close of the poem to the 'book of myths' which her diver consulted at the start of the venture, Rich's speaker notes that in it 'our names do not appear'. If our names do not appear in the myths, they have no reality for us. If we are male-female, female-male, then pure 'masculinity' is a myth; femininity likewise."

Here on the ocean floor the wreck is being explored. The speaker has returned to the source. Life on earth began as a unicellular organism in the sea and she is returning to the source, the primitive. The poem tells us that she 'came to see the damage that was done/ and the treasures that prevail'. Who inflicted that damage? Were the treasures that she discovered salvaged? These questions are not answered. The poem began with a solitary figure journeying towards the wreck and ends with an image of a figure and figures, the singular and plural, finding their way to this wreck and discovering there that the book of myths does not contain their names. Perhaps this would suggest that she and women like her have been excluded from the book of myths. The past is revisited, re-examined and rewritten.

In classical mythology the male hero frequently descended into the Underworld. In Rich's poem, a woman heroically enters into the darkness of her own being and discovers that the book of myths where men predominated and which was written by men do not contain the whole truth. This other truth which Rich is acknowledging here, the truth of her own being as a woman, is equally valid.

In lines 53/54 the speaker says 'The words are purposes./ The words are maps'. Such an interpretation of language alerts us to its power. The language that the book of myths is written in is male; Rich in this poem has forged her own understanding of her relationship with words and more importantly has forged her own language.

Neil Astley says of this poem that 'When Adrienne Rich goes beneath the surface . . . her underwater exploration is a metaphorical journey back through the mind which turns into a feminist argument with the poetic tradition she has emerged from.'

Rich herself has said [in a statement on the dust-jacket of *Diving Into the Wreck* (1973)] that she is 'coming-home to . . . sex, sexuality, sexual wounds, sexual politics.'

'Diving into the Wreck', a vivid, memorable, sensuous journey poem explores these issues and affirms woman's role, woman's courage, womanhood.

From a Survivor

This poem is dated 1972. In 1968 Rich's father died. In 1969 she and her husband separated and in 1970 he took his own life. Such difficult events inform this poem; the speaker charts the difficult stages of grief and survival.

It is an intensely personal poem. The speaker has survived the death of loved ones but as with so many of Rich's poems, the poem goes beyond the immediately personal and contains a universal emotional truth.

The word survivor has many meanings and reference points. What one individual survivor experiences emotionally, psychologically in a given situation can be compared to what another's experiences of survival are in a different situation.

The poem begins by looking back to the time when a man and a woman, in this instance the speaker and her husband, made a pact. The pact was a marriage and 'in those days' it was an 'ordinary pact'. A sorrow informs the opening lines. The passing of time has changed the speaker's life and her understanding of the marriage pact. She speaks of how he and she thought that they were different from other couples, that they might somehow not know 'the failures of the race'.

Twenty-four lines long, the poem is divided into ten parts which could be said to suggest fragmentation, loss, fragility, a feeling of tentativeness. The longest line, line 9, is tinged with youthfulness and sadness. There was a time when she viewed the world not in terms of disappointment or failure: 'we didn't know/ the race had failures of that order'.

The poem becomes increasingly personal. It begins with the legal, official word 'pact' but at line 10 the speaker addresses her dead husband, his physical self and the nature of their relationship. His body was once 'the body of a god'. Now the speaker, through experience, views life differently. The past, the present and the future are all referred to in the poem and the speaker thinks of an anniversary that will never be: 'Next year it would have been 20 years'. Rich had married in 1953 and 1973 would have represented a conventional anniversary but the marriage was not conventional. The speaker is acknowledging the distances between life as it might have been and life as it had to be.

Line 16 speaks of her husband who once had 'power over my life'. Such a detail gives us a glimpse into a strained marriage and also allows us to understand the subsequent course of events.

The image of the leap which the poet uses in line 19 conveys risk, adventure, imagination. Her husband 'might have made the leap' but instead is 'wastefully dead'. This is a clear-sighted comment on their complex relationship. It offers a glimpse of a happier future but he did not survive. She did. She changed and learned to cope with change and the poem ends with a quiet optimism. Though there is regret that her husband did not survive, there is also an awareness that the end of their marriage released her, made possible the new life she now lives.

They spoke of survival, of his making the leap but, when they talked of it, it was too late. She made the necessary leap but her life now is not lived 'as a leap' but as 'a succession of brief amazing movements'. This last description captures the speaker's grateful, calm state. The absence of the full stop here suggests survival and surviving, something that is on-going.

Power

This poem differs from the other Adrienne Rich poems on the Leaving Certificate course: the subject matter is a public, historical figure and it uses spaces between words in an interesting and effective way.

The opening line captures past and present:

> Living   in the earth-deposits   of our history

and the word earth-deposits reminds us of another time. The placing of the word between 'Living' and 'history' highlights the links between now and then. Line 1, on its own, is a meditative line. With 'Today', at the beginning of line 2, the speaker focuses on the immediate present, the here and now, the finding of the medicine bottle and what has prompted her to think of the past. This then leads to Marie Curie's story which she had been reading about 'Today'.

Lines 2–5 reflect on the modern and the old, the way they lived then and the differences between that time and this. A mechanical digger connects with a one-hundred-year-old medicine bottle, a 'cure for fever or melancholy a tonic'. Such cures are still being sought and the phrase 'the winters of this climate' describes the speaker's world as a bleak time.

The bottle has been found 'Today' and 'Today' the speaker has been reading about this woman scientist. The poet admires Marie Curie, physicist and chemist, for her great scientific discovery, which helped save many lives, achieved power. Yet Curie could not face the deleterious effects of radium on her own body and those of her associates. Ironically, Curie's discovery caused her own decline [and Curie's assistant Blanche Wittman lost an arm and both of her legs to radiation].

At the heart of the poem is this sense of contradiction. Words such as 'bombarded', 'cataracts', 'the cracked and suppurating skin' convey pain. Marie Curie would not admit that her research led to her illness and death; she 'denied to the end'. Curie devoted herself to a cause, to what she believed in and she refused to believe that it was destroying her. She denied the truth. Yet Curie was determined and though a scientist she symbolises every woman's struggle.

The poem presents the reader with two contradictory realities. Curie's position embodies contradictions, and these contradictions challenge the reader.

The poem, using a stream of consciousness technique, goes beyond narrative. The speaker focuses on the nature of power: 'her wounds came from the same source as her power'. The poet admires the scientific achievement but was the sacrifice too great? She was world-famous: 'She died a famous woman'. But the price she paid was high. The closing lines are more downbeat than celebratory.

'Power' is a sequence of observations and insights. The use of the long lines and the pauses within them create an effective rhythm. One has to stop, focus and consider particular words in the line.

'Diving into the Wreck' and 'Power', according to Eavan Boland, 'speak to the injustices of a society' and one of those injustices involves women. The injustice here is not immediately obvious perhaps. A woman is successful in a man's world but as Rich implies the price has been too high.

The first word in the poem is the poem's title 'Power' and 'power' is also the final word. Power has traditionally been associated with men and this poem looks at one woman's experience of power, its challenges and its demands.

Monument to Marie Curie in Warsaw, Poland.

William Wordsworth
(1770–1850)

The Overview

Much of Wordsworth's poetry was composed outdoors. He often composed while walking, speaking the words aloud, but he rarely wrote as a tourist. Wordsworth felt that he belonged to or lived in the places he describes and celebrates in his poetry and his poetry was startlingly original in its day. 'He painted place as it had never been painted before, and connected it in new ways with man's thought processes and moral being', says Margaret Drabble in *A Writer's Britain*. 'Wordsworth was a revolutionary in that his writings ultimately changed the way in which most of us now perceive the natural world', argues Ronald Sands. Dorothy Wordsworth, his sister, said of him that 'starlight walks and winter winds are his delight' and Wordsworth's love of nature marked a significant change from the preceding age, during which Dr Samuel Johnson pronounced that 'The man who is tired of London is tired of life'. For Wordsworth 'High mountains are a feeling, the hum of cities torture'.

William Wordsworth belongs to what is now known as the Romantic Age; the age preceding it was known as the Augustan. It is difficult to sum up the characteristics of each without being simplistic but the paintings, fashion and architecture from each period highlight the differences between them, as does the literature. In Augustan England, people wore wigs and dressed elaborately and social life centred on the city. The countryside was preferred when it had been tamed, arranged, controlled, ordered; buildings were ornate and landscaped gardens were very popular. Whereas the Augustan poets [e.g. Alexander Pope (1688–1744) and Samuel Johnson (1709–1784)] favoured heroic couplets – rhyming pairs of iambic pentameter lines – Wordsworth, for example, frequently wrote in blank verse, as in 'Tintern Abbey' and *The Prelude*. The Romantic poet focused on rugged, wild, untamed nature. The Romantic poet also focused on the imagination and, in Wordsworth's case, on how in nature we can discover our own nature. In *The Ascent of Man*, Jacob Bronowski says that the sight of nature, for Wordsworth, was 'a new quickening of the spirit because the unity in it was immediate to the heart and mind' whereas the Augustan writer preferred to view nature through a drawing-room window.

These nine poems by Wordsworth take place outdoors and, though nature is of vital importance, so too is our relationship with it and our understanding of it. He urges and invites his sister to come and enjoy the open air ('To My Sister'); he tells of his own deep relationship with nature in 'Tintern Abbey' and how that relationship can be everyone's; in *The Prelude* extracts he not only remembers with vivid and sensuous detail skating in winter and a dramatic episode with a boat, he also explores how he viewed nature as a mysterious and powerful presence; 'A Slumber did My Spirit Seal' expresses Wordsworth's belief that at death we, like the Lucy of the poem, not only are laid in earth but become part of earth's movement and continuity; in 'She dwelt among the untrodden ways', another one of the Lucy Poems, Wordsworth mourns someone precious and using imagery drawn from nature compares her to a violet and a star; the city of London is described in 'Composed Upon Westminster Bridge' but the poem celebrates nature and God's might; nature is also praised and the evening scene is wonderfully evoked in the sonnet 'It is a beauteous evening calm and free' but it is the relationship between himself and nature and the relationship between his daughter and nature that is of primary importance; in 'The Solitary Reaper' he immortalises the sad and beautiful song of a girl working in the fields and, as in many of his poems, Wordsworth praises the power of memory.

For Wordsworth, the poet is 'a man speaking to men'; he wanted a new immediacy for the language of poetry and he rejected what he called 'the gaudiness and inane phraseology' of many modern writers. He deliberately chose 'incidents and situations from common life, and wanted to relate or describe them . . . in a selection of language really used by men'. And yet Wordsworth, as Burton Raffel points out, is not a simple poet, not even in his language, as he sometimes liked to think. For example, Raffel says that there is nothing visibly complex about 'Five years have past; five summers, with the length/ Of five long winters!' but these opening lines of 'Tintern Abbey' capture what Raffel calls 'Wordsworth's sense of the measured passage of time' and a deep emotional response to nature. Phrases such as 'the still sad music of humanity' or 'to me was all in all' express Wordsworth's extraordinary empathy with nature. Past, present and future are intricately linked. When Wordsworth, for example in 'Tintern Abbey', revisits the banks of the River Wye, he is revisiting scenes that are precious to him, past and present merge and he is also aware of how the future will be affected by what he is experiencing now.

Though Pastoral poetry, a poetry celebrating the countryside and rural life, can be traced back to the third century B.C. (when Theocritus wrote of the Sicilian landscape of his childhood), Wordsworth writes about shepherds and beggars and ordinary people living ordinary lives in a fresh and original way. Margaret Drabble (in her book *Wordsworth*) says that for Wordsworth 'even the humblest and least sophisticated of men can have a true sense of the depth and meaning of life, and that the feelings of the humble are as important as those of the most famous and fortunate'.

In William Wordsworth's poetry, we are not only reminded of how nature affords us great pleasure but of how it also allows us to understand ourselves as creatures living in time and place. 'Tintern Abbey', one of Wordsworth's most important poems, contains Wordsworth's description of his growing up and how his relationship with nature developed and changed. First there was the physical response and boyish delight, then the 'aching joys' and 'dizzy raptures' of the young man and finally the combination of the senses and the intellect. The Norton edition sums it up as follows: 'All [Wordsworth's] knowledge of human suffering, so painfully acquired in the interim [between his last visit five years ago and his present visit], chastens him while it enriches the visible scene like a chord of music, and he has gained also awareness of an immanent "presence" which links his mind and all the elements of the external world. Here we glimpse how complex and changing that relationship was.' 'Growth is a central preoccupation for Wordsworth', writes John F. Danby, and it was Wordsworth's wife who subtitled *The Prelude* – 'Growth of a Poet's Mind', a poem which Stephen Gill sees as 'the most sustained self-examination in English poetry'.

William Wordsworth is sometimes known as the poet of childhood but 'to see Wordsworth as essentially the poet of childhood – a perception encouraged by Victorian illustrated editions of his work – is to misunderstand him completely', says Stephen Gill: 'Throughout his greatest period of creativity Wordsworth was interested in the development of the adult mind, the adult moral sense, and sought to demonstrate its evolution in one exemplary specimen – himself.' Seamus Heaney points out that 'Wordsworth, more than any writer before him, established how truly "the child is father of the man".' In other words, our early life determines our adulthood.

For Wordsworth, nature was the great teacher; in 'The Tables Turned' he wrote: 'One impulse from a vernal wood/ May teach you more of man;/ Of moral evil and of good,/Than all the sages can.' The following comments highlight Wordsworth's complexity and power: Stephen Gill says it was Wordsworth's conviction that 'love of nature led to love of man' and that 'creative power is a fundamental human attribute'; for Harold Bloom, 'Wordsworth invented modern or democratic poetry'.

Dr Johnson (1709–1784) defined the poet as 'An inventor; an author of fiction; a writer of poems; one who writes in measure'. Wordsworth's definition saw the poet as comforter, moral guide, prophet. Wordsworth believed that poetic, creative minds 'build up greatest things/ From least suggestions' and Stephen Gill identifies this as watchfulness, adding that Wordsworth 'was a poet who kept his eyes open and one who wanted to hear what people had to tell'. Wordsworth was, in Robert Woof's words, 'a poet who listened' and he is also a poet who shares with the reader and with the persons within the poems (his sister, his daughter) his understanding and insight.

Biographical Notes

William Wordsworth was born on 7 April 1770, in what is still the most impressive building in the main street in Cockermouth, Cumberland, a little town in the north west of England, in a region known as the Lake District. His young parents (John was twenty-nine and Ann was twenty-three) were well-off. Wordsworth's father worked as a law-agent to the most powerful man in the district, Sir James Lowther; the house where Wordsworth was born was owned by Lowther, but John Wordsworth and his family lived there rent free.

He was the second of five children, four boys and one girl (Richard, William, Dorothy, John, Christopher). Wordsworth's childhood was happy, wild and free and in the following lines, quoted by every biographer, he paints a picture of his young self playing on the banks of the River Derwent which bordered their garden:

> I, a four year's child,
> A naked boy, among the silent pools
> Made one long bathing of a summer's day,
> Basked in the sun, or plunged into thy streams,
> Alternate, all a summer's day, or coursed
> Over the sandy fields, and dashed the flowers
> Of yellow grunsel; or, when the crag and hill,
> The woods, and distant Skiddaw's lofty height,
> Were bronzed with a deep radiance, stood alone
> A naked savage in the thunder-shower . . .

These lines are from *The Prelude* which Wordsworth completed in 1799, when he was twenty-nine. It was first published in 1805 but Wordsworth reworked and revised the poem until 1839 and the final version was published immediately after his death in 1850.

William and Dorothy spent long periods of time with their maternal grandparents and the children received little formal education. While staying with his grandparents at Penrith, Wordsworth attended Ann Birkett's school where Mary Hutchinson, whom he married many years later, was also a infant pupil. Back home in Cockermouth, he attended Reverend Gilbank's grammar school and Wordsworth's father, we are told by his first biographer and nephew, Christopher Wordsworth, 'set him very early to learn portions of the works of the best English poets by heart, so that at an early age he could repeat large portions of Shakespeare, Milton and Spenser'.

Ann Wordsworth died of pneumonia in London in March 1778. The eight-year-old Wordsworth was staying with his grandparents at the time and when he came to write about it in *The Prelude* he said that her death 'left us destitute' and the family was deeply affected. In June 1778, Dorothy, then aged six, was taken to her mother's cousin's house in Halifax where she grew up and did not see William Wordsworth for nine years. In May 1779 Wordsworth and his brother Richard joined the grammar school at Hawkshead, a place he described twenty years later as 'Beloved Hawkshead'. He boarded with a local family, the Tysons, from 1779 to 1787 and Ann and Hugh Tyson, a childless couple, clearly provided a home for Wordsworth during the school terms. His three brothers and a cousin were also part of the Tyson household and the eight years that Wordsworth spent there were very happy.

Growing up in Hawkshead, he met the ordinary people of the district, the farm labourers, shepherds, blacksmiths, saddlers, cobblers, carpenters, quarrymen, charcoal-burners, shopkeepers, merchants, innkeepers, and the ferrymen on Lake Windermere and these, according to Stephen Gill, 'always seemed to Wordsworth to possess a stability and worth against which the sophisticated world could be tested'.

The school day was long but Wordsworth enjoyed living in the Esthwaite valley. He loved gathering nuts in the woods – 'I was an impassioned Nutter' – snaring woodcocks, discovering ravens' nests, fishing, skating and he loved wandering. Nearby, Coniston, Windermere, Yewdale and Tilberthwaite were explored and ''twas my joy/ To wander half the night among the cliffs' or to get up 'At the first hour of morning' and be at one with Nature.

School provided Wordsworth with a fine education. He studied Latin and Greek, mathematics, science and natural philosophy, English grammar and composition, French and dancing. During his school days, using his father's collection of books or the school library, the young Wordsworth read all of Fielding's works, *Don Quixote*, *Gulliver's Travels*, travel books, history and biographies. His two headmasters loved poetry and he was lent recent volumes by Cowper and Burns, becoming acquainted as a schoolboy with the contemporary works of Crabbe, Charlotte Smith, and Percy's *Reliques*. The young Wordsworth carved his name on his school desk – the signature is still visible today.

At grammar school, William Wordsworth was also encouraged to write. One of his earliest poems was inspired by the setting sun, written when he was fourteen years old. Wordsworth at seventy-three remembered his early composition and how he had been struck by 'the infinite variety of natural appearances which had been unnoticed by the poets of any age or country, as far as I was acquainted with them: and I made a resolution to supply in some degree the deficiency. I could not have been at that time above fourteen years of age'. He wrote poems celebrating the school's second centenary and in anticipation of leaving school. In March 1787, Wordsworth, a seventeen-year-old schoolboy, saw his poetry in print for the first time; the *European Magazine* published his poem 'Sonnet on Seeing Miss Helen Maria Williams Weep at a Tale of Distress'. It was signed 'Axiologus'. The very first poem in *The Poetical Works of Wordsworth* published by Oxford University Press is 'Extract – From the conclusion of a poem, composed in anticipation of leaving school' which was composed in 1786, when Wordsworth was sixteen, and published in 1815. Though a very early work, it contains Wordsworth's characteristic qualities – expressive feeling, his attachment to place, the importance of Nature:

Dear native regions, I foretell,
From what I feel at this farewell,
That, wheresoe'er my steps may tend,
And whensoe'er my course shall end,
If in that hour a single tie
Survive of local sympathy,
My soul will cast the backward view,
The longing look alone on you.

Thus, while the Sun sinks down to rest
Far in the regions of the west,
Though to the vale no parting beam
Be given, not one memorial gleam,
A lingering light he fondly throws
On the dear hills where first he rose.

Motherless from the age of eight, William Wordsworth was orphaned at thirteen. He and his brothers Richard and Christopher returned home to Cockermouth for Christmas 1783, only to discover that their father was very ill and he died, aged forty-two, on 30 December that year. The five homeless children were now under the guardianship of two uncles, Richard Wordsworth and Christopher Crackanthorp Cookson. At his death, his father's financial affairs were such that the children's representatives had to fight John Wordsworth's employer before a settlement was made and an inheritance granted, eventually, in 1804. The children had no base and their isolation intensified during this struggle to settle their claim. Stephen Gill says that the 'worst effect of their father's death, and again it was a lifelong shaping influence on Wordsworth, was that it deprived them of a home . . . all the strength of his later reverence for the values of rootedness, continuity, and sustained love, all originate now'.

Wordsworth, during the holidays, stayed with his maternal grandparents in Penrith but they felt put upon and the relationship was not a happy one. In 1787 Dorothy and William were reunited. Dorothy, now sixteen, and William, a year older, spent the summer rambling and they were joined by Mary Hutchinson, Wordsworth's future wife. Later that year, in October, Wordsworth left the Lake District for the first time in his life when he travelled to Cambridge and university.

During his five years at St John's College, Cambridge, Wordsworth disliked competitive examinations, spent more time socialising than studying and, at twenty-one, was awarded a pass degree in 1791. During his time there, however, he studied moral philosophy, Italian, recent English poetry, Euclid and Newton; he translated the Classics and composed poetic imitations based on them. Between 1787 and 1791, the long vacations were spent mainly at Hawkshead, sometimes at Penrith, and it was during the long holiday of 1789 with Dorothy and Mary Hutchinson at Penrith that he finished his poem 'Evening Walk', which was first published in 1793.

In 1790, Wordsworth embarked on a walking tour with his Welsh friend, Robert Jones, through France and Switzerland. They covered almost three thousand miles, almost two thousand on foot and covered twenty to thirty miles a day. They travelled light and spent only twelve pounds, though they had budgeted to spend twenty. In a letter to Dorothy, Wordsworth wrote that they carried their bundles 'upon our heads, with each an oak stick in our hands'. During the trip they rose early, sometimes walking twelve or fifteen miles before breakfast. They arrived in Calais on 13 July and as they travelled down through France they witnessed what Wordsworth later called a nation 'mad with joy' as it celebrated the first anniversary of Bastille Day, when the mob, during the French Revolution, stormed the Bastille on 14 July 1789. They crossed the Alps at the Simplon Pass, visited Lake Maggiore and Lake Como, and saw the glaciers of Chamonix. Wordsworth was so impressed by the Alps that he told his sister that 'Among the more awful [impressive, awe-inspiring] scenes of the Alps, I had not thought of man, or a single created being; my whole soul was turned to him who produced the terrible majesty before me'. For him these mountains were a religious and poetic experience.

Returning to Cambridge to complete his degree, Wordsworth, according to a memoir written by his nephew, spent the week before his Finals reading Richardson's novel, *Clarissa*. He was awarded a B.A. in January 1791 and, though his guardians hoped that Wordsworth would opt for a career in law or the church, both careers were rejected. In a letter to a contemporary at Cambridge, Wordsworth declared: 'I am doomed to be an idler throughout my whole life'. Still dependent on relatives for money, Wordsworth spent January to May (he was twenty-one on 7 April 1791) in London where he read, attended debates in the House of Commons and, because of the mood of dissent inspired by the French Revolution, became more politically aware. He then visited Richard Jones in Wales and they explored north Wales and one night climbed Snowdon, Wales's highest mountain (1085m/3561ft), in order to see the sun rise. In September Wordsworth returned to London and Cambridge, then travelled to Brighton to visit the poet and novelist Charlotte Smith and at the end of November left for France, where he intended to improve his French and assess for himself the effects of the 1789 Revolution.

He crossed the English Channel and landed at Dieppe on 26 November. First he visited Rouen and Paris; he reached Orleans on 6 December and there he moved in 'the best society this place affords'. In Orleans it is thought that he met Marie Anne, known as Annette, Vallon, a Catholic who was four years older than him, and by February had moved to Blois, her home town; very soon afterwards Annette was pregnant with Wordsworth's child. In letters written during 1792, Wordsworth never mentions Annette, not even in a letter to his brother Richard in which he asks him to send him money. By September, Wordsworth and Annette were back in Orleans where Wordsworth asked a close family friend of the Vallons, Andre-Augustin Dufour, a magistrate's clerk, to represent him at the child's baptism when the time came.

Meanwhile, Wordsworth left Annette and Orleans. At the end of October he was in Paris. His daughter, Anne-Caroline (called Caroline) Wordsworth, was born on 15 December 1792 and Wordsworth was back in London by the end of December. Some doubt surrounds Wordsworth's six-week stay in Paris. Why did he not stay by Annette's side? Why did he not return to England immediately in order to raise money with which he could support mother and child? Critics argue that Paris, in November 1792, was too interesting politically to be missed (in August King Louis XVI had been deposed and imprisoned) or that he was waiting on a passport. Wordsworth himself, in *The Prelude*, written twelve years later, claims that the drama unfolding in Paris prevented his leaving sooner: 'Reluctantly to England I returned/ Compelled by nothing less than absolute want/ Of funds for my support'. Though Annette expected Wordsworth to marry her, he did not and in her letters she longed for the father of her child to return. On 20 March 1793, for example, she wrote: 'Come, my love, my husband, and receive the tender embraces of your wife, of your daughter'. The outbreak of war between England and France and Annette's Catholic and Royalist background made a union between them difficult. Later, when Wordsworth married Mary Hutchinson, his relationship with Annette was fully known, so much so that before he married, Wordsworth, accompanied by Dorothy, travelled to France to meet Annette and Caroline and to make financial arrangements which would help support them.

In January 1793, King Louis XVI was guillotined. Wordsworth was twenty-two, a father and without an income, and he was staying with his brother Richard in London. That same month he published two poems, 'An Evening Walk' and 'Descriptive Sketches', but they did not receive good reviews or sell well. France, with its vision of freedom and its fight against oppression, was an inspiration and, although there was a Society for Constitutional Reform in England, the mood was different than that in France. England was opposed to revolution and on 1 February war was declared between England and France. Wordsworth now saw that the British government was intent on suppressing dissent and would oppose French liberalism. In a piece entitled *A Letter to the Bishop of Llandaff by a Republican*, Wordsworth denounced the Bishop for first encouraging, then denouncing, the French Revolution, arguing that not only the British Monarchy but the aristocracy should be abolished; this seditious Letter was never published during his lifetime. He was also worried about Annette, Caroline and their future, made doubly difficult because of the tension between the two countries.

In July 1793, Wordsworth borrowed five guineas from his brother Richard and set out with his friend William Calvert on a tour of the West Country. They spent a month on the Isle of Wight but the British fleet gathering for war and cannon fire at sunset depressed him. On leaving the Isle of Wight, their carriage was damaged in an accident and Calvert continued into the north on horseback, while Wordsworth walked on from Salisbury, into South and then through North Wales. He crossed Salisbury Plain, visited Stonehenge, travelled to Bath and Bristol and then followed the River Wye, stopping at Tintern Abbey, and continued on up through Wales until he reached Robert Jones's house (which he had visited in 1791).

Christmas 1793 was spent at Whitehaven and afterwards Wordsworth visited friends at Keswick and Armathwaite. By February he was reunited with Dorothy, who since 1788 had held various domestic positions, in Halifax, and they both went to Windy Brow, a farm above Keswick which William Calvert offered them. There, surrounded by natural beauty, they delighted in each other's company and lived simply: they drank milk, not tea, and their dinner, according to Dorothy, was 'chiefly of potatoes'. She was learning French and Italian, their lives were relatively stable and Wordsworth was rewriting and revising his poetry. It was during this period that Raisley Culvert, William Culvert's younger brother, seriously ill with tuberculosis and due his inheritance on his twenty-first birthday in September 1794, bequeathed William Wordsworth a substantial sum of £900 in his will. Raisley Culvert was dying. Wordsworth offered to accompany Culvert to Lisbon but he was too ill to travel and died in January 1795.

Culvert's belief in Wordsworth's poetic abilities was a significant boost but meanwhile there was little money, the bequest not being issued until October 1795 and always in small amounts. Wordsworth returned to London in February 1795 where he met with many radicals, including William Godwin, who supported the French Revolution. Dorothy, meanwhile, stayed with different friends until Wordsworth was given, rent free, Racedown Lodge, a house in North Dorset which was owned by a wealthy Bristol merchant John Pinney, whose sons John and Azariah befriended Wordsworth. It was also arranged that Wordsworth and his sister would look after a young boy named Basil Montagu, son of Basil Montagu, the illegitimate son of the fourth Earl of Sandwich. Wordsworth stayed at the Pinney home in Bristol until he and Dorothy were reunited. It was in Bristol that Wordsworth met Samuel Taylor Coleridge, then twenty-two, and a fellow radical, and their friendship was to have a lasting effect on them, both as men and poets. In September Dorothy joined her brother. They travelled to Racedown Lodge and there, with Basil Montagu in their care, they lived and worked happily, Wordsworth attending to the garden, Dorothy to the household. Visitors included Mary Hutchinson who stayed from November 1796 to June 1797. Dorothy wrote 'we are as happy as human beings can be' and the image of the three of them together became an image of their life to come. Brother and sister were never to be separated again during their long lives. While they were at Racedown, London witnessed protests by Liberals against the government – the King's coach was attacked as he was on his way to the state opening of Parliament and Wordsworth witnessed first hand wretchedly poor country people. In a poem, 'Imitation of Juvenal', one of many social protest poems being written at that time, he savagely attacked those who were powerful and wealthy but corrupt. He also composed *The Borderers*, a five-act play in blank verse which was rejected by Covent Garden, and he had little success in getting his work published.

From Racedown Lodge, they moved in July 1797 to Alfoxden House, a large, beautiful, spacious mansion near Nether Stowey, among the Somerset Hills. They had been visiting Coleridge, who lived with his wife and young family at Stowey, and had fallen in love with the place and also moved in order to live closer to him. Wordsworth, Coleridge and Dorothy soon became inseparable. Regardless of weather, they explored the locality and beyond. The three once set out on a walking tour at 4 o'clock in November. Wordsworth and Dorothy were close observers of nature. They went out at night, took notes on their observations and aroused the locals' suspicions, so much so that they were thought to be spies and this led to investigations by the Home Office. In the end, the Wordsworths were asked to leave Alfoxden House because of Wordsworth's political beliefs and his associations with Coleridge and other liberals, though Wordsworth and Coleridge by this time were no longer part of a radical movement.

They left Alfoxden in late June and spent the summer of 1798 at a friend's cottage near Bristol. Wordsworth and his sister spent much of the time exploring and averaged a twenty-mile walk every day. In July they walked to Tintern and it was this visit that inspired one of Wordsworth's best known poems. In August the Wordsworths travelled to London, where they said goodbye to Basil who was going to be looked after by an aunt. In September Coleridge and a friend, John Chester, joined them and they set sail for Germany where, in Wordsworth's words, 'we purpose to pass the two ensuing years in order to acquire the German language and to furnish ourselves with a tolerable stock of information in natural science. Our plan is to settle if possible in a village near a university, in a pleasant, and, if we can, a mountainous country.'

In terms of their poetic development 1797–1798 was a very important time for both Wordsworth and Coleridge and it marks the first great phase of Wordsworth's lyric development. In March 1798 Wordsworth wrote 'Lines Written in Early Spring' ['It is the first mild day of March']. The publication of the *Lyrical Ballads* on 4 October 1798 was a turning point in English poetry. The conversation between the two poets sometimes resulted in a form of collaboration. Many of the ideas in Coleridge's 'The Rime of the Ancient Mariner', for example, were suggested by Wordsworth and on 13 July 1798 Wordsworth wrote 'Tintern Abbey', which captures his total devotion to nature and which contains much of Coleridge's philosophy. Coleridge 'loved fields & woods & mountains with almost a visionary fondness' and Wordsworth's poetry expresses this. That said, the book was published anonymously because, as Coleridge declared, 'Wordsworth's name is nothing – to a large number of persons mine *stinks*'.

But the most significant thing to be said about the *Lyrical Ballads* is that the poems were unlike the poetry of the time. Wordsworth's friend William Hazlitt described them as having 'the sense of a new style and a new spirit in poetry . . . It had to me something of the effect that arises from the turning up of the fresh soil, or the first welcome breath of Spring'. Wordsworth clearly knew how different the *Lyrical Ballads* were and in an 'Advertisement' which serves as a Preface he states that the majority of the *Lyrical Ballads* 'are to be considered as experiments' and that, instead of the 'gaudiness and inane phraseology of many modern writers', the poems use the 'language of conversation' and 'a natural delineation of human passions, human characters, and human incidents'. No other book of poems in English, it has been said, announced a new literary departure. Nineteen of the twenty-four poems were by Wordsworth, including poems about beggars, a mad mother, and an idiot boy. Wordsworth's intention was that poetry like this would alter people's perceptions, not only of poetry but of how they viewed their fellow man.

●

Coleridge was intent on learning German but the Wordsworths lost interest and they went their separate ways. Coleridge immersed himself in German scholarship but Wordsworth and Dorothy were miserable in cheap lodgings and arrived back in England on 1 May. Wordsworth had been writing during his time in Germany, including Books I and II of *The Prelude*, in which he remembers the Stolen Boat and Skating episodes, many of the Lucy poems, including 'A slumber did my spirit seal' which is dated 1799. Coleridge returned in July and, though they still wanted to live close to Coleridge, the Wordsworths decided to return to their birthplace in the Lake District. Wordsworth and Coleridge went on a walking tour of the Lake District in November and by December 1799 Wordsworth and Dorothy had settled in Dove Cottage, Grasmere, rented for £8 a year. By doing so, Wordsworth, in Stephen Gill's words, was 'distancing himself from the political centre, from publishers, and the whole professional world of literature' and committing himself 'to an austere and dedicated life amidst the elemental forms of nature'.

Grasmere, with its hills, lakes and rivers, delighted the Wordsworths and they set about making the house their home. The poetry he was writing celebrated the local place names. They were joined by their brother John Wordsworth, a sailor, who had spent years at sea and in late February Mary Hutchinson came on a two-month visit.

By June, Coleridge and his family had moved to the Lake District, only half a day's walk from Dove Cottage, and a period of happiness and stability had begun.

In 1800, Wordsworth prepared another edition of the *Lyrical Ballads*, including some new poems, and a two-volume work was published in January 1801 with 'W. Wordsworth' on the title page. It included Wordsworth's now famous Preface and notes and Wordsworth excluded Coleridge from the project, which made for an uneasy relationship between them. In the Preface, Wordsworth tells of how the poems are inspired by 'Low and rustic life' and explore 'the primary laws of our nature' and reminds his reader that the *Lyrical Ballads* are unusual in their language, subject matter and emphasis. And, as Wordsworth said in a letter, dated 14 January 1801, to the politician Charles James Fox, these poems should 'shew that men who do not wear fine cloaths can feel deeply'.

Throughout his life Wordsworth revised his work continually. Stephen Gill puts it this way: 'Wordsworth could not bear the idea of finality. His manuscripts show just how hard he struggled throughout his life to bring poems into being . . . He revised his work for every new edition' and *The Prelude* 'remained in manuscript until Wordsworth's death [1850], but it was thoroughly revised at intervals after its apparent completion in 1805 . . . Wordsworth's revision was compulsive and it always brought him illness, fatigue, and sleepless nights.'

Their life at Dove Cottage consisted of reading, walking and gardening. In the spring of 1802, Wordsworth was falling in love with Mary Hutchinson and proposed marriage. That same spring Wordsworth wrote a short poem which sums up his belief in the beauty, power and importance of the natural world. It is dated 26 March 1802:

> My heart leaps up when I behold
>   A rainbow in the sky:
> So was it when my life began;
> So is it now I am a man;
> So be it when I shall grow old,
>   Or let me die!
> The Child is father of the Man;
> And I could wish my days to be
> Bound each to each by natural piety.

Mary's family disapproved of Wordsworth, who had no profession, but she accepted him. In May, Wordsworth's finances improved – over £10,000 was his when the family claim was eventually settled. Before they married, Wordsworth decided to travel to France to visit Annette and his daughter Caroline. Mary knew of his earlier relationship and Dorothy accompanied him on the journey. They set out in July and on the journey Wordsworth composed a sonnet inspired by London as seen from Westminster Bridge at dawn. Caroline, now nine, met her father for the first time at Calais, in August 1802. That same month Wordsworth wrote his sonnet 'It is a beauteous evening, calm and free', in which he expresses his feelings for Caroline, but little else is known of their relationship; on 31 August Wordsworth and Dorothy returned to England. [The Annette Vallon affair was omitted from the official biography published by Wordsworth's nephew, Christopher Wordsworth (1808–1885); the affair was not widely known about until the twentieth century.]

On 4 October 1802, Wordsworth married Mary Hutchinson at Brompton near Scarborough but Dorothy was unable to attend the actual ceremony. The night before the wedding, it is well-known that Dorothy wore the wedding ring and on the morning of the wedding, as she handed the ring to Wordsworth, he slipped it on her finger again for a brief moment and blessed her. She was so overcome that she lay on her bed 'neither hearing or seeing anything' while the early-morning marriage took place. Later that day, Mr and Mrs Wordsworth and Dorothy began their journey home to Grasmere.

The marriage between William and Mary was a very happy one and Dorothy became a second mother to their children. [John was born in June 1803, Dora in 1804, Thomas in 1806, Catherine in 1808, William in 1810]. Wordsworth's reputation was growing. In 1803 Wordsworth, together with Dorothy and Coleridge, set off on a tour of Scotland on an Irish jaunting-car. They visited Burns's home and grave and spent a week in Walter Scott's company. Scott's attachment to place was something which Wordsworth could identify with strongly. They witnessed dreadful poverty and heard Gaelic, a language they could not understand. Though the weather was bad and the travellers were often wet and cold, they still responded enthusiastically to Scotland. Wordsworth wrote some poems immediately but two years later, in 1805, he was, in his own words, to 'interrogate his memory' and write poems inspired by that Scottish tour, notably 'The Solitary Reaper'.

In 1803, Wordsworth not only met the novelist Scott but also George Beaumont, a landowner and artist. Beaumont was so impressed by the *Lyrical Ballads* and the man who wrote them that he gave Wordsworth a parcel of land at Applethwaite. Meanwhile the friendship between Wordsworth and Coleridge was, once again, troubled. Wordsworth was made uneasy by Coleridge's irresponsible attitude towards his family and the situation was not helped when Coleridge, thinking Wordsworth's long poems best, disapproved of his writing short poems. Coleridge's health broke down and he set off for the Mediterranean, where he stayed two years.

Wordsworth began 'Ode: Intimations of Immortality' in 1803, a great meditative poem in which he expresses many concepts central to his thought and feeling. For example, he writes that:

> Our birth is but a sleep and a forgetting:
> The Soul that rises with us, our life's Star,
>   Hath had elsewhere its setting,
>   And cometh from afar:
>   Not in entire forgetfulness,
>   And not in utter nakedness,
> But trailing clouds of glory do we come
>   From God, who is our home:
> Heaven lies about us in our infancy!
> Shades of the prison-house begin to close
>   Upon the growing Boy
> But He beholds the light, and whence it flows,
>   He sees it in his joy. . . .

Here, Wordsworth sees the child and childhood as special but he also realises that we become estranged from God at birth and that Nature reminds us of the creator. Later in the Immortality Ode poem he writes that:

> The innocent brightness of a new-born Day
> Is lovely yet

and ends, having praised the beauty of nature, with thanks:

> Thanks to the human heart by which we live,
> Thanks to its tenderness, its joys, and fears,
> To me the meanest flower that blows can give
> Thoughts that do often lie too deep for tears.

This period of Wordsworth's life [1802–1805] was a productive one. He began writing his long poem 'The Excursion' and once again he was working on *The Prelude* [Bks III–VII were written in April and May 1804; Bks VIII–XI between October and December 1804]. On 18 June 1803, John, his and Mary's first child, was born; on 16 August 1804, Dorothy (known as Dora) was born and it was in 1804 that Wordsworth wrote the poem that would make him famous throughout the world. It was untitled and, though the subject matter is the natural world, particularly daffodils, it is primarily a celebration of memory and is always worth re-reading. It illustrates the vital connection for Wordsworth between what we see before us, how we see again through the power of memory and imagination, and how the present moment can be stored up and can offer comfort in the future:

> I wandered lonely as a cloud
> That floats on high o'er vales and hills,
> When all at once I saw a crowd,
> A host, of golden daffodils;
> Beside the lake, beneath the trees,
> Fluttering and dancing in the breeze.
>
> Continuous as the stars that shine
> And twinkle on the milky way,
> They stretched in never-ending line
> Along the margin of a bay:
> Ten thousand saw I at a glance,
> Tossing their heads in sprightly dance.
>
> The waves beside them danced; but they
> Out-did the sparkling waves in glee:
> A poet could not but be gay,
> In such a jocund company:
> I gazed—and gazed—but little thought
> What wealth the show to me had brought:

> For oft, when on my couch I lie
> In vacant or in pensive mood,
> They flash upon that inward eye
> Which is the bliss of solitude;
> And then my heart with pleasure fills,
> And dances with the daffodils.

This poem also illustrates the very close relationship between brother and sister. Two years before Wordsworth drafted the poem, Dorothy had written in her Journal on 15 April 1802 the following:

> When we were in the woods beyond Gowbarrow park we saw a few daffodils close to the water side. We fancied that the lake had floated the seeds ashore and that the little colony had so sprung up. But as we went along there were many more and yet more and at last under the boughs of the trees, we saw that there was a long belt of them along the shore, about the breadth of a country turnpike road. I never saw daffodils so beautiful; they grew among the mossy stones about and about them, some rested their heads upon these stones as on a pillow for weariness and the rest tossed and reeled and danced and seemed as if they verily laughed and the wind that blew upon them over the lake, they looked so gay ever glancing ever changing.' [And Wordsworth told a friend that the best two lines, lines 21–22 ('They flash upon that inward eye/ Which is the bliss of solitude'), were composed by his wife Mary.]

By May 1805 Wordsworth had completed the first draft of *The Prelude*, which runs to almost eight thousand lines, and many Wordsworth specialists think that Wordsworth had written his greatest poetry by then. It is worth noting, perhaps, that all the poems chosen for study at Leaving Certificate were written by the younger Wordsworth, though he wrote throughout a long life and died aged eighty. Michael Schmidt says that for the last forty years of his life, Wordsworth 'wrote copiously and competently, but in the main dully'.

He lived most of his life in the Lake District where he was born. In 1808 he lived in Allan Bank and moved in 1813 to Rydal Mount, Grasmere, where he lived until his death. In 1812 two of his children died: Catherine, aged almost four, died in June, Thomas, aged six and a half, in December. In the sonnet 'Surprised by joy' he writes of his great pain on Catherine's death, which was made worse by Wordsworth's being in London at the time and not hearing the bad news until a week later when she had been buried. In 1813 Wordsworth was appointed Stamp-Distributor or Revenue Collector for Westmorland, which guaranteed him a steady income; in 1814 he toured Scotland and in 1815 a Collected Edition of his poems was published; in 1820 he toured Switzerland and the Italian Lakes, and in 1823 he toured the Netherlands. In 1828 he toured Germany with his daughter Dora and the following year Wordsworth took a five-week carriage tour through Ireland and visited many parts of the country including Kenmare and Killarney where, as recorded in his journal, he 'took the mountain of Carranthouel [sic] the highest in Ireland'.

One of his closest friends said that Wordsworth had 'a strong, but not a happy old age'. There were honours, but there were also many sorrows caused by illnesses and deaths. Durham and Oxford universities conferred honorary degrees, his poems were published in America and in 1843, at the age of seventy-three, he was appointed Poet Laureate. He was elected to the Royal Irish Academy in 1846. He had become a kind of national monument. There were many visitors, some invited, some not. There is a record of a conversation between a couple outside Wordsworth's gate in which the woman urges her partner 'to get on the wall & snatch a sprig of laurel, or anything; we must take something away'. But he had lost two children in 1812; Dorothy became ill in 1829 and never recovered and his daughter Dora died in 1847. In later life he was conservative, a churchgoer, the opposite to what he had been as a young man. Wordsworth, in Seamus Heaney's words, 'became more an institution than an individual'. But in some ways he had not changed. For example, he was planting trees well into his seventies, turned the grass at hay-making and continued to walk at all times of the year. In 1850 Wordsworth contracted pleurisy and lay ill for a month before he died on 13 April. Dorothy, who had been ill for years, died in 1855 and his wife Mary died in 1859. All three are buried in Grasmere churchyard, one of the world's most visited literary shrines.

POEMS

Poems

The poems, dated the year of their composition, are printed here in the order in which they were written. *The Prelude* was written over several years and first published in 1805 but these excerpts, from Book I, were composed in 1799. A revised edition of *The Prelude* was published posthumously in 1850 and it is the re-worked version that is used here.

To My Sister

It is the first mild day of March:
Each minute sweeter than before,
The redbreast sings from the tall larch
That stands beside our door.

There is a blessing in the air,   5
Which seems a sense of joy to yield
To the bare trees, and mountains bare,
And grass in the green field.

My sister! ('tis a wish of mine)
Now that our morning meal is done,   10
Make haste, your morning task resign;
Come forth and feel the sun.

Edward will come with you; and, pray,
Put on with speed your woodland dress;
And bring no book: for this one day   15
We'll give to idleness.

No joyless forms shall regulate
Our living calendar:
We from to-day, my Friend, will date
The opening of the year.   20

Love, now a universal birth,
From heart to heart is stealing,
From earth to man, from man to earth:
— It is the hour of feeling —

One moment now may give us more   25
Than years of toiling reason:
Our minds shall drink at every pore
The spirit of the season.

Some silent laws our hearts will make,
Which they shall long obey: 30
We for the year to come may take
Our temper from to-day.

And from the blessed power that rolls
About, below, above,
We'll frame the measure of our souls: 35
They shall be tuned to love.

Then come, my Sister! come, I pray,
With speed put on your woodland dress;
And bring no book: for this one day
We'll give to idleness.   40

📖 Glossary

Line 3 redbreast: the robin.

Line 3 larch: coniferous tree.

Line 6 a sense of joy to yield: to give a sense of joy.

Line 11 Make haste: hurry.

Line 11 task resign: give up/abandon your household chore/work.

Line 17 regulate: control, determine.

Line 26 years of toiling reason: years of mental hard work.

Line 32 temper: mood, outlook.

Line 35 measure: extent, rhythm.

This poem was composed in 1798 at Alfoxden and published that same year.
Wordsworth was then twenty-eight and on its first publication in the *Lyrical Ballads*
(1798) it was given the title: 'Lines written at a small distance from my House, and sent
by my little Boy to the Person to whom they are addressed'. The recipient was Dorothy
Wordsworth, the poet's twenty-seven-year-old sister, the little boy/messenger was
Basil Montagu whom the Wordsworths were looking after at the time [see biographical
note].

❓ Questions

1. The poem is an invitation from brother to sister. Do you find the invitation an attractive one? Why? Give reasons for your answer.

2. What is the effect of the opening lines in stanzas one and two? Comment on the movement of the line and on Wordsworth's use of rhyme. Which words, phrases, details, in your opinion, best capture the mood of the poem?

3. How would you describe the speaker's tone? Is it the same throughout?

4. How idle do you think they will be on this particular day? Which words and phrases best describe the day as Wordsworth sees it?

5. What gives this poem its immediacy? Consider the tone, the exclamation marks, the verbs.

6. What does the detail 'and bring no book' add to the poem? What does it say about poetry itself which is usually read in a book?

7. The poem celebrates the first mild day of March but it also goes beyond natural description. What do you understand by the lines: 'Love, now a universal birth,/ From heart to heart is stealing' and 'We'll frame the measure of our souls:/ They shall be tuned to love'?

8. Though the poem is spoken by one to another, do you feel excluded from the experience? Why? Why not?

9. In stanza seven (lines 25–28) the poet speaks of the present and the future. How are the present moment and the future linked? What do you understand by the lines 'We for the year to come may take/ Our temper from to-day'?

Tintern Abbey

Five years have past; five summers, with the length
Of five long winters! and again I hear
These waters, rolling from their mountain-springs
With a soft inland murmur.—Once again
Do I behold these steep and lofty cliffs,   5
That on a wild secluded scene impress
Thoughts of more deep seclusion; and connect
The landscape with the quiet of the sky.
The day is come when I again repose
Here, under this dark sycamore, and view   10
These plots of cottage-ground, these orchard tufts,
Which at this season, with their unripe fruits,
Are clad in one green hue, and lose themselves
'Mid groves and copses. Once again I see
These hedge-rows, hardly hedge-rows, little lines   15
Of sportive wood run wild: these pastoral farms,
Green to the very door; and wreaths of smoke
Sent up, in silence, from among the trees!
With some uncertain notice, as might seem
Of vagrant dwellers in the houseless woods,   20
Or of some Hermit's cave, where by his fire
The Hermit sits alone.
               These beauteous forms,
Through a long absence, have not been to me
As is a landscape to a blind man's eye:
But oft, in lonely rooms, and 'mid the din   25
Of towns and cities, I have owed to them,
In hours of weariness, sensations sweet,
Felt in the blood, and felt along the heart;
And passing even into my purer mind,
With tranquil restoration: —feelings too   30
Of unremembered pleasure: such, perhaps,
As have no slight or trivial influence
On that best portion of a good man's life,
His little, nameless, unremembered, acts

Of kindness and of love. Nor less, I trust,   35
To them I may have owed another gift,
Of aspect more sublime; that blessed mood
In which the burthen of the mystery,
In which the heavy and the weary weight
Of all this unintelligible world,   40
Is lightened: —that serene and blessed mood,
In which the affections gently lead us on,—
Until, the breath of this corporeal frame
And even the motion of our human blood
Almost suspended, we are laid asleep   45
In body, and become a living soul:
While with an eye made quiet by the power
Of harmony, and the deep power of joy,
We see into the life of things.
                                                    If this
Be but a vain belief, yet, oh! how oft—   50
In darkness and amid the many shapes
Of joyless daylight; when the fretful stir
Unprofitable, and the fever of the world,
Have hung upon the beatings of my heart—
How oft, in spirit, have I turned to thee,   55
O sylvan Wye! thou wanderer thro' the woods,
How often has my spirit turned to thee!

  And now, with gleams of half-extinguished thought,
With many recognitions dim and faint,
And something of a sad perplexity,   60
The picture of the mind revives again:
While here I stand, not only with the sense
Of present pleasure, but with pleasing thoughts
That in this moment there is life and food
For future years. And so I dare to hope,   65
Though changed, no doubt, from what I was when first
I came among these hills; when like a roe
I bounded o'er the mountains, by the sides

Of the deep rivers, and the lonely streams,
Wherever nature led: more like a man   70
Flying from something that he dreads than one
Who sought the thing he loved. For nature then
(The coarser pleasures of my boyish days,
And their glad animal movements all gone by)
To me was all in all.—I cannot paint   75
What then I was. The sounding cataract
Haunted me like a passion: the tall rock,
The mountain, and the deep and gloomy wood,
Their colours and their forms, were then to me
An appetite; a feeling and a love,   80
That had no need of a remoter charm,
By thought supplied, nor any interest
Unborrowed from the eye.—That time is past,
And all its aching joys are now no more,
And all its dizzy raptures. Not for this   85
Faint I, nor mourn nor murmur; other gifts
Have followed; for such loss, I would believe,
Abundant recompense. For I have learned
To look on nature, not as in the hour
Of thoughtless youth; but hearing oftentimes   90
The still, sad music of humanity,
Nor harsh nor grating, though of ample power
To chasten and subdue. And I have felt
A presence that disturbs me with the joy
Of elevated thoughts; a sense sublime   95
Of something far more deeply interfused,
Whose dwelling is the light of setting suns,
And the round ocean and the living air,
And the blue sky, and in the mind of man:
A motion and a spirit, that impels   100
All thinking things, all objects of all thought,
And rolls through all things. Therefore am I still
A lover of the meadows and the woods,

And mountains; and of all that we behold
From this green earth; of all the mighty world   105
Of eye, and ear, —both what they half create,
And what perceive; well pleased to recognise
In nature and the language of the sense
The anchor of my purest thoughts, the nurse,
The guide, the guardian of my heart, and soul   110
Of all my moral being.
                              Nor perchance,
If I were not thus taught, should I the more
Suffer my genial spirits to decay:
For thou art with me here upon the banks
Of this fair river; thou my dearest Friend,   115
My dear, dear Friend; and in thy voice I catch
The language of my former heart, and read
My former pleasures in the shooting lights
Of thy wild eyes. Oh! yet a little while
May I behold in thee what I was once,   120
My dear, dear Sister! and this prayer I make,
Knowing that Nature never did betray
The heart that loved her; 'tis her privilege,
Through all the years of this our life, to lead
From joy to joy: for she can so inform   125
The mind that is within us, so impress
With quietness and beauty, and so feed
With lofty thoughts, that neither evil tongues,
Rash judgements, nor the sneers of selfish men,
Nor greetings where no kindness is, nor all   130
The dreary intercourse of daily life,
Shall e'er prevail against us, or disturb
Our cheerful faith, that all which we behold
Is full of blessings. Therefore let the moon
Shine on thee in thy solitary walk;   135
And let the misty mountain-winds be free
To blow against thee: and, in after years,

When these wild ecstasies shall be matured
Into a sober pleasure; when thy mind
Shall be a mansion for all lovely forms,   140
Thy memory be as a dwelling-place
For all sweet sounds and harmonies; oh! then,
If solitude, or fear, or pain, or grief,
Should be thy portion, with what healing thoughts
Of tender joy wilt thou remember me,   145
And these my exhortations! Nor, perchance—
If I should be where I no more can hear
Thy voice, nor catch from thy wild eyes these gleams
Of past existence—wilt thou then forget
That on the banks of this delightful stream   150
We stood together; and that I, so long
A worshipper of Nature, hither came
Unwearied in that service: rather say
With warmer love—oh! with far deeper zeal
Of holier love. Nor wilt thou then forget   155
That after many wanderings, many years
Of absence, these steep woods and lofty cliffs,
And this green pastoral landscape, were to me
More dear, both for themselves and for thy sake!

📖 Glossary

Title: The full title reads 'Lines Composed A Few Miles Above Tintern Abbey, On Revisiting The Banks of The Wye During A Tour. 13 July 1798'. The poem was composed on that same day, 13 July 1798. Wordsworth said that 'No poem of mine was composed under circumstances more pleasant for me to remember than this. I began it upon leaving Tintern, after crossing the Wye, and concluded it just as I was entering Bristol in the evening, after a ramble of four or five days, with my sister. Not a line of it was altered, and not any part of it was altered, and not any part of it written down till I reached Bristol.'

Tintern Abbey: a ruined abbey in a wooded valley in Monmouthshire, Wales. It was founded by the Cistercians in 1131 but by 1536 Henry VIII had decided that all religious houses should be plundered for their wealth. Tintern Abbey, which had been the wealthiest abbey in Wales, was one of the victims. The lead used in roofing was removed and today, though roofless and in ruins, the tall abbey walls are still impressive.

Line 1 Five years have past: Wordsworth first visited the region in 1793 on a walking tour when he was twenty-three.

Line 3 These waters: the River Wye.

Line 4 With a soft inland murmur: The river is not affected by the tides a few miles above Tintern. [This is Wordsworth's own note, a note which emphasises that the poem does not focus on the site of the religious building.]

Line 5 lofty: very high.

Line 6 secluded: hidden, remote.

Line 6 impress: to produce a profound or deep effect upon.

Line 7 more deep seclusion: deeper solitude.

Line 9 repose: rest myself.

Line 11 orchard tufts: clusters or clumps of fruit-trees.

Line 13 hue: colour.

Line 14 groves: small wood.

Line 14 copses: woods of small growth.

Line 16 sportive: playful, growing luxuriantly.

Line 16 pastoral: shepherd.

Line 17 wreaths: spirals.

Line 20 vagrant: wandering.

Line 20 houseless woods: woods without buildings to dwell in.

Line 21 Hermit: one who lives a solitary life; a solitary, religious individual.

Line 30 restoration: recollection.

Line 37 sublime: majestic.

Line 38 burthen of the mystery: the burden or weight of life's mystery.

Line 42 affections: emotions.

Line 43 corporeal frame: body.

Lines 52/53 when the fretful stir / Unprofitable: the worrying, useless busyness (stir seems to be a noun here, meaning busyness).

Line 56 sylvan: rural, wooded.

Line 58 half-extinguished thought: half-forgotten memories.

Line 60 perplexity: bewilderment, confusion.

Line 67 roe: small species of deer.

Line 76 cataract: large waterfall.

Line 85 raptures: feelings of extreme delight.

Line 86 murmur: complain.

Line 92 Nor harsh nor grating: neither harsh nor grating.

Line 92 ample: abundant.

Line 93 chasten and subdue: restrain and reduce.

Line 96 interfused: imbued, mixed with.

Line 100 impels: drives forward.

Lines 106/107 both what they half create,/ And what perceive: Wordsworth here is referring to how one responds to the world: how the eye and ear sees and hears and the mind imagines.

Line 113 genial: genial means 'cheerful' but the word is related to genius and 'genial spirits' can also refer to creative powers.

Line 119 wild: excited.

Line 121 Sister: Dorothy Wordsworth (1771–1855). In his poem 'The Sparrow's Nest', Wordsworth writes of her importance:

> The Blessing of my later years
> Was with me when a boy:
> She gave me eyes, she gave me ears;
> And humble cares, and delicate fears;
> A heart, the fountain of sweet tears;
> And love, and thought, and joy.

Line 125 inform: give form to.

Line 131 intercourse: social exchange.

Line 132 prevail: gain victory.

Line 146 exhortations: urgings, strong advice.

Line 149 past existence: five years earlier.

Line 154 zeal: passionate feeling.

Wordsworth first visited the Wye Valley and the ruins of Tintern Abbey in Monmouthshire, Wales, in August 1793, when he was twenty-three years old.

'Tintern Abbey', in blank verse, was printed as the final poem in the *Lyrical Ballads*. 'I have not ventured to call this Poem an Ode', said Wordsworth, 'but it was written with a hope that in the transitions, and in the impassioned music of the versification would be found the principal requisites of that species of composition'.

Stephen Gill points out that Wordsworth 'passes over everything that gave the area its actual day-to-day character — the commercial traffic on the river, the charcoal-burners serving the iron furnaces along its banks.' Gill quotes Gilpin, who in his *Observations on the River Wye*, published in 1782, wrote of the smoke from the iron furnaces along the banks of the Wye 'issuing from the sides of the hills; and spreading its thin veil over a part of them' and also mentions the beggars at Tintern Abbey itself who lived in hovels.

? Questions

1. This long poem, almost one hundred and sixty lines in length, has been called 'an intricately organized meditation' and celebrates the natural world, the relationship between man and nature and the power of memory and the imagination. What was your first impression of it? How did you respond when you reread the poem?

2. What do we learn about Wordsworth in the opening section (lines 1–22)? How would you describe his mood here? Do you as a reader identify with what he is saying? Why? Why not? Give reasons for your answer.

3. Wordsworth is a central presence throughout. Comment, for example, on 'I hear', 'I behold', 'I again repose', 'I see', in the opening lines and on what they reveal of the poet. Does he respond only through the senses?

4. Who are the other people mentioned in lines 1–22? What is their relationship with Nature? Why do you think Wordsworth imagines 'vagrant dwellers', 'the Hermit'? What do such persons tell us about the natural world?

5. In lines 22–57, Wordsworth speaks of the intervening five years since he last visited this spot. What does he reveal about himself in this section? How does he illustrate that nature and the memory of nature allow us to 'see into the life of things'? Are you convinced? How would you describe his tone here, especially in lines 49–57?

6. The poem focuses first on the present, then on the past, and in lines 58–65 on the future. What is the significance of this, in your opinion?

7. Wordsworth speaks of his earlier response to nature (in lines 65–85) as one of 'aching joys' and 'dizzy raptures'. Which details best convey that sense of boyish delight? Choose three such details and justify your choice.

8. Though lines 85–111 capture Wordsworth's awareness of how his relationship with nature has changed, does he regret that the earlier 'aching joys' are no more? Why does he say that he is 'still/ A lover of the meadows and the woods'?

9. Wordsworth's language paints vivid and colourful pictures but it also expresses abstract and philosophical ideas. For example, reading 'the tall rock, / The mountain, and the deep and gloomy wood' (line 77/78) is a different experience from the language that we find in 'The still, sad music of humanity' (line 91). Examine the effect of both forms of language within the poem.

10. 'The sounding cataract/ Haunted me like a passion' (line 76/77). Such a line, says Stephen Gill, illustrates how William Wordsworth was 'utterly intoxicated by Nature'. Where else is this evident in 'Tintern Abbey' and in other poems by Wordsworth on your course?

11. In the poem's final section (lines 111–159), Wordsworth addresses his sister Dorothy. Comment of the presence of Dorothy. When is the reader first aware of her in the poem? Were you surprised when Wordsworth mentioned her? What would the poem lose if she was not mentioned at all?

12. Dorothy has been interpreted as representing the reader, everyone. What do you understand this to mean? How would you describe Wordsworth's prayer for his sister which begins at line 134: 'Therefore let the moon/ Shine on thee in thy solitary walk . . .' Why is 'solitary' an interesting detail here? Why is Dorothy such a comfort to Wordsworth?

13. Why are the closing two lines central to our understanding of Wordsworth?

14. 'Tintern Abbey' has 'a highly elevated, grand poetic style', says Margaret Drabble. What do you think she means by this? In your answer you should discuss several examples. Can you discover what gives this poem its momentum?

15. The poem contains many grim, realistic details (e.g. 'the din/ Of towns and cities'; 'evil tongues'; 'the sneers of selfish men'). Do you think such details strengthen Wordsworth's passionate argument? Write down those words that express Wordsworth's joy and delight.

16. Examine how Wordsworth, in this poem, combines an elegiac and a triumphant mood. Which, in your opinion, is the dominant mood in the poem? Discuss the significance of the past, the present and the future in the poem.

17. Professor Lorna Sage says of lines 122/123, 'Nature never did betray/ The heart that loved her . . .' —'Nonsense, of course, but wonderful nonsense.' Discuss!

18. 'Tintern Abbey' has been described as Wordsworth's 'impassioned ode to joy'. Is this an accurate description, do you think?

19. Others have visited the ruins of Tintern Abbey and have reflected on transience, mortality, but Jonathan Bate says that Wordsworth focuses not on death but on 'the life of things'. Discuss this view in relation to your reading and understanding of the poem.

20. 'Neither Tintern Abbey nor the River Wye is the subject of the poem. The poet himself is', says Stephen Gill. Discuss this view, supporting the points you make with quotation from or reference to the text.

from *The Prelude* Book 1
Childhood and School-time (lines 357–400)

The Stolen Boat

One summer evening (led by her) I found
A little boat tied to a willow tree
Within a rocky cave, its usual home.
Straight I unloosed her chain, and stepping in
Pushed from the shore. It was an act of stealth   5
And troubled pleasure, nor without the voice
Of mountain-echoes did my boat move on;
Leaving behind her still, on either side,
Small circles glittering idly in the moon,
Until they melted all into one track   10
Of sparkling light. But now, like one who rows,
Proud of his skill, to reach a chosen point
With an unswerving line, I fixed my view
Upon the summit of a craggy ridge,
The horizon's utmost boundary; for above   15
Was nothing but the stars and the grey sky.
She was an elfin pinnace; lustily
I dipped my oars into the silent lake,
And, as I rose upon the stroke, my boat
Went heaving through the water like a swan;   20
When, from behind that craggy steep till then
The horizon's bound, a huge peak, black and huge,
As if with voluntary power instinct
Upreared its head. I struck and struck again,
And growing still in stature the grim shape   25
Towered up between me and the stars, and still,
For so it seemed, with purpose of its own
And measured motion like a living thing,
Strode after me. With trembling oars I turned,
And through the silent water stole my way   30

Back to the covert of the willow tree;
There in her mooring-place I left my bark,—
And through the meadows homeward went, in grave
And serious mood; but after I had seen
That spectacle, for many days, my brain   35
Worked with a dim and undetermined sense
Of unknown modes of being; o'er my thoughts
There hung a darkness, call it solitude
Or blank desertion. No familiar shapes
Remained, no pleasant images of trees,   40
Of sea or sky, no colours of green fields;
But huge and mighty forms, that do not live
Like living men, moved slowly through the mind
By day, and were a trouble to my dreams.

📖 Glossary

Line 1 led by her: led by nature.

Line 4 Straight: quickly.

Line 5 stealth: theft, secrecy.

Line 17 elfin: small, mischievous (relating to elves).

Line 17 pinnace: small boat.

Line 17 lustily: vigorously.

Line 22 bound: boundary.

Line 23 instinct: charged, animated, imbued.

Line 31 covert: shelter.

Line 32 bark: boat.

Line 33 grave: serious.

Line 36 undetermined: unsettled.

Line 37 modes of being: states of being.

The Prelude was begun in 1799 and Wordsworth completed the poem in 1805. There were several versions but a revised version was finally published in 1850, just months after his death. It is the 1850 version which is prescribed here. Professor Frank Kermode says that 'Whether you prefer the early versions or the later depends partly on whether you want to see the poet's years "bound each to each", as he did, or prefer the younger Wordsworth before "mature reflection" disappointingly altered his character and dimmed his youthful fire. In the earlier version this extract begins

> One evening (surely I was led by her)
> I went alone into a shepherd's boat,
> A skiff that to a willow tree was tied
> Within a rocky cave, its usual home.
> 'Twas by the shores of Patterdale, a vale
> Wherein I was a stranger, thither come
> A schoolboy traveller, at the holidays.
> Forth rambled from the village inn alone,
> No sooner had I sight of this small skiff,
> Discovered thus by unexpected chance,
> Than I unloosed her tether and embarked.
> The moon was up, the lake was shining clear
> Among the hoary mountains; from the shore
> I pushed, and struck the oars and struck again
> In cadence, and my little boat moved on. . . .

? Questions

1. What is revealed of Wordsworth's relationship with Nature in the opening line of 'The Stolen Boat'?

2. How does the poet create a sense of drama in the opening lines? Pick out those details which create a dramatic mood. In your answer, consider verbs, rhythm, punctuation.

3. How would you describe the young Wordsworth as portrayed here? Is he a typical or an atypical boy? Give reasons for your answer.

4. The poet, as a boy, we are told, was 'led' by Nature. Is Nature an attracting force throughout the extract? Consider the significance of 'Strode after me'?

5. Examine how Wordsworth connects the boy's inner feelings with the surrounding landscape. Discuss the contrast between lines 18–20 and lines 32–34.

6. Nature, says Wordsworth (in 'Tintern Abbey'), is 'The guide, the guardian of my heart, and soul/ Of all my moral being'. How does it guide him in this instance? What has Wordsworth learned from the stolen boat episode?

7. How can one tell that stealing a boat has had a profound effect on Wordsworth? Quote from the text in support of your answer.

8. Stephen Gill, in his *William Wordsworth A Life*, asks 'Did Wordsworth really steal a boat on Ullswater and sense the mountain terrifyingly pursue him?' and adds that the question sounds ludicrous. The boat stealing episode is one of the best-known incidents in *The Prelude* and yet Gill adds that the only evidence we have is poetic evidence and, elsewhere in his poetry, Wordsworth changed the facts if it spoiled an imaginative work. Do you think it matters if the episode is true or not?

9. In the closing lines (39–44), Wordsworth writes about the familiar and the unfamiliar. Write a note on each as Wordsworth describes them.

from *The Prelude* Book 1
Childhood and School-time (lines 425–463)

Skating

   And in the frosty season, when the sun
Was set, and visible for many a mile
The cottage windows blazed through twilight gloom,
I heeded not their summons: happy time
It was indeed for all of us—for me   5
It was a time of rapture! Clear and loud
The village clock tolled six,—I wheeled about,
Proud and exulting like an untired horse
That cares not for his home. All shod with steel,
We hissed along the polished ice in games   10
Confederate, imitative of the chase
And woodland pleasures,—the resounding horn,
The pack loud chiming, and the hunted hare.
So through the darkness and the cold we flew,
And not a voice was idle; with the din   15
Smitten, the precipices rang aloud;
The leafless trees and every icy crag
Tinkled like iron; while far distant hills
Into the tumult sent an alien sound
Of melancholy not unnoticed, while the stars   20
Eastward were sparkling clear, and in the west
The orange sky of evening died away.
Not seldom from the uproar I retired
Into a silent bay, or sportively
Glanced sideway, leaving the tumultuous throng,   25
To cut across the reflex of a star
That fled, and, flying still before me, gleamed
Upon the glassy plain; and oftentimes,
When we had given our bodies to the wind,
And all the shadowy banks on either side   30

Came sweeping through the darkness, spinning still
The rapid line of motion, then at once
Have I, reclining back upon my heels,
Stopped short; yet still the solitary cliffs
Wheeled by me—even as if the earth had rolled   35
With visible motion her diurnal round!
Behind me did they stretch in solemn train,
Feebler and feebler, and I stood and watched
Till all was tranquil as a dreamless sleep.

📖 Glossary

Line 4 heeded not: ignored, paid no attention to.

Line 4 summons: call.

Line 7 wheeled: turned with a revolving motion.

Line 8 exulting: rejoicing.

Line 11 Confederate: bound together.

Line 15 din: loud noise.

Line 16 Smitten: struck.

Line 16 precipices: steep cliffs.

Line 19 tumult: noise, uproar.

Line 19 alien: different.

Line 23 Not seldom: Frequently.

Line 24 sportively: playfully.

Line 25 Glanced: moved rapidly.

Line 25 tumultuous: noisy.

Line 26 reflex: reflection.

Line 36 diurnal: daily.

Line 37 train: succession.

? Questions

1. 'The most immediately impressive thing about this passage is of course its amazing vitality', says Margaret Drabble. 'It is full of noise and movement and colour'. Which words best capture the noise, the movement, the colour? How does Wordsworth create the sense of winter, boyish gusto and the excitement and the rhythms of ice-skating in this passage? Pick out the words, phrases and images which, in your opinion, best capture the sensation.

2. Wordsworth makes you see; he also makes you hear. Examine the various sounds within the poem and their effect. What do you understand by 'an alien sound Of melancholy'?

3. In lines 8–9, the poet compares his boyhood self to an untired horse. Do you think it is an effective simile? Why? Why not?

4. There is a mood of exhilaration in the opening lines. How would you describe the mood in line 23 onward?

5. 'We hissed along the polished ice in games', writes Wordsworth in line 10. Is this a 'We' or an 'I' poem? Is Wordsworth part of a group or does he see himself as one apart?

6. How would you describe the relationship between Wordsworth and nature in this poem? Can the same be said of the other poems by Wordsworth on your course?

'A slumber did my spirit seal'

A slumber did my spirit seal;
    I had no human fears:
She seemed a thing that could not feel
    The touch of earthly years.

No motion has she now, no force;   5
    She neither hears nor sees;
Rolled round in earth's diurnal course,
    With rocks, and stones, and trees.

Glossary

Line 1 slumber: light sleep.

Line 1 spirit: consciousness; mind (Helen Vendler's interpretation).

Line 1 seal: enclose.

Line 7 diurnal: occurring daily; Stephen Logan suggests that it may be significant that 'diurnal' contains the word 'urn'; and Margaret Drabble comments that 'diurnal' is the only word in the poem with more than two syllables . . . the only literary word in the piece, and it is used with great care and effect. The heavy rolling of its syllables suggests the rolling of the earth, as the more usual word 'daily' could never have done, and its very unexpectedness adds immeasurably to the weight and gravity of the poem.

Wordsworth wrote this poem in 1799, in Germany, and sent it to Coleridge who thought it a 'most sublime Epitaph'. It is one of a group of poems known as 'The Lucy Poems'; Lucy's identity is unknown, though she is sometimes identified with his sister Dorothy. Harold Bloom thinks that the five Lucy poems probably elegise Margaret Hutchinson, the younger sister of Mary Hutchinson, who later became Wordsworth's wife. Margaret Hutchinson died in 1796, in her early twenties. Coleridge, in a letter written on 6 April 1799 to Thomas Poole, wondered 'whether it had any reality' but could not say and added 'Most probably, in some gloomier moment he had fancied the moment in which his Sister might die'. The five Lucy Poems focus on solitude and death.

Michael Schmidt, commenting on The Lucy Poems, says: 'It is not possible to relate the poems to specific incidents or a specific person, despite the theories that have been advanced. The loved and lamented one may be emblematic.'

? Questions

1. How would you describe the mood of the poem's opening lines and how does Wordsworth create that mood? Is the mood the same throughout?

2. What has happened between stanzas one and two? Why do you think Wordsworth changes from past tense to present tense, between one stanza and the other?

3. What is the poet's attitude towards the person he is writing about? Why did he have 'no human fears'? In stanza two what is his understanding of her?

4. What is nature's role in this poem? What interpretation of death emerges from your reading of it?

5. Why do you think Wordsworth speaks of her as a 'thing' in stanza one? A rock, a stone, a trees are things. What is the connection? Overall, how would you describe the poet's choice of words here? Comment especially on 'diurnal'.

6. Helen Vendler says that 'The poem would be very different — and almost inhuman — if the last line read, "With granite, stones, and rocks".' Do you agree? Why? Why not? Give reasons for your answer.

7. It has been suggested that the 'she' of the poem refers to the poet's spirit. Re-read the poem with this in mind. Do you think it a valid interpretation?

8. Commenting on this poem, Professor Leonard Michaels says that Wordsworth's very plain statement 'becomes melancholy and exhilarating at once'. What do you think is meant by this? What is melancholy or sad; what is exhilarating or joyful here?

9. Identify the references to stillness and motion in the poem and comment on how the poem's structure in stanza two is a movement from stillness to movement. Why is this significant?

'She dwelt among the untrodden ways'

She dwelt among the untrodden ways
 Beside the springs of Dove,
A Maid whom there were none to praise
 And very few to love:

A violet by a mossy stone   5
 Half hidden from the eye!
— Fair as a star, when only one
 Is shining in the sky.

She lived unknown, and few could know
 When Lucy ceased to be;   10
But she is in her grave, and, oh,
 The difference to me!

Glossary

Line 1 dwelt: lived.

Line 1 untrodden ways: paths and walkways that are seldom used.

Line 2 springs of Dove: small streams at Dove – which, as Margaret Drabble points out, is not a real place.

Line 3 Maid: girl, young woman.

This lyric poem was composed in 1799 and is one of the five 'Lucy Poems'.

? Questions

1. This short lyric tells of Lucy's life and death. Tell the story in your own words. How does it differ from Wordsworth's? How different would the poem be if stanza two were omitted?

2. How much do we learn about Lucy in this poem? What does Wordsworth choose to tell us about the girl? Comment on the images of the violet and star. What do such images suggest about Lucy?

3. How does Wordsworth feel about Lucy? How would you describe his mood? Which words are most effective in conveying Wordsworth's mood, do you think?

4. Wordsworth uses end-rhyme in this lyric poem (abab). Comment on its effect.

5. Does Lucy, as she is portrayed in the poem, strike you as a real person? An interesting person? Give reasons for your answer.

6. What part does time play in this poem? Is time viewed here in a similar or different way from other poems by Wordsworth on your course?

Composed Upon Westminster Bridge, 3 September 1802

Earth has not anything to show more fair:
Dull would he be of soul who could pass by
A sight so touching in its majesty:
This City now doth, like a garment, wear
The beauty of the morning; silent, bare,   5
Ships, towers, domes, theatres, and temples lie
Open unto the fields, and to the sky;
All bright and glittering in the smokeless air.
Never did sun more beautifully steep
In his first splendour, valley, rock, or hill;   10
Ne'er saw I, never felt, a calm so deep!
The river glideth at his own sweet will:
Dear God! the very houses seem asleep;
And all that mighty heart is lying still!

Glossary

Title: **'Composed Upon Westminster Bridge, 3 September 1802'**, though it was composed 31 July 1802 and first published in 1807. Wordsworth's own note reads: 'Written on the roof of a coach, on my way to France'. The sonnet's rhyming scheme is abbaabbacdcdcd.

Line 1 fair: beautiful.

Line 4 doth: does.

Line 6 towers, domes . . . temples: from Westminster Bridge, the Houses of Parliament, Westminster Abbey, several churches with steeples and the dome of St Paul's Cathedral can be seen.

Line 9 steep: saturate, imbue.

Line 12 sweet will: William Harmon points out that other poets named William (Shakespeare and Yeats) have used the phrase 'sweet will' [Shakespeare's 'Sonnet 135' and Yeats's 'Prayer for My Daughter'].

Commenting on this poem, Helen Vendler says that 'it is not London that we see in Wordsworth's "Composed upon Westminster Bridge", but rather "London-as-interpreted-by-Wordsworth" or "Wordsworth-turned-into-London". Because Wordsworth loved tranquil and sublime scenery, the bustle of daytime London repelled him; yet he found a way to discover "his" London, a London that could resemble him and his way of being. It was the London of dawn, when the air was free of smoke and the Thames was free of barges and the streets free of noise, when the architectural features of the city seemed almost like items in a natural landscape.'

? Questions

1. 'High mountains are a feeling but the hum of cities torture' says Wordsworth. Are you surprised that he wrote a poem about a city? What aspect of the city interests Wordsworth in this sonnet?

2. Why does he call the city majestic? What, in your opinion, gives this poem its power? Consider the images used, the rhythm. What is the effect of line 6?

3. How would you describe Wordsworth's tone here? Is the tone the same throughout? Why? Comment on Wordsworth's use of the present tense.

4. Wordsworth is known as a poet who celebrates nature. Is this city poem a nature poem?

5. Pick out particularly effective words and phrases and justify your choice. How can one tell that Wordsworth was surprised by the scene before him?

6. This has been described by Michael Schmidt as 'a love-poem addressed to a city'. Do you think that is a valid description? Give reasons for your answer.

7. In line 13, the poet addresses God. Is God's presence felt in the poem? Where? And how?

'It is a beauteous evening, calm and free'

It is a beauteous evening, calm and free,
The holy time is quiet as a Nun
Breathless with adoration; the broad sun
Is sinking down in its tranquillity;
The gentleness of heaven broods o'er the Sea: 5
Listen! the mighty Being is awake,
And doth with his eternal motion make
A sound like thunder—everlastingly.
Dear Child! dear Girl! that walkest with me here,
If thou appear untouched by solemn thought,   10
Thy nature is not therefore less divine:
Thou liest in Abraham's bosom all the year;
And worshipp'st at the Temple's inner shrine,
God being with thee when we know it not.

📖 Glossary

Line 1 free: open, unconfined.

Line 5 broods: meditates silently.

Line 9 Dear Child! dear Girl!: Wordsworth's nine-year-old daughter, Caroline.

Line 12 Abraham's bosom: the repose of the happy in death; in Luke XVI .22 there is a reference to the soul's final resting place in heaven – 'And it came to pass, that the beggar died, and was carried by the angels into Abraham's bosom'.

Line 13 Temple's inner shrine: the Temple is a sacred enclosure, the inner shrine was only entered by the sacred priests.

Wordsworth wrote this sonnet in Calais in August 1802 when he and his sister Dorothy went to France to see Annette Vallon, whom he was involved with years earlier, and their daughter Caroline. Dorothy, in her Journals, gives this account: 'The weather was very hot. We walked by the sea-shore almost every evening with Annette and Caroline or Wm and I alone . . . we had delightful walks after the heat of the day was passed away—seeing far off in the west the Coast of England . . . The Evening star and the glory of the sky. The Reflections in the water were more beautiful than the sky itself, purple waves brighter than precious stones for ever melting away upon the sands.'

? Questions

1. What is usually associated with evening? What aspects of evening does Wordsworth focus on in this sonnet? Pick out the details which best create, in your opinion, that evening scene. Comment on the use of sight and sound in the poem. Comment on the word 'broods'.

2. Trace the religious and spiritual references throughout the poem. What do such references suggest?

3. How would you describe the rhythm of the first five lines? What change takes place with 'Listen!' in line 6? What is Wordsworth's tone here? How would you describe the poet's mood?

4. How would you describe the poet's choice of words? Why do you think he uses words such as 'beauteous', 'doth', 'Thou liest'?

5. 'Tintern Abbey' ends with Wordsworth's address to his sister. This sonnet ends with Wordsworth addressing his daughter. How do the poems compare and contrast in terms of what Wordsworth says to both?

6. Is this a usual or an unusual father/daughter poem? Give reasons for your answer.

7. Why is nature so important to Wordsworth as revealed to us in this poem?

8. Which of the poem's two sections, the octet or the sestet, do you prefer? Give reasons for your answer.

9. How does the child's reaction to the 'beauteous evening' differ from Wordsworth's? How does the poet view the child's response?

The Solitary Reaper

Behold her, single in the field,
Yon solitary Highland Lass!
Reaping and singing by herself;
Stop here, or gently pass!
Alone she cuts and binds the grain,   5
And sings a melancholy strain;
O listen! for the Vale profound
Is overflowing with the sound.

No Nightingale did ever chaunt
More welcome notes to weary bands   10
Of travellers in some shady haunt,
Among Arabian sands:
A voice so thrilling ne'er was heard
In spring-time from the Cuckoo-bird,
Breaking the silence of the seas   15
Among the farthest Hebrides.

Will no one tell me what she sings?—
Perhaps the plaintive numbers flow
For old, unhappy, far-off things,
And battles long ago: 20
Or is it some more humble lay,
Familiar matter of to-day?
Some natural sorrow, loss, or pain,
That has been, and may be again?

Whate'er the theme, the Maiden sang   25
As if her song could have no ending;
I saw her singing at her work,
And o'er the sickle bending;—
I listened, motionless and still;
And, as I mounted up the hill,   30
The music in my heart I bore,
Long after it was heard no more.

📖 Glossary

Line 1 Behold her: Look at her.

Line 2 Yon: over there.

Line 6 strain: melody.

Line 7 Vale profound: deep valley.

Line 18 plaintive numbers: sad, mournful verses.

Line 21 lay: song.

Line 28 sickle: reaping hook with a curved blade and a short handle.

This poem was composed in November 1805, when Wordsworth was thirty-five, two years after his trip to Scotland in September 1803. Dorothy Wordsworth tells us that it was prompted by 'a beautiful sentence' in Thomas Wilkinson's *Tour of Scotland*. Wordsworth copied the sentence[s] into his commonplace notebook: 'Passed by a female who was reaping alone, she sung in Erse [the name given by the Lowland Scots to the language of the people of the West Highlands, as being of Irish origin] as she bended over her sickle, the sweetest human voice I ever heard. Her strains were tenderly melancholy, and felt delicious long after they were heard no more'.

The experience recorded here was not Wordsworth's own but, as John Purkis points out in his book *A Preface to Wordsworth*, 'The Solitary Reaper' is an example of a poem where Wordsworth assimilates other people's experiences and tells them as if they were his own. And Purkis adds that the 'I' of a Wordsworth poem 'may stand as a universal shorthand symbol with which the reader can equally identify'.

❓ Questions

1. How can the reader tell, from the outset, that Wordsworth is captivated? How would you describe the poet's tone in the first stanza? Why does he choose to use three exclamation marks in stanza one?

2. How does the second stanza contribute to the development of the idea in stanza one? Why is the girl's song similar to that of the nightingale and cuckoo?

3. The girl is alone and the song she sings strikes Wordsworth as a sad one. How would you describe the overall mood of the poem?

4. 'This is a poem about trying to understand what we hear' says William Harmon. In other words, it is a poem about interpretation. Does it matter that Wordsworth does not understand the words which the girl sings? Why? Why not? How does Wordsworth feel about his not knowing what she sings?

5. Why do you think Wordsworth chose to write this poem using a regular rhyming scheme?

6. What does this poem say about the importance and the power of memory?

7. Though Wordsworth wrote the poem two years after the event, do you think he captures the immediacy of the experience? Examine how the poem is structured and how it moves from 'description through reflection and speculation to remembrance'.

General Questions

A. William Hazlitt said of Wordsworth that 'it is as if there were nothing but himself and the universe; he lives in the busy solitude of his own heart, in the deep silence of thought'. Is this a fair assessment of Wordsworth's poetry, in your opinion? In your answer you should refer to the poems by Wordsworth on your course.

B. 'Wordsworth's poetry not only teaches us, it also engages our interest and moves us.' Would you agree with this view? Support the points you make by quotation or reference to the poems by Wordsworth on your course.

C. 'The people in Wordsworth's poetry are ordinary, humble, solitary characters and his poetry is all the more interesting because of this.' Would you agree with this assessment of Wordsworth's poetry? In your answer you should refer to the poems by Wordsworth on your course.

D. Wordsworth hoped that his poetry would teach us 'to see, to think and feel'. Is this how you responded to the poems by Wordsworth on your course? In your answer you should quote from or refer to the poems.

E. Wordsworth's poetry has been praised [by Matthew Arnold] for its 'healing power'. Would this be your response to the poems by Wordsworth you have studied? Support your discussion by reference to or quotation from the poems on your course.

F. What points would you make in a talk to a group of Leaving Certificate students on the topic: 'Why Wordsworth is worth reading'. In your answer you should refer to or quote from the poems by Wordsworth on your course.

G. Write an essay in which you outline your reasons for liking and/or not liking the poetry of William Wordsworth. Support your points by reference to the poetry of Wordsworth that you have studied.

Critical Commentary

To My Sister

The poem's title reveals the close relationship between Wordsworth and Dorothy, between brother and sister. It was written in 1798 when Wordsworth was twenty-eight and Dorothy, who was his constant companion, twenty-seven.

This poem is an invitation and an invitation one could hardly refuse. Fine weather, spring, the outdoor life have been enjoyed for centuries and any invitation which suggests freedom, enjoyment and escape from work can be understood immediately. The harshness of winter is over, there is a stretch in the evening and there is a delight in this part of the world when the weather turns gentler, softer.

The opening lines are casual and easy-going but there is also a feeling of gratitude and increasing pleasure:

> It is the first mild day of March:
> Each minute sweeter than before

The opening line, in its very vowel sounds, becomes more expansive as one reads through the line, imitating, as it were, the opening up of the year:

> **It is the first mild day of March**

The setting is ordinary; the scenery is not the spectacular scenery described elsewhere in Wordsworth's poetry but the birdsong, the tree, the door of the house make it all the more familiar. The reference to 'our door' gives the poem a sense of the particular, rooting the poem in a particular place, but it is the out of doors world that interests Wordsworth. We can understand, by the end of the first stanza, the feeling of happiness he is experiencing:

> It is the first mild day of March:
> Each minute sweeter than before,
> The redbreast sings from the tall larch
> That stands beside our door.

The short stanza, the regular line, the abab rhyming scheme throughout all contribute to the poem's attraction.

The poem issues an invitation which could be summed up in one line:

> Come forth and feel the sun

but the poem's forty lines offer a very persuasive argument and urge the listener to attend, respond and accept. The word 'blessing' in line 5 conveys a sense of Wordsworth's belief that for him nature was God's creation.

The voice is very immediate. This is achieved through the exclamation mark, the use of 'Now', the strong verbs 'Make haste', 'resign', 'Come' and 'feel':

> My sister! ('tis a wish of mine)
> Now that our morning meal is done,
> Make haste, your morning task resign;
> Come forth and feel the sun.

The mention of 'My sister' and 'Edward' are personal to Wordsworth. He is speaking to his sister and presumably refers to the little boy [real name Basil] whom they were looking after when the poem was written, but such personal details do not exclude the reader. The reader can easily enter into the scene proposed by Wordsworth. A day of idleness spent in the woodland is an attractive alternative to remaining indoors working or with a book. Wordsworth anticipates his sister's possible response that she has the young boy to look after:

> Edward will come with you; and, pray,
> Put on with speed your woodland dress;
> And bring no book: for this one day
> We'll give to idleness.

The world of the book is rejected this time; the mind is set aside and the senses are celebrated. Wordsworth expresses this clearly when he says:

> — It is the hour of feeling —

Stanza six marks a change in that the poem, which up until then tells of the lovely mild March day, now opens up to include all mankind. The beginning of spring is, for Wordsworth, the birth and awakening of Love in the hearts of men. The awakening world prompts a feeling of love in man's heart, and man's heart, in turn, looks on the world of nature with love:

> Love, now a universal birth,
> From heart to heart is stealing,
> From earth to man, from man to earth:
> — It is the hour of feeling —

But the poem also, in typical Wordsworth fashion, looks ahead to a time beyond the now, when memory of this happy moment will sustain and enrich. The use of 'we' in line 16 signals a shared joy, a shared experience, and Wordsworth speaks with conviction of how this day's joy and pleasure will influence the coming year.

In the poem's closing stanzas, Wordsworth speaks of the transformation 'the first mild day of March' makes possible. The change is deeply felt and long-lasting:

> Some silent laws our hearts will make,
> Which they shall long obey:
> We for the year to come may take
> Our temper from to-day.

The poem which began with such details ('each minute', 'redbreast', 'tall larch', 'our door') has given way to a cosmic or universal view of things where a great powerful presence is felt in 'our souls':

> And from the blessed power that rolls
> About, below, above,
> We'll frame the measure of our souls:
> They shall be tuned to love.

But in the closing stanza Wordsworth returns to the urgent tones of the opening lines. He repeats stanza four with a slight variation and the mood with which the poem ends is celebratory, happy, relaxed and forward-looking:

> Then come, my Sister! come, I pray,
> With speed put on your woodland dress;
> And bring no book: for this one day
> We'll give to idleness.

Much of the music of the poem is created through the very regular end rhyme throughout, the very regular rhythm of the lines and the happy, urging tones.

Tintern Abbey

[Lines Composed a Few Miles above Tintern Abbey, on Revisiting the Banks of the Wye During a Tour. 13 July 1798]

Very few great poems of sustained length are written in one day but 'Tintern Abbey' is one of them. It sums ups everything that there is to know about Wordsworth. 'Tintern Abbey' is, according to Harold Bloom, 'a history in little of Wordsworth's imagination'. In one hundred and fifty lines Wordsworth, though only twenty-eight at the time, has produced a very powerful and complex poem which focuses on the natural world, man's relationship with nature, man's relationship with his fellowman, the importance of memory and imagination, and the powerful presence, the mighty Being, which nature embodies.

A.C. Bradley argues that 'There have been greater poets than Wordsworth, but none more original. He saw new things, or he saw things in a new way' and 'Tintern Abbey' illustrates Wordsworth's seeing things in a new way. And yet, if Wordsworth's way of seeing seems familiar to us it is only because his poetry has coloured our way of thinking, even without our knowing it. People who have never read a line of Wordsworth relate to nature in a Wordsworthian way. Wordsworth, in Margaret Drabble's words, 'forged a new relationship between man and the natural world: he lived in a new communion' and when tourists for example visit the Lake District today it is 'through his eyes' that they see it.

For discussion purposes the poem can be divided into six sections:

I	lines 1–22	The present moment. The scene revisited.
II	lines 22–57	What this place has meant to him in the intervening years.
III	lines 58–65	This place, this moment in memory will sustain him in the future.
IV	lines 65–83	Wordsworth's boyhood relationship with nature.
V	lines 83–111	How his relationship has deepened since earlier days.
VI	lines 111–159	His sister's relationship with nature and his prayer for her.

Section I (lines 1–22). The opening lines create a feeling of time passing and passing slowly. Five summers and five long winters. The repeated 'five' and the exclamation mark create a melancholy feel to the line; the intervening years have known sorrow, but there is a sense of release, joy and ease in the words 'and again', a sense of delight in 'Once again':

> Five years have past; five summers, with the length
> Of five long winters! and again I hear
> These waters, rolling from their mountain-springs
> With a soft inland murmur.—Once again
> Do I behold these steep and lofty cliffs . . .

The description of the scene which follows, however, is a description not only of trees and landscape but of what the scene before him means to Wordsworth. 'I hear', 'I behold', 'I again repose', 'I view', 'I see' remind us of Wordsworth's presence. 'I' is one of the most important words in this intensely personal poem but it is an 'I' that invites us in rather than excludes. Margaret Drabble says of this opening section: 'it is the value and the meaning of the scene that he is trying to describe, not its outward appearance, not how many trees there were in the woods, or the colour of the sky, or the noise of the river. He is painting a picture not of a landscape with river and trees, but of something much more complicated; he is trying to describe the inner workings of his own mind.'

The pleasure Wordsworth feels on revisiting this scene is evident in the interest expressed in what he sees before him. The eye picks out different aspects of the rural scene: 'plots of cottage-ground, these orchard tufts', 'hedge-rows'. The scene affects him deeply, first through the eye (seeing) and then the mind (thinking):

> —Once again
> Do I behold these steep and lofty cliffs,
> That on a wild secluded scene impress
> Thoughts of more deep seclusion

The outer world makes possible an inner life of feelings.

The word 'again', which occurs in lines 2, 4, 9 and 14, also captures Wordsworth's quiet sense of relief. The immediacy of the moment is found in a line such as the following:

> Once again I see
> These hedge-rows, hardly hedge-rows, little lines
> Of sportive wood run wild . . .

where he qualifies the detail – 'hedge-rows, hardly hedge-rows' – and the reader senses the mind of the poet at work, searching for the more exact or appropriate description. This first section ends with Wordsworth wondering whether the 'wreaths of smoke/ Sent up, in silence, from among the trees' belong to 'vagrant dwellers' or 'some Hermit' living in the woods. Wordsworth imagines that the smoke from among the trees belongs to someone whose life is at one with the natural landscape, suggesting a harmony between man and nature.

The **second section (lines 22–57)** expands on the significance of this particular place which Wordsworth first saw in 1793, when he was twenty-three, and returns to now five years later. In the intervening years he has seen what he sees before him now in his mind's eye:

> These beauteous forms,
> Through a long absence, have not been to me
> As is a landscape to a blind man's eye

and it has given him great comfort. Wordsworth writes about the reality of loneliness and city life when he speaks of 'lonely rooms', 'the din/ Of towns and cities' and 'hours of weariness'. But memories of this place on the banks of the River Wye bring what he calls 'sensations sweet'. He has benefited from nature, continues to benefit because the experience lives on in his memory, and the effect is such that it touches Wordsworth physically, emotionally, intellectually and spiritually. This is seen when Wordsworth tells of how he

> Felt in the blood, and felt along the heart;
> And passing even into my purer mind,
> With tranquil restoration

These lines reveal what for Wordsworth was the 'living soul' where heart, mind, feeling and sense are integrated. In this second section, Wordsworth identifies three benefits that nature offers – it sustains him when he is lonely; it makes him a better person; and it helps him to understand the mystery of creation and man's part in it.

Wordsworth's memory has created sweet sensations. He also believes that 'little nameless, unremembered, acts/ Of kindness and of love' are made possible through a love of nature and nature creates a 'blessed mood' which allows Wordsworth a deeper understanding of what it means to be human. The language is different in section two, in that the poem becomes more philosophical, and this spiritual, heightened state is captured in the following lines where Wordsworth speaks of how nature helps him to cope with the 'heavy and the weary weight/ Of all this unintelligible world'. He achieves a 'blessed mood'

> In which the burthen of the mystery,
> In which the heavy and the weary weight
> Of all this unintelligible world
> Is lightened . . .

Wordsworth's tone here is one of gratitude and conviction and this tone intensifies as one moves through the passage. Wordsworth is recording a profound and significant change in himself, which his relationship with nature has made possible. One transcends the here and now and experiences a 'serene and blessed mood', so much so, that one is led on, entranced

> Until, the breath of this corporeal frame
> And even the motion of our human blood
> Almost suspended, we are laid asleep
> In body, and become a living soul

The movement here from body ('corporeal frame') to soul is of vital importance to Wordsworth. It is the body which responds initially to nature. The eye sees and responds to the natural world and in doing so the mind's eye, the imagination, the soul then sees

> into the life of things.

These simple words contain a complex truth. And it is significant that Wordsworth says 'we', not 'I':

> with an eye made quiet by the power
> Of harmony, and the deep power of joy,
> We see into the life of things.

The experience is one which everyone can share.

Harold Bloom says that 'To see into the life of things is to see things for themselves' and that it is 'memories of Nature's presence, which give a quietness that is a blessed mood, one in which the object world becomes near and familiar, and ceases to be a burden'. Bloom adds that a good way of explaining this is to think of the difference between being with a stranger or a good friend; Wordsworth viewed nature as a close friend.

This second section (lines 22–57) ends with a passionate expression, almost outburst, where Wordsworth wishes to prove that what he says and what he knows and what he has experienced is true. He has turned to nature often in times of unhappiness and despondency:

> If this
> Be but a vain belief, yet, oh! how oft—
> In darkness and amid the many shapes
> Of joyless daylight; when the fretful stir
> Unprofitable, and the fever of the world,
> Have hung upon the beatings of my heart—
> How oft, in spirit, have I turned to thee,
> O sylvan Wye! thou wanderer thro' the woods,
> How often has my spirit turned to thee!

This one sentence achieves momentum, not only through its length and structure, but in its repetitions and exclamations. The passionate tone is strengthened too in its direct, intimate address:

> How oft, in spirit, have I turned to thee . . .
>
> How often has my spirit turned to thee!

There is a shift of mood at the beginning of the **third section (lines 58–65)**. Wordsworth now focuses, once again, on the present moment and acknowledges that what he experiences now will sustain him in the future, just as that visit five years ago has sustained him in the intervening years. There is the 'present pleasure' and 'pleasing thoughts'

> That in this moment there is life and food
> For future years.

There then follows (**section IV: lines 65–85**) a flashback to Wordsworth's boisterous boyhood. He remembers a time of almost animal delight, aching joys and dizzy raptures and the memory is filled with sense impressions. Wordsworth, though claiming that 'I cannot paint/ What then I was', paints a vivid picture of wild and physical pleasures. He is driven towards nature, fleeing 'something that he dreads' and the experience is primarily pre-reflective. Nature then, he tells us

> (The coarser pleasures of my boyish days,
> And their glad animal movements all gone by)
> To me was all in all.—I cannot paint
> What then I was.

The waterfall haunted him; the mountain, rocks and trees, which he loved, fed the young Wordsworth's appetite:

> The sounding cataract
> Haunted me like a passion: the tall rock,
> The mountain, and the deep and gloomy wood,
> Their colours and their forms, were then to me
> An appetite

The boy differs from the man, however, in that the boy's response to nature was physical, unthinking and immediate, whereas the adult's response is more thoughtful and reflective. The boy felt and loved without thinking. The relationship between boy and nature was

> a feeling and a love,
> That had no need of a remoter charm,
> By thought supplied, nor any interest
> Unborrowed from the eye.

Section V (lines 83–111) marks another change in the ode. Wordsworth now describes how his boyhood is over ('—That time is past,/ . . . And all its dizzy raptures) and his boyhood relationship with nature has given way to a deeper response and understanding. He does not long for those earlier times, nor, he says, does he miss them, for 'other gifts/ Have followed'. The use of 'gifts' here reminds us of how Wordsworth viewed nature as a great, giving presence. In adulthood he tells us that he does not pine for or lament boyhood:

> For I have learned
> To look on nature, not as in the hour
> Of thoughtless youth; but hearing oftentimes
> The still, sad music of humanity

The phrase 'The still, sad music of humanity' is one of Wordsworth's most famous lines and also one of his most mysterious. Here Wordsworth finds in nature a quiet, sorrowful music and, for him, there is a link between the natural world and the human, in that Wordsworth often hears in nature a 'music of humanity'. Harold Bloom says that the music reminds him 'not only of man's mortality but of man's inseparable bond with Nature'.

The language here allows us to experience an emotion without, perhaps, fully understanding it. Wordsworth is expressing, through language, heightened emotions and intuitions in which he recognises the mutual relationship between the world of nature and his own mind. Nature's 'still, sad music of humanity' is neither harsh nor grating but it is, he tells us, 'of ample power/ To chasten and subdue'. Harold Bloom comments that 'The poet loves Nature for its own sake alone, and the presences of Nature give beauty to the poet's mind' and adds that the process, like a conversation that never stops, cannot be summed up or analysed.

Wordsworth elaborates on nature's influence and effect when he tells of how 'I have felt/ A presence that disturbs me with the joy/ of elevated thoughts; a sense sublime/ Of something far more deeply interfused . . .' Words such as 'elevated' and 'sublime' are key ideas here capturing, as they do, Wordsworth's heightened, exalted state. The phrase 'deeply interfused' reminds us that, for Wordsworth, nature and man are profoundly inter-connected, that a force or energy pours between or through man and nature. This section ends with a panoramic description of the beauty of the natural world. Wordsworth writes of 'setting suns', 'the round ocean', 'the living air', 'the blue sky' and, significantly, these are connected to 'the mind of man', illustrating, in Harold Bloom's words, that 'Nature disturbs the mind, sets it into motion, until it realises that Nature and itself are not utterly distinct, that they are mixed together, interfused'.

Within man and nature there is a living presence. Wordsworth loved nature as a boy and he continues to love 'the meadows and the woods,/ And mountains; and of all that we behold/ From this green earth'. As an adult he chooses to love nature which in turn becomes

> The guide, the guardian of my heart, and soul
> Of all my moral being.

and it is this mature response to nature which allows him to hear the 'still sad music of humanity' and which leads Wordsworth to love his fellow man.

Having spoken of his own intense relationship with nature, Wordsworth in the **final section (lines 111–159)** addresses his sister Dorothy, who is with him on the banks of this fair river. He has not hinted at her presence until now and yet her presence in the poem is vital, for in addressing Dorothy he is speaking to her but also to the reader. In her he recognises his younger self, his earlier relationship with nature and in her voice

>   I catch
> The language of my former heart, and read
> My former pleasures in the shooting lights
> Of thy wild eyes.

Nature delights us in childhood and sustains us in adulthood, leading us 'from joy to joy'. Nature, Wordsworth tells us, gives us 'quietness and beauty', feeding us with 'lofty thoughts'. The choice of 'feeds' reminds us of the absolutely essential and necessary part which Wordsworth believes nature plays in our lives.

Having spoken of the joys and pleasures of nature, Wordsworth then speaks of life's reality which he mentioned earlier in the poem (lines 25–26). Wordsworth is realistic in his awareness of sneers, selfishness, unkindness. He says that we all encounter, experience, endure 'evil tongues,/ Rash judgements', the 'sneers of selfish men', 'greetings where no kindness is' and what he terms 'The dreary intercourse of daily life'. Developing his argument carefully, Wordsworth believes that these negative, ugly realities will not prevail 'or disturb/ Our cheerful faith' because when we look on nature 'all which we behold/ Is full of blessings'.

It is this belief which leads Wordsworth to the poem's final movement **(lines 111–159)** which is, in effect, a prayer for Dorothy. The word 'Therefore' (line 134), with which he begins this prayer, illustrates Wordsworth's careful and detailed thinking. He asks that his sister be blessed on her life's journey and the image he creates is beautifully calm and atmospheric:

>   Therefore let the moon
> Shine on thee in thy solitary walk;
> And let the misty mountain-winds be free
> To blow against thee . . .

The adjective 'solitary' gives Dorothy's life an added poignancy but everyone's life is ultimately solitary. The moon, too, adds beauty and the image is of an individual alone but at one with nature. Harold Bloom thinks these 'the most beautiful lines' in the poem and the movement of walking and mountain-winds give the image a flowing, graceful feeling.

In imagining her life he is realistic enough to speak of 'solitude, or fear, or pain, or grief' but he also offers comfort through his own belief in the healing, sustaining power of nature. He also says that, though he may not always be beside his sister, his 'dear, dear Friend', he believes that she will remember this moment when they stood together 'on the banks of this delightful stream' and that his love of nature will lead Dorothy to love nature more and more.

The poem ends in a tone of deep conviction, heartfelt urging and the vocabulary used is religious. Wordsworth sees himself as a 'worshipper of nature' who turns to nature

> With warmer love—oh! with far deeper zeal
> Of holier love

and claims that 'these steep woods and lofty cliffs,/ And this green pastoral landscape' were important to Wordsworth not only for themselves but because of what they do mean and will mean to his sister. These closing lines bring together the world of nature and the human world and it is the relationship between both that is celebrated in the ode.

'Tintern Abbey' charts Wordsworth's deep and vital relationship with nature. This relationship was a complex one and Margaret Drabble identifies 'some of the many, various, and not wholly consistent attitudes towards nature that can be found in this one poem' in this order:

1. Nature as Comforter.

2. Nature as a doorway into a state of visionary trance-like insight. (The state in which, while contemplating nature, we 'are laid asleep in body, and become a living soul': a state of 'wise passiveness').

3. Nature as the object of appetite.

4. Nature as a source of and scene for animal pleasures, such as skating, riding, fishing, walking.

5. Nature as the home of the spirit of the world, or as the physical embodiment of God himself.

6. Nature as the union or meeting point of the inner and outer worlds. (The eye and ear both perceive and create what they sense, Wordsworth says; one of his most difficult concepts is his idea that the boundary between the outer world of nature and the inner world of the mind is a shifting boundary, not a fixed one.)

7. Nature as the source of and guide to human morality.

8. Nature as a source of simple joy and pleasure.

Stephen Gill says that in 'Tintern Abbey' Wordsworth gives 'an account of his own life, which took as its starting-point a profound gratitude that somehow, despite all loss, pain and discontinuity, he had survived, not just as a whole and joyful man, but as a creative being.'

The Stolen Boat

In this poem, written in 1799 when he was twenty-nine, Wordsworth is remembering a moment from boyhood which terrified and troubled him. Wordsworth responded strongly, physically, emotionally and imaginatively to nature from childhood and this extract from *The Prelude* illustrates his powerful relationship with the natural world. Nature has an attracting force which is clearly seen in the opening line:

> One summer evening (led by her) I found
> A little boat tied to a willow tree

Nature is sometimes referred to as Mother Nature and here the use of 'led by her' suggests that nature is a female presence with magnetic appeal. The poem begins hesitantly but then the moment is vividly evoked in gesture and physical movement:

> Straight I unloosed her chain, and stepping in
> Pushed from the shore.

The verbs move the lines forward, the placing of 'Pushed' at the beginning of the line being particularly effective in that it gives the line an energy which imitates the act itself. The pace with which the poem moves is determined by the rhythm and the movement creates its own mood.

Wordsworth is alone and the poem presents an image of a small boy in a small boat against the lake, the mountains and the vastness of the starry sky overhead.

It is a moment of quiet secrecy ('stealth') but also one of great pleasure and delight, captured in such descriptions as the 'Small circles glittering idly in the moon', 'sparkling light' or how 'lustily/ I dipped my oars into the silent lake' and 'my boat/ Went heaving through the water like a swan'. There is pleasure but there is also a feeling of unease:

> It was an act of stealth
> And troubled pleasure . . .

for nature, ultimately, is here seen by Wordsworth as threatening, disapproving, a moral force that reprimands him for stealing the boat.

Stephen Gill says that the structure of the piece is such that it begins with 'the wholeness of the scene – the water, the moonlight, the little ripples, the boat, the boy – but as soon as the frightening experience begins the poetry moves forward with a strong and powerful motion that simply demands that you follow the sense of the syntax right through to the last great statement – strode after me [line 29].' This feeling, of course, is all in the young Wordsworth's mind. Margaret Drabble points out that the word subconscious was unknown to Wordsworth [its first recorded use is in 1832] but, in effect, this poem describes the boy's psychological response to landscape and this is coloured by his having stolen the boat.

The 'huge peak, black and huge' is described as frightening, threatening:

> As if with voluntary power instinct
> Upreared its head . . .
> And growing still in stature the grim shape
> Towered up between me and the stars

John F. Danby thinks that 'the accent in this incident, however, is not on the sense of guilt so much as on the way the mountains assumed an independent being, a being not indifferent to the intruder, not accusing, but above all not subordinate.'

The pace is orchestrated in such a way that the lines describing the drama of excitement move to a different rhythm from those lines that capture the drama of fear.

The experience in his familiar surroundings has altered the boy; his relationship with nature has changed. The opening line speaks of how nature led him; later it appeared as if it strode after him. He is frightened ('I struck and struck again' and returns to the lake shore with 'trembling oars'). The familiar place has become strange:

> oe'r my thoughts
> There hung a darkness, call it solitude
> Or blank desertion. No familiar shapes
> Remained, no pleasant images of trees,
> Of sea or sky, no colours of green fields . . .

The speaker in the closing lines is haunted by how he thinks nature has responded to his stealing the boat. One episode has affected him 'for many days'. The familiar landscape has become dark, strange. The 'huge and mighty forms' remind him that he has done wrong. Nature here is a teacher and guide and the action of boat-stealing in itself is less significant than the boy's emotional, imaginative response.

Skating

This is a memorable moment from boyhood which the twenty-nine-year-old Wordsworth remembers and describes in an atmospheric and vivid way. The opening lines involve the senses. We imagine that we feel the cold, see the setting sun, see the warm glow of the cottage windows and feel their warmth:

> And in the frosty season, when the sun
> Was set, and visible for many a mile
> The cottage windows blazed through twilight gloom . . .

Here the outdoor life means excitement and freedom. Though it is getting dark, Wordsworth is not thinking of going indoors. Though the cottage windows call, Wordsworth tells us that

> I heeded not their summons

He expresses his own individual delight when he speaks of how happy all children are in such a season but he particularly enjoys it:

> happy time
> It was indeed for all of us—for me
> It was a time of rapture!

Yet, when he describes the skating, he uses 'we', which gives the experience a feeling of togetherness. The body in movement and the thrill of skating on the frozen lake are expertly captured. The rhythms, verbs and images all contribute to this overall effect. In the dictionary, 'kinaesthesia' is defined as 'a sense of movement and muscular effort' and these lines certainly have that kinetic quality. This rapturous time is signalled first by the sound of bells, then by the energetic 'wheeled', Proud', 'Exulting', the simile of the 'untired horse':

> Clear and loud
> The village clock tolled six,—I wheeled about,
> Proud and exulting like an untired horse
> That cares not for its home . . .

The age-old and ever-effective techniques of alliteration ['**s**hod with **s**teel'] and onomatopoeia ['hissed'] and the comparison of the group of vocal skaters to the hunt makes for a very alive and dramatic scene:

> All shod with steel
> We hissed along the polished ice in games
> Confederate

The strong feeling of togetherness is emphasised in Wordsworth's use of confederate [meaning grouped or leagued together] and, in Wordsworth's mind, the skaters become a loud pack of hounds chasing a hare to the sounds of the hunting, echoing horn:

> imitative of the chase
> And woodland pleasures,—the resounding horn,
> The pack loud chiming, and the hunted hare.

The poetry gathers greater momentum as the skating is being described. The sounds are crisp, metallic and echoing and, in the midst of this excitement and tumult, Wordsworth senses a different mood, 'an alien sound/ Of melancholy'. This is the sound of the 'far distant hills' which into the tumult sent this melancholic alien sound. Such an interaction between man and nature is frequently found in Wordsworth's poetry. The others, however, do not sense it, seem not to notice, and Wordsworth, having entered into the spirit of the fun and the exhilaration of skating, withdraws frequently ('not seldom') and becomes more reflective:

> while the stars
> Eastward were sparkling clear, and in the west
> The orange sky of evening died away.
> Not seldom from the uproar I retired
> Into a silent bay, or sportively
> Glanced sideway, leaving the tumultuous throng,
> To cut across the reflex of a star
> That fled, and, flying still before me, gleamed
> Upon the glassy plain

The sense of camaraderie, comradeship, is changing here. The 'I' voice, not the communal 'we', is beginning to be heard in these lines when Wordsworth mentions that 'I retired'. In the remaining lines of the extract there is a growing sense of the individual self who gives himself to the wind and the earth's motion and moves towards an extraordinary stillness and a tranquil state:

> and oftentimes,
> When we had given our bodies to the wind
> And all the shadowy banks on either side
> Came sweeping through the darkness, spinning still
> The rapid line of motion, then at once
> Have I, reclining back upon my heels,
> Stopped short; yet still the solitary cliffs
> Wheeled by me—even as if the earth had rolled
> With visible motion her diurnal round!

The lines have great force and energy ('sweeping', 'spinning', 'wheeled', 'rolled') and the speaker feels at one with the earth's diurnal round. Seamus Heaney comments that 'The exhilaration of the skating, the vitality of the verbs, "gleaming", "sweeping", "spinning", "wheeling", the narrative push, the *cheerfulness*, to use one of the poet's favourite positive words – all these things have their part to play in the overall effect of the writing'.

There is a heightened sense of excitement, but also of understanding, and the poem's closing lines achieve a calm communion between the observer and the observed, between Wordsworth and nature. He thinks of the 'solitary cliffs' and how

> Behind me did they stretch in solemn train,
> Feebler and feebler, and I stood and watched
> Till all was tranquil as a dreamless sleep.

The opening lines were not 'tranquil' and far from sleep but the poem has journeyed from energetic boyhood to the calm, quiet, mature understanding of the close.

Of the Skating episode from *The Prelude*, John F. Danby says: 'It is an experience of tumultuous excitement, and yet precisely controlled, verbally given. The foot goes into the hollow of 'shod', re-echoing against the feel of steel, and then the hiss and kiss and swish of the polished ice (with its cry of delight) in the games . . . There is every kind of concerted noise and motion, all issuing into a final silence.'

'A slumber did my spirit seal'

This little lyric poem is deceptive. Eight lines, only one unusual word ('diurnal'), a regular rhythm and rhyming scheme, and yet the poem expands to become a very profound and complex exploration of life, transience (the passing of time), death and eternity.

The poem begins with the poet himself. He tells of how in a slumber or light sleep he forgets his 'human fears'. These fears are not specified but, within the context of the stanza as a whole, it would seem that the speaker is, for a while, not aware of 'The touch of earthly years'. The inevitability of time passing, the loss of loved ones, the reality of death are all part of our human fears and in this slumbering state the woman whom he cares for and writes about seems as if she will not grow old and die. The word 'seemed' is important here:

> A slumber did my spirit seal;
>   I had no human fears:
> She seemed a thing that could not feel
>   The touch of earthly years.

Between stanza one and stanza two, however, there intervenes what Helen Vendler calls a 'white space' and Vendler argues that when we begin to read the second stanza 'we see that the girl has died between the two stanzas – that the white space represents her death. The first stanza was delusion; the second is reality.' Harold Bloom in *How to Read and Why* says that in the first stanza the young woman is described as a visionary being 'that could not feel/ The touch of earthly years' but that in stanza two the reader experiences a shock. She has died.

In stanza one it seemed that this woman was unaffected by mortality. Stanza two begins with a series of negatives which dispel the earlier thought that she 'could not feel/ The touch of earthly years':

> **No** motion has she now, **no** force;
>   She **neither** hears **nor** sees

Everything has been taken away from her – she has no motion, no force, no hearing, no sight. Now the speaker tells of how she has felt the 'touch of earthly years'. In stanza one it seemed as if it did not affect her; in stanza two we learn with a jolt that it did.

And yet her death is not seen in terms of trauma; rather she in death is among and at one with 'rocks, and stones, and trees'. What is also significant is that she, in fact, in death has motion, contrary to what is said in line 5. 'Trees' are living things and she is now part of that landscape, but even more significant is the mention that she is

> Rolled round in earth's diurnal course,
>   With rocks, and stones, and trees.

Therefore, in death she is part of the earth's very motion, its daily movement. The use of the present tense in this second stanza, despite a series of negative ('She neither hears nor sees'), also allows the reader to view her as part of nature's continuity.

In Margaret Drabble's words: 'She is nothing; she sees nothing, she hears nothing, she cannot herself move, she is beyond time, unchangeable, eternal. And yet, at the same time, she does move; she is not motionless, she moves with the movement of the whole world, as it turns in space, and this movement she almost seems to feel – certainly the poet feels it for her'.

'She dwelt among the untrodden ways'

This poem tells, in twelve lines, of the life and death of Lucy. 'She lived off the beaten track; she was not well-known; and now that she is dead the poet misses her very much' is how a summary of the poem would read. But the poem contains so much more.

The poet tells us very little about her, it would seem. Margaret Drabble says that there is a sense of vagueness, that Wordsworth 'tells us nothing practical, nothing factual about her at all. Even the "springs of Dove" that she dwelled beside are not a real place, which is odd only when one remembers what a passion Wordsworth had for using real places and real place names, and for giving his stories a detailed physical setting'.

And yet, we have a strong sense of Lucy from the images in stanza two. Imagery here is not decorative. Lucy is a violet and she is a star. These metaphors are developed and elaborated on and link Lucy to both earth and sky. The violet, a small and beautiful flower, is hardly seen; it is hidden. The star is all the more bright and special because it is the only one that can be seen:

> A violet by a mossy stone
>   Half hidden from the eye!
> —Fair as a star, when only one
>   Is shining in the sky.

The violet is hardly noticed, the star stands out and both qualities are attributed to Lucy.

The poem presents no difficulty in terms of meaning, but the poem's power and success can be found in the music it makes and the intense feelings that it expresses. The rhyme and rhythm are regular; the exclamation marks add intensity and the very simple vocabulary suits Lucy's life and nature.

The final two lines are particularly effective. Her death is somehow indicated in the use of the past tense in the opening line ('lived') but the punctuation and the predominantly monosyllabic words give the closing lines a depth of feeling:

> But she is in her grave, and, oh,
>   The difference to me!

The world does not know of Lucy's death but her death has made the world of difference to the speaker.

Composed Upon Westminster Bridge

This poem focuses on a specific time and place (though composed on 31 July 1802, the title dates it 3 September). But the sonnet goes beyond place and time and celebrates the timeless beauty of nature. Though Wordsworth did not care for cities, he finds London, at dawn, and empty of people and surrounded by fields and sky, a city that is as close as possible to nature. It is interesting that the London he admires and loves is London city when it is least like itself. He admires it because it is asleep.

The opening line displays extraordinary power and confidence. Eight words, seven of them strong monosyllables, spell out the speaker's conviction that

> Earth has not anything to show more fair

When a statement is as absolute as this, when a poet says that there is nothing more beautiful than this natural sight, the reader's attention is arrested and held.

Wordsworth believed that everyone would respond to such a beautiful sight and that if one did not, one had no soul:

> Dull would he be of soul who could pass by
> A sight so touching in its majesty

In attributing majestic qualities to the scene, Wordsworth is expressing the highest praise. Both the majesty of kingship and the majesty of God seem to be evident in the cityscape before him.

Having spoken of the city in general terms, Wordsworth then focuses on particular details and aspects. The word 'This' marks a more specific emphasis:

> This city now doth, like a garment, wear
> The beauty of the morning;

and the personification of the city – he sees it as a person wearing a beautiful garment, as clothed in beauty – helps us see a city on a human scale.

If this sonnet were a painting it would be sharp and bright, crystal clear and silent. He tells us that the panorama before him is 'silent, bare', and then he lists the various objects and different buildings of London and the River Thames, as seen from Westminster Bridge:

> Ships, towers, domes, theatres, and temples lie
> Open unto the fields, and to the sky;
> All bright and glittering in the smokeless air.

The first eight lines or octet describe the beautiful, early morning scene. The sestet, moving from outer to inner, focuses on the interior world, the poet's thoughts and feelings. Line 9, like the poem's opening line, uses a negative for emphasis:

> Never did sun more beautifully steep
> In his first splendour, valley, rock, or hill

Here Wordsworth imagines the first sunshine at the beginning of creation and all the beauty and freshness that that suggests. Then the sun shone on the natural landscape, not the man-made but Wordsworth is paying London the ultimate compliment when he says that London in this early morning sunshine is even more beautiful than when the world was first steeped in sunlight.

The sonnet then turns to the intensely personal voice of the poet. Earlier he had spoken of 'he' in line 2 meaning anyone; now, at line 11, Wordsworth uses 'I'. It is only used once in the poem but the closing lines, especially, express Wordsworth's own intense surprise and joy. Again he uses negatives for effect:

> Ne'er saw I, never felt, a calm so deep!

The calm outer world has made possible a calm inner world and the poem ends with an acknowledgement of the power of nature and God's power which are one:

> The river glideth at his own sweet will:
> Dear God! the very houses seem asleep;
> And all that mighty heart is lying still!

In the closing four lines, exclamation marks are used three times. The river is still free of man's presence, the busy commerce and traffic of the day have not yet begun and it can be itself. The houses, personified, 'seem asleep' and are not associated with the busy waking, living world. The inhabitants of the city are united in the poem's magnificent final image, that of a mighty heart. Wordsworth is not rejecting man but he prefers nature.

Commenting on this sonnet, Jonathan Bate says: 'Usually in Wordsworth the city is a place of alienation, but here it is transfigured because it is "calm" and "still" . . . In the smokeless light of a silent dawn, Wordsworth is able to imagine the very being of a city in which human institutions — "Ships towers, domes, theatres, and temples" — are not set against nature but open to it. When the houses are asleep, they rest upon their earthly foundations. In this moment, the human mode of being seems no different from that of other creatures who dwell upon the earth. But Wordsworth knows that such stillness can only be for a moment. When the day's work begins, the river will no longer glide at its own sweet will. The fields will be covered by new buildings and the sky blackened by smoke.'

'It is a beauteous evening, calm and free'

This sonnet was written in France in August 1802, when Wordsworth was thirty-two, and it is addressed to his nine-year-old daughter Caroline. The first eight lines describe the beautiful evening sunset and evening atmosphere; the remaining six lines focus on the relationship between the child and nature.

In the opening lines, in every line, many of the words suggest a great stillness:

> It is a beauteous evening, **calm** and free,
> The holy time is **quiet** as a Nun
> **Breathless** with adoration; the broad sun
> Is **sinking down** in its **tranquillity**;
> The **gentleness** of heaven **broods** o'er the Sea:

The time is 'holy' and the image of the Nun and the reference to heaven contribute to this sense of spirituality that Wordsworth recognises in the setting sun. These opening lines move slowly; the rhythm in this long, flowing sentence creates a solemn mood. The open vowel sounds in words such as 'calm', 'holy', 'adoration', 'broad', 'down', 'broods' create a stately music. The end rhymes also contribute to the harmony created within these lines: free/ Nun/ sun/ tranquillity/ Sea.

With line 6 there is a different music. The one word 'Listen' with an exclamation mark announces a new tone. Here Wordsworth is asking his daughter to listen to the sound of silence, for in the silence can be heard the mighty Being:

> Listen! the mighty Being is awake,
> And doth with his eternal motion make
> A sound like thunder—everlastingly.

In these lines Wordsworth achieves a sound that increases gradually and builds towards a crescendo. The poet senses a presence in the evening atmosphere. That this mighty Being is seen as having 'eternal motion' would suggest that for Wordsworth this Being is God and God in nature. That the sound he hears is compared to thunder suggests God's power and might.

The closing six lines or sestet move from the vast panorama of the evening sky and sea to the figure of the small child beside him. He does not address his daughter by name (even though 'Dear Caroline' would scan perfectly well in place of 'Dear Child! dear Girl!') and by calling her child and girl he is, in effect, speaking to all children. His feelings for her are intense – 'Dear Child! dear Girl!' – and, though he recognises that she does not respond to nature in the way that he does, if she does not have solemn thoughts on this occasion, it does not mean that she is untouched by the divine. Wordsworth believes his daughter is very close to God:

> Thou liest in Abraham's bosom all the year

In the Bible, Abraham's bosom is associated with a final resting place in heaven and perhaps Wordsworth is suggesting that his daughter beside him and all children are always close to heaven. In his poem 'Intimations of Immortality', Wordsworth says that 'Our birth is but a sleep and a forgetting' and that when we are born 'we come/ From God, who is our home'.

His daughter's special qualities are also found in the line which tells of how she

> worshipp'st at the Temple's inner shrine

which is a sacred enclosure where only sacred priests worshipped. These Christian references are clearly important to Wordsworth in this poem, which is not only a celebration of nature and God's presence but a blessing on his daughter.

The poem's closing line sums up something central to Wordsworth's understanding. In the opening lines he recognises God's presence but God can also be present even without our knowing it when we are with nature.

The words 'beauteous' in line 1, 'doth' in line 7, and 'Thy' and 'Thou liest' belong to an earlier vocabulary than Wordsworth's. It resembles the language of the Bible and lends the sonnet an added dignity and solemnity.

The Solitary Reaper

This begins directly: we are told to look and see a young woman. She is immediately before the reader, just as she was before the viewer when he saw her that day in September 1803 and before Wordsworth in his imagination and memory two years later when he wrote the poem. Stanzas one, three and four tell a story and stanza two tells through imagery something of what the experience meant to Wordsworth.

The poet is clearly captivated: 'Behold her', 'Stop here, or gently pass!' and 'O Listen!' in the opening stanza arrest the reader's attention. The Highland Lass is alone but she is part of nature. It is autumn and she is gathering in the harvest; the song she sings is of 'a melancholy strain' but Wordsworth does not understand the Scots Gaelic she sings and he can only sense its meaning. The mood is communicated; her voice is associated with grief or melancholy. Later, in the third stanza, he imagines that her song tells of 'old, unhappy, far-off things,/ And battles long ago' or, if not, a song that tells of contemporary matters but still sorrowful ones. It is as if human suffering and its continuity is expressed in the song she sings.

The power of her singing is deliberately exaggerated for effect:

> O listen! for the Vale profound
> Is overflowing with the sound.

In stanza two the young woman's voice is compared to birdsong, that of the nightingale and cuckoo. A very different world from Scotland is presented. A faraway world is evoked in the image of a desert in Arabia where travellers hear the nightingale's song. The voice of the cuckoo is another beautiful voice. It is one of renewal, a voice that announces the coming of spring. But, here, the human singing voice is preferred to the birds' song:

> No Nightingale did ever chaunt
> More welcome notes to weary bands
>
> A voice so thrilling ne'er was heard
> In spring-time from the Cuckoo-bird . . .

Mention of exotic Arabia and the Outer Hebrides makes the particular figure 'single in the field/ Yon solitary Highland Lass!' all the more special.

The woman's eloquent, beautiful voice seems never-ending and it is a song performed for its own sake. The Highland Lass is not singing for an audience; the poet overhears her singing while she works. The song, imperfectly understood and beautiful, in a sense symbolises a work of art. The song will live on from generation to generation; the poet remembers the song, which will live on in his memory, and it has been suggested that if the song of the bird is the voice of human nature, the girl's song could represent the voice of *human* nature itself.

It is as if there could be nothing more simple and directly beautiful than this one single human voice. And the solitary reaper herself is performing the function of the poet or chronicler. The title tells us that the reaper is solitary and in the first stanza 'single', 'solitary', 'by herself', 'Alone' remind us of this. Wordsworth, in writing the poem, passes on a human experience from generation to generation and the girl within the poem is doing something similar in her song.

William Butler Yeats
(1865–1939)

Contents	Page
The Overview	477
Biographical Notes	479
POEMS	487
Critical Commentary	527

IF I WERE FOUR-AND-TWENTY
BY
WILLIAM BUTLER YEATS.

THE CUALA PRESS
DUBLIN, IRELAND.
MCMXL

The Overview

Two poets, one American, one Irish, dominate English Literature during the first half of the twentieth century: T.S. Eliot and W.B. Yeats. So powerful is Yeats's distinctive poetic voice that his poetry has been described as 'magisterial', 'authoritative', 'commanding', 'formidable', 'compelling', 'direct', 'exhilarating', 'overbearing'. Before he died, Yeats arranged for an epitaph to be cut in stone 'by his command' and by then, Seamus Heaney says, that '"command" had indeed characterised the Yeatsian style'. But there is also in Yeats the voice of the dreamer and idealist. We see it in 'The Lake Isle of Innisfree', which he began writing when he was twenty-three. The life imagined on Innisfree is simple, beautiful and unrealistic and the longing for the ideal is also found in the sixty-one year old Yeats when he sails, in his imagination, to Byzantium.

Yeats lived in a time of extraordinary change. A world war was fought and Ireland struggled for and attained its Independence and went through civil war; his poetry charts the political turmoil of those times. Yeats writes of his private and his public life and sometimes those two aspects overlap. He is a public poet in a poem such as 'September 1913', where he becomes a self-elected spokesman in his condemnation of small-mindedness and the absence of vision. He played a public role, was committed to Ireland (he refused a knighthood in 1915) and was made a senator in 1922; one of his early ambitions, says the writer Michael Schmidt, was 'to reconcile the courteous Protestant heritage with the martyred, unmannerly Roman Catholic tradition in Ireland towards a political end.' In 'In memory of Eva Gore-Booth and Con Markiewicz' he touches on these themes. 'All his life,' wrote the scholar Augustine Martin, 'Yeats sought for a harmonious way of life as well as a perfect form of art and he re-invents himself several times during the course of his life and work.'

Yeats in these thirteen poems writes of the beauty of the natural world ('The Lake Isle of Innisfree'), his disillusionment with contemporary Ireland ('September 1913'), his heartbreak and his ageing self ('The Wild Swans at Coole'), war and patriotism and modern heroism ('An Irish Airman Foresees his Death'), political commitment, fanaticism, a crucial time in Ireland's history ('Easter 1916'), anarchy and breakdown ('The Second Coming'), nature versus art and the transforming power of art ('Sailing to Byzantium'), the bitterness of civil war and the continuity of nature ('The Stare's nest by My Window'), friendship, cultural legacy, choice ('In Memory of Eva Gore-Booth and Con Markiewicz'), determined, justified individuality ('Swift's Epitaph'), the ageing body, the ageing mind ('An Acre of Grass'), longing ('Politics'), poetry, Irish identity (from 'Under Ben Bulben'). Though similar themes recur, Yeats rarely repeated himself. In *Irish Classics* Professor Declan Kiberd identifies this aspect of Yeats's poetry and comments: 'The greatness of Yeats lay in his constant capacity to adjust to ever-changing conditions...As the years passed, he grew simpler in expression, using shorter lines dominated by monosyllables, with more nouns and fewer adjectives. He said himself that a poet should think like a wise man, but express himself as one of the common people.'

Poets frequently write on similar themes. When Yeats writes on his love of the ideal, nationalism, his preoccupation with the passing of time and the reality of growing old, his belief in the extraordinary power of art, it could be argued that thematically his poetry is not startlingly unusual, but it is the way he writes on such topics that makes him unique.

In a letter to Herbert Edward Palmer, dated 9 August 1922, Yeats offered Palmer some advice regarding style when he wrote, 'Examine your style, word for word, study the dictionary, study the most concentrated masters till writing grows very arduous and you will attain to a greater general height of accomplishment, to a steadier light, and yet not lose your flashes of lightning.' And, when he was old, Yeats wrote 'A General Introduction to My Work' where he says: 'I tried to make the language of poetry coincide with passionate normal speech. I wanted to write in whatever language comes most naturally when we soliloquise, as I do, all day long upon the events of our own lives or of any life where we can see ourselves for the moment . . .' Yeats, in that same piece, says 'I need a passionate syntax for a passionate subject matter', and so he accepted 'those traditional metres that had developed with the language'.

His tone can be harsh ('What need you, being come to sense'); regretful ('The ceremony of innocence is drowned;/ The best lack all conviction, while the worst/ Are full of passionate intensity.'); didactic ('An aged man is but a paltry thing,/ A tattered coat upon a stick, unless/ Soul clap its hands and sing, and louder sing/ For every tatter in its mortal dress'); prayer-like ('Come build in the empty house of the stare'); tender ('Dear shadows, now you know it all,/ All the folly of a fight'); defiant ('Grant me an old man's frenzy'); filled with longing ('But O that I were young again/ And held her in my arms!'); and authoritative ('Sing whatever is well made,/ Scorn the sort now growing up/ All out of shape from toe to top').

Imagery, especially his use of symbols, is another striking aspect of Yeats's work. Powerful, memorable images remain with the reader, such as the 'purple glow' of noon; the fumbling in 'a greasy till'; 'the hangman's rope'; the nine-and-fifty swans 'Upon the brimming water' and the 'bell-beat of their wings'; 'the stone in the midst of 'the living stream'; a creature 'somewhere in sands of the desert/ A shape with lion body and the head of a man'; 'sages standing in God's holy fire'; 'The bees build in the crevices/ Of loosening masonry'; 'Two girls in silk kimonos'; 'Shake the dead in their shrouds'; and 'Porter-drinkers' randy laughter'.

In 'Under Ben Bulben', written five months before he died, he praised the well-made poem and scorned and condemned the shapeless, badly made one. All his life he valued form and his mastery of rhythm, rhyme and the stanza are testimony to this; form contained and ordered his emotional, intellectual and imaginative outpourings. Yeats is intensely personal: he names names and writes about events and happenings that are recorded in newspapers and history books, but he knew that 'all that is personal soon rots, it must be packed in ice and salt'. The 'salt' and 'ice', in this instance, are the structures and techniques of the art of writing. The poems speak to us with great immediacy and directness but they do so in elaborate and musical forms.

'My poetry is generally written out of despair', said Yeats. As he grew older, he searched for ways to overcome his weakening body. He raged against old age, wrote about it with great honesty and accepted the inevitability of death. His poetry reminds us of the immortality of art, that 'Man can embody truth but cannot know it' and that 'we begin to live when we have conceived life as a tragedy'.

Biographical Notes

Though W.B. Yeats spent two-thirds of his life out of Ireland, it is with Ireland that he is most associated, especially Sligo and Dublin. He was born in a house called 'George's Ville' on Sandymount Avenue in Dublin on 13 June 1865, the first born of the family. His father John Butler Yeats was a well-to-do landlord who was reading for the Bar but who, in reality, preferred drawing; his mother Susan (Pollexfen) Yeats was the daughter of a wealthy Sligo family, the Pollexfens. Yeats's grandfather, a clergyman, was also called William Butler Yeats and his father, Yeats's great grandfather, a Reverend John Butler Yeats, had been appointed to Drumcliff in County Sligo.

In August 1866 a second child, Susan Mary Butler Yeats (nicknamed Lily), was born and soon afterwards John Butler Yeats, now a barrister, decided to give up law and go to London to study art. He moved to London early in 1867. His family meanwhile went to live with his wife's family in Sligo until he had found a place for them all to live in. In July 1867 the Yeatses were re-united in London and there they lived for the next five and a half years. Susan Yeats hated London, where Elizabeth (known as Lollie), Robert (Bobby) and John (Jack) were born. Her husband was having little success as an artist. John B. Yeats was becoming increasingly interested in Irish politics and he began to view James Stephens, who founded the Irish Republican Brotherhood, and John O'Leary with sympathy and understanding. He also admired the poetry of Walt Whitman and William Blake for their celebration of individuality and at one stage prevented his wife from teaching their children Church of Ireland prayers. They returned to Sligo every year for holidays but, in 1872, the Yeatses left London and settled once more in Ireland. Willie was seven years old. Years later Yeats wrote: 'I remember little of childhood but its pain.'

They stayed in Sligo for over two years. The Pollexfens lived in Merville, a house on sixty acres, but Yeats described it as a place where 'all was serious and silent'. Though seven years old, Willie did not know the alphabet; he did attend a local primary school but his spelling throughout his life was inconsistent and inaccurate. When his father visited, the young Yeats loved to hear his father read to him and Lily. In Sligo, Yeats grew up hearing many stories of the supernatural; fairies, banshees and ghosts were part of ordinary, everyday life in Sligo and it coloured his imagination. In autumn 1874, when Yeats was nine and a half, the family returned to London, but John Butler Yeats continued to have little success as an artist. Willie was homesick for Sligo and he later admitted that as a boy in London he 'longed for a sod of earth from some field I knew, something of Sligo to hold in my hand.'

In 1875, amidst the family's continuing financial difficulties, a sixth child was born but she died within a year. John Butler Yeats changed from portraiture to landscape painting. Susan and the younger children returned to Sligo and Willie joined his father at Burnham Beeches where he was painting. There John B. Yeats took his son's education in hand but in 1877, when the family was once more together in London, Willie was sent to Godolphin School in Hammersmith. He was eleven and a half and school reminded him of how different he was from other English schoolboys. He was mocked for being Irish and anti-Irish feeling was prevalent among the English, who governed a quarter of the earth's land surface at that time. A school report in 1877 placed him twenty-first in his class of thirty-one; his performance was 'only fair'. And yet he had a belief in himself and knew from an early age that, like his father, he would dedicate himself to his work (poetry) and make it his life.

In 1881, Willie left Godolphin School, where he was now known for his interest in science. The family returned to Ireland and settled at Howth and Willie's mind began to show strong intellectual ambition: he planned to write a book on the yearly cycle of a rock pool and read Darwin and others seriously. It was also at this time, between fifteen and sixteen, that he began writing poetry. He used to travel into Dublin on the train every morning with his father to his studio at 44 York Street and later at 7 St Stephen's Green. There John Butler Yeats would read to Willie passages from favourite poets, especially Shakespeare, Keats, Shelley, Byron and Rossetti. Willie enrolled himself at the Erasmus Smith High School in Harcourt Street, having been told by his father to do so. He was sixteen, was known to the other pupils as the 'insect collector' and later confessed that 'I was worst of all at literature, for we read Shakespeare for his grammar exclusively.'

The studio conversations were to have an important influence on Willie. It was there that ideas and literature were discussed and, gradually, the poet W.B. Yeats was born. As a young man, Yeats was attracted to the poetry of Spenser, Keats, Byron and Rossetti; his trips to Sligo continued to feed his imagination. There he heard tales of the supernatural and once, when he was walking with his cousin Lucy Middleton late one evening, passing a graveyard and abandoned village, they both believed they saw a flaming, brilliant presence moving towards them and then it disappeared and began to climb a mountain slope seven miles away. Yeats's fascination with the supernatural was lifelong.

Yeats left school in 1883. He was eighteen and had already written a verse play and his family were by then used to the sound of Yeats composing. He would murmur and hum aloud his verses in his room and he was determined to devote his life to writing. In November 1883 Yeats went to hear Oscar Wilde give a lecture in Dublin and in May 1884, academically too weak to go to Trinity College, he enrolled at the Metropolitan School of Art in Kildare St but he stopped attending the following summer and enrolled at the Royal Hibernian Academy. But overall Yeats was disillusioned and bored (years later he said that his artistic training was 'destructive of enthusiasm'.) He continued to write and he preferred verse drama and narrative to lyric poetry at first; in March 1885 he published two lyrics in the *Dublin University Review*, 'Song of the Faeries' and 'Voices'.

That year too, Yeats attended the newly formed Contemporary Club with his father, a club founded to discuss the social, political and literary topics of the time; another important influence on the young W.B. Yeats was his reading of a book entitled *Esoteric Buddhism* which his aunt Isabella Pollexfen had given him, a book that explored Eastern and Western religions. A third influence was Yeats's joining the Young Ireland Society, urged by John O'Leary, the Fenian journalist who had returned from exile in Paris at the beginning of 1885.

John O'Leary was a very influential figure in Yeats's life and poetry. When a student, O'Leary had abandoned medicine and had become a Fenian leader. He held nationalistic, romantic views and had been arrested in 1865 for his part in the Fenian movement. Condemned to twenty years in prison, he served five and had to spend the remaining fifteen years in exile. O'Leary was highly respected and Yeats later wrote that the meetings he attended at the Contemporary Club and the books O'Leary lent or gave him determined all that he subsequently set his hand to. Something else very important happened at this time in terms of Yeats's poetry and, in his *Autobiographies,* he explains how he realised that: 'We should write out our own thoughts in as nearly as possible the language we thought them in, as though in a letter to an intimate friend. We should not disguise them in any way for our lives give them force as the lives of people in plays give force to their words. Personal utterance, which had almost ceased in English literature, could be as fine an escape from rhetoric (and abstraction) as drama itself. But my father would hear of nothing but drama; personal utterance was only egotism. I knew it was not... I tried from that on to write out of my emotions exactly as they came to me in life, not changing them to make them more beautiful.' The Irish poet Eavan Boland says that 'it would be hard to overestimate the importance of that particular passage.' Yeats had made up his mind that he was going to take his life and use it as the raw material for his art. Boland adds that 'there have been a lot of poets since Yeats who have written about their lives. But Yeats lived at a time when it was believed you couldn't do that, at least not in that way. So Yeats was moving against the current; Yeats made his art out of his life and he did so deliberately.'

Yeats was friends with the poet Katherine Tynan and they attended a seance together. It was a frightening experience for them both; Yeats felt that his body experienced the supernatural, felt there was something 'very evil' in the room and he did not attend a seance again for many years. In April 1886, Yeats left art school and in October 1886 – he was twenty-one – published his first volume, *Mosada*, which did not impress Gerard Manley Hopkins, the poet and Jesuit priest, who thought it 'strained'. But already Yeats was finding new subject matter and themes: Irish settings and themes now began to figure in his writing and his well-known poem 'Down By the Salley Gardens', which was inspired by an old Sligo woman's song, belongs to this time. But in April 1887 the Yeats family were back in London where Yeats worked as a reviewer, made contacts in the literary world and visited Madame Blavatsky the theosophist, who encouraged Yeats's interest in myth and folklore. In August 1887, Yeats returned to Sligo to finish his poem 'The Wanderings of Oisin', a work which drew on myth and politics. Also in 1887 Yeats edited an anthology of poetry, dedicated to John O'Leary, which was published in

Dublin under the title *Poems and Ballads of Young Ireland*. Yeats finished his long narrative Oisin poem in Sligo and it was published in 1889 in a volume entitled *The Wanderings of Oisin and Other Poems* and reprinted that same year under the title *Crossways*. There are sixteen poems in all; the first eight are preoccupied with Indian, exotic themes; the final eight are inspired by Ireland.

Though Yeats described London as 'hateful', he met and became friends with William Morris, G.B. Shaw, Oscar Wilde and others. He carefully researched and edited a book called *Fairy and Folk Tales of the Irish Peasantry* and worked as a freelance journalist, but the financial situation at home was so serious that the entire family suffered hardship. It was in London, in December 1888, that Yeats was inspired to write what would become his most famous poem, 'The Lake Isle of Innisfree'. It was published in 1890 and was an immediate success. Robert Louis Stevenson wrote from Samoa and praised Yeats for a work 'so quaint and airy, simple artful, and eloquent to the heart'.

On 30 January 1889, a tall, beautiful, twenty-two year-old ardent Irish nationalist named Maud Gonne visited the Yeatses at their home in Blenheim Road. Though English born and the daughter of a British army colonel serving in Dublin, she had recently become involved in radical politics and insisted that Ireland be freed of British rule. Yeats's father was shocked by her outspoken nature but Yeats himself defended her and he was smitten. Maud Gonne invited Yeats to dine with her that evening and they also dined together on the next nine evenings of Gonne's London stay. Yeats had fallen in love. He was twenty-three years old and, many years later, he spoke of how it was at this time that 'the troubling of my life began'.

In 1891, Yeats founded the Irish Literary Society in London. He also returned to Ireland on a visit and while there asked Maud Gonne to marry him. She refused but Yeats continued to be fascinated by her and proposed to her several times. She had gone to Donegal to be with and to help the impoverished Irish. There, Gonne witnessed evictions, violence, death. She campaigned for the release of political prisoners and, when she asked Yeats to write a play for her on an Irish theme; he created his play *The Countess Cathleen*, which tells of a beautiful woman who sells her soul to the Devil in a bid to save the Irish people.

In 1896, Yeats had his first sexual relationship when he had a year-long affair with Olivia Shakespear. Also in 1896, Yeats met Lady Augusta Gregory, forty-five and a widow, who lived at Coole Park in County Galway. She had an enormous influence on Yeats. It was in 1897 that Yeats, with Lady Gregory and Edward Martyn, spoke of creating a theatre for new Irish plays and the idea of the Abbey Theatre, which opened on 27 December 1904, was born. In their book *W.B. Yeats and His World,* Micheal MacLiammoir and Eavan Boland wrote of Lady Gregory that 'It is impossible to over-estimate her influence on Yeats. She was his friend and counsellor, an understanding eye in the tumultuous and haunted places of his mind. She was to help him more than he had ever been helped in his life, chiefly, and most significantly, by offering him access to her house at Coole. This became Yeats's most important home; for more than thirty years he spent all his summers there, and often his winters.'

Yeats was interested in Buddhism, magic, spiritualism, astrology, and the Cabbala – a secret, traditional lore which allowed Jewish Rabbis to read hidden meanings in the Bible. He studied William Blake's work and co-edited an edition of Blake's poetry in 1893. To please Maud Gonne, Yeats joined the Irish Republican Brotherhood but he and she resigned from the organisation in 1900. Yeats was making his living at this time from journalism and he was very involved with the founding of the Irish National Dramatic Society which later became the Abbey Theatre.

Yeats and Maud Gonne had entered into a non-physical, "spiritual union". She played the title role in Yeats's 1902 play *Cathleen Ní Houlihan* and she converted to Catholicism around then because 'every political movement on earth has its counterpart in the spirit world'; she travelled Ireland, America and France fund-raising for the nationalist cause and addressed political rallies. Maud Gonne's marriage to Major John MacBride in 1903 (she and MacBride separated a few years later) upset Yeats but he continued to write poetry about her throughout his life. In a poem published in 1912, Yeats says of Maud Gonne: 'She lived in storm and strife,/ Her soul had such desire' .

In 1907 Yeats travelled to Italy with Lady Gregory and her son Robert where he saw the great Byzantine mosaics at Ravenna, mosaics which feature in Yeats's poem 'Sailing to Byzantium' (1926). Italian artistic achievements convinced Yeats that patronage played a vital role in the making of great art. When Sir Hugh Lane, Lady Gregory's nephew, offered the city of Dublin his collection of thirty-nine, very valuable, French Impressionist paintings if Dublin Corporation would house them and the Corporation refused, Yeats was enraged and wrote angry, political poems, including 'September 1913', denouncing the decision.

John MacBride was executed after the Easter 1916 Rising and Yeats once again proposed to Maud Gonne. She refused and Yeats then proposed to her twenty-year-old daughter Iseult, whose father was a French journalist and politician. Iseult Gonne refused him in 1916. In 1917 Yeats, again, asked Iseult Gonne to marry him and, on being rejected, proposed to an English woman Georgie Hyde Lees (born 1892). He was 52, she was 24 and they had first met in 1911. W.B. Yeats and Georgie Hyde Lees, known as 'George', were married in London, at the Harrow Road Register Office, on 20 October 1917.

Both husband and wife had an interest in the occult. Stephen Coote points out in his biography of Yeats that their wedding date had been chosen because the revolving planets moved into a position promising stability, inspiration, children, philosophic friendship and public acclaim for creative endeavour. During their honeymoon, George Yeats attempted automatic writing and later developed a gift for mediumship and they experimented in many occult practices. During the next few years George Yeats, in response to Yeats's questions, filled thousands of pages with automatic writing.

They lived in Oxford and London during the early months of their marriage and in 1918 the Yeatses moved to Ireland, first to Dublin and later to a Norman Tower, with two cottages attached, in Ballylee, County Galway, which Yeats had bought in 1917 for £35. The tower, known as Tur Bail' i Liaigh, was Anglicised by Yeats to Thoor Ballylee (something he did with all Irish names) and, having restored the tower, in 1919 they moved in. It became their summer home from 1919 until 1929 and Thoor Ballylee, four miles from Gort, a few hours' walk from Coole Park, was dedicated to George. Carved on a stone at Thoor Ballylee are the words:

> I, the poet William Yeats,
> With old mill boards and sea-green slates,
> And smithy work from the Gort forge,
> Restored this tower for my wife George;
> And may these characters remain
> When all is ruin once again.

A daughter, Anne, had been born in Dublin on 24 February 1919. In October the family went to America where Yeats read and lectured. In 1919 Yeats also published his seventh collection, *The Wild Swans at Coole*, which opened with the title poem. They returned to live in Oxford and in August 1921 a son, Michael, was born. In 1922 Yeats bought a house at 82 Merrion Square, Dublin. Micheal MacLaimmoir and Eavan Boland sum up this particular time in the Yeatses' life as follows: 'Yeats and his wife found themselves in an Ireland which was at once rebellious, active, joyous, defiant, up in arms, inflamed with love and hate, and deeply orthodox in terms of religious observance. To most Irishmen at the time, the preoccupation with the occult of Yeats and his wife must have seemed uncanny, obscure, cranky and heretical.' And yet Yeats was appointed to the Irish Senate of the Free State Government in 1922, a position he took up in January 1923, when he was fifty-eight. Yeats was also awarded the Nobel Prize for Literature in 1923 and, in a letter to Edmund Gosse, dated 23 November 1923, he wrote that 'I know quite well that this honour is not given to me as an individual but as a representative of a literary movement and of a nation and I am glad to have it so.'

In *A Vision* (1925), a prose work, Yeats produced a work of mystical philosophy based on his wife's automatic writings; in 1926 he translated Sophocles's play *Oedipus the King* for the Abbey, in 1927 Sophocles's *Oedipus at Colonus*. Early in 1928 poor health dictated a complete rest and Yeats with his wife and two children moved to Rapallo in Italy. In 1928 also he published his collection *The Tower* which included 'Meditations in Time of Civil War' (a sequence which includes 'The Stare's Nest by My Window') and 'Sailing to Byzantium.' It was a book which, in Micheal MacLiammoir and Eavan Boland's words, 'set him indisputably among the greatest living poets of the English language. His genius is at its height in these thirty-six poems, with their superb imagery, their perfection of form, and their ominous hatred of age and death.' Yeats thought Rapallo 'an indescribably lovely place' and, in a letter to Lady Gregory, confessed that he had re-read *The Tower*, was astonished by 'its bitterness' and intended to write 'amiable verses.'

Yeats and his family returned to Ireland in the spring of 1929 and the summer of 1929 marked his last visit to Thoor Ballylee. Winter found the Yeats family once again in Rapallo but he spent the winters of 1930 and 1931 in Ireland. His play, *The Words Upon the Window Pane*, featuring a seance, was performed at the Abbey and was very successful and he was awarded an honorary Doctorate of Letters by Oxford University.

Yeats spent the summer of 1931 at Coole, where Lady Gregory was ill; she died in May 1932. Yeats had once written in his diary [1909] that she 'has been to me mother, friend, sister and brother' and 'I cannot realise the world without her.' Late in 1932, Yeats gave a lecture tour in America in order to raise money for an Irish Academy of Letters which Yeats, George Bernard Shaw and AE [George Russell] had founded that year. By 1932, Yeats had also moved from Merrion Square to 'Riversdale', an early nineteenth-century house in Rathfarnham, his last home in Ireland.

In 1933, his tenth collection, *The Winding Stair and Other Poems*, was published; it opened with 'In Memory of Eva Gore-Booth and Con Markiewicz', a poem written in October 1927.

In April 1934, when he was sixty-nine, Yeats underwent a Steinach rejuvenation operation, which supposedly restored sexual potency. Whether or not the operation was a success, it certainly liberated his imagination. Yeats believed that he produced new poems which were 'among his best work'. In his final years there was what has been termed an astonishing revolution in Yeats's style and yet, during all this time, he was having difficulty with his health and suffered from lung congestion In 1936 he published *The Oxford Book of Modern Verse* and in 1938 travelled to the south of France, where he died of heart failure in Roquebrune on 29 January 1939, at the age of seventy-three. He was buried there, but in 1948 his remains were exhumed and brought to Sligo, though evidence now suggests that the wrong bones were exhumed, where he was buried in Drumcliff churchyard, as had been foretold by Yeats in his poem 'Under Ben Bulben', dated 4 September 1938:

> Under bare Ben Bulben's head
> In Drumcliff churchyard Yeats is laid.
> An ancestor was rector there
> Long years ago, a church stands near,
> By the road an ancient cross.
> No marble, no conventional phrase;
> On limestone quarried near the spot
> By his command these words are cut:
>
> *Cast a cold eye*
> *On life, on death.*
> *Horseman, pass by!*

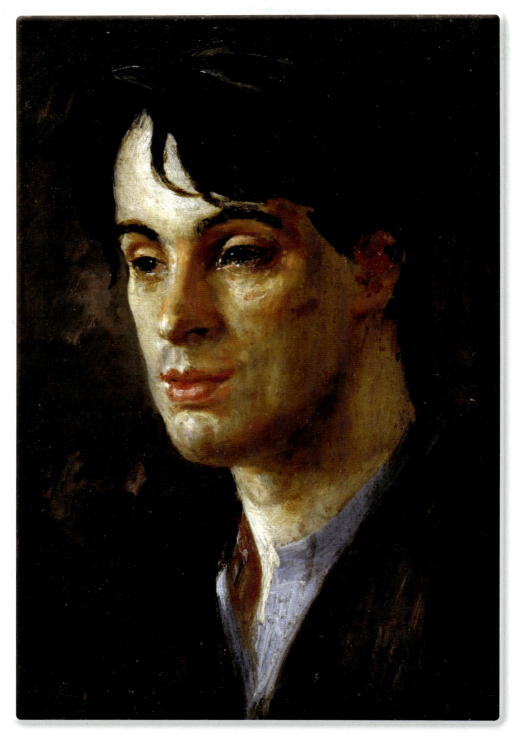

'W.B. Yeats' (1907) by Augustus John.

POEMS

Dates refer to the year in which these poems were first published in book form.

[Handwritten annotations top:] One of Yeats most celebrated poems. This is his lived experiences. Grew up in Dublin, used to visit was Sligo. It is an escape from Industrialisation and from other people. A beautiful poem that depicts a speakers longing to leave the city & spend time on the isle. He speaks of Innisfree in an idealistic way. Almost has magical qualities. Speaks about different times of day & overall peace he's going to achieve once he'll get there. wants to be alone.

[Handwritten left margin:] uses alliteration to emphasize he rlly wants to go Intentions are very clear

The Lake Isle of Innisfree

I will arise and go now, and go to Innisfree,
And a small cabin build there, of clay and wattles made: *build cabin*
Nine bean-rows will I have there, a hive for the honey-bee, *imagery*
And live alone in the bee-loud glade. *All about him solitude & Auditory*

[Handwritten:] Repetition: Reason for going.

And I shall have some peace there, for peace comes dropping
          slow,   5
          imagery
Dropping from the veils of the morning to where the cricket
          sings;
There midnight's all a glimmer, and noon a purple glow,
And evening full of the linnet's wings. *bird. Imagery. This is a daydream.*

I will arise and go now, for always night and day
wants up to hear sounds of waters & breaking along the shore.
I hear lake water lapping with low sounds by the shore;   10
we realise Yeats has been day dreaming. He wishes to escape a world
While I stand on the roadway, or on the pavements grey, *that is anything but*
what he imagine. Shan offer peace.
I hear it in the deep heart's core.

[Handwritten:] No Road or pave in Country so he's in the city
The poem ends on a very sombre note, The haunting images of lake isle are heard not only in his head but also in his heart. The speaker has left the reader unsure of whether he makes it to lake isle or not. To which he his long happiness reality.
Theme of nature is huge & longing to escape

Glossary

Title: Innisfree means the island of heather (from 'Inis' meaning island and 'fraoch' meaning heather) – hence the 'purple glow' of line 7.

Line 2 clay and wattles: (also known as wattle and daub) wattles are flexible rods and intertwined wattles were plastered with mud/clay and used as a building material.

Line 7 midnight's all a glimmer: in his essay on weather in the poetry of W.B. Yeats, John Holloway says that 'in such an open and unlighted place . . . on a cloudless and moonless night the stars will appear in astonishing brilliance' and he points out that Yeats's description is 'an understatement by far'.

Line 8 linnet's wings: the linnet, a songbird, is the common finch.

Line 10 lapping: rippling/splashing; can also mean caressing.

This poem began in London's Fleet Street. Yeats was standing on the pavement and looking at a little toy fountain in a shop window. The sound of the water reminded him of Sligo, where he spent his summer holidays.

This is how Yeats himself described the poem's origin: 'I had still the ambition, formed in Sligo in my teens, of living in imitation of Thoreau on Innisfree, a little island in Lough Gill, and when walking through Fleet Street very home-sick I heard a little tinkle of water, and saw a fountain in a shop-window which balanced a little ball upon the jet, and began to remember lake water. From the sudden remembrance came my poem "Innisfree"'.

The three stanzas rhyme abab; the first three lines in each stanza are hexameters, the fourth a tetrameter. Robert Louis Stevenson, author of *Treasure Island* and *Kidnapped*, wrote to Yeats on 14 April 1894 to say that he had been deeply moved by 'The Lake Isle of Innisfree'. Stevenson said of the poem that 'It is so quaint and airy, simple, artful, and eloquent to the heart — but I seek words in vain. Enough that "always night and day I hear lake water lapping with low sounds on the shore," and am, yours gratefully, Robert Louis Stevenson.'

In 2000, the *Irish Times* published its *Book of Favourite Irish Poems* which 3,500 readers had nominated. Yeats's poetry made up twenty-five per cent of the one hundred poems chosen and 'The Lake Isle of Innisfree' was voted number one.

Yeats included the first draft of 'The Lake Isle of Innisfree' in a letter he wrote to Katharine Tynan on 21 December 1888 and he prefaced the poem as follows: 'Here are two verses I made the other day: 'There is a beautiful Island of Innisfree in Lough Gill, Sligo. A little rocky island with a legended past' and added that 'to go away and live alone on that island' was 'an old daydream of my own'. The draft was as follows:

I will arise and go now and go to the island of Innis free
And live in a dwelling of wattles – of woven wattles and wood work made,
Nine bean rows will I have there, a yellow hive for the honey bee
And this old care shall fade.

There from the dawn above me peace will come down dropping slow
Dropping from the veils of the morning to where the household cricket sings.
And noontide there be all a glimmer, midnight be a purple glow,
And evening full of the linnet's wings.

In a recording, Yeats introduced his reading of the poem: 'I have gone to a lot of trouble to get into verse the poems that I am going to read and that is why I will not read them as if they were prose. I am going to begin with a poem of mine called "The Lake Isle of Innisfree" because if you know anything about me you will expect me to begin with it. It is the only poem of mine that is very widely known. When I was a young lad in the town of Sligo I read Thoreau's *Essays* and wanted to live in a hut on an island in Lough Gill called Innisfree which means Heather Island. I wrote the poem in London when I was about twenty-three. One day in the Strand I heard a little tinkle of water and saw in a shop window a little jet of water balancing a ball on the top. It was an advertisement, I think, for cooling drinks but it set me thinking of Sligo and lake water. I think there is only one obscurity in the poem: I speak of noon as "a purple glow." I must have meant by that the reflection of heather in the water.'

? Questions

1. How would you describe the particular appeal of this 'escapist' poem?

2. What is the effect of the opening words 'I will arise and go now' and their repetition in line 9? Why do you think Yeats opted for such formal language here?

3. Yeats wrote this poem in 1888–89. Do many details in the poem suggest the times he lived in, the contemporary? List the details which you would consider timeless and comment on their effect.

4. Why do you think Yeats chose a long line for this particular poem? Why is the final line in each of the three stanzas a shorter line?

5. Comment on how Yeats uses the senses to evoke a place. Identify how assonance and alliteration are used for particular effect, especially in the final stanza.

6. Robert Louis Stevenson said that the poem was both 'simple and artful'. Explain what you think he meant by this. Identify what is simple about the poem and artful.

7. How would your own version of Utopia compare with Yeats's?

September 1913

What need you, being come to sense,
But fumble in a greasy till
And add the halfpence to the pence
And prayer to shivering prayer, until
You have dried the marrow from the bone?   5
For men were born to pray and save:
Romantic Ireland's dead and gone,
It's with O'Leary in the grave.

Yet they were of a different kind,
The names that stilled your childish play,   10
They have gone about the world like wind,
But little time had they to pray
For whom the hangman's rope was spun,
And what, God help us, could they save?
Romantic Ireland's dead and gone,   15
It's with O'Leary in the grave.

Was it for this the wild geese spread
The grey wing upon every tide;
For this that all that blood was shed,
For this Edward Fitzgerald died,   20
And Robert Emmet and Wolfe Tone,
All that delirium of the brave?
Romantic Ireland's dead and gone,
It's with O'Leary in the grave.

Yet could we turn the years again,   25
And call those exiles as they were
In all their loneliness and pain,
You'd cry, 'Some woman's yellow hair
Has maddened every mother's son':
They weighed so lightly what they gave.   30
But let them be, they're dead and gone,
They're with O'Leary in the grave.

Glossary

Title September 1913: This poem, dated 7 September 1913, first appeared in the *Irish Times* on 8 September 1913, under the title 'Romance in Ireland (On reading much of the correspondence against the Art Gallery)'. Like Yeats's poem 'To a Wealthy Man who promised a Second Subscription to the Dublin Municipal Gallery if it were proved the People wanted Pictures', it was prompted in part by the controversy surrounding the Hugh Lane pictures. Lane's important collection of French Impressionist paintings was offered to Dublin on condition that they would be properly housed. Yeats and his friends tried to raise money for an art gallery but there was a poor response from the wealthy Catholic middle class. The owner of the *Irish Independent*, William Martin Murphy, publicly disagreed with Yeats on the issue. In 1913 also there was a workers' strike and lock-out in Dublin, which was led by Jim Larkin. William Martin Murphy opposed the workers and had the support of the Catholic Church and Yeats, together with many Irish writers and intellectuals, took the workers' side in the dispute.

Line 1 you: the Irish people, especially the Catholic wealthy middle class.

Line 2 greasy till: A. Norman Jeffares notes in his *Commentary on the Collected Poems of W.B.Yeats* that the image came from a speech Yeats made in July 1913. He wrote to Lady Gregory that he had spoken with Lane as well as possible subscribers to the Gallery in his mind: 'I described Ireland, if the present intellectual movement failed, as a little greasy huxtering nation groping for halfpence in a greasy till but did not add except in thought, "by the light of a holy candle"'.

Line 5 You have dried the marrow from the bone: destroyed everything essential to life.

Line 7 Romantic Ireland: an Ireland with vision, idealism.

Line 8 O'Leary: John O'Leary (1830–1907) influenced the young W.B. Yeats, especially because of his role in the struggle for Irish independence. He studied medicine but soon devoted himself to the struggle for Irish freedom. Between 1863 and 1865, O'Leary edited the *Irish People*, the Irish Republican Brotherhood newspaper, which openly promoted the overthrow of British rule. He was arrested in 1865 and sentenced to twenty years of penal servitude in Britain. He was released in 1871, as part of a general amnesty, but was not permitted to return to Ireland until 1885. He lived mainly in Paris and, on returning to Dublin in 1885, he met the twenty-year-old Yeats, who was deeply impressed by him.

Line 10 names: the names of Irish patriots.

Line 17 the wild geese: In Declan Kiberd's words, the Wild Geese were 'those Irish Rebels who sought training in the armies of Catholic Europe after 1691 in hopes of returning to expel the occupier.' These Irishmen served in French, Spanish and Austrian armies. After the Treaty of Limerick was signed in 1691, Patrick Sarsfield and 11,000 men went to France and fought with the French. In all, it was thought that 120,000 Wild Geese left Ireland between 1690 and 1730.

Line 20 Edward Fitzgerald: Lord Edward Fitzgerald (1763–1798), Irish republican politician; joined the United Irishmen in 1796 and went to France to arrange for a French invasion of Ireland. The plot was exposed and a price of £1,000 was placed on Fitzgerald's head; he was seized and was fatally wounded in Dublin.

Line 21 Robert Emmet (1778–1803): Irish republican, a member of the United Irishmen; his plot to seize Dublin Castle failed. He was tried for high treason and was hanged in 1803.

Line 21 Wolfe Tone (1763–1798): in 1791, he published a pamphlet, *An Argument on Behalf of the Catholics of Ireland*, and helped to found the Society of United Irishmen. He enlisted French help and, in September 1798, led a French force to Ireland; he was captured in Lough Swilly. In Dublin he was tried and condemned to be hanged as a traitor. It is said that he cut his own throat in prison.

*Line 22 **delirium***: fervour, selflessness.

*Line 28/29 **You'd cry, 'Some woman's yellow hair/ Has maddened every mother's son'***: 'the bloodless rabble, beholding the fervour of the old patriots, would find a banal explanation for it' is Daniel Albright's explanation of these two lines. Gus Martin says: 'Yeats suggests that people who were incapable of understanding the fervour of the patriotism of these men might be inclined to say that they were motivated by something, perhaps by love for a woman.'

*Line 30 **weighed***: calculated.

Micheál MacLiammóir and Eavan Boland in their book *W.B. Yeats and His World* comment: 'in "September 1913", Yeats looked about him at the country which he had served with such devotion and found nothing but disillusion. Seeing with sudden bitter clarity the littleness, the greyness, the meanness, the self-glorification, the prudish savagery and false piety gathering – as it seemed, incurably – over the face of the land and her people, he cried:

Romantic Ireland's dead and gone,
It's with O'Leary in the grave.'

? Questions

1. Who is Yeats addressing in this poem? How would you describe Yeats's tone in the opening stanza? Which words best describe that tone?

2. Examine how Yeats focuses on the present, the past, and the present again and comment on the significance of this.

3. Identify the sharp contrast between the men who 'were born to pray and save' (line 6) and those 'For whom the hangman's rope was spun,/And what, God help us, could they save?' (lines 13–14)

4. What is Yeats's idea of a Romantic Ireland? Why does the poet think 'Romantic Ireland's dead and gone'?

5. Is this a public or a private poem? Give reasons for your answer.

6. Comment on the use of rhyme, rhythm, repetition and questions throughout the poem.

7. Why do you think Yeats uses a question mark in every stanza except the final one? How would you describe the poet's tone in the line 'But let them be they're dead and gone'?

8. The didactic poem is a poem which instructs or teaches. Why is 'September 1913' considered a didactic poem and what does it teach?

9. Seamus Heaney says of W.B. Yeats that 'He never accepted the terms of another argument, but proposed his own.' Outline in your own words Yeats's argument in this poem.

wrote in 50s
subtly alludes to loss of love.

Reminds him of old life.

The Wild Swans at Coole

Poem sees speaker visiting Coole park in Ireland. Here he observes a large group of swans. He compares his visit to Coole park to his visit 19 years ago

consonace letter T alliteration The trees are in their autumn beauty, *✓ image* *✓ autumn*
The woodland paths are dry, *colours*
Under the October twilight the water *yellow brown* *October evening + Coole lake reflects the calme motioness sky above*
metaphore for later twilight years
Reflection of his life Mirrors a still sky; *years in life* *Sybilance + Alliteration*
Upon the brimming water among the stones *59 swans (lake almost overflowing)*
sts score for reader Are nine-and-fifty swans. 5
setting

The nineteenth autumn has come upon me *It was 19 years ago he was those first. Before, they flew above*
Since I first made my count; *his head* *In huge broken circles.*
I saw, before I had well finished, *Soaring around w noisy wings. Sibilance*
All suddenly mount 10
And scatter wheeling in great broken rings
Upon their clamorous wings.

I have looked upon those brilliant creatures, *looking at the birds now I*
And now my heart is sore. *feel heartache.* *Everything has changed since*
All's changed since I, hearing at twilight, *he first stood on shore of lake.* 15
The first time on this shore,
The bell-beat of their wings above my head,
Alliteration Trod with a lighter tread. *Younger when I came + used to walk w a lighter step (he's older)*

Repitition Unwearied still, lover by lover, *The swans are still as full of life as*
They paddle in the cold *they where the first time he saw them* 20
emphasis Companionable streams or climb the air; *In their loving pairs they paddle through the*
Their hearts have not grown old; *cold and fly through the sky. These hearts r still filled w passion*
Alliteration Passion or conquest, wander where they will, *are desires + free to do*
Attend upon them still. *whatever.* *↑ alliteration*

But now they drift on the still water, *Envious cos has alone. They havent aged.* 25
Mysterious, beautiful; *In the future I wonder where they'll build*
Among what rushes will they build, *there nest + other will see them (envious)*
By what lake's edge or pool *yeats is juxaposed against yeats. He'll grow old & they look beautiful in*
Delight men's eyes when I awake some day *their prime.*
To find they have flown away? *Rhetorical: uncertain future like swans* 30
Bring speaker bittersweet feelings
Alliteration→ shows power + gracefulness of swans
Speakers own life has changed irreversably by the onward PASSAGE of TIME. SWANS r symbol of power + beauty

📖 Glossary

Title Coole: Coole Park, Gort, Co. Galway, the home of Augusta Gregory, Yeats's friend and patron. The house was built circa 1770 and in 1927 the estate was sold to the Department of Lands, Lady Gregory being allowed to live there during her lifetime. In 1941, nine years after Lady Gregory's death, the house was demolished.

Line 5 brimming water: that autumn (October 1916), the water in Lough Corrib was particularly low; it had been one of the driest autumns on record. That did not prevent Yeats from altering the facts for poetic effect. Water, according to Curtis B. Bradford, is always a symbol of the sensual life in Yeats's poetry.

Line 12 clamorous: loud-sounding.

Line 15 All's changed: a reference perhaps to the political changes (World War I and the Easter Rising) and the personal (Yeats's own personal sorrow – his unrequited love for Maud Gonne, his growing old).

Line 19 lover by lover: swans mate for life and their being together highlights Yeats's solitariness.

Line 21 companionable: friendly.

Line 24 Attend upon them still: (Will) stay with them always.

The first draft of the opening lines reads as follows:

These/ The woods are in their autumn colours
But the Coole Water is low
And all the paths are dry under
And all paths dry under the foot
In the soft twilight I go…

In an earlier version of the poem, the final stanza was printed third. Yeats was fifty-one when he wrote 'The Wild Swans at Coole'. The rhyme scheme used here, abcbdd, is unusual for Yeats.

? Questions

1. What impresses Yeats about the swans? What do they stand for? What qualities of theirs does he admire? What differences does the speaker recognise between the swans and himself? Which details, in your opinion, express these best?

2. How do you think this poem achieves its slow and dignified rhythm? Look, for example, at the choice of words, the line length, the rhyme.

3. How might this poem be seen as a poem of regret and lament? How would you describe the speaker as he is portrayed in this poem?

4. Why do you think Yeats calls the cold streams 'companionable'? Explain what is meant by 'Passion or conquest, wander where they will,/ Attend upon them still.' What do these lines imply about Yeats?

5. Do you think Yeats has convinced the reader that the swans are 'Mysterious, beautiful'? What does this poem tell us about man's relation with nature?

6. How would you describe the mood in the closing stanza? Is it similar to or different from the mood elsewhere in the poem?

7. It has been said of this poem that Yeats expresses a universal state of mind and emotion and he does so in a diction and rhetoric that can rightly be called noble. Do you agree with this view? Give reasons for your answer.

An Irish Airman Foresees his Death

I know that I shall meet my fate *— Rhyme* *he knows he is going to die.*
Somewhere among the clouds above; *Doesn't hate the enemy*
Those that I fight I do not hate,
Those that I guard I do not love; *Doesn't love Britain either (neutral)*
My country is Kiltartan Cross, *highlights the senselessness of* 5
My countrymen Kiltartan's poor, *war. He knows his death will not change the*
No likely end could bring them loss *lives of the ppl. The outcome will not change their lives*
Or leave them happier than before.
Nor law, nor duty bade me fight, *He didn't have to fight,*
Nor public men, nor cheering crowds, *he didn't do it for glory* 10
A lonely impulse of delight *no body else will understand.*
Drove to this tumult in the clouds; *he's doing it for himself.*
I balanced all, brought all to mind, *Questions life.*
The years to come seemed waste of breath, *nothing else to live for*
A waste of breath the years behind 15
In balance with this life, this death. *Same idea.*

sense of urgency *Tone of detachment 'ready to die'*
Speaker is heroic.

Glossary

Title Irish Airman: Robert Gregory (1881–1918), Lady Gregory's only son, who died in action on the Italian front on 23 January 1918. He had trained as an artist and Yeats saw him as a Renaissance man, in other words a man of great learning, talent and accomplishment. Yeats wrote several poems in honour of Robert Gregory and in 1918 paid him the following tribute: 'I have known no man accomplished in so many ways as Major Robert Gregory, who was killed in action a couple of weeks ago and buried by his fellow-airmen in the beautiful cemetery at Padua… He had so many sides: painter, classical scholar, scholar in painting and in modern literature, boxer, horseman, airman – he had the Military Cross and the Legion d'Honneur. . .'

Line 3 Those that I fight: the Germans, in Italy.

Line 4 Those that I guard: the English; Gregory fought with the English army.

Line 5 Kiltartan Cross: crossroads near Coole Park, the Gregory home, in Co. Galway.

Line 12 tumult: commotion, din.

Line 13 I balanced all: Daniel Albright points out that the poem is a series of balances: enemies and friends (lines 3–4); loss and gain (lines 7–8); the past and the future (lines 14–15).

Yeats wrote this poem in 1918, the year Robert Gregory was killed.

? Questions

1. This poem is written in the voice of thirty-seven year old Major Robert Gregory. How does Yeats create a sense of the inevitable in this poem? In your answer, consider the title, the tone and rhythm of the lines.

2. Robert Gregory fought with the British against the Germans in Italy. Why does he say 'Those that I fight I do not hate,/ Those that I guard I do not love'? What is the significance of line 5: 'My country is Kiltartan Cross'? Do you think that there is a sense of confusion and contradiction in the speaker's mind?

3. What reasons does the speaker give for choosing to fight? Are they the usual reasons? What do you understand by 'A lonely impulse of delight'? Is there a recklessness in the poem? A futility? Where?

4. In the closing lines the speaker says 'I balanced all'. How do the lines themselves create a sense of balance in their very structure?

5. Is this a well-made poem? In your answer, you should consider the rhyming scheme and the regular, four-beat, eight-syllable line.

[Handwritten annotation at top:] This poem is a commemoration to the Irish rebels. WB Yeats is describing his torn emotions regarding the events of 1916. The uprising was unsuccessful in that. 14 of the Irish republicans were executed by Britain. This poem is an elegy (about those who died)

WILLIAM BUTLER YEATS

Easter 1916

I have met them at close of day *[annotation: Yeats says he's met them (foreshadowing of close of day)]*
Coming with vivid faces *[annotation: used to meet them on they way back from work]*
From counter or desk among grey *[annotation: work]*
Eighteenth-century houses. *[annotation: Imagery of Dublin street]*

I have passed with a nod of the head *[annotation: regarded them as normal ppl]* 5
Or polite meaningless words, *[annotation: and look down on them. Used to have]*
Or have lingered awhile and said *[annotation: Polite meaningless convos. He thought he]*
Polite meaningless words, *[annotation: was better than them. looked down.]*
And thought before I had done *[annotation: later he would make fun of them.]*
Of a mocking tale or a gibe *[annotation: at time Yeats was living in London, and thought Ireland was a circus.]* 10
To please a companion
Around the fire at the club,
Being certain that they and I
But lived where motley is worn: *[annotation: now everything is completely]*
All changed, changed utterly: *[annotation: different.]* *[annotation: repetition]* 15
A terrible beauty is born. *[annotation: 1916 event - Rising occurred + was highly destructive & helped bring ab change in Ireland.]*

[annotation: He describes the rebels (Countess marcovich tried to accomplish a positive change in Ireland.]
That woman's days were spent
In ignorant good-will,
Her nights in argument *[annotation: He speaks ab her life. before she]*
Until her voice grew shrill. *[annotation: got into politics she rode horses.]*
What voice more sweet than hers *[annotation: Pearg Pierce: was a teacher + poet:]* 20
When, young and beautiful,
She rode to harriers?
This man had kept a school
And rode our wingèd horse;
This other his helper and friend *[annotation: This guy helped Pierce become a poet. He believed Pearg would become famous for his poetry.]* 25
Was coming into his force;
He might have won fame in the end,
So sensitive his nature seemed, *[annotation: Describing P.]*
So daring and sweet his thought. 30
This other man I had dreamed, *[annotation: John McBride married Maude Gonn.]*
A drunken, vainglorious lout.

Major John
Yeats describes mcBride as a good for nothing
drunk. He was abusive towards his wife.

He had done most bitter wrong

To some who are near my heart, *Although Yeats hated him.*

Yet I number him in the song; *He must have huge respect for 135.*

He, too, has resigned his part *As this man completly tranformed*

In the casual comedy; *the easter rising.*

He, too, has been changed in his turn,

Transformed utterly:

A terrible beauty is born. *1916 rising brings change.* 40

Hearts with one purpose alone *Yeats is saying the stubborn rebels*
are being compared to a stubborn

Through summer and winter seem *stone.*

Enchanted to a stone *Speaker suggest ppl like the rebel*

To trouble the living stream. *dedicate all their life to one*

The horse that comes from the road, *activity or goal. can* 45

The rider, the birds that range *start to seem a bit inhuman.*

From cloud to tumbling cloud, *ppl become consumed in things*

Minute by minute they change; *they believe in. (freedom of Ireland)*

A shadow of cloud on the stream *even nature can change*

Changes minute by minute; *Over time. Stones are living* 50

A horse-hoof slides on the brim, *amonst nature & nature is*

And a horse plashes within it; *full of life but the stones are*

The long-legged moor-hens dive, *life less.*

And hens to moor-cocks call;

Minute by minute they live: 55

The stone's in the midst of all.

People who give up too much of
their lives,

Too long a sacrifice

Can make a stone of the heart.

O when may it suffice? *was all of it worth it?*

That is Heaven's part, our part *Im here to respect the people* 60

To murmur name upon name, *who've died.*

As a mother names her child *Did their death feel like going*

When sleep at last has come *to sleep at night but no night but death.*

On limbs that had run wild.

What is it but nightfall? 65

No, no, not night but death;

Was it needless death after all? *Speaker decides its not his*

For England may keep faith *Job to answer any of those*

For all that is done and said. *questions. Highlights the dead*

We know their dream; enough *deserve honour & respect.* 70

To know they dreamed and are dead;

And what if excess of love

Bewildered them till they died?

I write it out in a verse— *Lists rebels. Wherever Ireland*

MacDonagh and MacBride *gathers to celebrate their* 75

And Connolly and Pearse *country these men will be*

Now and in time to be, *honoured.* *& women*

Wherever green is worn, *In Yeats eyes the rebels*

Are changed, changed utterly: *identities have been*

A terrible beauty is born. *transformed from ordinary* 80

people to heros.

Rhyme: ABAB - + Theme of death & mourning

Glossary *Theme: Heroism + Bravery*

Date: Though dated specifically 25 September 1916 in *The Collected Poems*, Yeats in fact began working on the poem on 11 May 1916 and completed it on 25 September 1916.

Title Easter 1916: the Easter Rebellion in Dublin on 24 April 1916. Seven hundred of the Irish Republican Brotherhood took to the streets of Dublin and proclaimed Ireland a republic and no longer under British rule. British troops moved in and the uprising collapsed after five days. Fifteen of the leaders were executed between 3 and 12 May. In all, there were 450 dead and 2,614 wounded. Yeats was deeply moved by the event.

Line 1 them: the rebels, revolutionaries.

Line 2 vivid: intense, animated Latin (*vividus*, full of life).

Line 10 gibe: jeer, put-down.

Line 12 the club: Yeats was a member of the Arts Club.

Line 14 motley: clothing associated with fools; motley was a jester's particoloured dress.

Line 17 That woman: Constance Gore-Booth (Countess Markiewicz) who commanded a garrison at the College of Surgeons, St Stephen's Green, during the Rising. She was sentenced to death but that was commuted to penal servitude for life; she was eventually granted amnesty and released in 1917.

Line 23 harriers: pack of hunting hounds.

Line 24 This man: Patrick Pearse (1879–1916) – he founded a school for boys, St Enda's in Rathfarnham, where Irish language, culture and patriotism were promoted. Pearse was the chief of the Easter Rebellion; he was executed on 3 May.

Line 25 rode our wingèd horse: Pegasus a winged horse is a traditional symbol of poetic inspiration; here, the phrase means that Pearse wrote poetry.

Line 26 This other: Thomas MacDonagh (1878–1916) – poet, dramatist, taught English at UCD; he was executed in 1916.

Line 31 This other man: John MacBride (1865–1916), whom Maud Gonne had married in 1903; they separated in 1905. Mac Bride had fought against the British in the Boer War, was second-in-command at Jacob's Factory during the Easter Rising and was executed on 5 May 1916.

Line 34 some: Maud Gonne and Iseult Gonne.

Line 35 I number him in the song: this line and line 74, 'I write it out in a verse—' are not only self-conscious references to the making of the poem but acknowledge, perhaps, what Helen Vendler calls the 'numerological artifact' that is the poem. The Easter Rising began on 24 April 1916: stanza 1 is 16 lines long, stanza 2 is 24, stanza 3 is 16 and stanza 4 is 24.

Line 43 stone: the Yeats scholar A. Norman Jeffares says: 'hearts enchanted to a stone were Yeats's symbol for those who had devoted themselves to a cause without thought of life or love. The stone was a symbol of how politics had affected, in particular, Maud Gonne. To be choked with hate was the chief of all evil chances'.

Line 58 a stone of the heart: a reference to Maud Gonne's commitment to revolutionary ideals. Yeats sent a copy of 'Easter 1916' to Maud Gonne; she told Yeats 'I don't like your poem, it isn't worthy of you & above all it isn't worthy of the subject'. Terence Brown comments that Gonne 'was in no mood for a poem that could imagine England keeping faith' and 'She resented the idea that sacrifice could turn any heart to stone'.

Line 67 needless death: Yeats asks if these revolutionaries died in vain.

Line 68 England may keep faith: the British parliament passed the Home Rule Bill which gave Ireland some independence in 1913; the Bill was suspended at the outbreak of World War I. It was thought that the suspension would one day be lifted.

Line 76 Connolly: James Connolly (1870–1916) was Commandant in the General Post Office during the Rising. A trade union leader and author of *Labour in Irish History*. Severely wounded, he was arrested and executed on 12 May 1916, tied to a chair because he was unable to stand.

In 1938, the year before he died, Yeats wrote to Maud Gonne, who was writing her autobiography, *A Servant of the Queen*, to say that 'you can say what you like about me.' But he added: 'I do not however think that I would have said "hopeless struggle". I never felt the Irish struggle "hopeless." Let it be "exhausting struggle" or "tragic struggle" or some such phrase. I wanted the struggle to go on but in a different way.' (16 June 1938)

Commenting on this poem, Micheál MacLiammóir and Eavan Boland in their book *W.B. Yeats and His World*, write: 'It would seem to the single-minded imagination, unhampered by any legion of detailed facts, that the rising of the Irish Republican volunteers in Easter Week, 1916, was a direct answer to the melancholy challenge of Yeats's September poem ["September 1913"]. It is strange that his nostrils, usually sensitive to the approach of a storm as the nostrils of cat or horse, or of some nervous woman, seemed unaware of the gathering of the hosts of battle. But it was so: he sensed nothing at all. Nevertheless, the Easter Week Rising – from any point of view the most considerable of all Irish demonstrations of the ancient feud – certainly did take place, and when he heard of it the poet was deeply moved. His poem "Easter 1916", composed within a few weeks of the executions of the leaders of the rising, remains one of his finest. Its recurring couplet, with its insistent, irregular, beaten-out rhythm, like that of mournful bells, has become to Irish ears as familiar as a nightly prayer: 'All changed, changed utterly: A terrible beauty is born.'

? Questions

1. What atmosphere is created in the opening lines of the poem? Why do you think Yeats mentioned 'Eighteenth-century houses'? How did Yeats view the revolutionaries before the Easter Rising? Why did he speak 'polite meaningless words'?

2. What do you understand by the lines: 'All changed, changed utterly:/ A terrible beauty is born'?

3. Yeats initially thought the sacrifice of the leaders wasteful. In the second section, Yeats names those who fought and died for Irish freedom. Why has his tone of 'a mocking tale or a gibe' changed? How would you describe Yeats's tone in section 2? Do you admire Yeats's honesty here?

4. What do the words 'casual comedy' mean and what do they tell us about Yeats?

5. The third stanza marks a significant change in the poem. Descriptive detail of place and people is replaced by symbols – stone, stream, rider and horse, cloud, shadow, moor-hens, moor-cocks. What might each represent? Which ones are permanent? Which ones symbolise change? What is the effect of Yeats's use of symbols in the poem?

6. Stanza 3 begins and ends with the image of a stone. Yeats views those who fought as seeming to have hearts which changed to stone. What does such an image suggest? Is this related to the phrase 'terrible beauty'?

7. In the closing stanza, how does Yeats feel about the patriots? Why do you think he uses the word 'bewildered' (line 73)?

8. What is the significance of the image of a mother soothing and comforting her exhausted child? Do you think it is an effective image in the context of the poem as a whole?

9. What is Yeats's role as revealed in this poem? Look particularly at the final seven lines.

10. 'September 1913' and 'Easter 1916' are similar in some ways, different in others. Consider this and give your own view.

The Second Coming

Turning and turning in the widening gyre
The falcon cannot hear the falconer;
Things fall apart; the centre cannot hold;
Mere anarchy is loosed upon the world,
The blood-dimmed tide is loosed, and everywhere   5
The ceremony of innocence is drowned;
The best lack all conviction, while the worst
Are full of passionate intensity.

Surely some revelation is at hand;
Surely the Second Coming is at hand.   10
The Second Coming! Hardly are those words out
When a vast image out of *Spiritus Mundi*
Troubles my sight: somewhere in sands of the desert
A shape with lion body and the head of a man,
A gaze blank and pitiless as the sun,   15
Is moving its slow thighs, while all about it
Reel shadows of the indignant desert birds.
The darkness drops again; but now I know
That twenty centuries of stony sleep
Were vexed to nightmare by a rocking cradle,   20
And what rough beast, its hour come round at last,
Slouches towards Bethlehem to be born?

📖 Glossary

Title The Second Coming: Matthew, Chapter 24, verses 29–44, speaks of Christ's return to earth, a second coming, to reward the righteous and to establish the Millennium of Heaven on earth. Yeats, in this poem, saw the times he lived in as the end of the Christian era.

Line 1 gyre: for Yeats, a gyre was a cycle of history. Gyre is a spiral; a falcon is trained to fly in a spiralling motion, following the falconer's directions unless it flies so far away that it can no longer be controlled.

Seamus Heaney's comments on 'gyre' are detailed and interesting: 'A word of great potency in Yeats's vocabulary, suggestive of unstoppable process, of turbulent action that is part of a larger pattern. Yeats used the geometrical figure of two cones or vortices interpenetrating to represent the simultaneous processes of waxing and waning, rise and fall, which are necessarily at work at any moment in the life of an individual or a society. The extreme moment of risen, waxing life (the far-flung base of one cone) is also the moment when there arrives the original movement of new counter-swirling growth (the apex of the other cone, sharp-set at the centre of the wide base). So, when the 'widening gyre' reaches its fullest unwinding circumference, we are to expect a 'Second Coming', a new life which initiates an opposite motion. (Following upon this symmetrical pattern of antithesis, the 'rough beast' will replace the gentle Christ child at the same spot, in Bethlehem.)'

Line 2 The Falconer cannot hear the falconer: in Dante the falcon represents man and the falconer is Christ. Yeats, perhaps, is suggesting here that man has lost touch with Christianity.

Line 4 mere: nothing more than; 'mere' also used to mean absolute.

Line 4 anarchy: the absence of government; this frequently occurred after the First World War. In his book *A Vision*, Yeats wrote that anarchy and the adoration of violence are characteristic of the end of an historical era.

Line 5 blood-dimmed: war is seen as a flood of destruction.

Line 12 Spiritus Mundi: Spirit or Soul of the World; Yeats saw the spirit of the world as a universal consciousness or memory – something from which poets drew their images and symbols; the Swiss psychiatrist Jung called it the collective unconscious.

Line 14 lion body and the head of a man: the (Egyptian) sphinx.

Line 17 desert birds: birds of prey.

Line 19 twenty centuries: the time since Christ was born.

Line 20 vexed: harassed, distressed.

Line 22 Bethlehem: Christ's birthplace; the critic A. Norman Jeffares comments that the poem prophesies the arrival of a new god and adds: 'The location of the birthplace in Bethlehem, traditionally associated with the idea of the gentle innocence of infancy and maternal love, adds horror to the thought of the rough beast.'

Line 22 born: Yeats later wrote – 'Our civilisation was about to reverse itself, or some new civilisation about to be born from all that our age had rejected... because we had worshipped a single god it would worship many'.

The poem, in unrhymed iambic pentameter or blank verse, was written in January 1919, immediately after World War I ended. There are several references in the Bible to the end of the world: Daniel Ch 9 ('the end thereof shall be with a flood'); Matthew Ch 24 ('there shall be famines, and pestilences, and earthquakes, in divers places...'); and the Book of Revelation (the Apocalypse).

Yeats saw history as dependent on cycles of about 2000 years. The Graeco-Roman civilisation ended with the birth of Christ; now, it seems to Yeats that the Christian cycle is coming to an end. The next cycle, as predicted by Yeats, is not viewed with optimism.

In his edition of Yeats's Poems, Daniel Albright writes: 'According to orthodox Christianity, the faithful live in expectation that, after a Second Coming, Christ will establish on earth a kingdom of sanctity and bliss. The purpose of "The Second Coming" is to subvert that happy hope: the poet predicts that, at the end of the millennium, there will arise not Christ but Christ's opposite, a savage god whose reign will establish a system of behaviour antithetical to that recommended by Christ.'

The editor Maurice Wollman says that 'Yeats has a vision, a moment of insight into the future. It arises from a mood of doubt and despair, inspired by the anarchy of the world, the increase of bloodshed, and the growth of disbelief. He sees the present era as dying; the first two thousand years of Christianity have brought discord and strife because man has forgotten Christ. The new era that is about to be born is symbolised by the "rough beast," which is the antithesis of the gentle Bethlehem. It is not sought for or created: it comes uninvited, unwanted almost, upon the consciousness... It is Yeats's theory that a period of anarchy and violence follows a period of innocence and beauty.'

? Questions

1. Which details, do you think, best convey a sense of anarchy in the opening lines? What do you think Yeats meant by the phrase the 'ceremony of innocence'?

2. How would you describe Yeats's mood in the first stanza? Why does he praise 'conviction' and condemn 'passionate intensity'?

3. Does Yeats welcome the Second Coming? Is it possible to say? Look at lines 9–11. How would you describe Yeats's theme and overall mood in the poem?

4. How does Yeats view two thousand years of Christianity? What does 'nightmare' (line 20) suggest?

5. Is this a visual poem or a poem of ideas? Or does it combine both? If you were to paint this poem which images would predominate?

6. What evidence do you find in the poem to support the view that this poem 'foresees a future that, for all the horror of its approach, will offer a civilisation superior to that in which the poet lives'?

[handwritten top margin: An ancient Greek city · today Instanbul. The difficulty of keeping one's soul alive. The speaker is an old man who leaves behind the country of youth for on a quest to Byzantium. Yeats thought the young generation are so caught up with life that they fail to understand what the natural world has to offer. Escape from old age.]

Sailing to Byzantium

I

That is no country for old men. The young
In one another's arms, birds in the trees
—Those dying generations—at their song,
The salmon-falls, the mackerel-crowded seas,
Fish, flesh, or fowl, commend all summer long   5
Whatever is begotten, born, and dies.
Caught in that sensual music all neglect
Monuments of unageing intellect.

[handwritten right-side annotations I: (a wind sword, acre of grass) Old are not respected, no love. Old gen are dying out. Waters are swarmed w fish. Everything that is born dies. Everything in that world is so caught up in the moment that it pays no attention to the things that might outlive us (nature) Elderly are neglected by society.]
[handwritten left: world where young lovers embrace; connection w nature; is so caught up in the moment that it pays no attention to the things]

II

An aged man is but a paltry thing,
A tattered coat upon a stick, unless
Soul clap its hands and sing, and louder sing   10
For every tatter in its mortal dress,
Nor is there singing school but studying
Monuments of its own magnificence;
And therefore I have sailed the seas and come
To the holy city of Byzantium.   15

[handwritten annotations II: ② An old man in this world is nothing but a skinny rat or scarecrow unless he can keep his soul alive. The person who wants to keep their soul alive has to figure it out themselves. Therefore he wants to go to Byzantium. Assonance. imagery. Personification. metaphore. compares own body to a dress that'll go out of fashion.]

III

[handwritten: Sibilince ↓]

O sages standing in God's holy fire
As in the gold mosaic of a wall,
Come from the holy fire, perne in a gyre,
And be the singing-masters of my soul.   20
Consume my heart away; sick with desire
And fastened to a dying animal
It knows not what it is; and gather me
Into the artifice of eternity.

[handwritten annotations III: Oxymoron of being in Byzantium. metaphore (a dying animal) Enjambment. his soul is going to be trapped in a decaying body.]

IV

Once out of nature I shall never take
My bodily form from any natural thing,   25
But such a form as Grecian goldsmiths make
Of hammered gold and gold enamelling
To keep a drowsy Emperor awake;
Or set upon a golden bough to sing
To lords and ladies of Byzantium   30
Of what is past, or passing, or to come.

[handwritten annotations IV: wants to stay in Byzantium as it offers him eternity. Repetition. will be like a gold bird. Yeats yearns to leave his body behind & enters a spiritual and everlasting place.]

📖 Glossary

Title Byzantium: city founded in 660 B.C. It was known as Byzantium until A.D. 330, when it was re-named Constantinople; in 1930 it became Istanbul. Byzantium was the capital and holy city of Eastern Christendom from the late fourth century until 1453. Yeats never visited the city. The mosaics described in the poem are probably inspired by mosaics in the church of S. Apollinare Nuovo in Ravenna, which Yeats had visited in 1907. Yeats also saw Byzantine mosaics in the cathedrals at Monreale and Cefalu in Sicily in 1925.

Yeats in *A Vision* wrote: 'I think if I could be given a month of Antiquity and leave to spend it where I chose, I would spend it in Byzantium, a little before Justinian opened St Sophia and closed the Academy of Plato... I think that in early Byzantium, maybe never before or since in recorded history, religious, aesthetic and practical life were one, that architect and artificers... spoke to the multitude and the few alike.'

Line 1 That: Ireland – rejected by Yeats because it represents the temporal and natural world.

Line 3 dying generations: an effective rhetorical device known as an oxymoron.

Line 5 commend: praise, celebrate; 'Fish, flesh, or fowl' commend their life-cycle and death.

Line 7 sensual: worldly; not intellectual or spiritual.

Line 9 paltry: worthless, unimportant.

Line 10 tattered coat: an old man is like a scarecrow; in his poem 'Among School Children', Yeats says that old men are 'Old clothes upon old sticks to scare a bird'.

Line 10/11 unless/ Soul clap its hands and sing: poet William Blake (1757–1827) claims to have seen his brother's soul flying Heavenwards and clapping its hands for joy.

Line 13 Nor is there singing school but studying: the only singing school is studying.

Line 17 sages: wise men.

Line 19 perne in a gyre: spinning/whirling in a spiral, coiling motion, so that his soul may merge with the spiralling motion and thus enter a timeless world and leave behind the natural and historical world. Yeats made the word 'perne' from the Scots word 'pirn', meaning a reel, bobbin, spool. Augustine Martin, commenting on this line, wrote that Yeats 'asks the figures in the mosaic to come back to him through time and teach him the perfection of Byzantium and finally gather his soul into the eternity of art.'

Line 29 Emperor: 'I have,' wrote Yeats, 'read somewhere that in the Emperor's palace at Byzantium was a tree made of gold and silver, and artificial birds that sang.'

Line 32 past, or passing, or to come: Yeats, intensely aware of transience and mortality, longed for eternity; the golden bird, in eternity, sings of the passing of time.

'Sailing to Byzantium' is the first poem in Yeats's 1928 collection *The Tower*, a collection which, Yeats admitted, astonished him by its bitterness when he re-read it. MacLiammóir and Boland argue that what Yeats saw as 'mere bitterness was viewed by certain critics as an immortal fury against the tragedy of decay, the inevitability of death. And it is this emotion that evokes in his mind a bizarre, strangely assured speculation on life after death in 'Sailing to Byzantium'. There he celebrates what man can create, and rejects the way in which man himself has been created, the ill-starred slave of his inevitable passing into dust.'

Yeats has said of this poem that he was 'trying to write about the state of [his] soul, for it is right for an old man to make his soul'.

? Questions

1. Why do you think Yeats chose the word 'sailing' to describe the journey? Read the note on Byzantium and sum up in your own words why you think Yeats wants to go there.

2. If you were to edit out certain lines from the opening stanza, so that it read 'The young/ In one another's arms, birds in the trees... The salmon-falls, the mackerel-crowded seas ... all summer long... ', what impression would the reader be presented with? Now read the stanza as Yeats wrote it. What has happened to those beautiful, sensual images? Why does Yeats reject them?

3. Why does Yeats value 'monuments of unageing intellect' so highly? What is Yeats's view of Ireland and its destiny in relation to art?

4. Is it clear from the poem that the journey is a metaphorical or imagined one rather than an actual one? Give reasons for your answer.

5. Which details do you think emphasise Yeats's old age?

6. Music and singing are referred to in each of the four stanzas. Comment on this and its significance.

7. The poem has a very regular, patterned rhyme scheme. Is this obvious? What is the effect of the run-on line?

8. Yeats, in line 2, speaks of 'birds in the trees'; in the final stanza he speaks of a golden bird upon a golden bough. Compare and contrast these birds and say why one has replaced the other. Why should the golden bird, out of nature, out of time, sing of the passing of time? Are there similarities between the wild swans and the golden bird? Why has a city replaced the natural world?

9. The poet John Montague has praised 'Sailing to Byzantium' for its defiance and clangour. Discuss these qualities in the poem.

10. In 'The Lake Isle of Innisfree' and 'Sailing to Byzantium', Yeats imagines being in an ideal world. What are the essential differences between the two? Which one would you prefer and why?

from Meditations in Time of Civil War

VI

The Stare's Nest by My Window

The bees build in the crevices
Of loosening masonry, and there
The mother birds bring grubs and flies.
My wall is loosening; honey-bees,
Come build in the empty house of the stare.   5

We are closed in, and the key is turned
On our uncertainty; somewhere
A man is killed, or a house burned,
Yet no clear fact to be discerned:
Come build in the empty house of the stare.   10

A barricade of stone or of wood;
Some fourteen days of civil war;
Last night they trundled down the road
That dead young soldier in his blood:
Come build in the empty house of the stare.   15

We had fed the heart on fantasies,
The heart's grown brutal from the fare;
More substance in our enmities
Than in our love; O honey-bees,
Come build in the empty house of the stare.   20

📖 Glossary

Title Stare: starling, bird with blackish-brown feathers.

Line 3 grubs: larvae of insect, caterpillar, maggot.

Line 12 civil war: the Irish Civil War (1922–3) was fought between those who supported and rejected the Anglo-Irish Treaty (1922); the treaty stated that six counties would remain within the United Kingdom.

Line 13 trundled: wheeled, rolled.

Line 17 the fare: being fed (on fantasies).

Line 18 enmities: hatreds, hostilities, ill-will.

Meditations in Time of Civil War is a sequence of seven poems, each with a separate title: I Ancestral Houses; II My House; III My Table; IV My Descendants; V The Road at my Door; VI The Stare's Nest by My Window; VII I see Phantoms of Hatred and of the Heart's Fullness and of the Coming Emptiness. Poems II to VII were written at Thoor Ballylee during the Irish Civil War of 1922 and were first published in *The Dial* in January 1923.

Yeats, in a note to the poem 'The Stare's Nest by my Window', wrote: 'I was in my Galway house [Thoor Ballylee] during the first months of civil war, the railway bridges blown up and the roads blocked with stones and trees. For the first week there were no newspapers, no reliable news, we did not know who had won nor who had lost, and even after newspapers came, one never knew what was happening on the other side of the hill or of the line of trees. Ford cars passed the house from time to time with coffins standing upon end between the seats, and sometimes at night we heard an explosion, and once by day saw the smoke made by the burning of a great neighbouring house. Men must have lived so through many tumultuous centuries.

One felt an overmastering desire not to grow unhappy or embittered, not to lose all sense of the beauty of nature. A stare (our West of Ireland name for a starling) had built in a hole beside my window and I made these verses out of the feeling of the moment… Presently a strange thing happened. I began to smell honey in places where honey could not be, at the end of a stone passage or at some windy turn of the road…'

? Questions

1. Pick out those words in the opening stanza which you would consider negative and positive. Does a positive or negative feeling predominate?

2. What is Yeats's mood in line 5? The line is repeated three times. What is the effect of this?

3. In stanza 1, the poet looks at little details – crevices, grubs and flies, an empty nest. What happens in the second and third stanzas?

4. How does Yeats suggest a sense of fear, uncertainty, violence in lines 6–15? What is Yeats's reaction? Can it be summed up in the final line of each stanza?

5. In 'The Lake Isle of Innisfree', Yeats speaks of 'a hive for the honey-bee'. What do both poems say about the natural world? Is nature viewed the same or differently in both poems?

6. The final stanza focuses on fantasies and hatred. Why has the heart grown brutal, according to Yeats? Is he referring to something similar in 'Easter 1916' when he speaks in that poem of how hearts can turn to stone?

7. 'Come build... Come build... Come build.' What is the effect of 'O' in the final stanza, when Yeats writes 'O honey-bees,/ Come build in the empty house of the stare'?

8. 'There must be many millions all over the world who make the same prayer for honey-bees to come to the empty house', says the novelist Penelope Fitzgerald. What do you think she means by this?.

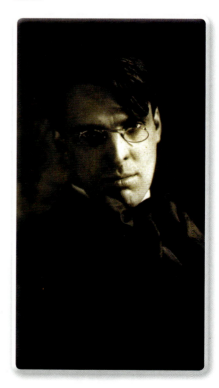

In Memory of Eva Gore-Booth and Con Markiewicz

The light of evening, Lissadell,
Great windows open to the south,
Two girls in silk kimonos, both
Beautiful, one a gazelle.
But a raving autumn shears   5
Blossom from the summer's wreath;
The older is condemned to death,
Pardoned, drags out lonely years
Conspiring among the ignorant.
I know not what the younger dreams—   10
Some vague Utopia—and she seems,
When withered old and skeleton-gaunt,
An image of such politics.
Many a time I think to seek
One or the other out and speak   15
Of that old Georgian mansion, mix
Pictures of the mind, recall
That table and the talk of youth,
Two girls in silk kimonos, both
Beautiful, one a gazelle.   20

Dear shadows, now you know it all,
All the folly of a fight
With a common wrong or right.
The innocent and the beautiful
Have no enemy but time;   25
Arise and bid me strike a match
And strike another till time catch;
Should the conflagration climb,
Run till all the sages know.
We the great gazebo built,   30
They convicted us of guilt;
Bid me strike a match and blow.

October 1927

Glossary

Title Eva Gore-Booth and Con Markiewicz: Eva and Constance Gore-Booth, sisters, were born into a world of privilege. Eva (1870–1926) became a political activist, an ardent socialist and poet. She moved to Manchester in 1922 and devoted herself to the women's trade union movement, feminism, socialism and pacifism. She died of cancer.

Countess Markiewicz: Constance Gore-Booth of Lissadell, County Sligo, Irish nationalist and first British woman MP, was born in 1868 in London. The family home was Lissadell in County Sligo and, though she was privileged and wealthy, she was unconventional. Stephen Coote, in *W.B. Yeats: A Life*, writes that Constance Gore-Booth 'was to play a wholly remarkable part in the struggle for Irish independence and, from her earliest days, when she invited the bare-footed peasant children home for tea, she had shown her instinctive defiance of convention and sympathy for the poor.'

A beautiful woman, she studied art in London and Paris, where she met and married the Polish count Casimir Markiewicz in 1900. They moved to Dublin in 1903 and in 1908 she joined Sinn Fein and became a friend of Maud Gonne. In 1916 Countess Markiewicz fought in the Easter Rising and was sentenced to death; the death sentence was reprieved in the 1917 amnesty. In 1918 she was elected Sinn Fein MP for the St Patrick's division of Dublin – thus becoming the first British woman MP – but she refused to take her seat, in line with Sinn Fein policy. In 1919 she was elected to the first Dáil and was appointed Minister for Labour. She was imprisoned twice. Following the Civil War she was a member of Dáil Éireann from 1923. She died in 1927. Yeats also writes about Countess Markiewicz in his poem 'On a Political Prisoner'.

Line 1 Lissadell: Lissadell House, a large Grecian-Revival house on the northern shore of Sligo Bay, was built 1830–1835 for Sir Robert Gore-Booth MP. During the Famine, Robert Gore-Booth mortgaged his estate so as to be able to feed everyone for miles around. Yeats first visited this ascendancy house in November 1894. Yeats was impressed by the aristocratic way of life, its grace and ease, but Constance and Eva were to leave that world behind when they became politically active as suffragettes and socialists.

Line 4 one a gazelle: Eva (a gazelle is a small, graceful, soft-eyed antelope).

Line 5 raving: howling, roaring.

Line 5 shears: cuts.

Line 7 The older: Constance was two years older than Eva.

Line 9 conspiring: plotting something unlawful; Constance was a political activist who trained the Fianna Scouts, worked with Fianna Fail Clubs and joined the Citizen Army in 1914.

Line 10 the younger dreams: Eva Gore-Booth studied philosophy and mystical literature.

Line 11 Utopia: an ideal world, an imaginary state (from ou, not, topos, a place).

Line 28 conflagration: great and destructive fire.

Line 30 gazebo: Seamus Heaney says: 'A summer house in the grounds of Lissadell; but equally important is the gazebo's association with a point of view that is spacious, contemplative and unconstrained.' Augustine Martin thinks 'gazebo' may refer to the decorative, non-utilitarian contribution of the Anglo-Irish to Irish life, for which some of them – not the Gore-Booths – were punished in the burning of their mansions by 'incendiary or bigot'.

Line 31 They convicted us of guilt: they, meaning the Catholics, felt the Protestant Ascendancy class should feel guilty for being Protestant.

This poem, the first in Yeats's 1933 collection *The Winding Stair and Other Poems*, has been described as 'a poignant recall of a passing time, its later ravages, the withering of dreams and the arrested pictures of young beauty' by Niall McCarthy in *Lifelines*. The Cork-based poet Thomas McCarthy also chose this poem by Yeats as his favourite in the same anthology. McCarthy praises the poem for 'its spectacularly beautiful opening images, the kimonos, the south-facing windows – but also for its maturity of insight and its underlying sadness'.

In a letter, dated 23 July 1916, to Eva Gore-Booth, Yeats wrote that 'Your sister and yourself, two beautiful figures among the great trees of Lissadell, are among the dear memories of my youth'. Eva Gore-Booth died in 1926 and Con Markiewicz died in August 1927. This poem is dated 21 September 1927 in manuscript but the date October 1927 is given in the *Collected Poems*.

Eva and Constance Gore-Booth when they lived at Lissadell.

? Questions

1. How does Yeats conjure up a magical and beautiful series of pictures in the opening four lines of this poem? Pick out those words which, in your opinion, are particularly effective. How is the feeling of leisure and ease conveyed? How different would it be if it were the light of morning?

2. What effect does Yeats achieve by the abrupt change at line 5?

3. A harsh reality is conveyed through sound and imagery in lines 7–13. Pick out those details which, in your opinion, best capture such harshness.

4. Is it possible to say how Yeats feels about what happened to these two beautiful women? Why does the image of the skeleton serve as an image of both Eva and her politics? Why does he want to seek out one or the other and speak of the past? Why should he prefer 'pictures of the mind' and to recall the past rather than the present?

5. If you were to paint pictures of the first twenty lines, what colours would you need? What movements? What settings?

6. 'Dear shadows, now you know it all' (line 21). What does this line tell us? How would you describe his tone towards the sisters here?

7. How would you describe this second stanza? How does it differ from the first? Look at the images. Why are lines 24–25 so important within the poem as a whole?

8. Yeats never took up arms. The Gore-Booth sisters did. How does Yeats view these women and what they dedicated their lives to? What does he ask their ghosts to do in the second stanza? What do you understand by his wish to burn time? Who is Yeats referring to when he says 'they' in line 31?

9. Yeats begins with the distancing phrase 'Two girls'; in line 21 he speaks to them as 'you'; in the closing lines Yeats switches to 'We'. What is the significance of this in your opinion?

10. Both 'Easter 1916' and 'In Memory of Eva Gore-Booth and Con Markiewicz' are elegies, one a public one, the other private, but in both Yeats speaks of politics and public involvement. Are his attitudes similar in both poems?

Constance Gore-Booth (Countess Markievicz) shortly before the 1916 rising.

Swift's Epitaph

Swift has sailed into his rest;
Savage indignation there
Cannot lacerate his breast.
Imitate him if you dare,
World-besotted traveller; he   5
Served human liberty.

📖 Glossary

Line Title Swift: Dean Jonathan Swift (1667–1745), satirist and clergyman, author of *Gulliver's Travels*. Born in Dublin of English parents, educated at Kilkenny Grammar School and Trinity College

Line Title Epitaph: an inscription for a stone or tomb (literally 'over a tomb'). Yeats considered Swift's epitaph the finest he knew.

Line 3 lacerate: tear, mangle, wound (Swift's Latin epigraph says that his body lies where 'saeva Indignatio/ Ulterius/ Cor lacerare nequit' – where savage indignation can no longer lacerate his heart').

This poem is a translation/version of the epitaph Swift wrote for himself, though Yeats added line 1 and the word 'World-besotted' (line 5) instead of 'Go Traveller', a literal translation of 'Abi Viator'. It can be seen in St Patrick's Cathedral Dublin, where Swift is buried:

Hic depositum est Corpus

IONATHAN SWIFT S.T.D.*

Hujus Ecclesiae Cathedralis

Decani,

Ubi saeva Indignatio

Ulterius

Cor lacerare nequit.

Abi Viator

Et imitare, si porteris,

Strenuum pro virili

Libertatis Vindicatorem

Obiit 19 Die Mensis Octobris

A.D. 1745 Anno Aetatis 78

* S[acrae] T[heologiae] D[octoris] – Doctor of Scared Theology

A literal translation of the above, by Elspeth Haren, reads as follows:

Here is laid the body

of JONATHAN SWIFT, Doctor of Theology,

of this cathedral church

Dean,

where furious disdain*

further

cannot rend the heart.

Go forth, traveller,

and imitate, should you be able,

one vigorous to his utmost

as a champion of freedom.

He died on the 19th day of the month of October

A.D. 1745 in the 78th year of his age.

* saeva Indignatio has been translated as 'savage indignation' by Yeats

? Questions

1. What qualities are being identified here by Swift in his own epitaph? Why do you think Yeats chose to translate it?

2. How would you describe the tone of this poem? Who is being addressed?

3. The first line is not a translation but Yeats's own. Why do you think Yeats added this line and chose to use the verb 'sailed'?

4. Yeats wrote this poem when he was sixty-five. Compare this epigraph by Swift with the one Yeats wrote himself for his own tombstone:

   Cast a cold Eye.
   On Life, on Death.
   Horseman, pass by!

Which one do you find the more personal? And the more interesting? Which one tells us more about the individual?

Jonathan Swift (1710) by Charles Jervas

similarly to the wild swans at coole — written in 1936. 3 b4 he ded
this poem talks about old age. In this poem yeats talks about
An unhappy life without dreams or desires. Rathfarnham
Dublin.

K piece of land

An Acre of Grass

alliteration

Picture and book remain,   *imagery. His house has been engulfed*
by old age. He moved + brought pic w him
An acre of green grass   *Reminds us of life. Green grass is juxtaposed*
For air and exercise,   *with his life.*
Alliteration
A
Now strength of body goes;   *The spirit of his body is gone.*
Midnight, an old house —   *Very quiet, sad image, on his own.*   5
Where nothing stirs but a mouse.   *fragile. His old age is v*
dark and lonely.

My temptation is quiet.   *He realises he has no temptations.*
Here at life's end   *Phase in life coming to an end.*
Neither loose imagination   *inability to focus*
imagery   alliteration   his minds   not   creative
Nor the mill of the mind   *Cognitive   mind   imagination   anything*   10
metaphore
Consuming its rag and bone,   *nothing left to give, no more*
Can make the truth known.   *material   as a poet*

Grant me an old man's frenzy,   *Sad at the thought of losing his*
Myself must I remake   *life now older. He wants to get*
Till I am Timon and Lear   *back to poetry like Timon + Lear.*   15
Or that William Blake   *He like (tried to keep) William Blake now how*
Who beat upon the wall   *easy was to lose ambition but kept going*
Till Truth obeyed his call;   *He's envious cas he cant do same.*
(copy)
Alliteration

A mind Michael Angelo knew   *Yeats wants emulate Michael.*
That can pierce the clouds,   *As he doesn't want to be forgotten*
by people.   20
Or inspired by frenzy
Shake the dead in their shrouds;   *Yeats will need the eye of*
Forgotten else by mankind,   *an eagle to come to grips with*
An old man's eagle mind.   *the reality of getting old. or*
he will be forgotten.

Very confessional poem. Theme of old age +
artistic revitalisation. Obsessed w getting old
but wants to write. Contrast between
acceptence of age + his determination to
be like Michael ext. wont accept he's old.
accepting at beginning then wants to get back
emphasizing loss + kindness of oldage.

Glossary

Title An Acre of Grass: this is a reference to Yeats's house in Riversdale in Rathfarnham, County Dublin. The acre in this instance is a garden containing tennis and croquet lawns and a bowling green. In letters written to Olivia Shakespear during the summer of 1932, Yeats described his new home as follows: 'apple trees, cheery trees, roses, smooth lawns'. … 'I shall have a big old fruit garden all to myself – the study opens into it and it is shut off from the flower garden and the croquet and tennis lawns and from the bowling-green.' The poem was written in November 1936 and was first published in April 1938 in *Atlantic Monthly and London Mercury*.

5 an old house: Riversdale, Rathfarnham, County Dublin.

13 frenzy: wild excitement; paroxysm of madness.

15 Timon and Lear: in Shakespeare's tragedies *Timon of Athens* and *King Lear,* the tragic heroes Timon and Lear ask questions about existence with a great raging anger. Augustine Martin, commenting on these lines, says that 'Timon and Lear question their place in the world with a ferocity and insistence akin to the "demonic rage" of such heroic artists as Blake and Michael Angelo.'

16 William Blake: English poet, painter, engraver and visionary (1757–1827).

19 Michael Angelo: Michelangelo di Lodovico Buonarroti Simoni (1475–1564), Italian sculptor, painter and poet.

22 shrouds: burial clothes.

Questions

1. What kind of life does Yeats describe in the first stanza? What mood is created in these opening lines?

2. How would you describe what Yeats discovers at his 'life's end'? Comment on Yeats's descriptions 'loose imagination' and 'the mill of the mind'.

3. Why do you think Yeats, in the third stanza, asks for a form of wild excitement or frenzy in his old age? Why does he find inspiration in the characters he names?

4. Explain in your own words what Yeats is saying in the closing two lines.

5. The poem begins quietly. Identify the words that give the poem a gathering sense of energy and momentum. Why is this appropriate to the poem's meaning?

6. Yeats believed that 'Man can embody truth but he cannot know it'. Is this reflected in this poem?

Politics

*'In our time the destiny of man presents its meaning
in political terms.' — Thomas Mann*

How can I, that girl standing there,
My attention fix
On Roman or on Russian
Or on Spanish politics?
Yet here's a travelled man that knows   5
What he talks about,
And there's a politician
That has read and thought,
And maybe what they say is true
Of war and war's alarms,   10
But O that I were young again
And held her in my arms!

📖 Glossary

epigraph: Thomas Mann (1875–1955), German novelist.

Line 10 alarms: sounds of danger.

Towards the end of his life, Yeats, in a letter to Dorothy Wellesley, dated 24 May 1938, wrote: 'There has been an article upon my work in the *Yale Review* which is the only article on the subject which has not bored me for years. It commends me above other modern poets because my language is "public". That word, which I had not thought of myself, is a word I want. Your language in "Fire" is "public", so is that of every good ballad . . . It goes on to say that, owing to my age and my relation to Ireland, I was unable to use this "public" language on what is evidently considered the right public material, politics. The enclosed little poem is my reply. It is not a real incident, but a moment of meditation.'

The version that Yeats included in that letter is as follows; a revised version appeared in *Last Poems*, published in 1939.

Politics

'In our time the destiny of man presents its meaning in political terms.'
(Thomas Mann)

Beside that window stands a girl;
I cannot fix my mind
On the analysis of things
That benumb mankind.

Yet one has travelled and may know
What he talks about;
And one's a politician

That has read and thought.
Maybe what they say is true
Of war and war's alarms;
But O that I were young again
And held her in my arms.

'Politics' was written on 23 May 1938 and was first published in January 1939 in the *Atlantic Monthly and London Mercury*. The day after he wrote it, Yeats explained the poem's origin in a letter to Olivia Shakespear. In Spring 1938, Archibald MacLeish, the American poet, had quoted Thomas Mann's words in his article 'Public Speech and Private Speech in Poetry'. Yeats was highly praised by MacLeish because his language was 'public' and Yeats, in his letter, says of the word 'public' – 'That word which I had not thought of myself is a word I want'. Then Yeats explains how the MacLeish article went on to say that 'owing to my age and my relation to Ireland, I was unable to use this "public" language on what it evidently considered the right public material, politics.'

In that same letter, dated 24 May 1938, Yeats says: 'The enclosed little poem is my reply. It is not a real incident, but a moment of meditation.' In a postscript, Yeats added 'No artesian well of the intellect can find the poetic theme', which shows, according to Daniel Albright, that 'Politics' is a meditation on the propriety of themes for poems. Yeats placed 'Politics' as the final poem in *Last Poems*, his 1939 collection; Albright adds that 'its placement at the end of Yeats's last volume of poems makes it a kind of valediction: and it fulfils this role, first by dismissing every topical theme in favour of the most universal, and second by its deliberate appeal to one of the oldest and most famous lyrics, the anonymous 'Westron Wind':

Westron Wind
Westron winde, when wilt thou blow,
The small raine downe can raine?
Christ if my love were in my armes,
And I in my bed againe.

? Questions

1. Why does Yeats dismiss politics and what does he choose to value instead?

2. In this poem, Yeats wishes for love and youth to return. Does he convince you that love and youth are all that matter?

3. Yeats was seventy-three when he wrote this poem, a year before he died. Does our knowing this cast a different light on the poem?

4. Why do you think Yeats quoted Thomas Mann's words? How do they influence your reading of the poem?

from Under Ben Bulben V, VI

V

Irish poets, learn your trade,
Sing whatever is well made,
Scorn the sort now growing up
All out of shape from toe to top,
Their unremembering hearts and heads 5
Base-born products of base beds.
Sing the peasantry, and then
Hard-riding country gentlemen,
The holiness of monks, and after
Porter-drinkers' randy laughter; 10
Sing the lords and ladies gay
That were beaten into the clay
Through seven heroic centuries;
Cast your mind on other days
That we in coming days may be 15
Still the indomitable Irishry.

VI

Under bare Ben Bulben's head
In Drumcliff churchyard Yeats is laid.
An ancestor was rector there
Long years ago, a church stands near, 20
By the road an ancient cross.
No marble, no conventional phrase;
On limestone quarried near the spot
By his command these words are cut:

> *Cast a cold eye*
> *On life, on death.*
> *Horseman, pass by!*

4 September 1938

📖 Glossary

Line 7/8 Sing the peasantry, and then/ Hard-riding country gentlemen: elsewhere in his poetry ('At Galway Races' and 'The Fisherman'), Yeats praises and addresses the horsemen and fisherman.

Line 16 indomitable: not to be overcome, stubbornly persistent.

Line 17 Under bare Ben Bulben's head: Yeats, in a letter dated 22 August 1938, wrote: 'I am arranging my burial place. It will be in a little remote country churchyard in Sligo where my great grandfather was the clergyman a hundred years ago. Just my name and dates and these lines: Cast a cold eye/ On life on death;/ Horseman pass by'.

Line 19 ancestor: Reverend John Yeats (1774–1846), Yeats's great-grandfather, was rector of Drumcliff, County Sligo, from 1805 until his death; he was a friend of Robert Emmet (1778–1803) who was hanged in 1803 for his involvement in the fight for Irish freedom.

Line 27 Horseman: in the first section of 'Under Ben Bulben', Yeats speaks of visionary horsemen; an old family servant, Mary Battle, claimed to have seen these figures and described them to Yeats. Daniel Albright says that 'It is significant that a poem that begins with supernatural horsemen should end with this address – almost a challenge. Yeats seems to have attained such a comprehensive view of life and death that he is on equal terms with the unearthly riders of Part I.' Albright also points out that much of 'Under Ben Bulben' is written in catalectic trochaic tetrameter, a metre proper to charms and incantations ('Eye of newt and toe of frog' – *Macbeth* [the witches' spell]).

These two sections, V and VI, are the final sections from a longer poem dated 4 September 1938 and which was first published on 3 February 1939 in the *Irish Times*, *Irish Independent* and *Irish Press*.

Stephen Coote in his biography of Yeats tells of how 'The night before Yeats left Ireland for the last time he read "Under Ben Bulben" aloud to F. R. Higgins. The evening came to an end and "we parted", Higgins recalled, "on the drive from his house. The head of the retiring figure, erect and challenging, gleamed through the darkness as I turned back; while on the road before me my thoughts were still ringing out with the slow powerful accents of his chanting".'

? Questions

1. In this poem, why does Yeats speak directly to Irish poets and why does he refer to contemporary poetry? Does the poem itself illustrate his ideas?

2. How would you describe Yeats's tone here? How does he view his Irishness?

3. What sense of time is created in these lines? What is the significance of 'seven heroic centuries' (line 13)?

4. This poem is written in a rhythm used for charms and incantations. Why do you think Yeats chose such a rhythmic pattern here?

5. What do we learn about Yeats the man and Yeats the poet in this poem? Do you think this poem a suitable and appropriate late poem?

6. Looking back over these poems by Yeats on your course, do you think that Yeats himself 'cast a cold eye on life, on death'?

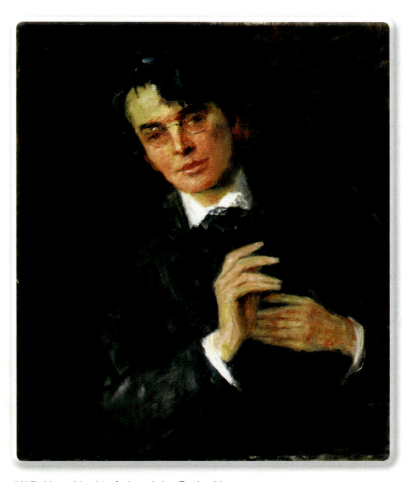

'W.B. Yeats' by his father John Butler Yeats

General Questions

A. 'In his poetry, Yeats explores public and private themes through powerful imagery.' Discuss this view in the light of your reading of the poems by Yeats on your course. Support the points you make with the aid of suitable quotation or reference.

B. 'Yeats is remarkable both for what he has to say and for the way he says it.' Would you agree with this view? In your answer, you should support the points you make with relevant quotation from or reference to the poems by Yeats on your course.

C. What would you consider the principal preoccupations of W.B. Yeats, as revealed to us in his poetry? Support your discussion by quotation from or reference to the poems you have studied.

D. In Yeats's poetry, 'the defiant self is pitted against hostile or disabling conditions'. Discuss this statement, supporting your answer by quotation from or reference to the poems by Yeats on your course.

E. 'Symbolism in Yeats's poetry is strong and memorable.' Discuss this view, supporting the points you make by relevant quotation from or reference to the poems by Yeats on your course.

F. According to Seamus Heaney, 'Command' has characterised the Yeatsian style. Examine how Yeats creates and achieves this tone of command in the poems on your course.

G. Write a short essay on those aspects of the poems by Yeats on your course that you found most interesting.

H. 'Though Yeats's poetry is rooted in the particular, it also achieves a universality.' Would you agree with this view? In your answer, you should support the points you make with quotation from or reference to the poems by Yeats on your course.

I. 'W.B. Yeats is both a personal and political poet.' Discuss this view, supporting your answer by quotation from or reference to the poems by Yeats on your course.

W.B. Yeats in old age.

Critical Commentary

The Lake Isle of Innisfree

Human nature is such that we have all known the desire to escape to a quieter, more beautiful world. For Yeats it is an island on a lake in Co. Sligo, but what is even more important than place is the feeling which the poem contains. Innisfree, as described by Yeats, is beautiful and tranquil but equally significant is the desire to be elsewhere.

The poem adopts a deliberately quaint, old-fashioned style. Yeats does not simply say 'I'll go to Innisfree'; he lends the occasion a ceremony and seriousness with the expression 'I will arise and go now, and go to Innisfree'. It has been pointed out that 'I will arise' are words spoken by the prodigal son in Luke xv. 18, and Yeats uses here this archaic expression, a type of language he soon abandoned. In a letter dated 30 November 1922, Yeats, looking back to 'Innisfree', told some schoolgirls that 'A couple of years later I would not have written that first line with its conventional archaism — "Arise and go" — nor the inversion in the last stanza', though in that same letter Yeats also admitted that 'Innisfree' was 'my first lyric with anything in its rhythm of my own music'.

There is a timelessness about the poem. Even though we know that Yeats was prompted to write the poem in a London Street in 1888, the only contemporary detail in the poem is 'pavements grey'. All other descriptions – the clay and wattle cabin, the bean-rows and bee hive, the birdsong cannot – date the poem to a particular century or age.

The long line gives the poem a stately, leisured tone: the opening words are formal, the repetition of 'go', the Latinate structure, for example, of line 2 (Yeats does not say 'I will build a small cabin there, made of clay and wattles'), the repeated 'there' in line 3, 'peace' in line 5, 'dropping' in line 6, and the very regular end-rhyme all create a very elevated, heightened, musical expression of longing. The voice is deliberate rather than casual.

The poem imagines Innisfree so vividly that the description dominates the poem. Everything, at first, is future tense: 'I will arise . . .'; 'will I have there'; 'I shall have some peace there . . .', but the world of Innisfree is so convincingly portrayed that the poet ends with the present tense. Though Yeats is standing on the 'pavements grey', he hears the lake water lapping. So deep is his sense of longing that he hears it deep in his heart.

Colour, sounds, textures combine to make the world of the poem. If there is a feeling of immediacy, of 'now', the present moment, in stanza 1, there is a sense of a never-ending time in the middle stanza, when Yeats describes the regular rhythm of the day, from dawn to noon to midnight. The eye sees only beauty; the ear hears only beautiful sounds.

The final stanza of the poem is atmospheric in its evocation of the sound of lake water and the contrast between Lough Gill and the London roadway or grey pavements is striking. Line 10 is an excellent example of how alliteration and assonance can achieve such effect:

> I hear **la** ke water **la** pping with l**o**w sounds by the sh**o** re

Yeats was in his early twenties when he began working on this poem. He wrote it in London, but it illustrates how Yeats's heart was in Ireland and how the imagination can create the ideal.

September 1913

This is a public poem prompted by a public event and Yeats is expressing a personal opinion in public. The title is factual and roots the poem in a particular time in Irish history. Yeats was deeply disillusioned by the Irish, especially the wealthy middle class, who had refused to support the housing of the Hugh Lane pictures and in general were mercenary, small-minded and without vision.

The opening stanza is scathing and ironic. The people he addresses are portrayed in an ugly light. They are without dignity or beauty; they are miserly and money, for them, is equated to prayer:

> What need you, being come to sense,
> But fumble in a greasy till
> And add the halfpence to the pence
> And prayer to shivering prayer, until
> You have dried the marrow from the bone?

Line 6 is deeply ironic:

> For men were born to pray and save

Yeats does not believe that men should give their lives to cautious praying and saving, saving their souls or saving their money or both. Perhaps Yeats intended to pun on pray/prey? These middle-class hoarders are, in the academic Alexander Davis's words, 'caught within an economy that, however much it breeds or saves, results in a form of death'.

An ideal Irishman, for Yeats, is John O'Leary and it is against such a figure that all others are measured. A romantic Ireland is an Ireland whose people are fired with ideas and idealism. In 1913, Yeats felt that there was no such energy or fiery optimism within the people; there were no individuals who would inspire and lead Ireland:

> Romantic Ireland's dead and gone,
> It's with O'Leary in the grave.

Yeats's tone is bitter and dismissive at the outset. The language is crisp, the images vivid. It is, in Eavan Boland's words, a poem of 'political disillusion' in which 'Yeats laments the loss of the Ireland he associated with the Fenian leader John O'Leary.' Boland also points out that part of the poem's power is in Yeats's use of the iambic tetrameter, a four foot, four stress line. It's the ballad metre, a very old form which is powerful in the telling of a story. Boland says that Yeats used it 'for the kind of poem which has a forceful argument but not a complicated idea behind it' and the poet has 'a lot of music, incantation and repetition'.

The idea is simple and straightforward: Yeats is deeply disappointed and disillusioned with the present and he compares the Ireland of now with the Ireland of the past. Having named John O'Leary, Yeats then opens up the past and offers a wide historical perspective to include Irish heroes over centuries and generations.

The simple word 'Yet' at the beginning of stanza 2 signals a different tone. Here, Yeats recognises a different kind of Irish man and regrets their passing. There were others, who, like John O'Leary, were willing to give their lives to Ireland.

> Yet they were of a different kind,
> The names that stilled your childish play

Here, Yeats does acknowledge that these heroes, their very names, once 'stilled' their 'childish play'; in other words, Ireland's past heroes once impressed, but the people of 1913 have, in Irish academic Terence Brown's words, 'lost their childhood capacity for wonder'. Once they were in awe of these heroic names; they were 'stilled'.

> Those heroes from the past were selfless and reckless:
> They have gone about the world like wind,
> But little time had they to pray
> For whom the hangman's rope was spun

The image of the wind catches the power and force of their commitment; the image of the rope being spun captures a sense of inevitability and destiny and sacrifice. And what Yeats emphasises here is the difference between them and those who are now so preoccupied with praying and saving. The colloquial, heartfelt, exasperated utterance in line 14:

> And what, God help us, could they save?

This highlights Yeats's despair, the implication being that those who died for Ireland were so giving that they were incapable of saving anything. What the academic Terence Brown calls the 'heady refrain' is repeated:

> Romantic Ireland's dead and gone,
> It's with O'Leary in the grave.

This gives the poem a momentum. The poet Eavan Boland identifies the rhymes and 'that strong artillery' of short lines' as qualities which make it 'a very catchy poem'. It is 'a bitter, cantankerous' poem, says Boland, but it is also a poem, she points out, which is very traditional and disciplined in its form.

The third stanza focuses on particular events and individuals whose story became Ireland's story. The Wild Geese, in their thousands, fought passionately for a cause; Edward Fitzgerald, Robert Emmet and Wolfe Tone lived and died for Ireland. The naming of names here gives the poem an energy and authenticity. Yeats's tone is incredulous ('Was it for this. . . . For this . . . For this . . .') and admiring. He names them with respect and admiration. These names from the history books focus the mind and Yeats's condemnation of the present is all the more strong.

The question asked in lines 17–22 is rhetorical:

> Was it for this the wild geese spread
> The grey wing upon every tide;
> For this that all that blood was shed,
> For this Edward Fitzgerald died,
> And Robert Emmet and Wolfe Tone,
> All that delirium of the brave?

In other words, the answer is implied and the repeated 'this' is indicative of Yeats's disappointment and disillusionment with the times.

Their passion and dedication is summed up in the line:

> All that delirium of the brave?

This is very different from the poem's opening line with its ironic reference to 'sense'. The poem measures sense against madness, caution against delirium and the fumbling, shivering individual versus the romantic hero. The structure of the poem also strengthens the poet's argument. Yeats first presents his reader with the dull and narrow present against a colourful and heroic past and by so doing emphasises Ireland's loss.

Having considered the present and the past, 'September 1913', in its final stanza, imagines a different present. Yeats asks how would those heroes be received if they were living now:

> Yet could we turn the years again
> And call those exiles as they were
> In all their loneliness and pain,
> You'd cry, 'Some woman's yellow hair
> Has maddened every mother's son':

Such heroic men would be mocked and denigrated, says Yeats, by the modern Irish middle class. Their noble motives would be misinterpreted and debased. Their 'delirium of the brave', their devotion, would be reduced to their infatuation with Ireland but belittled here in the image of a 'woman's yellow hair'.

Line 30 portrays Ireland's romantic visionaries as selfless and giving:

> They weighed so lightly what they gave.

They did not measure or weigh up what it was they were so willing to give. Their generosity of spirit did not allow them to view their lives in a calculating way.

The unforgettable refrain takes a different form in the closing lines. With John O'Leary, Romantic Ireland died; the others are also dead and perhaps it is best that they are 'in the grave'. Yeats's bitter, angry tone has given way to acceptance. Ireland has had a gloriously heroic past; the present is uninspiring; the future is not even mentioned.

The Wild Swans at Coole

The poem's title announces a natural grandeur: wild swans on Coole Lake in the west of Ireland is essentially a romantic image. Yeats wrote the poem in 1916, when he was fifty-one, and Yeats's own mood matches the autumn mood. The day is dying, the year is dying and the opening lines capture both the beauty and the sadness of autumn:

> The trees are in their autumn beauty,
> The woodland paths are dry,
> Under the October twilight the water
> Mirrors a still sky

The image of the trees is a stately, dignified one; the world is still; the rhythm is slow, the mood meditative. The poet observes in a detached, almost impersonal way:

> Upon the brimming water among the stones
> Are nine-and-fifty swans.

Counting is a mechanical activity but the 'nine-and-fifty' in this instance might prompt an emotional response in that fifty-eight of the swans are possibly paired and one is without a mate. Swans are magnificent and Michael Schmidt sums up their qualities when, speaking of the wild swans in Yeats's poem, he says that: 'They're natural, beautiful, powerful; most important, they return, they have a noble freedom and a noble permanence'.

Yeats's sadness is revealed indirectly in the first stanza in his being drawn towards twilight and the season, but stanza 2 introduces a more direct, personal note:

> The nineteenth autumn has come upon me
> Since I first made my count;
> I saw, before I had well finished,
> All suddenly mount
> And scatter wheeling in great broken rings
> Upon their clamorous wings.

Biographical detail tells us that when Yeats first visited Coole Park nineteen years before he was deeply depressed by his unhappy love affair with Maud Gonne. Now, at fifty-one, he is reminded of that earlier sorrow, a sorrow that has increased in the intervening years. The mood changes with the abrupt, sudden, unexpected movement of the swans. The strong, active verbs 'mount', 'scatter', the adjectives 'great broken' and 'clamorous' fill the poem with sound and serve as a striking contrast to the silence and stillness of stanza 1.

Yeats's description of himself in relation to the passing of time is passive in the line 'The nineteenth autumn has come upon me'; it is as if the years weigh upon him. The swans are active, powerful and filled with energy.

In the third stanza, the poet speaks of the great change in his life between his first visit to Coole and this visit. He is at his most personal:

> I have looked upon those brilliant creatures,
> And now my heart is sore.
> All's changed since I, hearing at twilight,
> The first time on this shore,
> The bell-beat of their wings above my head,
> Trod with a lighter tread.

He speaks of 'my heart', how 'All's changed'.
The sound of the swans' wings can be heard in that atmospheric line:

> The **bell-beat** of **their wings** above **my head**

This line has a strong and regular beat. Yeats remembers how nineteen years ago, when he first heard their bell-beat, he trod more lightly, his heart lifted.

For Yeats the swans represent or symbolise tireless continuity ('Unwearied still'), togetherness ('lover by lover'), youth ('their hearts have not grown old'), passion. What Yeats says indirectly here is that he himself is weary, old, alone. Passion and conquest will stay with the swans forever.

The final stanza offers a tranquil, calm picture of the wild swans upon the brimming water once again. Two words – 'Mysterious, beautiful' – sum them up:

> But now they drift on the still water,
> Mysterious, beautiful

And the poem ends with Yeats acknowledging that the swans will continue to delight. Their love will continue; others will witness it, even if Yeats will not:

> Among what rushes will they build,
> By what lake's edge or pool
> Delight men's eyes when I awake some day
> To find they have flown away?

Terence Brown says of these closing lines that Yeats imagines the swans 'in their freedom, flown away, leaving him'. Yeats is left with a heavier heart and in Brown's words 'the changes experienced in a personal autumn will be superseded by those of winter'.

Critical Commentary

An Irish Airman Foresees his Death

Yeats here is writing in the voice of a persona, that of thirty-seven year old Major Robert Gregory, who died in action on the Italian front in 1918. There is a tone of certainty and determination, a feeling of the inevitable from the outset. In the writer Stephen Booth's words, 'Yeats here presented a concise but evocative image of the war in the skies' and, according to Booth, 'There is a feeling that the speaker of the poem is already a partly disembodied spirit, a soul about to begin its "dreaming back"'.

Yeats is writing from hindsight, but Gregory did die in battle and this allows Yeats to allow his persona to speak with foresight. The four-foot line, the tetrameter, is used throughout, and this, together with the regular rhyme, gives the poem an urgency. From the poem's opening words:

> I know that I shall meet my fate

there is a sense of an individual confronting his destiny; that doom is his destiny is clear from the poem's title. The Irish airman is caught up in a war, but there is confusion in his thinking: he fights with the British against the Germans but claims that his real affiliation is with his native Galway. He does not hate the Germans; he does not love Britain. That he associates himself with a particular, local place and its people helps to create an image of Gregory as an unassuming and sympathetic man.

The pronoun 'I' is used six times in the opening four lines and is only used once again towards the end of the poem. This emphasis on himself gives way to a consideration of his allegiances, false and true; the repetition of 'My' reveals his true commitment. It also allows him to examine the reasons for his involvement in the war. Those whom he cares most about will be unaffected by the outcome:

> No likely end could bring them loss
> Or leave them happier than before.

This leads him to admit his reason for becoming an airman. First he rejects the more obvious reasons – 'law', 'duty', 'public men', 'the cheering crowd' – and then the speaker presents us with the haunting romantic explanation:

> A lonely impulse of delight
> Drove to this tumult in the clouds

The poem ends with a calculated, clear, understanding mind at work: 'I balanced all, brought all to mind' – the very balance of the lines acting out the balanced decision. The choice was a considered one, though it began as 'an impulse of delight'. The past and the future are seen as 'a waste of breath', the immediate repetition of the phrase stressing the futility felt. 'This life' is the life of young Major Robert Gregory. Losing one's life in battle is one thing, but that the speaker loses his life because he is drawn to a tumult in the clouds colours the experience differently. The final word in the poem is Gregory's final moment – 'death'.

Easter 1916

This poem is remarkable for many reasons, not least because it shows us that Yeats was not afraid to admit that he was wrong, that he could change his mind. In 'September 1913' he denounced the middle class for their cautious selfishness and argued that Romantic Ireland was 'dead and gone'; in 'Easter 1916' he takes that back and admits that he misjudged them. The Easter Rising was an apparent failure but signalled the beginning of modern Ireland and the making of a Republic. Yeats was not in Ireland at the time of The Rising and in a letter to Lady Gregory, dated 11 May 1916, he spoke of the 'Dublin tragedy' as 'a great sorrow and anxiety' and of how he 'had no idea that any public event could so deeply move me'. In that same letter, he confessed that 'I am very despondent about the future' and that he was 'trying to write a poem on the men executed – "terrible beauty has been born again"'.

The poem begins with a Dublin streetscape in which the poet passes those who were to fight in The Easter Rising and sacrifice their lives for Ireland. The backdrop is grey but their faces in the street are animated and 'vivid':

> I have met them at close of day
> Coming with vivid faces
> From counter or desk among grey
> Eighteenth-century houses.

These men and women have done their day's work, but they have within them a passion and enthusiasm for a cause that became clear when the rebellion took place. Their jobs and lives, it would seem, are routine; they work in shops or offices ('counter or desk') and there is no real understanding between Yeats and these people:

> I have passed with a nod of the head
> Or polite meaningless words,
> Or have lingered awhile and said
> Polite meaningless words

The deliberate repetition of 'polite meaningless words' captures the distance between him and them. The mood is bland, conventional, superficial. The mention of 'Eighteenth-century houses' is not only a background detail but it could also symbolise the British presence in Dublin. These houses were built for the colonists (Merrion Square, for example, was laid out in 1762 and by the end of the eighteenth century Dublin could boast very fine public and private buildings). Yeats makes clear his misreading of the situation when he confesses that, on meeting these men, he privately thought of some 'mocking tale or gibe' to entertain his companion at the club:

> And thought before I had done
> Of a mocking tale or a gibe
> To please a companion
> Around the fire at the club

Yeats tells this story against himself; he is honest in his portrayal of himself in a bad light and he clearly underestimated these people whom he met or passed in the street. There was some contact between the two worlds but it was essentially 'polite' and 'meaningless'. Yeats was convinced that he and his friends at the club were living among fools:

> Being certain that they and I
> But lived where motley is worn

The club becomes, in the poem, a symbol of privilege and separateness; the club is also frequently seen as a very English institution and Yeats with his background was closer to such a world than to those whom he passed on the streets of Dublin. In Terence Brown's words: 'The opening movement of "Easter 1916" magnanimously acknowledges how wrong he had been in thinking that the martyrs and he himself had inhabited a world of drab inconsequentiality, which would not change'.

The poem, which began in a matter-of-fact way, presents the reader with a powerful and paradoxical image by the end of its first stanza. It becomes a recurring image and one which captures Yeats's conflicting emotions. It becomes a key idea within the poem as a whole:

> All changed, changed utterly:
> A terrible beauty is born.

The line used in 'Easter 1916' is the trimeter, a speechlike, three foot line, with a simple and insistent rhyme scheme (abab). The subject matter of the poem is revolution, disturbing, chaotic events, but the form Yeats chose allows him to offer a measured, careful, considered exploration of these dramatic events and their consequences.

The division of the poem into four stanzas of 16-, 24-, 16-, 24-line sections matches, as Helen Vendler notes, the first day of The Rising, 24 April 1916.

The poem on the page therefore memorialises the day and the year (and indeed the month – April is the fourth month and there are four stanzas: 24/4/16), in a very deliberate way.

In stanza 2 and following, Yeats speaks individually of those who were active in the rebellion. First Countess Markiewicz. The phrase 'ignorant good-will' captures her supposed well-intentioned but uninformed nature and Yeats laments how her sweet voice grew shrill through political activism and argument. Patrick Pearse, Thomas MacDonagh and John MacBride are also featured in stanza 2. The rebels, who were only given anonymous 'vivid' faces in stanza 1, are now given qualities and attributes. Patrick Pearse is spoken of in his role as educator and poet:

> This man had kept a school
> And rode our wingèd horse;

Thomas MacDonagh, a fellow-poet and academic, his helper and his friend:

> Was coming into his force;
> He might have won fame in the end,
> So sensitive his nature seemed,
> So daring and sweet his thought.

Yeats's attitude towards John MacBride is more complex. As Maud Gonne's husband, he was jealous of him and the break-up of the marriage in 1905 is probably hinted at in the words 'bitter wrong'. She left MacBride on the grounds of 'cruelty, infidelity and drunkenness'. And yet Yeats admits that MacBride too must be included here:

> This other man I had dreamed,
> A drunken, vainglorious lout.
> He had done most bitter wrong
> To some who are near my heart,
> Yet I number him in the song.

Echoing an earlier idea where the times were viewed as clownish ('motley is worn'), Yeats highlights the reality of the uprising when he speaks of how MacBride and others gave themselves to the cause:

> He, too, had resigned his part
> In the casual comedy

Easter 1916 was neither terrible nor beautiful but gave birth to a complex 'terrible beauty'. MacBride himself was changed from 'drunken, vainglorious lout' and he was changed utterly:

> He, too, has been changed in his turn,
> Transformed utterly:
> A terrible beauty is born.

With stanza 3, line 41, Yeats introduces the symbol of the stone. Like 'terrible beauty', the stone heart is also paradoxical. The stone in the stream stands for resistance, persistence, and the stone heart could also symbolise the individual choked with hatred. It has also been pointed out that Yeats studied the work of the Celtic scholar Ernest Renan. Renan's work examines how the Celts once worshipped stones and the stone, therefore, could be interpreted to symbolise Irish belief. The single-mindedness of the revolutionaries seems to be summed up in lines 41–44:

> Hearts with one purpose alone
> Through summer and winter seem
> Enchanted to a stone
> To trouble the living stream.

The contrast between movement and stillness, between stasis and flux, is central here. If the living stream is time, the constant sense of change and unpredictability is captured in the imagery of the following lines:

> The horse that comes from the road,
> The rider, the birds that range
> From cloud to tumbling cloud,
> Minute by minute they change;
> A shadow of cloud on the stream
> Changes minute by minute;
> A horse-hoof slides on the brim,
> And a horse plashes within it;
> The long-legged moor-hens dive,
> And hens to moor-cocks call

Taken on their own these lines are remarkable for their constant movement, excitement, action, danger, unrest. A key word here is 'changes' (line 50) which, unlike the finality of 'changed' elsewhere in the poem (lines 15, 38, 79), implies possibility, potential, fluidity, and expresses Yeats's hope for progress without blood sacrifice. Details are sensuously evoked – 'tumbling cloud'; 'horse-hoof slides'; 'plashes'; 'dive'; 'hens to moor-cocks call' – and the repeated 'Minute by minute' gives the passage an immediate and living quality. Within 'Easter 1916', this passage, ostensibly describing the life of a stream, becomes an image for history and the deeds of humankind. There is uncertainty but there is also possibility. The stone, however, is static, inflexible, an inert presence. Is Yeats suggesting that those who sacrificed their lives are permanent presences in the living flow of time but that it need not have been like this? A diversity of life surrounds the stone; the stone is but one thing, one part of the stream, but the fanaticism of the rebels allows them to think and talk about only one thing. This third stanza offers neither judgement nor interpretation, but the stone in the stream becomes a simple and powerful image of political events.

'Easter 1916' explores the nature and meaning of heroism and Yeats reaches no one conclusion in the poem. He says what he thinks and what he feels; he asks questions; he wonders if it was needless to die. At line 56, however, Yeats seems to suggest that their sacrifice cannot be ignored when he says that 'The stone's in the midst of all' and the image of the stone heart begins, in fact, at the very centre of the poem on line 41.

Even the judgement with which Yeats begins the fourth and final stanza is qualified. If your sacrifice is too long, it can turn your heart to stone:

> Too long a sacrifice
> Can make a stone of the heart

What began as an almost comic world of noddings and superficial exchanges in the street changes and becomes a serious poem in which Yeats now marks their deaths. In death they are united by their heroic deed; their deaths have elevated them to a different order. Yeats, however, does not speak of their achievement; he does not dwell on how their deaths did not immediately achieve their aim.

The mystery of their sacrifice and death and how much must be sacrificed is impossible to understand:

> Too long a sacrifice
> Can make a stone of the heart.
> That is heaven's part

It is up to heaven to judge and he refuses to do so, but Yeats says that it is 'our' part to offer comfort. There is a tenderness in the image of mother and child but, unlike the sleeping child, the rebels are dead. The comparison of rebels to children, however, trivialises their gesture, according to Irish academic Declan Kiberd: 'The rebels (he implies) were children, and children are not full moral agents'. It is, therefore, an image of false comfort

> To murmur name upon name,
> As a mother names her child
> When sleep at last has come
> On limbs that had run wild

and Yeats recognises it as such:

> What is it but nightfall?
> No, no, not night but death

Then Yeats asks the startling question:

> Was it needless death after all?

And the poem becomes overtly political:

> Was it needless death after all?
> For England may keep faith
> For all that is done and said.

This is a reference to The Bill for Home Rule for Ireland which had been passed in 1913 but shelved at the beginning of the First World War. The poet, however, does not dwell on what the future might bring:

> We know their dream; enough
> To know they dreamed and are dead

But the unsettling question

> And what if excess of love
> Bewildered them till they died?

prompts the reader to think of wasted sacrifice, wasted lives. However, Yeats ends on a very authoritative and confident note. In the very act of making the poem, Yeats is granting these revolutionaries a permanent place in Ireland's history and in Irish poetry:

> I write it out in a verse—
> MacDonagh and MacBride
> And Connolly and Pearse
> Now and in time to be,
> Wherever green is worn,
> Are changed, changed utterly:
> A terrible beauty is born.

Here it is the men who are changed. The roll call of rebel names and descriptions in the first two stanzas and in stanza 4 becomes in its own way the living stream that flows by the stone. Yeats's act of naming them gives the poem a powerful resonance and The Rising, John Wilson Foster suggests, is 'like a stone in the midst of Irish history'.

Whether they were foolish and whether they died needlessly are no longer significant considerations. Yeats transforms the rebels into charismatic, immortal figures. He misread their vivid faces and had mocked them as 'motley'-clad players in a 'casual comedy', but by the poem's end they are tragic heroes. In the opening lines of the poem, he admitted to speaking 'polite, meaningless words', something a poet should never do. By the poem's closing lines, he has written profound, complex words which honour those who gave their lives for Ireland.

Writing in 1916, some months after the Easter Rising, Yeats said: '"Romantic Ireland's dead and gone" sounds old-fashioned now. It seemed true in 1913, but I did not foresee 1916. The late Dublin Rebellion, whatever one can say of its wisdom, will long be remembered for its heroism. "They weighed so lightly what they gave," and gave too in some cases without hope of success'.

The Second Coming

'September 1913' and 'Easter 1916', as evident from their titles, focus on particular events in time. 'The Second Coming' offers a very different temporal perspective, that of thousands of years. Here Yeats imagines Christ returning to earth, but in his stead there comes a slouching beast. The setting is different also in that there are no particular Irish references. The poem takes place, as it were, on a vast, world stage and it was written in 1919, at the end of the Great War. The absence of end-rhyme is appropriate in a poem that speaks of chaos and disorder.

The poem may have been prompted by a particular catastrophe, but the anarchy Yeats speaks of is not specified. The poem begins with a general sense of disorder, disconnectedness, break-down, a catalogue of disasters:

> Turning and turning in the widening gyre
> The falcon cannot hear the falconer;
> Things fall apart; the centre cannot hold;

The 'Turning', 'turning', 'widening' of line 1 charts an image of things spinning out of control and captures what Yeats feared: the collapse of civilisation. Yeats believed that history moves in cycles of birth-growth-decline-death and that the twentieth century would witness the collapse of Western civilisation.

Stephen Coote says, of the poem's opening lines, that 'The pitiless turning of the gyres has brought the democratic and self-effacing Christian period to a terrible climax. Now "The Second Coming is at hand". Far from being, as Christians believe, the period which will see the thousand-year rule of the godly, this era would be, Yeats thought, drawing on the deepest resources of his imagination, an aristocratic, physical, assertive and occult period of frightening primeval energies'.

> Mere anarchy is loosed upon the world,
> The blood-dimmed tide is loosed, and everywhere
> The ceremony of innocence is drowned.

The dramatic and active words – 'Turning and turning', 'fall apart', 'loosed' (repeated), 'drowned' – conjure up a chaotic, uncontrolled scene. The falcon is seen to circle further and further away from the falconer and this has been interpreted to mean that man has lost contact with Christ. Terence Brown reminds us that 'The Second Coming' has been seen as 'a prophetic anticipation of the monstrous unfolding of twentieth-century world history' but that the poem need not refer to a second coming in the Christian sense but to the birth of a deity.

The picture painted in the first stanza is one of anarchy. The pure and simple have been destroyed ('drowned') and the 'blood-dimmed tide', a tidal wave clouded or stained with blood, is an image of bloodshed on a vast scale. The first stanza ends with Yeats's opinion of humanity. Those who are 'best' (leaders, intellectuals?) have no energy or driving force or commitment and the 'worst' are fired with hatred and violence:

> The best lack all conviction, while the worst
> Are full of passionate intensity.

The second and longer stanza imagines the second coming. Yeats is so disillusioned with the present that he is certain that the birth of a new order is at hand:

> Surely some revelation is at hand;
> Surely the Second Coming is at hand.
> The Second Coming!

The tone of conviction, amazement and fear is clearly sensed and then slowly and dramatically the poet summons up a powerful image, not of the infant Christ who came and transformed the Greco-Roman civilisation, but of a sphinx-like creature with a blank and pitiless gaze:

> Hardly are those words out
> When a vast image out of *Spiritus Mundi*
> Troubles my sight

The desert landscape, the burning sun, the birds of prey and the darkness are harsh, unattractive, and the rough beast that the poet imagines will replace the divine child.

The movement in the opening lines of the poem changes in the poem's closing lines, from 'turning' and 'widening' to 'Reel', 'rocking', 'Slouches'. The beast moves slowly, while above are the contrasting frenzied movements of the desert birds:

> somewhere in sands of the desert
> A shape with lion body and the head of a man,
> A gaze blank and pitiless as the sun,
> Is moving its slow thighs, while all about it
> Reel shadows of the indignant desert birds.

This rough beast marks an end and a beginning. Yeats later said that the 'brazen winged beast' in 'my poem "The Second Coming" was 'associated with laughing, ecstatic destruction' and that 'Our civilisation was about to reverse itself, or some new civilisation about to be born from all that our age had rejected...; because we had worshipped a single god it would worship many.'

'The darkness drops again' may be an image of the dark, uncertain future. But Yeats is certain of one thing, that the birth of Christ and the Christian era would eventually lead to the present nightmare:

> but now I know
> That twenty centuries of stony sleep
> Were vexed to nightmare by a rocking cradle

In the final lines of this strange, haunting, powerful poem, Yeats, according to Seamus Deane, is asking if the rough beast can find 'a Bethlehem in which it can be born again as the demonic?' It is a poem whose symbolism will prompt many interpretations, meanings or understandings. Sixteen years after writing the poem, Yeats wrote to a friend and claimed that 'it foretold what was happening'. He was referring to the political barbarism throughout Europe. In Seamus Deane's words, the second coming 'became known as Fascism'.

Sailing to Byzantium

Yeats, in his poetry, often speaks in a voice that addresses public events but there are also poems where Yeats withdraws from the world and explores more personal themes. 'September 1913' is a public utterance; 'The Wild Swans at Coole' and 'Sailing to Byzantium' are preoccupied with his personal life, his disappointments, his growing old, his longing.

The title suggests a stately, graceful journey to an ancient and beautiful place. In Robert Pinsky's words, it 'denotes process'. 'Sailing', here, is a beautiful, timeless concept (substitute any other mode of transport and the image is somehow less attractive) and Byzantium, for Yeats, was an ideal place. The journey is an imagined, metaphorical one.

Yeats rejects Ireland in the opening line. Its strong, direct, dismissive tone is registered immediately in the first word. Yeats chose 'That' rather than 'This', distancing himself further from a country where he is no longer at ease. Ireland, here, symbolises the natural, temporal world; that country, therefore, is more the land of youth than Yeats's actual birthplace:

> That is no country for old men.

The country is teeming with youth and vitality and if the opening stanza read as follows

> The young
> In one another's arms, birds in the trees
>
> The salmon-falls, the mackerel-crowded sea,
> Fish, flesh, or fowl, commend all summer long

it would present a very attractive life-enhancing picture of young love and the never-ending riches of the natural world. It is old age, however, and the neglect of man's creative spirit by the young that cause Yeats to 'sail' to Byzantium. He dismisses Ireland but at the same time admits that it is attractive.

Though the first stanza begins and ends with negatives ('no country'; 'all neglect') there is, in the bird and fish, a sense of beginning. The salmon leap up-river in spring and the mackerel-crowded seas suggest energy and abundance.

A harsh, realistic, sombre note is struck in the striking description of fish, flesh and fowl as:

> Those dying generations.

In the midst of life, they are in the midst of death; they are 'caught' or trapped, but the 'young/ In one another's arms' are unaware of their mortality. Their lives are sensual, not intellectual, but the young will grow old too:

> Whatever is begotten, born and dies

The magnificent monuments of unageing intellect are neglected by the young and dying; ironically what they neglect is something outside of time and beyond time. Their lives are transient; the works of art are not.

The ageing Yeats realises that he is growing old, that old age is inevitable, but that art will allow him to escape this imperfect world and enter an immortal one. He wrote the poem in September 1926 when he was 61.

In stanza 2, Yeats focuses on himself and the reality of old age. He paints a grim picture:

> An aged man is but a paltry thing,
> A tattered coat upon a stick

Youth and its sensual music are no more and therefore Yeats believes it all the more important that the soul within the ageing body should sing out. Old age is empty and meaningless:

>   unless
> Soul clap its hands and sing, and louder sing
> For every tatter in its mortal dress

The soul defies its ageing, mortal body; the phrase 'and sing, and louder sing' gathers momentum through repetition and its strong sounds contrast with 'paltry', 'tatter'. The image of the soul clapping its hands is simple, childlike, spontaneous, delightful. This soul-singing, however, is best learned by studying great works of art; there is no way to learn to sing except by studying:

> Nor is there singing school but studying
> Monuments of its own magnificence

In stanza 1, the monuments of unageing intellect were being neglected by the young; it is vital that the old pay attention to such works for it is through art that their souls will achieve immortality. The stanza ends with the image of Yeats in old age, having made the journey to Byzantium, a journey of the imagination.

In stanzas 3 and 4, Yeats imagines himself in the holy city, a city of art, of magnificent monuments to the creative imagination and spirit. The tone is reverential and one of longing:

> O sages standing in God's holy fire
> As in the gold mosaic of a wall,
> Come from the holy fire, perne in a gyre,
> And be the singing-masters of my soul.

The soul is what is essential. The work of art (such as the gold mosaic) is the soul's creation and, if studied, such a work allows the viewer to enter the immortal world of art. Stanza 3 contrasts the heart and soul, the body and spirit, the sensual and the intellectual. Yeats speaks of his heart as sick with desire, his body as a broken, confused animal:

> Consume my heart away; sick with desire
> And fastened to a dying animal
> It knows not what it is; and gather me
> Into the artifice of eternity.

Though these are intensely personal lines ('my soul', 'my heart', 'gather me'), the reality of old age and the longing expressed in them are emotions that the reader can identify with.

By stanza 4, the poet imagines that he has been gathered 'into the artifice of eternity'. The natural world is left behind and the world evoked is ornate, privileged, ceremonious:

> Once out of nature I shall never take
> My bodily form from any natural thing,
> But such a form as Grecian goldsmiths make
> Of hammered gold and gold enamelling
> To keep a drowsy Emperor awake;
> Or set upon a golden bough to sing
> To lords and ladies of Byzantium
> Of what is past, or passing, or to come.

In 'The Lake Isle of Innisfree', Yeats longed to be part of the natural world. In 'Sailing to Byzantium', the natural world is rejected and he summons up an elegant civilisation. The 'birds in the tree' of line 2 become a bird of hammered gold and gold enamelling in line 28. The sensual music of stanza 1 has been rejected; Yeats rejects transience and sings of 'what is past, or passing, or to come'.

The immortal work of art is created by mortal man. The artist makes the gold mosaic; the Grecian goldsmith creates the bird; the old man makes the poem. The artist is mortal but art embodies or gives expression to man's soul and, in so doing, man becomes immortal. The very poem on the page becomes Yeats's monument of unageing intellect. 'Sailing to Byzantium' is, in Eavan Boland's words, 'a poem infatuated with the power of the imagination' and it shows us the imagination triumphing over the 'dying animal'. The vocabulary illustrates this tension between the two: 'dying' versus 'unageing'; 'tattered' versus 'Monuments'; 'gold mosaic' versus 'dying animal'; 'bodily form' versus 'hammered gold'.

And Boland also says: 'Yeats goes to Byzantium and there he hopes to enter the culture of art which will save him from the flux of life. He's not going to take his bodily form from any natural thing; he's going to become a work of art; he's going to become, in other words, what he himself can create – an immortal and timeless object'. The poem condemns 'the way in which man himself has been created' but 'celebrates what man can create'.

Though Eavan Boland thinks 'The Circus Animals' Desertion' is Yeats's greatest poem, she says: 'if I were to be asked which, in my opinion, is the best managed, best, most clearly written of all Yeats's poems, this ['Sailing to Byzantium'] is the one. It's not the most powerful; it's not the most haunting. But it has a wonderful command from stanza to stanza. There are only four stanzas, yet every one of them is a sort of magic box which you open to find out more. And the line lengths are beautifully managed.'

In a poem which praises and celebrates the importance of art, it is fitting that its form and structure are in themselves superb examples of a work of art. It is 'decorated' and 'artificial', as Eavan Boland described it.

Whenever we read we instinctively come up with a summary. This is a preliminary and important step and Elder Olson sums up 'Sailing to Byzantium' as follows: 'an old man faces the problem of old age, of death, and of regeneration, and gives his decision. Old age, he tells us, excludes a man from the sensual joys of youth; the world appears to belong completely to the young, it is no place for the old; indeed an old man is scarcely a man at all – he is a tattered coat upon a stick. But the young are so wrapped up in their sensuality that they are ignorant utterly of the world of the spirit. Hence if old age frees a man from sensual passion, he may rejoice in the liberation of the soul; he is admitted into the realm of the spirit; and his rejoicing will increase according as he realises the magnificence of the soul. But the soul can best learn its own greatness from the great works of art; hence he turns to those great works, but in turning to them, he finds that these are by no means mere effigies, or monuments, but things which have souls also; these live in the noblest element of God's fire, free from all corruption; hence he prays for death, for release from his mortal body; and since the insouled monuments exhibit the possibility of the soul's existence in some other matter than flesh, he wishes reincarnation, not now in a mortal body, but in the immortal and changeless embodiment of art.'

A paraphrase, obviously, cannot do justice to the poem being paraphrased but it does highlight the poem's special qualities and clarifies our thinking regarding not only what the poet says but more importantly how he says it.

The Stare's Nest by My Window

This is the sixth poem in a seven-poem sequence and the main title, 'Meditations in Time of Civil War', is an overtly political one. 'The Stare's Nest by My Window' is a political poem but its dominant image is a natural one, bees and birds, bees building and birds looking after the young in a nest.

The opening lines capture a sense of building up and breaking down:

> The bees build in the crevices
> Of loosening masonry, and there
> The mother birds bring grubs and flies.

Things are falling apart ('loosening masonry'), but there is also a sense of continuity. The poet speaks of 'My wall' and the repeated 'loosening' emphasises decay and destruction, but he also speaks of how the bees and the birds create. The poem begins with this activity of the world of nature and the man-made world is crumbling; the stanza ends with a plea that is repeated at the end of all the subsequent stanzas:

> Come build in the empty house of the stare.

Here, Yeats is addressing the honey-bees and creates what Eamon Grennan calls 'a context of maternal nurturing power in a context of violence and decay'. The birds' nest is now empty but Yeats, in wishing the bees to build a hive within the nest, is wishing for one positive, natural, instinctive life-force to replace another.

'The life that goes on' says Eamon Grennan, 'is a natural process independent of history, a gift of grace to the speaker'. But the speaker is fearful and uncertain. There is a feeling of claustrophobia, imprisonment, danger, helplessness, in stanza 2:

> We are closed in, and the key is turned
> On our uncertainty; somewhere
> A man is killed, or a house burned,
> Yet no clear fact to be discerned

He spoke of 'My Window', 'my wall' and now, though he speaks in the plural, 'We', meaning him and his family, the focus is still intensely private. The public world beyond the walls of Thoor Ballylee is a world of death and violence. Punctuation fragments the lines, but the final line is long and flowing when the speaker returns to his original prayer to the honey-bees:

> Come build in the empty house of the stare.

The third stanza lists the facts and there is a strong feeling of unrest. The speaker does not analyse nor does he offer judgement or solution but, against the backdrop of barricades and death, he returns to his hope and wish:

> Come build in the empty house of the stare.

The poet feels helpless. A detail such as 'Last night' brings the reality of the present moment alive, but all he can do is to renew his plea for nature to offer an image of the positive. The nest once contained birds. Now 'empty' captures the silence and the loss. He does not request the stares or starlings to return but asks for the bees to build there instead.

Yeats looks back in the final stanza and confesses how:

> We had fed the heart on fantasies,
> The heart's grown brutal from the fare

Everything springs from our own hearts and yet dreams have hardened the heart. In line 9, Yeats felt that there was 'no clear fact to be discerned' but he does end with the admission that hatred is now a stronger force than love. He addresses the honey-bees again, but this time an even stronger tone is captured in the expressive 'O':

> O honey-bees,
> Come build in the empty house of the stare.

This poem was written at Thoor Ballylee in 1922 and focused on a particular episode in Irish history and yet it achieves a relevance and universality today. Violence seems to be a permanent part of life, but the longing for a counterforce, for some fruitful activity, is also vital.

In Memory of Eva Gore-Booth and Con Markiewicz

Naming people in his poetry is frequent in Yeats. His life became the raw material for his art and his poems therefore chart his life, private and public. The lengthy and proper title lends the poem a dignity and formality. In this elegy he remembers the Gore-Booth sisters. Yeats had met them in 1894. He was thirty-one and they were in their twenties. He wrote the poem in late 1927; Yeats was sixty-two and the two sisters were dead. Eva died in 1926 and Constance died in August 1927.

Though their lives were troubled and difficult, in the opening lines Yeats remembers the two sisters in their youthful beauty. Like Lissadell itself, the lines are bathed in evening sunlight. The fine house, elegance and refinement are captured in the 'Great windows' and silk kimonos:

> The light of evening, Lissadell
> Great windows open to the south,
> Two girls in silk kimonos, both
> Beautiful, one a gazelle.

Each descriptive line presents a new different image from the past. Though distant and long ago, Yeats does not use a verb to distance the scene further. Instead, the images live again in memory.

The tranquillity and beauty are soon shattered at line 5. The poem shifts sudden y from past to more recent present and the change of mood is conveyed in the move from calm, summer evening light to harsh, autumn storms. 'But' signals this sudden and dramatic change:

> But a raving autumn shears
> Blossom from the summer wreath

The harshness of 'raving' and Yeats's use of the present tense ('shears') are forceful, and the image of the 'Blossom from the summer's wreath' suggests something beautiful and elegantly created. And all this is destroyed.

Their lives beyond Lissadell are portrayed as grim. Within eight lines, the poem has moved from elegant room to prison cell:

> The older is condemned to death,
> Pardoned, drags out lonely years
> Conspiring among the ignorant.

Yeats does not expand on their political involvement or campaigning but he regrets their involvement. 'Conspiring among the ignorant' and 'Some vague Utopia' suggests that Yeats did not believe in their social and political work; Eva's 'withered old and skeleton-gaunt body' symbolises for Yeats the futility of their efforts:

> I know not what the younger dreams—
> Some vague Utopia—and she seems,
> When withered old and skeleton-gaunt,
> An image of such politics.

Yeats leaves the harsh reality of their lives and returns to the beautiful world with which the poem began. The sisters are dead but Yeats speaks of them as if they are still alive, which of course, they are in his imagination:

> Many a time I think to seek
> One or the other out and speak
> Of that old Georgian mansion, mix
> Pictures of the mind, recall
> That table and the talk of youth,
> Two girls in silk kimonos, both
> Beautiful, one a gazelle.

The present is obliterated. Within stanza 1, the troubling, unsettling memory is framed by two gloriously beautiful ones. The world of Lissadell, with its civilised atmosphere, which Yeats wanted to return to, predominates.

The second stanza differs from the first in many respects. There are no golden, glowing images. The tone is tender at first. He addresses their ghosts, knowing that their deaths would bring them understanding and wisdom:

> Dear shadows, now you know it all

He looks at their lives and their strong convictions. He speaks of their struggle or fight as weakness ('All the folly of a fight'); they involve themselves with wrong or right issues, but the suggestion is that their involvement was unworthy of them and he gently laments that the only enemy these two innocent and beautiful girls had was time:

> The innocent and the beautiful
> Have no enemy but time

Yeats then speaks to these shades directly. He asks them to 'Arise and bid me strike a match'. The particular details of stanza 1 (house, setting, clothing, prison cell, conversation) now give way, in stanza 2, to one powerful symbol. Yeats imagines himself being told by these two women, who gave their lives to public causes, to set the world and time itself ablaze. The conflagration is a mighty, dangerous, destructive force. He imagines the great fire raging until such a time when the wise realise the significance of it:

> Arise and bid me strike a match
> And strike another till time catch;
> Should the conflagration climb,
> Run till all the sages know.

In the final sentence, the two girls, both beautiful, and Yeats are united as 'We'. He speaks of how they created something valuable and special and he speaks it with triumph:

> We the great gazebo built

However, he denounces those ('They') for resenting 'us' (the Gore-Booths, Yeats and others of their cultural inheritance):

> They convicted us of guilt

Those others felt that the privileged, ascendancy class should feel guilt for being who they are. Yeats, in a dramatic flourish, asks the shades once again to

> Bid me strike a match and blow.

This complex stanza is difficult to tease out but Yeats's imagination here is actively involved in honouring the memory of the Gore-Booth sisters. There was a beauty and a nobility in their lives but they never realised their dream. They worked with the common people but Yeats seems to say that he wishes that 'Dear shadows' would bid him bring about an end to everything.

A. Norman Jeffares says of this poem that it is 'an elegy for lost beauty, lost youth, the lost battle with time as well as a condemnation of the choices the sisters made about their lives'. But the closing lines also express a deep desire to bring about a change, in the dramatic image of the all-consuming conflagration. The mood is no longer elegiac but visionary and determined. The pleading tones – of 'Bid me strike...', 'And strike another...' – are a passionate expression of Yeats's admiration for everything Eva Gore-Booth and Con Markiewicz of Lissadell stood for.

Swift's Epitaph

Yeats had great admiration for Jonathan Swift and he considered Swift's epitaph 'the greatest . . . in history'. Yeats identified with the proud and solitary Swift and an Anglo-Ireland that both belonged to. Yeats translates Swift's Latin but line 1 is Yeats's own variation. The image of sailing in the first line offers an image of stately and dignified departure but, at the heart of the epitaph, is the sense of how Swift is now free from all anger and hatred that had been directed at him when he lived. This self-portrait by Jonathan Swift emphasises a fierce independence. The challenging tone of

> Imitate him if you dare
> World-besotted traveller

implies that Swift himself had travelled vast distances, intellectually and imaginatively, and that he could not be equalled. The epitaph's final line sums up his life's work. The commanding, confident tones in such a short piece and the compression of thought are impressive.

An Acre of Grass

This is Yeats at seventy-one. He begins with a calm, quiet, ordered description of his life at Riversdale in Rathfarnham. 'Picture and book' sum up his lifelong interest in art and literature. It is spacious – 'An acre of green grass/ For air and exercise' – but he realises that he is growing old in body. The references to 'midnight', 'old' house, the silence and absence of movement ('nothing stirs but a mouse') all create a picture of Yeats at 'life's end'.

In stanza 2, he speaks of how he is content ('My temptation is quiet') but also of how his own creative powers, the imagination and the mind, are failing him:

> Neither loose imagination,
> Nor the mill of the mind
> Consuming its rag and bone,
> Can make the truth known.

Here, he captures both the liberating ('loose imagination') and the workaday, mechanical nature ('mill of the mind') of the creative process. Though it is in the everyday and ordinary ('rag and bone') that truth can be found, he no longer seems to be able to capture and communicate that truth in his poetry.

The mood of quiet contemplation with which the poem began now changes dramatically at line 13. He defiantly breaks into an intense expression of desire:

> Grant me an old man's frenzy,
> Myself must I remake

He calls on Timon, Lear, William Blake and Michael Angelo, characters imagined and real, to inspire him. Yeats finds himself in need of their raging, death-defying energies. The word 'frenzy' and Blake beating upon the wall or Michael Angelo's mind piercing the clouds are powerful images of men forever searching, forever exploring.

When Yeats says 'Grant me an old man's frenzy', he is calling perhaps upon the Muse, the source of poetic inspiration. He wishes for the loose imagination and the mill of the mind to allow him, at the end of his life, full expression. The poem ends with a striking image of the force and power of the nature of man's mind. If 'inspired by frenzy', the effect is such that 'An old man's eagle mind' can 'Shake the dead in their shrouds'. The 'eagle mind' is an image of a sharp, focused mind. The poem, which began with an air of quiet acceptance, almost defeatism, ends with a rallying call by Yeats for renewed creative energies. Though 'An Acre of Grass' is one of Yeats's last poems, it is a poem that clings to life.

Politics

The title might lead one to expect a poem on civil government and its administration (in Greek, *polítikos* is citizen). Instead, Yeats dismisses politics in a mocking voice and longs instead for youth and love. The old man is distracted by 'that girl standing there' and he asks how a topic such as international politics could hold his attention.

The poem's theme is easily grasped: that the big, apparently important public events are not as important in the end as the universal experience of love. The questioning tone in the opening lines turns to mockery ('here's a travelled man', 'there's a politician'), then doubt ('maybe what they say is true/ Of war's and war's alarms') and eventually to longing:

> But O that I were young again
>
> And held her in my arms!

The rhyming even-numbered lines give the poem a rhythm and power and in two sentences Yeats gives his reader big and challenging ideas.

In her 1992 novel, *Jazz*, Toni Morrison says something similar: 'Whatever happens, whether you get rich or stay poor, ruin your health or live to old age, you always end up back where you started: hungry for the one thing everybody loses—young loving.'

from Under Ben Bulben V

Yeats was a formalist and this poem, appropriately, is in heroic couplets. In *The Making of a Poem,* Mark Strand and Eavan Boland identify the heroic couplet, with its progressing rhyme scheme (aabbcc, etc.), as 'a form in which a high subject matter could be written'. Yeats lived at a time when many poets (T.S. Eliot for example) favoured Free Verse, but he rejected this technique. If you look at Yeats's poetry, it is clear that he favoured traditional forms in metre, stanza structure, rhyme. In section V of 'Under Ben Bulben', Yeats begins in an authoritative, commanding voice in which he tells Irish poets to learn and practise a formal poetry, not 'the sort now growing up/ All out of shape from toe to top'. It is a proud rallying call for Irish poets to honour and continue their tradition and inheritance. Yeats calls on Irish poets to create for the people of Ireland an heroic and spiritual ideal. He speaks dismissively of those who have no sense of ceremony and history:

> Their unremembering hearts and heads
> Base-born products of base beds.

Yeats has been accused of snobbishness and of looking down on 'Base-born products', but he was also passionate about Ireland and its future. He includes the lowly and the privileged, the peasantry and the country gentlemen in his vision of Ireland; he includes the ascetic and the sensuous, Ireland's religious legacy and the randy laughter of porter drinkers. He is therefore inclusive rather than exclusive and wants Irish poets to write of all aspects of Irish life. Nor should we forget our long and troubled history:

> Sing the lords and ladies gay
> That were beaten into the clay
> Through seven heroic centuries.

His confidence, pride and patriotism are unquestionable:

> Cast your mind on other days
> That we in coming days may be
> Still the indomitable Irishry.

So is his belief in the power of poetry. He is addressing the present but it is only in remembering the past, that present and past can be understood, and the future made possible. This poem is a formal farewell. He completed the poem in September 1938 and it is not unlike a last will and testament. He died the following January.

from Under Ben Bulben VI

This is a stark and prophetic poem. The mood is solemn. The tone is once again authoritative and commanding, the heroic couplet fitting. Personal history is evoked and Yeats's individual, unconventional personality clearly emerges. Though his ancestor was a clergyman, he manages to cherish and break with that tradition. He wishes to be buried in Drumcliff churchyard but there is to be:

> No marble, no conventional phrase

The unconventional words on the tombstone, Yeats's own epitaph, challenge the reader to view life and death realistically. The poem's first section referred to a ghostly, supernatural horseman which Yeats heard about as a boy. Perhaps Yeats, in the closing line, is expressing his fearlessness of death; it could also be interpreted that the man on horseback who might pass by Yeats's grave should not concern himself with death but continue with the business of life.

Prescribed Poetry
at Leaving Certificate Higher Level

The "new" poetry course was first examined in 2001. Below are the eight poets prescribed, each year, since then. Names in bold indicate the poets on the exam paper that particular year. [In 2009, a Paper II exam paper was inadvertently handed out to a group of pupils when they ought to have been given Paper I. The four prescribed poets were seen by that group and as a result a substitute Paper II was sat on a Saturday morning and at a cost of one million euros. Originally the paper carried Larkin, Longley, Mahon and Rich. In the substitute paper, Longley was replaced by Montague.]

2001 **Bishop** Boland Dickinson Heaney **Keats Larkin Longley** Shakespeare.

2002 **Bishop Boland** Dickinson Heaney Keats Larkin **Longley Shakespeare**.

2003 Bishop **Donne Frost Heaney** Hopkins Mahon **Plath** Yeats.

2004 Dickinson Frost Heaney **Hopkins Kavanagh Mahon Plath** Wordsworth.

2005 **Boland Dickinson Eliot** Heaney Kavanagh Longley Wordsworth **Yeats**.

2006 **Bishop Donne** Eliot **Hardy** Hopkins **Longley** Plath Yeats.

2007 Bishop Donne **Eliot Frost** Kavanagh **Montague Plath** Yeats.

2008 Boland **Donne** Frost **Larkin Mahon** Montague Plath **Rich**.

2009 **Bishop Keats** Larkin [Longley*] Mahon **Montague*** Rich **Walcott**.

2010 Boland **Eliot Kavanagh** Keats Longley **Rich** Walcott **Yeats**

2011 **Boland Dickinson Frost** Hopkins Kavanagh Rich Wordsworth **Yeats**.

2012 Boland Heaney Frost **Kavanagh Kinsella Larkin** Plath **Rich**.

2013 **Bishop Hopkins** Kinsella **Mahon Plath** Rich Shakespeare Wordsworth.

2014 Bishop **Dickinson** Heaney Kinsella **Larkin** Mahon **Plath Yeats**.

2015 Dickinson Donne **Frost Hardy Montague Ní Chuilleanáin** Plath Yeats

2016 **Bishop Dickinson Durcan Eliot** Larkin Ní Chuilleanáin Plath Yeats

2017 **Bishop Boland Donne** Durcan Eliot Hopkins **Keats** Plath

2018 Boland Durcan **Frost** Hopkins Keats **Larkin Montague Ní Chuilleanáin**

2019 **Bishop** Heaney Hopkins **Kennelly** Lawrence Ní Chuilleanáin **Plath Yeats**

2020 Boland Dickinson Durcan Frost Lawrence Ní Chuilleanáin Rich Wordsworth

2021 Bishop Boland Durcan Frost Heaney Hopkins Keats Plath

2022 Bishop Dickinson Keats Kennelly Lawrence Rich Wordsworth Yeats

Questions from Past Papers

Elizabeth Bishop

- 'Bishop makes skillful use of a variety of poetic techniques to produce poems that are often analytical but rarely emotional.'

Discuss the extent to which you agree or disagree with the above statement. Develop your response with reference to the poems by Elizabeth Bishop on your course. [2019]

- 'From the poetry of Elizabeth Bishop that you have studied, select the poems that, in your opinion, best demonstrate her skilful use of language and imagery to confront life's harsh realities.'

Justify your selection by demonstrating Bishop's skilful use of language and imagery to confront life's harsh realities in the poems you have chosen. [2017]

- 'Bishop uses highly detailed observation, of people, places and events, to explore unique personal experiences in her poetry.'

Discuss this statement, supporting your answer with reference to the poetry of Elizabeth Bishop on your course. [2016]

- 'Bishop's carefully judged use of language aids the reader to uncover the intensity of feeling in her poetry.'

To what extent do you agree or disagree with the above statement? Support your answer with reference to the poetry of Elizabeth Bishop on your course. [2013]

- 'Elizabeth Bishop poses interesting questions delivered by means of a unique style.'

Do you agree with this assessment of her poetry? Your answer should focus on both themes and stylistic features. Support your points with the aid of suitable reference to the poems you have studied. [2009]

- 'Reading the poetry of Elizabeth Bishop.'

Write out the text of a talk that you would give to your class in response to the above title.
Your talk should include the following:
- Your reactions to her themes or subject matter.
- What you personally find interesting in her style of writing.

Refer to the poems by Elizabeth Bishop that you have studied. [2006]

- 'The poetry of Elizabeth Bishop appeals to the modern reader for many reasons.'

Write an essay in which you outline the reasons why poems by Elizabeth Bishop have this appeal. [2002]

- 'Introducing Elizabeth Bishop.'

Write out the text of a short presentation you would make to your friends or class group under the above title. Support your point of view by reference to or quotation from the poetry of Elizabeth Bishop that you have studied. [2001]

Emily Dickinson

- 'Dickinson's use of an innovative style to explore intense experiences can both intrigue and confuse.'

Discuss this statement, supporting your answer with reference to the poetry of Emily Dickinson on your course. [2016]

- 'The dramatic aspects of Dickinson's poetry can both disturb and delight readers.'

To what extent do you agree or disagree with the above statement? Support your answer with reference to both the themes and language found in the poetry of Emily Dickinson on your course. [2014]

- 'Emily Dickinson's original approach to poetry results in startling and thought-provoking moments in her work.'

Give your response to the poetry of Emily Dickinson in the light of this statement. Support your points with suitable reference to the poems on your course. [2011]

- What impact did the poetry of Emily Dickinson make on you as a reader?

Your answer should deal with the following:
- Your overall sense of the personality of the poet
- The poet's use of language/imagery

Refer to the poems by Emily Dickinson that you have studied. [2005]

John Keats

- 'Keats uses sensuous language and vivid imagery to express a range of profound tensions.'

To what extent do you agree or disagree with this statement? Support your answer with reference to the poetry of John Keats on your course. [2017]

- 'John Keats presents abstract ideas in a style that is clear and direct.'

To what extent do you agree or disagree with this assessment of his poetry? Support your points with reference to the poetry on your course. [2009]

- 'Often we love a poet because of the feelings his/her poems create in us.'

Write about the feelings John Keats's poetry creates in you and the aspects of the poems (their content and/or style) that help to create those feelings. Support your points by reference to the poetry by Keats that you have studied. [2001]

Brendan Kennelly

- Discuss how Kennelly's sensitive exploration of a range of emotions, and his imaginative use of a variety of characters, help to reveal the humanity intrinsic to his work. Develop your response with reference to the poems by Brendan Kennelly on your course. [2019]

D.H. Lawrence

Prescribed in 2019 and did not appear on the exam paper that year. Lawrence was also prescribed in 2020.

Adrienne Rich

- 'Rich's poetry communicates powerful feelings through thought-provoking images and symbols.'

Write your response to this statement with reference to the poems by Adrienne Rich on your course. [2012]

- 'Adrienne Rich explores the twin themes of power and powerlessness in a variety of interesting ways.'

Write a response to the poetry of Adrienne Rich in the light of this statement, supporting your points with suitable reference to the poems on your course. [2010]

William Wordsworth

Prescribed in 2004, 2005, 2011, 2013 and did not appear on the exam paper those years. Wordsworth was also prescribed in 2020.

W.B. Yeats

- 'Yeats's poetry is both intellectually stimulating and emotionally charged.'

Discuss the extent to which you agree or disagree with the above statement. Develop your response with reference to the themes and language evident in the poems by W. B. Yeats on your course. [2019]

- 'Yeats uses evocative language to create poetry that includes both personal reflection and public commentary.'

Discuss this statement, supporting your answer with reference to both the themes and language found in the poetry of W. B. Yeats on your course. [2014]

- 'Yeats can be a challenging poet to read, both in terms of style and subject matter.'

To what extent do you agree with this statement? Support your answer with suitable reference to the poetry on your course. [2011]

- 'Yeats's poetry is driven by a tension between the real world in which he lives and an ideal world that he imagines.'

Write a response to the poetry of W.B. Yeats in the light of this statement, supporting your points with suitable reference to the poems on your course. [2010]

- Write an article for a school magazine introducing the poetry of W.B. Yeats to Leaving Certificate students. Tell them what he wrote about and explain what you liked in his writing, suggesting some poems that you think they would enjoy reading. Support your points by reference to the poetry by W.B. Yeats that you have studied. [2005]

The Unseen Poem
Part II

Part II

Approaching the Unseen Poem

Every poem, to begin with, is an unseen poem. When approaching a poem, it is useful to ask some very basic questions, such as: Who is speaking in the poem? What is being said? What prompted the poet to write the poem? What struck you first about this particular poem? What do you think of the opening? The Ending? Does the poet use unusual words, images or repetition?

The following is an outline of a step by step approach to the unseen poem on the page.

The shape of the poem on the page

This is often the very first thing you will notice about the text. Certain forms are recognised immediately, for example the fourteen-line sonnet or the sestina. Other poems may have a less definite shape, and that is also an important aspect of those poems. George Herbert (1593–1633) used very specific designs in some of his poems:

Easter Wings

Lord, who createdst man in wealth and store,
Though foolishly he lost the same,
Decaying more and more
Till he became
Most poor:
With thee
O let me rise
As larks, harmoniously,
And sing this day thy victories:
Then shall the fall further the flight in me.

My tender age in sorrow did begin;
And still with sicknesses and shame
Thou didst so punish sin,
That I became
Most thin.
With thee
Let me combine,
And feel this day thy victory;
For, if I imp my wing on thine,
Affliction shall advance the flight in me.

A modern writer who uses the same device is the American poet John Hollander. His poem 'Swan and Shadow' would lose its impact if it were printed as follows:

Dusk Above the water hang the loud flies Here O so gray then What a pale signal will appear When Soon before its shadow fades Where Here in this pool of opened eyes. . .

This is how it should be:

Swan and Shadow

<pre>
                    Dusk
                 Above the
             water hang the
                   loud
                   flies
                   Here
                   O so
                   gray
                   then
               What   A pale signal will appear
               When   Soon before its shadow fades
               Where   Here in this pool of opened eye
               In us   No Upon us As at the very edges
                 of where we take shape in the dark air
                    this object bares its image awakening
                      ripples of recognition that will
                          brush darkness up into light
   even after this bird this hour both drift by atop the perfect sad instant now
                      already passing out of sight
                    toward yet untroubled reflection
                  this image bears its object darkening
                  into memorial shades Scattered bits of
               light   No of water Or something across
               water   Breaking up No Being regathered
               soon   Yet by then a swan will have
               gone   Yes out of mind into what
                   vast
                   pale
                   hush
                   of a
                   place
                    past
               sudden dark as
                 if a swan
                   sang
</pre>

Shape here is so obviously of particular importance, but every poem has been shaped in a special way by means of line number, line length, rhyme and so on. Shakespeare wrote a 154 sonnet sequence; when Romeo and Juliet meet for the very first time in Shakespeare's play, they speak a sonnet between them. Elizabeth Bishop's 'The Prodigal' consists of two sonnets.

The Title

After the look of the poem on the page, the title is the next thing to be noticed. The American poet Emily Dickinson wrote 1,775 poems, but gave none of them titles. However, most poems have a title. What does the choice of title tell us about the poem? When we get to know the poem better we can then think about how effective and suitable the title is. Michael Longley's poem 'Carrigskeewaun' celebrates the place of the title, but each stanza is also given a title.

Consider the following titles. What do they reveal, or not reveal, suggest, imply, announce? Does the title win the reader's attention?

'The Dream of Wearing Shorts Forever' (Les Murray); 'Finale' (Judith Wright); 'Red Roses' (Anne Sexton); 'Red Sauce, Whiskey and Snow' (August Kleinzahler); 'Death of an Irishwoman' (Michael Hartnett); 'Hitcher' (Simon Armitage); 'Fifteen Million Plastic Bags' (Adrian Mitchell); 'For Heidi with Blue Hair' (Fleur Adcock); 'Wanting a Child' (Jorie Graham); 'SOMETHING FOR EVERYONE!!!' (Peter Reading); 'Phenomenal Woman' (Maya Angelou); 'The Hunchback in the Park' (Dylan Thomas); 'Depressed by a book of Bad Poetry, I walk Toward an Unused Pasture and Invite the Insects to Join me' (James Wright); 'Logan' (Catherine Phil MacCarthy); 'Ode on a Grecian Urn' (John Keats); 'Love' (George Herbert and Eavan Boland); 'The Armadillo' (Elizabeth Bishop); [r-p-o-p-h-e-s-s-a-g-r] (E E Cummings); 'Tea at the Palaz of Hoon' (Wallace Stevens); 'Church Going' (Philip Larkin); 'The Black Lace Fan My Mother Gave Me' (Eavan Boland); 'From a Conversation During Divorce' (Carol Rumens)

Language/Vocabulary

The language of poetry is the language of the age in which the poem is written. If someone today wrote a poem using 'thee' and 'thou' it would not convince; if someone today wrote exactly as Keats did, that poem would be dismissed as inauthentic. The poet writes in a language different from his or her predecessors and the poet today is less restricted in terms of subject matter. There is no word today, no emotion, no topic deemed unsuitable for poetry. Sylvia Plath once said that she wanted to get the word 'toothbrush' into a poem, meaning that she felt that there was nothing too ordinary or mundane for the poet to write about.

Yet the magic of poetry is such that each of the poets in this collection – though they span four centuries and all write in English – has a distinctive, unique voice. Their choice of words is part of this unique quality.

Ask yourself how you would describe a poet's vocabulary, his or her choice of words? This may be difficult to do at first. The task is easier if you look at opposites: is the language unusual or ordinary? Formal or colloquial? Does the poet invent new words? And, if so, what does this tell us about the poet? Is the language concrete or abstract? Are the words drawn from Anglo-Saxon, Latin, Anglo-Irish? Are there words on the page from the world of Greek Myth / Science / The Bible? Are there particular words that you would associate with particular poets? And how is the language of poetry different from the language of prose?

The following illustrates some interesting differences between the language of prose and the language of poetry. The first is a newspaper article which, according to his biographer Lawrance Thompson, inspired Robert Frost's poem 'Out, Out—'. The second is the poem itself. A discussion of the similarities and differences between the two should sharpen an awareness of language.

Sad tragedy at Bethlehem
Raymond Fitzgerald, a Victim of fatal accident

Raymond Tracy Fitzgerald, one of the twin sons of Michael G. and Margaret Fitzgerald of Bethlehem, died at his home Thursday afternoon, March 24, as a result of an accident by which one of his hands was badly hurt in a sawing machine. The young man was assisting in sawing up some wood in his own dooryard with a sawing machine and accidently hit the loose pulley, causing the saw to descend upon his hand, cutting and lacerating it badly. Raymond was taken into the house and a physician was immediately summoned, but he died very suddenly from the effect of the shock, which produced heart failure . . .

(From *The Littleton Courier*, 31 March 1901)

'Out, Out —'

The buzz saw snarled and rattled in the yard
And made dust and dropped stove-length sticks of wood,
Sweet-scented stuff when the breeze drew across it.
And from there those that lifted eyes could count
Five mountain ranges one behind the other
Under the sunset far into Vermont.
And the saw snarled and rattled, snarled and rattled,
As it ran light, or had to bear a load.
And nothing happened: day was all but done.
Call it a day, I wish they might have said
To please the boy by giving him the half hour
That a boy counts so much when saved from work.
His sister stood beside them in her apron
To tell them 'Supper'. At the word, the saw,
As if to prove saws knew what supper meant,
Leaped out at the boy's hand, or seemed to leap —

He must have given the hand. However it was,
Neither refused the meeting. But the hand!
The boy's first outcry was a rueful laugh,
As he swung toward them holding up the hand
Half in appeal, but half as if to keep
The life from spilling. Then the boy saw all —
Since he was old enough to know, big boy
Doing a man's work, though a child at heart —
He saw all spoiled. 'Don't let him cut my hand off —
The doctor, when he comes. Don't let him, sister!'
So. But the hand was gone already.
The doctor put him in the dark of ether.
He lay and puffed his lips out with his breath.
And then—the watcher at his pulse took fright.
No one believed. They listened at his heart.
Little — less— nothing! — and that ended it.
No more to build on there. And they, since they
Were not the one dead, turned to their affairs.

The importance of vocabulary is also clearly seen in the following two poems.
They share the same title and they both say something similar. One was written
– the original spelling is retained – at the beginning of the sixteenth century (and
supposedly tells of Thomas Wyatt's sorrow on being forsaken by women friends,
including Anne Boleyn, who left him for Henry VIII); the other was first published in
1979.

They flee from me, that somtime did me seke

They flee from me, that somtime did me seke
With naked fote stalkyng within my chamber.
Once have I seen them gentle, tame, and meke,
That now are wild, and do not once remember
That sometyme they have put them selves in danger,
To take bread at my hand, and now they range
Busily sekyng in continuall change.
   Thanked be fortune, it hath bene otherwise
Twenty tymes better: but once especiall,
In thinne aray, after a pleasant gyse,
When her loose gowne did from her shoulders fall,
And she me caught in her armes long and small,
And therwithall, so swetely did me kysse,
And softly sayd: deare hart, how like you this?
It was no dreame: for I lay broade awakyng.
But all is turnde now through my gentlenesse,
Into a bitter fashion of forsakyng:

And I have leave to go of her goodnesse,
And she also to use newfanglenesse.
But, sins that I unkyndly so am served:
How like you this, what hath she now deserved?

– Thomas Wyatt (1503–42)

They flee from me that sometime did me seek

At this moment in time
the chicks that went for me
in a big way
are opting out;
as of now, it's an all-change situation.
The scenario was once,
for me, 100% better.
Kissing her was viable
in a nude or semi-nude situation.
It was How's about it, baby?
Her embraces were relevant
and life-enhancing.

I was not hallucinating.
But with regard to that one
my permissiveness
has landed me in a forsaking situation.
The affair is no longer on-going.

She can, as of now, explore new parameters
How's about it? indeed!
I feel emotionally underprivileged.
What a bitch!
(and that's meaningful).

– Gavin Ewart (1916–95)

Punctuation

All poets are wordsmiths and punctuation is an aspect essential to poetry. Sometimes its absence is deliberate, as in the poems by Emily Dickinson. The frequent use of the full-stop will naturally slow down a line. In his poem 'Laertes', Michael Longley uses only one full-stop and that is at the end because, in his own words, he 'sustained the sentence from the first word right the way through'. Philip Larkin's 'MCMXIV' is also a one-sentence poem.

The full-stop, comma, colon, exclamation mark, question mark, dash, bracket, ellipsis and italics are just some examples of punctuation and their use are important aspects of a writer's style. You will meet with all of these in the prescribed poems. If you are aware of their importance and significance when you come to read the ten Emily Dickinson poems on your course, for example, consider the significance of how each poem ends: two with a full-stop, seven with a dash, one with a question mark. A poem that ends with a full-stop achieves a sense of closure; the dash often creates the opposite effect.

Rhyme

Rhyme, for centuries, has been one of the most distinguishing characteristics of poetry, though poetry without a regular rhyming scheme is not necessarily a poem without music. Blank verse, which is unrhymed iambic pentameter, for example, achieves rhythm and cadence without end rhyme. Internal rhyme and cross rhyme are also important features in poetry.

The run-on line is deceptive in that often a very rigorous and regular rhyming scheme is not apparent. 'Child of Our Time' by Eavan Boland has a very disciplined and regular end rhyme, but Boland's mastery of rhythm and the flowing line is such that a careless reader might think that the poem has no rhyming scheme.

Rhythm

Rhythm is movement. We are all familiar with rhythm. The individual day, the seasons of the year, the sound of the sea all have their own rhythm or movement. The Dublin poet Paula Meehan believes that our sense of rhythm dates from the time spent in the womb – the regular heartbeat of the mother and our own heartbeat give us an inbuilt rhythmic pattern.

Cadence

Cadence, a musical term, is difficult to define, yet it is easily recognised. A dictionary definition speaks of the rise and fall of words. If you consider the following short extracts, you can hear this rising, falling sound and it is a very effective means of capturing a mood:

> Brightness falls from the air,
> Queens have died young and fair,
> Dust hath closed Helen's eyes.

(from 'Song' by Thomas Nashe, 1567–1601)

> It was evening all afternoon.
> It was snowing
> And it was going to snow.

(from 'Thirteen Ways of Looking at a Blackbird'
by Wallace Stevens, 1879–1955)

> Only the groom, and the groom's boy,
> With bridles in the evening come.

(from 'At Grass' by Philip Larkin, 1922–85)

The cadence here creates a mood: in the first an elegiac feeling, in the second a melancholy one, the third a peaceful, tranquil one. The sounds of the words, the arrangement of the words in the line, the use of repetition, for example, create these cadences.

Line break and line length

These are other important aspects of the total impact of the poem. It would be a worthwhile and interesting exercise to think about line break in a poem you are not already familiar with. Here are two poems called by William Carlos Williams minus capital letters, punctuation, line break. How do you think it ought to be arranged on the page?

the red wheelbarrow

so much depends upon a red wheelbarrow glazed with rain water beside the white chickens

to a poor old woman

munching a plum on the street a paper bag of them in her hand they taste good to her they taste good to her they taste good to her you can see it by the way she gives herself to the one half sucked out in her hand comforted a solace of ripe plums seeming to fill the air they taste good to her

The poet Denise Levertov says that 'there is at our disposal no tool of the poetic craft more important, none that yields more subtle and precise effects, than the linebreak if it is properly understood'. Levertov illustrates her point by taking four lines from the William Carlos Williams poem 'To a Poor Old Woman', mentioned above, in which the old woman has been eating plums:

> They taste good to her
> They taste good
> to her. They taste
> good to her.

Each word here has a special emphasis because of its place in the line. If Williams had written of the plums that:

> They taste good to her
> They taste good to her
> They taste good to her

it would be a very different and less effective piece. Levertov's commentary (see below) on the four lines from Williams is worth reading, for it shows a mind keenly alert to the power of language.

But first, look again at the four lines that Williams wrote:

> They taste good to her.
> They taste good
> to her. They taste
> good to her.

Levertov observes: 'First the statement is made; then the word good is (without the clumsy overemphasis a change of typeface would give) brought to the center of our (and her) attention for an instant; then the word taste is given is given similar momentary prominence, with good sounding on a new note, reaffirmed – so that we have first the general recognition of well-being, then the intensification of that sensation, then its voluptuous location in the sense of taste. And all this is presented through indicated pitches, that is, by melody, not by rhythm alone.'

The nuts and bolts of poetic language belong in the study of metre, which is the study of sound patterns and measured sounds. Every syllable is long sounding or short and the way such sounds are arranged is an intrinsic part of poetry. When you come to read Shakespeare's sonnets, you will discover that each one is written in a five foot line, each foot consisting of one unaccented syllable followed by an accented one (the iambic pentameter). This is not as complicated as it sounds. The glossary at the back of this book provides a detailed note on metrics.

Imagery

If you say the words traffic-jam, strobe lighting, town, river, hillside, elephant, images form one after the other in your mind, all in a matter of seconds. Many of the words in the English language conjure up an image on their own. Every noun does, for example. However, there is a difference between the image prompted by the word 'tiger' and the phrases 'roaring like a tiger', and 'he's a tiger'. Here tiger becomes simile and metaphor. Symbol is another familiar and powerful technique and symbol occurs when something in the poem such as a tiger in a cage is both actual and means something beyond itself. For example, a caged animal is just that, but it can also stand for the death of freedom. 'The Armadillo' in Elizabeth Bishop's poem of the same name is both actual and symbolic.

And in 'The Harvest Bow' Seamus Heaney writes of how the bow made by his father is an actual object, but it also becomes a symbol of his father's life and work as a farmer, the season itself, and a work of art.

Tone

What is being said and how it is being said are very important. Think for a moment of the sentence: 'Please leave the room'. Tone, or the attitude of the speaker, can make a huge difference here. First try saying that sentence four different ways simply by emphasising a different word each time. Then, if you introduce a note of anger or exhaustion or apathy or urgency into your voice, the sentence takes on a different meaning. In poetry, tone is the attitude the poet/speaker has towards the listener or reader. Tone can be formal or casual/off-hand, serious or tongue-in-cheek, superior or prayer-like, profound or simple and so on.

Mood

A tone can create a mood or atmosphere. Mood is the feeling contained within the work and the feeling communicated to the reader. In 'Sonnet 29' by Shakespeare, the mood at first is one of loneliness and dejection. The speaker feels worthless: 'I all alone beweep my outcast state'. However, the mood is triumphant and exultant in the closing couplet. Shakespeare, remembering his friend and the love that they share, feels an immense emotional richness. In Eavan Boland's poem 'This Moment', the mood throughout is one of expectation and mystery.

Allusion

This is when one writer refers to another writer's work, either directly or indirectly. When an allusion is used, it can enhance or enlarge a topic or it can serve as an effective contrast. When Keats mentions 'the sad heart of Ruth' in 'Ode to a Nightingale', he is referring to a sorrow from a very different time. The moment in the Bible and the moment that the poem focuses on are brought together, one enriching the other, through allusion.

Onomatopoeia

Listen out for the sounds. Read the poem aloud and the onomatopoeic words will clearly reveal themselves. Keats's 'Ode to a Nightingale' contains one of the finest examples of words imitating the thing they describe: 'The murmurous haunt of flies on summer eves'.

Other Aspects To Keep In Mind

Beginnings and Endings

Think about the following examples of opening and closing lines. What do these openings reveal to us of the poets? The situation in which they find themselves? Their tone/mood? Does the poet use the run-on line or punctuation in an interesting way?

Beginnings

'This Italian earth is special to me
because I was here in a war
when I was young and immortal.'

– Harvey Shapiro, 'Italy 1996'

The sunset's slow catastrophe of reds
and bruised blues
leaches the land to its green and grey.

– Robin Robertson, 'Tryst'

That God-is
Light smile of your arms
One second before
I'm in them.

– Ruth Padel, 'Being Late to Meet You at the Station'

never in all my life have I seen as handsome a rat as you.

– Christopher Logue, 'Rat, O Rat . . .'

Endings

And I let the fish go.

– Elizabeth Bishop, 'The Fish'

Never such innocence again.

– Philip Larkin, 'MCMXIV'

To the children, to a bewildered wife,
I think 'Sorry Missus' was what he said.

– Michael Longley, 'Wounds'

And reaching into my pocket in Dublin for busfare home
I found handfuls of marvellous, suddenly worthless coins.

– David Wheatley, 'Nothing to Declare'

For thy sweet love remembered such wealth brings,
That then I scorn to change my state with kings.

– William Shakespeare 'Sonnet 29'

Responding to the Unseen Poem

A Blessing

Just off the highway to Rochester, Minnesota,
Twilight bounds softly forth on the grass.
And the eyes of those two Indian ponies
Darken with kindness.
They have come gladly out of the willows   5
To welcome my friend and me.
We step over the barbed wire into the pasture
Where they have been grazing all day, alone.
They ripple tensely, they can hardly contain their happiness
That we have come.   10
They bow shyly as wet swans. They love each other.
There is no loneliness like theirs.
At home once more,
They begin munching the young tufts of spring in the darkness.
I would like to hold the slenderer one in my arms,   15
For she has walked over to me
And nuzzled my left hand.
She is black and white,
Her mane falls wild on her forehead,
And the light breeze moves me to caress her long ear   20
That is delicate as the skin over a girl's wrist.
Suddenly I realise
That if I stepped out of my body I would break
Into blossom.

James Wright (1927–80)

It is important that we re-read the poem a few times. A poem usually consists of sentences or sections and, having read the poem through several times, it might be useful to approach the poem a sentence or a line or two at a time.

The shape of the poem seems to be irregular. There is no obvious rhyming scheme. The poem contains twelve sentences, some long and flowing, others equally effective because they are short. The lines are of uneven length and the final line is the shortest.

Wright calls his poem 'A Blessing' not '*The* Blessing', which would imply something more specific. If the moment that he writes about is 'a' blessing, it means that there are other such moments also. The blessing experienced in this particular moment, however, is the particular focus of this poem. A blessing has religious and holy connotations and it is a special moment for the poet, though the setting is not a place associated with a conventional religious experience.

The poem begins in a matter-of-fact way – 'Just off the highway' – and the American city and state are named. A 'highway' suggests reinforced concrete, the man-made, busyness, speed, but the second line is soft and natural and beautiful, capturing, as it does, a world 'Just off the highway'. It is twilight, a time of fading light and shadows; the quaint, old-fashioned phrase 'softly forth' contains gentle sounds and the grass contrasts with the highway itself.

The use of the word 'And' at the beginning of line 3, which is also the beginning of a new sentence, leads us further into the poem. The first thing that Wright tells us about the ponies is that their eyes 'darken with kindness' and that they are Indian (Native American) ponies. Their mystery and their nature are conveyed in the words 'darken' and 'kindness'; that they are Indian might be significant. Modern America as symbolised by the highway is very different from the Native American traditions.

'Gladly' and 'welcome' suggest how Wright feels as both he and his friend are approached by the ponies.

The human and the animal world meet when 'We step over the barbed wire'. Wright speaks of the ponies being alone. Their happiness is vividly conveyed in a phrase: 'They ripple tensely'.

There is no sound mentioned. The image Wright uses – 'They bow shyly as wet swans' – is elegant and graceful and beautiful. The three short sentences in lines 11–12, each following the other, are effective. They are both the poet's accurate observation and his conclusions:

> They bow shyly as wet swans. They love each other.
> There is no loneliness like theirs.

The loneliness that the poet speaks of here is a different kind of loneliness, a loneliness that does not frighten or destroy.

The moment passes and the ponies are 'At home once more', happy to be visited and happy to feel at ease 'munching the young tufts of spring in the darkness', a phrase that contains sensuous, evocative details.

The final part of the poem, the last three sentences, focuses on the speaker. 'I', absent from the poem so far, is now used four times. 'I would like to hold the slenderer one in my arms' is Wright's response when his left hand is nuzzled ('ripple';'munching';'nuzzle' add to the sensuousness of the experience). It is clearly a very personal and beautiful moment that the poet is recording. He moves from the very emotional/subjective response to objective description in the lines:

> She is black and white,
> Her mane falls wild on her forehead

He then returns to the intense emotion of 'the light breeze moves me to caress her long ear'. The image of the 'skin over a girl's wrist' is echoing the earlier image of the swans. Both are graceful and slender and delicate. The moment of insight comes and it comes 'suddenly':

> Suddenly I realise
> That if I stepped out of my body I would break
> Into blossom.

The final image is inspired by the natural world and, just as a blossom unfolds naturally and beautifully, Wright, in choosing this image, is giving us a very vivid description of a complex, metaphysical/spiritual moment. It is a poem of longing and here the word 'break', so often associated with destruction, is used with opposite effect. The word 'break' is also placed appropriately at the line break.

•

The above is but a beginning. However, gradually, with each re-reading, you can enter more fully into the poem. If, for example, you focus on the mood of the poem would one word sum up the mood or does the mood change and how would you describe that changing mood? What is the dominant mood of this poem?

Are the verbs or adjectives or sound of particular importance? What if the images were removed? What would the poem lose?

Your own response to a poem on the page should focus on **Theme** and **Technique**. Hundreds of poems may share a similar theme, but every true poet has his or her own individual way of viewing and expressing an idea, his or her own individual way of mastering technique.

Sample Answer on the Unseen Poem

Your response need not be long, but it must be personal. You must engage with the text. And quote little details throughout your answer to support the points you make. The examiner is told to watch out for FOUR things: the candidate's awareness of the poem's

- **Pattern** (or structure)
- **Imagery** (the word pictures painted by the poet and the impact/effect such images have on you, the reader)
- **Sensuousness** (the world as evoked or brought to life through sight, smell, hearing, taste, touch)
- **Suggestiveness** (what personal thoughts, ideas, feelings are prompted by this particular poem)

And, yes, the first letter of the four aspects listed here, as outlined by the Examinations Commission, form an unfortunate and unforgettable acronym: P.I.S.S. But there you go. Did the powers that be think of that at the time?

Here is a poem that could appear as an Unseen Poem and there follows an answer written in exam conditions that earned twenty marks out of twenty.

In this poem, Alistair Elliot celebrates the ordinary things in life.

A Northern Morning

It rained from dawn. The fire died in the night.
I poured hot water on some foreign leaves;
I brought the fire to life. Comfort
spread from the kitchen like a taste of chocolate
through the head-waters of a body,
accompanied by that little-water-music.
The knotted veins of the old house tremble and carry
a louder burden: the audience joining in.

People are peaceful in a world so lavish
with the ingredients of life:
the world of breakfast easy as Tahiti.
But we must leave. Head down in my new coat
I dodge to the High Street conscious of my fellows
damp and sad in their vegetable fibres.
But by the bus-stop I look up: the spring trees
exult in the downpour, radiant, clean for hours:
This is the life! This is the only life!

Question

Write a personal response to this poem, highlighting aspects of it that you liked and/or disliked.

Answer

(Written by Bethany Hart, a Leaving Cert pupil in exam conditions)

On first reading this poem, I did not particularly like it but when I looked closer, the poem opened itself to me, and I can now see that it is intelligent, lyrical and atmospheric. I think the first three lines have a beautiful rhythm; the words are mostly monosyllabic and Elliot creates a steady pace, which suits the relaxed mood of the poem. I liked the image of pouring 'hot water on some foreign leaves' because I found it quirky and different. It seems that in order to celebrate the ordinary things in life, the poet is exaggerating and lyricising them so that making a cup of tea sounds like a beautiful song.

I like how the poet uses rich images such as 'a taste of chocolate' and 'I brought the fire to life' to create a warm atmosphere. The poem is very sensuous in this way; the poet wants to engage his reader's senses with these images.

In the second stanza the poet brings a contrast to the warm feeling previously created. He comments on the happiness that the human race experiences 'with the ingredients of life', describing the world as 'lavish' and 'the world of breakfast as easy as Tahiti'. It seems to me that the poet wants us to return to basics and appreciate the little things. He describes the people around him as 'damp and sad', which not only contrasts with the previous stanza but also with the statement that 'people are peaceful in a world so lavish'. I think the poet is commenting on the fact that possessions do not affect how long happiness lasts.

The final moment in the poem is my favourite moment. It is a sentence of complete exultation and celebration. Elliot describes 'the spring trees' in the 'downpour', as at their best, at their highest, at the moment when the rain is feeding them and bringing life to them. I think he means to tell us that we should be like these spring trees and exult in the things that make us 'radiant' and bring us life.

© Bethany Hart 2011

Appendices/Glossary
Part III

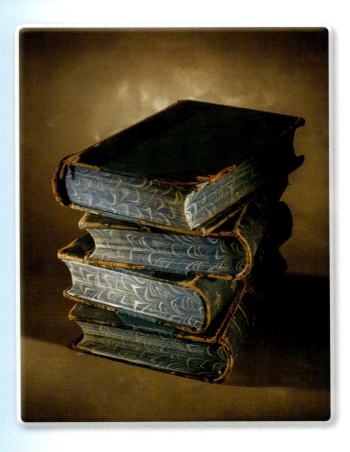

Contents	Page
Appendix I	582
Appendix II	584
Glossary	589

Appendix I

Responding to a Poem – Some Exercises and Strategies

Some Questions to Ask

- Who is speaking? (the poet/a persona/an inanimate object/an animal?)
- What is being said?
- What occasion prompted the poem/why was it written?
- How does the poem begin?
- How does it end? (Write down the opening and closing lines and comment on the style)
- Which line/section captures the gist of the poem?
- Which image is the most effective/striking/memorable?
- What struck you first about a particular poem?
- What struck you while re-reading the poem?
- Comment on the shape of the poem.
- Are the lines regular in length?
- Comment on the stanza divisions.
- Does the poem belong to a particular genre? – sonnet/sestina/ballad/lyric/epic/ode...?
- Comment on the punctuation in the poem. What would the page look like if only the punctuation remained? (e.g. poet's use of question marks, dashes, commas, and where these occur in the line)
- Ask if the poet uses (i) alliteration (ii) assonance (iii) onomatopoeia (iv) end-rhyme (v) internal rhyme (vi) metaphor (vii) simile (viii) repetition (ix) rhyme scheme (x) run-on lines.
- Comment on the title of the poem.
- If you were to paint this poem, what colours would you use?
- If this poem were a piece of music, how would you describe it? Which musical instrument(s) would suit it best?
- Draw three pictures or images that you see with your mind's eye when reading or thinking about this poem.
- Say from which source the poet has drawn these images – from nature, art, mythology, science . . .
- Which is the most important word/line in the poem? Justify your choice.

Some General Guidelines

- You will need to know the poems well if you are to discuss them and write about them intelligently and in detail. You cannot read these poems too often. When you've made them your own, then you will have the confidence of your own thoughts and opinions about the texts.

- If you know the poems in your head and in your heart, then you will be able to summon up the necessary detail when discussing an aspect of the work. Another way of entering into a close relationship with the text is to write the poems out for yourself. Professor Helen Vendler, of Harvard University, says: 'I know no greater help to understanding a poem than writing it out in longhand with the illusion that one is composing it – deciding on this word rather than another, this arrangement of its masses rather than another, this prolonging, this digression, this cluster of senses, this closure.'

- If you read through the collected poems of any poet, it is as if you are looking at, as Wallace Stevens puts it, a globe upon the table. It is a complete and unique world. For example, the poems by John Donne on your course (and they include his finest work) are by a distinctive voice. If we were given an unsigned poem by Donne, we should be able to recognise some of the characteristics which make his poetry memorable and unique: vocabulary, sentence structure, the poetic form, thematic preoccupations and so on.

Appendix II

How to Write a H1 Answer

We all have a lot of faff and fluff and nonsense in our heads. However, whatever else you can say about the poetry on your course, you have to admit that it is intelligent. And having *intelligent* things to think about and discuss is a *good* thing. Think positive from the outset. It's the only way to go.

Every year, poor unfortunates sit down to mark hundreds and hundreds of Leaving Certificate English exam scripts. First, they've had to drive up or down or across to Athlone to collect the scripts, then drive home with a boot full of paper and, secondly, they must then mark and mark and mark, and finish the lot to a deadline. How do they do it? And what is the biggest complaint year after year? What do most English examiners say afterwards? Well, more often than not, it is, 'If only the candidates answered the question . . .' There's definitely a market out there for the T-shirt that reads, 'Answer the bloody question!' It would serve as a useful *aide-memoire*.

It is truly extraordinary, frustrating and disappointing that so many Leaving Cert candidates, again and again, ignore or misinterpret a question's main topic or focus. This is an exam and, therefore, you really must do what you are invited to do. Suppose you love the poetry of Joe Bloggs and could write a brilliant five-page essay on the imagery in that poet's work, and the question on the exam paper invites you to discuss the tone and mood in Joe Bloggs's poetry. Then you simply *must* focus on tone and mood, and nothing else. Obviously, the images may convey or capture a mood, but you must adapt your material on the day of the exam and think things through all over again.

Prepare. Prepare. Prepare.

Someone said, 'If you don't know it, you can't say it.' This means that you simply have to know the poems – five or six per poet at Higher Level. Otherwise, you haven't a chance. Ideally, you should read the poems repeatedly until you know them well in your head and in your heart. One of the best things you can do is to write out the poems in your own handwriting. This, of course, is a really stupid thing to do if you do it without thinking. But if you take every poem, line by line, and write out every word, your relationship with that poem will be an up-close-and-personal one. Pay attention to what you are doing. You will notice such details as line length, the choice of words, how the poem is punctuated, the use of similes, repetition, etc. Obviously, some lines are more important than others; some lines are well worth quoting if you want to illustrate a point you are making.

You might also have read a biographical note on the poet you are studying. This is undoubtedly useful, but watch that you don't just lob in a biographical detail for the sake of it. Again, in the exam hall, you must decide what is *relevant* to the question you are answering. For example, if you are writing an answer on, say, 'Eavan Boland and the world of her poetry', it is significant and worth mentioning that she and her husband moved to the suburbs in the early 1970s and that they have called Dundrum home ever since. And it is also worth quoting Declan Kiberd's remark that Boland 'is one of the very few Irish poets to describe with any kind of fidelity the lives now lived by half a million people in the suburbs of Dublin.' Or if you're writing on Wordsworth and exploring how he saw nature as a guide and guardian, it could be mentioned that Wordsworth's mother died when he was eight and his father when he was thirteen. Likewise, if you are focusing on Emily Dickinson's eccentric, unique style it might be relevant to say that her poems, when first published, were altered to make them look less odd or extraordinary.

When you think about any poet, ask yourself:

- What makes that particular poet unique?
- What does that poet say?
- How does that poet say it?

Bear the following in mind:

- *What* the poet says is the poet's **theme**.
- *How* the poet is saying it is **style**.

Most questions allow for a discussion and analysis of both what is being said and how it is being said.

SAMPLE ANSWER

'The poetry of William Wordsworth appeals to the twenty-first century reader for many reasons.'

Write an essay in which you outline the reasons why poems by William Wordsworth have this appeal.

Life today is busy and uncertain: Facebook, Twitter, iPhones, the recession, the doom and gloom, the pressure of exams, the threat of unemployment all make for a heady mix. Wordsworth, born 1770, is a world away and yet, I think that the poems by Wordsworth that I've read [and re-read] speak to us today. His poetry is important for what it says and for the way it's said.

Wordsworth was ahead of his time. He would have been an environmentalist; he is an eco-poet; he loves the great outdoors and he knows that being part of nature makes us better and happier in ourselves.

In 'To My Sister' he issues a wonderful invitation that any Leaving Cert pupil would love. Put away your books, says Wordsworth, and come outside – the weather is beautiful. The opening line opens up and relaxes into a beautiful idea:

> It is the first mild day of March:
>
> Each minute sweeter than before

There is 'a blessing in the air' and Wordsworth says that 'the blessed power that rolls/ About, below, above' can be felt on this lovely day, a day he calls 'the opening of the year'. It is a poem that people could enjoy in 1798 when it was written and in the early 21st Century when it is still being read. It appeals to the senses, to the imagination and he repeats the delicious idea: 'And bring no book: for this one day/ We'll give to idleness.' And the musical way the poem moves is very appealing, it flows along like a stream.

'Tintern Abbey' is a symphony of a poem. It is complex and philosophical and very rewarding but I think that the modern reader can find something in the poem even on a first reading. Wordsworth's description of the landscape and river valley before him on 13 July 1798 in high summer is very attractive. With Wordsworth, we hear 'These waters, rolling from their mountain springs/ With a soft inland murmur'; we see the hedge rows, the farms 'green to the very door'; we imagine someone sitting by a fire and the wreath of smoke rising. It is a world apart. More people now on planet earth live in urban rather than rural areas so these descriptions by Wordsworth are even more appealing and special.

But there is something else going on. Margaret Drabble says that Wordsworth 'painted place as it had never been painted before, and connected it in new ways with man's thought processes and moral being.' I agree with her. And the 21st Century reader sees in 'Tintern Abbey' not only a poem about place but we are also given a description of how Wordsworth responded emotionally, intellectually and spiritually to nature. We are being shown how Wordsworth processed his experiences and this, I think, is very appealing to a modern reader who is very in tune with the psychological workings of the mind.

Many readers can connect with 'Tintern Abbey' because it traces Wordsworth's own journey from what he calls 'the coarser pleasure of my boyish days' and 'their glad animal movements', a time of 'aching joys' and 'dizzy raptures' to a more mature stage where he experiences 'elevated thoughts' and says that 'I have learned to look on nature, not as in the hour of thoughtless youth; but hearing oftentimes the still sad music of humanity.'

His energy and his enthusiasm for nature are very appealing and another thing that impresses a modern reader is the fact that Wordsworth composed this long poem on a walking tour and wrote it down without altering a word. There aren't many minds today that see so deeply and think so interestingly and speak so well. The blank verse format flows so easily and sounds so natural that reading the poem becomes a very personal experience.

But the thing that appeals to me most, a reader in the 21st Century, is Wordsworth's realism. In 'Tintern Abbey' he writes honestly about being lonely, he writes of times when 'the fever of the world,/ Have hung upon the beatings of my heart'. He knows of 'the dreary intercourse of daily life' of 'greetings where no kindness is'; that 'solitude, or fear, or pain, or grief' can be part of our lives and he also knows that nature can help us through those dark days.

'Tintern Abbey' ends with a prayer for his sister. Wordsworth tells her that nature 'through all the years of this our life' can lead us from 'joy to joy'. If you worship nature, it will not let you down. This is an important and relevant message. It was for Wordsworth then and it is for us now. We need to cherish planet earth now more than ever. And when he prays 'Therefore let the moon/ Shine on thee in thy solitary walk' the words themselves are so beautiful that it is easy to see why Wordsworth is so appealing. He is a kind and caring and loving brother but he wants everyone to believe what he believes because it has brought him so much joy.

Though 'The Stolen Boat' is filled with fear and guilt it is still an appealing poem for many reasons. It teaches us that our actions have consequences and it illustrates very dramatically and effectively a young boy's imagination. It's a very atmospheric poem from the moment he steals 'a little boat tied to a willow tree/ Within a rocky cave'. Nature, here, is a powerful presence. This is nature as a guide and what he calls in 'Tintern Abbey', the 'soul of all my moral being'. Every reader, in every age, will benefit from this poem. It reminds us to be honest and that if we do wrong we will feel bad about it. Wordsworth imagines a 'huge peak, black and huge' striding after him and the boy's response is troubled and strikes me as real. I think this poem tells us that our past will always catch up with us – an important lesson now and then.

In the 'Lucy' poems Wordsworth writes about someone whom he loves and who has died. Lucy was what would be crassly termed in our celebrity-obsessed culture: a nobody. But the poem appeals to me for its tender tone and its beautiful images. Lucy is compared to 'a violet by a mossy stone' and she is as 'fair as a star, when only one is shining in the sky'. Death is a difficult subject but Wordsworth writes about it in a gentle and comforting was. In 'A slumber did my spirit seal', though only two stanzas long, Wordsworth moves from what Harold Bloom calls delusion to reality. The young woman has died. Wordsworth does not avoid reality but even in death there is something appealing in the way she is described:

> Rolled round in earth's diurnal course
>
> With rocks, and stones, and trees.

Though dead she is part of earth's continuing movement. And the last word in the poem is 'trees' – definitely an appealing idea. I associate trees with growth and rebirth.

Finally, 'Upon Westminster Bridge'. This is the odd-one-out in that the setting is urban, not rural. Wordsworth disliked cities – for him 'High mountains are a feeling and the hum of cities torture'. This sonnet appeals to the modern reader in that the cityscape is a familiar image for real or on television screens. In so few words Wordsworth creates a panorama: 'Ships, towers, domes, theatres and temples'. London, in this instance, strikes Wordsworth as a most beautiful place. 'Earth has not anything to show more fair'. It is early morning, it is quiet, it is pollution free. The modern reader is invited to think about city life. Nature is the hero here, not the man-made world. 'Never' says Wordsworth 'did sun more beautifully steep/ In his first splendour, valley, rock, or hill' and he is clearly moved by the spectacle before him in the early morning. This is a poem before its time and it's a poem fcr our time. This poem could be used to promote the environmental movement and environmental awareness! It appeals to the eyes and the ears and reminds us that Mother Nature is a powerful, vital force.

Of all the poets on the course I found Wordsworth the most appealing. Even though he is over 250 years old he speaks to me. The Blank Verse in 'Tintern Abbey' and 'The Stolen Boat' sounds natural and yet it is musical and special. I see him as a friendly voice and what he has to say about nature and friendship and life and death is important, more important now than ever.

Glossary of Literary Terms

ACROSTIC: this is when the first letter in each word at the beginning of a line or stanza spells out a word, name or title. For example:

Man
Is
Never
Dead

ALLEGORY: the word allegory comes from Greek *allos*, 'other', and *agoreuein*, 'to speak'. In literature, an allegory is a work which has a surface meaning and another, deeper, meaning; in other words it can be read at two levels. An example would be George Orwell's *Animal Farm*. It is a story about a group of animals and can be read as such, but it also charts certain events in Eastern European and Russian politics.

ALLITERATION: when two or more words in close connection begin with the same letter or sound and affect the ear with an echoing sound. Examples include the childhood doggerel, 'Betty bought a bit of butter but the butter Betty bought was bitter'. Dickinson uses alliteration as in 'Berries of the Bahamas – have I –/But this little Blaze . . .'; or Larkin in 'The Whitsun Weddings' - 'A slow and stopping curve southwards we kept'; or Seamus Heaney's 'to the tick of two clocks'.

ALLUSION: this is when a writer deliberately introduces into his/her own work recognisable elements from another source. This may be a reference to a well-known character, event, or place or to another work of art. For example, in her poem 'Love', Eavan Boland never names Virgil's Aeneas but the reader is expected to identify 'the hero . . . on his way to hell' as an allusion to Book VI of *The Aeneid*.

AMBIGUITY: when language is open to one or more interpretations based on the context in which it occurs. Ambiguity can be intentional or unintentional. An example would be the opening line of Keats's 'Ode on a Grecian Urn': 'Thou still unravished bride of quietness' – where the word 'still' can mean 'without movement, silent' or 'as before, up to the present time'.

ANAGRAM: this is when a rearrangement of the letters in one word or phrase results in a new word or phrase, as in 'listen' into 'silent', 'now' into 'won'.

ANAPHORA: when a word or phrase is repeated for effect at the beginning of lines, clauses or sentences. The Bible contains many examples, as in the Book of Ecclesiastes: 'A time to be born, and a time to die. A time to plant, and a time to pluck up that which is planted.' In Shakespeare's Sonnet 66, ten of the fourteen lines begin with 'And'.

ANTITHESIS: in Greek, 'antithesis' means 'opposition'. Antithesis occurs when contraries are placed side by side, as in T.S. Eliot's 'We are the hollow men/We are the stuffed men' from 'The Hollow Men'; or Samuel Johnson's 'Marriage has many pains, but celibacy has no pleasures'; or in Shakespeare's Sonnet 116 'Whose worth's unknown, although his height be taken'.

ARCHAISM: in Greek, the word means 'old-fashioned', and an archaism is when a writer or speaker deliberately uses a word or phrase no longer in current use, for example, 'oft', 'morn', 'thy'. Keats's use of 'faery' in 'Ode to a Nightingale' is an example.

ARCHETYPE: the word comes from Greek meaning 'original or primitive form' and archetypes can take the form of symbols, characters, images or events which we respond to in a deep and meaningful way. For example fire, the dark, the sun, the father, the mother, snake, birth, death, the young man setting out on a journey, the young man from the country first arriving in the city all come under the heading archetype.

ASSONANCE: in Latin, 'assonare' is 'to answer with the same sound'. Assonance is when vowel sounds are repeated in a sequence of words close to each other. For example, in W. B. Yeats: 'I hear lake water lapping with low sounds by the shore'.

AUBADE: in French, 'aubade' means 'dawn'. The aubade is a celebratory morning song or a lament that two lovers must part.

BALLAD: a simple and memorable song that tells a story in oral form through narrative and dialogue. It is one of the oldest forms of literature and was originally passed on orally among illiterate people. Ballads often tell of love, courage, the supernatural. Ballads usually are written in four-line stanzas with an abcb rhyme, and often have a refrain. The first and third lines are usually four stress iambic tetrameter, the second and fourth lines are in three stress iambic trimeter. For example:

> There lived a wife at Usher's Well
> And a wealthy wife was she
> She had three stout and stalwart sons,
> An sent them o'er the sea.

Other examples of ballad include Keats's 'La Belle Dame sans Merci' and the anonymous 'Frankie and Johnny'.

BLANK VERSE: this is unrhymed iambic pentameter and is often used in long poems and dramatic verse. One of the earliest examples of blank verse in English is to be found in Henry Howard Surrey's translation of Virgil's *Aeneid*, which was published in 1540. Shakespeare, Milton, Wordsworth, Robert Frost all wrote in blank verse.

CADENCE: the word 'cadence' means 'the fall of the voice' and refers to the last syllables in a pattern of words. Cadence is difficult to define, and yet it is easily identified or, more accurately, easily heard. When Philip Larkin writes at the end of 'At Grass

> With bridles in the evening come

we know that the sounds have been arranged in a particularly effective way on the page. For example, he puts the verb at the end which is not usual in English (it is a Latin form), but the effect is musical and beautiful and very different from 'Come with bridles in the evening', which says exactly the same thing. Cadence is found especially in Biblical poetry, free verse, prose poetry. Ezra Pound in *Make It New* (1934) urged poets to 'compose in the sequence of the musical phrase, not in sequence of a metronome'.

CAESURA: a caesura is a pause which usually occurs in the middle of a line and is caused by rhyme, punctuation or syntax. For example, Boland uses the caesura for effect in the closing lines of 'The Pomegranate':

> The legend will be hers as well as mine.
> She will enter it. As I have.
> She will wake up. She will hold
> the papery flushed skin in her hand.
> And to her lips. I will say nothing.

CARICATURE: from an Italian word meaning 'to exaggerate'. When a character's personality or physical feature is portrayed in a distorted manner, the result is a caricature. The cartoonist's work is almost always a caricature.

CLICHÉ: a phrase which has through overuse become familiar and jaded. The word cliché originally referred to a plate used in printing which produced numerous identical copies. Clichés were once original and interesting uses of language but now, though it is difficult to do so, they are best avoided. Examples include 'a clear blue sky', 'go haywire', 'hard as a rock', 'stand up and be counted', 'tough as nails'.

CLIMAX: climax comes from a Greek word meaning ladder and a climactic moment is one when there is intensity. In a Shakespearean play, for example, there is often a climax in Acts III and V, when the audience's interest is at its height. In Shelley's sonnet 'Ozymandias' the lines 'My name is Ozymandias, King of Kings,/Look on my Works, ye Mighty, and despair!' form a climax.

CLOSURE: the way a poem, novel, play, etc. ends and how the author achieves the sense of an ending. For example, Shakespeare in his sonnets uses a rhyming couplet; Philip Larkin in 'The Explosion' places a single line between eight three-line stanzas.

COMPARATIVE LITERATURE: the study of the relationships and similarities between different literatures by writers from different nations or peoples – e.g. you can read *Great Expectations* by Charles Dickens and *Cat's Eye* by Margaret Atwood and examine and analyse both as 'coming of age' novels or *Bildungsroman* (an upbringing or education novel) – one about a boy in the nineteenth-century in England, the other about a girl growing up in Canada in the twentieth century. Ian Reed states that 'Unless we compare things, we cannot see things either wholly or fully'; and Michael Lapidge says: 'The comparative approach is instinctive to human intelligence. From our very infancy we learn by comparing like with like, and by distinguishing the like from the nearly like, and the other.'

CONCEIT: conceit comes from a Latin word meaning 'to seize' and the literary conceit occurs when a writer expresses an idea in which an interesting connection is made between two distinct things. For example, when a writer compares his state of love to that of a ship in a storm or when John Donne (1572–1631) likens the souls of two lovers to a compass:

> If they be two, they are two so
>   As stiffe twin compasses are two,
> Thy soule, the fixt foot, makes no show
>   To move, but doth, if the other doe.

Dr Johnson described the conceit most associated with the seventeenth-century Metaphysical poets as 'a kind of *discordia concors* [a harmony of opposites]; a combination of dissimilar images, or discovery of occult resemblances in things apparently unlike . . . The most heterogeneous ideas are yoked by violence together'. In Seamus Heaney's poem 'Valediction', the poet uses the conceit of a ship at sea to express his own inner feeling.

COUPLET: two lines of rhymed or unrhymed verse which follow the same metre. Eavan Boland's 'The War Horse' is written in couplets. The heroic couplet is made up of iambic pentameter lines which rhyme in pairs.

CRITICISM: the evaluation, interpretation and discussion of a work

CROSS RHYME: (or interlaced rhyme) this occurs when a word at the end of a line rhymes with a word in the middle of a following line.

ECPHRASIS: also spelt *ekphrasis* (meaning 'description' in Greek); it is a poem that describes a work of art, e.g. Keats's 'Ode on a Grecian Urn' or Bishop's 'Poem' or Derek Mahon's 'Courtyards in Delft'.

ELEGY: elegy comes from the Greek word meaning lament. The elegy is usually a long, formal poem that mourns the dead. Gray's 'Elegy in a Country Churchyard' is one of the more famous. Also, Whitman's elegy for Abraham Lincoln, 'When Lilacs Last in the Dooryard Bloom'd' and W. H. Auden's 'In Memory of W.B. Yeats'.

ELISION: this occurs when a syllable is omitted or when two syllables are slurred together to form one. For example, in Shakespeare's sonnet:

> Th' expense of spirit in waste of shame

Or in Elizabeth Bishop's 'Questions of Travel':

> blurr'dly and inconclusively

END RHYME: this is when the words at the end of lines rhyme.

ENJAMBMENT: also known as the run-on line, enjambment occurs when a line ending is not end stopped but flows into the following line. For example these lines from Michael Longley's 'The Greengrocer':

> He ran a good shop, and he died
> Serving even the death-dealers
> Who found him busy as usual
> Behind the counter, organised
> With holly wreaths for Christmas,
> Fir trees on the pavement outside.

EPIGRAM: a short witty well-made poem. Coleridge defined the epigram as follows and the definition is itself an epigram.

> 'What is an epigram? A dwarfish whole
> Its body brevity, and wit its soul'

Another example would be the epigram called 'Coward' by A. R. Ammons: 'Bravery runs in my family.'

EPIPHANY: a moment of illumination, beauty, insight. For example, the closing lines of Elizabeth Bishop's 'The Fish' or the final stanza of Seamus Heaney's 'Sunlight'.

EYE RHYME: (also known as sight-rhyme) eye-rhyme occurs when two words or the final parts of the words are spelled alike, but have different pronunciations as in 'tough/bough', 'blood/mood'.

FEMININE ENDING: (also known as 'light ending') the feminine ending is an unstressed syllable at the end of a regular metrical line and is added for its musical quality. This feminine ending makes for a falling foot.

FEMININE RHYME: words of two (or more) syllables which rhyme. Shakespeare's sonnets 20 and 87 use feminine end rhymes throughout.

FOOT: a metrical unit of measurement in verse and the line can be divided into different numbers of feet as follows:

one-foot line	:	monometer
two-foot line	:	dimeter
three-foot line	:	trimeter
four-foot line	:	tetrameter
five-foot line	:	pentameter
six-foot line	:	hexameter
seven-foot line	:	heptameter
eight-foot line	:	octameter

Once a line is divided into feet, each foot can then be identified as containing a distinctive metrical pattern. For example, if a foot contains one weak and one strong stress (U –) that foot is an iamb or an iambic foot. If there are five iambic feet in a line, it is known as an iambic pentameter. The following are the most common forms of metrical foot – the stress pattern is given and an example:

iamb (iambic)	:	$\cup$ – (hello)
rochee (trochaic)	:	– $\cup$ (only; Wallace; Stevens)
anapest (anapestic)	:	$\cup$ $\cup$ – (understand)
dactyl (dactylic)	:	– $\cup$ $\cup$ (suddenly; Emily; Dickinson)
spondee (spondaic)	:	– – (deep peace)

FREE VERSE: on the page, free verse is unrhymed; it often follows an irregular line length and line pattern and is unmetered. Free verse depends on rhythm, repetition or unusual typographical and grammatical devices for effect.

FULL RHYME: (also known as perfect rhyme or true rhyme) when the sound or sounds in one word are perfectly matched by the sounds in another. For example, soon and moon, thing/spring, mad/bad, head/said, people/steeple, curious/furious, combination/domination.

HAIKU: the word 'haiku' in Japanese means 'starting verse', and the haiku is a sixteenth-century Japanese form of lyric poem of seventeen syllables in three lines of five, seven and five syllables respectively. Originally, the haiku had to follow certain rules: it had to have nature imagery, a reference to a season, a reference to a religious or historical event; had no rhyme; had to create an emotional response in the reader; and it had to capture the essence of its theme in an insight. The seventeenth century Japanese poet Basho wrote many fine haikus. Here are some modern ones:

> 1.1.87
> Dangerous pavements.
> But I face the ice this year
> With my father's stick.
> – Seamus Heaney

> This is a haiku.
> Five syllables and then foll
> ows seven. Get it?
> – John Cooper Clarke

> To write a haiku
> In seventeen syllables
> Is very diffic.
> – John Cooper Clarke

HALF RHYME: (also called slant-rhyme, near-rhyme, off-rhyme, half-rhyme, partial rhyme, imperfect rhyme) half-rhyme occurs when two words have certain sound similarities, but do not have perfect rhymes. Half-rhymes often depend on the same last consonant in two words such as 'blood' and 'good' or 'poem' and 'rum'. Emily Dickinson, Hopkins, Yeats, Dylan Thomas, Elizabeth Bishop and many other poets use half-rhyme.

HYPERBOLE: in Greek, the word 'hyperbole' means 'an overshooting, an excess' and hyperbole is the deliberate use of exaggeration or overstatement for dramatic or comic effect. For example, in 'The Daffodils' Wordsworth is using hyperbole in 'Ten thousand saw I at a glance'. The opposite of hyperbole is litotes.

IAMB: the iamb is a metrical foot made up of one unaccented syllable followed by an accented one (‿ –). The word 'today' or 'forget' or 'hello' are examples of the iamb.

IAMBIC PENTAMETER: the word pentameter is Greek for five measures and is used to describe a line of verse containing five metrical feet. The iambic pentameter is the most commonly used meter in the English language and there's a very simple reason for this: the length of an iambic pentameter line is the length of time most of us can hold our breath. Blank verse, which Shakespeare used in his plays, is unrhymed iambic pentameter. There is a old girls' skipping chant which goes 'I must, I must, I must, improve my bust' and it is a perfect example of iambic pentameter. So too is a sentence such as 'You make me sick, you make me really sick' or 'My birthday is the twenty-sixth of May'. The iambic pentameter could be represented as follows:

daDA daDA daDA daDA daDA or (‿ – | ‿ – | ‿ – | ‿ – | ‿ –)

Obviously, when you read a line of iambic pentameter, you do not exaggerate the stress, just as we do not exaggerate the stress on a vowel sound in our everyday speech. In the poem, however, the underlying structured pattern creates a music and a flow that is heard in the ear. If you look at and read lines such as the following from Eavan Boland's 'The Pomegranate', you will see and hear them as iambic pentameters:

I climb the stairs and stand where I can see (line 26)

The rain is cold. The road is flint-coloured (line 43)

Not every line in a poem that is written in iambic pentameter will follow the iambic pentameter pattern. If that were the case, the sequence of stresses could have a crippling effect. The rule for poets seems to be that they will use a rule, knowing that it can be broken or abandoned when necessary. The best judge, in the end, is the ear rather than a book on metrics.

IMAGE: in literature, an image is a picture in words, and similes, metaphors and symbols all offer the reader word-pictures as in

'his brown skin hung in strips
like ancient wallpaper,
and its pattern of darker brown
was like wallpaper:
shapes like full-blown roses . . .'
– Elizabeth Bishop 'The Fish'

> '. . . where the ocean
> Like a mighty animal
> With a really wicked motion
> Leaps for sailor's funeral . . .'
> – Stevie Smith 'Deeply Morbid'

Ezra Pound defined the image as 'an intellectual and emotional complex in an instant of time' and this definition reminds us that the image involves the head and the heart. Our intellect creates the picture and our emotions are also involved in determining our response to it, and all of this takes place in an instant of time. Single words such as 'snow', 'rat', 'velvet', 'isolation' and so on present us with images of our own making. The poet, in creating a successful image, allows the reader to see something in a new and interesting way.

IMAGERY: the pictures presented in a work of literature which communicate more fully the writer's intention. For example, the predominant imagery in a play by Shakespeare may be light and darkness and these images become powerful ways of portraying characters, moods, the play's structure.

IN MEDIAS RES: in Latin, the phrase means 'in the middle of things', and, when a work is said to begin immediately or abruptly and without introduction, then it is said to begin *in medias res*. For example, Seamus Heaney's poem 'St Kevin and the Blackbird':

> And then there was St Kevin and the blackbird.

INTERNAL RHYME: this is a rhyme which occurs within the line to create a musical or rhythmical effect, as in Elizabeth Bishop's 'Filling Station', where 'taboret' (American pronunciation) and 'set' and the repeated color form an internal rhyme:

> Some comic books provide
> the only note of *color* —
> of certain *color*. They lie
> upon a big dim doily
> draping a tabor**et**
> (part of the s**et**), beside
> a big hirsute begonia.

INTERTEXTUALITY: the term was coined by Julia Kristeva in 1966. It refers to the interdependence of literary texts; any one text does not exist in isolation, but is linked to all the texts which have gone before. All texts define themselves against other texts, either through differences or similarities.

IRONY: there are two kinds of irony: verbal irony, when something is said and the opposite is meant; and irony of situation, the classic example being the story of Oedipus.

KENNING: a word invention frequently found in Old Norse and Anglo-Saxon or Old English in which two ideas are joined to form a condensed image. For example, 'whale road' or 'swan's path' for sea; 'sky-candle' for the sun. Gerard Manley Hopkins uses kennings in his poetry, calling the kestrel a 'windhover', for example.

LITOTES: litotes is the technique whereby you say something positive by contradicting a negative. A famous example is when Saint Paul said of Rome: 'I am a citizen of no mean city'; in other words he is saying that he is a citizen of a magnificent and great city. If you say of someone that he/she is not bad-looking' you are using litotes.

LYRIC: from the Greek word for lyre, a stringed musical instrument. The lyic poem was originally sung and accompanied by the lyre. Lyric now means a personal, concentrated, musical, short poem. Helen Vendler says 'Lyric is the genre of private life: it is what we say to ourselves when we are alone.' Examples include Ben Jonson's 'Song: To Celia', 'Fern Hill' by Dylan Thomas, Michael Longley's 'Amish Rug'.

MASCULINE RHYME: when stressed monosyllabic words rhyme.

METAPHOR: when a direct link is made between two things without using 'like' or 'as'. Metaphors are often more powerful than similes. 'You're an angel' is more effective than 'You're like an angel'; 'He blazed a trail through the town' is a metaphor which gives a vivid image of a person directly compared to fire — colourful, exciting, dangerous.

METRE: the word metre comes from the Greek word for measure and there are different ways of identifying the metre in a poem:
   (a) by the number of stressed syllables in a line: STRONG-STRESS METRE
   (b) by the number of stressed and unstressed syllables in a line: ACCENTUAL-SYLLABIC METRE
   (c) by the number of syllables in a line: SYLLABIC METRE
   (d) by the duration of short and long syllables in a line: QUANTITATIVE METRE
Do not worry overmuch about the technicalities of metre. I. A. Richards compared metre in a poem to a frame around a painting. It is obviously important but the poem can be appreciated and understood without a thorough knowledge of every technical term in the book. Metre can appear too artificial if overemphasised. When you speak or write, you do not always plan a metrical pattern in your speech, yet the words you speak and the order in which you speak them often make for an effective sound-pattern. The metrical pattern is important, but your ear and your command of language allow you to communicate effectively. In poetry, metre is very important; it is one of poetry's most distinguishing features.

METRICS: the composing or study of the rhythmic pattern in verse. The theories relating to these.

MOOD: this is the feeling contained within a poem and the feeling communicated to the reader. If someone walked into a room containing several people and angrily shouted at you to 'Get out of here at once!', the TONE of voice used would be an ANGRY, COMMANDING one and the MOOD within the room might be one of UNEASE. Do not confuse TONE and MOOD. Tone has to do with the expressing of an attitude; mood has to do with feeling.

MOTIF: motif comes from Latin and means 'to move'. Motif means a theme, a technique, an event, a character which is developed and repeated in a work. For example, in Shakespeare's *Macbeth*, light and darkness become a motif. In literature in general, there are certain motifs such as the *Carpe Diem* (Seize the Day) motif, which means to make the most of a situation. In Michael Longley's poetry, the relationship between father and son, be it between Longley and his own father or that between Odysseus and Laertes, becomes a motif.

MYTH: a story of strange, unusual, supernatural happenings of unknown authorship which was passed on to future generations in an effort to explain origins and natural events.

NEAR RHYME: (also known as slant-rhyme, partial-rhyme, oblique-rhyme, half-rhyme) near-rhyme occurs when two words sound approximately the same and are placed within the poem for musical effect. Emily Dickinson frequently used near-rhyme such as in 'song'/'tongue'.

NEGATIVE CAPABILITY: a phrase used by John Keats (1795–1821) in a letter dated 21 December 1817; it refers to a power of sympathy and a freedom from self-consciousness. In the letter he wrote that the true poet is one who is 'capable of being in uncertainties, Mysteries, doubts, without any irritable reaching after fact and reason'. Keats, by way of illustration, spoke of a sparrow picking among the gravel outside his window, and his observation of the sparrow was so intent and interested that he became that sparrow.

OBJECTIVE CORRELATIVE: the term was first used by Washington Allston in 1850 in *Lectures on Art* and later by T. S. Eliot in his study of *Hamlet*. The phrase refers to how the objective or external world can produce an emotion in the viewer; how there is a correlation between the object and the viewer. Similarly, if a writer uses certain details, descriptions in his/her work, a specific emotional response will be evoked in the reader.

OCTAVE/OCTET: an eight-line stanza. In a Petrarchan sonnet, the fourteen lines are divided into octet and sestet. The octet often poses a question and this is answered in the sestet.

ODE: a poem of celebration and praise. John Keats wrote some of the most famous odes in the English language.

ONOMATOPOEIA: in Greek, 'onomatopoeia' means 'the making of a name' and onomatopoeia refers to words whose sounds imitate what is being described. For example, 'buzz', 'slap', 'cuckoo', 'gargle'.

OTTAVA RIMA: an Italian eight-line stanza in iambic pentameter with an ababab cc rhyming scheme.

OXYMORON: (in Greek, the word means foolishness) oxymoron refers to a figure of speech in which contradictory and opposite aspects are linked. It is similar to paradox, but the oxymoron is contained within a phrase, the paradox within a statement. Examples of oxymoron include 'cruel kindness' and 'thunderous silences'.

PALINDROME: in Greek the word palindrome means 'running back again'. A palindrome is a word, a line of verse or a sentence which reads the same way backwards and forwards: e.g. 'Dad'; 'noon'; 'Madam, I'm Adam'; 'Was it a cat I saw?'. The following refers to Napoleon: 'Able was I ere I saw Elba'. Other examples are: 'Sums are not set as a test on Erasmus'; and 'A man, a plan, a canal – Panama!'

PARADOX: a paradox is when language expresses a truth in what seems, at first, to be a contradiction. For example, Wordsworth's 'The child is father of the man' or Shakespeare's line in *Julius Caesar*: 'Cowards die many times before their deaths'.

PARODY: this is when a well-known work is deliberately imitated in a mocking or humorous way. The reader is expected to be familiar with the original work, if the parody is to be effective.

PATHETIC FALLACY: this term was coined by John Ruskin in 1856 and it refers to the writer's technique of attributing human feeling or behaviour to nature. For example, in 'Lycidas' John Milton says of the flowers 'And Daffadillies fill their cups with tears'.

PATHOS: the word *pathos* in Greek means 'suffering' or 'passion'. Pathos is a deep, sympathetic feeling which the writer summons up in the reader or audience. The final line of Seamus Heaney's poem, 'Mid-term Break' is an example: 'A four foot box, a foot for every year.'

PENTAMETER: this is a line of poetry which is made up of five metrical feet. The iambic pentameter (∪ –/∪ –/∪ –/∪ –/∪ –) is the most commonly used meter in the English language.

PERIODS OF ENGLISH LITERATURE: the following is an outline of the periods into which English literature has been divided by literary historians, though the exact dates sometimes vary:

450 – 1100	Old English or Anglo-Saxon period
1100 – 1500	Middle English or Medieval English period
1500 – 1660	The Renaissance
1558 – 1603	Elizabeth the First's reign Elizabethan
1603 – 1625	Jacobean (after James I)

1625 – 1649	Caroline age
1649 – 1660	Commonwealth period/Puritanism
1660 – 1798	Neo–Classical period
1660 – 1700	The Restoration
1700 – 1745	Augustan Age (the Age of Pope)
1745 – 1798	Age of Sensibility (the Age of Samuel Johnson)
1798 – 1832	Romantic Period
1832 – 1901	Victorian period
1901 – 1914	Edwardian
1910 – 1936	Georgian
1914 – 1970s	Modern English
c. 1970s –	Postmodern

PERSONA: in Latin, the word *persona* means person or mask, and the persona is the speaker in a work such as poem or play who is different from the poet or playwright. The list of characters in a play used to be given under the heading *Dramatis Personae* (the dramatist's persons). In Michael Longley's poem 'Self-Heal' and in 'Wedding-Wind' by Philip Larkin, the voice is that of a female persona.

PERSONIFICATION: this occurs when a writer gives human qualities to inanimate objects or abstractions. For example, if one said that the clouds were in a rage that would be personification.

POETIC LICENSE: when rules are broken, when facts are ignored, when logic is abandoned all for the sake of the overall effect. Emily Dickinson abandons conventional grammatical rules with poetic license. Or Eavan Boland mixes Greek and Latin names in her reference to the myth of Ceres and Proserpine/Demeter and Persephone.

PUNCTUATION: in Latin, the word *punctus* means 'to point' and punctuation indicates speed, flow, emphasis, direction, the emotional charge of language and so on. The following are the more familiar forms:

comma	,	a slight pause
semicolon	;	a longer pause or a division between clauses
colon	:	a long pause; introduces a list, explanation or quotation
full-stop	.	indicates a full stop at the end of a sentence; also used at the end of certain abbreviated words (e.g. Prof. and ad. but not Mr because Mr in the abbreviated version ends with the same letter as the word in full does)
ellipsis	...	indicates that something is missing or is being omitted
dash	—	used to indicate a break in a sentence or elsewhere
hyphen	-	connects compound words
quotation marks	' '	are used to indicate quoted material
	" "	indicate a quotation within a quotation or something of a false or spurious nature
slash	/	indicates a line ending
exclamation mark	!	used for emphasis or to express emotion
question mark	?	suggests puzzlement, confusion, a need for information

parentheses	( )	used in an aside
brackets	[ ]	indicates an editorial comment
italics	*italics*	used for emphasis, foreign words

PUN: a play upon words alike or nearly alike in sound, but different in meaning. A famous example is the dying Mercutio's line in *Romeo and Juliet* (III i): 'Ask for me tomorrow and you shall find me a grave man.'

QUATRAIN: in French, 'quatrain' means a collection of four, and quatrain, in English, refers to a poem or stanza of four lines, usually with alternating rhyming schemes such as abab, aabb, abba, aaba, abcb.

REPETITION: repeated sounds, words, structures is a feature of all poetry to a lesser or greater degree. Repetition has many effects such as emphasis, music, surprise, predictability. Paul Durcan's use of repetition in 'Going Home to Mayo, Winter, 1949' or Elizabeth Bishop's use of repetition in the closing lines of 'The Fish' are significant and effective.

RHYME: when a sound is echoed creating a music and order within the work.

RHYME SCHEMES:

Couplet	aa
Triplet	aaa
Ballad stanza	abab
Limerick	aabba
Ottava Rima	abababcc

RHYTHM: the work in Greek means 'flowing'. Rhythm refers to how the words move or flow.

ROMANTICISM: Romanticism and the Romantic Movement belong to a period in English Literature in the late eighteenth century and the beginning of the nineteenth. Some date the beginning of the movement from the beginning of the French Revolution in 1789; others from 1798 when Wordsworth and Coleridge published *Lyrical Ballads*. The movement ended in the 1830s (Victoria became queen in 1837). The movement began as a reaction to the formality and restraint of neo-classicism in the preceding age. The Romantic Movement focused on the individual's feelings and imagination. The child was valued for its innocence and society was regarded as a corrupting influence. The Romantic poet wrote about his own thoughts and feelings (Wordsworth, speaking of *The Prelude*, said that 'it was a thing unprecedented in literary history that a man should talk so much about himself') and celebrated nature over city life and civilisation. Samuel Johnson, in the eighteenth century, had said that 'The man who is tired of London is tired of life'; the Romantics often found their inspiration in nature.

RUN-ON LINE: this is the same as enjambment. See above.

SARCASM: not to be confused with IRONY, sarcasm is a crude and obvious method of expressing apparent praise when the opposite is meant.

SENSIBILITY: the sensitivity and quality of a person's mind, the capacity of feeling or emotion.

SENTIMENTALITY: an expression of feeling which is excessive, indulgent, immature.

SESTET: a group of six lines, usually the final six lines in a sonnet where the fourteen line poem is divided into eight (octet) and sestet.

SESTINA: a complicated poetic form in which the poem consists of six stanzas of six lines each followed by three-line stanza. The same six end-words occur in each of the first six stanzas and form a definite pattern. The final stanza also contains the six key-words. Elizabeth Bishop's 'Sestina' is an example.

SIMILE: from the Latin word for 'like', the simile is a figure of speech in which one thing is compared to another, using the words 'like', 'as', 'as if'. For example:

> When I was small I swallowed an awn of rye.
> My throat was like standing crop probed by a scythe.
> – Seamus Heaney 'The Butter-Print'

SONNET: a fourteen line poem, usually in iambic pentameter.

STREAM OF CONSCIOUSNESS: the phrase was invented by the nineteenth-century American psychologist William James to describe the writer's attempt to imitate or capture every thought, impression, memory, feeling and so on in an individual consciousness, as they happen. The most famous example of stream of consciousness is found in the closing forty pages of James Joyce's *Ulysses*. Here Joyce has entered into Molly Bloom's consciousness. Her thoughts and ideas flow through the reader's mind, and Joyce abandoned all conventional punctuation to give the passage immediacy. Here is an excerpt:

> I love flowers Id love to have the whole place swimming in roses God of heaven theres nothing like nature the wild mountains then the sea and the waves rushing then the beautiful country with fields of oats and wheat and all kinds of things and all the fine cattle going about that would do your heart good to see rivers and lakes and flowers all sorts of shapes and smells and colours springing up even out of the ditches primroses and violets nature it is as for them saying theres no God I wouldnt give a snap of my two fingers for all their learning why dont they go and create something I often asked him atheists or whatever they call themselves go and wash the cobbles off themselves first then they go howling for the priest and they dying and why why because theyre afraid of hell on account of their bad conscience ah yes I know them well who was the first person in the universe before there was anybody that made it all who ah that they dont know neither do I so there you are they might as well try to stop the sun from rising tomorrow the sun shines for you he said the day we were lying among the rhododendrons on Howth head in the grey tweed suit and his straw hat the day I got him to propose to me yes first I gave him the bit of seedcake out of my mouth and it was leapyear like now yes 16 years ago my God after that long kiss I near lost my breath . . . . .

STYLE: the manner of writing or speaking, e.g. the way a writer uses words may be direct or convoluted or vague or inaccurate or florid . . . . 'Style most shows a man, speak that I may see thee' (Ben Jonson)

SUBJECT MATTER: this refers to the actual material spoken of in the work. For example, a poet might write about a cluttered room which is the subject matter of the poem, but the theme of the poem could be the confusion felt because a relationship has ended. In Elizabeth Bishop's poem 'Filling Station', the subject matter is an oily, dirty, petrol (gas) station but the poem's theme is human endeavour, dignity, love.

SUBLIME: in Latin, this means high, lofty, elevated. The sublime in literature refers to moments of heightened awareness, intense feeling. The closing lines of James Wright's poem 'A Blessing' are sublime.

SURREALISM: Surrealism is a movement in art and literature which sought to release and express the creative potential of the unconscious mind. It frequently contains the irrational juxtaposition of images. The Uruguayan-born French writer Isidore Lucien Ducasse's (1846–1870) description of 'the chance meeting on a dissecting-table of a sewing machine and an umbrella' has been frequently quoted as a definition of surrealism. Salvador Dali's paintings are examples. The surreal is literally 'above the real'. In writing, the surreal occurs when conventional modes are broken, and dreamlike or nightmarish or seemingly unrelated images are juxtaposed. In Michael Longley's poem 'The Linen Workers', the opening lines have a surreal quality: 'Christ's teeth ascended with him into heaven:/ Through a cavity in one of his molars/The wind whistles; he is fastened for ever/By his exposed canines to a wintry sky.'

SYMBOL: a symbol is a word, phrase or image which represents something literal and concrete, but also suggests another source of reference. In everyday life, a piece of coloured cloth is just that, but that same cloth can be a country's flag. It is both object and symbol. Similarly in literature: in Shakespeare, the King is a male character, but he is also the symbol of power, authority and God's presence on earth. The use of symbol is a powerful device because of its rich, complex associative qualities. In Michael Longley's poem 'The Civil Servant', the smashing of the piano is a symbolic act.

SYNAESTHESIA: in Greek, *synaesthesia* means 'to feel or perceive together', and it is when one sensory perception is expressed in terms of a different sense. For example, when an image is experienced through two senses at the same time, as in:

> a loud red coat
> purple stained mouth

SYNECDOCHE: this is a figure of speech in which a part stands for the whole. For example, 'sail' stands for ship; 'hired hands' or 'all hands on deck' means hired persons.

TETRAMETER: the word *tetrameter* in Greek means four measures and the tetrameter is a four foot, four stress line. These feet can be iambic, trochaic and so on. The iambic tetrameter is the second most widely used form in English poetry, the most common being the iambic pentameter.

THEME: theme comes from a Greek word meaning 'proposition', and the theme of a work is the main or central idea within the work. Theme should be distinguished from subject matter. For example, the subject matter of Philip Larkin's 'Church Going' is visiting churches, but the theme of the poem is our natural fascination with religion, its power, effect and future.

TONE: the tone is the attitude conveyed by the writer. From the writer's tone of voice, the reader can identify the attitude of the writer towards his/her subject matter and/ or audience. A tone can be reverent, angry, disrespectful, cautious, dismissive, gentle, reserved, slangy, serious.

TRIMETER: the word *trimeter* in Greek means 'three measures' and the trimeter line is a three foot line. The trimeter is used in nursery rhymes and in many songs, such as Sir Thomas Wyatt's 'I will and yet I may not'.

TROCHEE: the trochee is a two syllable foot. The first syllable is long or stressed, the second is short and unstressed (⌣ –). Examples are 'pushing', 'running'. It is known as the falling foot, opposite to the iambic foot, which is a rising foot.

VERSE: verse comes from the Latin word 'to turn' or 'a line or row of writing'. Verse can now refer to a line in a poem, a stanza, a refrain or a passage from the Bible. Verse can also refer to an entire poem based on regular meter or a poem that is lacking in profundity.

VILLANELLE: the word comes from Italian *villanella*, a rustic song or dance. At first, a villanelle was called such because of its pastoral subject and the use of a refrain. Later, the villanelle followed a strict pattern and became a poem of five three-line stanzas and a concluding quatrain, with only two rhymes throughout. The intricate rhyming scheme is as follows: aba, aba, aba, aba, aba, abaa. Examples of the villanelle are Dylan Thomas's 'Do Not Go Gentle Into That Good Night' and 'One Art' by Elizabeth Bishop.

VOICE: this is the distinctive utterance of a writer; it is the sounds we hear when we read or listen to the poem. In other words, a writer's ability to use words in such a way that a reader can recognise that writer's unique quality. T. S. Eliot identified three voices in poetry:

1. the poet in silent meditation
2. the poet addressing an audience
3. the voice of a dramatic character or persona created by the poet

The publishers would like to thank the following for permission to reproduce copyright material in this book.

Poems

Bloodaxe Books and Brendan Kennelly for 'Begin', 'Bread', 'Dear Autumn Girl', 'Poem from a Three Year Old', 'Oliver to his Brother', 'I See You Dancing, Father', 'A Cry for Art O'Leary', 'Things I Might Do', 'A Great Day', 'Fragments', 'The Soul's Loneliness', 'St Bridgid's Prayer'. Brendan Kennelly, *Familiar Strangers: New & Selected Poems 1960-2004* (Bloodaxe Books, 2004)

The Poems of Emily Dickinson: Reading Edition, edited by Ralph W. Franklin, Cambridge, Mass.: The Belknap Press of Harvard University Press, Copyright © 1998, 1999 by the President and Fellows of Harvard College. Copyright © 1951, 1955 by the President and Fellows of Harvard College. Copyright © renewed 1979, 1983 by the President and Fellows of Harvard College. Copyright © 1914, 1918, 1919, 1930, 1932, 1935, 1937, 1942 by Martha Dickinson Bianchi. Copyright © 1952, 1957, 1958, 1963, 1965 by Mary L. Hampson.

'A Blessing' from *The Branch Will Not Break* ©1963 by James Wright. Published by Wesleyan University Press and reprinted with permission.

Yale Representation Limited for 'Swan and Shadow' by John Hollander. Reproduced with permission of the Licensor through PLSclear.

New Directions Publishing Corporation for 'The Red Wheelbarrow' and 'To a Poor Old Woman' by William Carlos Williams from The Collected Poems: Volume I, 1909-1939 © 1938.

'The Voice You Hear When You Read Silently' from *New & Selected Poems* by Thomas Lux. Copyright © 1997 by Thomas Lux. Reprinted by permission of Houghton Mifflon Harcourt Publishing Company.

Penguin Random House for *The Complete Poems* by Elizabeth Bishop. Published by Chatto and Windus. Reprinted by permission of The Random House Group Limited © 2004.

The publishers have tried to make every effort to trace and acknowledge the holders of copyright materials included in this book. In the event of any copyright holders having been overlooked, the publishers will be pleased to come to a suitable arrangement at the first opportunity.

Notes

Notes

Notes

Notes

Notes

Notes

Notes